Contents

Section One:
Healing Division, Forging Transition

Section Two:
In the Midst of Battles Old, New and Recurring

Section Three:
The Struggles of Democratic Consolidation

Through Fire with Water:
The Roots of Division and the
Potential for Reconciliation in Africa

Edited by Erik Doxtader and Charles Villa-Vicencio

Institute for Justice
and Reconciliation

Africa World Press, Inc.

P.O. Box 1
Trenton, N

Africa World Press, Inc.

P.O. Box 1892

Trenton, NJ 08607

P.O. Box 48

Asmara, ERITREA

Cover photograph of Luanda, Angola by Charles Villa-Vicencio
Maps by John Hall
Typography by Helanna Typesetters
Cover design by Odette Marais
Origination by House of Colours
Printed and bound by ABC Press, Cape Town

Library of Congress Cataloging-in-Publication Data

Through fire with water : understanding the roots of division and
assessing the potential for reconciliation in Africa : 15 case studies /
edited by Erik Doxtader and Charles Villa-Vicencio.
   p. cm.
Includes bibliographical references and index.
   ISBN 159221083X – ISBN 1-59221-084-8 (pbk.)
   1. Africa–History, Military–Case studies. 2. Africa–Politics and government–Case
studies. 3. Africa–Social conditions–Case studies. 4. Violence–Africa–Case studies.
   5. Social conflict–Africa–Case studies. 6. Peace movements–Africa–Case studies.
   7. Reconciliation– Case studies. I. Doxtader, Erik. II. Villa-Vicencio, Charles.

DT21.5.T48 2003
967.03'2–dc21

2003000128

Published in South Africa by David Philip Publishers, an imprint of New Africa Books
(Pty) Ltd, 99 Garfield Road, Claremont 7700, South Africa

Preface

JUSTICE RICHARD GOLDSTONE

Africa is a complex continent. Its peoples speak hundreds of languages and comprise thousands of ethnic groups each with its own history and culture. The boundaries of the countries surveyed in this unusual publication were drawn by colonial powers with scant regard to the indigenous people. Newly independent governments were faced with the often-unenviable task of ruling over disparate groups. Inevitable problems emerged and are still bedevilling a large number of African countries. There are many mental and physical scars left by colonial rulers. This was manifested at the 2002 World Summit for Sustainable Development (the Johannesburg Conference) during which the still deep negative feelings of Africans were vented against leaders of the former colonial powers. By the same token, there was a tendency by some to rally to the support of some unfortunate African leaders who faced stringent and justifiable criticism.

These problems are peculiar to the countries concerned. They do not lend themselves to general and simplistic solutions. While foreign assistance may be constructive and even crucial, the problems have to be resolved by the people themselves. The history and current pathology of the situations in fifteen South and Central African countries are described in profiles contained in this book. The reader will immediately recognise the staggering nature of the problems facing those nations as well as their significant differences. As the editors point out in their introduction, the variation in the country profiles is "significant and instructive. It illustrates both the diverse nature of violence in Africa and the different approaches that are being employed to build peace and promote reconciliation."

The thrust of this collection is the quest for solutions to what often appear to be intractable problems. There is a significant focus on reconciling differences between people many of whom have long histories of enmity if not hate towards each other. Perhaps the most intractable situation is that faced by Rwanda even now, some eight years after the genocide which wiped out about one-seventh of the population of that small country in little more than one hundred days. Much has been written about the *gacaca* system of justice now under way in Rwanda. This is a system of tribal justice that runs counter to accepted modern norms of criminal justice and respect for fundamental human rights. However, the

Rwandan government is faced with a huge, overcrowded prison population of some 120 000 people, all of whom are suspected of involvement with the crimes of 1994. It is not politically possible to simply release these prisoners – there are too many victims crying for justice. I understand the criticisms of the *gacaca* system but have yet to be told of a more acceptable alternative.

In considering the problems facing so many African countries one is struck by the failure of our leaders to establish effective regional bodies to assist in the search for solutions. The Organisation of African Unity (the OAU) has now been dissolved in a state of financial and political bankruptcy. I would suggest that a serious problem on our continent is the reluctance of our leaders to criticise their peers. Again, this reluctance is understandable but comes with a heavy price. One can but hope that the African Union, which has replaced the OAU, will be more forthright in coming down on members who do not live up to the standards contained in the Charter of the African Union.

In this same context, the African Union should give attention to strengthening the African Commission on Human and Peoples' Rights. The European Community has demonstrated how much can be achieved if there is sufficient political will. The European Court of Human Rights has made a remarkable contribution to the protection of human rights in all of Europe. Impressive progress has also been made in the Americas. More African and Asian countries have been setting up national human rights commissions. With good leadership these bodies can make a significant contribution to preventing, as well as solving problems.

There has also been welcome progress in the more frequent and efficient use of global justice – international criminal tribunals, truth and reconciliation commissions and the recognition of universal jurisdiction by domestic courts. The work of the United Nations ad hoc tribunals for the former Yugoslavia and Rwanda led to the highly successful meeting in Rome in the middle of 1998 and the adoption of the Rome Statute for the International Criminal Court. An agreement between the government of Sierra Leone and the United Nations in Freetown on 16 January 2002 has, in turn, resulted in the formal establishment of a special court to try those people who bear the greatest responsibility for the commission of war crimes under international law and Sierra Leonean law. The Sierra Leonean Truth and Reconciliation Commission has also been established. Its primary task, as stated in a supplement to the *Sierra Leone Gazette*,[1] is

---

1 Vol. 131, No. 9, dated 10 February 2000.

"to create an impartial historical record of violations and abuses of human rights and international humanitarian law related to the conflict from 1991 to the signing of the Lomé Peace Agreement [in 1999], to address impunity, to respond to the needs of the victims, to promote healing and reconciliation and to prevent a repetition of the violations and abuses suffered".

The importance of the International Criminal Court that will soon open its doors for business with the election, early in 2003, of the judges and prosecutor, cannot be over-emphasised. The fight against impunity for war criminals is making significant progress notwithstanding the unfortunate opposition from Washington.

The global community is without question in a new era that began with the attacks in the United States on 11 September 2001. There is now an uncomfortable tension between the fight against international terrorism and the protection of human rights. I am concerned that the balance is tilting heavily against the latter and there is a special obligation on the leaders of the democratic nations to be vigilant and to ensure that civil liberties are not unnecessarily compromised. There are concerns in this area for Africa where in many countries a culture of human rights is still in its infancy.

In concluding this preface to an especially welcome and useful book I would like to refer to another positive African development – the concern for exposing and recording the truth and, with it, the acknowledgment of the victims of serious human rights violations. In my view, the most important gift of our Truth and Reconciliation Commission has been the recording of a single history of those violations that occurred during the apartheid era. The inevitable consequence of the official and efficient recording of the truth is that it reduces the denials of the violations. The Nuremberg Trials similarly made the work of the Holocaust deniers all the more difficult and so, too, the trials held by the United Nations war crimes tribunals for the former Yugoslavia and Rwanda. A problem in Rwanda is that earlier crimes against the Hutu people are largely being ignored. As it was put by Mahmood Mamdani:

[History in Rwanda] comes in two versions: Hutu and Tutsi. Ever since the colonial period, the cycle of violence has been fed by a victim psychology on both sides. Every round of perpetrators has justified the use of violence as the only effective guarantee against being victimized yet again. For the unreconciled victim of yesterday's violence, the struggle continues. The continuing tragedy of Rwanda is that each round of violence gives us yet another set of victims-turned-perpetrators.[2]

This book makes an important contribution towards the all-important understanding of the history and factual context in which the diverse problems facing the fifteen African countries must be approached. There is still cause for concern but also for optimism.

2 In *When Victims Become Killers: Colonialism, Nativism and the Genocide in Rwanda* (Princeton: Princeton University Press, 2001), 267–68.

Contributors

Adewale Segun Banjo teaches in the Department of Political Science at Lagos State University, Nigeria. Recently, he concluded work at the University of Cape Town as a UNESCO/MINEDAF Fellow in the Department of Political Studies. In 2000, he received his doctorate in Political Science from the University of Idaban. He has taught at Anambra State University and Lagos State University. His research and publications are on the themes of conflict and peace policy studies.

Shupikayi Blessing Chimhini is a lawyer with the Zimbabwe Human Rights NGO Forum, where he is Programme Manager of the legal unit. His work involves interviewing victims of organised violence, instituting legal proceedings and doing advocacy work on their behalf. He is also a past Fellow in the Justice in Transitional Societies: Africa and Southeast Asia Fellows Programme, jointly sponsored by the International Centre for Transitional Justice and the Institute for Justice and Reconciliation.

Erik Doxtader is a Senior Research Fellow at the Institute for Justice and Reconciliation and an Assistant Professor of Rhetoric at the University of Wisconsin-Madison, USA. A former Social Science Research Council-MacArthur Fellow (1999–2000), he has published a number of essays on the South African transition and is now completing the manuscript for a book on the history and practice of reconciliation in South Africa. He is the co-editor of a forthcoming volume on the history and politics of South African amnesty.

António da Costa Gaspar graduated in international relations and has a master's degree on Peace and Development from Gothenburg University, Sweden. He is Deputy Director and Head of the Department of Peace and Security at the Centre for Strategic and International Studies (CEEI) of the Higher Institute for International Relations (ISRI) in Maputo, Mozambique and is also a lecturer in Peace and Conflict Studies at ISRI. Previously he was an officer in the Mozambican Armed Forces.

Manelisi Genge is a graduate of Michigan State University, USA, where he earned a PhD in African history specialising in the history of Swaziland. He also has a master's degree from Ohio University, USA. He has taught history at the University of the North, South Africa and was Acting Director of the Africa Institute of South Africa based in Pretoria. He is presently the Director of the Policy, Research and

Analysis Unit in the Department of Foreign Affairs of the South
African government.

Gape Kaboyakgosi is an Assistant Research Fellow at the Botswana
Institute for Development Policy Analysis. His major research
interests are in the area of public policy analysis, with emphasis on
structural changes in the Botswana economy. He is a graduate of
Syracuse University's Maxwell School of Citizenship and Public
Affairs.

Ricky Khaukha is completing an advanced degree in politics at the
University of Cape Town, where he served as a founding member and
first Vice Chairman of the Political Science Students Association
(POLSSA) and the East African Students Society (EASS). He has
also worked as a volunteer with People Living with HIV/AIDS in
Swaziland and Uganda. He had a short spell with Médecins Sans
Frontières as a researcher in Chad and worked at the Institute for
Justice and Reconciliation in 2001.

Iraê Baptista Lundin is a social anthropologist and political geographer.
She worked for seven years (1984–91) at Eduardo Mondlane
University, Maputo as a lecturer in social anthropology and thereafter
spent six years (1992–98) as advisor to the Minister of State
Administration in Mozambique. At present, she is Head of the
Department of Socio-Political and Cultural Studies at the Centre for
Strategic and International Studies (CEEI) of the Higher Institute
for International Relations (ISRI) in Maputo, Mozambique and is
also a lecturer in Methodology of Research in Social Sciences at ISRI.
She is the author of *Reflections on the Dynamics of a Nation building
Process under Stress: the Case of Mozambique 1993–1998, Illustrated
with Five Articles*. She is also a member of the UNDP team responsible for the National Human Development Report for Mozambique
(1998, 1999, 2000 and 2001).

Yeki Mosomothane is a Research Associate at the Institute for Justice and
Reconciliation. He is currently completing an advanced degree in law
at the University of Cape Town.

S'fiso Ngesi simultaneously studied French and English at the University
of South Africa. Thereafter, he gained a BA and French Honours
degree from the University of Cape Town. In June 2001, he obtained
a Master of Philosophy degree (cum laude) in Rhetoric Studies with
a dissertation on *A Rhetorical Study of the Open Democracy Bill: A
Perelmanian Approach*. He is currently pursuing his PhD in Rhetoric
Studies in France.

Mokete Lawrence Pherudi is a DPhil from Free State University, Bloemfontein. He specialises in the contemporary history of Lesotho. He has written a number of articles in accredited journals on Lesotho and is currently a Senior Lecturer in the School of Historical Sciences at the University of the North-QwaQwa Campus, South Africa.

Joseph Rahall is a leading human rights defender in Sierra Leone and is currently the Chairman of the Board of Directors of the National Forum for Human Rights, a federation of human rights organisations in that country. He is also the Executive Director of Green Scenery, an organisation that campaigns for the environment, human rights, leadership and peace. He was involved in the unfolding Truth and Reconciliation Commission process in his country.

Tyrone Savage is currently Africa Programme Co-ordinator at the Institute for Justice and Reconciliation. Following studies at the University of Cape Town, he was awarded a Fulbright Fellowship for graduate studies in Conflict Mediation. He is a graduate of Syracuse University's Maxwell School of Citizenship and Public Affairs. His publications include *Rwanda and South Africa in Dialogue: Addressing the Legacy of Genocide and a Crime Against Humanity*.

Susanne Streleau studied law at the University of Marburg, Germany and the University of Paris, France. After she completed her internship, including four months at the High Court of Windhoek, Namibia, she took the German legal examination. In 1999, she attained her doctorate with a dissertation on anti-competition restraints on the managing directors of closely held corporations. In 1999, she was admitted as an attorney in Germany and took a position with the international law firm of Shearman & Sterling. In 2000 she took a leave of absence to read law at the University of Cape Town and in 2001 obtained an LLM degree focusing on transitional law in Africa.

Edmond Tiku was born in Mamfe, South West Province (one of Cameroon's two English-speaking provinces). He is a member of the Social Democratic Front and the Southern Cameroon National Council, organisations that seek a return to the federal system of government, protect the identity of the minority Anglophones and want the institutionalisation of democratic principles in the United Republic of Cameroon. He obtained a "Licence en Droit" (Bachelor of Law degree) from the University of Yaoundé, Cameroon in 1991 and in 1992 obtained a "Maitrise en Droit" degree from the University of Yaoundé. He has published in the area of criminal law and is now studying for an LLM in International and Human Rights law at the University of the Western Cape.

Charles Villa-Vicencio is Executive Director of the Institute for Justice and Reconciliation, based in Cape Town. He was formerly the National Research Director in the Truth and Reconciliation Commission. Prior to that he was Professor of Religion and Society at the University of Cape Town. He was appointed a Fellow of that university in 1994. He has published widely in the area of South African affairs and issues of transitional justice.

Introduction: Profiling Violence and the Potential for Reconciliation

ERIK DOXTADER AND CHARLES VILLA-VICENCIO

Africa has indeed been through the fire. For many of her peoples, the flames still rage. Colonialism and other forms of institutionalised racism, genocide, economic deprivation, famine, civil war, opportunistic dictatorship, HIV/Aids and a host of other wounds have been seared into consciousness and left indelible scars on the body. Still, all is not only or always wrong in Africa, conclusions that have justified paralytic Afropessimism and legitimised too many misguided interventions. There is greatness and great hope across Africa. The call for an African Renaissance, the launch of the African Union and the development of the New Partnership for Africa's Development (NEPAD) are signals of the desire and growing ability of a continent to confront its problems and devise not only solutions but also opportunities. Moreover, frequently overlooked in the rush to diagnose and remedy, Africa is endowed with a tremendous strength and spirit of everyday life – the joys of family, celebrations of community, traditions of political participation, pride of place and bonds of love. Drawn from a Xhosa proverb, the title of this volume expresses just this complex state of affairs, a time when past trouble brings the question of how to use the resources of the present to make a better future. Expressed and expressible in so many ways, freed from the obstacles of undue cynicism or abstract idealism, this art of invention holds much potential for Africa.

This book has very much to do with finding and inventing potential. It is composed of 15 essays, each of which profiles a conflict situation in Africa and the ways in which violence and instability within these situations contain the potential for transition, peace-building and reconciliation. Viewed together, from the brutal hot war in the Democratic Republic of Congo to the clashes taking place during Burundi's first steps of transition, to the problems that have appeared with Mozambique's efforts to consolidate democracy, the profiles address a range of conflicts. The variation is significant and instructive. It illustrates both the diverse nature of violence in Africa and the different approaches that are being employed to build peace and promote reconciliation.

The decision to produce this book was made in response to a number of problems, conversations and questions. Each year, the Institute for Justice and Reconciliation receives numerous requests for information and undertakes work with actors interested in data about the form and history of conflicts within Africa. Some of the queries come from ordinary citizens, people wanting to know about a particular conflict and seeking recommendations about what they might read to better understand where a country has been and where it might be going. For these people, the desire is for more than a newspaper or magazine exposé and for less than a full course of study. Others inquire because they are interested in undertaking certain kinds of work, frequently efforts related to building peace in war-torn nations or entering into co-operative agreements with civil society groups striving to build and consolidate democracy. For this group, there is a need for substantive background material and a clear picture of the current situation.

This book addresses the question of how countries across Africa are defining, promoting and achieving reconciliation. In light of the role that reconciliation played in South Africa's transition, there is tremendous interest in this matter. What is reconciliation? How is it best promoted and achieved? Does it work? What are its limits? Relative to South Africa, however, the issue is not whether there is a formula for reconciliation. Rather, the concern is to better grasp how reconciliation shaped South Africa's move from apartheid to democracy and the ways in which it has been used to bridge deep historical divisions. Reconciliation is now part of the discourse of transitional justice and democracy-building. This does not mean that it is a necessary element. Rather, it is an option, a path that many are choosing to explore and which some are working to implement.

From the beginning, it was clear that a volume with these aims could not hope to cover the entirety of Africa. This is partly to say that this work marks the start of an ongoing series. In this volume, decisions about which countries to include and which to leave for later were based on a number of factors, including accessibility of resources, apparent or expressed interest in reconciliation and opportunities to consult with local actors in the development of the profiles. Viewed as a whole, the volume's contents are oriented towards, but not exclusively concerned with, countries located in southern and central Africa. The focus is not intended to slight or create the impression that these are the only places where there is concern for transition and the promotion of reconciliation. Indeed, the work presented here does well to show just how much more remains.

In brief, each chapter in the volume offers readers a clear, well-researched and concise profile of a particular conflict. While conscious that borders are fluid, highly permeable and frequently imposed, the essays in this volume are country-specific, tending to a kind of "national" focus. Within this domain, each profile surveys the current state of violence and conflict, the historical roots of these clashes and efforts that are being made to promote peace and foster reconciliation. Each of the profiles includes an annotated set of resources for further reading and study. While produced with a variety of research materials, the volume as a whole is a testament to the growing amount of information about Africa that exists on the World Wide Web. Overall, our hope is that this small offering can make a difference to raising consciousness and promoting collaboration between brothers and sisters who have not always had the time to fully understand what is going on "over there" or "down there" or even just "around the corner". One lesson of this volume is that we have much to learn from one another. Where some have been, others are headed. A vital first step is taking the time to ask about and better understand what is happening in different places and why. Reconciliation begins when we ask questions, demonstrate genuine concern and offer to roll up our shirt-sleeves and set to work.

Profiling Questions

What is a profile? What exactly does it mean to profile a violent situation and the ways in which those involved are struggling for its resolution? What is the risk of such work? These are important and frequently ignored questions. Ideally, a profile is a sketch or a picture that stops well and consciously short of attempting to fill in the lines of that which it endeavours to represent. A profile is not the whole. When it pretends otherwise, losing a sense of its contingency and incompleteness, a profile devolves to a caricature that can easily become the basis for a stereotype. In the wake of the 2001 attack on the World Trade Centre, there are many air travellers who can testify to the risks and insults that come when the act of profiling piously takes one quality (skin colour, national origin, quality of luggage) for another (threat, hostility, intent to harm). A profile of any sort is only as useful as its ability to convey that it is an outline of something or someone that has a much richer and fuller face.

Done well, profiles have significant value. They are condensation symbols that allow us to gain vital information about people and events that we would like to know better. In this sense, profiles are substantive introductions that afford the chance to form intelligent and incisive questions. They provide descriptive and critical information that allow us to see both the shape and variable nature of things, human interests and states of affairs. In this sense, a profile offers a reference point for our questions, information that can help support queries about what is happening and why. For instance, the profile of South Africa does not and cannot detail all of the ways in which reconciliation has played a role in the transition from apartheid. But, what it does do very well is indicate that reconciliation has appeared in many contexts and fostered important debates. Thus, it offers information that provokes us to ask about the different means and modes by which reconciliation can help and sometimes hinder a society struggling to heal the pain of the past. Such questions are the stuff of conversation and a gateway to collaboration.

Aside from spurring questions, profiles have a number of other uses. Detailed profiles, like many of the ones offered in this volume, can help us survey literature about a conflict that has many different sides and whose meaning admits to a wide range of interpretations. Some profiles use this kind of review to engage in synthesis and support policy-making. Indeed, there are a number of profiles on African conflicts that conclude with detailed proposals for what ought to be done to solve a set of general and particular problems. While these sorts of profile have their value, they are not the focus of this collection.

One common aim of a profile is to "tell it like it *is*". While this concern to detail the "essential" elements of a situation is important, it can and frequently does come at the expense of understanding how many situations of violence and conflict are characterised by diverse and competing perceptions about what the conflict is about, why it is occurring and how it is best resolved. To ignore these perceptions or to cast them off as so much propaganda is to risk our ability to ask questions that are sensitive to context. The desire to understand what is real, really true or absolutely certain can obscure the changing appearances and diverse interpretations of reality that both foster and help overcome violence. When political science aspires more to the scientific than the political, the question of what people say about the conflict in which they are involved becomes less important, an accessory if not a hindrance to understanding what is *really* going on and what surely should be done about it.

Whether one reads Hannah Arendt or Steve Biko, the lesson remains the same: perceptions are important to the matter of how violence develops and gives way to peace. People use speech to express their interests and opinions. These expressions are not always heard. They can and do take the form of propaganda, statements issued without a corresponding intention to listen. In many cases, however, combatants, government institutions, citizens and civil society groups find one another only as they are able to both express themselves and hear the position of their counter-parts. This is very much the stuff of reconciliation; not what *is* the conflict but what are the ways that participants describe it and is there room to forge common ground from within these different and often opposed perceptions? The point is made well in the profile of the tremendous difficulties confronting Zimbabwe. Many do not want to hear what Robert Mugabe's government has to say, writing it off as misguided, anti-democratic and potentially evil. This may be true. But, the profile shows that Mugabe's claims are tied to a historical discourse about the colonial legacy of land ownership, a problem that has appeared and reappeared over the course of Zimbabwe's history. Thus, the point may not be to accept Mugabe's characterisations of the situation but to grasp the ways in which they shape the playing field, defining positions of power and the grounds that determine whether there can or should be any sort of negotiated solution to a growing crisis.

Overall, the profiles that compose this volume take pains to grasp the various and variable features of their "object". To greater and lesser degrees, they detail what people involved in the particular conflict are say-ing about the situation and its meaning. This perceptual focus has obvious limits. It is not possible to canvas all actors. Hearing from a distance can prove very difficult. However, the profiles do pause to listen. They offer something of a chance to grasp the complexity of rationales for violence and various declarations about ways that it might be brought to an end. For all its limitations, this sort of profile offers ground for developing questions in situations where the answers are not always obvious.

Arguments of Content

Profiles can be designed and written in different ways. Many take a nar-rative form, weaving together facts and descriptions to provide readers with a clear sense of an event's basic history and characteristics. In study-ing violence and conflict, this narrative approach shows significant value. As they work from beginning to middle to end, such profiles offer both a sense of context and direction, a view of what has been and what it may mean for the future. However, the seamless nature of many narratives can make it easy to forget that profiles make arguments. Indeed, the very act and art of profiling involves argumentation. This is true regardless of whether a particular profile advances claims about the meaning of key events, the factors that cause or sustain violence and the ways in which particular groups or nations might build peace.

Like other forms of analysis, profiles are selections of reality, carefully constructed attempts to represent a situation, event or collection of activities. However, this reflection of reality is always partial if not partisan, a function both of the representational limits of language and the predisposition of an author as she or he goes about researching, sorting and interpreting data about a situation. In many cases, this interpretative work is most difficult when one is standing in and surrounded by the events to be profiled. While this is a matter for debate, the larger point is that a profile's selection of reality will also be a deflection, an exclusion of those elements that are deemed "not to fit" or judged less important than what is chosen for inclusion in the profile. Thus, while a pleasant sentiment and noble aspiration, it is not especially meaningful to say things like "we tried our best to include everything in our profile". The more important issues are what does the profile include and exclude and were these choices made with care. Answers to these questions have much to do with the underlying purpose that motivates the creation of profiles.

Each profile in this volume works toward a similar set of ends. To begin, each profile details the nature and extent of certain kinds of violence within the particular country to which it is addressed. Here, the general goal is to grasp something of the big picture. Where relevant, this includes consideration of systemic, cross-cultural and institutional forms of violence. Sometimes, as in the case of civil war, the terms of this violence are readily apparent. In others, evident within the investigation of Namibia, the matter is a bit fuzzier and requires inquiry into such things as the dynamics of electoral politics and relative levels of tolerance among government institutions. Thus, violence does not mean the same thing from profile to profile. A hot war is not the same thing as clashes that occur during periods of transition and consolidation. HIV/Aids, which is addressed in some profiles, is a kind and source of violence. The same is true of economic deprivation and undue exploitation of the environment. Overall, however, the profiles here remain within the orbit of armed conflict and certain other structural forms of violence. By necessity, detailed analysis of local-communal conflict has been set aside. It is also clear from the standing research that much more work needs to be done on gender-based violence and its implications for fragmented and transitional societies.

A second aim of the profiles is to offer limited explanations of the causes and historical precursors of violence within particular countries. This work takes the form of both historical narrative and documentation of the perceptions espoused by some of those who are involved and implicated in violence. As noted already, a key premise of this project is that accounts of the nature, causes and meaning of particular conflicts need to be routed through the expressed opinions of those involved. This work has been frustrating even as it has paid important dividends. For instance, the ability of authors to record and compare opinions has been hampered routinely by the fact that in many conflicts, one or more sides do not have ready access to (frequently state controlled) media. Nevertheless, many of the authors have spent long days in the library, pouring over newspapers, primary documents and reports from the internet to better understand the perceptions of those engaged in struggle. When set into the larger historical tapestry, the inclusion of these voices does make a difference. They are instructive precisely because they show some of the ways in which conflicts come to have two, three, four and sometimes five sides. In these terms, the profiles offer historical explanation but stop well short of isolating singular cause. In many cases, it is just this reductive gesture that motivates and sustains violence.

Finally, the profiles are concerned to understand what if any opportunities exist for countries to move from violence toward peace-building and reconciliation. We will return to the matter of reconciliation in a moment. For now, the important point is that the profiles examine both historical and present-day efforts to end violence. In many cases, this analysis is centred on the terms and relative success of formal peace talks. Thus, the concern is not so much for the ways in which communities are working to resolve disputes but how national-level actors have entered into, concluded and broken negotiated settlements. The two are tied in many cases. The investigation into the Rwandan *gacaca* court system does well to illustrate some of the ways in which broad-based agreements shape the terms of communal and individual life. Overall, the work of profiling peace negotiations always involves difficult choices. Inevitably, decisions have to be made about how much of the actual process to record. As in the discussion of Burundi's fragile peace process, the profiles are intended to open the door to more extensive and detailed study of how sworn enemies come to the table and reach agreements.

In planning this volume and considering its purpose, the decision was made to develop profiles that share a common form. Where necessary, due largely to the kind of conflict being investigated, modifications were made to enhance the readability and content of the profile. In the end, however, most profiles are composed of four sections: The Face of Conflict; The Historical Roots of Violence and Division; Prospects for Peace-building; and Present and Future Opportunities for Reconciliation. Some will wonder about the order of the first two sections. Why not start with the historical case and move to the present day? While this is an option, we found that leading with the historical narrative can create a sense of singular cause or inevitability when it comes to diagnosing the current state of affairs. Thus, the disjunction is intentional, a reminder that what is happening now has both a relationship to and distance from what has come before.

Assessing the Potential for Reconciliation

The profiles collected here work toward the question of whether and how particular conflicts contain the potential for reconciliation. For a variety of reasons, clear answers are not easy to come by. Reconciliation is elusive in a number of ways. Its meaning changes from context to context. It can take a number of different forms. Sometimes it is institutionalised in truth and reconciliation commissions. In other situations, it takes place at local levels or in interpersonal interactions that are difficult to see and assess. In any case, what remains clear is that reconciliation matters. While it may be a relatively new kid on the democratisation theory block, calls for reconciliation can be heard throughout Africa. Part of this interest can be tied to the apparent success of the South African reconciliation experience. Its appeal is also related to both the form and dynamics of conflict in Africa and an increasing awareness of how deep divisions can carry over time, coming back to re-ignite old disputes.

What is reconciliation? Thousands of pages have been devoted to this issue. The oldest definitions hold that reconciliation is an exchange that transforms enmity into friendship. This is and is not helpful. What kinds of conflicts admit to reconciliation? How does it occur? What are its outcomes? The profiles here devote substantial attention to just these questions. Viewed together, they show that reconciliation is an increasingly important aspect of peace-building and a relational good that takes shape in direct response to the kind of conflict being waged, the interests of combatants and the contextual demands of transitional justice. They also show that there is no formula for reconciliation. This means that the profiles do not propose specific frameworks for reconciliation. There is no heavy-handed attempt to argue that reconciliation must or should occur. Too, the profiles do not presuppose that the model employed by the South African Truth and Reconciliation Commission (TRC) can be packed up and exported. Rather, the profiles begin with the question of how institutions, publics and citizens are talking about reconciliation and its potential value. Evident in the profile on Lesotho, this involves nuanced analysis of whether calls for reconciliation have been advanced in particular conflicts, the terms of these proposals and the degree to which they are supported by key stakeholders. In some instances, as in Burundi and Somalia, there appears to be a substantial push for reconciliation, efforts that directly acknowledge and repair the wounds of history. This may involve the creation of TRC-style initiatives. In other situations, the notion of reconciliation is being combined in innovative ways with war trials and other kinds of programmes designed to promote individual and collective healing.

In many conflicts where there is growing support for reconciliation, there is a need for resources and an interest in collaboration. Many of those who contact the Institute for Justice and Reconciliation seek information about such matters as designing amnesty legislation, facilitating programmes that inculcate respect for human rights and ways to promote reconciliation from the highest levels of government to the smallest communities. As there is not a certain answer, the task becomes one of learning from one another, using different experiences and insights to design programmes that promote reconciliation in the direct light of the violence and conflict that has occurred. Such collaboration has much promise. It is also hard work with a slow pay-off. Each of the profiles in this volume contains detailed information about local and international organisations that are striving across Africa to build peace and promote reconciliation. For those interested in such work, this volume provides resources and insights that allow for the development of good questions, queries that build relationships and help create opportunities for reconciliation and justice. For others, the volume offers the chance to see and learn something about the experience of neighbours, communities and nations that are struggling, building and hoping. The fires continue to burn. Within each of us there is water to help douse the flames.

Acknowledgements

When one undertakes to develop a set of political profiles, there is never quite enough time. As the moments of writing and editing pass, circumstances change, necessitating revision and careful tracking of where a country is going and might go in the next months. While the circle is potentially endless, the experience itself is enriching, a lesson in precisely that which cannot and ought not to be "captured" by the word. In part, this is to say that the time for this project has been a very good one, a period of intense work, collegiality and collaboration. The authors of the profiles endeavoured and sometimes struggled with the task of summarising that that cannot be summarised. They made vital suggestions about the design of the volume, shaped its purpose and undertook revision with dedication and care.

There are a number of individuals who supported and helped turn the potential of a good idea into the actuality of the present volume. S'fiso Ngesi appeared at a pivotal moment, donning the hats of both author and editorial assistant. A man of great integrity, compassion and intellect, S'fiso has worked long hours and given great energy to this work. Moira Levy has been wonderful to work with and instrumental in bringing the project to completion. We are grateful for her help.

Every project needs a home, a place of comfort and structure for growth. For this, we owe a great debt to the entire staff at the Institute for Justice and Reconciliation – Carol Esau, Fanie du Toit, Nyameka Goniwe, Debbie Gordon, Paul Haupt, Karin Lombard, Thapelo Mokushane and Zola Sonkosi. Their individual insights, comradely ethos and hard work have inspired and shaped the volume. As editors, we worked closely together in complementing one another's work.

From Erik Doxtader's perspective, Charles Villa-Vicencio has been a wonderful and tireless colleague. His vision and commitment to reconciliation runs throughout this volume. Charles' generous invitation to direct the project has come to pay dividends that I could not have predicted. I am grateful for his faith and friendship.

From Charles Villa-Vicencio's perspective, this volume would simply not have made it into print without the tireless work of Erik Doxtader. Erik's name ought to have appeared on several essays as joint author. He wrote and rewrote large sections of many essays. He was a mentor to many young writers and scholars, teaching the value and importance of words. From the beginning this was an Institute project, involving student interns and research fellows, as well as associates of the Institute who are established scholars in their own right. Erik's contribution to this Institute and collegiality to me is huge.

Collectively, it is our hope that the contents of this volume afford some insights and avenues for action, bridges that help close the divides that have done so much harm to so many.

We acknowledge with great appreciation the financial subvention of this publication, made available through the Swiss Agency for Development and Co-operation. We are particularly grateful to Gerhard Pfister and Remy Duiven for their support and encouragement for the project. This volume is the fruit of the Fellows and the Interns Programme, which is part of the Institute's infrastructure funded by the Royal Danish Embassy and the Norwegian Embassy. This too, along with support from the Social Science Research Council, we acknowledge with gratitude.

Cape Town, July 2002

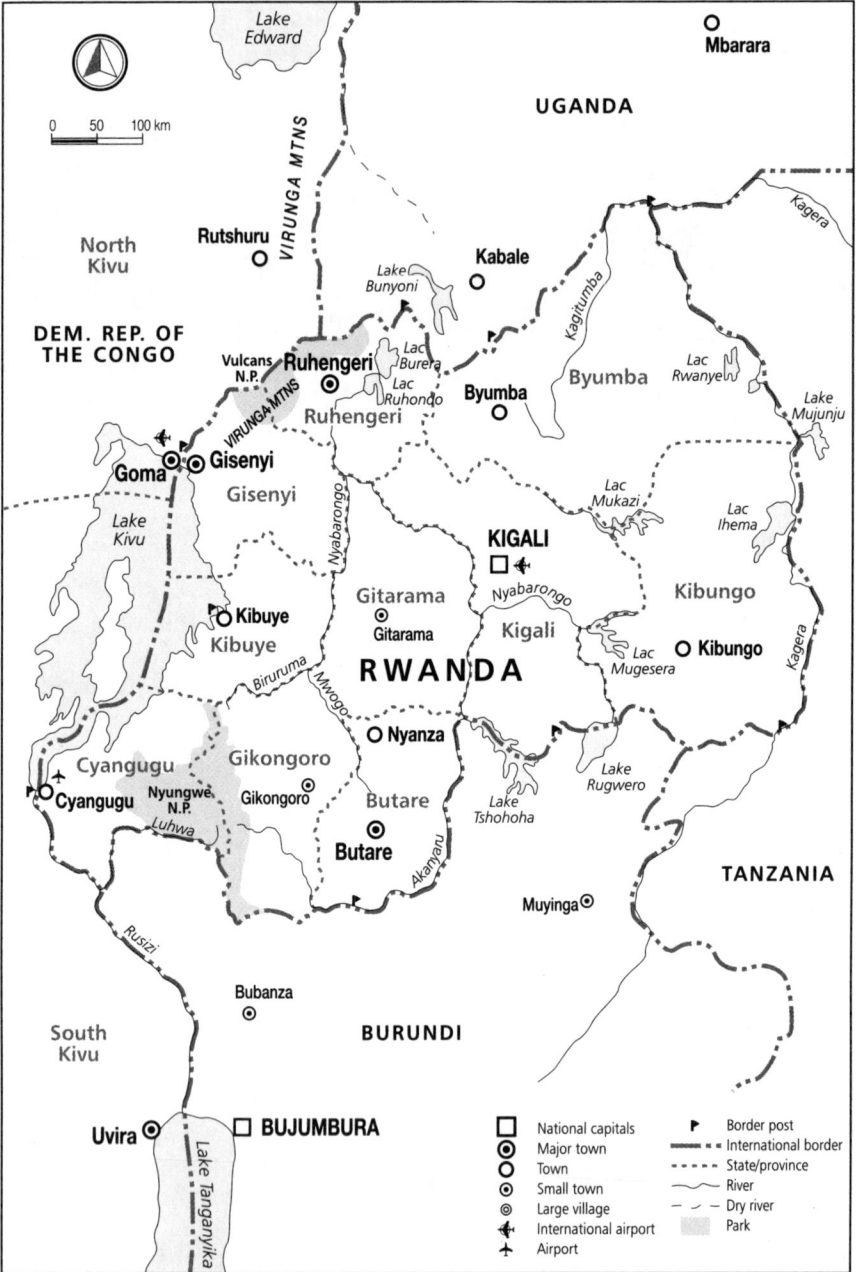

Lake Edward

Mbarara

UGANDA

VIRUNGA MTNS

North Kivu

Rutshuru

Lake Bunyoni

Kabale

Kagera

DEM. REP. OF THE CONGO

Vulcans N.P.

Ruhengeri

Lac Burera

Byumba

Kagitumba

Lac Rwanye

Lake Mujunju

VIRUNGA MTNS

Ruhengeri

Lac Ruhondo

Byumba

Goma

Gisenyi

Gisenyi

Lac Mukazi

Lac Ihema

Lake Kivu

Nyabarongo

KIGALI

Gitarama

Nyabarongo

Kibungo

Kibuye

Kibuye

Kigali

Lac Mugesera

Kibungo

Gitarama

RWANDA

Biruruma

Mwogo

Nyanza

Cyangugu

Gikongoro

Butare

Lake Rugwero

Cyangugu

Nyungwe N.P.

Gikongoro

Lake Tshohoha

TANZANIA

Luhwa

Butare

Akanyaru

Kagera

Rusizi

Muyinga

South Kivu

Bubanza

BURUNDI

Uvira

BUJUMBURA

Lake Tanganyika

0   50   100 km

National capitals
Major town
Town
Small town
Large village
International airport
Airport

Border post
International border
State/province
River
Dry river
Park

Chapter 1

Rwanda: Balancing the Weight of History

S'FISO NGESI AND CHARLES VILLA-VICENCIO*

Approximately 75% of the Rwandan population of seven million people were killed, displaced or driven into exile by the 1994 genocide. An entire nation was brutalised and traumatised. They are, in their own phrase, "the walking dead".[1] It was perhaps the most intimate and devastating genocide in recent memory, effected by an enraged population, enticed by a fearful and desperate government. General Romeo Dallaire, head of the United Nations peace-keeping force at the time, argues that "the Rwandan extremists were far more efficient at genocide than the Nazis".[2] Close to a million people (mostly Tutsis) were killed in less than three months – the vast majority in face-to-face slaughter, with machetes and clubs. When the genocide "ended" on 18 July 1994, the situation in Rwanda was as grim as anything previously witnessed anywhere. In the words of Jeff Drumtra, a United States Committee of Refugees (USCR) policy analyst, "Rwandans have been through a national nightmare that almost defies comprehension. Theirs is a post-genocide that has also experienced civil war, massive refugee displacement, a ruthless [post-genocide] insurgency . . . deep physical and psychological scars that are likely to linger for decades . . . and economic ruin so extensive that it is now one of the two least developed countries in the world."[3]

This was the context in which the victorious Rwandan Patriotic Front (RPF) launched its Government of National Unity, led by President Pasteur Bizimungu, in 1994. The tattered social fabric had to be repaired. There were no funds, save a trickle from the outside world. An infrastructure had to be rebuilt. The economy needed massive reconstruction just to return to its previous precarious state. A legacy of violence and a culture of impunity had to be transformed. A criminal justice system had to be restored so that the guilty would be punished to deter others, while their expected contrition would make forgiveness possible for their victims. International actors had to be satisfied. The immediate physical and psychological needs of violated women and traumatised children had to be met.[4]

* The initial research of Wynoma Michaels is gratefully acknowledged.

The Face of Conflict

Developments in 1994–2000

By July 1994, Rwanda was a wasteland. Apart from those killed, two million people were displaced internally and a further two million became refugees, mostly in neighbouring countries.[5] Many of those who remained had suffered greatly. Large numbers had been tortured and wounded. Many women had been raped and humiliated, some infected with HIV/Aids.[6] Rwandans were, indeed, "the walking dead". The economy was depleted. Per capita GDP was a mere $95, a decline of 50% in one year.[7] Inflation stood at 40%.[8] More than 70% of Rwandans lived below the poverty line. There was a country but no state. When the Government of National Unity was formed, only two members of the Cabinet had any experience of running a government. Most members of government had never actually lived in Rwanda.[9] Most of the educated, skilled and professional Rwandans who had lived inside the country were dead or in exile.

The change in government persuaded some 800 000 long-time Tutsi refugees to return home during 1994–96. Hundreds of thousands of Hutu refugees suddenly returned in late 1996 under controversial circumstances precipitated by civil war in the Democratic Republic of the Congo (DRC). Another 200 000 Hutu refugees returned to Rwanda during 1997. More than 30 000 additional Hutu refugees gradually returned during 1998–99.[10] The returnees often brought with them much-needed capacity – skills, talent, drive, leadership – that played an indispensable role in the creation of the new state.

Despite promising signs of national unity in the early days of Bizimungu's government, by 2000 there was some high-profile instability in the upper ranks of the government. The Speaker of Parliament, Joseph Sebarenzi, a Tutsi, resigned and soon after fled the country. He was variously accused of mismanagement, abuse of office, supporting the return of the former king and inciting soldiers to rebel against the government.[11] No charges were substantiated and he denied culpability. Some reports suggested that Sebarenzi had fled the country to avoid assassination.[12] In February 2000, Prime Minister Pierre-Celestin, a Hutu, resigned amid accusations of financial impropriety and corruption. He too denied the accusations.[13] A few days later, Assiel Kabera, a Tutsi and an advisor to President Bizimungu, was murdered. He was a prominent member of the genocide survivors' association, a group that had been highly critical of the government. In March, Bizimungu himself resigned and Paul Kagame became president.[14] Bizimungu was a Hutu who had joined the RPF after his brother, an army colonel, was assassinated, apparently on the orders of the previous government.[15] He was the most public symbol of a government that claimed to represent all Rwandans. Bizimungu's reasons for his resignation were that he was mistreated and marginalised within government.

These resignations attracted much criticism from observers. They led to a Cabinet reshuffle that gave 10 out of 18 seats to the RPF, which was perceived as a violation of the Arusha Accords of 1993.[16] Some have argued that from the very first, real power in the government has consistently been monopolised by a small group of Tutsis, even though Hutus were formally well represented. This conclusion was echoed by the International Panel of Eminent Personalities (IPEP) of the Organisation of African Unity (OAU) which was charged with investigating the 1994 genocide in Rwanda.[17]

The Tutsis, who comprise 15% of the Rwandan population, control the Government of National Unity. Cabinet, ministerial general-secretaries, district prefects and burgomasters are mainly Tutsis. The "Tutsisation" of the judicial apparatus is evident in the Supreme Council, which is mainly Tutsi.[18] The government is one of "national unity", but on terms that many Hutu leaders in the diaspora completely reject.

Rwandan authorities have disputed these objections. Joseph Karemera, for example, a former Minister of Health and Education and currently Ambassador of Rwanda to South Africa and other southern African countries, challenged the statistics pertaining to the Cabinet and the armed forces when he argued, "Presently [2001], three-quarters of the Cabinet is composed of Hutus. More than half the members of the Rwandan Armed Forces (police, army and prisons) are Hutu."[19]

Regarding the resignation of President Bizimungu, Gerald Gahima, the prosecutor general of the Supreme Court of Rwanda and the Rwandan representative to the United Nations Commission on Human Rights, had certain questions to ask: "What do you do with someone who chooses to resign? He chose to resign because he could not reach agreement with his colleagues in the RPF. Now if the political party in the accepted legal system decides not to have so and so as its president or he decides not to be its president what do you do to him? Do you allow somebody to hold a whole country to ransom?"[20]

Whether President Bizimungu's resignation was ethnically-related is difficult to establish, as it could have been linked to the issue of corruption. Government ministers have publicly warned that "the evil of corruption" has become a serious problem in the country. The National Assembly itself has been engaged in an ongoing effort to expose government corruption. In 1999 it summoned ministers to explain alleged misdeeds, and forced the resignations of three ministers.[21] In order to emphasise its commitment to ethnic harmony, the government passed an anti-discrimination law criminalising segregation among Rwandans in October 2001.[22]

The RPF and Human Rights Violations

There have been accusations of human rights violations levelled against the ruling RPF and former Rwandan Armed Forces (FAR) members before, during and after the genocide. After scrutinising all the sources at its disposal, the IPEP confirmed in its report that, indeed, both parties had committed human rights abuses.[23] The International Commission on Human Rights Abuses in Rwanda declared that the RPF was responsible for a number of serious human rights violations, starting with their 1990 invasion of Rwanda, which began the civil war. The Hutus consistently claim that the RPF soldiers have killed hundreds of thousands of Hutus in Rwanda in the past decade, constituting what they call a "second genocide". However, there is no hard evidence to justify this accusation.[24] A UN fact-finding commission has indicated the possibility of RPF forces being guilty of genocide in the DRC in 1997 – a notion that is today gaining credence.[25]

The RPF's determination to win the civil war resulted in the killing of many civilians. They sought to establish their control over the local population through numerous executions and wholesale massacres. Thousands of Hutus fled the advancing RPF troops, while many who remained were driven into refugee camps. Kagame, the first vice-president of the 1994 Government of National Unity, defended the RPF's actions on Radio Rwanda in late July 1994: "Harmful elements were hidden in bushes and banana plantations," he said. "Therefore a cleansing was necessary, especially to separate the innocent people from the killers."[26] The problem then and since, as both former president Bizumungu and President Kagame conceded in their meeting with the IPEP, is that it was not always easy to distinguish between "innocent" and "guilty" Hutus.

It is difficult to determine the extent of human rights violations by the RPF in Rwanda. From its evidence, Human Rights Watch believes the RPF may have killed tens of thousands of civilians between April and July 1994.[27] They also conclude that RPF abuses occurred so often and in such similar ways that they must have been directed by high level officers. "It is likely that these patterns of abuse were known to and tolerated by the highest levels of command of the RPF forces."[28] These findings are in stark contrast with the African Rights' assertion, two months after the conflict ended, that "no conflicting evidence has yet been produced to show that the RPF has a policy of systematic violence against civilians".[29] To complicate the subject further, another knowledgeable observer, Gerard Prunier, revised his own views on this issue between the first and second editions of his book *The Rwanda Crisis: History of a Genocide*. Prunier had initially agreed with Human Rights Watch estimates, yet after further research he concluded that the figures might be even greater than previously calculated.[30]

It has been held that some RPF human rights violations were in retaliation to atrocities committed by ex-FAR soldiers, by the armed group known as the Interahamwe and by their various allies. Examples of these atrocities include the abuse of Tutsi women in 1996, and attacks on schools and missionaries, as well as on witnesses called to the 1995 Arusha International Criminal Tribunal for Rwanda. In 1997–98, there was a major, organised insurgency in the northwest of the country, a full-scale military operation led by ex-FAR officers with close ties to the exiled Hutu leadership. Thousands of civilians were killed. Schools, health centres, bridges and municipal offices were all deliberately targeted as part of their strategy to paralyse government operations and demonstrate the RPF's incapacity to run the country.[31] The government responded to each of these attacks with its own reprisals and revenge killings.

The level of internal violence against civilians has decreased in the last few years, as the activities of the Interahamwe and counter-insurgency operations by the Rwandan military have increasingly been restricted to the eastern DRC.[32] However, a number of unarmed civilians have been killed, some by members of Rwandan security forces, others by armed opposition groups and yet others by unidentified assailants. Members of the Local Defence Forces (LDF), armed but unpaid and poorly trained civilian forces recruited to protect local communities, were also responsible for killing civilians and other abuses. In addition, some detainees who had been acquitted of genocide charges or conditionally released were killed.[33]

Beyond Rwanda itself, there is a quite separate, post-genocide history of human rights abuses by the RPF in the DRC. The Rwandan government became embroiled in the DRC due to the fact that tens of thousands of armed ex-FAR and Interahamwe forces had fled to that country after the genocide, where they established refugee camps. Government forces viewed the camps as launching pads for the armies of the Hutu Power movement to conduct raids across the border, kill Tutsis, co-operate with and incite local Hutus in Rwanda, destroy infrastructure and undermine confidence in the government so they could finish the "work" begun during the 100 days of the genocide.[34] President Mobutu Sese Seko's DRC government helped the ex-FAR soldiers to rearm and persistently refused to co-operate with the International Criminal Tribunal for Rwanda in apprehending and extraditing persons indicted for genocide.[35]

Time and again, RPF leaders insisted that if the international community failed to disarm ex-FAR forces, they would do so themselves. Kagame told an American journalist that he had travelled to Washington in August 1996 to meet with officials of the Clinton administration. "I was looking for a solution from them. They didn't come up with any answers, not even suggestions." A State Department official confirmed that Kagame had been unequivocal. If the UN did not dismantle the camps, "somebody else would have to do it".[36] Consequently, in October 1996, the Rwandan Patriotic Army (RPA), leading an informal coalition of groups that formed the anti-Mobutu Alliance, attacked the Hutu Power-dominated camps of eastern Zaire.

Rwanda's involvement in the DRC was further motivated by the plight of the Zairian Tutsis who had been supportive of the RPF after the 1990 invasion, providing recruits, weapons and money. Mobutu wanted to strip these ethnic Tutsis of their citizenship and drive them from the country.[37] This sparked the rebellion. Rwanda's government seized on the uprising as an opportunity to disband the Hutu refugee border camps and destroy the ex-FAR and Interahamwe forces. Gross human rights violations were clearly committed by both the RPA and the ex-FAR and Interahamwe forces.[38]

The RPF's Kagame has acknowledged that the Rwandan government planned and directed the rebellion that toppled Mobutu in 1997, while Rwandan troops and officers led the rebel forces.[39] Mobutu's overthrow did not stop Rwanda's engagement in the DRC. In August 1998, Rwanda supported a second military campaign in an attempt to topple the new president, Laurent Kabila. In response, Kabila incited his followers on Congolese state radio: "People must bring a machete, a spear, an arrow, a hoe, spades, rakes, nails, truncheons, electric irons, barbed wire, stones and the like, in order, dear listeners, to kill the Rwandan Tutsis."[40] The broadcast drove Congo's terrified Tutsis into hiding. The Rwandan government then accused Kabila of instigating genocide against the Tutsis in the DRC and providing rebel training for Rwandan Hutu rebels.

In 2000, the RPA and forces of the Rwandan-backed Congolese armed opposition groups, the Goma-based *Rassemblement congolais pour la démocratie* (RCD-Goma), Congolese Rally for Democracy, continued to control large areas of the eastern DRC. Units of both forces were responsible for widespread human rights abuses, in particular the murder of unarmed civilians and torture, including rape.[41] Torture and ill-treatment were routine in Rwandan and RCD-Goma detention centres, and numerous cases of "disappearance" were reported. Congolese human rights defenders and civil society activists were singled out by the Rwandan and RCD authorities for harassment and worse. Many suffered arbitrary arrest and unlawful detention.[42]

Rwanda claims the right to deploy forces inside the DRC (in particular in the Kivu and Katanga provinces) in pursuit of armed perpetrators. This could have long-term implications beyond any cease-fire. It involves the mining, expropriating and exporting of minerals from the DRC, including diamonds, gold and rare metals such as coltan or columbite-tantalite, used in the manufacture of computer chips, fibre optics, jet engines and mobile phones.[43] This engagement has sustained Rwanda's military co-operation with armed militia groups in the DRC such as the RPA and RCD, enabling President Kagame to refer to Rwanda's war in the DRC as "a self-sustaining war".[44]

Although the security situation inside Rwanda itself can be said to be fairly stable, various incidents were reported in 2001. In May, the RPA killed about 40 rebels of the Hutu extremist Interahamwe militia in the northwestern Ruhengeri area. According to Rwanda's Presidential Defence Advisor, Lt-Colonel Charles Kayonga, the rebels had fled from the war-torn DRC.[45] In June, a Rwandan army spokesman, Lt-Colonel Jean-Bosco Kazura, held that the Rwandan army had killed 150 rebels and captured 32 in "fierce battles" on 5 and 6 June.[46]

Attempts at Democratisation

Despite the setbacks to the creation of a peaceful environment, it may be argued that the Rwandan government has taken certain steps to bring about stability and democracy in the country. On 6 March 2001, Rwanda held communal (local, district) elections, although no political parties were allowed to contest the elections and campaigning was forbidden. The National Electoral Commission (NEC) reported that 98% of the electorate had registered to vote.[47] The UN Special Representative for Human Rights in Rwanda, Michel Moussali, described the elections as an important step in the country's democratic process. He stated that he was impressed by the massive turnout for the polls. Nearly 90% of adult Rwandans voted, although there are allegations that soldiers and civilian authorities used force and threats to compel people to vote.[48]

However, some observers did not view the process as genuinely "democratic". Peter Takirambudde, the Executive Director of the Africa Division of Human Rights Watch, argued, "This election has been flawed from the beginning, and those flaws far outweigh the few election-day irregularities that have been reported . . . Contests with a single contender are no contests at all."[49] The report further stated that in some sectors where more than one candidate ran, the balloting was expected to confirm choices that had been dictated by higher authorities. The Human Rights Watch criticism was countered by the Rwandan chairman of the NEC, who argued that the allegation was "so encompassing it left one speechless".and that "such generalisation had hidden agendas".[50]

Another observer, the International Crisis Group, applauded the NEC for supervising and delivering "superbly organised polls". Nonetheless, it held that the elections were far from satisfactory when assessed by normal democratic standards.[51]

The anti-government Rwandan diaspora organisation, Rally for the Return of Refugees and Democracy in Rwanda, branded the elections "non-free and unfair municipal elections under the new brand of tyranny known as the 'no party' system, imported to Rwanda from Uganda by the RPF".[52]

Democratisation in Rwanda will always be in dispute as long as there is an unelected national government. This sentiment was expressed explicitly by IPEP in its report: "It is not realistic to expect reconciliation so long as an unelected minority rules. Majority rule must be respected. No majority will forever accept minority rule. The government will not relinquish power unless minority rights are guaranteed and ironclad. A majority government that excludes or discriminates against a minority is not democratic."[53]

The government has postponed, for the second time, the national elections agreed to in the Arusha Accords. This, says Aloisea Inyumba, the head of the National Unity and Reconciliation Commission, is because the Arusha agreement had prevented the establishment of political parties for five years, but this date was subsequently extended by the Rwandan government for a further four years. The elections are now scheduled for 2003 – nine years after the genocide and the accession of the RPF. The high level of mistrust between political groupings continues. The tight political control exercised is partly explained by the fact that Rwanda remains a country at war. Although the Rwandan civil war has been largely exported to the DRC since 1994, the security threat is not only external. The ex-FAR and Interahamwe militias recruit inside Rwanda, and launch attacks across the border. Some segments of the population still share the Hutu Power ideology that exploded in 1994 into the campaign to exterminate the country's minority Tutsi population.[54]

There is much of the past that continues to contaminate the nation. It is seen in the mono-ethnic nature of the national armed forces. The autocratic tendency of the government has intensified the Hutu-Tutsi divide and impaired the restoration of law and order. The violent conflict between the Tutsi-led national army and the Hutu militias continues. One of the main threats to stability in Rwanda is the Hutu insurgency in the northwest of the country by people who are members of ex-FAR and Interahamwe militias. The rebels operate under the name of the Liberation Army of Rwanda (ALIR). Their political wing is known as the Armed People for the Liberation of Rwanda (PALIR). Their hit-and-run actions target Tutsi survivors of the genocide and local Hutu politicians, foreign human rights monitors and aid workers.[55] The military-led economic exploitation of minerals in the DRC by the Rwandan government simply adds fuel to these conflicts. The Rwandan and Great Lakes conflicts are complex and have no obvious short-term solutions.

The Historical Roots of Violence and Division

The Roots of the Genocide

A pertinent question is how a small political elite could have instigated such a vast section of the population to kill, maim and destroy their neighbours? Mahmood Mamdani's words are important in this regard: "If the violence from below could not have spread without cultivation and direction from above, it is equally true that the conspiracy of the tiny fragment of *genocidaires* could not have succeeded had it not found resonance from below . . . The response and initiative from below involved multitudes and presents the true dilemma of the Rwandan genocide."[56]

To begin to understand the violence, it needs to be situated within the categories and myths of Rwandan and more specifically colonial and postcolonial rule. The conflict is old, running through the pre-colonial, colonial and independence periods. It extends across the country's borders, where close ties and animosities link Rwandans and their neighbours. This said, the singular cause of the genocide is also a symptom, an expression of a contested history that continues to motivate violence. Moreover, an increasing number of analysts refuse the assumption that the roots of the conflict and genocide lie exclusively in the domain of racism, a position that has been used to obscure a number of ideological and structural dynamics in which race, ethnicity and power have intertwined and shifted over time. This does not deny that, against the backdrop of pre-colonial rivalry, tensions between Hutus and Tutsis owe much to the systems of discrimination and privilege that were brought and imposed by the colonial powers that occupied Rwanda.

Forerunners of the people who are now known as Hutus, Tutsis and Twas organised themselves in small groups based on lineage or loyalty to a leader. During the second half of the nineteenth century, Tutsi king Rwabugiri's administration (1860–95) imposed a harsh regime on the formerly semi-autonomous Tutsi and Hutu lineages through the confiscation of their land, which resulted in breaking their political power. Rwabugiri amplified feudal labour systems, in particular the *ubretwa*, which involved labour in return for access to land. This system was restricted to Hutu peasant farmers, exempting the Tutsis. Rwabugiri also manipulated social categories and introduced an "ethnic" differentiation between Hutus and Tutsis based on historical social positions. Tutsi was used to describe the status of a person rich in cattle. Tutsi became the term that referred to the elite group. Hutu was used to describe a subordinate or follower of a more powerful person. It was used to refer to the mass of ordinary people. Briefly stated, a social structure was already in place when the colonialists first arrived in Rwanda at the turn of the twentieth century.[57]

The colonialists entrenched, exploited and expanded this to their own advantage. The process began almost invisibly when Rwanda was awarded to the Germans at the Berlin Conference in 1885. It was a development about which no Rwandan, including the king, was so much as informed. For years the Rwandans lived as a colonised people, without even knowing it. Later, the Germans showed little interest in the colony, losing it to Belgium after World War I. The Belgians were different. They exploited the tribal demography of Rwanda, which is less complex than elsewhere and therefore easier to manipulate. The Congo, for example, has 300 tribes and Nigeria 250, while Rwanda consists of Hutu farmers (85%), Tutsi cattle owners (14%) and the Twa group (1%). Despite the porous nature of the ethnic divisions in Rwanda, which allowed for upward mobility and transition from one class to another, the Belgians viewed the Tutsis as an aristocratic people with a natural aptitude to rule. They identified them as "Europeans under a black skin", confirming the prevailing western belief in the inherent inequality of the races. They were appointed in large numbers to leading positions in the colonial administration, while the Hutus were entrenched as a class of workers and subsistence farmers.

Committed to maximising profit without serious regard for the Rwandan people, the Belgians aimed to reorganise the Rwandan state in the name of administrative efficiency. They eliminated the traditional hierarchies and regrouped the country into administrative "chiefdoms" and "sub-chiefdoms" of uniform size. They used force to install state officials in the autonomous enclaves, destroying the power of the heads of lineages and of local small states. The Belgians allowed the Tutsis to become administrative officials, which systematically removed Hutus from positions of power. The Hutus were excluded from higher education, which closed all possible career opportunities within the Belgian administration. This enabled the Belgians to impose a Tutsi monopoly of public life not just for the 1920s and 1930s, but for the next generation too.

It is important to recognise the complicated and shifting nature of race and ethnicity in Rwanda, dynamics that render it very difficult to isolate the exact causes of historical violence. In his recent analysis of the genocide, Mamdani argues that "Hutu and Tutsi have changed political identities along with the state that has enforced these identities". Mamdani's analysis culminates in an argument as to how Hutu were defined as "native" while Tutsi were held to be "alien". Moreover, he holds that the claim that there is "no difference" between Hutu and Tutsi has been historically aligned with Tutsi power while the view that there is a difference has fed the growth of Hutu power. The matter must be politically understood. Cultural identity is routed through forms of political development.[58]

Belgium continued its support of the Tutsis until the 1950s, when the socially privileged Tutsis began to see themselves not only as superior to the Hutus but equal to the Belgians. With this the colonisers shifted policy in favour of the Hutu majority, who won the first elections in 1962, with the Parmehutu Party receiving 78% of the vote and Grégoire Kayibanda being elected president. The new republican government continued to label all Rwandans as Hutus, Tutsis or Twas. The identity cards that had served to guarantee privileges to the Tutsis during Belgian rule, now served to discriminate against them in both employment and education.[59] Ethnic and political violence erupted and tens of thousands of Tutsis fled the country.

Over the following years, the Parmehutu leaders eliminated Hutu rivals as well as the once powerful Tutsis. In July 1973, General Juvénal Habyarimana established the Second Republic through a coup. Early on, the change seemed to portend a more inclusive Rwanda, particularly as Tutsis were "redefined" from being an alien race to an indigenous ethnicity. Then in 1975, Habyarimana turned Rwanda into a single-party state under the National Revolutionary Movement for Development – *Mouvement Revolutionnaire National pour le Développement* (MRND) – which Habyarimana ruled for 21 years until his death in a plane crash on 6 April 1994. For at least two-thirds of his presidency, the country was stable and relatively peaceful, although the Tutsis were not equal to the Hutus.

Under Habyarimana, identification cards, ethnic quotas and spheres of exclusive ethnic concentration remained hallmarks of Rwandan society. Power at every level was still monopolised by the Hutus. There was only a handful of Tutsi officers in the entire army, and officers were discouraged from marrying Tutsi women. Control was an obsession for the regime, and the fate awaiting those Rwandans who did not accept the rules was clear to all, which intensified the flight of Tutsis to neighbouring countries. Dissenters were few and far between, and the few nonconformists were subjected to arbitrary arrests, torture and long stretches in wretched prisons without benefit of trial. The justice system was independent in name only and press freedom was tightly controlled. Job loss was the price of speaking out.

Habyarimana was opposed to the mainly Tutsi exile community returning, claiming that Rwanda's economy was unable to sustain the large exiled community. By the late 1980s, the exile community had swelled to approximately 600 000 people. The majority lived in the countries surrounding Rwanda. In 1982, however, Uganda expelled thousands of refugees who returned to Rwanda only to be forced back across the border shortly after crossing. In 1986, the Rwandan authorities declared that the country was too overpopulated to permit the return of refugees. At a meeting in Washington in 1988, Rwandans in exile affirmed their right to return home, if necessary by force. The Rwandan government then formed a commission in 1989 to deal with the refugee problem. The commission met thrice with the Ugandan authorities in 1990, and appeared to be making some progress in clearing the way for refugees to return until the RPF proclaimed that its goals were not just to achieve the return of refugees, but to oust Habyarimana and establish a democratic government.

In the 1970s and 1980s, Habyarimana attracted substantial foreign assistance, which was used to construct an impressive infrastructure. The economy performed better than others in the region for the first decade. At the end of the 1980s, however, coffee prices dropped sharply. Coffee accounted for 75% of Rwanda's foreign exchange. In conjunction with the

1989 drought, which reduced harvests in the south and left substantial numbers of people short of food, the drop in coffee prices caused the economy to contract rapidly. The economic decline and increasing corruption within the Habyarimana government resulted in increasing demands for political reform, some of which were backed by donor nations who believed that political reform was necessary for economic progress. In July 1990, Habyarimana agreed to discuss change and announced that a national commission would be formed to examine the question of reform.[60] Rumours of a planned RPF attack circulated in both Uganda and Rwanda from mid-September 1990 as Rwanda embarked on reforming its political system.

The RPF Invasion and the Genocide

On 1 October 1990 the RPF invaded Rwanda to try to seize power. Civil violence erupted against the Tutsi minority and critics of the regime as RPF forces advanced.[61] A report by the UN Commission on Human Rights and an independent international commission of inquiry suggested that the killings portended genocide. Additional reports indicated that Hutu extremists were organising and arming themselves to massacre "internal enemies". The creation of death squads, death lists and hate propaganda provided warnings of a potential genocide. However, the UN Commission took little notice of their own and other reports.

The civil war which began with the 1990 offensive appeared to come to a halt in 1993. Under international pressure, Habyarimana's government and the RPF started negotiations in the town of Arusha in Tanzania, under the auspices of the OAU and Tanzania. The Arusha Accords provided for the establishment of a Broad Based Transitional Government (BBTG), the repatriation of refugees, the integration of all military forces into one national army and the holding of democratic elections in 1999.

The UN assumed formal responsibility for overseeing the implementation of the Arusha Accords, but failed to make adequate use of the OAU and local African states. As a consequence, there was a disjuncture between the mediation and implementation phases of the Accords, a gap that contributed to their failure. The Arusha Accords led to the exclusion of Hutu extremists from key positions within the BBTG and marginalised them in the political process. Hutu extremists within the government and the army refused to accept the power-sharing proposal and prepared to derail the negotiation process to retain their power and financial privilege.[62]

In the months preceding the genocide, many additional signs indicated that the implementation of the Arusha Accords was faltering and that massive violence was being planned. Unequivocal warnings reached the UN Secretariat in January regarding the planned coup, an assault on the UN forces to drive them out, provocations to resume the civil war and detailed plans for carrying out genocidal killings in the Rwandan capital. The UN Secretariat questioned the validity of the information, prepared no contingency plans for worst-case scenarios and failed to provide adequate guidance to the members of the Security Council.[63] Belgium withdrew its forces from the UN peace-keeping initiative after 10 Belgian soldiers were killed, and it also championed the total withdrawal of UN forces. The US, having lost 18 soldiers in Somalia in October 1993, was unwilling to participate in any new peace-keeping missions to Rwanda. It undermined any possibility of the UN Security Council authorising any serious intervention in Rwanda, either with or without US participation. France actively supported the Francophone Habyarimana regime's campaign against the Anglophone Tutsi "interlopers" from Uganda. France's chief contribution was the notorious *Opération Turquoise,* which established a safe zone in the southwest of Rwanda ostensibly for refugees fleeing the genocide, but which served as a corridor into Zaire (now the DRC) for the genocidal regime, soldiers and militia. "Not one country on Earth came to stop this thing. The western world provided me with nothing,"[64] lamented General Dallaire, head of the UN peace-keeping force at the time. Many hold that the intervention of Belgium, France and the US at the UN Security Council could have prevented or reduced the genocide. Nigeria's Permanent Representative to the UN, Ambassador Ibrahim Gambari, said: "Without a doubt, it was the Security Council, especially its most powerful members, and the international community as a whole, that failed the people of Rwanda in their gravest hour of need."[65]

The genocide itself began to unfold on 6 April 1994, after the downing of the aircraft that carried President Habyarimana. Speculation was rife as to whether Hutu extremists or the RPF shot it down. Whatever the cause, it was the trigger that unleashed the genocide. A major role in the events that followed was played by the Interahamwe militia, which consisted of young Hutu men armed with machetes and clubs. The RPF also stepped up its military campaign. The events of the "100 days" are well known, particularly what caused the bloodletting and how much of the situation was known by international actors. The killings were well planned in some cases. In others, the impetus to slaughter was based on suspicion. Between 800 000 and a million people were killed. Over two million people fled the country, leaving behind decimation and a nation split to the core. In July 1994, the RPF succeeded in defeating the government and its army, putting an end to the genocide. The Government of National Unity was established with Pasteur Bizimungu, a Hutu, as president. General Kagame, the mastermind of the civil war, took the key positions of vice-president and minister of defence. Several Hutu ministers resigned in late 1995, claiming that the new government was dominated by Tutsis and served Tutsi interests.

The cycle of violence did not end when the RPF came to power. A spate of killings occurred in November 1996 following the repatriation of some 600 000 refugees from the DRC, including ex-FAR and Interahamwe forces. The returnees attacked civilians and soldiers. The RPF responded by killing civilians, including Hutu refugee returnees, through counter-insurgency operations.[66]

The continuing conflict in Rwanda cannot be divorced from the racial and ethnic division that exists between the Hutus and the Tutsis. However, there are other factors that contribute to the civil war in Rwanda, each of which increases the complexity of the conflict.

First, the Tutsi and Hutu communities are far from homogeneous and united. Tutsi families returning to Rwanda included those who fled to neighbouring countries at the time of the genocide, those who left 35 years prior to the genocide and those born in exile. Many among them were setting foot on Rwandan soil for the first time. This has contributed to an almost new Tutsi people emerging in Rwanda after the war. The Hutus are also divided, particularly with respect to who did what during the genocide.[67]

Second, behind the ethnic strife between the Hutus and Tutsis lies a conflict over access to Rwanda's limited resources. As distribution has much to do with one's relationship to power, there is substantial tension around allocation of land, housing and employment.[68] Since the genocide, the Hutus have, in many instances, been marginalised politically and eco-nomically. Conflict over property has intensified. Tutsi exiles who returned to Rwanda after the new government came to power occupied the land and houses of Hutus who had fled Rwanda before the RPF offensive. The Tutsis justified their action by arguing that the land was stolen from them between 1959 and 1964. The Hutus who did not flee Rwanda continued to be subsistence farmers – while in many instances the land now for-mally belongs to Tutsi landowners and government agencies. The dynamic shows a significant resemblance to the colonial dynamic – a cycle of occupation, displacement and reoccupation that serves to fuel conflict. The Rwandan government has proposed a policy of recreating villages for the homeless. Although aimed at assisting all Rwandans, it is mostly Hutu refugee returnees and genocide survivors who inhabit the new settlements, a situation that threatens to fuel the kind of ghettoisation that has contributed to the ongoing tension.[69] Third, the history of Rwanda's involvement in the DRC (discussed earlier) continues to impact on the present.

In an effort to move the country beyond the genocide, the government has sought to downplay divisions by removing ethnic references from identity cards. Legislation entitles landowners to regain possession of their land – which has itself raised disputes about lawful ownership. Many Hutu landowners and business proprietors are afraid to reclaim their properties and government officials are accused of not doing enough to impose laws pertaining to ownership.[70]

The government has not done enough to broaden its political power base and promote power sharing. It has excluded political opponents from important political and judiciary positions, and has failed to hold national elections as promised. The government has, however, made efforts to build national unity and reconciliation within Rwanda. Some of the initiatives include the repatriation of refugees, the creation of a Commission of National Unity and Reconciliation and the formation of a National Human Rights Commission. Still, government officials have been accused of exploiting the genocide to get new homes and shares in the high-rise buildings being constructed in Kigali. As a consequence, many dismiss the government's reconciliation initiatives as little more than a sophisticated public relations exercise. Newspapers have exposed widespread practices of corruption, embezzlement, favouritism and illegal expropriation of land. Some Rwandans who are critical of government policies have fled Rwanda in fear of their lives, others have been imprisoned. The government insists that it seeks to promote democratic debate in the precarious context of a society that, according to Minister of Justice Jean de Dieu Mucyo, lives in the wake of a genocide that could reoccur.[71]

Prospects for Peace-building and the Promotion of Reconciliation

The Arusha Accords

Efforts to bring about peace in Rwanda can be traced back to the Arusha Accords of August 1993. Arusha was an African initiative in which both the OAU and several African states played a pivotal role. The former president of Tanzania, Julius Nyerere, was the facilitator of the process. Belgium, Germany, France and the US also participated, as well as the UN and the UN High Commission for Refugees. In a series of negotiations, the following issues were agreed upon: the establishment of the rule of law and a culture of human rights, power-sharing in all public institutions, the transitional arrangements that would lead to elections, the repatriation of refugees, the resettlement of internally displaced persons and the integration of the armies.[72]

When the RPF came to power in 1994, it prioritised power-sharing. Both the Hutus and the Tutsis were represented in government. But the resignation of the three top government officials in early 2000 raised many questions about the commitment of Kagame's government to implementing the Accords.[73] The possibility for power-sharing has also been challenged in connection with Tutsi and Hutu representation in the army and the judiciary.[74] There is great concern about the postponement of the general elections that were supposed to have taken place five years after the signing of the Arusha Accords.

In an endeavour to inculcate a culture of human rights, Rwanda has established the National Human Rights Commission. Some are sceptical about its ability to succeed. The Human Rights Watch has stated:

> It is too early to tell whether the Commission will function independently enough to help improve the situation of human rights in Rwanda. Given the strong governmental links of the majority of its members, it may prefer to work through personal contacts behind the scenes rather than through public criticism of abuses. While this may help resolve individual cases, it will do little towards developing real respect for human rights in Rwanda.[75]

However, Gasana Ndoba, the president of the Commission, reported to the Rwanda News Agency that the Commission has exposed cases of "illegal arrest and detention of suspects by state security agents" in its annual report. The report also criticised the Rwandan judicial system, citing cases of judges knowingly or unknowingly making decisions that infringe on the rights of aggrieved parties.[76]

As far as the resettlement of the internally displaced people and the repatriation of refugees are concerned, the USCR reported that more than 200 000 Rwandans were uprooted at the end of 2000, including some 150 000 who were internally displaced, and more than 55 000 refugees and asylum seekers who lived in a number of countries.[77] USCR also stated that nearly 10 000 Rwandans fled to Tanzania during 2000, joining 20 000 Rwandan refugees already living there. Sources gave different reasons why the new asylum seekers fled the country. Many who fled said they feared arbitrary arrests and abductions.[78] Some international observers, however, reported that Rwandans were fleeing drought or land disputes, or because they feared implementation of local judicial proceedings against genocide suspects by the newly installed *gacaca* community courts.

There are widely divergent estimates of the number of internally displaced Rwandans because various humanitarian and human rights agencies have used differing definitions of "displacement". Estimates range from as few as 3 000 to as many as 300 000. The wide discrepancy is partly due to the government's controversial policy of *villagisation*, which required up to 600 000 rural Rwandans – Hutus and Tutsis – to relocate into 180 or more newly established village sites since 1997.[79] Government officials argued that *villagisation* would ease land pressures in Africa's most densely populated country and enable residents to benefit from schools, health centres and other economic opportunities while maintaining access to nearby farmland. Critics charged that the relocation policy was a coercive security measure by the government.[80]

Approximately 25 000 Rwandan refugees were repatriated during 2000, including about 22 000 from the DRC and about 2 000 from Tanzania. Approximately 60 000 refugees have returned to Rwanda since 1999, virtually all of them Hutus.

The Lusaka Accords

The next important step in peace-making came with the Lusaka Accords, signed in 1999 by select representatives from the DRC, Rwanda, Zimbabwe, Angola, Namibia and Uganda. They were intended to partly redress some of the underlying dynamics that have continued to promote violence in Rwanda. The agreement contained several components reflecting the national, regional and international dimensions of the conflict.[81] The armed militias operating in the regions were seen to constitute major threats to their respective governments: ex-FAR and Interahamwe for Rwanda, FDD for Burundi, UNITA for Angola, and several that have used the DRC as a base against Uganda. None of these groups were part of the Accords, although all are associated with one or another of the signing governments.[82] Among other steps, the Accords require the governments to honour their commitment to disarm ex-FAR and Interahamwe allies in their countries, as a precondition for Rwanda abandoning its military activities in the DRC.

The Lusaka Accords have encountered problem after problem. Some signatories have accused each other of failing to comply with the terms. In a letter dated 13 July 2001, the DRC representative at the UN accused Rwanda and its rebel ally, RCD-Goma, of having a hidden agenda in the eastern DRC and of trying to "annexe" the territory.[83] A Rwandan permanent representative to the UN, Anastase Gasana, responded in a letter dated 9 August by saying that, "Launching such a virulent attack on two of the signatories to the Lusaka peace agreement on the basis of delusions of secession, constitutes a deliberate attempt to thwart the implementation of the Lusaka peace agreement that we all have signed voluntarily".[84] In brief, the Lusaka Accords have failed to deliver on their promises.

The International Criminal Tribunal

The UN established the International Criminal Tribunal for Rwanda (ICTR) in November 1994 in a further attempt to bring closure to the Rwandan conflict. In December 1994, Kagame argued that there could be no durable reconciliation as long as those who were responsible for the massacres were not properly tried. The ICTR, based in Arusha, Tanzania, is intended to prosecute those who were responsible for the genocide. Eight years after its creation and more than four years since the beginning of the first trial, the ICTR has handed down verdicts in only nine cases. There has been one acquittal and eight convictions. Of approximately 75 indicted suspects, 60 have been arrested.[85] Four of the alleged masterminds of the genocide, Colonel Théoneste Bagosora, Lt-Colonel Anatole Nsengiyumva, Major Aloys Ntabakuze and Brigadier-General Kabiligi, appeared before the ICTR on 22 April 2002. Some of the masterminds of the genocide, whether indicted by the ICTR or not (due to lack of evidence), are said to be walking free in many countries, including the DRC, Gabon, Kenya, France and Belgium.

With more than 800 employees, three trial chambers presided over by nine judges and a budget of around US$90 million, the performance of the ICTR is depicted by the International Crisis Group as "lamentable".[86] Between July 1999 and October 2000, the only substantial case heard was the trial of a single accused, Ignace Bagilishema, the former mayor of the village of Mabanza. Five judges out of nine have spent more than a year and a half without hearing a substantial case and one of them had managed by March 2001 to attain a record 28 months without hearing a substantial matter.

In 2000, an estimated 125 000 detainees were being held in Rwanda's detention centres and prisons. The majority were accused of participation in the genocide. Many had been held for years without trial or evidence against them. The overcrowding, poor hygiene and medical care, and insufficient food within the prisons had caused widespread disease and thousands of deaths. Torture and ill-treatment of detainees was widely alleged, especially in local detention centres and military sites.[87]

According to a report by the International Crisis Group, the ICTR does not seem to have much popular support.[88] Nevertheless, the report highlights the tribunal's achievement:

> It has provided indisputable recognition of the Rwandan genocide and has politically neutralised the "Hutu Power" movement's agenda of Tutsi extermination. However, seven years on, it has still not been able to shed light on the design, mechanisms, chronology, organisation and financing of the genocide, nor has it answered the key question: who committed the genocide?[89]

The tribunal has been accused of mismanagement and corruption. Consequently, in June 2001, the ICTR introduced a series of measures designed to prevent abuse of its legal aid system and to protect the integrity of its judicial system. The move followed the release in February 2001 of a report by a UN oversight committee which detailed alleged irregularities at the ICTR, including fee-splitting arrangements between some supposedly poverty-stricken clients and lawyers retained by the tribunal on their behalf.[90]

The Gacaca Community Courts

The genocide and massacres committed in Rwanda between 1 October 1990 and 31 December 1994 have left the country with major challenges. Eradicating impunity is a prerequisite for peaceful coexistence in the wake of the genocide. The enormity of the problem facing the judicial system and its activities in a country that desperately needs social cohesion means adapting procedural laws created for normal periods. This has given rise to the passing of Organic Law No. 8/96 of 30 August 1996.[91]

In an effort to relieve the burden of existing courts in dealing with alleged *genocidaires*, the Rwandan government introduced a court based on the *gacaca* community courts.[92] Derived from the Kinyarwanda words *gacaca* or *urucaca* or even *umucaca*, meaning a patch of grass usually under a tree where people meet to discuss or settle disputes between community members,[93] the word captures a sense of community participation in the sentencing and healing process. The *gacaca* court system is a system where the retributive (punitive) aspect of justice is less important than the reparatory (restitutive) function. While the classical justice system attempts to establish guilt or innocence, the participatory system aims to reconcile parties and, by appropriate compensation, (re)create the social harmony that preceded criminality.

Like other courts, the *gacaca* courts are guided by the principles that allow them to reach their goals. These principles can be summed up as follows: Firstly, *gacaca* court representatives must be honest individuals. They have to be elected by the population on the basis of their honesty or concern for justice. These elections were held on 4 October 2001. At least 90% of eligible voters cast their ballots to choose the judges and other officials who would serve in *gacaca* courts.[94] In terms of the legislation, *gacaca* court representatives will be replaced if they do not remain honest during their term of office. Second, the *gacaca* courts will have to prosecute individuals completely independently. For this reason, *gacaca* court members cannot hold certain posts. They cannot be officials of the state, political activists, soldiers or members of the national police, religious groups or non-governmental organisations. Independence is also assured through the secret nature of deliberations. Finally, as genocide trials are mainly based on evidence, the organic law includes provisions that punish individuals who refuse to give evidence regarding acts they saw, or individuals who give false evidence.[95]

Following the example of the organic law that currently serves as a framework for prosecuting and sentencing people suspected of having committed genocide and crimes against humanity, the new system categorises the perpetrators into four categories:

❑ Genocide planners, organisers, supervisors and those who oversaw the carrying out of these crimes or used their authority to incite the crimes. This category also includes notorious killers and individuals who committed acts of sexual torture and rape. Category one individuals will be tried and sentenced by common law courts and the ICTR. The *gacaca* system can only provide evidence and identify people belonging to this category.

❑ People suspected of being authors of voluntary homicides, serious attacks that resulted in the death of victims and authors of injuries or serious acts of violence committed with the intention of killing their victims. Accused individuals in this category will be prosecuted and sentenced by district *gacaca* courts. The accused can appeal against their sentence before provincial *gacaca* courts.

❑ People suspected of causing serious harm but without intending to cause the death of victims are in the third category. These people will be subject to trial by the *gacaca* courts. They can appeal to the *gacaca* courts of the appropriate district.

❑ People suspected of damaging property are in the fourth category.

These people will be allowed to appeal before *gacaca* courts of the appropriate area.[96]

All the *gacaca* courts have the power to conduct investigations, prosecute and try people classified in the categories under their authority. Moreover, they can prosecute and try people who neglect or refuse to give evidence about what they saw or what they know, as well as those who make false or slanderous denouncements.

The sentence applied by the *gacaca* courts will hinge on the category to which the accused belongs. Furthermore, the organic law on *gacaca* courts distinguishes different kinds of sentences within the same category, depending on whether the accused confesses or not. Thus, category two people will receive a prison sentence of 25 years to life if they choose to confess and plead guilty; 12 to 15 years if they only resort to confession after being accused during a trial; 7 to 12 years if they confess before the *gacaca* courts draw up the list of perpetrators of violations. The same system applies to category three people whose prison sentences range from five to seven years, from three to five years and from one to three years respectively.[97] Category four prisoners will only be sentenced to civil compensation for damages caused to the property of others. This option, created to punish any violation, will also allow the prisoner to return to society after a certain period provided the prisoner demonstrates that he or she has been rehabilitated.

Notwithstanding the aforementioned guidelines, serious questions have been raised regarding the capacity of *gacaca* to operate fairly and efficiently. Some survivors' groups have expressed fears that this mechanism amounts to a form of disguised amnesty. They are concerned that a category two suspect (a person guilty of intentional homicide or of a serious assault causing death) might confess and, as a consequence, be released after a short prison term. Fears have also been expressed that *gacaca* may be used to settle personal scores through some form of collusion between defendants and local inhabitants, especially in the rural areas with large Hutu majorities.[98]

Another area of concern is related to expertise and competence. Judges will be expected to understand complex legal issues, and without the benefit of legal training or legal argument they will be expected to distinguish between genuine and false testimonies. In addition, they will have to deal with the problems caused by the delays in the matters coming to trial, and the poor quality of dockets and witness statements, where these exist.[99] It is also a matter of concern that untrained judges will be expected to hand down heavy sentences, including life imprisonment. Observers have also expressed the concern that the accused in *gacaca* trials will not be allowed representation by defence counsel. Consequently, they contend that "this system would not conform to international standards of fairness".[100]

While acknowledging the deficiencies of the *gacaca* court system, Des Forges is essentially correct: "The system has flaws, but it provides the only real hope for trials in the foreseeable future for more than 100 000 persons now detained in inhumane conditions."[101] The IPEP agrees, while suggesting that: "speed and efficiency, important as they are, must also be accompanied by fairness. Basic human rights must not be sacrificed either to productivity or local participation."[102] This cardinal point was recognised in the Dakar Declaration, adopted in September 1999, following the Seminar on the Right to Fair Trial in Africa, organised by the African Commission on Human and Peoples' Rights: "It is recognised that traditional courts are capable of playing a role in the achievement of peaceful societies and exercise authority over a significant proportion of African countries. However, these courts also have serious shortcomings, which result in many instances in a denial of fair trial. Traditional courts are not exempt from the provisions of the African Charter relating to fair trial."[103]

The tensions inherent in the *gacaca* courts are captured in a story from the Gitarama province where Agnes was elected a judge. A Tutsi, she was married to a Hutu. Her family was murdered in 1994. Her husband was able to save her life, but was accused of taking part in the genocide and sent to jail after the new Tutsi government came to power. Agnes may see her husband, the man who saved her life, accused by her neighbours in a court of which she is part.[104] Such are the dilemmas that are part of this alternative to an established court system that, in the Rwandan situation, would take more than a century to deal with the cases of the accused in prisons across the country. Lin Rusekampunzi too is a judge in a *gacaca* court. In most countries, this 48-year-old mechanic would have been excluded from judicial service as being incapable of delivering objective judgement. Eight years ago roving gangs of killers killed his parents, his wife, their four children and nineteen other relatives. "How can people judge others when they have vengeance in their hearts?" asked a Hutu man. "In the first years I wanted revenge," Rusekampunzi responded. "But the fire has died down. If the people who killed my family admit they did wrong, I'll forgive them." The *gacaca* courts will never satisfy everyone, nor will they meet the demands of all their critics. And yet, according to Antoine Mugesera, president of the main survivors' group, *Ibuka* (which means "to remember"), most survivors support *gacaca* as a way of dealing with the past.[105]

Reconciliation

Initiatives to "reconcile" Rwandans are also being attempted through the work of local churches, indigenous women's organisations and some international aid agencies. However, "reconciliation" is a sensitive topic among those who continue to grieve and seek justice for the loss of loved ones. "Anybody wanting to intervene to make sure it [genocide] never happens again has to understand the attitudes . . . You cannot just talk to the adult generation about 'loving each other'," explained an aid official engaged in reconciliation work. A young member of the *Ibuka* told a South African visitor: "Reconciliation may work in South Africa. In Rwanda we need justice and time to bury our dead. We may then be able to consider reconciliation."[106] Reconciliation is a difficult word for many who have suffered. Unless seen as the *beginning* of a tentative process that can lead to a transformed and better future for victims and for the nation as a whole, it will be met with instinctive resistance. It is not about pretending that things were other than they were. It involves facing up to reality and doing what is possible to redress the past.

The failure of the Roman Catholic Church to acknowledge collective responsibility for the genocide has contributed to the lack of healing in Rwanda. "The Church continues to use the word 'reconciliation' but it has no substance," explains a Rwandan who managed to escape the genocide.[107] Many clerics were accessories to the genocide, including being active accomplices of the *genocidaires*, accusing Tutsi rebels of provoking the bloodshed and blaming the atrocities on "both sides". The Pope appealed for peace after the slaughter began, but failed to have his representatives in Rwanda pressurise the killers to stop their deadly work. The Rwandan government has repeatedly demanded a formal apology from the Vatican, but has not had any success. Many argue that it is not too late for the Church to apologise for its role in the genocide. This could constitute a major contribution to healing in the country.[108]

Overall, the attempt by government counsellors and district executives to embrace a spirit of "national unity and reconciliation" may contain risks. If it is used to constrict political freedom and vigorous dissent, the RPF risks eroding the very foundations of its own policies and dampening hopes for Rwanda's recovery. Rwandans have shown, for example, by their acceptance of community development committees, that they are willing to take over management of their own communities when given the opportunity, training and resources. The power of internal security services and the monolithic political control in the name of national goals need to be relaxed. Government opponents are being driven out of the country, fuelling the external threat that the government seems to fear most.[109] The crucial challenge facing Rwanda today concerns the continuing struggle over the meaning and legacy of the genocide. The RPF demands that the genocide be recognised as the defining event in Rwandan history. Conversely, Hutu radicals refuse to acknowledge that there even was a genocide.[110] The RPF leaders sometimes claim that anywhere between one and three million Hutus directly or indirectly participated in the genocide. The implication is that all Hutus are *genocidaires* and all Tutsis are potential victims. From the Hutu perspective, this assertion means that all Tutsis are potential revenge-seekers. Perhaps, "the notion of collective guilt is the principal obstacle to national reconciliation".[111] Unless agreement is first reached on this basic premise, it may be argued that no peace will ever come to the soul of what remains a deeply troubled country.

The major internal challenge facing Rwanda is the need for democratic elections. For this to happen a new level of inter-ethnic trust needs to develop. The fear of democracy degenerating into tribal politics continues to persuade many an African leader to favour a one-party state. The Tutsis fear that democracy could lead to a revival of Hutu power. The Hutu fear that the absence thereof will mean continued subjugation. To quote Mamdani, "After 1994, the Tutsi want justice above all else, and the Hutu democracy above all else. The minority fears democracy. The majority fears justice. The minority fears that democracy is a mask for finishing an unfinished genocide. The majority fears the demand for justice is a minority ploy to usurp power forever."[112] Future options for peace are likely to be determined by how these fears are negotiated and assuaged.

Related to this internal challenge is the external reality of the military involvement of Rwanda in the DRC. This is most forcibly symbolised in a recent case filed at the International Court of Justice in The Hague in which the DRC accused Rwanda of "genocide against more than 3.5 million people" in the DRC by engaging in "killing, slaughter, rape, throat-slitting and crucifying" in South Kivu and Katanga Orientale provinces. The Rwandan Special Envoy for the DRC, Patrick Mazimhaka, has denied these charges, saying that Rwanda has no case to answer, and arguing that the people in question have died of neglect, poverty and disease.[113] As recognised in the Lusaka Accords, national conflicts have the most severe implications for other countries in the region. There can be no lasting peace in any one country without addressing the challenges of the region.

It is in this context that the signing of the peace pact between Rwanda and the Democratic Republic of the Congo on 30 July 2002 must be viewed as a vital first step in the restoration of peace in the Great Lakes region.[114] The agreement is the culmination of the talks that began on 18 July 2002 between President Kabila and President Kagame at the naugural summit of the African Union. Central to those discussions – brokered by the South African President, Thabo Mbeki – was the proposal to create a security zone along the DRC-Rwanda border to prevent Hutu rebel incursions into Rwanda.

In terms of the agreement, the DRC undertook to round up, disarm and repatriate Rwandan Hutu rebels based in the east of the DRC within 90 days – by 27 October 2002. Rwanda, in turn, agreed to withdraw some 20 000 troops from DRC soil within the same time limit.[115] The pact was criticised by some as being unrealistic both in terms of timelines and scope. Clearly, there were problems with the pact, not least regarding the need for all foreign troops to be withdrawn and all armed groups to co-operate. However, the pact clearly represented the best chance for peace in the region for decades. In the words of a leading analyst, "it simply must be made to work".

NOTES

1 Amnesty International, "Civilians Trapped in Armed Conflict, 19 December 1997." Reprinted at www.amnesty.org (accessed 7 November 2000); "Ending the Silence, 25 September 1997." Reprinted at www.amnesty.org (accessed 7 November 2000); "Alarming Resurgence of Killings, 12 August 1996." Reprinted at www.amnesty.org (accessed 7 November 2000); "The Hidden Violence: 'Disappearances' and Killings Continue, June 1998." Reprinted at www. amnesty.org (accessed 7 November 2000).

2 "UN could have stopped Rwandan genocide," *The Sunday Independent*, 23 June 2002.

3 Jeff Drumtra, "Life after Death: Suspicion and Reintegration in Post-genocide Rwanda." Reprinted at http://129.41.41.28/world/articles/rwanda_wrs98.htm (accessed 27 November 2001).

4 OAU, "IPEP to Investigate the 1994 Genocide and the Surrounding Events." Reprinted at www.oau-oua.org/document/ipep/report/rwanda-e/EN-17-CH.htm (accessed 22 November 2001).

5 OAU, "IPEP to Investigate the 1994 Genocide and the Surrounding Events."

6 Ibid.

7 World Bank Group, "Rwanda: Country Assistance Strategy – Progress Report, June 1999." Reprinted at www.worldbank.org/pic/cas/cpin21.htm (accessed 27 November 2001).

8 OAU, "IPEP to Investigate the 1994 Genocide and the Surrounding Events."

9 Ibid.

10 United States Committee for Refugees, "Country Information: Rwanda."

Reprinted at http://129.41.41.28/world/countryrpt/africa/rwanda.htm (accessed 27 November 2001).

11 Amnesty International, "Amnesty International Report 2001: Rwanda." Reprinted at www.web.amnesty.org/web/ar2001.nsf/webafrcoun (accessed 23 November 2001).

12 Human Rights Watch, "The Search for Security and Human Rights Abuse, April 2000." Reprinted at www.hrw.org/reports/2000/rwanda (accessed 21 November 2001).

13 Integrated Regional Information Network (IRIN), "Rwanda: Premier Resigns, 28 February 2000." Reprinted at www.irinnews.org/report.asp (accessed 21 November 2001).

14 Reliefweb, "IRIN-CEA Weekly Round-up 12 Covering the period 18–24 March 2000: Rwanda: President Resigns." Reprinted at www.reliefweb.int/w/rwb.nsf/s (accessed 28 November 2001).

15 OAU, "IPEP to Investigate the 1994 Genocide and the Surrounding Events."

16 Human Rights Watch, "Human Rights World Report 2001: Rwanda: Human Rights Developments." Reprinted at www.hrw.org/wr2k1/africa/rwanda.html (accessed 28 November 2001).

17 OAU, "IPEP to Investigate the 1994 Genocide and the Surrounding Events: Chapter 23." It is important to note that the findings of the IPEP report were described as "biased" by the Rwandan government. See IRIN, "Rwanda: Government Condemns OAU Genocide Report, 18 September 2000." Reprinted at www.irin-news.org/report.asp (accessed 23 November 2001).

18 OAU, "IPEP to Investigate the 1994 Genocide and the Surrounding Events: Chapter 23."

19 Charles Villa-Vicencio and Tyrone Savage, eds., *Rwanda and South Africa in Dialogue: Addressing the Legacies of Genocide and a Crime Against Humanity* (Cape Town: IJR, 2001), 93.

20 Ibid, 95.

21 IRIN, "Rwanda: Meeting Tackles Corruption, 18 January 2000." Reprinted at www.irinnews.org/report.asp (accessed 21 November 2001).

22 IRIN, "Parliament Passes Anti-discrimination Law, 24 October 2001." Reprinted at www.irinnews.org/report.asp (accessed 21 November 2001).

23 OAU, "IPEP to Investigate the 1994 Genocide and the Surrounding Events: Chapter 22."

24 Gerard Prunier, *The Rwanda Crisis: History of a Genocide* (Columbia: Columbia University Press, 1997), 339.

25 OAU, "IPEP to Investigate the 1994 Genocide and the Surrounding Events: Chapter 23."

26 Ibid: Chapter 22.

27 Alison Liebharsky Des Forges, "Leave None to Tell the Story: Genocide in Rwanda." Reprinted at www.hrw.org/reports/1999/rwanda (accessed 27 November 2001).

28 Ibid.

29 OAU, "IPEP to Investigate the 1994 Genocide and the Surrounding Events: Chapter 22."

30 Prunier, *The Rwanda Crisis*, Chapter 10.

31 OAU, "IPEP to Investigate the 1994 Genocide and the Surrounding Events: Chapter 22."

32 Amnesty International, "Amnesty International Report 2001: Rwanda."

33 Ibid.

34 OAU, "IPEP to Investigate the 1994 Genocide and the Surrounding Events: Chapter 20"; also see Gerald Gahima, "Genocide: Its Unique and Common Identity," in *Rwanda and South Africa in Dialogue*, eds. Charles Villa-Vicencio and Tyrone Savage (Cape Town: IJR, 2001), 21.

35 Human Rights Watch, "Human Rights Watch World Report 1998: Democratic Republic of Congo (Formerly Zaire): Human Rights Developments." Reprinted at www.hrw.org/worldreport/Africa-04.htm (accessed 29 November 2001).

36 OAU, "IPEP to Investigate the 1994 Genocide and the Surrounding Events: Chapter 20."

37 Human Rights Watch, "Human Rights Watch World Report 1998: Democratic Republic of Congo."

38 OAU, "IPEP to Investigate the 1994 Genocide and the Surrounding Events: Chapter 22."

39 John Pomfret, "Rwanda Admits to Toppling Mobutu." Reprinted at www.mg.co.za (accessed 11 July 1997).

40 *The Mail and Guardian*, "No peace without security for Tutsis, 21 August 1998." Reprinted at www.mg.co.za (accessed 15 January 2000).

41 Amnesty International, "Amnesty International Report 2001: Rwanda."

42 Human Rights Watch, "Human Rights Watch Report 2001: Rwanda: Human Rights Developments."

43 See Tyrone Savage, "To Protect or to Profit? An Inquiry into the *Logique de Guerre* of Rwanda's War in the Congo," unpublished paper.

44 United Nations Security Council, "Report of the Security Council Mission to the Great Lakes Region," 15–26 May 2001, S/2001/521; par. 114.

45 IRIN, "Rwanda: Army kills 40 rebels, 23 May 2001." Reprinted at www.irinnews.org/report.asp (accessed 23 November 2001).

46 IRIN, "Rwanda: Heavy Fighting in Northwest as Militiamen kill Gorilla, 7 June 2001." Reprinted at www.irinnews.org/report.asp (accessed 23 November 2001).

47 IRIN, "Rwanda: Kagame Lauds 'Significant Step for Democratisation,' 7 March 2001." Reprinted at www.irinnews.org/report.asp (accessed 19 November 2001).

48 Jeremy Sarkin, "Promoting Justice, Truth and Reconciliation in Transitional Societies: Evaluating Rwanda's Approach in the New Millennium of Using Community Based Gacaca Tribunals to Deal with the Past." *International Law Forum* 2 (2000): 112–21.

49 Human Rights Watch, "No Contest in Rwandan Elections: Many Local Officials Run Unopposed." Reprinted at www.hrw.org/press/2001/03/rwanda0309.htm (accessed 19 November 2001).

50 IRIN, "Rwanda: Election Chairman Defends Local Polls, 13 March 2001." Reprinted at www.irinnews.org/report.asp (accessed 19 November 2001).

51 International Crisis Group, "Consensual Democracy in Post Genocide Rwanda: Evaluating the March 2001 District Elections." Reprinted at www.crisisweb.org/projects/showreport.cfm?reportid=453 (accessed 19 November 2001).

52 IRIN, "Rwanda: Diaspora Body Rejects 'No Party Elections,' 8 March 2001." Reprinted at www.irinnews.org/report.asp (accessed 19 November 2001).

53 OAU, "IPEP to Investigate the 1994 Genocide and the Surrounding Events: Chapter 23."

54 International Crisis Group, "Consensual Democracy in Post Genocide Rwanda."

55 Monique Mekenkamp, Paul van Tongeren and Hans van de Veen, eds., *Searching*

for Peace in Africa: An Overview of Conflict Prevention and Management Activities (Utrecht: European Platform for Conflict Prevention and Transformation, 1999).

56 Mahmood Mamdani, *When Victims Become Killers: Colonialism, Nativism and the Genocide in Rwanda* (Princeton: Princeton University Press, 2001), 7.

57 IRIN, "Lessons from the Rwandan Experience: Historical Perspective," *Journal of Humanitarian Assistance*. Reprinted at www-jha.sps.cam.ac.uk/policy/pb025c.htm (accessed 8 November 2000).

58 Mamdani, *When Victims Become Killers*.

59 Prunier, *The Rwanda Crisis*.

60 OAU, "IPEP to Investigate the 1994 Genocide and the Surrounding Events: Chapter 4."

61 Jean-Paul Kimonyo, "The Rwandan Experience," in *Rwanda and South Africa in Dialogue*, eds. Charles Villa-Vicencio and Tyrone Savage, 36.

62 Mekenkamp et al., *Searching for Peace in Africa*.

63 OAU, "IPEP to Investigate the 1994 Genocide and the Surrounding Events: Chapter 15."

64 "UN could have stopped Rwandan Genocide." *The Sunday Independent*, 23 June 2002.

65 Ibrahim Gambari, "Guns over Kigali: A Review Article on the Rwandan Genocide." *West Africa* 19 (1998): 747.

66 Gerard Prunier, "Rwanda: The Social, Political and Economic Situation." Reprinted at www.unhcr.ch/refworld/country/writenet/menu.htm (accessed 8 July 1997).

67 Gerard Prunier, "Rwanda: Update to End of February 1998." Reprinted at www.unhcr.ch/refworld/country/writenet/menu.htm (accessed 10 March 1998).

68 Mekenkamp et al., *Searching for Peace in Africa*.

69 Jeremy Sarkin, "The Necessity and Challenges of Establishing a Truth and Reconciliation Commission in Rwanda." *Human Rights Quarterly* 21 (1999): 667–823.

70 Drumtra, "Life after Death: Suspicion and Reintegration in Post-genocide Rwanda."

71 South Africa-Rwanda Dialogue, February 2001.

72 OAU, "IPEP to Investigate the 1994 Genocide and the Surrounding Events: Chapter 8."

73 Amnesty International, "Amnesty International Report 2001: Rwanda"; IRIN, "Rwanda: Premier resigns, 28 February 2000"; Reliefweb, "IRIN-CEA Weekly Round-up 12 covering the period 18–24 March 2000: Rwanda: President resigns."

74 OAU, "IPEP to Investigate the 1994 Genocide and the Surrounding Events: Chapter 23."

75 Human Rights Watch, "Protectors or Pretenders: Government Human Rights Commissions in Africa." Reprinted at http://store.yahoo.com/hrwpubs/protorpretgo.html (accessed 10 September 2001).

76 IRIN, "Rwanda: National Human Rights Group Opens Provincial Offices, 10 July 2001." Reprinted at www.irinnews.org/report.asp (accessed 23 November 2001).

77 United States Committee for Refugees, "Country Information: Rwanda."

78 Ibid.

79 Ibid; Human Rights Watch, "Human Rights Watch Report 2001: Rwanda: Human Rights Developments."

80 Human Rights Watch, "Human Rights Watch Report 2001: Rwanda: Human Rights Developments."

81 OAU, "IPEP to Investigate the 1994 Genocide and the Surrounding Events: Chapter 20."

82 Ibid, Chapter 20.

83 IRIN, "Rwanda: DRC Undermines Lusaka Peace Agreement – Rwanda Envoy, 24 July 2001." Reprinted at www.irinnews.org/report.asp (accessed 23 November 2001).

84 Ibid; IRIN, "Rwanda: Government Responds to DRC claims, 13 August 2001." Reprinted at www.irinnews.org/report.asp (accessed 23 November 2001).

85 International Criminal Tribunal for Rwanda, "Press Briefing by the ICTR Spokesman, Arusha 25 March 2002." Reprinted at www.ictr.org/wwwroot/ENGLISH/pressbrief/2002/brief9-13-21.htm (accessed 20 June 2002).

86 International Crisis Group, "International Criminal Tribunal for Rwanda"; IRIN, "ICTR's Performance is 'Lamentable,' think tank says, 8 June 2001." Reprinted at www.irinnews.org/report.asp (accessed 23 November 2001).

87 Sarkin, "The Necessity and Challenges of establishing a Truth and Reconciliation Commission."

88 International Crisis Group, "International Criminal Tribunal for Rwanda."

89 Ibid.

90 IRIN, "Rwanda: New ICTR Rules Intended to Curb Abuses, 18 June 2001." Reprinted at www.irinnews.org/report.asp (accessed 23 November 2001).

91 Jean de Mucyo, "Gacaca Courts and Genocide," in *Rwanda and South Africa in Dialogue: Addressing the Legacies of Genocide and a Crime Against Humanity*, eds. Charles Villa-Vicencio and Tyrone Savage, 49.

92 IRIN, "Rwanda: Gacaca Courts Ruled Constitutional, 16 February 2001." Reprinted at www.irinnews.org/report.asp (accessed 19 November 2001).

93 De Mucyo, "Gacaca Courts and Genocide," 50.

94 IRIN, "Rwanda: 90 Percent of Electorate Vote for Traditional Judges, 5 October 2001." Reprinted at www.irinnews.org/report.asp (accessed 19 November 2001).

95 De Mucyo, "Gacaca Courts and Genocide," 49f; Jeremy Sarkin, "Gacaca Courts and Genocide," in *Rwanda and South Africa in Dialogue: Addressing the Legacies of Genocide and a Crime Against Humanity*, eds. Charles Villa-Vicencio and Tyrone Savage, 54f.

96 De Mucyo, "Gacaca Courts and Genocide," 51.

97 Ibid, 52.

98 OAU, "IPEP to Investigate the 1994 Genocide and the Surrounding Events: Chapter 18."

99 Sarkin, "Gacaca Courts and Genocide," 80.

100 Amnesty International, "Amnesty International Report 2001: Rwanda."

101 Human Rights Watch, "Rwanda: Elections May Speed Genocide Trials: But New System Lacks Guarantees of Rights, 4 October 2001." Reprinted at www.hrw.org/press/2001/10/rwanda1004.htm (accessed 6 December 2001).

102 OAU, "IPEP to Investigate the 1994 Genocide and the Surrounding Events: Chapter 18."

103 Sarkin, "Gacaca Courts and Genocide," 82.

104 "Justice on the Grass," *The Economist*, 8–14 June 2002.

105 *The Sunday Independent*, 2 June 2002.

106 Kigali, June 2000.

107 Kigali, June 2000.

108 Prunier, *The Rwanda Crisis*.

109 International Crisis Group, "Consensual Democracy in Post Genocide Rwanda:

Evaluating the March 2001 District Elections."

110 OAU, "IPEP to Investigate the 1994 Genocide and the Surrounding Events: Chapter 23."

111 Ibid.

112 Mahmood Mamdani, *When Does a Settler Become a Native?: Reflections on the Colonial Roots of Citizenship in Equatorial and South Africa* (Cape Town: University of Cape Town, 1998).

113 IRIN, "Rwanda Accused of Genocide Against 3.5 Million People, 30 May 2002." Reprinted at www.irinnews.org/report.asp (accessed 24 June 2002).

114 Mariette le Roux, "DRC and Rwanda take first step to peace," *Independent Online*, 30 July 2002. Reprinted at www.iol.co.za (accessed 31 July 2002).

115 Ofeibea Quist-Arcton, "Kabila and Kagame Sign Ambitious Congo Peace Deal." Reprinted at http://allafrica.com/stories/200207300621.html (accessed 31 July 2002).

RESOURCES

Books, Articles, Media Reports

De Mucyo, Jean. "Gacaca Courts and Genocide." In *Rwanda and South Africa in Dialogue: Addressing the Legacies of Genocide and a Crime Against Humanity*, edited by Charles Villa-Vicencio and Tyrone Savage. Cape Town: IJR, 2001.

Des Forges, Alison Liebharsky. "Leave None to Tell the Story: Genocide in Rwanda." Reprinted at www.hrw.org/reports/1999/rwanda (accessed 27 November 2001).

Dorsey, Learthen. *Historical Dictionary of Rwanda*. London: Scarecrow Press, 1994.

Drumtra, Jeff. "Life after Death: Suspicion and Reintegration in Post-genocide Rwanda." Reprinted at http://129.41.41.28/world/articles/rwanda_wrs98.htm (accessed 27 November 2001).

Franche, Dominique. "There's Only One Ethnic Group in Rwanda: Rwandan." *Le Monde Diplomatique/The Guardian Weekly*, 24 November 1996.

Gambari, Ibrahim. "Guns over Kigali: A Review Article on the Rwandan Genocide." *West Africa* 19 (1998).

Gourevitch, Philip. *We Wish to Inform You that Tomorrow we will be Killed with our Families: Stories from Rwanda*. New York: Farrar, Straus, and Giroux, 1998.

Heusch, Luc de. "Rwanda: Responsibilities for Genocide." *Anthropology Today* 11 (1995). *The Mail and Guardian*, "No peace without security for Tutsis, 21 August 1998." Reprinted at www.mg.co.za (accessed 15 January 2000).

Mamdani, Mahmood. *Citizen and Subject: Contemporary Africa and the Legacy of Late Colonialism*. Princeton: Princeton University Press, 1996.

———. *When Does a Settler Become a Native?: Reflections on the Colonial Roots of Citizenship in Equatorial and South Africa*. Cape Town: University of Cape Town, 1998.

———. *When Victims Become Killers: Colonialism, Nativism and Genocide in Rwanda*. Princeton: Princeton University Press, 2001.

McGreal, Chris. "Chaos at Genocide Tribunal, 14 February 1997." Reprinted at www.mg.co.za (accessed 14 September 2001).

Mekenkamp, Monique, Paul van Tongeren and Hans van de Veen, eds. *Searching for Peace in Africa: An Overview of Conflict Prevention and Management Activities*. Utrecht: European Platform for Conflict Prevention and Transformation, 1999.

Pomfret, John. "Rwanda Admits to Toppling Mobutu." Reprinted at www.mg.co.za (accessed 11 July 1997).

Prunier, Gerard. *The Rwanda Crisis: History of a Genocide*. Columbia: Columbia University Press, 1997.

———. "Rwanda: The Social, Political and Economic Situation." Reprinted at www.unhcr.ch/refworld/country/writenet/menu.htm (accessed 8 July 1997).

———. "Rwanda: Update to End of February 1998." Reprinted at www.unhcr.ch/refworld/country/writenet/menu.htm (accessed 10 March 1998).

Reyntjens, Filip. "Rwanda: Background to a Genocide." *Bulletin des Séances de l'Académie Royale d'Outre-Mer* 41 (1995): 281–92.

Sarkin, Jeremy. "The Necessity and Challenges of Establishing a Truth and Reconciliation Commission in Rwanda." *Human Rights Quarterly* 21 (1999): 667–823.

———. "Promoting Justice, Truth and Reconciliation in Transitional Societies: Evaluating Rwanda's Approach in the New Millennium of Using Community

Based Gacaca Tribunals to Deal with the Past." *International Law Forum* 2 (2000): 112–21.

———. "Gacaca Courts and Genocide." In *Rwanda and South African Dialogue: Addressing the Legacies of Genocide and a Crime Against Humanity*, edited by Charles Villa-Vicencio and Tyrone Savage. Cape Town: IJR, 2001.

Uvin, Peter. *Violence, Aid and Conflict: Reflections from the Case of Rwanda*. Helsinki: United Nations University and World Institute of Development Economics Research, 1996.

———. *Aiding Violence: The Development Enterprise in Rwanda*. West Hartford, CT: Kumarian Press, 1998.

Government, Intergovernmental Bodies, Political Parties

International Panel of Eminent Personalities (IPEP) was established under the banner of the OAU to investigate the 1994 genocide in Rwanda and the surrounding events: http://www.oau-oua.org/document/ipep/ipep.htm

Organisation of African Unity (OAU) was established on 25 May 1963 to promote the unity and solidarity of African states; defend sovereignty of members; eradicate all forms of colonialism; promote international co-operation having due regard for the Charter of the UN and the Universal Declaration of Human Rights; co-ordinate and harmonise member states' economic, diplomatic, educational, health, welfare, scientific and defence policies: http://www.oau-oua.org

Rally for the Return of Refugees and Democracy in Rwanda (RDR) is an anti-government Rwandan diaspora organisation: http://www.rdrwanda.org

Rwandan Patriotic Front (RPF) is the ruling party in Rwanda

International NGOs

Amnesty International provides reports and news about human rights practices in Rwanda: http://www.amnesty.org

Human Rights Watch is an independent non-governmental organisation, supported by individuals and foundations worldwide to prevent discrimination, uphold political freedom, protect people from inhumane conduct in wartime and to bring offenders to justice: www.hrw.org

Integrated Regional Information Network (IRIN) is part of the UN Office for the Coordination of Humanitarian Affairs: http://www.irinnews.org

International Crisis Group (ICG) is a private multinational organisation committed to strengthening the capacity of the international community to anticipate, understand and act to prevent and contain conflict: http://www.crisisweb.org

Reliefweb is a project of the United Nations Office for the Coordination of Humanitarian Affairs: http://www.reliefweb.int/w/rwb.nsf

United States Committee for Refugees was established in 1958 to help refugees get the protection and assistance they need to survive: http://129.41.41.28/world/countryrpt/africa/rwanda.htm

World Bank Group is one of the world's largest sources of development assistance: http://www.worldbank.org

Rwanda Country Information

Geography
Location: Central Africa, east of the Democratic Republic of the Congo.
Cities: *Capital*: Kigali (est. pop. 236 000). *Other cities:* Gitarama, Butare, Ruhengeri, Gisenyi.

People
Nationality: *Noun:* Rwandan. *Adjective:* Rwandan.
Population (1997 est.): 7 600 000.
Population growth rate: Over 3%.
Ethnic groups: Hutus 85%, Tutsis 14%, Twas 1%.
Religions: Christian 80%, traditional African 10%, Muslim 10%.
Languages: French, English, Kinyarwanda.
Education: *Years compulsory:* 6. *Attendance:* 70% (prewar). *Literacy:* 50%.
Health: *Infant mortality rate:* 123/1 000. *Life expectancy:* 50 years. *HIV infection rate:* 12.75%.
Workforce: Agriculture: 92%. Industry and commerce, services and government: 8%.

Economy
GDP (1996 est.): 425 billion Rwandan francs.
GDP real growth rate (1996 est.): 13%.
Per capita income (1997 est.): $234.
Inflation rate (1996 est.): 9%.
Natural resources: Cassiterite, wolfram, methane.
Agriculture (1996 est.): 35% of GDP. *Products:* coffee, tea, cattle, hides and skin, pyrethrum. *Arable land:* 48%, 90% of which is cultivated.
Industry (1996 est.): 17% of GDP. *Types:* beer production, soft drink, soap, furniture, shoes, plastic goods, textiles, cigarettes, pharmaceuticals.
Trade (1996 est.): *Exports:* $68 million: coffee, tea, hides and skins, cassiterite, pyrethrum. *Major markets:* Germany, Belgium, Netherlands, Pakistan. *Imports:* $275 million: food, consumer goods, capital equipment, petroleum products. *Major suppliers:* Belgium, US, Tanzania, Kenya, France.
Official exchange rate: Approx. 300 Rwandan francs = $1 (fluctuates daily).

Military
Military expenditure: Dollar figures: $92 million (FY99).
Military expenditure: Percent of GDP: 3.8% (FY99).

Demographic information is drawn from that compiled by the United States Department of State. See http://www.state.gov/r/pa/ei/bgn

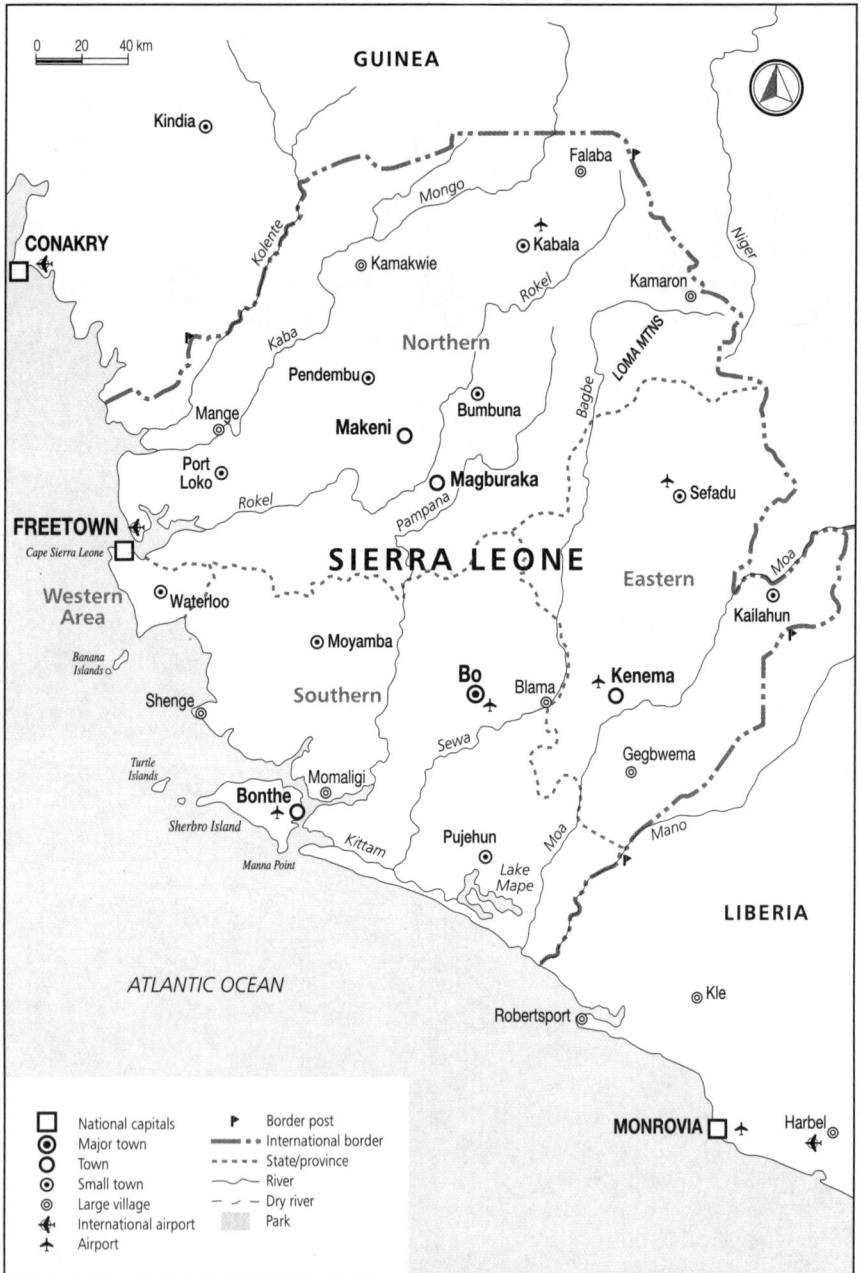

Map of Sierra Leone

0   20   40 km

GUINEA

Kindia

CONAKRY

Falaba

Kabala

Kamakwie

Kamaron

Kolente

Mongo

Rokel

Niger

Northern

LOMA MTNS

Pendembu

Bumbuna

Bagbe

Mange

Makeni

Magburaka

Port Loko

Sefadu

Kaba

Rokel

Pampana

FREETOWN

Cape Sierra Leone

SIERRA LEONE

Eastern

Western Area

Waterloo

Moyamba

Bo

Blama

Kenema

Kailahun

Moa

Banana Islands

Shenge

Southern

Sewa

Gegbwema

Turtle Islands

Momaligi

Bonthe

Sherbro Island

Manna Point

Kittam

Pujehun

Lake Mape

Moa

Mano

LIBERIA

ATLANTIC OCEAN

Kle

Robertsport

MONROVIA

Harbel

□ National capitals
◉ Major town
○ Town
◉ Small town
◎ Large village
✈ International airport
✈ Airport

► Border post
▬▬ International border
- - - - State/province
— River
– · – Dry river
░ Park

Chapter 2

Sierra Leone: History Hidden by Horror

TYRONE SAVAGE AND JOSEPH RAHALL

In early April 2001, a report emerged that the Sierra Leone rebels, the Revolutionary United Front of Sierra Leone (RUF), had declared an end to the war that they had been conducting against the government for a decade. Senior rebel commander Gibril Massaquoi indicated that the United Nations peace-keeping force, UNAMSIL, was free to operate throughout Sierra Leone. The declaration of peace was significant. At the very least, it suggested a weariness among the insurgent forces. In as much as it reflected a will to demobilise, it represented an interval of opportunity in a brutal war that had claimed over 20 000 lives, displaced over 1.5 million people, seen the capital sacked twice, and become notorious for the scale and patterns of its atrocities.[1]

In the peace that emerged, Sierra Leone held presidential and parliamentary elections in May 2002. These passed relatively peacefully and successfully, resulting in a consolidation of the rule of former United Nations diplomat Ahmed Tejan Kabbah. Kabbah won 70% of the vote, against 22% for his nearest challenger, and a mere 1.7% for the RUF candidate. In this context, Sierra Leone is now embarking on processes of truth and reconciliation that include both a national commission as well as an international tribunal. The present historic moment represents a juncture of stability and hope, set against the backdrop of an appalling civil war.

The profile developed here takes March 1991 – the date RUF militia entered the small village of Bomaru, Eastern Sierra Leone, from Liberia with the declared goal of overthrowing the neo-colonial regime – as a starting point for analysing the present conflict. In the ensuing war, the grievances initially articulated by the RUF have been obscured by atrocities perpetrated by the movement. As a result, local, regional and international attempts to resolve the conflict have generally been directed at addressing the immediate hostilities rather than the deep-running political, social and economic frustrations that have shaped contemporary Sierra Leone. However, conflict resolution and sustainable reconciliation may be possible only when the conditions that occasioned the conflict are redressed. Accordingly, after describing the face of the conflict, discussion will home in on the structural problems that have shaped the historical course of the conflict in Sierra Leone – the ongoing role of neo-colonialism, the continual recourse to military solutions and the problematical attempts at civilian rule. Thereafter, the profile turns to the potential for peace-building and the task of reconciliation in the aftermath of the conflict.

The Face of Conflict

In March 1991, an armed, insurgent movement calling itself the Revolutionary United Front of Sierra Leone entered Sierra Leone from Liberia, launching a civil war that would become notorious for its atrocities. "This is not a war in which civilians are accidental victims," one international commentator has noted, "this is a war in which civilians are the targets."[2] Survivors and witnesses of gross human rights violations committed by the insurgent RUF speak of physical mutilation such as amputations by machete of one or both hands, limbs, buttocks and fingers, lacerations, the gouging of eyes, rape, gunshot wounds, burns, injections with acid, and ruthless beatings, among other atrocities. Human Rights Watch has received unconfirmed reports of mutilation of breasts and genitalia.[3] The RUF has terrorised victims by forcing them to participate in their own mutilation, making them decide, for example, which arm or leg they want to have amputated.

The war in Sierra Leone is a war in which terror has been deployed by the insurgents as a means of gaining social, political and military control. The declared reason for revolt was frustration at the neo-colonial, one-party dictatorships that have governed Sierra Leone since independence.[4] The conditions out of which the rebel movement emerged will form an integral part of this profile's discussion of the underlying causes of the conflict.

Resistance emerged as early as the mid-1970s against policies that curtailed government expenditure on the basic needs of Sierra Leoneans in favour of cultivating relationships with foreign investors. Beginning at the level of ideas, the revolt drew on, among other sources, Muammar Gaddafi's *Green Book*, a call for African youth to resist continued exploitation by colonial powers. As the conflict has progressed, however, atrocities have obscured the legitimacy of the claims, and an increasingly complicated battlefield has undermined the prospect of a viable revolution.

On the eve of the March 1991 insurgency, the manifesto of the RUF, *The Basic Document of the Revolutionary United Front of Sierra Leone (RUF/SL): The Second Liberation of Africa*, originally drafted as an agenda for democratic transition, was reworked to justify armed action.[5] Abdel-Fatau Musah notes that the document was "tinged with radicalism and populism", depicting the RUF as "the Sierra Leone wing of a Pan-African liberation umbrella army fighting to overthrow the neocolonial system and replacing it with people's governments".[6]

There is some debate over the meaning of the initial attack. Some commentators view the event as part of a larger African resistance to neocolonialism. Some see it as the return of democratic forces that had been exiled by a corrupt, one-party state. Others have argued that it was a de facto invasion by Charles Taylor's National Patriotic Front of Liberia (NPFL). A variety of motivations for NPFL intervention are possible, among them, retaliation for Sierra Leone having provided an operational base for the West African peace-keeping force, the Economic Community of West African States Monitoring Group (ECOMOG), during the NPFL uprising in 1989. Charles Taylor has also been accused of attempting to gain access to the diamond mining areas of Sierra Leone through the RUF, as well as attempting to extend his control beyond the official borders of Liberian territory, thus claiming the southeastern part of Sierra Leone.[7] This view is rooted in the notion held by some Liberians that there is a "greater Liberia", which includes the diamond and timber-rich areas situated in the border region of the two countries.[8] What is certain is that the attackers presented themselves as the RUF, fighting under the leadership of Foday Sankoh, and benefited from the logistical and military support of the NPFL.[9]

The invasion caught the national army, the Republic of Sierra Leone Military Force (RSLMF), off-guard. After establishing a one-party state in 1978, President Siaka Stevens had sought to minimise the threat of a military coup by downsizing and demobilising the military and expanding his internal police force, the Internal Security Unit, later renamed the State Security Department. Thus, at the time of the invasion, Stevens' successor Joseph Momoh, who had previously been the head of the military, had a national army comprising a mere 3 000 ill equipped and badly trained personnel. Lacking firepower, Momoh instigated an anti-Charles Taylor movement in Liberia. Momoh encouraged and harboured a faction of the warring parties in Liberia. The United Liberian Movement for Democracy (ULIMO) was made up of supporters of Liberia's former President Sam Doe and members of the Doe regime's national army, the Armed Forces of Liberia (AFL). At home, Momoh hurriedly conscripted recruits into the RSLMF, boosting its numbers to 14 000 soldiers within two years. However, the conscripts were sent to the frontlines with little training.

They lacked equipment, as well as logistical and medical support.[10]

In April 1992, a group of RSLMF soldiers, led by Captain Valentine Strasser, arrived in Freetown from the frontlines, initially, it seems, to demand better conditions for soldiers. Their demands became a protest and, in turn, a revolt that led to the overthrow of Momoh's regime. Strasser convened a military junta, the National Provisional Ruling Council (NPRC), the bulk of which was made up of military officers. While maintaining that the NPRC was committed to the multi-party system, Strasser nevertheless suspended the 1991 constitution, dissolved the House of Representatives, imposed a state of emergency and temporarily closed all access to the country. Relations between the junta and the RUF rapidly worsened, largely due to the dashing of the RUF's expectation of joining the NPRC to form a government. The RUF had claimed that it was responsible for the political consciousness of the NPRC. The war escalated after Sankoh accused the "rebel NRPC" of being a vestige of the previous regime.

The end of 1992 brought events that changed the shape and extent of the war. Specifically, the RUF wrested economic targets from government control in the diamond-rich Kono district in the east. These gains augured several shifts and altered the stakes of the conflict for the rebels, shifting its grounds from an ideological, social platform to a contest for resources. In January 1995, the RUF overran the Sierra Leone Rutile titanium and SIEROMCO bauxite mines, two of the largest employers in the country. A further consequence of the RUF seizure of Kono was a change in the RUF's relations with the rural populace. Musah observes:

> This trade provided the RUF with an extended economic space, thus greatly reducing its dependence on the rural population for supplies. Had RUF manoeuvrability been confined only to Sierra Leone . . . where it was restricted to only weapons and logistics it could acquire from its interrelationships with the rural dwellers, it would have been compelled to harmonize relations with the peasants.[11]

As the stakes heightened and its position deteriorated, the NRPC government called for a revival of traditional warrior institutions, such as local paramount chiefs, men's secret societies and traditional hunters/warriors. The Gbethis and Donsos were the first warrior institutions to be invoked and used to fight alongside the junta. The project was short-lived for several reasons, one of which was the erosion, as the numbers of their casualties grew, of the invincibility myth surrounding these warrior institutions. These groups emerged ostensibly to ensure local security and were known collectively as the Civil Defence Force (CDF). The most significant group among them is the Kamajors.[12] Described by one commentator as "the façade of national pride", the Kamajors have been accused of some of the worst abuses during the war. A Kamajor leader, Sam Hinga, currently occupies the post of Deputy Defence Minister and, under the auspices of the ECOMOG, the Kamajors have been deployed in co-operation with foreign troops from Nigeria and Guinea.

A second strategy deployed by the failing junta was to contract with foreign mercenaries. In early 1995, Strasser enlisted the military assistance of the Gurkha Security Guards (GSG), and following that the South African-based Executive Outcomes (EO). GSG's venture was short-lived, but EO, willing to engage in actual combat, linked its military operations to a share of the diamond fields it was employed to re-take. EO was effective and costly. Abdel-Fatau Musah, in *Mercenaries: An African Security Dilemma,* describes their impact as follows:

> Within nine months of their arrival, EO had led the anti-RUF coalition to recapture all major mining centres including the Kono diamond mines . . . The coalition had also formed a *cordon sanitaire* around the capital, Freetown, checking the advance of RUF guerrillas and permitting a semblance of normalcy to return. The RUF guerrillas were forced to retrace their steps along bush paths into the forest to regroup, their war machine having been greatly weakened.[13]

So successful was EO in providing security and stability, that some commentators have drawn specifically on the Sierra Leone example to argue for the "strategic advantage and cost effectiveness" of deploying mercenaries.[14] The hidden costs of looking to mercenary organisations for security and stability are vast, however. In Sierra Leone, such costs would become evident as the course of the war unfolded. Musah explains, "the hidden cost of corporate intervention in current wars in Africa, besides the mortgaging of natural resources, is sovereignty".[15] In Sierra Leone, intervention by private military forces secured only temporary victory for the hiring party. Moreover, the eventual departure of these mercenaries precipitated an upsurge of hostilities. However, the momentary stability did allow for negotiation. The non-governmental organisation International Alert facilitated discussion between the RUF and the United Nations, the OAU and the Economic Community of West African States (ECOWAS). The negotiations led to the Abidjan Peace Accord, signed in July 1996.

Signatories to the accord agreed to the demobilisation and resettlement of combatants; the transformation of the RUF into a political party; the withdrawal of foreign forces, and in particular the mercenaries; a Citizens Consultative Conference to chart a course to democratic politics; the holding of elections; and a series of socio-economic reforms.[16] Under pressure from civil society and the international community to establish a constitutional government, Sierra Leone moreover prioritised the holding of elections, albeit "in the midst of a raging war, without prior attempts at any meaningful cease-fire or demobilization of combatants".[17] With the RUF boycotting the electoral process, and threatening to kill anyone in or near a voting station, the first multi-party elections in three decades went ahead in early 1996. Though the elections were marred by heavy attacks that left an estimated 27 people dead, a significant commitment to democratic processes became evident among Sierra Leoneans. Many defied the threats and voted. Some reportedly protected the ballot boxes with their bodies during transportation to the counting centres, to prevent rebels from destroying them.

Ahmed Tejan Kabbah of the Sierra Leone People's Party drew almost 60% of the votes, despite having spent more than two decades abroad.[18] On assuming the presidency, Kabbah sought to establish a broad-based government from among the leading political parties, and included members of the People's Democratic Party (PDP) in his cabinet. The RUF, having refused to participate in the elections, was excluded. Accordingly, the primary parties to the conflict remained in a state of war, unsure how to implement those sections of the peace accord that centred on disengagement. Musah describes the outcome of the elections ominously:

> By holding elections first and thinking later about key elements of conflict settlement such as demobilization, reintegration and rudimentary reconstruction, further progress in the peace process became contingent upon the goodwill and selflessness of the incoming administration. Lacking both, the newly installed civilian administration soon became a party to the conflict.[19]

Though the Abidjan Accord called for the withdrawal of foreign troops and the dismantling of all sub-state militia, President Kabbah, unsure of the loyalty of the national armed forces (RSLMF), chose to renew EO's contract. This flagrant violation of the accord was intended to allow the mercenary outfit to co-ordinate the expansion and strengthening of the Kamajors into a 20 000-member standing army. Like his predecessors,

Kabbah chose to prioritise regime security over reconciliation.

The consequences of this choice became evident, however, when the International Monetary Fund (IMF), "alarmed by the staggering pay-offs in cash and mineral concessions to EO and its partners, made the termination of the outfit's contract a precondition for bailing out the collapsed economy".[20] Caught between mercenary forces and foreign funders, Kabbah's government was overtaken – in less than 100 days – by its own military.[21] The Armed Forces Revolutionary Council (AFRC), under the leadership of Major Johnny Paul Koroma, seized power. President Kabbah and his government retreated into neighbouring Guinea.

During the nine months it ruled, the AFRC claimed it had secured peace with the RUF and formed an alliance with the rebels. Instead of peace, however, the AFRC/RUF junta instituted what Human Rights Watch called "a regime characterized by serious human rights violations and a complete breakdown of the rule of law".[22] The regime was met with resentment and active resistance, however. The widespread view both in the international community and among Sierra Leoneans was that the democratically elected leader of Sierra Leone had been deposed. Civil protest surged in Sierra Leone as trade unions, women's groups, students and civil servants opposed the military regime and brought the entire country to a standstill. Moreover, ECOWAS, the OAU and then the United Nations placed stringent embargoes on Sierra Leone. These were enforced by the Nigerian-led peace-keeping force, ECOMOG, resulting in drastic shortages of food, crude petroleum and other essential commodities. ECOMOG occupied the sea around Freetown but was unable to wrest it from AFRC/RUF control. A military stalemate emerged.

In this context, the president-in-exile continued negotiations under ECOWAS auspices, ostensibly seeking out, as the rightful head-of-state, a political solution. Behind doors, however, he accepted a proposal by the British High Commissioner to Sierra Leone, Peter Penfold, to engage the services of a mercenary outfit affiliated with EO, Sandline International.[23] Sandline provided a shipment of 35 tons of AK-47 assault rifles, ammunition and mortars. On 18 February 1998, the combined forces of Nigerian troops, the Kamajors and about 200 Sandline mercenaries retook Freetown in a single day. Against the historical backdrop of coup and countercoup, the multi-party elections had given Sierra Leone its first democratically elected leader in 30 years. Accordingly, the return and restoration of Ahmed Tejan Kabbah was greeted with jubilation, and widely recognised as a triumph for democracy. The means by which democratic restoration had been secured, however, came with a price.

In late 1998, as mercenary presence decreased and local attempts to restore order grew, RUF leader Foday Sankoh, having been extradited by Nigeria where he had been detained on charges of the possession of arms, was convicted of treason and sentenced to death. The RUF and AFRC reacted viciously, overwhelming government forces and its allies and eventually engaging in a three-week long sacking of Sierra Leone's capital. Human Rights Watch described the events:

> As the rebels took control of street after street, they turned their weapons on the civilian population. By the end of January, both government and independent sources estimated that several thousands of civilians had been killed. The rebels dragged entire family units out of their homes and murdered them, hacked off the hands of children and adults, burned people alive in their houses, and rounded up hundreds of young women, took them to urban rebel bases, and sexually abused them. As the ECOMOG forces counterattacked and the RUF retreated through the capital, the rebels set fire to neighbourhoods, leaving entire city blocks in ashes and 51 000 people homeless.[24]

For the second time in a year, Sierra Leone's capital had been turned into the arena of a vicious battle. After three weeks, the government forces and ECOMOG managed to gain control.

In May 1999, a cease-fire was established, leading to negotiations in the Togolese capital, Lomé, and the signing of a peace agreement.[25] The Lomé Agreement granted rebels full amnesty and various posts in government. Not without irony, Foday Sankoh was appointed chairman of the Strategic Minerals Commission. The United Nations presence was significantly expanded to allow for adequate policing of the peace agreement. UN forces began arriving in the latter months of 1999.

Implementing the Lomé Agreement posed an array of difficulties. Relations with the RUF deteriorated drastically, culminating in the abduction of 50, and then several hundred UN peace-keeping troops. The breakthrough in that series of events appears to have been the citizen's arrest of Foday Sankoh early one morning in the streets of Freetown, when the RUF leader apparently attempted to visit home. In the window of opportunity provided by the capture of the RUF's leader, negotiators secured the progressive release of the peace-keepers.

In the absence of Foday Sankoh, a split has emerged in the RUF. Agence France-Presse (AFP) has quoted the spokesperson of the RUF, Gibril Massaquoi, as acknowledging a split, and as having said that 90%

of the rebels refused to recognise the designated interim leader, General Issa Sesay. They opted, he said, for taking orders from Brigadier-General Maurice Kallon, the RUF battle group commander in the northern part of the country. Massaquoi, however, later denied this, claiming that he made no such statement.[26]

The disarray apparent in the RUF has, moreover, been evident as Sierra Leone has pressed forward in its commitment to democracy. In May 2002, general elections were held, passing relatively peacefully (one major violent incident occurred but was contained) and successfully. The results consolidated the presidency of Ahmed Tejan Kabbah, who won 70% of the vote, against 22% for his nearest challenger, and a mere 1.7 % for the RUF Party candidate, Alimamy Pallo Bangura. The RUF Party moreover did not gain a single seat in parliament, as against Kabbah's Sierra Leone People's Party, which won 83 of the 112 seats being contested.

In this context of growing democratic stability, Sierra Leone is now embarking on processes of truth and reconciliation that include both a national commission as well as an international tribunal. This profile examines these developments in the sections on prospects for peace-building and reconciliation.

A new chapter has clearly opened in Sierra Leone, a new chapter in which democratic elections and processes of truth and reconciliation have taken hold. But a chapter in which the questions that have shaped the story persist. What middle path is possible between urgent security needs and the development of democratic processes? What role should foreign forces have in it? What role is there for African neighbours, neo-colonial and former colonial powers? How useful – and how potentially counter-productive – are multi-party elections in the context of a raging war? Where war has become institutionalised, what does peace even look like? And how might outsiders interact helpfully with Sierra Leone's courageous civil society? Whatever becomes of the resistance, the conditions that have produced Sierra Leone's conflict will remain, prolific and pernicious, unless the systemic patterns of frustration are addressed.[27]

The Historical Roots of Violence and Division

Sierra Leone, in the words of Abdel-Fatau Musah, "symbolizes the complex, usually torturous relationships between Africa and the trans-Atlantic, beginning with the holocaust of the slave trade and followed by colonization; these exploitative relations continue today through post-independent neo-colonial economic arrangements".[28] This is to say that Sierra Leone is a deeply divided society. Its ethnic groupings can be understood in terms of waves of migration that began with movements of various coastal peoples. In the 1200s, the ruling group in Mali, the Mandinka, entered Sierra Leone as merchants and Islamic scholars, and gradually integrated with the local people. In 1462, the Portuguese explorer, Pedro da Sintra, arrived in the region and called it the Serra Lyoa (Lion Mountain). For the next two centuries, Portuguese activities impacted on local life, as merchants and sailors took up residence in Sierra Leone. A mix of African and Portuguese culture developed, producing a Creole people the Portuguese called Filhos da Terra (Native Sons).

The development of the slave trade significantly altered the demographics of Sierra Leone. The British dominated the trans-Atlantic trade in human cargo in the eighteenth century, transporting more captives than all the other European powers combined. From about 1750, British companies operated out of Bunce Island in Freetown harbour, specialising in supplying slaves to South Carolina and Georgia. The eventual success of the abolitionist movement in Britain brought about a variety of changes that would impact on the Sierra Leone region, most notably in the establishment of Freetown as a settlement for former slaves. Four distinct groupings arrived, the first, in 1787, following the banning of slavery by British courts. Former North American slaves who fought for the British during the American Revolution came five years later, and escapees who had been recaptured in the mountains of Jamaica came in 1800. The last group were the "Recaptives", who were taken off slave ships seized by the British Navy after 1807, when the British parliament prohibited the Atlantic slave trade. The people who formed this last group comprised more than 50 000 West Africans, mostly from Nigeria. The four groups settled along the coast, and enjoyed various forms of exchange with foreigners, gradually merging in what became known as the Krio community.

In 1808, the British declared Freetown a Crown Colony. Colonial administrators, teachers and missionaries arrived in the region, giving preference to former slaves when filling positions in colonial civil service, clergy and various other professions. In public life, locals imitated British society, but domestically, Krio culture comprised a mixture of European and African influences. British policy was, however, premised on a system of preference that divided former slaves and indigenous groups of the interior – a widening gulf that would still be evident well into the following century when the struggle against British rule would emerge primarily from the hinterland.[29]

In 1896, amid European scrambling for portions of Africa, the British declared a "protectorate" over the hinterland. To account for the costs of providing such "protection", the British instituted a tax on locals, precipitating an uprising that became known as the "Hut Tax War".[30] The conflict took several forms. Warriors from several kingdoms embarked on a series of hit-and-run attacks on British forces, while others struck civilian targets – including British, American and Krio missionaries and traders – in an effort to purge the country of the foreign presence. Full-scale rebellion persisted for 10 months before it was finally quashed by British forces.

Fifty years later, as Britain lost control of its colonial possessions, authorities in Sierra Leone introduced constitutional proposals aimed at creating a unified administration for the Crown Colony (Freetown) and the Protectorate (the hinterland). The proposals provided for a Legislative Council that would rule both the Crown Colony and the Protectorate. Most of the council was to be made up, however, of representatives from the Protectorate, who accounted for 98% of the population of the combined colony and protectorate. The Krio community, accustomed to having significant sway in running the colony, feared domination from the majority and for several years fought a losing battle to retain political prominence.

In 1961, Sierra Leone claimed its independence, opting for a Westminster-style government. The history of Sierra Leone since independence is marked by patterns of military coup and problematical civilian rule. Throughout these extremes, a mix of allegiance to and dependency upon the former colonial power has been evident. Britain has accordingly been able to influence the country's policies to its own benefit. The Sierra Leonean economy has in consequence been shaped around the export of the country's natural resources, including diamonds, shipbuilding timber, vegetable oils, palm produce, bauxite and chromate. The constraints and incentives imposed by foreign interests have, in turn, shaped the patterns of governance, producing a series of regimes dependent on the favour of external parties rather than the will of Sierra Leoneans for its survival.

The first prime minister was Sir Milton Margai, from the Protectorate. His time in power was largely free of political confrontation. The mood changed abruptly with his death in 1964, when his brother Albert, as leader of the Sierra Leone People's Party (SLPP), became prime minister. Albert Margai's rule is widely remembered for its deterioration of public accountability and his attempt to amend the constitution to create a one-party state. Albert Margai and the SLPP lost the 1967 general election to the All People's Congress (APC), led by Siaka Stevens. Before Stevens could assume office, however, a coup was staged, aimed at restoring the status quo ante. A counter-coup a few hours later installed a military government that would rule until another counter-coup the following year brought Stevens back from exile and restored civilian government.

The instability continued, however, culminating in an attempted coup in March 1971. The coup was suppressed with the aid of troops from Guinea.[31] It was in this attempted coup that the future RUF leader, Foday Sankoh, was implicated and sentenced to seven years' imprisonment. A month later, a republican constitution was introduced, with Stevens as executive president. In the 1977 general elections, the SLPP offered no candidates and Stevens served a further presidential term. In 1978, a well-orchestrated referendum established a one-party state. It was in the aftermath of this turn of events that civil resistance would emerge in Sierra Leone.

The rule of Siaka Stevens is widely regarded as having precipitated Sierra Leone's spiral into conflict. Not only did Stevens quash civilian opposition, he consciously dismantled the army and created a parallel force in the police known as the Internal Security Division, later renamed the State Security Department. By the onset of hostilities in 1991, the national army numbered a mere 3 000 personnel. Moreover, by the time of his retirement in 1985, Sierra Leone's GDP had shrunk to US$965 million – one of the lowest in the world – and would shrink further, with the onset of civil war. The chief reason for this was the effect of hosting the OAU conference in 1980, when the state ran into huge debt as it financed projects prior to and during the summit. By 1994, the GDP was down to US$646 million.[32] Moreover, government spending on Sierra Leoneans' basic needs had dropped significantly. In the 1974/75 financial year, 15.6% of government spending went into education, 6.6% into health and 4.8% into housing; by the year before the outbreak of hostilities, the numbers were down to 8.5%, 2.9% and 0.3%, respectively. "The levels of impoverishment, social and generational exclusion," comments Abdel-Fatau Musah, ". . . fuelled social unrest, and state repression had reached alarming proportions."[33]

In 1985, Stevens handed the APC party leadership and the presidency to Major General Joseph Saidu Momoh, a cabinet minister and commander of the armed forces. Though handpicked by Stevens and the sole candidate nominated for the positions, Momoh promised a "New Order" in national life. Initially, he enjoyed widespread support among Sierra Leoneans. His seven years in office generated further disillusionment, however, when reform efforts failed to materialise. The country's foreign donors, in turn, demanded structural adjustments. The economy, already strained by years of corruption, collapsed. Civil service salaries went unpaid and government offices were stripped bare of typewriters and furniture. In 1990, Momoh supported a return to multi-party democracy and the writing of a new constitution. Most of the new parties entering the political process were led by corrupt former APC ministers who sought to protect their privileges through shrewd use of the multi-party system. The new order thus offered little change from the old. External exploitation continued, as it had throughout the colonial and post-colonial era, along with socio-economic mismanagement, graft and rent-seeking politics. The result was worsening impoverishment and instability.[34] At this point, resistance in Sierra Leone shifted from civil activism to armed uprising.

Amid the deteriorating socio-economic conditions that marked the mid-1970s, the first phase of civil activism in Sierra Leone took the form of student opposition to the neo-colonialism that had blighted Sierra Leone since independence. By 1982, student-led demonstrations had became widespread and extremely vocal in denouncing the one-party system introduced by Siaka Stevens and perpetuated by Momoh. In 1984, student activism spread to the acclaimed Fourah Bay College, where it coalesced into a populist movement called the Mass Awareness and Participation (MAP). Under a regime that would not tolerate opposition, student activism was banned on campuses. "This only led," in Musah's words, "to a more qualitative stage in mass awareness as the centres of resistance shifted to the mines, factory floors and the recreational centres (*potes*)."[35]

The *potes* were peri-urban relaxation venues which generally drew those most affected by government's dwindling expenditure on education and social services, namely restless, unemployed, male youth. Their marginal position had changed in the 1970s when *potes* became part of a popular urban culture, attracting middle class youth and in particular students from Fourah Bay College. The venue developed into a site for political socialisation. An exchange occurred in which *rarray man dem* – petty criminals, pimps and hitmen for political patrons and criminal bosses – learned about politics from the educated middle class youth, and students became acutely aware of the suffering of Sierra Leone's underclasses and increasingly disgruntled by the corruption and nepotism that had marked the post-colonial era.[36]

A number of students were expelled from Fourah Bay College and went into exile in Ghana, where they were offered opportunities to study at Legon University. Among them were Alie Kabba, Rashid Mansaray and Abu Kanu, founder of the Future Shock club, a group that played an integral role in the establishment of the RUF. These exiled students began developing theoretical and logistical plans for armed insurrection, including an initial training phase in Libya, which drew recruits from Freetown and the hinterland and began in 1987.[37] Foday Sankoh was among them. The movement shared a collective type of leadership and when they later surfaced as a rebel movement, Sankoh emerged as the official spokesperson. In 1992 and 1993, Kanu and Mansaray were respectively executed for their opposition to the indiscriminate violence beginning to proliferate in the name of revolution.[38] Having begun as a movement committed to resisting neo-colonial exploitation and unaccountable, undemocratic governance, the RUF was drifting toward the use of violence that would obscure the legitimacy of its complaints.

Abdel-Fatau Musah observes that inquiries into the conflict in Sierra Leone have generally centred on the lack of a positive vision among RUF leaders as well as the prevalence of crime-prone elements among RUF recruits. Factors such as the disintegration of the national negotiation process, relationships within the region, mismanagement of the economy and the barriers to peaceful change have pushed thousands of youth, peasants and workers to the fringes of society.[39] In seeking a sustainable peace in Sierra Leone, it will be necessary to step out of the atrocities of the past, ensuring that the oppressive conditions out of which the RUF grew do not reappear.

Prospects for Peace-building

The current interval of stability in Sierra Leone has, in many ways, been made possible through foreign military intervention. This small country on the west coast of Africa is host to the largest United Nations peacekeeping deployment anywhere. Moreover, since intervening when the RUF took UN soldiers hostage, the British Army has become increasingly entrenched in Sierra Leone's security arrangements. Currently, the British Army is putting together a new military for the country comprising screened members of the warring factions, as well as new recruits. It is widely acknowledged that such military intervention has been indispensable in creating conditions within which to build peace in Sierra Leone.

However, throughout Sierra Leone's history, the stability that comes from military force has been transitory. Worse still, it has contributed to a militarised culture in which the problems that led to the uprising 10 years ago have worsened. Per capita income is less than $150 per year. It is estimated that only 15% of adults are literate. In this context, young rebels who possessed very little prior to the war have developed options for themselves based on terror and an ability to pillage the country's diamond fields. In the event of a permanent cease-fire, the predicament of these former combatants could actually worsen. Not only have they become accustomed to the benefits of illicit diamond trading, their activities have disconnected them politically, socially and psychologically from the larger community. *Africa Confidential*, in a report entitled *Sierra Leone: Precarious Calm*, commented that "the fighters are disarming and demobilising fast but the much tougher job of rebuilding the peace remains to be done".[40] Given the RUF Party's poor showing in the 2002 elections, the members of this military movement turned political party may find themselves without satisfactory options.

In themselves, disarmament and demobilisation will not bring lasting peace. Though the atrocities of the past decade have made firm action against the rebels urgent, unless the history of discontent that motivated the war is addressed, Sierra Leone will remain trapped in cycles of frustration and rage. Sustainable peace would necessarily entail acknowledging the country's history of extreme poverty in the hinterland, government corruption, neo-colonial economic relations and the consistent failure of successive regimes to translate the country's significant economic resources into productive, peaceful options for Sierra Leoneans. In addition to recognising the role of this history in the present crisis, the incentives that made waging war possible and continue to make it a lucrative option will need to be acknowledged. In a paper entitled *The Heart of the Matter: Sierra Leone, Diamonds & Human Security*, Partnership Africa Canada notes that the appalling violence is not the result of Sierra Leone's lack of integration in a modern world; on the contrary, such violence has been sustainable only by the economic opportunity provided by the breakdown in law and order. It further asserts that "the point of the war may not actually have been to win it, but to engage in profitable crime under the cover of warfare".[41] Such profiteering is, in short, made possible by the way that the diamond trade is conducted. It is not merely that trade in diamonds has fuelled the war; rather, war itself has become useful and lucrative, providing the necessary conditions for the illicit exports of diamonds through intermediary states in the region to Antwerp.

It was the RUF's link-up with Charles Taylor, Liberia's warlord-turned-president, that led to a chaotic, brutal war. In exchange for supporting the rebels, Taylor has gained significant access to Sierra Leone's diamonds. As a result, though Liberia's annual diamond mining capacity is between 100 000 and 150 000 carats, the organisation that regulates the Belgian diamond industry, the *Hoge Raad voor Diamant* (HRD), recorded

Liberian imports into Belgium of over 31 million carats between 1994 and 1998 – an average of over six million carats a year. A sustainable, productive peace will be impossible in Sierra Leone unless it addresses the diamond interests of neighbouring Liberia.

Cognisant of the potential blight Taylor represents to peace in Sierra Leone, the international community's efforts have focused on disarmament and demobilisation in the mineral rich regions. By mid-2001, UN peace-keepers had made significant headway in wresting control from rebels in these areas. Although it represents a breakthrough in terms of the regional balance of power, this success is not in itself a sustainable peace. Rather, it provides an interval of stability in which structural reforms can be developed. In particular, reform of the ways in which the HRD does its business is long overdue. The HRD is at once the lobbying institution for the Belgian diamond industry as well as the government-designated monitor of imports and exports. This dual role poses a conflict of interests and violates international norms of accountability. Moreover, this body still records the origin of a diamond as the country from which the diamond was last exported. Diamonds from Sierra Leone may be officially imported and registered as originating in Liberia or Guinea, depending on their journey from one trading centre to another. It is a direct consequence of this arrangement that Liberian diamond exports to Belgium between 1994 and 1998 were 40 times the country's mining capacity. Many people now argue that the HRD should be required to use diamond "fingerprinting" technology in order to identify a diamond's origin. Without reform in the HRD, it appears that the incentives for conflict will continue, hampering demobilisation and development efforts on the ground.

In addition to addressing the transnational arrangements that presently make illicit exporting of diamonds possible and lucrative, the current culture of unaccountability within Sierra Leone itself will need to be rooted out for lasting peace to become a possibility. After the Lomé Agreement of July 1999 provided rebels posts in government and assurances that they would not be prosecuted for war crimes, it became evident that the conflict of the past decade would not be so easily forgotten: blanket amnesty and posts in government that even included Foday Sankoh as chairman of the Strategic Minerals Commission were not sufficient incentive to maintain peace. In August 2000, the United Nations Security Council voted in favour of setting up an international court to try Sierra Leone rebels accused of war crimes. In contrast to Lomé's attempt to put the past behind, the Special Court represents an attempt to establish transitional justice by recognising wrong and seeking redress. Moreover, the court will differ from the tribunals set up at The Hague and at Arusha in that it will include judges from Sierra Leone. The inclusionary approach of this transitional institution, it is hoped, will increase participation by Sierra Leoneans themselves in finding a resolution to the conflict.

In January 2002, a few months ahead of the general elections, officials from the United Nations and the Sierra Leone government signed an agreement setting up the war crimes tribunal. Coming at a time when demobilisation and disarmament had begun to take firm hold, the prospect of a tribunal has not been welcomed by former RUF combatants. It is moreover widely rumoured that Foday Sonkah will be a special target of the court.[42] Be that as it may, the tribunal represents an opportunity for Sierra Leone to develop a culture of accountability in the present interval of stability and to depart from historical patterns of pursuing change through coercion and military force.

Present and Future Opportunities for Reconciliation

The present stability in Sierra Leone is not only the result of international military intervention. This intervention itself was made possible – credible to the international community and among locals – by a groundswell of civil resistance to the patterns of repressive rule that have marked post-independence Sierra Leone and by the emergence of a real commitment to democratic processes. As the war worsened and governance became increasingly repressive, culminating in the formation of the AFRC/RUF military junta, organisations developed and called for civil liberties, human rights and democratically accountable governance. Organisations that have emerged include the Women's Movement for Peace, the National Commission for Democracy and Human Rights and a local division of Amnesty International. Concerned Youths for Peace (CONYOPA) has been active since 1996, sharing ideas, information and resources through symposia, seminars, workshops, lectures and conferences and publishing materials on peace issues and youth development. The National Forum for Human Rights serves as secretariat for more than 30 human rights organisations in Sierra Leone. The Sierra Leone Association of Non-Governmental Organisations (SLANGO) provides an umbrella for local non-governmental organisations.

In this context, calls for reconciliation have become a leitmotif in Sierra Leonean public life. At the same time, questions abound. What reconciliation will be possible in the aftermath of the atrocities that have overwhelmed Sierra Leone for the past decade? What role would there be for justice in bringing the nation together? What justice is possible? What can reconciliation look like in such a context?

The prospect of a truth and reconciliation commission in Sierra Leone was first touted in the 1999 Human Rights Committee of Sierra Leone. It was later given a place in the 1999 Lomé Peace Agreement. Drawing on the experiences of truth commissions elsewhere, the Truth and Reconciliation Commission Act homes in on the particular needs of Sierra Leoneans. It defines the aim of the proposed commission as the creation of an impartial historical record of violations and abuses of human rights related to the armed conflict in Sierra Leone, from the beginning of the conflict in 1991 to the signing of the Lomé Peace Agreement. It also addresses the problems of impunity, the needs of victims and ways that the country might take steps to ensure the past does not repeat itself.

A national workshop was held in Freetown in November 2000 to discuss the proposed Truth and Reconciliation Commission.[43] Participants at the event noted that lasting peace would require the healing of Sierra Leonean society and that only such healing could lead to the reconstruction of the whole nation. A commission could form an integral part of such a process. It would need to be a national project supported by significant resources, technical assistance and extensive campaigning to raise awareness among citizens in the hinterland as well as within refugee communities outside of Sierra Leone.

Since 2000, a groundswell of support has developed around Sierra Leone's Truth and Reconciliation Commission. Local and international partners including the government of Sierra Leone, combatants, traditional leaders, religious leaders and various parts of civil society, including the NGO community, have affirmed this development. Loosely modelled on the South African Truth and Reconciliation Commission, Sierra Leone's Truth and Reconciliation Commission may help open up and heal divisions caused by a decade of brutal civil war. Moreover, the commission has the potential to contribute significantly to other elements in the peacebuilding process in Sierra Leone such as the Disarmament, Demobilisation and Reintegration (DDR) process and the Resettlement, Reconstruction and Rehabilitation (RRR) process.

The most significant obstacle facing the commission is a lack of resources. The executive secretary of the commission, Yasmin Jusu-Sheriff, has indicated that "the Commission and the Commission's staff . . . want to go to the communities where this war was fought, they want to bring about reconciliation, they want to give people a chance to tell their stories. But no matter how committed we are we cannot walk around Sierra Leone. And if we are not able to hire sufficient people to take the statements, then we will not be able to do the work."[44] The commission has so far been granted US$1 million, against a projected budget of approximately US$9 million. Rachel Harvey comments that "there is a real danger that Sierra Leone's efforts to bring about a lasting peace will be thwarted – not because of a shortage of will to confront the past, but because of a shortage of hard cash".[45]

One further area of potential difficulty has to do with the relationship between the Truth and Reconciliation Commission and the Special Court. Clearly, they are not intended as a substitute for one another. However, in practice, difficulties would emerge if testimony given in confidence in one were to inform or be required for investigations in the other. There remains a need for a process to work out the relationship between the Truth and Reconciliation Commission and the Special Court. Particular attention needs to be given to how they will work at the same time. Such a consultative process should draw upon the views of experts with previous experience in respect to the relationship and interaction between courts and truth commissions and of relevant parties in Sierra Leone. It is also recognised that there is a need for a comprehensive public awareness and education campaign to explain the purposes, goals, workings and benefits of the Truth and Reconciliation Commission and to illustrate its different roles and independence from the Special Court.

A number of local and international organisations are active among traumatised children and youth. All As One (AAO), founded in 1997, currently has two interim care centres for orphaned and abandoned children, providing them with schooling, food, shelter and medical care. The Children's Relief Trust of Sierra Leone and the Children's Rights Council of Sierra Leone (CRCSL) also focus on children's needs. The Nehemiah Project is a rehabilitation project that addresses the needs of traumatised ex-child combatants. The project is currently run by LifeLine West Africa. International DOVE (Development, Orphanages, Vocational Education) is a non-denominational Christian organisation that cares for orphans in war-torn countries in the world. Numerous organisations engaged in relief and development work have operations in Sierra Leone. CAUSE Canada (Christian Aid for Under-Assisted Societies Everywhere) has been active in Sierra Leone since 1989. Current projects include rehabilitation and reintegration of war amputees and women and children impacted by the war. Medical Emergency Relief International (MERLIN) is a British medical charity which provides emergency relief in disaster zones around the world. In Sierra Leone, MERLIN is currently providing nutritional feeding to over 350 severely malnourished and 1 300 moderately malnourished children in hospitals in Kenema and Blama, running an 80-bed tented children's hospital for emergency treatment and nutritional feeding in Freetown, re-establishing and restocking one hospital and 32 health centres in Kenema and Bo districts in eastern Sierra Leone, and running four mobile teams to provide basic aid.

The Centre for Alternative Development Strategies (CADS) Global Network is a Sierra Leonean initiative, which attempts to enable the less privileged to overcome deprivation, misery and suffering using practical alternative development strategies as instruments of social change. CADS provides a forum for collective reflection and encourages a dialogue on development issues at all levels. The programme was founded to create a network – including its membership and chapter organisations across Africa, and in Europe and North America – which links individuals and institutions. International organisations active in Sierra Leone include the International Rescue Committee (IRC), which works in Freetown, Bo and Kenema. Italian NGO *Cooperazione Internazionale* (COOPI) has been active in Sierra Leone since 1967. COOPI focuses on the vulnerability of poor people in emergency situations generated by war, civil conflict and natural disaster. COOPI also helps trace children's families or establish them in new homes. Friends of Sierra Leone (FOSL) was established by former US Peace Corps volunteers and endeavours to educate people in the US about Sierra Leone. Shelter for Africa is a German-based NGO which produces building materials such as roofing, wall and floor tiles, clay bricks and concrete toilets and water-tanks using intermediate or appropriate technology.

Sierra Leone is currently engaged in the challenges posed by an interval of stability of the sort described by Hannah Arendt when she spoke of a moment in history determined neither by the past nor a pre-determined future:[46] demobilisation is underway among Sierra Leoneans, the president is democratically elected and enjoys international support, and civil society has surged prolifically, reflecting a growing commitment among Sierra Leoneans to address the effects of the country's conflict-ridden history. The most significant obstacle to peace and reconciliation may be the structural one of a diamond economy that has hitherto thrived in the appalling conditions of war.

NOTES

1 Abdel-Fatau Musah, "A Country Under Siege: State Decay and Corporate Military Intervention in Sierra Leone," in *Mercenaries: An African Security Dilemma*, eds. Abdel-Fatau Musah and J. 'Kayode Fayemi (London: Pluto Press, 2000), 76. On the ground interviews by staff of the Institute for Jushze and Reconciliation suggested that the number of deaths resulting from the war may be closer to 200 000.

2 Peter Takirambudde, "Sierra Leone Government Bombing Causes Civilian Deaths." Reprinted at www.hrw.org/press/2000/07/sl0711.htm (accessed 19 September 2001).

3 Human Rights Watch, "Sowing Terror: Atrocities against Civilians in Sierra Leone." Reprinted at www.hrw.org/reports98/sierra (accessed 19 September 2001); Amnesty International, "Sierra Leone: Towards a Future Founded on Human Rights." Reprinted at www.web.amnesty.org/ai.nsf/index/AFR510051996 (accessed 19 September 2001).

4 Posthumus Bram, "Seeking a Way out of the Abyss: Sierra Leone," in *Searching for Peace in Africa: An Overview of Conflict Prevention and Management Activities,* eds. Monique Mekenkamp, Paul van Tongeren and Hans van de Veen (Utrecht: European Platform for Conflict Prevention and Transformation, 1999), 373. Sierra Leone gained its independence in 1968.

5 Paul Richards, *Fighting for the Rainforest: War, Youth and Resources in Sierra Leone* (Oxford: The International African Institute in association with James Currey; Portsmouth, N. H.: Heinemann, 1996).

6 Musah, "A Country Under Siege," 85.

7 Between 1998 and 2000, the value of official annual diamond exports by Sierra Leone halved to $30 million. In the same period, diamond exports by Liberia, which possesses relatively few diamond fields, rose to $300 million. David Bamford, "Foday Sankoh: Rebel Leader." Reprinted at http://news.bbc.co.uk/hi/english/world/africa/newsid_737000/737268.stm (accessed 19 September 2001).

8 Ibrahim Abdullah, "Bush Path to Destruction: The Origin and Character of the Revolutionary United Front of Sierra Leone." *Journal of Modern African Studies* 36 (1998): 203–235.

9 Newafrica.com, "Post-Colonial History of Sierra Leone." Reprinted at www.newafrica.com/history/sierraleone (accessed 19 September 2001).

10 Cry Freetown, "A Brief History of Sierra Leone." Reprinted at www.cryfreetown.org/history.html (accessed 25 September 2001).

11 Musah, "A Country Under Siege," 86.

12 The Kamajors and the CDF only came into being when the Sierra Leone People's Party (SLPP) came on to the political stage. The movement gathered momentum when the SLPP was overthrown by the AFRC/RUF in 1997.

13 Musah, "A Country Under Siege," 89.

14 David Shearer, "Private Armies and Military Intervention, Adelphi Paper 316, IISS, 1998." Reprinted at www.iiss.org/pub/prap316.asp (accessed 21 September 2001).

15 Musah, "A Country Under Siege," 92.

16 Musah, "A Country Under Siege," 90.

17 Ibid.

18 Conciliation Resources, "Profiles: Sierra Leone." Reprinted at www.c-r.org/accord9/profiles.htm (accessed 20 September 2001).

19 Musah, "A Country Under Siege," 90.

20 Ibid, 91; *Africa Confidential* reports that EO was charging US$1.8 million a month, in addition to alleged diamond concessions, "Chronology of Sierra Leone: How Diamonds Fuelled the Conflict." Reprinted at www.africa-confidential.com (accessed 20 September 2001).

21 Musah cites a conversation with Michael Grunberg in which Grunberg claims that EO warned Kabbah that his government would be overthrown within 100 days if he went through with the decision to expel them. Kabbah was overthrown on the 95th day. Musah, "A Country Under Siege," 100.

22 Human Rights Watch, "Sowing Terror: Atrocities Against Civilians in Sierra Leone."

23 House of Commons, "Select Committee on Foreign Affairs-Second Report: Sierra Leone." Reprinted at www.publications.parliament.uk/pa/cm199899/cmselect/cmfaff/116/11603.htm (accessed 21 September 2001). Newafrica.com, "Post-Colonial History." On 6 March 1998, *Africa Confidential* published a report that revealed detailed planning between Sandline, Kabbah and Nigerian forces pointing to Penfold as a key player in the planning. *Africa Confidential* said that the means by which Koroma had been ousted had belied Foreign Secretary Robin Cook's "ethical foreign policy" as well as its ban on military co-operation with the Abacha regime. Later that day the Foreign Office confirmed that Penfold had met with Sandline about Sierra Leone.

24 Human Rights Watch, "Sierra Leone: Getting Away With Murder, Mutilation and Rape." Reprinted at www.hrw.org/reports/1999/sierra (accessed 19 September 2001).

25 Sierra Leone Web, "Lomé Peace Accord: Peace Agreement Between the Government of Sierra Leone and the Revolutionary United Front of Sierra Leone." Reprinted at www.sierra-leone.org/lomeaccord.html (accessed 19 September 2001).

26 Sierra Leone Defence Force website. Reprinted at www.slcdf.org (accessed 19 September 2001).

27 Bram, "Seeking a Way Out of the Abyss: Sierra Leone." International Crisis Group, "Sierra Leone: A Brief Overview." Reprinted at www.intl-crisis-group.org (accessed 19 September 2001); Human Rights Watch, "Sowing Terror: Atrocities Against Civilians in Sierra Leone."

28 Musah, "A Country Under Siege," 78.

29 Newafrica.com, "Pre-Colonial History of Sierra Leone." Reprinted at www.newafrica.com/history/sierraleone/post_colonial.htm (accessed 19 September 2001).

30 Ibid.

31 Ibid.

32 UNDP figures cited by Musah in "A Country Under Siege", 82.

33 Musah, "A Country Under Siege," 82–83.

34 Ibid, 79.

35 Ibid, 84.

36 Abdullah, "Bush Path to Destruction: The Origin and Character of the Revolutionary United Front of Sierra Leone," 203–235.

37 Ibid.

38 Ibid.

39 Musah, "A Country Under Siege," 84–85.

40 "Sierra Leone: Precarious Calm," *Africa Confidential* 42 (2001).

41 Quoted in Ian Smillie, Lansana Gberie and Ralph Hazleton, "The Heart of the Matter: Sierra Leone, Diamonds and Human Security." Reprinted at www.sierra-leone.org/ heartmatter.html (accessed 20 September 2001).

42 Mark Doyle, "Leone War Crimes Tribunal Set Up." Reprinted at http://news.bbc.co.uk/hi/english/world/africa/newsid_1763000/1763957.stm (accessed 8 November 2001).

43 Sierra Leone Web, "Final Communiqué: Truth and Reconciliation Commission Workshop, Freetown, November 2000." Reprinted at www.sierra-leone.org/trc1100.html (accessed 8 November 2001).

44 In Rachel Harvey, "Sierra Leone TRC to Begin Work." Reprinted at http://news.bbc.co.uk/hi/english/world/africa/newsid_2106000/2106390.stm (accessed 17 July 2002).

45 Ibid.

46 Hannah Arendt, *Between Past and Future: Six Exercises in Political Thought* (New York: Viking Press, 1961), 9.

RESOURCES

Books, Current Media Reports, Articles

Abdullah, Ibrahim. "Bush Path to Destruction: The Origin and Character of the Revolutionary United Front of Sierra Leone," in *Journal of Modern African Studies* 36 (1998): 203–235.

Alie, Joe A. D. *A New History of Sierra Leone*. New York: St. Martin's Press, 1990.

Bamford, David. "Foday Sankoh: Rebel Leader." Reprinted at http://news. bbc.co.uk/hi/english/world/africa/newsid_737000/737268.stm (accessed 19 September 2001).

Bram, Posthumus. "Seeking a Way out of the Abyss: Sierra Leone," in *Searching for Peace in Africa: An Overview of Conflict Prevention and Management Activities*, edited by Monique Mekenkamp, Paul van Tongeren and Hans van de Veen. Utrecht: European Platform for Conflict Prevention and Transformation (1999), 372–382.

Cilliers, Jackie and P. Mason, eds. *Peace, Profit and Plunder: The Privatisation of Security in War-Torn African Societies*. New York: Institute for Security Studies, 1999.

Conteh-Morgan, Earl and Mac Dixon-Fyle. *Sierra Leone at the End of the 20th Century: History, Politics, and Society*. New York: Peter Lang, 1999.

Doyle, Mark. "Leone War Crimes Tribunal Set Up." Reprinted at http:// news.bbc.co.uk/hi/english/world/africa/newsid_1763000/1763957.stm (accessed 8 November 2001).

Harvey, Rachel. "Sierra Leone TRC to Begin Work." Reprinted at http:// news.bbc.co.uk/hi/english/world/africa/newsid_2106000/2106390.stm (accessed 17 July 2002).

Hayner, Priscilla. "Reflections on the Sierra Leone Truth and Reconciliation Commission." Reprinted at http://www.article19.org/docimages/728.htm (accessed 17 July 2002).

Human Rights Watch. "Sierra Leone: Getting Away With Murder, Mutilation and Rape." Reprinted at www.hrw.org/reports/1999/sierra (accessed 19 September 2001).

———. "Sowing Terror: Atrocities against Civilians in Sierra Leone." Reprinted at www.hrw.org/reports98/sierra (accessed 19 September 2001).

Musah, Abdel-Fatau. "A Country Under Siege: State Decay and Corporate Military Intervention in Sierra Leone," in *Mercenaries: An African Security Dilemma*, edited by Abdel-Fatau Musah and J. 'Kayode Fayemi. London: Pluto Press, 2000.

National Commission for Democracy and Human Rights, Sierra Leone. "The TRC at a Glance" Series No. 7, 2001. Reprinted at http://www.sierra-leone.org/trcataglance.html (accessed 17 July 2002).

Reno, William. *Warlord Politics and African States*. Boulder: Lynne Rienner, 1998.

Richards, Paul. *Indigenous Agricultural Revolution: Ecology and Food Production in West Africa*. London: Hutchinson; Boulder: Westview Press, 1985.

———. *Rebellion in Liberia and Sierra Leone: A Crisis of Youth*. London: Tauris, 1995.

———. *Fighting for the Rainforest: War, Youth and Resources in Sierra Leone*. Oxford: The International African Institute in association with James Currey; Portsmouth, N. H.: Heinemann, 1996.

Shearer, David. "Private Armies and Military Intervention, Adelphi Paper 316, IISS, 1998." Reprinted at www.iiss.org/pub/prap/316.asp (accessed 21 September 2001).

Smillie, Ian, Lansana Gberie and Ralph Hazleton. "The Heart of the Matter: Sierra Leone, Diamonds and Human Security." Reprinted at www.sierra-leone.org/heartmatter.html (accessed 20 September 2001).

(no author indicated) "Truth and Reconciliation in Sierra Leone." A booklet about the Truth and Reconciliation Commission. Reprinted at http://www.sierra-leone.org/trc-documents.html (accessed 17 July 2002).

Primary Documents

Cry Freetown, "A Brief History of Sierra Leone." Reprinted at www.cryfreetown.org/history.html (accessed 25 September 2001).

House of Commons, "Select Committee on Foreign Affairs – Second Report: Sierra Leone." Reprinted at www.publications.parliament.uk/pa/cm199899/cmselect/cmfaff/116/11603.htm (accessed 21 September 2001).

Sierra Leone Web provides an updated, online bibliography of books and publications on Sierra Leone: www.sierra-leone.org/bibliography.html

United States Institute of Peace Library. Peace Agreements Digital Collection: Sierra Leone. http://www.usip.org/library/pa/sl/sierra_leone_07071999annex.html

Government, Intergovernmental Bodies and Political Parties

Economic Community of West African States (ECOWAS): http://www.cedeao.org

The National Unity Party of Sierra Leone: http://www.nupsl.org

The Political Alliance for Development and Democracy in Sierra Leone: http://www.salonepaddy.org

The Revolutionary United Front (RUF) Party: http://rufp.org

Sierra Leone Defence Force website: http://www.slcdf.org

Sierra Leone Government news and information website: http://www.sierra-leone.gov.sl

Sierra Leone Web: http://www.sierra-leone.org

The Sierra Leone People's Party: http://www.slpp.ws

Truth and Reconciliation Commission: http://www.sierra-leone.org/trc.html

United Nations inter-agency appeals from 1995 to 1998, including a breakdown of contributions and major donors of humanitarian assistance: http://www.reliefweb.int/fts/fin98sle.html

United Nations Mission to Sierra Leone (UNAMSIL): http://www.un.org/Depts/dpko/unamsil/body_unamsil.htm

Local NGOs

The Campaign for Good Governance works to facilitate the full participation of all Sierra Leoneans in the political, social and economic processes of development in Sierra Leone: http://www.slcgg.com

Sierra Leone Live provides a network that links Sierra Leoneans throughout the world by posting information, news, discussion forums, and a message board for making inquiries about lost friends and relatives: http://www.sierraleonelive.com

International NGOs

African Centre for the Constructive Resolution of Disputes (ACCORD) is an international civil society organisation working throughout Africa to bring appropriate African solutions to the challenges posed by conflict on the continent: http://www.accord.org.za

Conciliation Resources endeavours to support sustained practical activities of those working at the community and national levels to prevent or transform violent conflict into opportunities for social, political and economic development based on more just relationships: http://www.c-r.org

The International Rescue Committee (IRC) works in Freetown, Bo and Kenema, as well as in Guinea and Liberia: http://www.theirc.org/whatwedo/westafrica/sierra-leone.cfm

Lawyers Committee for Human Rights protects and promotes fundamental human rights. Its work is impartial, holding all governments accountable to the standards affirmed in the International Bill of Human Rights: http://www.homestead.com/lchrsl/index.html

Partnership Africa Canada (PAC) is a coalition of Canadian and African NGOs working together on issues of human rights, human security and sustainable development. In collaboration with its members and other organisations, PAC undertakes research and policy dialogue initiatives on issues affecting Africa: http://www.partnershipafricacanada.org

SIERRA LEONE COUNTRY INFORMATION

Geography
Location: Western Africa, bordering the North Atlantic Ocean, between Guinea and Liberia.
Cities: *Capital:* Freetown.

People
Nationality: *Noun:* Sierra Leonean(s). *Adjective:* Sierra Leonean.
Population (July 2000 est.): 5 232 624.
Population growth rate: 3.67%.
Ethnic groups: 20 indigenous African tribes 90% (Temne 30%, Mende 30%, other 30%), Creole 10% (descendants of freed Jamaican slaves who were settled in the Freetown area in the late 18th century), refugees from Liberia's recent civil war, small numbers of Europeans, Lebanese, Pakistanis and Indians.
Religions: Muslim 60%, traditional African 30%, Christian 10%.
Languages: English (official, regular use limited to literate minority), Mende (principal vernacular in the south), Temne (principal vernacular in the north), Krio (English-based Creole, spoken by the descendants of freed Jamaican slaves, a lingua franca and a first language for 10% of the population but understood by 95%).
Education: *Literacy:* total population that can read and write English, Mende, Temne or Arabic 31.4%; male 45.4%, female 18.2%.
Health (2000 est.): *Infant mortality rate:* 149/1 000. *Life expectancy:* 45.25 years. *HIV infection rate:* 3.17%.
Workforce (1989 est.): 1 369 000 – no figures available on sectors.

Economy
GDP (1999 est.): $2.5 billion.
GDP real growth rate: 10%.
Per capita income: $500.
Inflation rate: 30%.
Natural resources: Diamonds, titanium ore, bauxite, iron ore, gold, chromite.
Agriculture: 52% of GDP. *Products:* rice, coffee, cocoa, palm kernels, palm oil, peanuts; poultry, cattle, sheep, pigs; fish.
Industry: 16% of GDP. *Types:* mining (diamonds); small-scale manufacturing (beverages, textiles, cigarettes, footwear); petroleum refining.
Trade (1998): *Exports:* $41 million: diamonds, rutile, cocoa, coffee, fish. *Major markets:* Benelux, Spain, US, UK. *Imports:* $166 million – foodstuffs, machinery and equipment, fuels and lubricants, chemicals. *Major suppliers:* UK, Côte d'Ivoire, Benelux, US.
Economic aid: Recipient (1995) of $203.7 million.
Debt – external (1998): $1.15 billion.

Military
Military expenditure: Dollar figures: $46 million (FY96/97).
Military expenditure: Percent of GDP: 2% (FY96/97).

Demographic information is drawn from that compiled by the United States Department of State. See http://www.state.gov/r/pa/ei/bgn

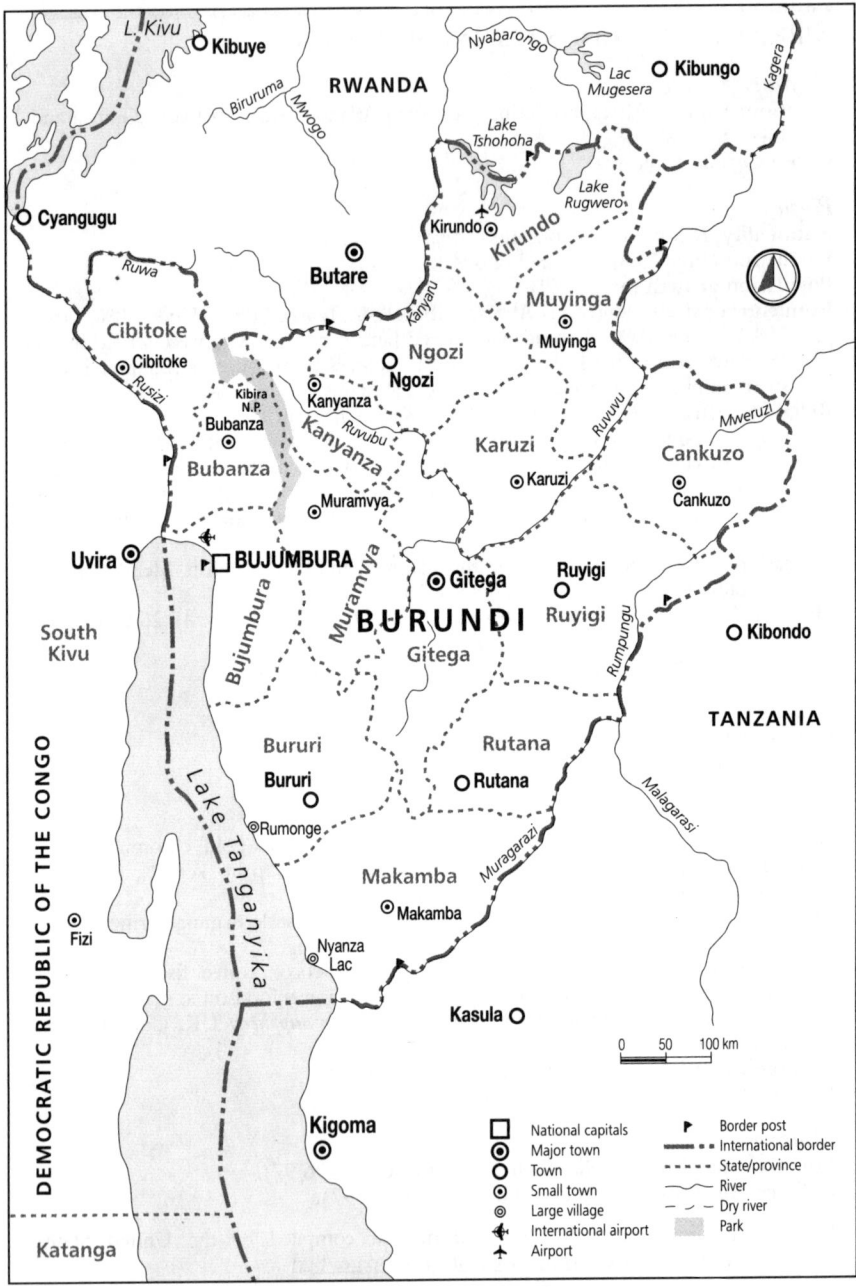

Map of Burundi showing provinces and neighbouring countries: RWANDA, DEMOCRATIC REPUBLIC OF THE CONGO (South Kivu, Katanga), and TANZANIA.

Locations shown include:

L. Kivu, Kibuye, Nyabarongo, Lac Mugesera, Kibungo, Kagera, Biruruma, Mwogo, Lake Tshohoha, Cyangugu, Ruwa, Kanyaru, Butare, Kirundo, Lake Rugwero, Kirundo, Muyinga, Muyinga, Cibitoke, Cibitoke, Ngozi, Ngozi, Rusizi, Kibira N.P., Kanyanza, Bubanza, Ruvubu, Kanyanza, Karuzi, Ruvuvu, Mweruzi, Cankuzo, Cankuzo, Karuzi, Bubanza, Muramvya, Uvira, South Kivu, Bujumbura, BUJUMBURA, Muramvya, B U R U N D I, Gitega, Gitega, Ruyigi, Ruyigi, Kibondo, Rumpungu, Bururi, Bururi, Rutana, Rutana, Rumonge, TANZANIA, Malagarasi, Fizi, Makamba, Makamba, Muragarazi, Nyanza Lac, Kasula, Lake Tanganyika, Katanga, Kigoma

Scale: 0 50 100 km

Legend:
□ National capitals
◉ Major town
○ Town
⊙ Small town
◎ Large village
✈ International airport
✈ Airport
▶ Border post
International border
State/province
River
Dry river
Park

Chapter 3

Burundi: Permanent Deadlock or Tentative Peace?

ERIK DOXTADER AND YEKI MOSOMOTHANE

The sheer number and intensity of conflicts in Africa's Great Lakes region continues to concern the world. In the Rwandan genocide and the "first African world war" in the Democratic Republic of the Congo (DRC), atrocity has built on atrocity. Rivers of blood have flowed unimpeded. Throughout, the violence has shown with great clarity how ethnicity and identity can fuel crimes against humanity and gross violations of human rights. It is against this backdrop that the Burundian civil war finds its place, a conflict characterised by great brutality and with an as yet unknown outcome. There are signs of hope and signals of danger; the difference is not always substantial.

What may make Burundi's civil war different from those of its neighbours is a sense that there is now a chance to forge a deep and lasting peace agreement. As one prominent observer has noted, "at a stage when virtually all other countries in the Great Lakes Region are in various degrees involved in conflicts with no sign that their leadership are even willing to consider talks or negotiations with their armed opponents, Burundi is the only country that has actively engaged and is willing to negotiate with all political groupings whether armed or not".[1] Led by Nelson Mandela, the most recent peace talks seem to have paid dividends. In late June 2001, an agreement was reached which appeared to resolve key disputes about the nature and form of a transitional government. On 1 November that year, a transitional government was installed, an event that many have hailed as a defining moment in the peace-building process.

However, some have expressed dissatisfaction with Mandela's "intrusion" into Burundian affairs. Also, the terms of an inclusive cease-fire remain elusive. Key rebel groups in the country, the factions with the most firepower and who have not participated in the negotiations, continue to resist a settlement. In a recent report, Jan van Eck warned that continued conflict has the potential to unravel the transitional agreement and the Arusha Accord of 2000.[2] Thus, the conflict is not yet over, and it is a war with disastrous effects for the warring parties, the people of Burundi and the region.

For peace and reconciliation, the agreements will have to be signed by all parties and disputes over who will lead the transition will need resolution. Regional stability will also play a crucial factor in the country's future. If the DRC re-ignites, most believe that chances for peace in Burundi will fade quickly. Even if this is avoided, there are many who believe that the international community will need to play a substantial role in the process of democratic institution-building and economic reconstruction. It also appears that the people of Burundi will need to find ways of healing the wounds of the past, many of which stem from ongoing mistrust between Hutus and Tutsis. There is hope in Burundi. There is also a legacy of violence and atrocity that may easily confound the move to democracy and peace.

The Face of Conflict
The present conflict in Burundi has been bloody and complicated. Multiple parties are vying for power in an atmosphere poisoned by fear and deep division. While the Arusha Accord offers a viable way forward, negotiations have been slowed by disputes between parties at the table and by disagreements among those willing to negotiate and those who are not. The negotiated form of the country's transition from civil war has been both celebrated as an immense step forward and condemned as a blatant violation of Burundi's sovereignty. As several key armed rebel groups have yet to sign the agreement, there remains much unfinished work. Some analysts see signs that the parties are using talks to cover rearmament and preparation for the next onslaught. In a country that has the world's second largest internal refugee population, human rights abuse is widespread. Confidence-building has to take place in a country that well remembers and fears genocidal violence.

Most trace the current phase of conflict to the events of 1993, the year of Burundi's first democratic presidential elections.[3] After a new constitution was adopted, Melchoir Ndadaye was elected president, thus ending several decades of minority Tutsi rule. An ethnic Hutu, Ndadaye was head of the popular *Front pour la démocratie au Burundi* (FRODEBU). The election of a Hutu president and majority government did not sit well with a Tutsi elite that had long held power, controlled the military and enjoyed substantial privilege during Burundi's colonial years. Disillusion and fear thus helped inspire an attempted coup in October 1993, an attack that resulted in Ndadaye's death. Massacres ensued, with violence born partly out of the fear that past Tutsi violence against Hutus was about to repeat itself. The violence escalated, with all sides, including the Tutsi-dominated army, playing a role in the atrocities. An estimated 150 000 people lost their lives. Almost a million individuals were displaced, many fleeing to Rwanda, Tanzania and the DRC.[4]

The violence drew widespread international condemnation. Inside the country, opposition to the coup, coupled with the ethnic violence it inspired, reduced the military's support for the new government, then operating as the National Committee for Public Salvation. With little military backing, the committee disbanded on 25 October 1993. The return of civilian government did little to halt the ethnic clashes, especially in the rural areas. The deteriorating security situation and the diminishing influence and capacity of the government set the country on edge.

President Sylvestre Ntibantunganya, an ethnic Hutu appointed after Cyprien Ntaryamir was killed in a plane crash, failed to resolve the crisis. In July 1996, the army led a successful and relatively bloodless coup, claiming that it was provoked by the Ntibantunganya government's willingness to supply arms to Hutu extremists accused of participating in massacres designed to undermine the inter-ethnic power-sharing arrangement known as the Convention of Government. Other reasons were cited, including the request by President Ntibantunganya for an international intervention force composed of troops from neighbouring states to provide protection for politicians, civil servants and crucial installations. Although the request for such a force had received support at a regional OAU summit, there was no attempt to consult Burundi's armed forces. Thus, differences of interpretation appeared around the purpose and mandate of the force. Political leaders of mainly Tutsi political parties rejected the intervention force and criticised Ntibantunganya for encouraging external interference in Burundi's domestic affairs.[5] More precisely, the possibility of intervention raised fears that the Tanzanian-led force would have little interest in departure. This perceived threat, coupled with the internal rebellion, continued massacres and increasing institutional chaos, fed the drive for the July coup.

The successful coup had a number of immediate effects on Burundian society.[6] Most notably, it effectively ended the inter-ethnic power sharing arrangement, the 1994 Convention of Government. This structure, created by all major political parties after the death of President Ndadaye, was the closest thing Burundi had to a peace settlement in the wake of the 1993 violence. While not perfect, the arrangement was an important stopgap in a situation where it was not yet possible to hold general elections. In the midst of ethnic violence, it detailed plans for a transitional government and provided for the creation of a national security council to address the clashes that had precipitated the initial crisis. However, many believed that the arrangement was destined to fail. As it gave the opposition significant power, the convention appeased the Tutsis but provoked the Hutus, cementing the perception that the majority governance was a façade. It was also clear that many did not want the arrangement to work. After three months, the mainly Tutsi party, the Union for National Progress (UPRONA), withdrew from the coalition government, accusing FRODEBU of complicity in the 1993 violence.

The coup ended hopes for transitional power-sharing. It also returned to power the current president, Pierre Buyoya, who in 1987 had staged a successful coup against Jean-Baptiste Bagaza. Buyoya's recovery of the presidency was met with diverse reactions.[7] Some saw in it a glimmer of hope for democratic reforms. Others questioned Buyoya's integrity and his role in a number of ethnic clashes during the 1980s. Many Hutus were critical of Buyoya's decision to accept the military's offer of power, especially those who believed that he was co-operating with a military regime that had been responsible for the death of Melchoir Ndadaye. While countries such as the United States and Belgium were willing to negotiate with the Buyoya regime, neighbouring African countries were quick to impose sanctions after the president dissolved the national assembly and banned political parties.[8] Although economic sanctions had an impact, Buyoya's return to power did seem to stabilise the situation within the country, especially as it appeared to rein in Tutsi extremists and militias.

Over the next few years, the Buyoya administration adopted a number of approaches to the conflict. The government also endeavoured to mobilise the population through "consciousness-raising". Specifically, the government sought to discredit rebel forces by pointing out their links with the ex-FAR and Interahamwe factions involved in the Rwandan genocide. By emphasising these ties, in part to rally international and national opinion, the government helped marginalise and discredit the Hutu rebels by condemning their so-called "barbaric methods" and ideology of genocide. By labelling the rebels as terrorists, the government sought to present itself as the source of the people's security. This strategy appeared to be successful at first. However, it has failed to produce conclusive international support for the Buyoya regime and what it has defined as a just war. At the same time, Buyoya expressed a willingness to negotiate with opposition and rebel groups.[9] The Arusha talks were thus an indicator that the government was not necessarily committed to a military solution. However, some argue that the shift has more to do with economic sanctions than a change of heart. Publicly, Buyoya claimed that his foremost desire was to reunite Burundi's people.

The present conflict in Burundi defies singular explanation. It has its basic roots in a legacy of ethnic-based violence and a long-standing struggle for political and economic power. All sides point to the events of 1993 as a key turning point.[10] Coupled with events in Rwanda, some Tutsis fear for their wellbeing, if not life. On the other side, the Hutu population holds many of the same concerns, mindful of past Tutsi domination and violence. In the run of history, the blame for atrocity can be laid at many doors. However, the sheer number of groups involved in the peace process complicates the conflict in Burundi. The war does not pit one monolithic ethnic bloc against another equally homogeneous group. Rather, the players show a varying range of interests and opinions about the prospects and terms for peace. Led by Buyoya, the government is supported and opposed by various Tutsi and Hutu groups. In 1998, the government entered into a partnership agreement with two large political parties, the Tutsi-dominated UPRONA and the Hutu-aligned FRODEBU, the party that controls the national assembly. However, there is also a group of aligned Tutsi-oriented parties, known collectively as the G-10, and a set of Hutu counterparts, the G-7. Within and between each, there are substantial differences of opinion about the nature of the Burundian conflict and Buyoya's ability to lead the country into the future.[11] Across this spectrum, there are a number of different and competing accounts of the current conflict and its meaning.[12] Locally the rebels are said to have lost support, largely due to the fact that they have launched attacks on unarmed civilians.[13] Internationally, the rebels' refusal to negotiate has earned them condemnation and blame for the continuation of the war.

There are three main armed "rebel" movements actively involved in the current phase of the Burundian conflict. The *Parti pour la libération du peuple hutu* (PALIPEHUTU) is one of the country's oldest Hutu political groups.[14] It has declared repeatedly that it is motivated by a desire to end "Tutsi dominance" over the majority of Burundi's citizens. Led by Kosan Kabura, this group's armed wing is known as the *Forces nationales de libération* (FNL). However, there is substantial tension between the PALIPEHUTU and PALIPEHUTU-FNL. For instance, the former is represented in the Arusha process while the latter is not.[15] Linked to the PALIPEHUTU is the *Front de libération nationale* (FROLINA), with its armed wing, the *Forces armies du peuple* (FAP), and the *Union pour la libération nationale* (ULINA), with its armed wing, the *Forces de libération nationale* (FALINA).

The National Council for the Defence of Democracy (CNDD), with its armed wing, the Forces for the Defence of Democracy (FDD), is perhaps the largest, best organised and most active of the Hutu rebel movements.[16] Leonard Nyangoma, Interior Minister in the Ndadaye government, formed the CNDD in exile. Although the support base of the CNDD is largely Hutu, the CNDD executive has included a number of Tutsis. At its inception, the CNDD was opposed to Buyoya's regime on the grounds that it was a military government that did not represent the people of Burundi.[17] Recently, internal division has wracked the organisation, with Colonel Jean-Bosco Ndayikengurukiye ousting Leonard Nyangoma from his leadership position only to be ousted himself. The changes have been justified on the grounds that many within the CNDD-FDD resented the Tutsi presence in the organisation's leadership struggle.[18] As a result, the CNDD-FDD under Ndayikengurukiye was not involved in the Arusha peace process although the larger CNDD, still led by Nyangoma, has entered the talks.

The conflict in Burundi has come at tremendous cost. It is estimated that more than 250 000 civilians have lost their lives in the current round of violence, many caught in the crossfire between government troops and various rebel factions. Deaths are attributed to all sides. Many of those killed have been women and children. There are indications that some of these deaths have been the result of direct and pre-planned attacks. One report has described the killing of Hutu civilians by government forces as retribution against Hutu-aligned rebels who have allegedly killed Tutsi civilians.[19] There are also indications that unarmed civilians are targeted by government soldiers if it is believed that they are assisting rebel forces.

The war has brought substantial atrocities and human rights violations that range from murder, torture and rape to dislocation and forced removal. Government forces have reportedly responded to rebel activity with great brutality. There are reports of widespread torture and the "disappearance" of civilians accused of collaborating with rebel factions. According to Amnesty International, the methods of torture used by the security forces include severe and prolonged beatings with electric cables, sticks and heavy implements on the joints, the soles of the feet and genitals.[20] The rebel groups have also committed violations of human rights. They are reported to have targeted unarmed civilians in the course of the fighting. These attacks appear to be aimed at those Hutus and Tutsis thought to collaborate with the government.

Large numbers of human rights violations have been reported in government regroupment camps. Established in 1996, the camps were intended to deprive the rebels of potential support. Their creation entailed the removal of an estimated 300 000 people, mostly Hutus who were living in and around areas of rebel activity.[21] Conditions inside the camps are said to be appalling and overcrowded, with few facilities and shortages of water, food and medical supplies. Predictably, cholera and other diseases are common.[22] There are widespread reports of summary executions, disappearances, rapes and forced labour. Rebel factions have objected strongly to the camps, going so far as to attack them. There are reports that the rebels, just like the government forces, have made use of child soldiers and looted vacant homes left by people forced into the regroupment camps.[23] Overall, human rights violations have had a lasting impact on ordinary citizens, not only in relation to the extent of the trauma suffered, but also with respect to perceptions regarding relations between Hutus and Tutsis. According to one report, the destruction of homes and the regrouping of the Hutu population has reinforced segregation between the different ethnic groups.[24] Throughout the country, lack of personal security, continued war and extensive human rights violations have combined to create a highly volatile situation.

Human rights violations in Burundi have shaped international perceptions of the government's role in the conflict and its commitment to peace. In general, the world community has directed its criticism more to the government than the rebel groups. This is due to perceptions that the government has failed to obey a number of international treaties that speak to the treatment of civilians in internal conflicts. Human Rights Watch claims that the government has consistently violated the principle of civilian immunity. The displacement of people is also prohibited under international law, especially by Article 17(1) of Protocol II of the Geneva Convention, except where such a displacement is in the interest of those being moved or is militarily necessary. In this case, however, the forced removals meet neither of the exceptions. Even if they did, the actions of government forces within the camps appear to violate international law. The world community has condemned the camps and urged their closure. To date, the process has been slow, with many people still behind the fences.[25]

The killing of civilians by government forces has dented Buyoya's international credibility and undermined the government's claims that its violence is justified. Thus, while the Burundian government might perceive itself as the conduit of change, much of the outside world views the government as a minority regime unwilling to share power.[26] The international community, especially the United States and the European

Community, has maintained sanctions, despite the decision in early 2001 by regional actors to resume interaction. In any case, existing sanctions do not appear to be hindering the government's ability to wage conflict.[27] The rebel movements appear to receive support from forces in the DRC. This has had implications, within and outside Burundi, for the movements' image. According to some reports, the DRC government has recruited Hutu rebel groups to fight with it. The FDD are said to have bases in Eastern Congo in return for helping government troops, but the FDD has denied this charge. There are also reports that the rebels are being financed by ex-FAR and Interahamwe factions in Rwanda and that there is continuing support from the Tanzanian government.[28]

The fate of the Burundian conflict is inextricably linked to the conflict and (ethnic) tensions in the DRC and Rwanda. The conflict in the DRC has had a profound impact on the whole Great Lakes region, especially as more countries have been drawn into the fighting. The increasingly ethnic overtones of the Congolese war, adopted especially by the forces of the late DRC President, Laurent Kabila, and the hard-line attitude of his allies against the Tutsi regimes of Burundi, Rwanda and Uganda, has had the effect of dividing the region into Hutu and Tutsi camps.[29] As Tutsi governments fear violent opposition from forces in the DRC, the entire region remains unstable. The slow pace of implementing the Lusaka Accords has and will continue to have an impact on the Burundi conflict.[30] This is of even greater concern given reports that Burundian troops have intervened in the conflict in the DRC on the grounds that they must secure the country's border. It is important to mention that the current DRC president, Joseph Kabila, unlike his late father and predecessor, has committed himself to ending the conflict. While this might be a step in the right direction, at the time of writing there was not yet a clear sense of whether these developments would have a lasting impact on regional stability. The Burundian conflict has also led to strained relations between Burundi and Tanzania, largely due to claims of reported cross-border insurgencies launched by the Burundian rebels using the refugee camps in Tanzania as their bases.

In sum, Burundi labours under the toll of ongoing war even as it is buoyed by the hope for a transition that appears to contain the basis for long-term peace and reconstruction. Monitoring agencies reported substantial violence in the run-up to the installation of the new transitional government, conflict that demonstrates that the country stands at the beginning, not the end, of a long road. The legacy of distrust weighs heavily, a problem of history that has much to do with the future.

The Historical Roots of Violence and Division

Burundi is home to some six million people, 85% of whom are Hutus (Bantu), 14% Tutsis (Hamitic) and roughly 1% Twas. Although the groups share a language, religions and a kinship system, they have long been defined as separate groups. Prior to German colonisation in 1894, the country was a long-standing and stable monarchy. Nonetheless it was the Tutsis, the group that formed the warrior-aristocracy of traditional Burundian society, who were dominant.[31] In the pre-colonial period, Tutsi privilege was social rather than tribal. Status rather than ethnicity was the principal determinant of rank and privilege. With colonialism, the Germans and later the Belgians installed a system of indirect rule that concentrated power in the hands of the Tutsis, the group that received access to education, economic resources and employment. It has been argued that the Germans and the Belgians were impressed with the Tutsis' "European-like features" and thus considered them more suitable for rule.[32] This did much to cement the ethnic divide, creating rigid identity categories and polarisation between groups that spoke the same language.

In 1962, the rifts between the two ethnic groups were evident when the country gained its independence from Belgium. At that time, two political parties emerged. The *Union pour le Progrès National* (UPRONA) was led by Prince Rwagasore, who aimed to unite the country through his nationalist movement. UPRONA won the legislative elections in 1961, but the prince was assassinated two weeks later in a plot orchestrated by the opposition party, the *Parti Démocrate Chrétien* (PDC). The death of Rwagasore was a turning point in Burundi's history. Without its leader, a figure who represented the people and seemed able to bridge the country's divides, UPRONA splintered along ethnic lines. With neighbouring Rwanda as an example, the Tutsi elite increased their opposition to democratic institutions in order to secure the terms of power.[33]

After full independence, the situation did not improve. King Mambutsa tried to maintain the country's stability by ensuring equal representation of Hutus and Tutsis in the government. However, ongoing ethnic violence in Rwanda forced thousands of refugees into Burundi. The assassination of the Hutu Prime Minister, Pierre Ngendadwe, by a Rwandan refugee in 1965, came at a time of heightened Hutu political consciousness, especially with respect to political representation and access to power. In 1965, Hutu elements within the army staged a coup attempt, an action that was brutally repressed and resulted in a number of Hutu deaths, mostly members of the army or politicians. This early violence is a basic symbol of the divide between Hutus and Tutsis, a rift central to the communal and ethnic conflict that defines Burundi's post-independence political history. It created perceptions that are still evident in the current situation. It also exposed the vulnerability of each group, as both sides had the capacity to attack if not decimate the other.[34]

Hutu-Tutsi antagonism led to two brutal massacres, both of which continue to shape politics and attitudes. In 1972, a deadly attack by Hutu militants in Southern Burundi led to fears of a larger uprising, spurring Tutsi gangs and soldiers to massacre between 80 000 and 100 000 civilians, mostly younger, educated Hutus. According to some observers, Tutsi leaders attempted to eradicate the episode from the country's collective consciousness. In 1988, another massacre occurred. This time, in the wake of attacks by PALIPEHUTU activists, the Tutsi-led army killed thousands if not tens of thousands of Hutus.[35] Thus, Burundi's independence period comprises a series of coups, attempted coups and inter-communal clashes. The resulting culture of violence has been hard to dissolve. To most Hutus, Burundi's history is a legacy of Tutsi oppression, discrimination and massacre. The discourse of ethnic inequality is firmly entrenched and used frequently, a politics of identity that breeds distrust and grounds Hutu calls for majority rule.[36] For their part, Tutsis have been unmoved by charges of ethnic dominance and have frequently denied the existence of a Hutu-Tutsi problem.[37] No official enquiry was ever conducted by Michel Micombero's government into the events or causes of the 1965 and 1972 massacres. It was only during President Buyoya's first term in the presidency, following the 1988 massacres, that a Commission for National Unity was established to investigate the terms and extent of the violence. Although there were claims that the Commission conducted a shallow and inefficient inquiry, it was a sign of the government's willingness to at least recognise the connection between ethnicity and violence.

The proffered official history – that Tutsis have long been subject to Hutu violence – has been used by the minority to instil a fear of Hutu political power. This sentiment is firmly entrenched in some circles, a problem that threatens the trust-building needed to carry out negotiations and implement formal peace agreements and power-sharing plans.[38] Indeed, while all the major political groupings have committed themselves publicly to the peace process, these dynamics remain powerful factors. Analysts complain that the difference between what is apparent and real is not always obvious, especially when one or more of the parties appeal to ethnic fear to justify their case.

Political and ethnic conflict in Burundi is fed by a number of material and demographic problems. Burundi is a small, resource-poor country with a highly underdeveloped manufacturing sector. The country's economy is agriculture-based, with approximately 90% of the population dependent on subsistence farming. The armed conflict has had a devastating impact on the economy, in both the rural and urban areas. According to the World Bank, the impact of the conflict on the agricultural economy has been felt through the widespread destruction of farms and crops, coupled with population displacement. In urban areas, the conflict has caused substantial unemployment and dramatically degraded the country's infrastructure. Overall, the competition for scarce resources has heightened real and perceived inequalities between Hutus and Tutsis. The colonial advantage of the Tutsis over the Hutus continues to appear in the economic arena and in competition for jobs. As one of the least developed and highly indebted countries, scarcity is a fact of life in Burundi. The government remains the main repository of wealth, power and privilege. It is thus at the very centre of conflict over the terms of economic security.

The current structures of governance play a clear role in fuelling the conflict. Burundi is considered a de facto authoritarian state as a result of the 1996 military coup that handed power to Buyoya. Upon taking control of the country, Buyoya banned political parties and restricted press freedom. After a time, political parties were reinstated with the proviso that they needed to make a "positive" contribution to national life. While this declaration aimed to create a picture of normality, permitting some political opposition was also a way for the state to claim that sanctions were no longer justified. When the powers of the national assembly were restored, Buyoya issued an order that prohibited the assembly from dismissing the government. In June 1998, however, an internal partnership was formed between the government of President Buyoya and the large Hutu party in Burundi, FRODEBU. The partnership saw the appointment of about 12 Hutus in Buyoya's reshuffled cabinet. While it has been perceived as an attempt simply to legitimise the Buyoya regime, the arrangement has helped create some trust between the leadership of the two groups. It did not, however, lead to an all-out acceptance of the Buyoya regime by FRODEBU.

The voice of civil society is not often heard in Burundi. Most observers have noted that the conflict and the peace talks at Arusha have focused on accommodating political elites with little corresponding engagement with the rest of civil society.[39] Civil society remains outside the current political dynamics, a situation that some see as risky, because civil society will need to play a crucial role in popularising a peace agreement. At present, there are limited civil society organisations within Burundi. The Human Rights

League and the Apostles for Peace are among the organisations working in the areas of conflict resolution and reconciliation, offering education, training, dissemination of basic civic values and respect for human rights. Traditionally the Catholic Church in Burundi has provided a significant voice for civil society, serving as a counterweight to and potential rival of the government by educating, and providing medical treatment to, poor citizens.[40] However in the 1980s there was a vigorous effort by then president Bagaza to silence the Catholic Church, a campaign that was perceived as an attempt to undermine Hutus who, despite widespread discrimination, maintained significant influence in church affairs.

Prospects for Peace-building

The vast range of actors, coupled with generations of ethnic animosity and the memory of past atrocities, make it difficult to build peace in Burundi. At the time of writing, the chances for a lasting peace agreement appear to have increased as parties recommitted themselves to the terms of the Arusha Accord. In July 2001, an agreement was signed that called for a two-phase transition in which President Buyoya would lead the country for 18 months, after which a Hutu, Domitien Ndayizeye, would take over for the second half of the transition. With the installation of this framework in November 2001, Burundi may be ready to turn the page. The new transitional government is a coalition of Tutsi and Hutu actors who appear ready and willing to share power. Tutsis were handed the defence, finance and foreign affairs portfolios while Hutus received interior and public security as well as a number of others. Foreign troops, including a substantial South African contingent, were brought in to smooth the transition and help ensure the safety of those returning from exile. However, there is substantial work left undone. The two major armed rebel groups have yet to sign. There is also evident displeasure over Mandela's role in the process and continued uncertainty over whether Buyoya will fulfil his commitments as outlined in the Arusha agreement.

The Arusha peace process began in July 1998. It was preceded by the formation of the internal partnership for peace, a transitional agreement that reinstated Burundi's constitution and created an alliance between the government and FRODEBU. Sponsored and led by former Tanzanian President, Julius Nyerere, the first Arusha meetings were attended by 17 of Burundi's political parties. Several groups did not attend. The FDD, the military branch of the CNDD, announced that it was not bound by any agreement that flowed from the talks, a declaration that complicated assessments of whether it was possible to negotiate a cease-fire and clouded the question of who Hutu parties would support for the transitional presidency.[41] The initial meeting nonetheless demonstrated concrete progress, showing that parties were willing to talk about how to resolve the issues that stood between them.

Under Nelson Mandela, the process made significant strides, culminating in an agreement signed by 19 parties in August 2000. Much of the success has been credited to the former South African president, who helped build trust while creating a necessary sense of urgency.[42] The agreement called for the formation of a transitional government that would hold power until full elections could be held. This interim structure has been installed. However, there are significant obstacles still to clear. One of the fault lines that divided the parties was the question of who should lead the new government.[43] Both Tutsi and Hutu groups, the G-10 and G-7, showed internal division over the question of who is best suited to lead the country through the transition. Across ethnic lines, there are many who oppose Buyoya's leadership. For now, he will lead the country for the first half of the transition. This does not necessarily mean that everyone is happy with the arrangement. During the talks, representatives from a set of pro-Hutu parties threw their support behind Colonel Epitace Bayaganakande and argued that support for the Buyoya-Ndayizeye leadership arrangement was tantamount to "treason". Increasingly, this view has appeared with the claim that Mandela's involvement in the peace process "violated [Burundi's] national sovereignty".[44]

The transitional government has taken power before the creation of a cease-fire agreement, something that Buyoya long opposed and which has created significant pressures during the early days of his administration. The new government still lacks the support of the FDD and FNL, the two major armed rebel groups. There is still dispute over whether they are even willing to negotiate in good faith. The current prognosis is mixed, with conflicting reports about whether South African-sponsored cease-fire talks will yield results. In fact, contradictory reports of respective progress and ensuing failure appear monthly. In May 2002, it appeared that the FNL was increasingly interested in entering the cease-fire talks. A month later, it seemed that deadlock had returned except for some progress in talks with the FDD. The International Crisis Group, a private multinational organisation, has recently argued that part of the problem lies in the fact the various sides do not all want the same cease-fire. International monitoring groups have called on FRODEBU to put pressure on the rebels. The success of such action may depend partly on whether it is possible to reduce the support that the rebels are receiving from sources inside the

DRC. Other monitoring groups have recommended that international and regional pressure be applied to all warring parties and their foreign sponsors. In any case, the promise of the Arusha Accords remains at substantial risk.

The agreement forged at Arusha contains a number of strict provisions, all of which Buyoya has pledged to implement. These include assurances that all signatories will be represented in the government and that the transitional authorities will work with the United Nations High Commissioner for Refugees (UNHCR) to repatriate refugees and strive to open the political process to all parties and citizens. The Implementation Monitoring Committee for the accord has raised questions about the government's pending legislation on the prevention of genocide and crimes against humanity, an issue that will be pivotal in moving from transition to consolidation. Along with the creation of political rights and respect for human rights, it is apparent that the success of the transition will turn partly on the ability of the government to effect material and economic change. International NGOs have called for the UN and western powers to invest in the reconstruction process or see it fail. Burundi's Minister of the Peace Process, Ambroise Niyonsaba, has argued that the end of the war will open substantial economic opportunities. However, a plan for economic reconstruction is not yet on the table.

There are several domestic and international NGOs engaged in efforts to boost peace in Burundi. International Alert was the first foreign organisation to try to implement peace preventative programmes in Burundi. In 1995, it established an initiative that saw prominent figures within Burundian society coming to South Africa to hear of South Africa's peaceful transition to democracy and the Truth and Reconciliation Commission (TRC) process. The organisation also established a Burundi Steering Committee and an International Steering Committee for Burundi. Both bodies aimed to co-ordinate peace-building initiatives taken by NGOs, the UN and representatives of donor countries.[45]

Another prominent international NGO working toward peace-building and reconciliation in Burundi is Search for Common Ground. This American-based NGO opened a field office in Burundi in 1995 and has initiated programmes aimed at reconciling the different ethnic groups in Burundi. Its programmes include the creation of a radio station in Burundi (Studio Ijambo) that produces and distributes a wide variety of reconciliation-oriented material and the establishment of a women's peace centre in the capital, Bujumbura. Other programmes launched by the organisation include the establishment of a Great Lakes Policy Forum, a coalition of concerned NGOs, government agencies and international organisations that meet monthly and focus on the crisis in the Great Lakes region. There is also now a youth project that teaches conflict resolution skills to ethnically mixed groups of young leaders.[46]

The International Crisis Group is another organisation that is actively involved in Burundi, focusing mainly on fact-finding missions, early warning, training, lobbying and media-focused activities to help bring about peaceful resolution to the conflicts. This organisation, which is based in Belgium, has in the past proposed a TRC initiative in Burundi modelled on the South African example.[47] The Centre for Conflict Resolution, based in Cape Town, has also continued to play an active part in facilitating peace and reconciliation in Burundi. This has been largely due to the involvement of Jan van Eck who, as Senior Consultant for the Great Lakes region, continues to be involved in peace initiatives by engaging with all parties involved in the peace process and bringing the South African experience of transitional politics to the peace process.

Present and Future Opportunities for Reconciliation

With the possibility of a sustained and stable political transition comes the chance for Burundians to consider whether and how to undertake local and corporate forms of reconciliation, efforts that might heal deep division and contribute to the consolidation of democracy. At present, in the light of ambiguities around the credibility of transitional leadership and whether there can be a lasting cease-fire, the problem of reconciliation is a delicate one, raising issues of trust and accountability that have the potential to create new controversy. However, for those who favour reconciliation, the form of the negotiations is itself a cause for hope. Under Mandela, the top-down peace process in Burundi shows substantial similarity to the one developed in South Africa. They are certainly not identical. Jan van Eck's report underscores the point that reconciliation in Burundi will have to take into account that the war was not a formal liberation struggle but a crisis born in a "common legacy of blood".[48] This means that reconciliation will need to address the question of ethnicity. Still, the structure of the negotiating committees and the call to offer a temporary amnesty that would allow exiles to return and participate in the transition has obvious parallels with the negotiations that took place during the early 1990s in South Africa. In this light, the call for amnesty – temporary or otherwise – may open up space for actors in Burundi to take up the question of what reconciliation might mean and the ways that it could help redress the wounds of the past. The international community has already begun to weigh in on the matter, offering suggestions that range from all-out trials for crimes against humanity to a South African-like TRC. Voices within Burundi are somewhat softer, perhaps reflecting the fragile state of the transition talks. In any event, it is clear that the nature and object of reconciliation will need to develop out of the consensus forged in the peace process and collective debate over how to define and redress the wounds of history.

What is there to reconcile in Burundi? This question is a source of controversy, especially given long-standing taboos that prevent discussion of the violence and ethnic hatred that has dominated Burundian society. In May 2000, the CNDD-FDD petitioned the UN for recognition that the 1965 and 1972 killings amounted to genocide. In fact, the UN investigations of the events did affirm this conclusion. However, the declaration is risky at a number of levels. As it offers clear standing for indictments and trials, it may provoke political reactions that run contrary to the spirit of consensus that is needed to carry out the transitional agreement. Mistrust and fear still run deep. Together, these problems weave a tight web. The causes and extent of ethnic violence are not fully known or explained in Burundi. The ethnic rift has the potential to blossom into new conflict if not adequately addressed.

Inside and outside Burundi, there is substantial literature suggesting that "impunity" is one key cause of the violence. This finding has brought calls to prosecute those responsible for atrocities. These external calls for how Burundi *should* deal with its past come with certain problems. The country's judiciary is neither robust nor trusted. It does not appear to have the capacity to try significant numbers of perpetrators. In addition, if history is any indication, many would doubt the fairness of the proceedings. Over the last three years, there have been trials convened for those implicated in the 1993 coup and the assassination of President Ndadaye. Amnesty International has noted that these trials have fallen short of international standards of fairness. It has noted that although some military personnel were found guilty, the trials were marked by an apparent unwillingness to elucidate facts and responsibilities. There was little if any attempt to identify the instigators of the coup and thus those behind substantial violence have not been called to account.[49]

Overall, Burundi confronts a complex situation, a transitional period in which there appears to be a need to build democratic institutions through a spirit of compromise while simultaneously creating programmes that assure accountability and generate respect for the rule of law. This line between pragmatism and duty is a fine one and there is not yet a clear proposal in Burundi for how it might be walked. The major political parties have both agreed to the creation of a Commission of Inquiry to investigate the 1972 and 1993 violence. The precise mandate of the body has yet to be established. To be successful, it will need to address perceptions that past inquiries have neglected many issues and appeared to favour Tutsi interests.

The terms of the Arusha peace process may open the way towards a Truth and Reconciliation Commission, a body that has been advocated publicly by President Buyoya. Measured largely in the light of South Africa's experience, the value of such a body may turn on its ability to facilitate the recovery of lost history, and to recognise victims and the interaction between victims and perpetrators. Official truth-seeking may also help cement respect for the rule of law by making it difficult for parties to deny the extent and nature of past violence. Given the South African involvement in the peace process, there may be opportunities for productive collaboration on how to set up and design a commission.[50] However, there is not yet a clear indication that the Burundians have resolved to take this approach. If it were modelled on the South African system, the country confronts the problem of whether conditional amnesty is an acceptable outcome of the transition. If not, this may spur further calls to convene international tribunals to prosecute key perpetrators, a process that may or may not help build the trust needed to overcome ethnic-based fear and mistrust.

While high-level initiatives remain tentative, this has not stopped some local actors from undertaking efforts designed to promote reconciliation. In collaboration with traditional local authorities (*Abashingantahe*), groups like the Apostles for Peace have begun programmes across the country. The *Abashingantahe*, said to recall traditional pre-colonial groups renowned for their sense of justice, have apparently succeeded in reconciling families and individuals.[51] The *Abashingantahe* have received the support of the government, with the issuing of a decree in 1997 establishing a National Council of *Bashingantahe*, consisting of 40 individuals, drawn from all ethnic and social groups, tasked to discuss issues related to the country's future. It is not clear what effect this debate is having on citizens. However, as a traditional dispute-resolution mechanism, the National Council of *Bashingantahe* may be able to hear certain kinds of cases related to past violence. Similar to the Rwandan *gacaca* initiative, community-level trials could have a number of advantages. The trials would allow local actors to establish the facts and decide the fate of those accused, while at the same time addressing possible reconciliation objectives such as trust-building, restitution and reintegration. However, it is not easy to build fair and efficient hearing structures, especially in a situation already characterised by ethnic and inter-communal tensions.[52]

Economic peace-building can be another means to promote national reconciliation in Burundi. Broad-based economic peace-building is an essential requirement because peace and reconciliation will be to no avail for ordinary citizens if economic opportunities are absent.[53] It seems highly unlikely that any meaningful policy of addressing the material inequalities between rich and poor will be adopted by any new Burundian government on its own. This is due to the fact that while there are some Tutsis who have held power over the government and the economy of the country, the benefits of such power have only been available to a relatively few, while the rest of the population, Hutu and Tutsi, have continued to live in relative squalor. Thus an economic peace-building initiative within Burundi would depend upon the support of the international community, donor agencies and countries providing material assistance for future programmes in Burundi aimed at democratic institution-building and pro-viding economic opportunities for combatants once the conflict is finally over.[54] The recent pledge, therefore, by donor countries to make funds available to support the peace process should help facilitate such a process.

The signs are hopeful in Burundi. Many of the pieces of transition are in place and there is now an opportunity to begin the hard work of building and consolidating democracy. Much of this work will involve addressing the legacies of distrust and violence that have divided Burundi's citizens and fractured its politics. On both levels, the task of reconciliation may well need to begin with the negotiation of a sustain-able cease-fire.[55] This work will take time and is likely to proceed in fits and starts. If it succeeds, larger opportunities for reconciliation will follow, chances to build the nation in a way that both accounts for the past and recognises the importance of the future. The line will be fine. For now, there is both deadlock and peace in Burundi. The coming months and years will prove decisive.

NOTES

1 Jan van Eck, "Burundi Report," 1999. Reprinted at http://ccrweb.ccr.uct.ac.za_burundi_reports/burrep-april99.html (accessed 29 November 2000).
2 Integrated Regional Information Network (IRIN), "IRIN Focus on Ceasefire

Talks in Pretoria," 3 May 2002. Reprinted at www.reliefweb.int (accessed 10 June 2002).

3 Edward Nyankanzi, *Genocide: Rwanda and Burundi* (Rochester, V. T.: Schenkman Books, 1998), 43.

4 Mike Dravis and Anne Pitsch, "Hutu and Tutsi in Burundi," 1998. Reprinted at www.bsos.umd.edu/cidcm/mar/burundi.htm (accessed 23 November 2000); Réné Lemarchand, *Burundi: Genocide Forgotten, Invented and Anticipated* (Centre for African Studies: University of Copenhagen, 1996), 8.

5 New Africa, *Burundi Country Profile 2000*. Reprinted at www.newafrica.com/profiles/burundi.htm

6 International Crisis Group, "Burundi Under Siege." Reprinted at www.crisisweb.org/projects/cafrica/reports/bu05e_2.htm (accessed 2 August 2000).

7 Jos Havermans, "Burundi: Peace Initiatives Help Stem the Violence," in *Searching for Peace in Africa: An overview of Conflict Prevention and Management Activities*, eds. Monique Mekenkamp, Paul van Tongeren, Hans van de Veen (Utrecht: European Platform for Conflict Prevention and Transformation, 1999), 198.

8 Dravis and Pitsch, "Hutu and Tutsi in Burundi."

9 International Crisis Group, "Burundi Under Siege."

10 John Prendergast and David Smock, "Postgenocidal Reconstruction: Building Peace in Rwanda and Burundi." Reprinted at www.usip.org/oc/sr/sr990915.html (accessed 27 July 2000).

11 IRIN, "G-6 points to link between Arusha and Bujumbura Violence." Reprinted at www.reliefweb.int/IRIN/cea/countrystories/burundi/20010307.phtml (accessed 6 March 2001).

12 Van Eck, "Burundi Report"; International Crisis Group, "Burundi Peace Process: Tough Challenges Ahead." Reprinted at www.crisisweb.org/burundi/reports.htm (accessed 30 August 2000).

13 Jan van Eck, "Mandela Breathes New Life into Burundian Peace Process." Reprinted at http://ccrweb.ccr.uct.ac.za/burundi_reports/burrep-feb2000.html (accessed 13 November 2000).

14 IRIN, "Glossary of the main rebel groups operating in the Great Lakes Region." Reprinted at www.reliefweb.int/IRIN/cea/countrystories/drc/19990630a.htm

15 Van Eck, "Mandela Breathes New Life into Burundian Peace Process."

16 Frederick Ehrenreich, "Burundi: The Current Political Dynamic." Reprinted at www.usip.org/grants/burundi/burehren.html (accessed 14 November 2000); Van Eck, "Burundi Report."

17 See letter addressed to UN Secretary General Koffi Anan by Nyangoma in 1997. Reprinted at www.club.euronet.be/pascal.karolero/cndd.burundi/nyangonu.htm (accessed 16 November 2000).

18 Ehrenreich, "Burundi: The Current Political Dynamic."

19 Human Rights Watch, "Burundi Human Rights Development 2000 Report." Reprinted at www.hrw.org/wr2k/Africa-01.htm (accessed 14 November 2000).

20 Amnesty International, "Burundi 2000 Annual Report." Reprinted at www.webamnesty.org/ar2000web/countries.htm (accessed 14 November 2000).

21 Human Rights Watch, "Human Rights Watch condemns targeting of civilians in Burundi's Civil War." Reprinted at www.hrw.org/hrw/press98/aprl/burproxy.htm (accessed 24 November 2000).

22 Amnesty International, "Burundi 2000 Annual Report."

23 Human Rights Watch, "Burundi Human Rights Development 2000 Report."

24 International Crisis Group, "Burundi Under Siege."

25 Human Rights Watch, "Emptying the Hills – Regroupment in Burundi." Reprinted at www.hrw.org/wr2k/africa-01.htm (accessed 14 November 2000).

26 Prendergast and Smock, "Postgenocidal Reconstruction."

27 Van Eck, "Burundi Report."

28 Prendergast and Smock, "Postgenocidal Reconstruction."

29 Van Eck, "Mandela Breathes New Life into Burundian Peace Process."

30 International Crisis Group, "Burundi Peace Process: Tough Challenges Ahead."

31 Réné Lemarchand, *Burundi: Ethnic Conflict and Genocide* (Cambridge: Cambridge University Press, 1996), 1; Jakes Gerwel, "Reconciliation in Burundi and South Africa." Reprinted at www.ijr.org.za/jakes1.htm (accessed 4 December 2000).

32 Dravis and Pitsch, "Hutu and Tutsi in Burundi."

33 Ibid.

34 Lemarchand, *Burundi: Ethnic Conflict and Genocide*, 15.

35 Lemarchand, *Burundi: Genocide Forgotten, Invented and Anticipated*, 6–7.

36 Lemarchand, *Burundi: Ethnic Conflict and Genocide*, 16.

37 Dravis and Pitsch, "Hutu and Tutsi in Burundi."

38 Prendergast and Smock, "Postgenocidal Reconstruction"; Ehrenreich, "Burundi: The Current Political Dynamic"; Van Eck, "Mandela Breathes New Life into Burundian Peace Process."

39 Van Eck, "Burundi Report."

40 Dravis and Pitsch, "Hutu and Tutsi in Burundi."

41 Havermans, "Burundi – Peace Initiatives Help Stem the Violence," 203.

42 Van Eck, "Mandela Breathes New Life into Burundian Peace Process."

43 CNN, "Mandela promises aid in search of Burundi Peace." Reprinted at www.cnn.com/2000/WORLD/africa/11/27/burundi.peace/index.html (accessed 29 November 2000).

44 IRIN, "FRODEBU faction rejects Buyoya-Ndayizeye Team." Reprinted at www.reliefweb.int/IRIN/cea/countrystories/burundi/20010716.phtml (accessed 16 July 2001).

45 Havermans, "Burundi: Peace Initiatives Help Stem the Violence," 203.

46 Search for Common Ground. Reprinted at www.sfcg.org/locations.cfm (accessed 14 November 2000).

47 Havermans, "Burundi: Peace Initiatives Help Stem the Violence," 205.

48 Jan van Eck, "Burundi Report October 2001: Relative Success of Transitional Government Essential for the Next Phase of the Burundi Peace Process." Reprinted at www.up.ac.za/academic/cips/burundi2/html (accessed October 2002).

49 Amnesty International, "Burundi 2000 Annual Report."

50 Gerwel, "Reconciliation in Burundi and South Africa."

51 Havermans, "Burundi: Peace Initiatives Help Stem the Violence," 203.

52 Prendergast and Smock, "Postgenocidal Reconstruction."

53 Van Eck, "Mandela Breathes New Life into Burundian Peace Process."

54 Prendergast and Smock, "Postgenocidal Reconstruction."

55 On the eve of this publication going to press, a cease-fire agreement was signed between Burundi's government, represented by President Pierre Buyoya, and Pierre Nkurunziza, the leader of the Forces for the Defence of Democracy (FDD). Early reports indicated that the agreement addressed one of the rebels' key concerns, the composition of the army. Throughout the negotiations, the FDD held that sharing political power between the two main ethnic groups, Hutus and Tutsis, would be meaningless while the army was still dominated by Tutsis. At the time of going to press, it was not yet clear how this obstatcle had been overcome.

RESOURCES

Books, Articles, Media Reports

Boraine, Alex. "Criminal Prosecutions in the Wake of Mass Violence: Alternatives and Adjuncts to Criminal Prosecutions." Reprinted at www.polity.org.za/govdocs/speeches/1996/sp0720.html (accessed 10 September 2001).

Dravis, Mike and Anne Pitsch. "Hutu and Tutsi in Burundi." Reprinted at www.bsos.umd.edu/cidcm/mar/burundi.htm (accessed 23 November 2000).

Ehrenreich, Frederick. "Burundi: The Current Political Dynamic." Reprinted at www.usip.org/grants/burundi/burehren.html (accessed 14 November 2000).

Gerwel, Jakes. "Reconciliation in Burundi and South Africa." Reprinted at www.ijr.org.za/jakes1.htm (accessed 4 December 2000).

Havermans, Jos. "Burundi: Peace Initiatives Help Stem the Violence." In *Searching for Peace in Africa: An Overview of Conflict Prevention and Management Activities,* edited by Monique Mekenkamp, Paul van Tongeren and Hans van de Veen. Utrecht: European Platform for Conflict Prevention and Transformation, 1999.

Lemarchand, Réné. *Burundi: Ethnic Conflict and Genocide.* Cambridge: Cambridge University Press, 1996.

————. *Burundi: Genocide Forgotten, Invented and Anticipated.* Centre for African Studies: University of Copenhagen, 1996.

Nyankanzi, Edward L. *Genocide: Rwanda and Burundi.* Rochester, V. T.: Schenkman Books, 1998.

Prendergast, John and David Smock. "Postgenocidal Reconstruction: Building Peace in Rwanda & Burundi." Reprinted at www.usip.org/oc/sr/sr990915.html (accessed 27 July 2000).

Van Eck, Jan. "Mandela Breathes New Life into Burundian Peace Process." Reprinted at http://ccrweb.ccr.uct.ac.za/burundi_reports/burrep-feb2000.html (accessed 13 November 2000).

————. "Burundi Report." 1999. Reprinted at http://ccrweb.ccr.uct.ac.za_burundi_reports/burrep-april1999.html (accessed 29 November 2000).

————. "Burundi Report October 2001: Relative Success of Transitional Government Essential for the Next Phase of the Burundi Peace Process." Reprinted at www.up.ac.za/academic/cips/burundi2.html (accessed October 2002).

Government, Intergovernmental Bodies and Political Parties

Government of the Republic of Burundi: http://www.burundi.gov.bi
Conseil National pour la Défense de la Démocratie (CNDD)/Inama y'Igihugu Igwanira Demokarasi (National Council for the Defence of Democracy): http://club.euronet.be/pascal.karolero/cndd.burundi

Local NGOs

Ligue Burundaise des Droits de l'Homme (ITEKA) is a broad-based NGO concerned particularly with the protection of human rights. ITEKA's web page has an excellent overview of the human rights situation and a list of contact details for other NGOs. Address: Avenue de la Mission, n° 29, B. P. 177, Bujumbura. Tel: 228636 or 211623. E-mail: iteka@cbinf.com. Website: http://www.ligue-iteka.bi

Search for Common Ground Burundi is a branch of the New York-based conflict resolution group. The Burundi organisation is dedicated to peace-building at all levels of society. Address: Old East Building, Avenue des États-Unis, Place de l'Indépendence, Bujumbura, Burundi. Tel: 257 241 944/216 332. Email: shamil@cni.cbinf.com. Website: http://www.sfcg.org/mainbur.htm

International NGOs

Amnesty International provides reports and news about human rights practices in Burundi: http://www.amnesty.org/ar2000web/countries

Centre for Conflict Resolution seeks to contribute towards a just peace in South Africa and elsewhere in Africa by promoting constructive, creative and co-operative approaches to the resolution of conflict and the reduction of violence: http://ccrweb.ccr.uct.ac.za

Human Rights Watch: http://www.hrw.org/reports/2000/burundi2/Bur008.htm

Initiative on Conflict Resolution and Ethnicity (INCORE) is a joint initiative between the University of Ulster and the United Nations University aimed at addressing the management and resolution of conflict via a combination of research, training and other activities which inform and influence national and international organisations working in the field of conflict: http://www.incore.ulst.ac.uk/cds/countries/burundi.html

International Alert is an NGO based in the UK which aims to identify and address the root causes of violence and contribute to the just and peaceful transformation of internal conflict: http://www.international-alert.org

International Crisis Group is a private multinational organisation committed to strengthening the capacity of the international community to anticipate, understand and act to prevent and contain conflict: http://www.crisisweb.org

BURUNDI COUNTRY INFORMATION

Geography
Location: Central Africa, bordering Tanzania, the Democratic Republic of the Congo, Rwanda.
Cities: *Capital:* Bujumbura (pop. 300 000). *Other:* Cibitoke, Muyinga, Ngozi, Bubanza, Gitega, Bururi.

People
Nationality: *Noun:* Barundi (sing. and pl.). *Adjective:* Burundian(s).
Population (June 2000): 200 000.
Population growth rate (1999 est.): 3.54%.
Ethnic groups: Hutus 85%, Tutsis 14%, Twas 1%.
Religions: Roman Catholic 62%, Protestant 5%, traditional African 32%, Muslim 1%.
Languages: *Official:* Kirundi, French. *Other:* Kiswahili, English.
Education. *Years compulsory:* 6. *Attendance:* 55% male, 45% female. *Literacy:* 35.3%.
Health (1999 est.): *Life expectancy:* 44 years men, 47 years women. *Infant mortality rate:* 99/1 000. *HIV infection rate:* 8.3%.
Workforce (1997 est.): Agriculture: 58%. Industry: 18%. Services: 24%.

Economy
GDP (1998 est.): $4.1 billion.
GDP real growth rate (1998 est.): 2%.
Per capita income (1998 est.): $740.
Inflation rate (1998): 17%.
Central government budget (1999): *Receipts:* $138.7 million. *Spending:* $186.8 million.
Natural resources: Nickel, uranium, rare earth oxides, peat, cobalt, copper, platinum deposits not yet exploited, vanadium.
Agriculture (1998 est.): 49.4% of GDP. *Products:* coffee, tea, sugar, cotton fabrics, oil, corn, sorghum, sweet potatoes, bananas, manioc (tapioca), beef, milk, hides, livestock feed, rice. *Arable land:* 44%.
Industry (1998 est.): 19.1% of GDP. *Types:* sugar refining, coffee processing, telecommunications, pharmaceuticals, food processing, chemicals (insecticides), public works construction, light consumer goods, assembly of imported components.
Services (1998 est.): 31.5% of GDP.
Natural resources: Commercial quantities of alluvial gold, nickel, phosphates, rare earth, vanadium and other; peat mining.
Trade (1998): *Exports:* $49 million: coffee (88% of export earnings), tea, sugar, cotton fabrics, hides. *Major markets:* UK, Germany, Benelux, Switzerland. *Imports:* $102 million: food, beverages, tobacco, chemicals, road vehicles, petroleum and products. *Major suppliers:* Benelux, France, Germany, Saudi Arabia, Japan.
Debt external (1997): $247 billion.

Military
Military expenditure: Dollar figures: $25 million (FY93).
Military expenditure: Percent of GDP: 2.6% (FY93).

Demographic information is drawn from that compiled by the United States Department of State. See http://www.state.gov/r/pa/ei/bgn

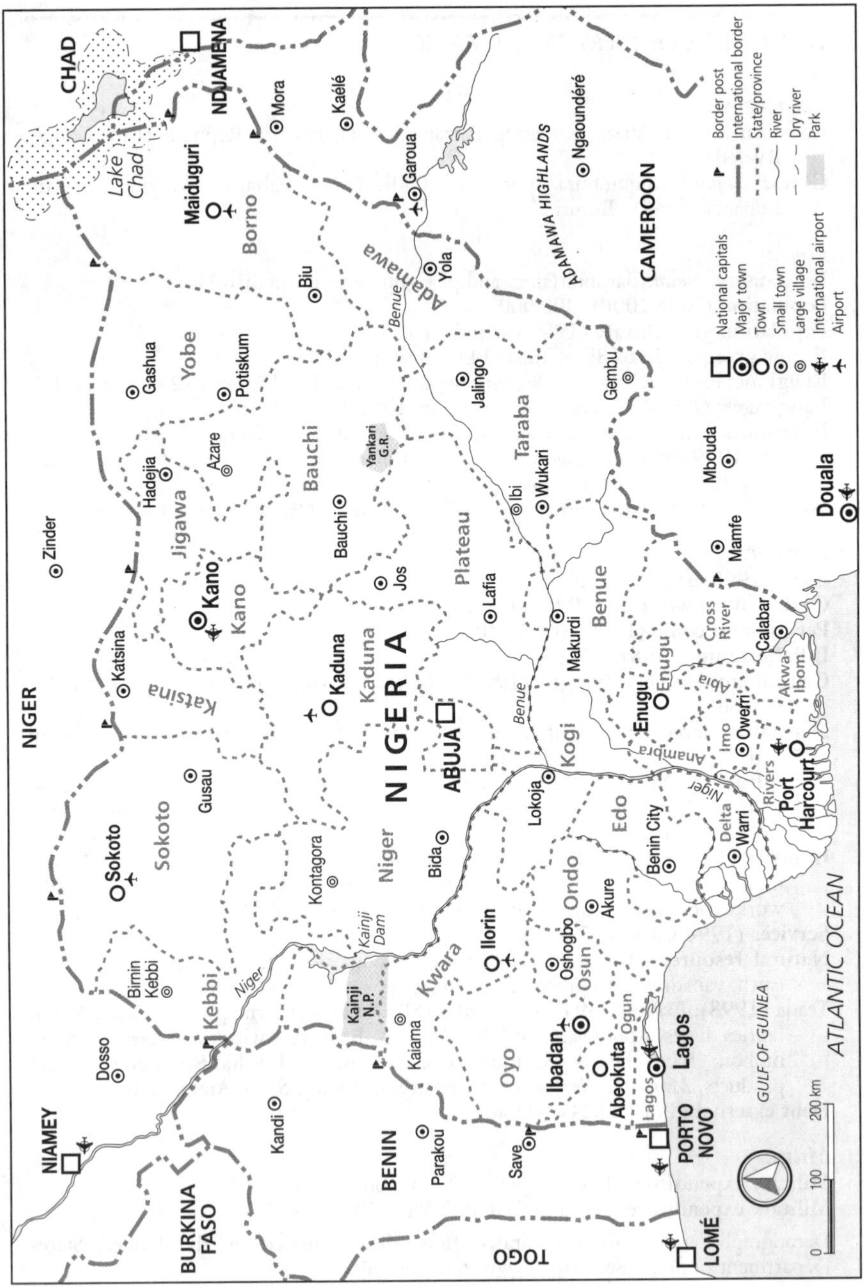
CHAD
Lake Chad
NDJAMENA
Maiduguri
Borno
Mora
Kaélé
Garoua
NIGER
Zinder
Gashua
Yobe
Potiskum
Biu
Yola
Adamawa
Benue
ADAMAWA HIGHLANDS
Ngaoundéré
CAMEROON
Hadejia
Azare
Bauchi
Yankari G.R.
Jalingo
Taraba
Gembu
Jigawa
Kano
Bauchi
Ibi
Wukari
Mbouda
Douala
Katsina
Jos
Plateau
Lafia
Mamfe
Kaduna
NIGERIA
Makurdi
Benue
Cross River
Calabar
ABUJA
Enugu
Abia
Akwa Ibom
Sokoto
Gusau
Kogi
Anambra
Imo
Owerri
Port Harcourt
Rivers
Niger
Lokoja
Edo
Delta
Warri
Benin City
Kontagora
Bida
Ondo
Akure
Birnin Kebbi
Kebbi
Kainji Dam
Ilorin
Oshogbo
Osun
Kainji N.P.
Kwara
Ogun
Ibadan
Kaiama
Dosso
Oyo
Abeokuta
Lagos
GULF OF GUINEA
ATLANTIC OCEAN
NIAMEY
Kandi
BENIN
Parakou
Save
PORTO NOVO
BURKINA FASO
TOGO
LOMÉ
0 100 200 km
National capitals
Major town
Town
Small town
Large village
International airport
Airport
Border post
International border
State/province
River
Dry river
Park

Chapter 4

Nigeria: An Overview of a Multifaceted Conflict

ADEWALE SEGUN BANJO

Nigeria, the most populous nation in Africa, is in West Africa. Covering a total area of about 923 770 square kilometres, it is bounded in the north by the Sahara Desert and in the south by the Gulf of Guinea, an arm of the Atlantic Ocean. Its climate is equatorial in the south, tropical at the centre and arid in the north. In terms of topography, the southern lowlands merge into central hills and plateaux and there are savannah plains in the north.[1]

Archaeological records suggest that parts of the country have been inhabited by humans since the Palaeolithic or Old Stone Age (500 000–9 000 BC). According to the 1952/53 census, there are more than 250 ethnic groups in Nigeria, most of whom have distinct customs, traditions and languages. The larger and politically dominant groups include the Yoruba (about 20 million), the Igbo (about 17 million) and the Hausa/Fulani (20 million).

The Yoruba, in addition to their linguistic homogeneity, share common traditions and a common ancestor called Oduduwa. Although the Yoruba are predominantly an agricultural people, they have a long-standing tradition of living in towns. They occupy a large area in southwest Nigeria. The Yoruba stand out as deeply religious (mostly Christian and Muslim) and place heavy value on respect for their elders and their superiors. The Yoruba group is extremely independent, diplomatic and resentful of despotic leadership, qualities that were clearly expressed in pre-colonial days and are well-known Yoruba qualities in post-independence Nigerian politics.

The Igbo can be found in the east of the lower Niger Valley. They have never organised themselves into larger states or kingdoms like those of the Yoruba. Rather, the largest political unit tends to be the village group, typically with a population of only a few thousand people. This highly decentralised political organisation of the eastern forest people has earned them the description of "stateless societies".

The Hausa/Fulani group is the largest and most politically powerful group in the open grassland area of the Nigerian Sudan. It was after the

Fulani Jihad, led by Usman dan Fodio in 1804, and the subsequent conquest of Hausaland that Islam became widely adopted as a way of life.
Today, most Hausa/Fulani are Muslim and both their political and socio-
economic life, including their land tenure and legal systems, are influenced
by Islamic principles. Hausaland is also the home of the Fulani of Nigeria,
probably the only ethnic group in Africa without a distinct territory.[2]

Other prominent but smaller groups include the Binis, the Ibibios of the
southeastern region, the Tiv of Benue Valley, the Nupe of the Middle
Niger Valley and the Kanuris of the Lake Chad basin. The large concentration of the smallest ethnic groups in the middle-belt where there are
more than 180 different groups is a significant feature of the distribution
of ethnic groups in Nigeria.[3] Despite the fact that each ethnic group occupies a distinct and considerable territory, most of the smaller groups have
significant trade and cultural contacts with the major grassland groups, the
Hausa/Fulani, the Nupe and the Northern Yoruba. In the forest belt, a
long-standing line has existed between the Binis of Edo kingdom and the
Yoruba of Ife and Lagos. With its attendant clashes, these early contacts
between the middle-belt groups (with their small fighting forces) exposed
them to the mercy of the larger and more powerful groups from the north
and the south. The result was that the middle-belt became a major source
region for slaves traded both across the Sahara and the Atlantic.[4]

It was the advent and course of colonialism that brought the various
groups inhabiting Nigeria under one government. The process, which
started from 1898, involved a number of important measures, including
the removal of all visible African opposition to the imposition, expansion
and consolidation of British central authority over the territory. According
to Tekena Ntonye Tamuno: "To secure central direction of policy and pool
economic resources, the British Government from 1898 adopted the
policy of gradually amalgamating its various administrative units in
colonial Nigeria."[5]

In May 1906, on the recommendation of the 1898 Niger Committee
headed by Lord Selborne, Lagos Colony and Protectorate was amalga-
mated with the Protectorate of Southern Nigeria to form the Colony and
Protectorate of Southern Nigeria. It is important to note that the government did not seek the views of Nigerians in the two territories before the
amalgamation. Neither did the British seek the opinions of Nigerians
before amalgamating the Northern and Southern Protectorates in January
1914, creating a single entity called Nigeria. Thus, Nigeria between 1914
and 1939 resembled a federation of two groups of provinces. However,
from 1 April 1939 the British colonial authorities divided the Southern

Protectorate into the Eastern and Western Provinces. This administrative step, taken by Governor Bernard Bourdillion, created a tripartite division within Nigeria that was to last until independence in 1960.[6]

Nigerian politicians and nationalists, who were increasingly given the chance to discuss and modify the constitutions from 1949, were however not able to alter the tripartite administrative foundations of the Nigerian state until 1967. This is because the constitutions that followed embodied the results of deliberations involving Nigerian and British representatives during several constitutional conferences inside and outside Nigeria. One of these was the General Conference at Ibadan in 1950, which preceded a major constitutional change in 1951. Other constitutional conferences followed, in Lagos and London, to sort out critical issues before independence was granted in October 1960. However, it has been observed that the pre-independence constitutions of the 1922–54 era were less controversial than those since 1960 (1963, 1979, 1989 and 1999). This is not altogether surprising in a federation comprising over 250 ethnic groups, over 400 distinct languages (as against dialects) and a number of religious belief-systems (Christianity, Islam and adherents of African traditional religions).[7] Since the amalgamations of 1914, the inheritors of Nigeria have struggled amidst violent secessionist movements to consolidate the weak foundations laid by generations of British colonial rule.

Though the majority of Nigerians have come to associate themselves with the colonial behemoth called Nigeria, the understanding that it was the *interests* of colonial administrators rather than the *choices* of Nigerians that brought Nigeria into being has left a deep mark on Nigerian history and contemporary political process. The former Nigerian president Ibrahim Babangida tried to recast a new image and a sense of oneness in Nigerians by stating: "If in the pursuit of their interest the British created Nigeria, today Nigeria has come to have a different meaning for us. If Nigeria used to be a mere geographical expression, it is now an organic state."[8] In response, one of Nigeria's foremost intellectuals has argued: "If the above statement represented the truth and nothing but the truth, the pains, the groaning, contemporary fires and terrorism prevalent in Nigerian cities and towns . . . would not have featured prominently as they have done in print and electronic media . . . under an organic state, peace, security, stability, prosperity would have been achieved at lesser cost."[9]

Nigeria has a long history of violent conflict coupled with gross human rights abuse. The Attahiru rebellion of 1903 in Sokoto, the Aba women's riot of 1929–30, the general labour strike of 1945 and the Egba women's demonstration of 1948 were all examples of violent crises in Nigeria even before it became an independent country. Though Nigeria's independence was achieved without bloodshed or the stress of liberation or guerrilla wars, the pattern of political, ethno-religious conflict with attendant violations of human rights was set by the TIV riots of 1964, which were followed by the western region Agbekoya killings of 1965. Thuggery and vandalism became an integral part of inter-ethnic relations in that period as evidenced by the Ibo (Igbo) massacre of 1966, which led to Biafra's succession and civil war of 1967–70. It was the ethnic friction that characterised Nigerian public life that led to civil war. In the mostly Hausa-dominated north, resentment against the more prosperous, educated and predominantly Christian Igbo minority triggered the violence. In September 1966, 10–30 000 Igbo people were massacred in the northern region and about one million fled back to the Igbo-dominated east. A total of one million Ibo people perished during the civil war.[10]

Post-civil war, the relative stability that characterised the latter part of General Yakubu Gowon's administration was shattered by the military coup of July 1975, while the assassination of General Murtala Muhammed raised again the spectre of ethnic tension. Furthermore, the Bakolari killings of 1980, the Maitatsine (an Islamic sect) riots of 1980–82, the military coups of 1983 and 1985, the student riots of 1986, Gideon Orkar's coup of 1990, the TIV-Jukun violence of 1990–92, the Kataf-Hausa violence of 1992, the riots of 12 June 1993, and the pro-democracy riots of 1994 serve as critical examples of the deep ethno-religious, social and political upheavals and conflict in Nigeria. Lately, however, the religious, ethnic and economic/environmental character of these conflicts has become more profound. This is with specific reference to the religious violence in the north, the conflict in the Niger Delta and the intra/inter-ethnic crisis in the southwest.

Religious unrest and riots have become the setting for playing out class, political and ethnic relations in post-independence Nigeria. The beginning of inter-faith (particularly Islam versus Christianity) confrontations can be traced to the Hausa-Igbo ethno-religious riots in Jos in 1945. The relative absence of major religious conflict during the first 15 years of independence (apart from the 1967–70 civil war, which was caused purely by ethnic and political differences) gave the impression that religious conflict was not likely to be one of Nigeria's social and political headaches.[11] However, the abortive but tragic Dimka coup of 13 February 1976 left in its wake a clear impression that religious belief was being internally and externally manipulated. In addition, there was the Sharia debate of 1977–78 in the constituent assembly. This was soon followed by a series of intra-faith

(Islam–Islam) clashes between the Izala, Kadiriya and Tijaniya movements. These events point to the presence of deep religious/sectarian divides in Nigeria, especially as the profile of religious conflicts in Nigeria has been very broad, particularly in the 1980s and 1990s.

As if to make up for its late arrival, in the last 20 years religion has outdone all traditional causes of political tension in Nigeria. The 1980s opened with Maitatsine religious violence in Kano, the first religious shock to the national psyche. Subsequent Maitatsine riots occurred in the Bullum–Kutu area of Borno State on 16 October 1982 and Rigassa Village in Kaduna State on 20 October 1982. Jimeta and Yola also experienced Maitatsine disturbances in 1984. The Gombe riots of April 1985 and the Funtua riots in January 1993 were all cases of Maitatsine-induced religious violence that threatened the security of the state and engaged the material and human resources of the security forces to their utmost.[12]

The national debate about Sharia law versus secular law has been particularly divisive. During the Obasanjo-led transition to the Second Republic, the constituent assembly failed to reach agreement on the Sharia law debate. The Sharia controversies raged fiercely during the drafting of the 1979 constitution. In April 1979 protesters took to the street in Zaria and Kaduna towns with such banners as "Sharia, No peace . . . No Nigeria". The burning of churches in Kano in 1982 was the first open and violent religious conflict between Christians and Muslims. Early in 1986, Nigeria was reported to have joined the Organization of Islamic Countries (OIC). In the heat of the OIC crisis, trouble also erupted on the campus of the University of Ibadan in 1986. The Kafanchan/Kaduna crisis of 1987 also started as a religious conflict. Other cases of religious conflict are the Decree Six crisis of 1989, the Pro-Bali Christian demonstrations of 1990 and the Kano, Kastina and Bauchi riots of 1991. The Zagon-Kataf bloodbath of 1992, the Akaluka crisis of 1994, the Zaria riots of 1996, D-8 controversies, the anti-bible knowledge riots of 1998 in Maiduguri and finally the Sharia crisis of 2000 were all cases of religious violence in Nigeria.

Sharia is as old as Islam in Nigeria, though it was not until the Usman Oan Fodio Jihad of 1804 that an attempt was made to create an Islamic state based on Sharia. However, when the British completed the imposition of their authority over the northernmost part of Nigeria in 1903, the application of Sharia law was halted. The British did not directly recognise Sharia as the law in the emirates that they had conquered. The first major challenge to the status of Sharia came in 1947 when the appeal trial of Tsofo Gubbia prevented the imposition of a death penalty for homicide, as provided by Sharia but disallowed by the British criminal code. The

British were convinced that, as in most other parts of the Muslim world, a separation should be made between Sharia courts which deal with personal status and family law and civil courts which deal with criminal law applicable to all Nigerians.

However, the origin of the contemporary religious tension in Nigeria can be traced firstly to the 1978 constituent assembly debate and secondly to the 1988 constituent assembly Sharia debate. The 1988 constituent assembly provides the best possible instrument for measuring the heat of this battle by Muslims to gain legal recognition of their faith. According to Muslims:

> The Sharia courts in the North and even in the South are legitimate Constitutional rights of Moslems in Nigeria. Sharia is for Moslems alone and will not necessarily affect non-Moslems. The present Nigerian judicial set-up is not only un-Islamic but also favours Christianity. The Islamic Sharia is superior to the English common law and to Nigerian customary law in sovereignty, sources, justice, in judicial procedure, in legal-moral dichotomy and in volition of victim in deciding the fate of the offender. That Moslems are in [the] majority, both in Nigeria as a whole and the South in particular. That Nigeria is not a secular country. That all opposition to Sharia is based on ignorance and/or prejudice and intolerance.[13]

For their part, Christians argue that it is unconstitutional and unjust to deploy the scarce resources of the country for the propagation and practice of only one religious faith; practical experiences have proved that non-Muslims have been forced to abide by Sharia injunctions and such encounters have been disastrous for them. Nigeria is a secular country and Christians are in the majority. In addition, the Christians in Nigeria believe very strongly that most regimes favour Islam.

The Face of Conflict

Violent conflict in Nigeria was frequently centred on the Niger Delta. The image evoked at any mention of the Delta is still one of battle scenes, machetes flying, booming guns and blood everywhere.

Recent reports of hostilities in Ondo State between the Ilaje and their erstwhile cordial neighbours, the Arogbo-Ijaws, and indications that hundreds have already perished, only serve to reinforce this profile of violence in which the immense natural resources of the Niger Delta region are the cause of intense animosity. Add to that the confounding dimensions of the

Warri crisis in which thousands of men, women and children from the three contending ethnic groups died between May and June 1999. The three ethnic groups, the Itsekiri, Urhobo and Ijaws, are caught in a decades-old supremacy bid for ownership of portions of Warri, which past court cases and blood-letting episodes have not succeeded in resolving.[14] Currently, Warri and its surrounding communities lie prostrate under enforced peace. It is not clear if the turmoil is truly indicative of an agenda to prevent the rest of the country from benefiting from resources whose proceeds constitute the major revenue source for the country. Indeed, they account for at least 40% of Gross Domestic Product, about 80% of government revenues and expenditures and 96% of total export receipts.

Environmental lawyer and leader of the Pan-Niger Delta Chikoko Movement, Oronto Douglas, has dismissed the tag of terrorism hung on groups and individuals actively pursuing an end to what he described as the political marginalisation and economic exploitation of the ethnic nationalities of the Niger Delta.[15] This perception of terrorism held by some within and even outside these shores was a source of concern to the reported 5 000 youths from about 40 clans in the Ijaw nation which met on 11 December 1998 at Koiyama, Bayelsa State. The youths deliberated on the issue of survival for the Ijaws within Nigeria. They noted that, "we are tired of gas flaring, oil spillage, blow out and being labeled saboteurs and terrorists. It is a case of preparing the noose for our hanging. We reject this labeling."[16]

Informed observers of the developments in the Niger Delta have discerned a political perspective to the ongoing crisis in the region. The activities of organised groups active in the Niger Delta have always been peaceful. On the contrary, the panicky response by government, acting mostly in concert with oil firms operating in these areas, has been severely repressive. Beatings, shootings, detentions and constant hounding of activists have been commonplace and have contributed to destabilisation.

The issue at the centre of what is commonly referred to as the Niger Delta crisis is aptly captured in a report by Human Rights Watch which states that "conflict in the Niger Delta is directly related to debates about the structure of the Nigerian polity. It can be assumed that there would have been disputes as to the relationship between the centre and periphery in Nigeria in any economic circumstances, given the complexity of the country and the lack of established nationwide democratic institutions at independence. Yet, the addition of oil production and oil wealth to the difficulties already posed by the problem of ruling a country of at least 250 ethnic groups, each with its separate historical traditions of government, has greatly increased the potential for conflict and the stakes at play in the conflict."[17]

It has been argued that there are more fundamental issues that must be addressed. Prominent is the so-called national question. For the people of the oil-producing communities, it is a question of empowerment – who should control the oil produced from their soil and how should the proceeds be distributed? These concerns have galvanised the various peoples of the Niger Delta toward action to determine their destiny within the larger Nigerian nation. On 10 January 1999, the Egi clan of Ogba ethnic nationality of Rivers State met at Aklaka, their ancestral headquarters, and issued the *Aklaka Declaration*. In a related development, over 5 000 Ijaw youths met on 11 December at the historic riverside town of Kaiama in the Bayelsa State and came up with the *Kaiama Declaration*, which was the result of extensive deliberations. In addition, other groups in the Niger Delta have similar documents: the Ogbas have the *Ogba Charter*; the Urhobos of Delta State have the *Resolutions of the Urhobo Economic Summit*.[18]

A common strand that runs through each of these documents is the demand for resource control, calls for an end to the political exclusion of the minority peoples of the Delta and an end to the ecological devastation caused by four decades of oil exploration and exploitation. Indeed, the 1990s marked a renaissance of the century-old battle between ethnic nationalities to exert control over territory and natural resources, a control they lost following British colonial and economic manipulation. This awakening, manifested in the mostly peaceful demonstrations in various oil communities, was nowhere more eloquently expressed than in the plays, novels and speeches of the late Ken Saro-Wiwa.

The official response to this rebirth of consciousness by the government and oil multinationals was evident unease.[19] In response to the Niger Delta crisis, in early 1994 a team was put together by the military government of General Sani Abacha. This team undertook a tour of major parts of the oil-producing communities and decided, as noted in its reports, that "a new and increasingly dangerous awareness and sensitivity is sweeping through the oil producing communities across the country. It is in the interest of the oil industry and the nation that urgent and lasting solutions be put in place to prevent the situation from getting worse."[20]

The solution offered in the face of this "increasingly dangerous awareness and sensitivity" for the oil-producing communities was a massive clampdown. Vocal proponents of an end to the ecological devastation and economic exploitation of the oil-producing communities were hounded all over the Niger Delta. In particular, the vocal Ogonis, even before the ministerial team's visit, had begun to face informal repression in the form of conflict with neighbouring communities with whom they had lived, intermarried and traded for hundreds of years. Bloody clashes flared up between the Ogonis and the Adonis as well as the people of Okirika. In 1993, security operatives funded by the multinational oil company Shell shot and killed several people in the Ogoni community of Korokoro. Increasingly, tensions within the Ogoni community gave way to unrest, culminating in the May 1994 killing of four members of the Ogoni. A flawed judicial process led to the conviction and eventual hanging of writer Saro-Wiwa and eight other Ogonis on 10 November 1995.[21]

Long before the Ogoni problem, other oil-producing communities had a taste of the government and oil company's response to the growing consciousness in the oil-producing region. A reportedly peaceful protest by the people of Umuechem in Rivers State in October 1990 was met with a brutal reprisal by a mobile police force team invited by Shell. At the end of a dawn attack, hundreds of Umuechem people had been killed and over 400 houses burned down. The scars of the Umuechem massacre remain today. No compensation worthy of mention has been paid to the community. After the brutal repression of growing agitation in Umuechem there were punitive acts at Ekeremorsion, Ikenya, Uzere, Opia and elsewhere.

The demand by the oil-producing communities for a fundamental restructuring of the polity to ensure their participation in the processes affecting their survival as a people continues. The "Ogoni treatment" did not stop the Ijaws from taking steps to end the destruction of their environment and the waste of vital resources needed for the development of their forgotten portion of the earth in December 1999. In an operation tagged "operation climate change", communities in Bayelsa State and other Ijaw-speaking areas closed down a flow station, effectively shutting down gas flares, some of which had burned endlessly for 40 years spewing toxic gases into the Niger Delta.

The issues that constitute the Niger Delta crisis are captured in various bills, declaration charters and resolutions. The *Kaiama Declaration* noted, for instance, that "the violence in Ijawland and other parts of the Niger Delta area, sometimes manifesting in intra and interethnic conflict, are sponsored by the state and transnational oil companies to keep the communities of the Niger Delta divided, weak and distracted from the causes of their problems". The *Ogba Charter* avers that "successive governments have offered us no hope, alternating, as they have, between military dictatorships, which have decreed away our rights and seized our property, and supposedly democratic civilian regimes which have been unyielding in their intent to press democracy to the service of exploitation and oppression". The *Aklaka Declaration* states: "The Egi people condemn the human rights violence on the Egi people and on the people of the Niger Delta, by the military dictatorship in conjunction with the oil companies." The Ogonis in their "bill of rights" also affirm that "we cannot sit idly by while we are, as a people, dehumanized and slowly exterminated and driven to extinction even as our rich resources are siphoned off to [provide for the] exclusive comfort and improvement of other communities and the shareholders of multinational companies".[22]

Many have argued that the opening up of a democratic space will reduce some of the agitation in the oil-producing Niger Delta, buttressing their position with the arguments that the heavy-handed response to agitation in the area in the last few years could only have occurred under military dictatorship. The fact that nothing has changed for the struggling ethnic nationalities and will not change without a restructuring within the polity was brought home when President Obasanjo, during a visit to the Niger Delta in early June 2000, clashed with leaders of the Ijaw Youth Council at Government House, Port Harcourt. The youths presented him with their demands as contained in the *Kaiama Declaration*, apparently offering a way out of the Niger Delta crisis. Obasanjo launched a verbal attack on the leaders. He lectured them on how he had liberated their fathers from the Biafran enclave. An Ijaw youth observed, "It is doubtful if liberation from war necessitates economic slavery. What we are agitating for is liberation from economic enslavement perpetrated by the operation of oppressive laws that deprive us our rights."[23] The Ogonis registered their displeasure that Obasanjo failed to meet and talk with them.

President Obasanjo has since gone on to create a Nigeria Delta Development Commission (NDDC), modelled on that proposed by the Willinks Commission over 40 years ago. But the question the people of the Niger Delta still ask is why decisions affecting their lives continue to be taken at Abuja without consulting them. The Nigerian state is clearly set for a long period of unrest in the Niger Delta as there is as yet no indication that the present administration will set in motion the restructuring needed to bring peace to the distressed Niger Delta area.

Beyond the Delta, since the restoration of civil rule in Nigeria on 29 May 1999, there have been deaths and mindless destruction of property caused by increasing ethnic conflicts. In the eastern part of Nigeria, the Aguleris-Umuleri communal conflict has devastated parts of Nigeria; the Ife/Modakeke war erupted again and led to the death of more than 7 000 people and the destruction of more than 4 000 buildings in Ife-East. The Ilajes-Ijaw conflict, which lasted for over a year, was ignited by the fact that oil was discovered in commercial quantities at an unmarked boundary of the two communities. There was also the Takum/Wukari crisis, precipitated by historical claims to territory boundaries. Of these crises, the Odua People's Congress (OPC) crisis deserves fuller discussion.

In October 1999, the Hausa and Yoruba engaged in bloody clashes because it was alleged that a Hausa woman desecrated the Yoruba's traditional beliefs in Sagamu town. The Sagamu crisis centred on the validity of traditional practices in some states of the Federal Republic of Nigeria. One question that has been asked repeatedly is whether it is justifiable for some cultures to infringe on other people's fundamental human rights. Or put in another way, should the life of a human being be taken with impunity in the name of a traditional taboo? At the time, nobody seemed willing to venture a reply to these questions. The government kept its lips sealed. The only organisation that did speak out made a plea. The Movement for a Greater Nigeria (MGN), which has Hausas as its major members in different parts of the world, wrote rather mildly that, "we must plead with all custodians of various Nigerian ethnic traditions to review cultural and custom practices and rituals that justify the murder of human beings".[24] MGN, which traced the root of the crisis to the killing of a woman in Sagamu on account of the Oro cult, said it condemned in unequivocal terms the loss of many lives as well as the wanton destruction of property. It further noted: "It is especially tragic to lose a single life. To lose several in such circumstance is simply a national catastrophe. The emotional and financial implications inflicted on many Nigerian families as a result of the carnage is too colossal to quantify."

The MGN restrained itself from fault-finding, as it would have been an exercise in futility, yielding more aggravation and heightening tension among feuding groups. The National Association of Yoruba Descendants (NAYD) in North America was no less disapproving. According to the association, the Sagamu clash began as a result of a flagrant disrespect for the customs and religious beliefs of Sagamu people by non-indigenous people living in the town. The association cautioned people of other nationalities who decide to live on Yoruba land to learn to respect Yoruba traditions and customs. It went on to say, "the events leading to the Sagamu incident were not the first in the nation's history where those who are contemptuous of tradition were dealt with severely, regardless of their ethnic background".[25]

This statement, credited to Egbe Omo Oduduwa who was living

abroad, has been seen as a blanket invitation for lawlessness. Perhaps responding to this statement, the OPC, a militant group fighting for the Odua (Oduduwa or Yoruba) nation, clashed with other ethnic groups in Lagos. In the ensuing confrontation, triggered by the allegation of armed robbery against an Ijaw, several lives were lost.

The OPC is an ethnic militia made up of Yoruba youths. According to its founder, Fredrick Fasheun, the OPC is a socio-cultural, non-political organisation set up to promote the interest of the Yoruba people and redress the gross and glaring marginalisation Yoruba have suffered in Nigeria. According to Gani Adams, the leader of the militant faction of the OPC, the OPC stands for self-determination and social emancipation, regional autonomy, self-government and self-management, economic reconstruction and control, the reunion of all Yoruba in Kwara and Kogi States with those in southwest Nigeria, an independent army, police force and judiciary, a sovereign national conference and the creation of the Odua Republic.[26]

However, the OPC has been perceived differently by diverse sections of the Nigerian population. Some perceive it as a conglomeration of vandals and social misfits, others see it as an organisation of true patriots. For some it is a civil rights organisation and its members are civil rights activists. Others describe it as an ethnic movement made up of die-hard tribalists. Again some see it as a militant secessionist group, while others perceive it as a cultural organisation and even a peace movement. By and large, the state police view the OPC as a repressive movement, a view that they support by pointing to violence committed by the group.

The Search for Peace, Justice and Compensation

From the foregoing it is obvious that much of the conflict in Nigeria has been blamed on the prolonged military rule and the wrongs visited on some ethnic groups during the military dictatorship. However, every time violent confrontation has occurred, there have been efforts to seek justice and reconciliation. These efforts have often been described as a façade.

The government often set up ad hoc judicial investigative panels to probe the recurring ethno-religious conflicts in northern Nigeria. Such commissions are often mandated to determine the causes, course and consequences of the crisis. They are also charged to determine who ought to be punished and which victims deserve restitution. For instance, the Justice Akanbi Commission was established by the federal government to probe the Maitatsine riots of 1980. In 1987, following the Kaduna ethno-religious bloodbath, the federal military government headed by Babangida set up the Justice A. G. Karibi–Whytte Commission/Tribunal. While the Tribunal dealt with criminal aspects of the tragedy, an administrative board of inquiry, headed by Justice Donli, assessed and documented the extent of damage and destruction caused by the riots. The John Shagaya Commission was set up to probe the Organisation of Islamic Conference membership crisis of 1986 while the Ambassador Bashir Wali Commission probed the ethno-religious violence in Sokoto in 1995. In addition, the Justice I. M. Zango Special Civil Disturbances Tribunal was established to probe the Bauchi (Sayawa-Fulani) riots of 1995.

The state government responded to the various OPC-induced violent confrontations in Lagos State, by instituting the Justice Famakinwa Commission to unravel the extent of destruction and provide suggestions on how to reconcile the opposing ethnic militias in Lagos.

Successive federal administrations have initiated rather insincere efforts to tackle the continuous killings and conflicts in the Niger Delta. The problem identified over 40 years ago by the Willinks Commission remains. Early in 1999, General Abdusalami Abubakar announced a proposed N15.3 billion development project for the Niger Delta. A panel, headed by Major General Oladapo Popoola, took charge of the funds and projects, but sustained criticism by members of the communities in the Niger Delta led to the proposals being shelved. As the military prepared to hand power back to civilians on 29 May 1999 some hope was raised for the resolution of the marginalisation of these communities by the prospect of the opening up of a democratic space. But this did not amount to much; apathy greeted the 1998/99 elections in the majority of the oil-producing areas.

In a significant achievement for the promotion of human rights and reconciliation after the return to civil rule, one of President Obasanjo's first acts was to set up the Human Rights Violation Investigation Commission headed by a retired Supreme Court Judge, Justice Chukwudifu Oputa. The Commission was modelled on South Africa's Truth and Reconciliation Commission. It was charged with establishing the causes, nature and extent of human rights violations, and identifying the individuals, authorities or organisations responsible and their motives. The panel also sought to hear the stories of victims to determine whether the violations were the product of deliberate state policy and if there were judicial, legislative or other measures that could redress past injustices and prevent their reoccurrence. The Commission was initially asked to investigate the period from 1984 to May 1999, covering four military governments, but this period was later extended back to 1966, the year of the first military coup following independence.

The Commission invited petitioners to submit complaints. It received more than 11 000, many concerned with human rights violations in the Niger Delta in the mid 1990s. At the hearings, some witnesses gave evidence of ill-treatment and torture under successive military administrations. The Commission also heard pleas by relatives of people believed to have been executed by state agents for non-violent political activities or for their relationship to critics of the government. Some witnesses demanded medical treatment for injuries resulting from torture or ill-treatment or compensation for the loss of property seized by security forces. However, some victims and their lawyers expressed a lack of faith in the Commission. These included those who lacked the means to bring complaints to the Commission and others who saw little hope of obtaining justice in the absence of admissions by the perpetrators.

From the foregoing it is apparent that Nigeria is a conflict-ridden state, but also a nation struggling to prevent and redress human rights violations and violence. Though the federal and state authorities have adopted the practice of investigating violent conflicts, it is evident that the sincerity necessary for ensuring justice and reconciliation has been lacking. This is especially true of the process of constituting investigative commissions that have the power to issue findings that will shape policy-making. Finally, few actors, save the federal government, have shown a significant commitment to the promotion of truth and justice in Nigeria. Thus, the chance for national reconciliation may remain elusive and the effort to achieve it may remain largely cosmetic.

NOTES

1 Obaro Ikime, ed., *The Groundwork of Nigerian History* (Ibadan: Heinemann, 1980).

2 Tekena Ntonye Tamuno, *Nigeria: Its People and Its Problems* (Lagos: University of Ibadan Press, 1989), 11–12, 46.

3 Tamuno, *Nigeria*, 12.

4 Tekena Ntonye Tamuno, *The Evolution of the Nigerian State: The Southern Phase, 1898–1914* (London: University of Ibadan Press, 1972).

5 Ibid, 41.

6 Ibrahim Babangida, *Federalism and Nation Building in Nigeria*, presidential speech, Abuja, 1993, 1.

7 Kunle Amuwo, Adigun Agbaje, Rotimi Suberu and Georges Herault, eds., *Federalism and Political Restructuring in Nigeria* (Ibadan: Spectrum Books, 1998).

8 Ibid, 11.

9 Ibid, 21.

10 Tekena Ntonye Tamuno, *Peace and Violence in Nigeria* (Ibadan: Nigeria Since Independence History Project, Ibadan University Press, 1991), 402–7.

11 Leonard Plotnicov, "An Early Nigerian Civil Disturbance: The 1954 Hausa-Ibo Riots in Jos," *Journal of Modern African Studies* 9 (1971), 297–305.

12 Chinedu N. Ubah, "Religion and Nigerian Unity," *Sunday Voice*, 22 February 1987, 13.

13 David D. Laitan, "Sharia Debate and the Origins of Nigeria's Second Republic," *Journal of Modern African Studies* 20 (1983); Martin J. Dent, "Dangers of Polarity in Religious Matters," *West Africa*, 24 April 1978.

14 *The Punch*, 20 July 2001, 1–2.

15 Tunde Olakunle, "Death in the Land," *The Liberty*, November 1999, 24.

16 Ibiba Don Pedro, "Crisis in the Niger Delta," *The Liberty*, November 1999, 12–13.

17 Human Rights Watch, "The Price of Oil: Corporate Responsibility and Human Rights Violations in Nigeria's Oil Producing Communities." Reprinted at www.hrw.org/reports/1999/nigeria/Nigew991.01.htm#P190_8265 (accessed 14 February 2002).

18 In August 1990, the Movement for the Survival of the Ogoni People (MOSOP) adopted an *Ogoni Bill of Rights*. The Movement for the Survival of the Izon (Ijaw) Ethnic Nationality (MOSIEND) adopted an *Izon's People Charter* in November 1992. The Movement for Reparation to Ogbia (MORETO) adopted a charter of demands of the Ogbia people. These various declarations are discussed in the Human Rights Watch report entitled "The Price of Oil".

19 Adewale Segun Banjo, *Oil and Intra-Ethnic Violence in South-Eastern Nigeria: The Internationalization of Ogoni Crisis* (Ibadan: Emmi Press, 1996).

20 Dent, "Dangers of Polarity in Religious Matters."

21 For details of the Ogoni crisis and the trial of Ken Saro-Wiwa see Human Rights Watch, "The Ogoni Crisis: A Case Study of Repression in South-Eastern Nigeria." Reprinted at www.hrw.org/africa/nigeria.php (accessed 14 February 2002).

22 Douglas Oronto and Doife Ola, "Defending Nature, Protecting Human Dignity and Conflicts in the Niger-Delta." In *Searching for Peace in Africa: An Overview of Conflict Prevention and Transformation*, eds. Douglas Oronto and Doife Ola (Utrecht: Africa Centre for Constructive Resolution of Disputes, 1999), 332.

23 Human Rights Watch, "Permanent Transition: Current Violations of Human Rights in Nigeria." Reprinted at http://hrw.org/reports/1996/Nigeria.htm (accessed 14 February 2002).

24 Olakunle, "Death in the Land."

25 *Tell Magazine* (Lagos), 31 January 2000.

26 *The Guardian on Sunday* (Lagos), 13 January 2000.

RESOURCES

Books, Articles, Media Reports

Amuwo, Kunle, Adigun Agbaje, Rotimi Suberu and Georges Herault, eds., *Federalism and Political Restructuring in Nigeria*. Ibadan: Spectrum Books, 1998.

Banjo, Adewale Segun. *Oil and Intra–Ethnic Violence in South-Eastern Nigeria: The Internationalization of Ogoni Crisis*. Ibadan: Emmi Press, 1996.

Dent, Martin J. "Dangers of Polarity in Religious Matters." *West Africa*, 24 April 1978.

Elarigwu, J. I. Isawa. "The Shadow of Religion on Nigeria Federalism: 1960–1993." National Council on Intergovernmental Relations (NCIR) Monograph Series 2, 1993.

Laitan, David D. "Sharia Debate and the Origins of Nigeria's Second Republic." *Journal of Modern African Studies* 20 (1983).

Muhammadu, Tuvi and Haruna Mohammed. *The Making of the 1979 Constitution in Nigeria since Independence*. Ibadan: Heinemann, 1989.

Olakunle, Tunde. "Death in the Land." *The Liberty*, November 1999, 24.

Oronto, Douglas and Doife Ola. "Defending Nature, Protecting Human Dignity and Conflicts in the Niger-Delta." In *Searching for Peace in Africa: An Overview of Conflict Prevention and Transformation*, edited by Douglas Oronto and Doife Ola. Utrecht: Africa Centre for Constructive Resolution of Disputes, 1999.

Pedro, Ibiba Don. "Crisis in the Niger Delta." *The Liberty*, November 1999, 12–13.

Plotnicov, Leonard. "An Early Nigerian Civil Disturbance: The 1954 Hausa–Ibo Riots in Jos." *Journal of Modern African Studies* 9 (1971): 297–305.

Tamuno, Tekena Ntonye. *The Evolution of the Nigerian State: The Southern Phase, 1898–1914*. London: University of Ibadan Press, 1972.

———. *Nigeria: Its People and Its Problems*. Lagos: University of Ibadan Press, 1989.

———. *Peace and Violence in Nigeria*. Ibadan: Nigeria Since Independence History Project, University of Ibadan Press, 1991.

Ubah, Chinedu N. "Religion and Nigerian Unity." *Sunday Voice*, 22 February 1987, 13.

Local NGOs

African Peace Research and Strategies Studies Group (AFSTRAG): NIIA, Kofo Abayomi, Victoria Island, Lagos. Director: Prof L. S. Aminu.

African Research Bureau: 2 Olufemi Folami Crescent, opposite Voice of Nigeria, Itasin, Ebute, Ikorodu, Lagos.

Centre for Peace and Conflict Studies: Department of Political Science, University of Idaban. Director: Prof Bayo Adekanye.

Peaceworks/Academic Associates: 14 Isaac John St, Ikeja, Lagos. Director: Dr Judith Asuni.

NIGERIA COUNTRY INFORMATION

Geography
Location: West Africa.
Cities: *Capital:* Abuja (pop. est. 100 000). *Other cities:* Lagos (12 million), Ibadan (5 million), Kano (1 million), Enugu (500 000).

People
Nationality: *Noun:* Nigerian(s). *Adjective:* Nigerian.
Population (1999 est.): 100 000 000.
Total fertility rate (avg. number of children per woman): 6.
Ethnic groups: (250) Hausa/Fulani, Igbo and Yoruba are the largest.
Religions: Muslim, Christian, traditional African.
Languages: English (official), Hausa, Igbo, Yoruba, others.
Education: *Attendance (secondary):* male 32%, female 27%. *Literacy:* 39%, 51%.
Health: *Life expectancy:* 56 years. *HIV infection rate:* 4.12%.

Economy
GDP (1998 est.): $36 billion.
GDP real growth rate (2000): 2.7%.
Per capita income (1999 est.): $300.
Inflation (2000 est.): 6.6%.
Natural resources: Petroleum, natural gas, tin, columbite, iron ore, coal, limestone, lead, zinc.
Agriculture: *Products:* cocoa, palm oil, yams, cassava, sorghum, millet, corn, rice, livestock, groundnuts, cotton.
Industry: *Types:* textiles, cement, food products, footwear, metal products, lumber, beer, detergents, car assembly.
Trade (1997): *Exports:* $15.2 billion: petroleum (98.4%), cocoa.

Military
Military expenditure: Dollar figures: $23 million (FY99).
Military expenditure: Percent of GDP: 0.7% (FY99).

Demographic information is drawn from that compiled by the United States Department of State. See http://www.state.gov/r/pa/ei/bgn

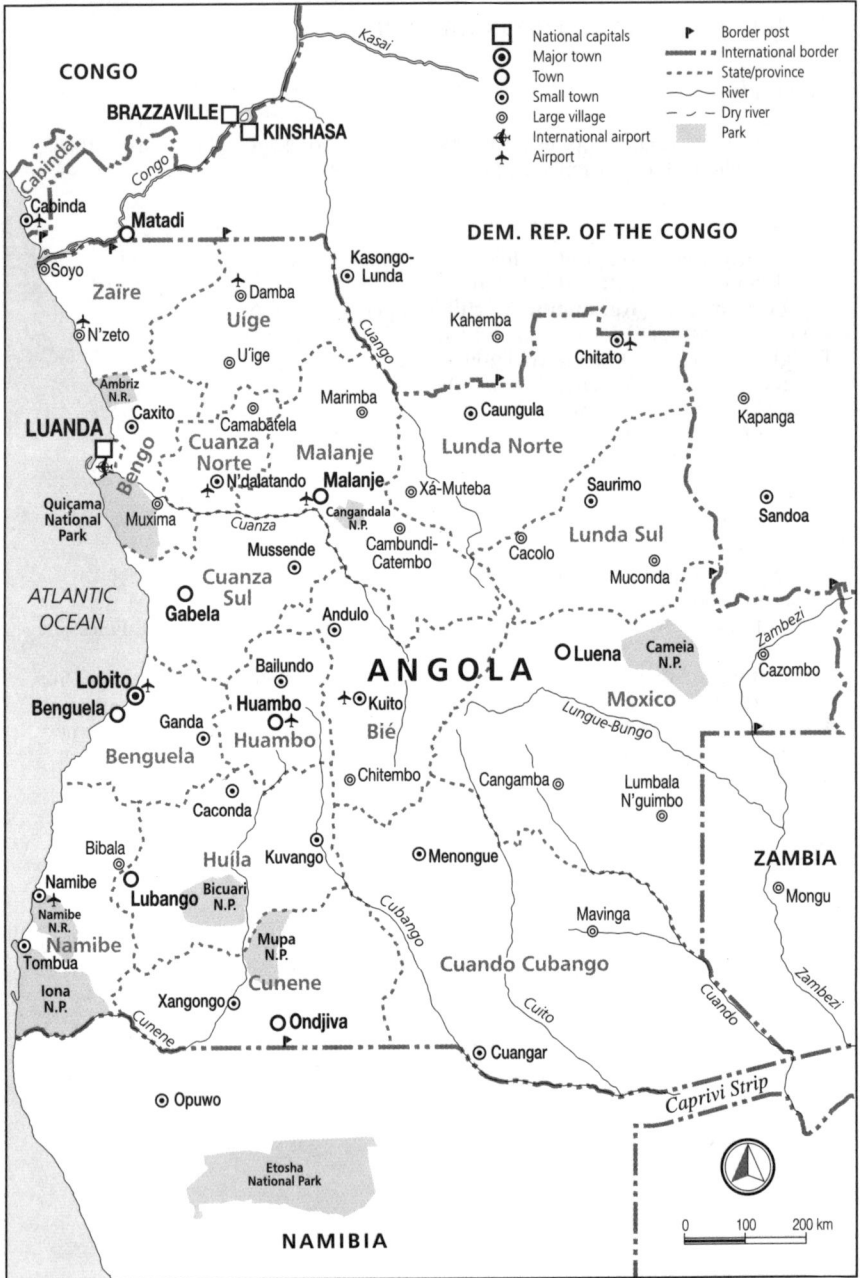

CONGO

Kasai

BRAZZAVILLE

KINSHASA

Cabinda

Congo

Cabinda

Matadi

Soyo

Zaïre

DEM. REP. OF THE CONGO

Kasongo-
Lunda

Damba

N'zeto

Uíge

U'ige

Kahemba

Chitato

Kapanga

Ambriz
N.R.

Caxito

Marimba

Camabatela

Caungula

Cuango

LUANDA

Bengo

Cuanza
Norte

Malanje

N'dalatando

Malanje

Xá-Muteba

Lunda Norte

Saurimo

Sandoa

Quiçama
National
Park

Muxima

Cuanza

Cangandala
N.P.

Cambundi-
Catembo

Cacolo

Lunda Sul

Muconda

*ATLANTIC
OCEAN*

Mussende

Cuanza
Sul

Gabela

Andulo

A N G O L A

Zambezi

Cazombo

Bailundo

Luena

Cameia
N.P.

Moxico

Lobito

Benguela

Huambo

Ganda

Huambo

Kuito

Bié

Lungue-Bungo

Cangamba

Lumbala
N'guimbo

Benguela

Chitembo

Caconda

Bibala

Huíla

Kuvango

Menongue

ZAMBIA

Mongu

Namibe

Lubango

Bicuari
N.P.

Mavinga

Namibe
N.R.

Namibe

Mupa
N.P.

Cubango

Cuando Cubango

Tombua

Cunene

Cuito

Cuando

Zambezi

Iona
N.P.

Xangongo

Ondjiva

Cunene

Cuangar

Caprivi Strip

Opuwo

Etosha
National Park

NAMIBIA

	National capitals		Border post
	Major town		International border
	Town		State/province
	Small town		River
	Large village		Dry river
	International airport		Park
	Airport		

0   100   200 km

Chapter 5

Angola: The Beginning of Hope for Peace

ERIK DOXTADER AND RICKY KHAUKHA

When speaking of Angola, optimism is not a word that comes readily to mind. The country lies in shambles, its infrastructure destroyed, its citizens brutalised by colonialism, war and political conflict. Repeatedly, Angola has been voted the worst place in the world to be a child. Hunger and displacement are the norm. In mid-2002, it was estimated that over half a million people were confronting starvation. Since 1990, an estimated 300 000 have been killed or maimed. Many more have lost their homes, their communities and their livelihoods. This is but part of the whole. With Angola, history and violence are nearly synonymous.

Today, there is cause for optimism in Angola. Increasingly, citizens speak to a cautious hope, a sense that the country may soon turn a corner, moving from the past to a future in which reconstruction and prosperity are at least a possibility. The sentiment has much to do with the events of 22 February 2002, the day that National Union for the Total Independence of Angola (UNITA) leader Jonas Savimbi was killed in fighting with government troops. The demise of this magnetic, shrewd and altogether stubborn character was mourned by some and celebrated by many.

Whether a hero or a criminal, Savimbi's death has changed the face of Angola's political landscape. A cease-fire agreement has been in place since April. It appears that UNITA is committed to disarmament and taking a seat at the political table. With this said, it is also true that Angolans now face the Herculean struggle of rebuilding and moving forward. In a real sense, Savimbi's death exposed rather than solved the problems. Hundreds of thousands if not millions may yet perish. The path to recovery is fraught with obstacles that will demand yet more sacrifices from Angola's citizens and a concerted effort by members of the international community, a community that has much blood on its hands and that also claims to be aidweary. The beginning of Angola's future has begun, but only barely.

The Face of Conflict

Angola presently sits squarely between a devastating civil war and an opportunity for peace-building. Savimbi's death neither ensures the end of conflict nor guarantees that Angola will be able to rebuild its tattered infrastructure. This is a tenuous time, a moment in which political leaders and citizens are moving between a conflict that has extracted a great toll and a potential transition that can set the stage for reconstruction and democratisation. To understand the dynamics within this situation, it is necessary to move back and forth between the events that preceded Savimbi's killing and those that followed.

At the time of Savimbi's death, the conflict in Angola was an episodic but very real "hot" war. After the further breakdown of the Lusaka Peace Accord in 1998, fighting increased, an escalation that was largely blamed on UNITA. While the government enjoyed substantial international support, it was far from clear that the government had the tools and resources to win its desired military victory. As it was a guerrilla war, UNITA's capabilities were difficult to find and destroy.[1] What is more, UNITA appeared to have a viable support base in the rural areas. Still, the government was having some military success. In recent years it had captured former UNITA strongholds like Bailundo, UNITA's former headquarters, and Andulo, Savimbi's hometown in central Angola. These victories lent credence to the government's claim that its military position was improving.[2]

In the late twentieth century, the conflict in Angola has taken a largely bi-polar form. In 1975, however, after a long war for independence against the Portuguese, the country was torn between three different political movements that represented different ethnic groups and which served different international constituencies. The division proved disastrous. On one side, the National Front for the Liberation of Angola (FNLA) was led by Roberto Holden and aimed to restore the glory days of the Kongo Kingdom. On another side, the Popular Movement for the Liberation of Angola (MPLA) was a largely urban movement, grounded mostly in Luanda and led initially by Agostinho Neto. Founded in 1966, UNITA has long been dominated by the Ovimbundu people of central and southern Angola. Supported by largely rural constituents, UNITA aimed to secure recognition of Angolans' indigenous rights.[3]

By the mid-1990s, internal disputes and divisions, some of which appeared to be engineered by the government, had weakened UNITA's political power. According to *Africa Confidential*, there have been five different political groups that claim to represent UNITA's vision: UNITA Savimbi, UNITA Luanda, UNITA Autonome, UNITA Renovada and UNITA International.[4] Each has asserted its moral authority over UNITA and each articulates a different hope for Angola's socio-economic and political future. The fault lines have weakened UNITA's power. Though

the different "parties" claim independence from the government, there
have been reports by local and international media that the government
deliberately set out to weaken UNITA by dividing it. For example,
UNITA Renovada ("Renewed") is an officially recognised partner in the
MPLA government. It represents the bulk of UNITA's non-military leadership, individuals who refused to recognise Savimbi as the leader of
UNITA, since he rejected both the results of the 1992 elections and the
terms of the Lusaka Peace Accord.[5]

The reasons for the current conflict are various and variable. In all cases,
they have much to do with power and ideology. The perceptions of the
government and UNITA are tied directly to their history of conflict and
its relationship to colonialism. Each has a different vision for Angola's
future, perceptions that rarely intersect and which make it difficult to
assess the nature, meaning, necessity and significance of the conflict.
According to James Ciment, the MPLA has always defined itself as a van-
guard party. Like the former Communist Party in the Soviet Union, it
strives for the total reconfiguration of Angolan society.[6] This mission
shapes the party's perspective about its conflict with UNITA. For the
MPLA, the war is a fight against counter-revolutionary forces with a dangerous socio-political and economic agenda.[7] The struggle against UNITA
is vital to ensure that Angola retains the inclusive values that the MPLA
pioneered, an ideal of national identity designed to reverse the colonial
legacy of ethnic and racial division. According to the MPLA, UNITA's
agenda represents the antithesis of this goal, a return to the structures and
inequities of colonialism.[8] The MPLA also saw Savimbi as a morally suspect figure, incapable of leading Angola to a better future. Citing
Savimbi's long history of alleged opportunism, multiple failures to comply with signed treaties and his lack of a consistent political vision for the
country, the MPLA argued that all his campaigns needed to be resisted at
every turn.

Historically, UNITA has defined its political goals more in terms of
what it opposes rather than what it envisions for Angola. UNITA has a
long tradition of defining itself in direct opposition to the MPLA.[9]
However, UNITA has also consistently emphasised the centrality of traditional African values in reforming the post-colonial Angolan state. Citing
the MPLA's revolutionary programme, an agenda that de-emphasises the
role of traditional authority in the rural areas, UNITA criticised the
MPLA's failure to define its politics in relation to ordinary Angolans. In
large measure, UNITA has defined the conflict as a struggle of the rural
peasant majority against the urban elite who are out of touch with the

needs and aspirations of most citizens. UNITA claims to defend the interests of the largest group in Angola, arguing that the Ovimbundu have historically been marginalised.

The international community's perceptions about the conflict have been shaped by a desire to end the civil war and relieve the long-suffering Angolan people. This is the primary position taken by international organisations like the UN, foreign countries from all around the world and international NGOs like Amnesty International and Human Rights Watch. This unanimity in the international community has led to numerous efforts to broker peace agreements. Over the last decade, three such attempts have failed. The Bicesse Accord of 1991 paved the way for the election of 1992, which was then disputed; the United Nations Verification Mission II (UNAVEM II) was intended but failed to rescue the results of the 1992 elections. UNAVEM III attempted to rehabilitate the terms of UNAVEM II and the 1994 Lusaka Accord.[10] At best, the parties persistently failed to resolve the fundamental demands that began the war. UNITA never accepted the MPLA as a "true" or legitimate representative of the Angolan people.[11]

In assessing why various peace proposals have failed, most international stakeholders blame UNITA.[12] Organisations like the Southern African Development Community (SADC) have been very critical of UNITA. Before his death, Savimbi was declared a war criminal by some organisations, a status that has led many to revoke their recognition of his organisation and its aims. International sanctions followed. On the other side, the MPLA government has received military assistance and co-operation from SADC countries like Namibia and Zimbabwe.[13] Its war against UNITA was perceived as a "just" action, acknowledgement that served to bolster and sustain its effort.

UNITA's very survival is something of a testament to its founding purpose. It still has the support and loyalty of many Angolans. It is alleged that it long enjoyed covert support from some former cold war allies. Some in the UN and the Angolan government claim that several African countries, namely Uganda, Zambia, Togo and the Ivory Coast, have provided support to UNITA, in part by channelling blood diamonds that sustain its capacity to fight.[14] However, by early 2002, it was clear that UNITA's power was dwindling. Attacks became more sporadic and there was evidence that UNITA troops were increasingly unable to survive in the bush.[15]

The conflict in Angola has come at incredible cost. Over the course of the civil war it is estimated that there have been more than 800 000 war-related casualties, nearly 10% of the country's population. Another 2.6 million individuals have been internally displaced by the fighting and there is a substantial refugee population in neighbouring states. It is believed that there are between 9 and 15 million landmines still planted in Angola, spread throughout the country, a threat that will haunt its citizens for decades to come. Aid organisations hold that there have been 70 000 mine-related amputations in the last decade, many of these children under the age of 15. Malnutrition and disease are widespread. Education and infrastructure lie in ruin. The country's HIV/Aids infection rate is estimated to be one in four.

The human rights situation in Angola is complicated by entrenched institutional interests, many of which have worked against the emergence of a civil society that can support reform. For instance, a report by Alex Vines highlights the important role that NGOs will need to play within an atmosphere characterised by "elite domination, using the almost perpetual state of war as an excuse".[16] In effect, civil society in Angola operates in an atmosphere where war has been used by the government to repress what it feels is against its interests. The Angolan government has been accused of censoring the press.[17] One editor has summarised the state's attitude towards the independent media by noting how the authorities in Luanda "have invaded newsrooms, stopped journalists from leaving the country, passed judgements on them, and taken other 'measures'".[18] The independent press has not been the only victim in civil society. The government's attempt to silence those it deems a threat to its interests has led to tension between the government and the church. This perceived hostility towards civil society can be traced to what Vines calls the MPLA's history as an "orthodox Marxist-Leninist" party, a past in which civil society was thought to flourish only under the auspices of the state.

The legacy of the war in Angola has been destabilisation, general stagnation and the deterioration of other facets of life. According to *The Economist*, Angola is "one of the fastest growing countries in Africa and will receive 3.5 billion dollars of investments from the international oil industry".[19] However, this picture is misleading, since it gives the impression that Angola as a whole is prospering. A World Bank report highlights that Angola's debt burden is 100% of its GDP.[20] In essence, the economy is stagnant in all sectors except the oil and diamond industries. War has also collapsed the rural economy. The economic decline has had a significant impact on life expectancy and child mortality.[21] Economic stagnation is further compounded by a culture of graft and mismanagement. According to one British NGO, "a lack of . . . transparency has encouraged massive official corruption, impoverishing people and obstructing peace initiatives".[22] Additionally, there is a "major problem in the transparent use of growing oil revenues by the Angolan government, leaving a war-torn population with little benefit from massive expected investments".

The complexion and complexity of the situation in Angola has changed dramatically since Savimbi's death. Much appears to hang in the balance. In the weeks after Savimbi was killed, UNITA forces continued to launch sporadic attacks against mainly civilian targets. With Savimbi's successor also missing, and later found dead, the organisation faced a leadership vacuum along with shortages of supplies and food for troops. Some have argued in the aftermath that without Savimbi, UNITA lost its "cause". Others hold that the organisation was simply without the means to survive. In either case, the government's unilateral cease-fire in March was a show of good faith that opened a space for dialogue. After a series of talks, the details of which are explained below, a formal cease-fire agreement was signed on 4 April. Since then, UNITA troops have largely been seen to give up, reporting to camps where they can be disarmed and hopefully reintegrated into Angolan society. Whether this process can succeed remains to be seen. The camps are reported to lack supplies and food. Indeed, the latter appears to be a significant concern throughout the country. The end of open fighting has lifted a curtain on the country's vast crisis. Almost one-third of Angola's population has been displaced by war. Given the decimation of the agricultural sector, international agencies predict that without substantial aid, several hundred thousand citizens will starve in the coming months. Whether the humanitarian crisis has the potential to upset the peace process is not clear. What is certain is that stability and security will remain elusive goals.

The Historical Roots of Violence and Division

The contemporary civil war in Angola can be traced first to the violence of colonialism and then to a liberation struggle in which three leaders came to believe that their own movements had legitimate claims to the post-colonial state. While the war has ethnic implications, many agree that it has been driven less by such animosity than differences over how to define and implement the politics of self-determination. Over time and at significant cost, the protagonists were reduced from three to two. This did not relieve the crowding on the stage, however. Angola's war has been a wholly international affair, a central feature of the cold war and a clash with a southern neighbour intent on keeping a corridor between apartheid South Africa and the rest of Africa.

The Portuguese presence in Angola began around the fifteenth century when the Portuguese made contact with the centralised kingdom of the Bakongo (the Kongo Kingdom). The kingdom controlled a large territory, running from present-day northern Angola to southern Congo.[23] Portuguese colonialism took shape in two time periods: the slave trading period that started in the fifteenth century and ended when slavery was abolished in the 1880s and the formal colonial period that began around 1885, when Portuguese administrative networks were introduced into the country.

For 350 years, the Portuguese engaged in the slave trade in Angola. This continues to have an impact on the population of Angola today. The slave trade established a pattern of "exploitation and relative advantage" for some groups in Angola, largely because of their location near the heart of the trading centres.[24] For example, the Mbundu-speaking people are still viewed by some as having a collaborationist relationship with the Portuguese, in part because of their proximity to colonial settlements near the coastal plains. With the conquest of the Angolan interior, the Portuguese imposed a formal colonial network between 1890–1930.[25] Portuguese settlements were often located at the Angolan coast in cities like Luanda and Benguela. This led to interaction and intermarriages between indigenous Angolans and the Portuguese. The results were new "racial" and cultural categories of people, groups that were held to be distinct from indigenous Angolans. These are categories of people called *Mestizos* and *Assimiliados*. The political status of these individuals continues to be one of the factors fuelling the conflict.[26] There is widespread belief by UNITA that the *Mestizos*, who have historically dominated the MPLA movement, are illegitimate in the sense that, as a minority, they have neither the right nor legitimacy to dominate national politics.

Resistance to Portuguese rule took clear shape in the 1950s and 1960s. Led by Neto, the MPLA was formed in 1956 and came to prominence by claiming to lead an attack on Angola's political prisons in 1961. From the early days, the MPLA espoused both a vision of African nationalism and a commitment to Marxism. With links to the Angolan Communist Party, it argued that the struggle against colonialism had to be geared towards the need for self-determination and economic independence. The goal, in short, was the "complete destruction of the colonial machinery and all forms of domination". While equally committed to African nationalism, the FNLA disavowed its counterpart's Marxism. In 1962, as it emerged from the Union of the Peoples of Angola (UPA), an organisation that worked largely within the lines to produce economic and political gains, the FNLA was largely based in the Congo. It struggled to convince many that it did represent the interests of ordinary Angolans, a problem that was tied both to its external location and its concern to resurrect the northern-based Kongo Kingdom. Led by Roberto Holden, it argued early on that Angola needed to be united and that this work required a fervent anti-communism.[27]

In 1966, Jonas Savimbi founded UNITA after breaking away from the FNLA. Initially in coalition with the Portuguese against the MPLA, Savimbi appealed to a rather small constituency with his Maoist doctrines.[28] Throughout its history, UNITA has variously portrayed its ideology to maximise support for its struggle. Initially, it showed a social-ist face.[29] In its structures and programmes, UNITA used language and phrases associated with socialist thinking of the 1960s. Nevertheless, this identification was made in the context of increased collaboration with the Portuguese colonial administration in the first half of 1970.[30] UNITA was consequently viewed by some as ideologically bankrupt, intent on amass-ing political power through violence and ready to co-operate with any group that would help further its goals. While advancing the ideology of anti-imperialism, and fashioning itself as a third world movement fighting Western exploitation, UNITA pursued a policy of co-operation with South Africa. Minter concludes that Savimbi has variously portrayed him-self as "nationalistic, Marxist, Maoist, Pro-Western and socialist" and that he has "demonstrated an extraordinary skill in presenting different images to different people".[31] The ideology that has remained throughout UNITA's history has been its "championing" of the rights of the indige-nous peoples (mostly the Ovimbundus) of Angola.

Angolan independence followed rather quickly after the Portuguese coup in April 1974. After a period of uncertainty, the parties met in Alvor, Portugal to sign an agreement that called for a transitional government and elections that would lead quickly to independence. What followed was an intense struggle for power, one in which each of the liberation move-ments vied for the support of the Portuguese and the key players in the cold war. Fighting ensued and it quickly became clear that the negotiated arrangements were being supplanted by a struggle over who would lead the country. Guimaraes' picture of the transformation is remarkable, a sit-uation in which relatively rag-tag movements were armed to the teeth by the United States, the Soviet Union and South Africa.[32] Supported by the Soviets, the MPLA came to draw the upper hand against the US and Chinese-backed FNLA. Open fighting between the groups began in early 1975, a conflict that UNITA initially eschewed, claiming that it supported the Alvor arrangement. With the FNLA in control of the north and the MPLA fixed in the capital and southern areas, conflict escalated, in part due to an overall "disintegration of authority". UNITA began to receive arms from the US and support from South Africa. The latter conducted multiple raids into Angola in the mid-1970s. In league with the FNLA, it sought to defeat the MPLA in what it hoped would be a set of decisive and short battles. Intense fighting occurred in the ensuing months, including a battle for the capital that amounted to a significant and largely fatal loss for the FNLA. Backed by Cuba, the MPLA was in a position of control and turned its sights on defeating UNITA.[33]

With the 1980s came continued fighting between MPLA and UNITA forces, with greater and more destructive South African intervention. With State President P. W. Botha's "Total Strategy" came troops, thousands of infantry who first struck SWAPO units based in Angola and then Angolans themselves. Sabotage of Angolan assets became more frequent and destructive. Throughout most of 1980, South African forces occupied sections of the Cuando Cubango province. In 1984, South African agreements to reduce violence were signed and then largely ignored. Meanwhile, conflict between UNITA and MPLA forces continued, particularly in the countryside.

In 1988, agreements over Namibian independence were tied to the withdrawal of Cuban forces in Angola. This move brought an opportunity to resolve the civil war or at least reduce its intensity. Talks continued through 1988 and 1989, efforts that appeared to gain momentum as both Savimbi and Angolan President Eduardo dos Santos tentatively agreed to a cease-fire and concrete discussions about political normalisation. After disagreements over whether elections would feature multi-party competition or the incorporation of UNITA into existing political structures, a cease-fire was concluded on 1 May 1990. Elections were held 18 months later, with the MPLA winning a slim majority of seats. Savimbi refused to accept the outcome of the plebiscite, a decision that signalled a return to war.

Prospects for Peace-building and Reconciliation

Angola's history is littered with broken and contested peace agreements. In 1994, the Lusaka Protocol appeared to offer the best opportunity in Angola's post-independence history to end the war. The protocol was intended to create a single national security structure, thus removing a key source of violence. It sought an alliance of the opposing forces to create a government of national unity. Sponsored by international and multilateral actors it seemed to open the door to peace-building, especially as its success ensured an influx of reconstruction and development resources. However, the war resumed in 1998 when UNITA broke from the accord, an action that it claimed was necessary due to government intransigence. In 2002, the death of Savimbi has brought new life to the troubled Lusaka Protocol. Coupled with the government's offer of amnesty to all UNITA forces, it is the centrepiece of the April cease-fire and the basis for rebuilding Angolan politics. However, the precise outcome of the process is not yet certain. Internal splits in UNITA, along with a vast humanitarian crisis, portend a potentially rough ride. In this sense, it is likely that peace and stability will need to precede the promotion of reconciliation in Angola.

The Lusaka Protocol provided for a cease-fire, the integration of UNITA troops and government forces to create a unified army, repatriation of mercenaries and creation of a unified police force and intelligence agency. Politically, the agreement included a framework to complete the democratisation process started by the 1992 general elections. This included instituting the results of the 1992 elections, installing a government of national unity and the provision of material benefits for UNITA's top officials. Notably, the agreement declared that "competent institutions will grant amnesty, in accordance with Article 88(h) of the Constitutional Law, for illegal acts committed by anyone prior to the signing of the Lusaka Protocol, in the context of the current conflict".[34] In short, prosecutions would not follow amnesty. For one, those involved in negotiating the accord felt that prosecution was not possible given the extended nature of the conflict and the resentment that would be generated by trials. For some, this meant that the protocol was a first step toward reconciliation. Others argued that amnesty would bring an end to the war at the cost of justice. Explicitly, the agreement was offered in a "spirit of national reconciliation" wherein "all Angolans should forgive and forget the offences resulting from the Angolan conflict and face the future with tolerance and confidence".

The Lusaka peace process had substantial foreign involvement. It was co-ordinated by the UN. Additionally, there was the "Troika" group – the US, Russia and Portugal – that was historically involved in the conflict. These were supposed to serve as general facilitators and guardians of the peace process, using their "authority" to persuade the combatants to accept and implement the protocol. International pressure from the UN, the Troika nations, SADC states and international NGOs has led some to suspect that the agreement was signed prematurely. Foreign pressure, insensitive to the need for consultation and inclusion of Angolan interests from across the political spectrum, has been offered as an explanation for why the protocol failed.[35] What is more, efforts to implement the Lusaka peace process may have been one-sided.[36] There was commitment by the government, for example, to create the necessary institutional framework for an effective peace process by appointing UNITA members to state positions. President Dos Santos resisted pressure to review the concessions given to UNITA until after the agreement was implemented. Later, he was pressured by the Angolan military and top MPLA leaders to limit these benefits. However, the government appeared serious in its desire for peace, going so far as to implement a government of national unity even before UNITA had fully implemented its side of the bargain.

When discussing the previous failures of the Lusaka Protocol, most analysts focus on UNITA's role in the peace-building process and its "intransigence" toward the protocol. The international community condemned UNITA's withdrawal. The UN, in addition to criticising UNITA's role in the failure of the peace process, accused the Angolan government of "a lack of political tolerance and an unwillingness to engage in mutual accommodation".[37] The UN's sentiments were echoed by UNITA's allegations against the government's role in the 1997 violence, conflict that included the detention and killing of some of its members and supporters. UNITA claims the implementation phase of the protocol had the effect of weakening it politically. It holds that the government undertook "a systematic attempt to annihilate its forces".[38] Facing such action, UNITA argues that it had no choice but to withdraw from the protocol. A UNITA press release dated 17 November 1997 states that the "normalisation of state authority in areas which until recently were administered by UNITA is having effects contrary to the spirit of national reconciliation". This is because "Government Police, and the Angolan Armed Forces are destroying UNITA party structures in areas where state administration has been normalised".[39] In contrast to the spirit of the protocol, which emphasised peace and mutual understanding, UNITA contends that the government has exhibited the opposite by harassing UNITA forces. UNITA lists many examples of gross human rights abuse against its armed forces and supporters. The statements issued during the period just before the resumption of the conflict in 1998 can be read as UNITA's expressed rationale for revoking its commitment to the peace treaty.

In 2001, public statements released by UNITA suggest that it was hoping for a new peace process. According to a UNITA spokesman, Justinho Jofre, the goals of the Lusaka peace process were unattainable because of new military and political dynamics in Angola. UNITA held that the balance of power shifted in a way that required a new negotiation process. It also pointed to the introduction of Namibian troops in the conflict as a reason to remake both the form and content of talks. The organisation also contended that the effects of sanctions require a different approach to the question of reconstruction. Politically there are also new actors in the conflict. Civil society organisations and political parties that did not feature in the original process must be represented in future negotiations.[40]

The history of the Lusaka Protocol is important in understanding its current potential. With Savimbi's death and subsequent talks between the government and UNITA leaders, there is now a firm commitment to amnesty and what appears to be a workable cease-fire. Both took shape in early April of 2002. Just prior to the signing of a formal truce, the Angolan parliament unanimously passed legislation that offered all UNITA forces the chance to lay down arms in exchange for indemnity. Tied to the terms of the 4 April cease-fire, the agreement stipulates that the UNITA members will report to one of 33 cantonment areas for purposes of demobilisation, vocational training or reintegration into the Angolan military. However, the conditions within the camps remain a potential source of trouble. Under-staffed and under-resourced, particularly given the numbers of soldiers and their families who are suffering from the effects of starvation and malnutrition, there is some worry that the quartering stations will become death camps. All stakeholders agree that international aid will be a crucial factor in the process. However, such assistance has been slow to arrive and severely hampered by a lack of infrastructure and an inability to move aid to where it is needed most.[41] There is also concern that a substantial number of larger weapons remain outstanding, hidden in the bush or in the possession of private citizens.

Politically, the cease-fire set the stage for Angola's return to the terms of the Lusaka Protocol. For his part, the MPLA's President Dos Santos has proposed to resume the interrupted 1992 elections process, as well as take steps to ensure that UNITA is able to reorganise itself into a viable and recognised political party that may take its place in parliament. UNITA representatives are also slated to receive several cabinet posts, governorships and ambassadorial positions. An election date has yet to be worked out and appears somewhat contingent on whether and how UNITA redresses its own internal divisions. In this matter, there is conflicting evidence. Some have argued that the organisation appears less divided than ever before, in part due to the pragmatic need to end the war. Others have predicted that there will continue to be divisions for the foreseeable future. At present, Lukamba Paulo Gato heads UNITA. In several statements, he has pledged to help "build a lasting peace and genuine national reconciliation". He has also argued that for the transition to succeed it will be necessary to convert a culture of violence into "one of dialogue and consultation".[42] For its part, the so-called dissident arm of UNITA has named a committee to undertake discussions with the larger organisation, a move that was accompanied by claims about the need to uncover the history of inter-UNITA strife and killings. Whether this pre-condition will be met remains to be seen.

International commentators have voiced substantial approval for the way in which talks have proceeded in recent months. The Troika of observers has pledged support for the demobilisation process and offered to help in further implementing the terms of the Lusaka Protocol. There is also the matter of assisting with the immense task of repatriating some 400 000 refugees who are currently living in various southern African countries. As of July 2002, however, the most daunting task involves feeding the people of Angola. The UN estimates that 500 000 are at risk of starvation if not assisted "immediately". The ways and means of this support remain uncertain.

At present, the government, UNITA officials and international observers are each calling for Angola to undertake a process of national reconciliation. The precise meaning of this call varies and lacks precision. The Namibian-based National Society for Human Rights has recently called for the formation of an Angolan Truth and Reconciliation Commission that could deal with the atrocities of the past, including those committed during colonial rule, the struggle for independence and the civil war. This move may follow logically from the amnesty agreement, particularly if Angola is to avoid inculcating a culture of impunity. However, it is still early days and the question of a truth commission hinges on the larger matter of fostering basic peace and political stability.

Along with various TRC-style proposals, many argue that Angolans must enter into sustained dialogue and that this exchange must develop at local and national levels. In late 1991, it appeared that such efforts were having a tangible effect on the conflict. However, a report by the United States Institute of Peace concludes that civil society groups in Angola face a daunting task in trying to influence the peace process.[43] Apart from the church, most have influence in only one area of the country and are unable to operate across the lines of conflict. The problem is also historical. Since independence, the state has been suspicious of independent NGOs and civil society. It has continued to undermine institutions that contradict its thinking. The most affected stakeholders in Angola, its citizens, are represented by a civil society that does not yet possess the capacity to independently pressurise the government and UNITA into resolving their differences. However, there are some hopeful signs that there may now be a chance for new initiatives. In part, this opportunity stems from the fact that many in the country are increasingly war weary, exhausted and ready to move from conflict to talk.

The search for peace will likely have to involve a coalition of forces. Many reports have highlighted the relative weakness of the local NGO sector in Angola.[44] The United States Institute of Peace concluded that apart from the large presence of international NGOs, advocacy groups and humanitarian organisations, local independent organisations are emerging in select areas but do not have "a tradition to sustain their development". This is because they possess limited human and financial resources, factors that constrain their power. The report adds: "There are few NGOs in Angola . . . what can be termed as civil society hardly exists in the country."[45] The key NGO network is sustained by church associations and church-affiliated organisations. "Churches are the most important independent organisations, with the Catholic church being the largest and most important, followed by Methodist, Congregationalist, Kimbangoist Churches, and others." According to the report, although they are independent, the churches are often reluctant to confront the government. To demonstrate the church's access to all sectors of the country, the Angolan Lutheran Church periodically organises reconciliatory meetings between women from UNITA and MPLA-dominated areas. These efforts signify a yet unrealised potential to build networks for reconciliation that bridge deep division.

Most NGOs have limited access to the citizens of Angola, partly because they are perceived to favour one side or the other in the conflict. For example, the Association for Rural Development and the Environment (ADRE) is hampered because it cannot operate in the UNITA areas, which are mostly rural. UNITA rejects its presence because of its alleged close association with the government in Luanda.

International NGOs based in Angola have a larger scope of operation: "Many international NGOs, such as Africare, World Vision, Catholic Relief Services, Caritas, and Save the Children, operate effectively in Angola. However, they generally avoid addressing the issues of peace and reconciliation. One source of their hesitation is fear of alienating either the government or UNITA authorities and, in turn, jeopardizing access to areas where they currently operate."[46] International NGOs have taken the opportunity presented by a liberalised registry regime for civil society groups to support the building of a domestic civil society. For example, the International Republican Institute aims to help build and strengthen political parties in Angola. The Association of Western European Parliamentarians for Africa organises workshops to promote local understanding of the Lusaka Protocol.

All told, the situation in Angola is extremely fragile. There is great danger and there is also the possibility for significant change. There is an increasing recognition by the authorities in Luanda that citizens want and expect peace. In a speech delivered recently, President Dos Santos concluded: "The word peace must be the most used word in the country at this moment. There is not a single Angolan who does not wish to see his or her country pacified with urgency. However, if we ask all of them what is the path to reach this peace, the response will be different. On this subject, as in almost all others, the government defines its position bearing in mind the will of the majority of the population, especially those that some call 'Deep Angola'."[47] All sides appear to have recognised that it is time for the war to end. The road to peace will not be easy and it will require more than token assistance from those countries that bear substantial responsibility for the atrocities of the past. While they may grow slowly, what is clear is that the seeds of peace have been sown.

NOTES

1 *Africa Confidential*, "Angola." Reprinted at www.africa-confidential.com/country.asp (accessed 9 April 2001); Amnesty International, "World Report 2000: Angola." Reprinted at www.rights.amnesty.org/ailib/aireport/ar99/afr12.htm (accessed 5 April 2001).

2 *Africa Confidential*, "Angola: Who Blinks First? Government and UNITA Rebels Edge Reluctantly Towards a Cease-fire and New Negotiations in One of Africa's Longest-running Wars." Reprinted at www.africa-confidential.com/news (accessed 1 June 2001).

3 James Martin, *A Political History of the Civil War in Angola 1974–1990* (London: Macmillan, 1992), 46.

4 *Africa Confidential*, "Angola: Who Blinks First?"

5 Ibid.

6 James Ciment, *Conflict and Crisis in the Post-cold War World: Angola and Mozambique. Post-colonial Wars in Southern Africa* (New York: Facts on File Inc, 1997), 158–60.

7 Ibid, 160.

8 Martin, *A Political History of the Civil War*, 61.

9 Ciment, *Conflict and Crisis in the Post-cold War World*, 160–61.

10 Richard Cornwell and Jackie Potgieter, "Angola: Endgame or Stalemate? ISS Paper No. 30, April 1998." Reprinted at www.iss.co.za/pubs/PAPERS/30/paper30. html (accessed 9 April 2001).

11 William Minter, *Account from Angola: Unita as Described by Ex-participants and Foreign Visitors* (Uppsala: African-European Institute, 1991), 36–37.

12 Integrated Regional Information Network (IRIN), "Oxfam Voices Concern about IDP." Reprinted at www.reliefweb.int/IRIN/sa/countrystories/angola/ 20010726.phtml (accessed 15 October 2001).

13 Tangeni Amupadhi, "Namibia's Secret Battles with UNITA." Reprinted at www.mg.co.za/news (accessed 6 August 2001).

14 UN Security Council, "Sanctions on UNITA's Activities by the United Nations." Reprinted at www.un.org/news/ossg/sanctions.html#Angola (accessed 14 April 2001).

15 UN Security Council, "Security Council Resolution 10943 on Angola." Reprinted at www.un.org/sanctions/angola (accessed 14 April 2001).

16 Alex Vines, *Angola Unravels: The Rise and Fall of the Lusaka Peace Process* (New York: H. R. W., 1999), Chapter 11.

17 *Mail & Guardian*, "Savimbi Interviewed by Luanda Newspaper." Reprinted at www.mg.co.za/mg/news/2000may1/11may-angola.phtml (accessed 15 June 2001).

18 Vines, *Angola Unravels*, Chapter 11.

19 *The Economist*, "Oil, Diamonds and Danger in Angola, January 13, 2001." Reprinted at www.economist.com/displayStory.cfm?story_ID=s (accessed 9 November 2001).

20 The World Bank Group, "Angola Data Profile." Reprinted at www.worldbank. org/external/dgprofile.asp (accessed 25 April 2001); Cornwell and Potgieter, "Angola: Endgame or Stalemate?"; Minter, *Account from Angola*, 6.

21 IRIN. "Angola: Humanitarian Update, 20 March 2001." Reprinted at www.reliefweb.int/IRIN/archive/angola.phtml (accessed 20 August 2001).

22 Global Witness, "Global Witness Report on Angola." Reprinted at www. globalwitness.org (accessed 25 April 2001).

23 Cornwell and Potgieter, "Angola: Endgame or Stalemate?"; Lawrence Henderson, *Angola: Five Centuries of Conflict* (Ithaca: Cornell University Press, 1970), 37–40.

24 Cornwell and Potgieter, "Angola: Endgame or Stalemate?"

25 Douglas Wheeler and Renee Perlissier, *Angola* (London: Pall Mall Press, 1971), 81.

26 Martin, *A Political History of the Civil War in Angola*, 64.

27 An excellent history of the development of the MPLA and FNLA can be found in Fernando Anreson Guimaraes, *The Origins of the Angolan Civil War: Foreign Intervention and Domestic Political Conflict* (London: Macmillan, 1998), 31–57.

28 Michael Wolfers and Jane Bergerol, *Angola: On the Front Line* (London: Zed Press, 1983), 194.

29 Minter, *Account from Angola*, 40.

30 Wolfers and Bergerol, *On the Front Line*, 197–201: This work highlights evidence of Savimbi and Unita's collaborationist activities with the Portuguese. Though UNITA denied that it was involved in joint activities with the Portuguese against the MPLA, retired Portuguese officials have confirmed the collaboration.

31 Minter, *Account from Angola*, 40–41.

32 Guimaraes, *The Origins of the Angolan Civil War*, 95–113.

33   For accounts of the roles taken by various foreign actors in Angola see William Minter, *Apartheid's Contras: An Inquiry into the Roots of War in Angola and Mozambique* (Johannesburg: Witwatersrand University Press, 1994), 11–35.

34   Angolan Government website, "The Lusaka Peace Protocol." Reprinted at www.angola.org/politics/p_annex6.htm (accessed 7 May 2001).

35   Vines, *Angola Unravels*, Chapter 11.

36   Ibid, 20–27.

37   UN website, "Secretary General's Report to the Security Council on the Situation in Angola." Reprinted at www.un.org/Docs/sc/reports/1999/s199949htm (accessed 15 June 2001).

38   Kwacha UNITA Press, "The Political and Diplomatic Page." Reprinted at www.kwacha.com/19/english/epoli2.htm (accessed 3 May 2001).

39   Most of these communiqués date from 1997, at the time when UNITA, according to many sources, was preparing for a new war by rearming, retraining, etc. However, a search for more contemporary releases from UNITA has been unsuccessful, perhaps demonstrating the recent losses incurred by UNITA and the capture of some of its bases.

40   IRIN, "Unita Questions Legitimacy of Lusaka Process." Reprinted at www.reliefweb.int/IRIN/sa/countrystories/angola/20010712.phtml (accessed 14 August 2001).

41   Action for Southern Africa, *Angola Peace Monitor* No. 9 (May 2002). Reprinted at www.reliefweb.int (accessed July 2002).

42   US Department of State, "New UNITA Head Sees Prospects for Lasting Peace in Angola," 14 June 2002. Reprinted at www.reliefweb.int (accessed 18 June 2002).

43   United States Institute of Peace, "NGOs and the Peace Process in Angola." Reprinted at www.usip.org/oc/angola.html#ngos (accessed 7 May 2001).

44   United States Institute of Peace, "NGOs and the Peace Process in Angola."

45   Ibid.

46   Ibid.

47   Angolan Government website, "Address by his Excellency Jose Eduardo Dos Santos at the International Conference on Law, Democracy, Peace and Development." Reprinted at www.angola.org/reference/speeches/dossantos/050201E.html (accessed 7 May 2001).

RESOURCES

Books, Articles, Media Reports

Bender, Gerald. "Angola: Left, Right, and Wrong." *Foreign Policy* 43 (1987): 53–67.

Ciment, James. *Conflict and Crisis in the Post-cold War World: Angola and Mozambique, Post-colonial Wars in Southern Africa.* New York: Facts on File Inc, 1997.

Cornwell, Richard and Jackie Potgieter. "Angola: Endgame or Stalemate?" ISS Paper No. 30, April 1998. Reprinted at www.iss.co.za/pubs/PAPERS/30/paper30.html (accessed 9 April 2001).

———. "Angola: At the Precipice." ISS Paper No. 32, July 1998. Reprinted at www.iss.co.za/pubs/PAPERS/32/paper32.html (accessed 9 April 2001).

Guimaraes, Fernando Anreson. *The Origins of the Angolan Civil War: Foreign Intervention and Domestic Political Conflict.* London: Macmillan, 1998.

Henderson, Lawrence. *Angola: Five Centuries of Conflict.* Ithaca: Cornell University Press, 1970.

Martin, James. *A Political History of the Civil War in Angola 1974–1990.* London: Macmillan, 1992.

Minter, William. *Account from Angola: Unita as Described by Ex-participants and Foreign Visitors.* Uppsala: African-European Institute, 1991.

———. *Apartheid's Contras: An Inquiry into the Roots of War in Angola and Mozambique.* Johannesburg: Witwatersrand University Press, 1994.

United States Institute of Peace. "NGOs and the Peace Process in Angola." Reprinted at www.usip.org/oc/sr/angola.htm#ngos (accessed 7 May 2001).

Vines, Alex. *Angola Unravels: The Rise and Fall of the Lusaka Peace Process.* New York: H. R. W., 1999.

———. "Mercenaries, Human Rights and Legality." In *Mercenaries: An African Security Dilemma*, edited by Musah Abdel-Fatau and Kayode Fayemi. London: Photo Press, 2000.

Wheeler, Douglas and Renee Perlissier. *Angola.* London: Pall Mall Press, 1971.

Wolfers, Michael and Jane Bergerol. *Angola: On the Front Line.* London: Zed Press, 1983.

Primary Documents

Angolan Mission Observer is a bi-monthly publication of the Permanent Mission of the Republic of Angola to the United Nations: www.angola.org/news/mission/index.html

Angola Peace Monitor is produced monthly by Action for Southern Africa (ACTSA), the successor organisation to the British Anti-Apartheid Movement: www.anc.org.za/angola

Institute for Security Studies: http://www.iss.co.za/pubs/PAPERS

Integrated Regional Information Network (IRIN) is part of the UN Office for the Coordination of Humanitarian Affairs that offers daily news briefings from Angola: www.reliefweb.int/IRIN/sa/countrystories/angola

Lusaka Protocol. Full text of the 1994 peace agreement between the government of the Republic of Angola and UNITA: www.usip.org/library/pa/angola/lusaka.html

Pensador is a newsletter published by the embassy of Angola in the United States. It gives regular updates on Angolan politics: www.angola.org/news/pensador/index

Political resources on Angola on the internet, with information on elections, the leadership and a number of the political parties: http://www.agora.it/politic/angola.htm

Government, Intergovernmental Bodies and Political Parties

Angolan government news and information website: http://www.Angola.org UNITA: http://www.kwacha.org/english

International NGOs

Amnesty International is a global human rights organisation that advocates basic human rights and monitors human rights developments in most countries in the world: http://www.rights.amnesty.org/ailib/aireport/ar99/afr12.htm

Global Witness is an organisation that monitors good governance in a country, concentrating mainly on highlighting corruption in the third world. It has a base in Angola: http://www.globalwitness.org/Africa/Angola

Human Rights Watch is a global human rights NGO that monitors human rights developments in most countries in the world: http://www.hrw.org/wr2kr/Africa/Angola.html

ANGOLA COUNTRY INFORMATION

Geography

Location: Southern Africa, bordering the south Atlantic Ocean, between Namibia and the Democratic Republic of the Congo.

Cities: *Capital:* Luanda. *Other towns:* Bengo, Benguela, Bie, Cabinda, Cunene, Huambo, Huila, etc.

People

Nationality: *Noun:* Angolan(s). *Adjective:* Angolan.

Population (July 2000 est.): 10 145 267.

Population growth rate: 2.15%.

Ethnic groups: Ovimbundu 37%, Kimbundu 25%, Bakongo 13%, Mestizo (mixed European and native African) 2%, European 1%, other 22%.

Religions (1998 est.): Traditional African 47%, Roman Catholic 38%, Protestant 15%.

Languages: Portuguese (official), Bantu and other African languages.

Education (1998 est.): *Literacy:* total population of people aged 15 and over who can read and write 42%; male 56%, female 28%.

Health: *Infant mortality rate:* 196/1 000 (2000 est.). *Life expectancy:* 38.31 years. *HIV infection rate:* 2.12%.

Workforce: 500 000. Agriculture: 85%. Industry and services: 15%.

Economy

GDP (1999 est.): $11.6 billion.

GDP real growth rate (1999 est.): 4%.

Per capita income (1999 est.): $1 030.

Inflation rate (1999 est.): 270%.

Natural resources: Petroleum, diamonds, iron ore, phosphates, copper, feldspar, gold, bauxite, uranium.

Agriculture: 13% of GDP. *Products:* bananas, sugar cane, coffee, sisal, corn, cotton, manioc (tapioca), tobacco, vegetables, plantains, livestock, forest products, fish.

Industry: 53% of GDP. *Types:* petroleum, diamonds, iron ore, phosphates, feldspar, bauxite, uranium, gold, cement, basic metal products, fish processing, brewing, tobacco products, sugar, textiles.

Trade (1998/99): *Exports:* $5 billion: crude oil, diamonds, refined petroleum products, gas, coffee, sisal, fish and fish products, timber, cotton. *Major markets:* US, Benelux, China, Chile, France. *Imports:* $3 billion: machinery and electrical equipment, vehicles and spare parts, medicines, food, textiles, military goods. *Major suppliers:* Portugal, US, South Africa, Spain, Brazil, France.

Economic aid: Recipient (1995) $493.1 million.

Debt – external (1999 est.): $10.5 billion.

Military

Military expenditure: Dollar figures: $1.2 billion (FY97/98).

Military expenditure: Percent of GDP: 25% (FY97/98).

Demographic information is drawn from that compiled by the United States Department of State. See http://www.state.gov/r/pa/ei/bgn

128

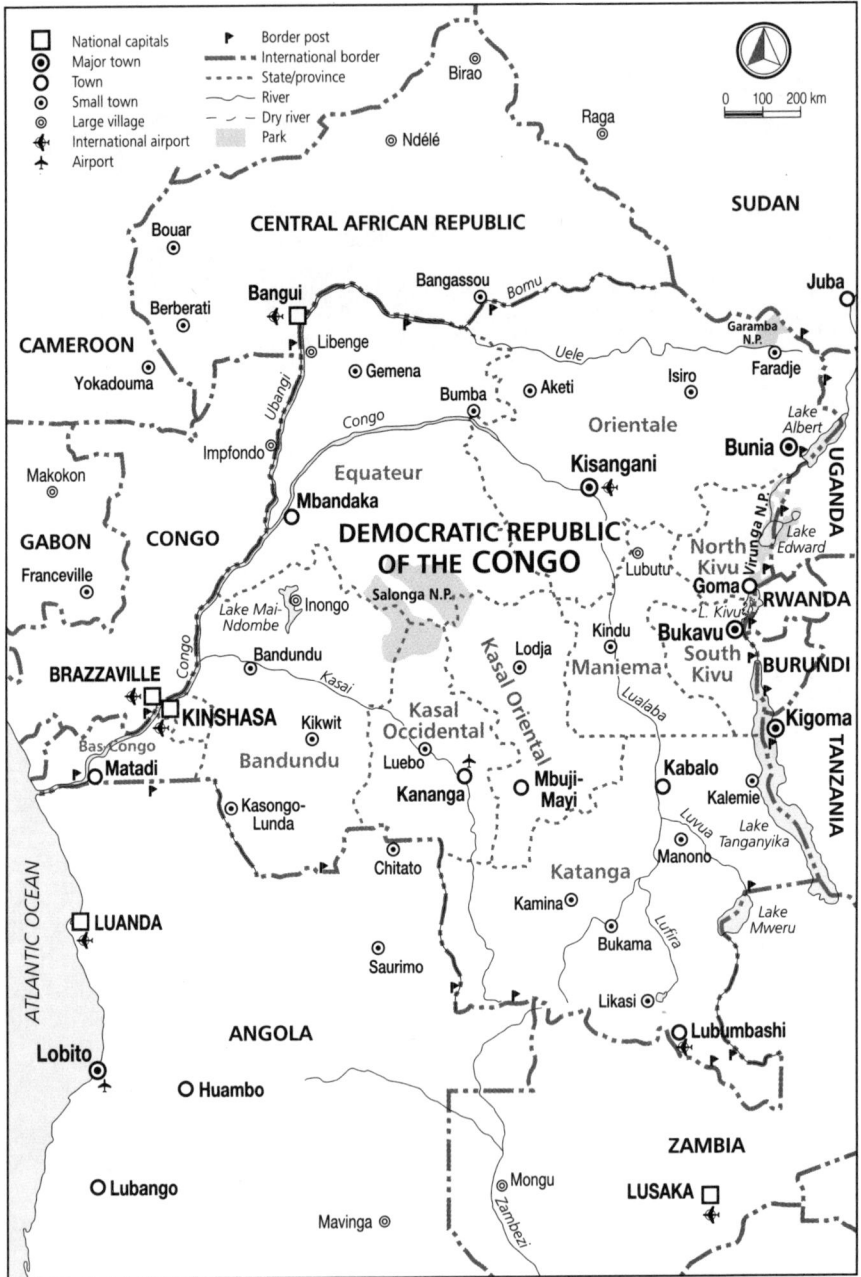

The Democratic Republic of the Congo: Inchoate Transition, Interlocking Conflicts

TYRONE SAVAGE*

The dialogue that has opened up in the war in the Democratic Republic of the Congo (DRC) since Joseph Kabila became president holds a promising but fragile moment of opportunity in a war composed of numerous interlocking conflicts, in a country that is yet to extricate itself from the grasp of a brutal history. In the sixteenth and seventeenth centuries, European merchants conducted trade in slaves in the region. In 1885, King Leopold II of Belgium established a fiefdom that, by some estimates, resulted in the deaths of 10 million Africans.[1] Many others were mutilated in coercive tactics designed to ensure cheap labour for Leopold's rubber plantations. The Belgian colonial rule that followed Leopold perpetuated, albeit in less glaring forms, the patterns of plunder and paternalism. A few days into its hard-won independence, the country's first democratically elected prime minister, Patrice Lumumba, was killed, reportedly with the collusion of Belgium and other western powers. In the aftermath of Lumumba's death, the United States helped install military chief Mobutu Sese Seko and, over the next 30 years, provided more than $300 million in weapons and $100 million in military training to a kleptocratic regime notorious for its human rights abuses.[2]

Led by Laurent Kabila, the overthrow of Mobutu in 1997 by a wide-ranging coalition of forces carried with it hopes of democratic transition, accountable governance and peace in the region. Kabila's rule, however, was marked by a worsening of conditions both within the country and in its relations with others in the region. In August 1998, within days of Kabila's dismissal of Rwandan advisors, war again broke out and the largest country in sub-Saharan Africa fell victim to a variety of interconnected regional and local conflicts. According to the International Rescue Committee, over two million people died as a result.[3] In this context, the assassination of Laurent Kabila in January 2001, and the installation of his son Joseph as president, has been both worrying and welcome – worrying

* The initial research of Wynoma Michaels is gratefully acknowledged.

in that his appointment was based on lineage rather than any democratic principle but welcome in that, within days of assuming office, Joseph Kabila reopened the prospect of democratic transition and negotiations. In recent months, these negotiations have shown progress but also the deep distrust that lies beneath the conflict. Tentative agreements between some parties have led others to withdraw from the talks and to accusations that the Kabila government is not interested in fully representing the interests of Congo's citizens. At the end of July 2002, the DRC and Rwandan governments reached an agreement that sets the stage for peace between the two countries. The settlement appears genuine and is currently being implemented, but it does not fully address the internal troubles that continue to motivate armed clashes. In the short-term, peace is likely to remain more a possibility than a reality.

In the first section, this profile discusses the inchoate transition and brutal conflict that have emerged in the post-Mobutu period. The second section examines the historical roots to the present conflict, tracing its causes from pre-colonial times to the failed transition from colonialism. The final section highlights the complex challenges currently facing efforts to establish peace and reconciliation in the DRC.

The Face of Conflict

In May 2001, a report by the International Rescue Committee on mortality rates in the war-torn eastern DRC noted that between August 1998 and April 2001 there had been about 2.5 million deaths over and above those that would be expected under normal circumstances.[4] Most of the deaths have been due to malnutrition and disease among communities fleeing the fighting. Some 350 000 of the excess deaths were, however, from directs acts of violence. About 40% of these were women and children. This pernicious war broke out in the midst of a failed transition within the DRC. Against the historical backdrop of colonial plunder and decades of dictatorship under Mobutu, military victory in 1997 by the wide-ranging alliance led by Laurent Kabila restored hopes of democratic transition, accountable governance and peace in the region. Kabila's rule disappointed, however. The demise of the Mobutu regime came as a result of many domestic and international factors, among them worsening poverty, growing unrest over Mobutu's dictatorship, the termination of cold war alliances – in particular the loss of US military support – and various changes in the balance of forces within the region.[5] This section charts the onset of conflict in the post-Mobutu period, noting in particular the interaction between several factors: embattled domestic transition, competing international interests, ethnic conflict and economic resources.

The event that has been pivotal for the stability and course of conflict throughout the entire region was the Rwandan genocide of 1994. The ethnic composition in the eastern parts of the DRC (then Zaire) altered significantly in the aftermath of the genocide. When the safe haven established by *Opération Turquoise* created a corridor into Zaire for the genocidal regime, more than a million Hutu refugees fled Rwanda, fearing reprisals from the Tutsi-led Rwandan Patriotic Front (RPF). Two years later, in September 1996, the deputy governor of South Kivu province issued an ultimatum to the Banyamulenge, a Tutsi group opposed to then President Mobutu, to leave the region. The Banyamulenge resisted and their rebellion, in turn, gathered into a coalition of forces committed to overthrowing the Mobutu regime. The coalition, the *Alliance des forces démocratiques pour la libération du Congo-Zaire* (AFDL), was led by Laurent Kabila, but comprised a range of very diverse interests, not least those of Rwandan advisors concerned with apprehending *genocidaires* who had taken refuge in the DRC. Rwandan interests as well as anti-Tutsi sentiment would play a significant role in the second – and much larger – conflict that was to unfold.

Military victory over Mobutu was rapid and the installation, on 17 May 1997, of Laurent Kabila as president of the newly named DRC was widely hailed as an opportunity for democratic transition and peace in the region. To the disappointment of Congolese citizens and the international community, Kabila postponed democratic reform and proceeded to centralise executive, legislative and military power in himself. Of the previously existing institutions only the judiciary was not disbanded. However, it had been weakened by decades of corruption and neglect and it was unable to safeguard basic freedoms. Nor did it provide any significant check on the actions of security agencies. The Kabila regime systematically intimidated political opposition, the press, the country's civil society and human rights movements. Politically active civilians were tried in military courts and subjected to cruel, inhumane or degrading treatment, torture and even execution.

As the promised transition failed to materialise, opposition to Kabila's rule became wide-ranging, both internationally and among the Congolese themselves. Disaffected military officers, Mobutu supporters and opposition politicians developed a coalition called the Congolese Democratic Movement (RDC). Its leader was Ernest Wamba-dia-Wamba. In August 1998, the RDC declared that its goal was to oust Kabila. Kabila, in turn, sought to consolidate his regime, and expelled the Rwandan military officers who had helped bring him to power. Within days, the Congo was at war; within weeks most of it was occupied by foreign forces.

In an ironic repeat of the events that led to the downfall of Mobutu the previous year, alliances developed between local opposition groups and foreign forces in opposition to the regime in Kinshasa. In the weeks leading to the loss of the Congo's third largest city, Kisangani, to Rwandan troops, the provincial governor in that city, with the active collaboration of senior local officials, waged a public hate campaign against Congolese Tutsis that resulted in the killing of at least 100 people. Similarly, as the insurgents besieged Kinshasa, Kabila publicly encouraged the civilian population to identify and expose possible rebels and rebel sympathisers. Numerous summary executions ensued. Commentators such as Horace Campbell have pointed out that, whatever Kabila's previous credentials, he lost all possible legitimacy as Congolese leader when he incited citizens to turn against each other.[6]

The uprising reached the gates of the capital, but was repelled when troops from Zimbabwe and Angola intervened. This left Rwandan, Ugandan and insurgent Congolese forces stretched across this vast country to turn their failed assault into a war of ongoing occupation and attrition. The Kabila alliance that withstood the assault on Kinshasa, in turn, was unable to project its influence deep into the Congo. The outcome was that central government controlled about half the country, from the Equateur region in the northwest to mineral-rich Katanga in the southeast. Insurgent groups comprising Rwandan, Ugandan and Congolese rebel forces controlled the remainder.

In this stalemate, the RDC splintered into two factions, a militant faction led by Emile Ilunga and supported by Rwanda, and a faction loyal to Wamba. The Wamba faction has repeatedly dissociated itself from the prospect of a military solution and is looking for resolution by political means. Through all this, Wamba has, however, enjoyed the protection of Ugandan forces. A third rebel force, the Congolese Liberation Movement (MLC) of Jean-Pierre Bemba, also receives military support from Uganda. The MLC controls vast portions of the northern Equateur region. With such links evident between Congolese opposition movements and the armed forces of neighbouring states, Kabila argued that resistance to his administration was a mere front for a foreign invasion. On this basis, he rallied support around himself and indicated that the primary precondition for negotiations was the withdrawal of all foreign forces from the DRC.

The Great Lakes countries have, however, claimed throughout that their military presence in the DRC was necessary for their national security against extremist militia operating from safe havens in the DRC. Rwanda has insisted on its right to pursue the forces of the genocidal regime, the Interahamwe militia and members of the former Rwandan Armed Forces (FAR), wherever they may be. Uganda has declared its presence in the DRC necessary in its war against the Sudan-based Alliance of Democratic Forces (ADF), which uses the porous borders in the northeast of the DRC as a corridor into Uganda. The Burundian government has asserted its right to defend its border against rebels operating out of the DRC. In addition to the forces of the Great Lakes countries, Angola's support for Kabila drew its adversary, the National Union for the Total Independence of Angola (UNITA), into loose and often clandestine arrangements with anti-Kabila forces, resulting in an expansion and escalation of the Angolan civil war. It is rumoured that Uganda, for example, has provided a channel into world markets for illicit diamond exports by UNITA. Other armed forces active in the DRC include Zimbabwe, which has over 10 000 troops fighting in support of Kabila, and numerous ethnically based, local militia movements. Most notable among these is the Mayi Mayi, a loose association of traditional Congolese local defence forces. In short, the war that broke out in August 1998 has rapidly developed into a jigsaw puzzle of interlocking conflicts inextricable from the security needs of the Great Lakes countries, Angola, Congolese ethnic groups and the central government of the DRC.[7]

After numerous attempts to establish a cease-fire failed, extensive mediation by Zambian president Frederic Chiluba led to an agreement in the Zambian capital of Lusaka in July 1999. Unlike previous attempts to stop the fighting, the Lusaka Peace Accords were signed by the heads of state of Angola, the DRC, Namibia, Rwanda, Uganda and Zimbabwe and over 50 rebel leaders. The cease-fire agreement provided for a cessation of hostilities, the withdrawal of all foreign forces, the disarmament of armed groups not party to the agreement, the deployment of a peace-keeping force and open political dialogue to culminate in the establishment of a new dispensation.

Implementation failed, however, as a result of mistrust. The various signatories suspected each other of a double game and used their suspicions to justify their own duplicity. Instead of leading to the establishment of terms for peace, the cease-fire had the effect of freezing the armies in their positions. The result was a steady deterioration within the various zones. Crises of governance worsened as remaining administrative controls and infrastructure were sucked into the conflict; ethnic militarism grew, transforming the eastern regions into a patchwork of warlords' fiefdoms; and the Rwanda and Uganda alliance fragmented, precipitating sporadic, lengthy battles in Kisangani and elsewhere.

As hopes about the Lusaka Accords faded and living conditions worsened drastically throughout the DRC, Kabila resuscitated the notion of an "Inter-Congolese Dialogue" – a national debate on issues such as constitutional reform, legitimatisation of power and liberalising of political activity. Like Mobutu a decade earlier, however, Kabila used this democratising institution to stall democratic transition. In April 2000, he postponed promised elections. Fighting began again, particularly in the southeastern regions, leading to the eventual fall of Pweto to insurgent forces, and with that, clashes between Kabila and his military command. With war worsening and democracy postponed, Kabila was assassinated on 16 January 2001.

In a move that resembled a dynastic transition, the Congolese military installed Laurent Kabila's son, Joseph, as president. In the days and weeks that followed his installation as president, Joseph Kabila made several pointed departures from Laurent's positions. In his first week in office, he signalled an unconditional willingness to seek a negotiated solution to the wars being waged in the DRC. He accepted the OAU-designated facilitator of the Inter-Congolese Dialogue, Sir Ketumile Masire, and, in a flurry of diplomatic activity, he travelled to France for consultations with French president, Jacques Chirac, and then to Washington. In the US, he met President George Bush as well as his leading adversary in the conflict, Rwandan President Paul Kagame. Kabila also addressed a meeting of the UN Security Council and urged all combatants to hold peace talks with him. He also called for a precise timetable for the deployment of UN troops in the DRC and the withdrawal of foreign troops from the country.

His overtures were well received. In late February, Ugandan and Rwandan troops began pulling thousands of troops back from the frontline as a good faith gesture toward the peace process. This, in turn, allowed the UN to enter rebel-held regions. The following month, the UN Security Council sent a diplomatic mission on a 10-day visit to the Great Lakes region. The leader of the mission, Jean-David Levitte, indicated that the mission was taking place "because a new stage had been reached in implementing the Lusaka agreement".

At home, Joseph Kabila has revived hopes for a democracy, talking consistently of his presidency in transitional terms. He has indicated a firm commitment to holding elections, and in this climate, civil society and public life has reawoken. Among many others, Etienne Tshisekedi, veteran leader of the Union for Democracy and Social Progress (UDPS), has returned to Kinshasa. On 7 May 2001, at the first round of the Inter-Congolese Dialogue, the DRC government and armed opposition groups reached agreement on a set of principles to guide negotiations for peace and a new political dispensation in the country. The government, with the *Mouvement de libération du Congo* (MLC), the *Rassemblement congolais pour la démocratie* (RCD-Goma) and the *Rassemblement congolais pour la démocratie-Mouvement de libération* (RCD-ML), signed the "Declaration of Fundamental Principles of the Inter-Congolese Political Negotiations". Wamba, the leader of the non-militaristic RCD-ML, hailed the declaration as a turning point.

The most recent round of the Inter-Congolese Dialogue was held in February and March 2002 in Sun City, South Africa. Over 300 representatives attended. Bemba initially declined to attend, arguing that the composition of the negotiating teams was not representative of the conflict's stakeholders. Attacks and fighting in the eastern part of the country slowed the talks and caused the government to pull out of the meetings for a short time. With their resumption, disputes began to emerge over the precise purpose of the dialogue and whether its participants had the power to craft an agreement that would replace the current dispensation. Bemba initially held that his participation was contingent on Kabila stepping down within six weeks of the meetings, a demand that the government rejected. Behind this dispute, the larger issue was whether and how to create a transitional government in the run-up to the elections. As the talks dragged on, South African president Thabo Mbeki entered the fray, offering a proposal for power-sharing in which Kabila would remain in power but would be joined by a prime minister and a Cabinet for National Reconciliation. The RCD immediately rejected the plan while Bemba showed more interest.

In early April, the government and the MLC agreed to a version of the Mbeki proposal, a decision that the RCD roundly criticised and which led several commentators to predict renewed fighting in the eastern part of the country. Shortly thereafter, the RCD entered into a coalition with several other groups opposed to the arrangement. Informal talks in South Africa continued, but at the time of writing the outcome was still largely inconclusive, a fact that was evidenced by renewed military clashes in Gomu and the surrounding area. What is more, the government and the MLC have been slow to agree on how to implement the new agreement.

In the midst of these promising domestic and regional developments, reports have begun to emerge that substantiate rumours about the vested interests warring parties have in the war. These suggest the war provides access to the DRC's abundant mineral resources. In April 2001, a UN panel of inquiry accused Rwanda, Uganda and Burundi of systematically plundering the DRC's mineral resources and recommended sanctions on their trade in minerals. The report noted the establishment of the mining company, *Société minière des Grands Lacs* (the Mineral Society of the Great Lakes or SOMIGL), as evidence of Rwandan and Ugandan economic interests in the DRC. In the debates that have followed, several UN Security Council members have noted that the report did not spell out the role of Zimbabwe, which refused to co-operate with the panel, or of large private companies.[8] The recent DRC-Rwanda agreement, discussed below, may provide a way of alleviating some of these troubles.

While the clamour for economic resources may have become an obstacle to peace in the eastern DRC, conflict in the post-Mobutu period, as we have noted, has been precipitated by an embattled domestic transition to democracy, regional security concerns and the fears of local ethnic groups in the war zones. In order to grasp more fully this mix of inchoate transition and interlocking conflict, it is necessary to inquire into the history of collaboration between external and domestic forces that has marked the country's failed transition from colonial rule to democracy and nationhood.

The Historical Roots of Violence and Division

The ecological conditions prevailing in the tropical rainforest of the area today called the DRC made state-building difficult in the pre-colonial period. Small-scale segmented societies, organised into village communities, were typical as corporate groups that combined social and economic functions among small numbers of people formed the dominant mode of organisation. Among such groups, exchange took place through trading activities and reciprocal gift-giving. In time, social interactions produced a measure of cultural homogeneity among otherwise distinct communities, including Bantu and Pygmy. Bantu communities absorbed and intermarried with their Pygmy clients, who brought their skills and crafts into the culture.

From the fifteenth to the seventeenth centuries, several state systems did emerge. The most important were the Kongo Kingdom in the west and the Luba and Lunda empires in the east. All three developed elaborate political structures, supported by military force and the symbolism of kingship. Typically, power emanated from the centre to the outlying areas through the mediation of appointed chiefs or local clan heads. Adam

Hochschild describes the Kongo's "sophisticated and well developed state" as follows:

> The ManiKongo [the monarch] appointed governors for each of some half-dozen provinces, and his rule was carried out by an elaborate civil service . . . Although they were without writing or the wheel, the inhabitants forged copper into jewelry and iron into weapons, and wove clothing out of fibers stripped from the leaves of the raffia palm tree. According to myth, the founder of the Kongo state was a blacksmith king, so ironwork was an occupation of the nobility. People cultivated yams, bananas, and other fruits and vegetables, and raised pigs, cattle and goats. They measured distance by marching days, and marked time by the lunar month and by a four-day week, the first day of which was a holiday. The king collected taxes from his subjects and, like many a ruler, controlled the currency supply: cowrie shells found on a coastal island under royal authority.[9]

Competition for the kingship often led to civil strife, however. With the development of slave-trading activities a new source of instability was injected into regional politics. The history of the Kongo peoples in the sixteenth century is largely the story of how the Atlantic slave trade created powerful vested interests among provincial chiefs, in time greatly lessening the capacity of the kingdom to resist the encroachments of its neighbours. By the late sixteenth century, the Kongo Kingdom had virtually succumbed to the attacks of warriors from the east. Two centuries later the Lunda and Luba peoples underwent a similar process of internal fragmentation followed by attacks from various interlopers eager to control the trade in slaves and ivory. On the eve of the European conquest, local political institutions were both fractious and oppressive. The relative ease with which Congolese societies yielded to the European conquest bears testimony to the profound internal dislocations most of them had experienced in the course of previous centuries.

As European interests in Africa grew, Henry Morton Stanley charted the course of the Congo River. His explorations were made possible by the supply, from his benefactor King Leopold II of Belgium, of "a powerful private army, equipped with a thousand quick-firing rifles, a dozen small Krupp canons, and four machine guns".[10] At the Berlin West Africa Conference (1884–85), Leopold gained international legitimacy, and thus used the African International Association to exert his influence in the area he named the Congo Free State. Hochschild describes the mood at Berlin in ominous terms:

> More than anyone, Stanley had ignited the great African land rush, but even he felt uneasy about the greed in the air. It reminded him, he said, of how 'my black followers used to rush with gleaming knives for slaughtered game during our travels.' The Berlin Conference was the ultimate expression of an age whose new-found enthusiasm for democracy had clear limits, and slaughtered game had no vote. Even John Stuart Mill, the great philosopher of human freedom, had written, in *On Liberty*, 'Despotism is a legitimate form of government in dealing with barbarians, provided the end be their improvement'. Not a single African was at the table in Berlin.[11]

To the outside world, Leopold depicted his activities in the Congo as magnanimous. Within the Congo, Leopold's regime was notorious for its illtreatment of local inhabitants. Forced labour was used for gathering wild rubber, palm oil and ivory. Lashings and taking hostages were techniques used to force villages to meet rubber quotas. Mutilation of limbs was a common form of punishment used by the Belgians, even for minor offences. In 1890, a visitor from the US, George Washington Williams, wrote an open letter to Leopold, in which he provided evidence of Leopold's infamy.[12] Instead of inhibiting the slave trade, Williams revealed, "Your Majesty's Government is engaged in the slave trade, wholesale and retail. It buys and sells and steals slaves."[13] He debunked Leopold's claim that he was providing wise government and public services as a sham and showed how the military bases established along the Congo River had generated a wave of destruction. White officers frequently engaged in brutal activities, such as torture, whippings and the use of ox-chains to imprison the wives of rubber workers, thereby ensuring that the workers returned. The harsh conditions of the Leopold regime in the Congo Free State left a legacy of anti-western sentiment on which subsequent generations of nationalists were to capitalise.

Under a barrage of international criticism, the Belgian parliament eventually voted in favour of annexation in 1908. Notwithstanding the elimination of the more brutal aspects of its rule in the Congo Free State, Belgian colonial rule reiterated the patterns of its Leopoldian predecessor: paternalism, profiteering and a firm commitment to political control remained the basis of Belgian rule. As decolonisation movements swept through central Africa and constitutional reforms were introduced in neighbouring French-speaking territories, social unrest in the Congo developed into nationalist sentiment and activity. In 1956, an elite group of educated Bakongo affiliated with an association called the *Alliance des Bakongo* (ABAKO) published a political manifesto calling for immediate independence from Belgium. Under the leadership of Joseph Kasavubu, ABAKO became a major vehicle for anti-colonial protest. Nationalist sentiment quickly spread through the lower Congo region, and, in time, reached into the rest of the colony. ABAKO's appeal was mainly limited to Bakongo, however, and scores of self-styled nationalist movements sprang up almost overnight. Amid the plethora of political parties that developed, the Congolese National Movement (*Mouvement National Congolais*, MNC), led from 1958 by Patrice Lumumba, stood out as the most powerful vector of territorial nationalism.

In early January 1959, with protest against colonial occupation growing, the Belgian government formally recognised independence as the ultimate goal of its policies in the Congo. It moderated this shift, however, by saying that the goal was to be reached "without fatal procrastination, yet without fatal haste". By then, however, nationalist agitation had reached a threshold that made delay impossible. Amid turbulence, the Belgian government convened a round table conference in Brussels in January 1960 and invited a broad spectrum of nationalist organisations. Belgium's declared aim was to work out the conditions of a viable transfer of power; the outcome, however, was a process for speedy decolonisation. Six months later, on 30 June 1960, the Congo formally gained independence. Kasavubu was named president and Lumumba, prime minister.

Within days, Congolese hopes for a successful transition floundered. First, units of the "Force Publique" – the national army – mutinied. Then, a few days later, the country's richest province, Katanga, declared itself independent. In the chaos, Belgium declared itself obliged to intervene, ostensibly to protect the lives of Belgian citizens. To the surprise of the newly installed Congolese government, however, the Belgian troops landed in Katanga and proceeded to support the secessionist regime. Lumumba claimed that Brussels was trying to reimpose its authority on its former colony, and on 12 July he and Kasavubu appealed to UN Secretary-General Dag Hammarskjöld for UN security assistance.

In this quandary, a further problem emerged. Kasavubu and Lumumba disagreed on the role and limitations of the UN peace-keeping force. Lumumba insisted that the UN should use force if necessary to bring Katanga back into the domain of central government; Kasavubu was adamantly opposed to this option, preferring to entertain the possibility of allowing a measure of local autonomy in the provinces. Disappointed by the international response, Lumumba then turned to the Soviet Union for logistical assistance in the Katanga, at which point the Congo crisis became inextricably bound up with the cold war.

Amid this dissension, the machinery of government ground to a halt. Kasavubu relieved Lumumba of his duties. Lumumba contested the legality of his dismissal and responded by dismissing Kasavubu. In the ensuing constitutional impasse, two groups claimed to be the legal government. Moreover a process of fragmentation set in motion by the Katanga secession grew, resulting in the break up of the country into four separate areas (Katanga, Kasai, Orientale Province and Léopoldville).

On 14 September 1960, Congolese army leader Colonel Joseph Mobutu (later Mobutu Sese Seko) announced that the army, with the help of a caretaker government, would henceforth rule the country. He later reached a working agreement with Kasavubu and in October 1960 the UN General Assembly recognised Kasavubu's government. In a bizarre story, the details of which are only now fully emerging, the ousted Lumumba was apprehended by Kasavubu's forces and arrested. On 17 January 1961, he was handed over to the Katanga secessionist regime where he was murdered, reportedly with the collusion of Belgian officers and the authorisation of US president, Dwight Eisenhower. Kasavubu's surrender of Lumumba to the Katanga secessionists was supposedly intended as an exchange for a reintegration of the province into the ambit of central government. However, it was not until January 1963 that the secession was decisively crushed – and even then only after a violent showdown between the Belgian-trained Katanga gendarmerie (police force) and UN forces.

In Léopoldville, a new civilian government was installed, headed by Cyrille Adoula, on 2 August 1961. From January to August 1964, rural insurgencies engulfed five of the 21 provinces, raising the ominous prospect of a total collapse of the central government. Former leader of the Katanga secession, Moise Tshombe, replaced Adoula as prime minister on 10 July 1964, and formed another short-lived administration. On 24 November 1965, for the second time Mobutu seized control of government. This time, however, Mobutu consolidated his rule. The country's sole legal political party, the Popular Revolutionary Movement (*Mouvement Populaire de la Révolution*, MPR) became the primary instrument of Mobutu's control. Officially described as "the nation politically organised", the MPR was a weakly articulated patronage system, supported by a single-party state and Mobutism as a legitimising formula.

Mobutu drafted a new constitution, which provided for centralised executive powers: Mobutu was head of state, head of government, foreign policy chief and commander-in-chief of the armed forces and the police. Cabinet ministers' sole function was to execute the president's programmes and decisions in their respective departments. Similarly, the provincial governors and the court judges, including those in the Supreme Court of Justice, were subject to Mobutu. His hegemony was absolute and extended to every level of government.

Mobutu's rule was based on bonds of personal loyalty between himself and his cohorts. Some western powers, most notably France and the US, propped up his regime. During the cold war, the US alone provided more than $300 million in weapons and $100 million in military training to Mobutu, leaving a trail of arms that have outlived their original recipients and ended up being used by local Congolese militia in the current welter of wars.[14] On two occasions, governments friendly to his regime saved Mobutu. In 1977 and 1978, the country's main opposition movement, the Congolese National Liberation Front (*Front de la Libération Nationale Congolaise*, FLNC), operating from Angola, instigated two major invasions into Shaba. On the first occasion, Morocco came to Mobutu's rescue; on the second, France.

It was not until the end of the cold war that, under pressure from opposition parties and foreign donors, Mobutu was forced to declare an end to the one-party state and introduce measures designed to allow for the growth of political pluralism. Within days of the announcement in April 1990, almost 400 political parties sprang up, most notably the *Union des Fédéralistes et Républicains Indépendants* (UFERI) led by Nguza Karl-i-Bond, the *Parti Démocrate et Social Chrétien* (PDSC) led by Joseph Illeo, the Union for Democracy and Social Change (UDPS) led by Etienne Tshisekedi and the umbrella organisation, *Union Sacrée de l'Opposition Radicale* (USOR), which consisted of 130 smaller parties. Ten days after making the announcement, Mobutu announced that political parties did not legally exist and were therefore not authorised to hold marches or public meetings.

In May 1990 protesting students and security forces clashed at the University of Lubumbashi, resulting in a death toll estimated by international human rights organisations to be somewhere between 30 and 150 students. The incident and the subsequent refusal of Mobutu to allow an international inquiry resulted in strong international censure, suspension of aid and growing opposition at home. In this context, Mobutu acceded to demands for a national conference that would debate constitutional reform and the transition to a new democratic form of government. In August 1991 the national conference on political reform known as the Sovereign National Conference (CNS) was convened. It encompassed 2 800 political, religious and civic leaders. The following month, Mobutu and the opposition agreed to form a transitional coalition government. Under the accord, Mobutu named UDPS leader Tshisekedi as prime minister and agreed that the cabinet would contain five Mobutu loyalists and six opposition leaders. Tshisekedi was fired after one week in office over a dispute over ministerial portfolios. In late November 1991, Mobutu formed another transitional government, this time with a Tshisekedi rival, Nguza Karl-i-Bond. This development led to a resumption of the CNS. On 12 December, Laurent Monsengwo Pasinya was elected president of the CNS. Monsengwo's election and support by all the opposition parties was a blow for the Mobutu camp whose candidate was soundly defeated. Delegates at the conference voted that the CNS had sovereign powers to draft a new constitution, legislate a multiparty system and make constitutionally binding decisions.

In August 1992, the CNS passed a Transitional Act allowing for a provisional constitution and a transitional government. According to the act, the government would be composed of four branches: a figurehead president as head of state; a High Council of the Republic (HCR) to serve as a provisional legislature and to oversee new elections; a prime minister elected by the CNS as head of government with full executive powers; and an independent judiciary. Tshisekedi was elected transitional first state commissioner and appointed a transitional government of "national union" with no Mobutu supporters. In December 1992, the HCR began its work of formulating and adopting the new constitution and organising legislative and presidential elections. At this point, Mobutu refused to accept the authority of the transitional authorities or the legitimacy of any constitution it might formulate. He reconvened his abolished legislature, tasking it with drafting a rival constitution to his liking.

The transitional government was never able to govern effectively because of its inability to limit Mobutu's powers. Mobutu continued to use his control of key military units to obstruct the functioning of the transitional government, intimidate critical opposition leaders, promote anarchy and chaos and incite violence. Some 35 years after the country's independence and nearly nine decades after the demise of the Congo Free State, the Leopoldian quality of the Mobutist state remained evident in its thoroughly centralised power apparatus, highly personalised style of governance and readiness to use force.

It was with the country caught in this inchoate, arrested transition that Mobutu left Zaire for cancer treatment in Europe. In the four months he was away, his authority declined significantly. A caretaker government was left to confront the rapid escalation of violence in the east when what initially appeared to be a regional movement by the Banyamulenge seeking to protect the Tutsi population in South Kivu quickly gathered momentum. The local movement became a national rebellion against the Mobutu regime. With the support of Rwanda, the *Alliance des forces démocratiques pour la libération du Congo-Zaire* (AFDL) swept through Zaire, culminating in transitional negotiations mediated by President Mandela. Mobutu refused to resign, however, even when Kinshasa was threatened. In May 1997, Mobutu was forced to flee Kinshasa for Morocco, where he died that September.

The 32 years of the Mobutu regime – and a century of Leopoldian plunder, profiteering and coercive rule – was finally over. Expectations were high that democracy would follow and peace would be established in the region. The ghost of Leopold would not be that easily exorcised, however, and the newly renamed DRC continued to be faced with the challenges left by its inchoate transition out of the brutalities of Belgian rule and the interlocking conflicts this failure had spawned.

Prospects for Peace-building

Several interconnected elements have shaped the current conflict in the DRC. Neighbouring countries' interests, economic resources, ethnic division and the country's ongoing history of embattled domestic transition will need to be addressed if realistic possibilities for conflict resolution and peacemaking are to be developed.

Neighbouring states' interests in the DRC's minerals have long been rumoured to be an obstacle to peace. The country is rich in diamonds, gold and other rare minerals such as niobium and tantalum. Kivu has deposits of precious minerals used in cutting-edge industries, such as electronics, aeronautics and nuclear medicine. These include niobium (15% of the world's reserves are to be found in Africa, 80% of these in the Congo) and tantalum, associated with coltan. The potential role of vested interests in the war economy that has developed, most notably in the eastern DRC, is an emerging area of inquiry. Since the 2001 publication of the UN report, "The DRC: Using the War Pretext to Loot Resources and Violate Human Rights", discussion has grown about this clandestine industry. The report notes that, in the context of lawlessness and weak central authority, the DRC's mineral wealth is "appealing and hard to resist". Top military commanders from various countries needed and continue to need this lucrative conflict for temporarily solving some internal problems in those countries as well as allowing access to wealth.

While the clamour for economic resources may well have proved to be an obstacle to peace in the eastern DRC, the conflict, as we have noted, has been triggered by the security concerns of neighbouring states, the fears of local ethnic groups in the war zones and inchoate domestic transition. Rwandan president Paul Kagame has repeatedly stated that a complete withdrawal of Rwandan troops from Congo will only happen when the forces of the genocidal regime, the Interahamwe militia and members of the former FAR, no longer pose a threat to Rwanda. Kagame's willingness to sign the July 2002 agreement with his counterpart, Kabila, signifies a departure from the conflict's standing logic. Uganda is under threat from the Sudan-based ADF, which uses the porous borders in the northeast of the DRC as a corridor into Uganda. Unless the legitimate concerns of the Great Lakes countries with regard to extremist militia operating from safe havens in the DRC are recognised, it is unlikely that any withdrawal from the DRC will be thoroughgoing.

Joseph Kabila's administration has taken significant steps in this regard. In September 2001, the DRC's security minister, Mwenze Kongolo, indicated that authorities in the DRC had disarmed 3 000 Rwandan Hutu rebels and handed them over to the United Nations Observer Mission in the DRC. The fighters, Kongolo said, had been fighting alongside DRC troops in the recent wars as part of a group called the Democratic Liberation Forces of Rwanda (FDLR). He insisted they had never been part of the Interahamwe militia or the ex-FAR contingents responsible for the 1994 Rwandan genocide. The handing over, said Kongolo, removed any possible grounds for continued Rwandan military presence in the eastern DRC. "There are no longer any armed Rwandans on DRC territory under government control, and the disarmament of the FDLR is an important step in our quest for peace. Rwanda has used the presence of armed rebels in DRC as an excuse to justify its occupation of part of our country," the minister was reported as saying.[15]

The withdrawal of forces by the Great Lakes countries may not be sufficient for local Congolese, however. Human Rights Watch issued a report in March 2001 that alleged that the Ugandan army had "fuelled political and ethnic strife in eastern Congo with disastrous consequences for the local population". Moreover, they had "attacked local people thought to have aided the Mayi-Mayi, killing civilians and laying waste their villages". As a result, Congolese locals in areas under Ugandan control felt that ending the war would not be enough to resolve the conflict. Justice still has to be done, in their view, and soldiers responsible for abuses have to be identified and punished.[16]

The importance of including local, ethnically based militia movements in any peacemaking process became evident after a cease-fire established at Windhoek in January 1999 failed because the agreement was between heads of state and did not include non-state actors. With this in mind, the architects of the Lusaka Accords shuttled, over several months, between representatives of local militia to avoid a state-to-state agreement that would function at the expense of the interests of eastern Congolese minorities. Fifty rebel leaders, along with the heads of state of the DRC, Zimbabwe, Namibia, Angola, Rwanda and Uganda, eventually signed on. Though all sides violated the Lusaka Accords, the agreement did result in a scaling-down of hostilities in numerous flashpoints: fighting was less intense, and frequently contained. Currently, it forms the fragile but only widely accepted point of reference for peace in the region.

The Lusaka Accords provide for an urgent cessation of hostilities and the delivery of humanitarian assistance through the opening of aid corridors. They also make provision for establishing a Joint Military Commission (JMC), comprising two representatives from each party under a neutral chairman, and a separate ministerial-level committee tasked with investigating reported cease-fire violations, working out mechanisms to disarm militia groups, verifying the disarmament of Congolese civilians and monitoring the withdrawal of foreign forces. The Accords call for the deployment of UN peace monitors and the peace-keeping force, the United Nations Observer Mission, tasked with collecting weapons from civilians; scheduling and supervising the withdrawal of all foreign forces; providing protection and humanitarian assistance to displaced persons; and handing over suspected *genocidaires* to the International Criminal Tribunal for Rwanda in Arusha, Tanzania. Finally, the Lusaka Accords bolster the prospect of political negotiations that might lead to the establishment of a new dispensation in the DRC.

The first step toward such negotiations took place in May 2001. At the first round of the Inter-Congolese Dialogue, a forum designed around the prospect of domestic transition, the DRC government and armed opposition groups reached agreement on a set of principles to guide negotiations for peace and a new political dispensation within the country. The signatories reaffirmed the Lusaka agreement as the basis of the principles, which include the following: the sovereignty and territorial integrity of the country; peace, security and stability in the region; a restructured, integrated national army; utilisation of the country's natural resources to improve the lives of the Congolese people; strict observance of human rights; support for humanitarian assistance across the country; elections that are "free, democratic and transparent"; and national reconciliation as the basis for rebuilding a country in which people can be "united, reconciled and free of tribalism, regionalism, ethnicism and all forms of hatred".[17]

While these agreements do count as progress, recent developments show that the country still has a distance to travel. There remain deep and decisive disputes over how to design a transitional government and how to establish a viable framework for elections. The Government-MLC agreement in April 2002 left significant groups out of the mix and appears to have funded renewed fighting. Kabila remains firm in his commitment not simply to step aside but to demand a clear order to the transition. This will be difficult given the international scope of the conflict. However, a potentially major step toward peace was taken on 31 July 2002. Meeting in Pretoria, Kabila and Rwandan president Paul Kagame signed a treaty that calls for the DRC to disarm and repatriate thousands of the Hutu Interahamwe that are now in Congo. For its part, Rwanda has actually begun to withdraw its troops from the DRC. There are principled and practical obstacles that stand in the way of the agreement. The militias are unlikely to disarm voluntarily and the timeframe for completing the agreement is very short. While supported by the RCD, the deal does not appear to address its demands for continued negotiations about the country's internal situation.[19]

Present and Future Opportunities for Reconciliation

In the context of emergent peace, reconciliation has become a priority both for the national government and local communities in the DRC. In the conflict-torn eastern parts of the country, the *Conseil Régional des Organisations Non-Gouvernementales de Développement/Nord Kivu* (CRONGD/Nord Kivu) has emerged as an umbrella organisation that brings together local NGOs organised along ethnic lines. The main goal of CRONGD/Nord Kivu has been to create dialogue between the ethnic communities in the region. Also in the northeastern DRC, rival Hema and Lendu communities have sought possibilities for reconciliation, and in February 2001 held a joint ceremony celebrating peace between them.[18] And in Kinshasa, the *Association Africaine de Défense des Droits Humaines*/African Association for the Defence of Human Rights (ASAD-HO) has survived three regimes in a decade of political and military turmoil to develop an apolitical defence of human rights as the basis of reconciliation and sustainable peace in the country.

Prior to the present interval of stability and hope, reconciliation efforts in the DRC were continually undermined by outbreaks of fighting. The priority among Congolese organisations committed to reconciliation has been the establishment of conditions that stem the complicated, interconnected patterns of conflict that have marked the country's transition. Against this background, and in response to the emerging inter-Congolese dialogue, representatives from a broad cross-section of Congolese civil society met in Kinshasa in September 2001. In the ensuing discussions, the organisations placed reconciliation in the context of extensive institutional transformation. The organisations observed that gaining consensus on a number of issues would be crucial in establishing a new political order and national reconciliation in the country. The first of these issues, the delegates agreed, is the nature and the objectives of the transition. The transitional government should be designed around non-partisan, consensually agreed upon principles, especially in electoral procedures, respect of human rights, rights of assembly and the welfare of the citizens. The objectives of the transitional government should firstly be to organise a constitutional referendum and elections. It should implant democratic, transparent institutions that will engender peaceful, free and fair elections in the country. Thirdly, it should rehabilitate the state itself. Particular attention should go to the functions, authority, good governance and sovereignty of the state. In addition, the transitional government should have as its objective stimulating and guiding socio-economic redress among the Congolese people. Furthermore, the transitional government should pursue a policy of national reconciliation by promulgating and reinforcing laws to this effect.

A second issue identified by the meeting of Congolese civil society as crucial to the transition is the constitution governing the transitional period. The principles of the constitution should provide for sovereign institutions on the one hand and constitutional institutions of the transitional government on the other. The gathering proposed that with regard to sovereign institutions, there should be a presidential council, composed of members democratically designated from the parties that constitute the national dialogue, namely the RCD, the MLC, political parties, civil society and representatives of Congolese in the diaspora. There should also be a head of state, appointed by the presidential council, and several vice presidents, charged with supervising the political and administrative affairs, economic and financial affairs, social, humanitarian and cultural affairs, and technical and national reconstruction. Other sovereign institutions should include a transitional parliament, a government of national unity, the High Council of Judiciary and the Congolese national army. Special institutions during the transitional period should include a national electoral commission, a national defence commission, a commissioner responsible for relations with the UN peace-keeping force, and a military command charged with unification of the national military.

The gathering of civil society also saw the need for the creation, in stages and according to certain principles, of a new Congolese national army. The staggered, principled unification of the military would need to reform the army and the gendarmerie, and then locate, disarm and allow for the rehabilitation of former soldiers in the Zairian army and the local militia identified by the Lusaka peace agreements. The civil society gathering, moreover, proposed an institutional approach for disarmament, demobilisation and reintegration programmes. These programmes should come into being with the consent of all the parties to the national dialogue and, with gradual implementation, it should be carried out in the entire country. The programmes should have the capacity to respond in the event of large-scale demobilisation, in which vast numbers of former combatants would seek reintegration into civilian life. The National Commission for Social Rehabilitation (CONARES) should be composed of representatives of the combatants themselves as well as civil society.

Further issues identified by the meeting of Congolese civil society as crucial to the transition are reunification of the public service; the social and economic welfare of the country, as well as pressing humanitarian engagement; and establishing policies for reconciliation within the nation as well as throughout the region.

In the dialogue that has opened up in the DRC in 2002, a promising but fragile moment of opportunity has appeared. It is an interval in which the present is determined neither by an inescapable future nor by its tortured past. It is a brave opening in which, against the backdrop of a century of coercive rule, intervention by international and local organisations committed to reconciliation has become possible.

NOTES

1 Adam Hochschild, *King Leopold's Ghost: A Story of Greed, Terror, and Heroism in Colonial Africa* (Boston: Houghton Mifflin, 1998), 225–34.

2 William Hartung and Bridget Moix, "Deadly Legacy: U.S. Arms to Africa and the Congo War." Reprinted at www.worldpolicy.org/projects/arms (accessed 31 January 2002).

3 International Rescue Committee, "Mortality Study, Eastern Democratic Republic of Congo." Reprinted at www.intrescom.org/mortality.cfm (accessed 11 December 2001).

4 Ibid.

5 Hartung and Moix observe that the US continued its military support to Zaire for many years despite credible reports of widespread abuses. It was only when the Mobutu regime defaulted on loan repayments that the US stopped supplying arms and training to Mobutu. Hartung and Moix, "Deadly Legacy."

6 Horace Campbell, "The Assassination of Laurent Kabila." Reprinted at www.prairienet.org/acas/campbell.htm (accessed 11 December 2001).

7 International Crisis Group, "Africa's Seven Nation War." Reprinted at www.crisisweb.org (accessed 11 December 2001).

8 United Nations Security Council, "Report of the Security Council Mission to the Great Lakes Region," 15–26 May 2001, S/2001/521.

9 Hochschild, *King Leopold's Ghost*, 9.

10 Hochschild, *King Leopold's Ghost*, 71.

11 Ibid., 84.

12 George Washington Williams, *An Open Letter to His Serene Majesty Leopold II, King of the Belgians and Sovereign of the Independent State of the Congo, by Colonel Honourable Geo. W. Williams, of the United States of America*, cited in Franklin, John Hope, *George Washington Williams: A Biography*. Chicago: University of Chicago Press, 1985.

13 *An Open Letter*, quoted in Hochschild, *King Leopold's Ghost*, 111.

14 Hartung and Moix, "Deadly Legacy."

15 Integrated Regional Information Network (IRIN), "Kinshasa Presents 3,000 Disarmed Hutu Rebels to UN, 13 September 2001." Reprinted at www.irinnews.org/report.asp (accessed 11 December 2001).

16 IRIN, "Ugandan Presence Has 'Fuelled Strife' in Congo, 27 March 2001." Reprinted at www.irinnews.org/report.asp (accessed 11 December 2001).

17 "Declaration of Fundamental Principles of the Inter-Congolese Political Negotiations signed by the Congolese Parties to the Agreement for Ceasefire in the Democratic Republic of Congo." May 2001.

18 IRIN, "Rival Ethnic Groups Hold Reconciliation Ceremony, 22 February 2001." Reprinted at www.irinnews.org/report.asp (accessed 11 December 2001).

19 At the time of going to press, three further, salient developments were becoming evident. Congolese participants in the peace process reportedly perceived South Africa's intervention as hasty and rushed. Secondly, international relations with countries in the region were altering rapidly. Most notably, France, previously understood to be an ally of the DRC, was now mending its relations with Rwanda. The US and Britain, previously viewed as allies of Rwanda, were cultivating their respective relationships with the DRC. These developments gave rise to the view that a unified international effort in the region may increasingly become possible. Finally, the situation on the ground in the conflict-torn eastern half of the DRC was proving even more complex than previously thought, as the number and variety of organisations with claims seemed to be growing rapidly.

150   SAVAGE

RESOURCES

Books, Articles, Media Reports

Ajibewa, Aderemi. "The Civil War in Zaire (now Democratic Republic of Congo)." Reprinted at www.ccsu.edu/afstudy/archive.html (accessed 11 December 2001).

Anstee, Margaret Joan. *Orphan of the Cold War: The Inside Story of the Collapse of the Angolan Peace Process, 1992–93.* New York: St. Martin's Press, 1996.

Austin, Kathi. "Hearts of Darkness," *Bulletin of Atomic Scientists* 55 (1999). Reprinted at www.thebulletin.org/issues/1999/jf99/jf99austin.html (accessed 31 January 2002).

Boutwell, Jeffrey and Michael T. Klare. *Light Weapons and Civil Conflict: Controlling the Tools of Violence.* Lanham: Rowman & Littlefield, 1999.

Campbell, Horace. "The Assassination of Laurent Kabila." Reprinted at www.prairienet.org/acas/campbell.htm (accessed 11 December 2001).

Cilliers, Jakkie and Peggy Mason. *Peace, Profit or Plunder? The Privatisation of Security in War-torn African Societies.* Halfway House: Institute for Security Studies, 1999.

Clapham, Christopher. *African Guerrillas.* Oxford: James Currey, 1998.

Hartung, William and Bridget Moix. "Deadly Legacy: U.S. Arms to Africa and the Congo War." Reprinted at www.worldpolicy.org/projects/arms (accessed 31 January 2002).

Havermans, Jos. "Africa's Most Worrying Battlefield." In *Searching for Peace in Africa: An Overview of Conflict Prevention and Management Activities,* edited by Monique Mekenkamp, Paul van Tongeren and Hans van de Veen. Utrecht: European Platform for Conflict Prevention and Transformation, 1999.

Hochschild, Adam. *King Leopold's Ghost: A Story of Greed, Terror, and Heroism in Colonial Africa.* Boston: Houghton Mifflin, 1998.

Kanza, Thomas. *Conflict in the Congo: The Rise and Fall of Lumumba.* Harmondsworth: Penguin, 1972.

Mazrui, Ali Al'Amin. *Africa's International Relations: The Diplomacy of Dependency and Change.* London: Heinemann; Boulder: Westview Press, 1977.

Musah, Abdel-Fatau and J. 'Kayode Fayemi. *Mercenaries: An African Security Dilemma.* London: Pluto Press, 1999.

Nkrumah, Kwame. *Challenge of the Congo.* New York: International Publishers, 1967.

Renner, Michael. "Small Arms, Big Impact: The Next Challenge of Disarmament." *Worldwatch Paper* 137 (1997).

Rodney, Walter. *How Europe Underdeveloped Africa.* With a postscript by Abdul R. M. Babu. Washington, DC: Howard University Press, 1974.

Schatzberg, Michael G. *The Dialectics of Oppression in Zaire.* Bloomington: Indiana University Press, 1988.

———. "Mobutu or Chaos?" in *The United States and Zaire, 1960–1990.* Lanham: University Press of America, 1991.

———. "Beyond Mobutu: Kabila and the Congo," *Journal of Democracy* 8 (1997).

Schearer, David. "Africa's Great War," *Survival* 41 (1999).

Tomlinson, Chris. "Troops Withdraw from Congo, 28 February 2001." Reprinted at www.intl-crisis-group.org/projects/showreport.cfm?reportid=257 (accessed 15 March 2001).

Turner, Thomas. "War in the Congo," *Foreign Policy In Focus* 5 (2000). Reprinted at www.foreignpolicy-infocus.org/briefs/vol15/v5n10congo.html (accessed 15 March 2001).

Willame, Jean-Claude. "The 'Friends of the Congo' and the Kabila System," *Issue: A Journal of Opinion* 1 (1998): 27–30.
Young, Crawford and Thomas Turner. *The Rise and Decline of the Zairian State*. Madison: University of Wisconsin Press, 1985.

Local NGOs

African Association for the Defence of Human Rights in Congo (ASADHO) is the largest human rights organisation in Kinshasa and has been critical both of violations under Joseph Kabila's regime as well as by occupying forces and Congolese rebel movements.

The **Conseil Régional des Organisations Non-Gouvernementales de Développement/Nord Kivu** (CRONGD/Nord Kivu) is an umbrella organisation operating in North-Kivu, which works with local NGOs committed to dialogue, peace and reconciliation.

International NGOs

International Crisis Group (ICG) conducts research and reports on the conflict in the region: http://www.crisisweb.org

International Human Rights Law Group is engaged in advocacy, strategic human rights lawyering and training around the world: http://www.hrlawgroup.org

Integrated Regional Information Network (IRIN) for central and eastern Africa is part of the UN's office for the Coordination of Humanitarian Affairs that offers daily news briefings from central and eastern Africa: http://www.reliefweb.int/IRIN

International Rescue Committee (IRC) operates in the conflict zones of the Great Lakes region: http://www.intrescom.org

THE DEMOCRATIC REPUBLIC OF THE CONGO COUNTRY INFORMATION

Geography
Location: Central Africa. Bordering nations: Angola, Burundi, Cameroon, Central African Republic, Republic of the Congo, Sudan, Rwanda, Tanzania, Uganda, Zambia.
Cities: *Capital:* Kinshasa (pop. 6.55 million). *Regional capitals:* Bandundu, Bukavu, Goma, Kananga, Kindu, Kisangani, Lubumbashi, Matadi, Mbandaka, Mbuji-Mayi.

People
Nationality: *Noun:* Congolese. *Adjective:* Congolese.
Population (1997): 47 700 000.
Population growth rate (1997): 3.1%.
Ethnic groups: More than 200 ethnic groups; Bantu 80% of which Luba (18% of total population), Kongo (16.1%) and Mongo (13.5%) are largest groups.
Religions: Roman Catholic 50%, Protestant 20%, Kimanguist 10%, Muslim 10%, other syncretic sects and traditional beliefs 10%.
Languages: *Official:* French. *Widely used:* Lingala, Kingwana, Kikongo, Tshiluba.
Education (1995 est.): *Literacy:* 77.3% in French or local language.
Health (1998 est.): *Infant mortality rate:* 120/1 000. *Life expectancy:* 49 years. *HIV infection rate:* 4.35%.

Economy
GDP (1997): $6.1 billion. **GDP growth rate (1997):** 5.7%.
Per capita income (1997): $350.
Natural resources: Copper, cobalt, diamonds, gold, other minerals; petroleum; wood; hydroelectric potential.
Agriculture: *Cash crops:* coffee, rubber, palm oil, quinquina, cocoa, sugar. *Food crops:* manioc (tapioca), corn, legumes, plantains, peanuts. *Land use:* agriculture 3%; pasture 7%; forest/woodland 77%; other 13%.
Industry: *Types:* processed and unprocessed minerals; consumer products, including textiles, plastics, footwear, cigarettes; metal products; processed foods and beverages, cement, timber.
Trade (1997): *Exports:* $1.396 billion: diamonds, cobalt, copper, coffee, petroleum. *Major markets:* Belgium, France, Germany, Italy, Japan, South Africa, UK, US. *Imports (1997):* $1.022 billion. *Major markets:* consumer goods i.e. food, textiles; refined petroleum products. *Major suppliers:* Belgium, China, France, Germany, Italy, South Africa, UK, US.
Debt external (1997): $14.38 billion.

Military
Military expenditure: Dollar figures: $250 million (FY97).
Military expenditure: Percent of GDP: 4.6% (FY97).

Demographic information is drawn from that compiled by the United States Department of State. See http://www.state.gov/r/pa/ei/bgn

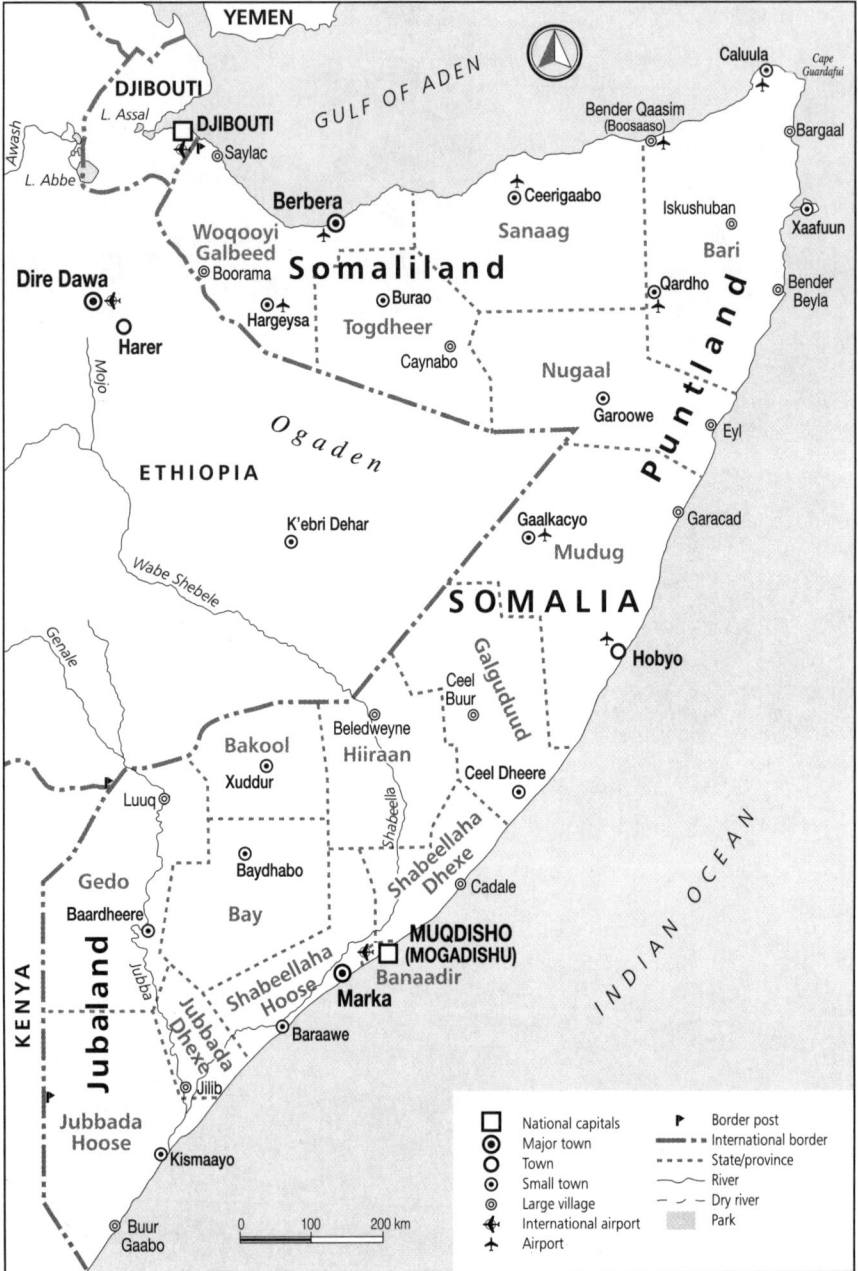

Chapter 7

Somalia: Beginning the Journey from Anarchy to Order

SUSANNE STRELEAU AND S'FISO NGESI

In the past decades, the Horn of Africa has been host to some of the world's most prolonged, complex and devastating conflicts. Sudan, Ethiopia and Eritrea have each endured protracted war. The same is true of Somalia, a country in the Horn of Africa that has been devastated by civil war, a clash that has produced a huge percentage of the world's refugees and clouded the country's future.

In the twenty-first century, most people living in Somalia are still nomadic pastoralists. Their way of life has not significantly changed during the past hundred years. This stands in stark contrast to the political situation. After 60 years of colonial domination, 30 years of self-rule, and 10 years of fighting between warlords, Somalia appeared set for self-destruction.[1] Recently, however, there has been cause for hope. In the summer of 2000, a wide cross-section of Somalia's political parties gathered in Djibouti for five months of negotiations, the aim of which was to establish an interim parliament, elect a president and write a national charter. These moves produced substantial change. Today, Somalia has a 245-member transitional parliament, a national government and an interim presidency. The new president, Abdikassim Salat Hassan, and his prime minister, Ali Khalif Galeyr, have spent considerable time attempting to gain the support of the international community and forging ties with international organisations such as the United Nations (UN), the Organisation for African Unity (OAU) and the Inter-Governmental Authority on Development (IGAD).[2]

While there has been substantial change, the future of Somalia remains uncertain. On the one hand, there is a realistic chance that the new government can bring peace and stability to the country. Success hinges largely on the question of whether Somalia's new leaders can reach out and embrace the combatants and factions who did not participate in the Djibouti peace conference and who continue to oppose the government. On the other hand, the current process of unification and integration may well be out of phase with the realities of Somalian politics. Ten years of civil war have brought deep division. Faction leaders still have significant power, especially in Mogadishu, where they have established the so-called Somali Reconciliation and Restoration Council (SRRC). The SRRC does not recognise the current government and has declared that its aim is the creation of a 'legitimate transitional government'. Also, the self-declared independent state of Somaliland has been unwilling to participate in the peace process. All in all, the new government is under great pressure to "achieve" in circumstances that are difficult in the extreme. High expectations could turn quickly to disappointment. As a result, it will be tempting for the interim president, Salat Hassan, to rely on supporters – his sub-clan, Hawiye-Ayer, and the business community – to strengthen his position. The test, however, will be whether he is able to reach out to new constituencies in the name of creating security, national unity and reconstruction.[3] At the same time, there is growing international pressure on Somalia, largely the result of perceptions of unstable governance making the country a haven for terrorists.

Reconciliation in Somalia is both overdue and potentially premature. There is a growing concern that the country must deal with its past, examining the motives of past violence and the extent of human rights abuses. This has led some to propose the creation of a South African-style truth commission. At a larger level, however, the question of reconciliation between political factions, communities and neighbours may depend first on the creation of the rule of law. To this end, the government recently established a peace and reconciliation committee, which aims to smooth the transition to a federal system. Also charged with addressing property and land issues, the committee is to mediate between the government and the faction leaders and between the government and Somaliland and Puntland.[4] However, this effort, along with a number of such similar institutions, has been rejected by those faction leaders who oppose the government and who have used the SRRC to create their own reconciliation body. At this stage, the government's reconciliation committee has been rejected by both Somaliland and Puntland. In light of this, the first task may be to establish a judiciary system that can stop the culture of impunity that has grown out of the civil war. Equally important is the need for programmes to disarm militias, improve education, train journalists and rehabilitate Somalia's youth.

The Face of Conflict

Somalia's conflict is intricate. It is a complex interaction rooted in clan-based factionalism and a struggle for political power. The new government

continues to face opposition from numerous faction leaders and established breakaway administrations in Somaliland, in the northwest of
Somalia, and Puntland in the northeast. The country has been ruled by
warlords who controlled clan-based fiefdoms, backed by heavily armed
militias. For the past 10 years, Somalia's recurring political crises have
been exasperated by floods, drought, famine and disease.

While bound by similar ethnicity, religion and language, Somalis are
split into six major clans.[5] In the agricultural south there are two clan
families, the Digil and the Rahawayn. Among the pastoralists, there are
four dominant clans – Darod, Dir, Hawiye and Issaq. These clans are further divided into smaller sub-clans and hundreds of lineages. The Darod
clan family, for instance, includes the Dolbahante, Majerteen, Mareehan
and Ogadeni sub-clans. The Hawiye clan comprises six sub-clans, two of
which are sharply divided, namely the Abgal led by Ali Mahdi Mohamed
and Hussein Mohamed Aidid's Habr Gedir clan.[6] In the precolonial era,
the clan system was a basis for mutuality and interaction among people
who lived under harsh environmental conditions. Today, many sense that
the system is abused by almost all combatants in the name of amassing
political power, money and natural resources such as pastures, water
points, urban property and markets.[7] These problems are especially acute
in Mogadishu, where the traditional system has given way to hostility that
threatens both stability and national unity.[8]

After Somalia's independence in 1960, irredentist movements prevailed
among ethnic Somalis in Kenya, Djibouti and the eastern regions of
Ethiopia. Later, however, the focus changed from incorporating these territories into the Somalia Republic to overthrowing the increasingly personal and repressive rule of President Siad Barre, a member of the
Majerteen sub-clan. Opposition to Barre developed from several sources:
the Somali Salvation Democratic Front (SSDF), a faction tied to
Majerteen and Darod clans in the northeast, and the Somali National
Movement (SNM), an Issaq-based group from the Somaliland region
with ties to the Ethiopian government,[9] and the United Somali Congress
(USC).[10] After the successful expulsion of President Barre, the groups
were left without a common goal and Ali Mahdi Mohamed's attempt to
form a new government failed. Although he was appointed interim president by the USC, he was checked by his rival Aidid. Following a major
split within the USC, Aidid founded his own movement, the Somali
National Alliance (SNA). This move portended chaos, a situation in
which roughly two dozen major armed factions entered into warfare.

Unlike Ethiopia, where the Ethiopian People's Revolutionary

Democratic Front (EPRDF) took power in 1991, conflict in Somalia was complicated by the fact that there was no state to take over. Looting and killings dominated daily life; civil servants were either conscripted into the factional forces or scared away; the new provisional president had no operating budget; army morale was low. These problems were complicated by the need for demobilisation. The faction leaders had mobilised their clans for military services, wrongly assuming that after Siad Barre was ousted, they would resume their pastoral or agricultural activities. But the militias, mostly from the pastoralist Hawiye clan, had established ties with the city, especially as it afforded opportunities for power. Thus, violence escalated. The distinction between combatants and criminals became increasingly blurry. The situation in the north was even worse. In 1993, two years after the end of Siad Barre's regime, there were still large areas in ruins. These could not be cleared due to landmines that Barre's troops had laid in 1991. The self-declared Somaliland government lacked everything from pens and paper to electricity and telephones. In general, it can be said that none of the factions in Somalia represented a political force that could effectively maintain law and order and bring the state back to life.

Between the fall of Siad Barre in 1991 and the establishment of the transitional government of Salat Hassan in 2000, Somalia had no formal government. The Transitional National Assembly (TNA) was inaugurated on 13 August 2000. It elected Salat Hassan as the new president on 26 August and approved the appointment of the prime minister, Ali Khalif Galeyr, on 9 November 2000. However, several members of the new government have been assassinated and violence remains the order of the day in Mogadishu. Attempts to gain legitimacy have been more successful internationally than within the country. The government is still weak. President Hassan and Prime Minister Galeyr have travelled to almost all neighbouring countries, including Ethiopia, Kenya, Libya and Djibouti. They also reformed a number of regional organisations, including the IGAD.

Within Somalia itself, there has been little reconciliation between Mogadishu faction leaders. Specifically, the relationship between the transitional government and these leaders is complicated by the fact that not all factions were involved in the Djibouti peace process. Indeed, most of the faction leaders were not even officially invited to the conference.[11] As a result, many are critical of its outcome. One of the main Mogadishu faction leaders, Hussein Mohamed Aidid, leader of the SNA, said in November 2000 that there was still no government in Somalia.[12] He warned that the outcome of the Arta conference would be renewed fighting and accused Djibouti of interfering in Somalia's internal affairs. This statement was made despite the fact that Aidid signed a reconciliation agreement with President Salat Hassan in September 2000. The accord was the result of Muammar Kadhafi's efforts to facilitate national reconciliation and restore peace.

Another Mogadishu faction leader, Muse Sudi Yalahow,[13] is also opposed to the new government and has mobilised his militia in response to police and army recruiting by the transitional government. The government has called for former soldiers of the Somali national army to "serve and defend" their country. The faction leaders Osman Hassan Ali "Atto" and Hussein Haji Bod, each of whom controls parts of Somalia's capital, see this behaviour as a threat and claim that it may lead to renewed fighting. Outside of Mogadishu, the government faces equally troublesome challenges. In order to oppose the new government more effectively, the president of Puntland, Abdullahi Ahmed, and 17 faction leaders of southern Somalia have established the SRRC. In public statements, the group has indicated that it plans to convene a national reconciliation conference inside of Somalia and set up a broad-based government.[14] Altogether, the political landscape in Somalia is difficult to map. After years of statelessness it may not be enough to base a government on the remains of the old Republic. The developments of the last 10 years might even, to some extent, be irreversible.

It is not easy to pinpoint the cause or the causes of the Somali conflict. Nonetheless, it may be argued that Siad Barre's regime left a troublesome legacy. Barre ruled Somalia in a dictatorial style. He maintained power often by suppressing critics, detaining opponents, playing on clan interests and rivalries. He took the natural resources that had previously been in the hands of local communities and he redistributed them to friends and potential allies.[15] The regime's control of natural resources and access to them was not uncontested. Organised opposition to Barre's autocratic rule began in the aftermath of the abortive Ogaden campaign and continued to grow through the 1980s until virtually every region and clan had produced an anti-Barre movement.[16]

What enabled Siad Barre to resist opposition for so long were the forces at his disposal. Weaponry provided until 1977 by the Soviets and subsequently by the Americans gave his state a capacity for repression that had hitherto been unthinkable.[17] Barre's later years were marked by the unbridled use of force against the civilian population. Force was met with force. As the regime's opponents took over urban and rural assets from the dictator's followers, they replaced his force with their own. With the end of the cold war, Barre's calls for foreign military and economic assistance fell on deaf ears. Human rights abuses, long known to international human rights organisations, now served to justify the end of US aid to his regime.

Following the overthrow of the dictator, the civil war showed patterns of clan warfare as old scores were settled and members of clans privileged by the deposed regime were systematically hunted down. But below the surface of militia mobilisation was a struggle to secure resources in an increasingly resource-poor country. However, it may be argued that the conflict in Somalia today is not just about competition for scarce resources. It is also about power and legitimacy, especially in the matter of which leader from which clan has the right to lead a reconstituted Somali state. And like all civil wars, the issues provide the occasion for some individuals and groups to redress past grievances, humiliate old enemies and plunder or provide for kin. This is exemplified by the argument of Somaliland president, Ibrahim Egal. Referring to the investigation of the mass graves discovered in Somaliland, he contended: "We would have to start with the admission of error. *The people of the south think that we are telling a tall tale.* They have no guilt about it." Although this statement can be interpreted as an endeavour to establish the truth or justice that may lead to reconciliation, it can also be perceived as an attempt by Egal to justify the legitimacy of the "independence" of Somaliland. Subsequently, he made an explicit reference to that point: "But the history of the Somali people is [that] they have never had a central authority. We were independent tribes and we lived together in equality."[18] Like others, Egal questions the legitimacy of the unified Somalia.

Conversely, the interim prime minister of the Transitional National Government (TNG), Ali Khalif Galeyr, has his version of Somali history: "Puntland and Somaliland are administrative entities which we realise were created with some good reasons. In the case of Puntland, the idea was an attempt to manage its own affairs until a central government was formed. A central government is in place now, and the majority of the people in the northeast are very much supportive of the TNG. . . . In the case of the northwest, again, we know there were some good reasons why that entity was created – there have been a lot of grievances on the part of that particular territory."[19] In a nutshell, Galeyr argues that Puntland and Somaliland form part of a greater Somalia. The conflict of opinions among Somali leaders, especially with regard to the status of self-declared states, is one of the problems that hinders reconciliation. This problem is compounded by the fact that some faction leaders oppose the leaders of the self-declared states if the latter engage in dialogue with the Transitional

National Government, for example the SNM. One of its leaders, Awale, stated this unequivocally: "After that, Egal, with bad intentions, began fighting with the SNM, because he saw SNM was uncompromised regarding Somaliland's independence. He was aware that it may block his way back to Somalia unification."[20]

Somaliland and Puntland contain over a third of Somalia's overall population but have not played a substantial role in the Djibouti peace process.[21] In the northwest, Somaliland declared its independence and proclaimed the Somaliland Republic in 1991, shortly after Siad Barre's ousting. International recognition of this move has not been forthcoming. Although Mohamed Ibrahim Egal,[22] the leader of Somaliland, has not ruled out the possibility of a reunification, he says that it could never be imposed on the Somaliland region, but that Somalia and Somaliland must interact as equals.[23] Compared with the rest of Somalia, Somaliland has enjoyed relative peace. At present, Somaliland's government includes a bicameral parliament with elders exercising a traditional role under the 1997 constitution.[24] Popular support for independence appears to be substantial.

Similar in many respects is the recently self-designated Federal State of Puntland. Puntland does not appear to desire secession. However, in June 1998, after continuing civil war in Somalia, it elected a regional administration, led by Abdullahi Yussuf Ahmed. It has declared that the appointment of a national government is a direct threat to local peace and stability. Indeed, the region's non-participation in the Djibouti talks has complicated its internal politics and worsened relations with Hassan's government.[25]

In this complex situation, the new Somali government has received support from "Somali businessmen, the donor community and the friends of Somalia".[26] The new government sees itself as working towards the reconstruction of Somalia. The government has stated that it is willing to discuss the situation with the Mogadishu faction leaders, if mediated by Yemen president Ali Abdullaha Saleh, and that this is an option only if the new constitution, the present parliament and the new president are accepted as legitimate.[27] However, most of the faction leaders in Somalia, especially in Mogadishu, feel that too many of Siad Barre's followers have been allowed into the new government. The current president himself served in vital cabinet positions under Barre and a key member of parliament was a former military commander. As such, many of the faction leaders remain opposed to the peace process and do not recognise the new government and the interim president. The faction leaders believe that there is little to gain by joining the peace process. Mogadishu faction leaders Muse Sudi Yalahow, Hussein Aidid, Osman Hassan Ali "Atto" and

Hussein Haji Bod reject the government as hostile and dangerous. They sense a regime that wants to wage war against its rivals and have announced that government initiatives will lead to renewed inter-clan fighting. Most of the faction leaders, as well as the president of Puntland, support the SRRC led by Hussein Aidid. The SRRC has challenged the new government, which it calls the "Arta group" (named after the host town of the peace conference in Djibouti), by preparing another peace and reconciliation conference, this time within Somalia. Although opposed to the government, it acknowledges that convening such a conference requires the participation of both the new government and Somaliland.

Despite its claims, there appears to be a deep-seated wariness in the international community about throwing substantial weight behind the new government of Somalia. After 10 years of devastating civil war, there is a feeling that the new government has to "prove itself". When the interim president was inaugurated in Djibouti on 27 August 2000, heads of state from Ethiopia, Eritrea, Sudan and Yemen attended, along with senior representatives from Kenya, Egypt, Libya, France, the United Nations and the European Union. President Salat Hassan was later fêted by the Arab League conference in Cairo, the UN Millennium Summit in New York, and received in Saudi Arabia, Egypt and Libya. However, most states appear to be maintaining some contact with other Somali faction leaders. The overall caution displayed internationally with regard to any substantial support, financial or otherwise, makes the government's task very difficult. One regional diplomat is quoted as saying: "It's a real 'chicken and egg' situation. Can the government get anything done without international funding? And can it get international funding before it gets anything done?"[28]

According to regional experts, an important factor in Somalia's relationship with the international community will be its ties with Arab countries. Although vital for financial support, such an association is likely to make the west uneasy. This seems especially significant against the backdrop of the American intervention in 1991. Little humanitarian assistance has entered the country since, with international and local staff deterred by a climate of lawlessness. After his election, President Salat Hassan was met with criticism that he was too closely associated with "Islamic fundamentalism" – a US foreign policy preoccupation. Supporters include Egypt, which initially was disengaged from the Djibouti peace initiative and was accused, like Ethiopia, of smarting from the fact that its own peace attempts during the civil war had failed. Support has also been declared by Libya, although Khadafi's role in the development of Somalia is seen as unpredictable. Backing both Puntland and southern politicians, Khadafi seems to have established future friends no matter how it all might end. Recently, in trying to support President Salat Hassan, Khadafi even made generous offers to the rival warlords in Mogadishu to win their endorsement for the new president. Despite extensive meetings in Libya and the signing of a reconciliation agreement, Hussein Aidid declared that he recognised President Salat Hassan as just another "local leader".[29] Other neighbouring countries – Djibouti, Kenya and Yemen – also seem to support the fragile new government although some of them have noted concerns. The United Nations has followed the peace process and appears to welcome Somalia's new government.

Some states that back the new government appear to be promoting their own interests rather than endorsing President Salat Hassan. To gain the support of neighbouring states, the Somali president gave, for example, assurances to Ethiopia that his government would do everything to remove all elements that use Somali territory as a springboard to threaten Ethiopian security. Within the context of Somali-Ethiopian relations, this refers to the fundamentalist Al-Itihad group which, operating from Somalia, engages in destabilisation activities in the Ogaden area of eastern Ethiopia. Ethiopian security forces have in the past entered Somalia's territory to protect the Ethiopian border and pursue armed Al-Itihad groups.[30] In addition, Ethiopia has shown concern over the lack of contact between the new president, opposition faction leaders and the administrations in Somaliland and Puntland. The governments of other countries, notably Kenya and Libya, share these concerns, especially with regard to the faction leaders, and are pressurising the new government to co-operate with them.[31]

The face of Somalia's conflict is complex. The country has been brought into its present situation by several factors, both internal and external. Within Somalia, a number of faction leaders have inflamed the country with violence in the hope of winning their struggle for political power. Meanwhile the north of Somalia has tried to reach stability through independence (Somaliland) or independent administration (Puntland). In many ways, however, the current conflict is not new. Its origins and motives have deep roots in Somalia's colonial history and the ensuing legacy of internal struggle.

The Historical Roots of Violence and Division

Until the 1850s, Somalia had no determined borders. Its population was composed primarily of nomadic pastoralists who occupied territory from the Indian Ocean coast deep into what is now Ethiopia and from northeastern Kenya to Djibouti at the mouth of the Red Sea. In the second half of the nineteenth century, the European colonial powers expanded their interests in this part of the Horn. The British, having already established a Crown Colony in Aden, Yemen, set up a protectorate in what is now northern Somalia. They later extended their territories by claiming land inhabited by Somalis in northeastern Kenya.[32] France soon did the same in today's Djibouti, creating French Somaliland. In 1893 Italy established Italian Somaliland along the coast of the Indian Ocean. The splitting up of traditional Somali lands was completed by Ethiopia's annexation of the Ogaden region. Throughout the colonial era, Somalia was divided and pulled in different directions: the internal demands of a social structure suited to a decentralised pastoral lifestyle sat in a basic tension with the artificial boundaries of the colonial powers and a centralised, externally-orientated market system. Imperialism and commercialisation led to a corrosion of the Somali moral and socio-political order.[33]

At independence in 1960, two parts of the five Somali territories were combined: British and Italian Somaliland. The other three territories, regarded by the independent government as part of Somalia, were not incorporated. The Ogaden region remained the possession of Ethiopia, Somali areas of Kenya remained part of that state when it became independent in 1963 and French Somaliland became the independent state of Djibouti in 1977. These territories were the concern of irredentist movements that struggled to incorporate them into Somalia. For nine years, Somalia had the basic appearance of a modern state. A stable parliamentary democracy, it had a unicameral national assembly elected by proportional representation on a list system. This system was chosen on the view that it would promote a greater balance between the regions and the clans than the British first-past-the-post system. The assembly then elected the president, who appointed the prime minister. Then a combination of poor economic performance, unresolved domestic issues (like choosing a national written language), the intense rivalry between clan-based parties, the tendency for politicians to fill their own pockets at the public's expense, and the assassination of President Abdirashiid Ali Shermaarke by the police force, all contributed to a bloodless military coup in October 1969, led by Major General Mohamed Siad Barre.[34]

At first, the Somalis welcomed Siad Barre and his Supreme Revolutionary Council (SRC). The SRC selected an official orthography for the Somali language and promoted programmes for the development of adult literacy. It also helped settle populations displaced by drought and worked to empower the status of women in Somali society. On the other hand, it abrogated the constitution, banned political parties and brooked no dissent. In part, the new regime was carried by the Soviet Union, which was looking for facilities to support its naval aspirations in the Indian Ocean. When the tensions between Somalia and Ethiopia intensified in 1974, clans involved in the SRC urged Siad Barre to risk war. In 1977, Somalia attacked Ethiopia to regain the Ogaden region. In the same year, the Soviets shifted their support to Ethiopia, which had declared itself a Marxist state, and abandoned their Somali hosts, intervening in the conflict on Ethiopia's side with equipment and troops. The Ogaden war, which was supposed to shore up Barre's flagging popularity, ended in defeat. Instead of successful expansion, Somalia saw the return of clan rivalry as historical frictions, especially around land issues and political power, multiplied. Although now western-backed, Barre's support continued to dwindle. By the end of the 1980s, he relied more and more on terror and the manipulation of clan identity to stabilise his power. Apart from internal problems, Somalia had also become a fertile arena for proxy war and regional interference. In an attempt to restore control over the situation, Siad Barre signed a "live and let live" accord with Ethiopia's President Mengistu in April 1988 in which it was agreed that Somalia and Ethiopia would each stop supporting the other's enemies.[35] Barre hoped that this move would give him the opportunity to step up the fight against the Somali National Movement (SNM). In turn, the SNM staged assaults in an attempt to capture the major cities of Hargeysa, Burao and the port of Berbera. With great brutality, the revolt was quashed by Barre's son-in-law, Mohamed Siad Hersi. Thousands were killed. More than 300 000 people fled to Ethiopia. The army regained control of the cities but the SNM kept control of the countryside. With groups and clans turning against Siad Barre, conflict spread throughout the country.

In 1989, Siad responded by stepping up the use of force, especially against civilians. By mid-year, the army was splintering and more clans were forming their own political factions. All were bound by the common objective of defeating Siad Barre. Especially in Mogadishu, the situation escalated, producing a situation ripe for the abuse of human rights. Public demonstrations, riots, looting, arrests and repression were commonplace. In January 1991, Siad Barre left Mogadishu and fled south shortly before the forces of the United Somali Congress captured the presidential palace. Days later, Ali Mahdi declared himself interim president, without consulting his military counterpart Mohammed Farah Aidid, who was still busy fighting remnants of the Barre regime in southern Somalia. As a result,

supporters of Ali Mahdi and Farah Aidid turned Mogadishu into a battlefield, firing at anything that moved. Somaliland meanwhile declared its
independence and separated from Somalia. As discussed earlier, the presidency of Ali Mahdi had little popular legitimacy and no other faction
managed to gain power, so Somalia remained without a government until
the summer of 2000.[36]

As politics turned to chaos, human and material suffering became the
order of the day. Not only Somalis in the refugee camps abroad but also
those in the country have suffered human rights violations at the hands of
the armed militias. These include abductions, hostage-taking, forced
recruitment of child soldiers and rape. Militias have deliberately and arbit-
rarily killed unarmed civilians. As Somalia has not had a functioning court
system or judiciary since 1991, human rights abuses occurred with
impunity. Often Islamic courts were themselves involved in gross human
rights violations. None of the factions have complied with the rules of the
Geneva Convention which comprise the principles of international
humanitarian law regulating the conduct of armed conflict and the protection of civilians.[37]

The escalation of conflict corresponded with a sharp economic downturn. The 1980s brought a decline in export prices due to stiffening competition for the Saudi market (accounting for more than 90% of the
Somali exports). As a result, the country endured an increase of between
500% and 800% in the inflation rate, the decay if not complete disappearance of social services, sky-rocketing unemployment and debt. In the
early 1990s, not long after the outbreak of the war, Somalia suffered an
almost complete collapse of economic activity.[38] These economic problems
have had lasting effects. For instance, there has been a sharp increase in
food prices and prices of local construction materials as a result of the continuing devaluation of the Somali shilling. In addition, there is a limited
availability of foreign exchange in Mogadishu.

Communities within the country have been severely affected by 10 years
of civil war and economic crisis. Due to conflict, drought and flood,
Somalia's population suffers from a lack of proper medical care, food insecurity, and a lack of water and sanitation facilities. Undernourished children and mothers are especially susceptible to diseases and respiratory
infections; malaria and diarrhoeal diseases account for more than half of
all child deaths. Somalia also has one of the highest maternal mortality
rates in the world, which is worsened by the widespread practice of female
genital circumcision. There is a high incidence of tuberculosis and cholera.
Estimations of Somalis in need of humanitarian assistance vary between

526 000 in a best case scenario and 1.5 million in the worst.

The crisis has devastated the educational and environmental sectors. The impact of the civil war on education has been dramatic, indeed the system has come close to total collapse – Somalia has one of the poorest enrolment rates in the world. The majority of schools were damaged, educational records and materials were lost, and subsequently many teachers left the country. Almost two entire generations of Somali children have suffered a severe, if not total, interruption of their education. A survey of primary schools throughout Somalia conducted by UNICEF in 1997 revealed that only a fraction of the schools operated and that almost none of them offered the full primary cycles of grades 1 to 8. This situation is compounded by generally poor conditions and standards in the schools, as well as a significant gender imbalance in that twice as many boys as girls attend school.

The absence of a central government has had a major impact on the environment of Somalia. In addition to the perennial problem of overgrazing, a major concern in certain areas is deforestation related to firewood and charcoal production. Although this is a concern throughout Africa, in Somalia it is occurring on an unprecedented scale. Another serious worry for the various communities within Somalia, especially in the Somaliland and Puntland regions, is the threat of landmines and other unexploded weapons. Surveying and demining has begun in a few locations with the support of the UN Development Programme (UNDP). However, there have been few donors interested in supporting this work in Somalia.[39]

The current government in Somalia is the result of the peace conference held in Djibouti in 2000. More than 2 000 Somalis, a cross-section of numerous clans, gathered in Arta, Djibouti for five months of negotiations dedicated to creating an interim parliament, electing a president and writing a national charter. The 245-member Transitional National Assembly (TNA) was chosen along clan lines. When the clan representatives negotiated power, the Hawiye, who control the capital, were given the presidency, largely due to the belief that it was the only way to re-establish peace and security in Mogadishu. So far, the government has had to depend largely on backing from the local business community. This crucial financial support, as well as remittances from North America, Europe and the Arab states, has enabled the government to begin a demobilisation programme. However, this funding will ultimately have its limitations, and has the potential to become politically uncomfortable.[40]

Somalia's new government is still finding its feet. Whether it can achieve peace, security and national unity will depend heavily on how it deals with Somaliland and Puntland and whether it can reach an agreement with the faction leaders in Mogadishu. After his election, Salat Hassan said some "warlords" would be ignored and dialogue would be established with others. A meeting with SNA leader Aidid in Libya seems not to have been successful, but apparently the Islamic courts want to back the new government by providing protection through their own security services, which were another armed militia group during the 10 years of civil war. To placate or, as many perceive it, to undermine the leader of Somaliland, Mohamed Ibrahim Egal, President Hassan has appointed two northerners from Somaliland as prime minister (Ali Khalif Galeyr) and minister of foreign affairs (Ismail Mahmoud Hurre).[41] In addition to its old opponents (Somaliland, Puntland and individual faction leaders), the new Somali government perceives a threat in the form of the SRRC. The chief Somali faction leaders have organised themselves to "prepare the ground for setting up a new government with popular support at the grassroot level". They want to convene a national reconciliation conference where the kind of "regional autonomy and democratic system to be established in a federal set-up of a representative government of national unity" can be decided.[42] They reject the current government as illegitimate, because, according to the faction leaders, this government was formed outside of Somalia under the influence and in the interest of Djibouti.

Whether the new government or the SRRC is successful remains to be seen. Both will have to face the problem of a culture of impunity which has developed in Somalia over the last decade. Part of the problem has to do with the histories of those who now occupy government positions. In addition, the country faces the problems of demilitarisation and refugee settlement. There are no reliable figures on the number of militia in the country, but aid workers and residents put the number in the tens of thousands. In the hope of bringing security and stability to the country, the new Somali government established a National Demobilisation Committee. The goal of the committee is to begin demobilisation and reintegrate up to 75 000 militia over the next three years by providing them with basic education, religious and civics instruction and job training. According to a survey by the UN Development Programme, 493 out of 500 militia members in Mogadishu would be willing to leave their armed groups and participate in the programme. Somali refugees pose another problem. Civil strife in Somali has resulted in substantial population displacement. More than a million Somalis are internally displaced. In addition almost 300 000 Somali refugees are spread all over the Horn of

Africa and the East African region. With 124 000, Kenya hosts the biggest group of refugees, mainly from southern Somalia, in the Daadab refugee camps. The United Nations High Commissioner for Refugees intends to promote the repatriation of Somali refugees from the south as soon as the situation in Somalia becomes relatively peaceful. Repatriation of refugees from the north to Somaliland and Puntland is already in progress. Meanwhile, insecurity in the Kenyan Daadab camps increases. Women in particular are in danger. From January until October 2000, 72 rape cases had been reported. Furthermore, armed attacks are frequent and the camps are probably used to traffic arms.

Prospects for Peace-building

Unlike many other African countries, Somalia is not divided along ethnic or religious faultlines. Somalis speak the same language, Somali, and share the same religion, Sunni-Islam, a variation of the Islamic faith. Nevertheless, in 1999, the international organisations involved in Somalia advocated peace-making through a "building block" approach. This meant that instead of rebuilding Somalia as a whole, peace within different regions would be supported and promoted. It was widely argued that the only road ahead was for other parts of Somalia to follow the example set by Somaliland and Puntland, namely to establish peace and stability on a regional and local level by creating independent administrations.[43] As there was an opportunity to set up a national government, those plans were set aside. However, the Djibouti peace process brought mixed results. In light of past peace-building efforts, many are taking a wait-and-see attitude to the recent reforms.

Since the beginning of civil war in 1991, some 15 peace initiatives directed toward either faction leaders or clan elders have been undertaken. Respectively hosted or convened by the United States, the UN, Ethiopia or Egypt, none succeeded.[44] Since 1991, just after Siad Barre was toppled, the major political Somali leaders have assembled twice in Djibouti. This resulted initially in the self-appointment of a new president, Ali Mahdi Mohamed, the first in a series of rival leaders. Although it has been several years since the last president claimed to represent the entire nation, it has become clear that the naming of individuals to this position has not helped to solve problems. Indeed, it has sometimes served to create new rivalries and instability. But it must be admitted that in 1991 the UN failed to support Djibouti's plans to convene peace-talks for the country. Nor did the League of Arab States, the OAU, the Islamic Conference, the United States or the European Community offer help.

If they had made serious efforts to negotiate peace in 1991, almost 10 years of civil war may have been averted.[45]

The UN did take an interest in early 1992, when Aidid's and Ali Mahdi's forces had paralysed Mogadishu and the situation in Somalia appeared increasingly desperate. However, when UN representative Mohamed Sahnoun arrived in Mogadishu to start the UN Somalia operations, he relied on traditional structures to promote reconciliation and conflict settlement. Sahnoun managed to negotiate a largely successful cease-fire and plan confidence-building measures between the Somali faction leaders and Ethiopia. He came to a separate agreement with Somaliland regarding its role in the peace process and the terms of its future autonomy. However, his approach seemed, in light of the increasing famine in Somalia, too slow for the UN Secretary-General, Boutros Boutros Ghali, and the US, who favoured a more radical solution in the form of a large military intervention. This tension led to the replacement of Sahnoun and the adoption of Security Council Resolution 794 of 3 December 1992, authorising the deployment of a Unified Task Force (UNITAF) under Chapter VII of the UN Charter. For the first time in the history of the UN, the Security Council allowed enforcement actions to interfere in the domestic affairs of a sovereign state. The US-led Operation Restore Hope began on 9 December 1992. It involved about 24 000 American soldiers and another 20 000 troops from all over the world. In spite of the military presence, the UNITAF forces did not, apart from some half-hearted attempts in January 1993, disarm Somali militias. To the contrary, the mission was an abject failure and outright embarrassment for the international community. It most certainly entrenched the conflict.

1997 saw another effort to bring peace and stability to Somalia. At a peace conference in Cairo, attended by Hussein Aidid's SNA and 25 other factions, it was decided again to base future solutions to the Somali conflict on the principle of regional self-administration. The idea was inspired by the situation in Ethiopia, but hampered by quarrels among the faction leaders. Finally, Aidid withdrew. However, this approach was adopted by the UN in 1998. Focusing its attention on the development of regional administrations in areas like Puntland and Jubaland in the southwest, the UN attempted to create an agreement that would organise the country on a federal model.

The Transitional National Government of Somalia, viewed internationally as the only possible vehicle to bring peace and reconciliation to Somalia, is the culmination of the initiative launched by the president of Djibouti, Ismail Omar Guelleh, in 1999. The first formal move to implement the Djibouti initiative was the March 2000 Technical Consultative Symposium, hosted by the government of Djibouti. President Guelleh emphasised that the symposium was not a decision-making body but a means of providing advice to the government of Djibouti in its preparations for the conference. The symposium was attended by about 60 Somalis, invited in their individual capacities, from all parts of the country and from the diaspora. The UN was represented by Kofi Annan's Special Advisor.

The symposium recommended, *inter alia*, that the negotiations process should be as inclusive as possible by allowing the participation of faction leaders who desired peace and by enhancing the role of civil society within Somalia. On the future structure of the government, the symposium recommended a decentralised arrangement as well as consolidation of peace in areas where stability had been restored; the establishment of a human rights commission to monitor violations of the peace process; the departure of Somalis occupying the lands and properties of others; the reaffirmation of Mogadishu as the capital of Somalia, with the possibility of establishing a temporary capital for a future provisional government; and the demobilisation of militia members. If necessary, the transitional government could call for an international force to assist in matters of security. The delegates also recommended stricter enforcement of the Security Council arms embargo on Somalia, stressed the need for international support for a future agreement by the Somalis and called upon Djibouti to send delegations to Somalia to prepare for the Somali National Peace Conference.

On 2 May 2000, the first phase of the Somali National Peace Conference, a meeting of traditional and clan leaders, was formally opened in the town of Arta, Djibouti. Participants included elders from most of Somalia's clans and from all parts of the country. In addition to working on reconciliation issues among the clans, the conference prepared for the second phrase by drawing up an agenda and lists of delegates who would represent clans. The delegates included political, business, and religious leaders, as well as representatives of civil society.[46] President Guelleh formally inaugurated the second phase on 15 June 2000. After deliberating in committee and plenary sessions for a month, the delegates overwhelmingly approved the Transitional National Charter for governance in a three-year transitional phase that would culminate in elections. The charter provides for regional autonomy, based on the 18 regions that existed at the end of the Siad Barre regime. It also sets out structures for executive, legislative and judicial powers, as well as the rights of individuals. These include, for the first time in Somali history, a specific requirement that 25 seats in parliament be set aside for women. A representation of 24 seats for minority clans was also agreed upon. The charter will be the supreme law until a definitive federal constitution for Somalia is adopted at the end of the transition.

The results of the Arta Conference produced mixed feelings. Almost all the attendees were unanimous that the peace conference was inclusive and representative.[47] Non-attendees thought otherwise. Some of them felt that the conference consisted of "remnants of the Siad Barre regime, religious extremists and Somali exiles".[48] Consequently, the faction leaders organised their own conference under the banner of the Somali Reconciliation and Restoration Council, a body that has not yet convened. The leaders of the self-declared states of Somaliland and Puntland felt that their administrations were not treated with "due respect". These differences are key to understanding disruptions in the peace process. However, it must be emphasised that the Djibouti peace accord has the backing of the international community. It may well be the only possible avenue that can bring peace to Somalia. It has made some inroads by bringing on board some of the faction leaders who were initially opposed to it. For example, on 16 October 2001, a peace deal was signed between two rival clans, the Marehan and Muhammad Zubayr, in the port city of Kismaayo. The Muhammad Zubayr clan had supported the SRRC, while the Maheran supports the Transitional National Government (TNG). Under the agreement, the two sides will join forces in support of the TNG.

The President of the TNG constantly appeals to the opponents of the TNG to join hands with his government. Nonetheless, there is a feeling that there is a lack of progress in Somalia's peace process. Owing to this, the UN Secretary-General is considering establishing a "Committee of Friends" for the war-torn country. Annan intends to consult with all the concerned parties on setting up a committee that could bring together interested countries and organisations in the search for a lasting peace, and to help mobilise funds for rehabilitation and development. Moreover, a number of western countries have recently established a framework for opposition groups to gather and discuss their disagreements with the government. To be held in Nairobi in late 2002, these reconcilation talks have been on again, off again in recent months. At planning meetings in April 2002, representatives from all sides indicated that part of the diffuclty was how to define the agenda and procedures for the meetings.

The status of Somaliland continues to play a central role in efforts to build a stable peace. It has taken no part in any of the 20 or so "peace agreements" that southern factions have signed throughout the war, peace agreements that begin with the phrase "The unity of Somalia is sacred". Somaliland's economy has gradually improved and its political stability is admirable when set against the ruins of the former capital. However, this reality has not impressed many southerners who, in an environment of increasing disparity, have found cause to rally against Somaliland. To believe the assessment of some Somalis, the region's secession is the cause of the south's suffering. While Puntland has officially expressed its willingness to be part of a future federal Somalia, it too is seen as an impediment to the re-emergence of a united Somali Republic.[49]

From the arguments advanced by the leaders of Somaliland, Puntland and some faction leaders, the unification of these self-declared states with Somali is unforeseeable. These leaders have a profound distaste for unification. The president of Somaliland, Mohamed Ibrahim Egal, argues that this feeling stems from the fact that the Somali people led by the Transitional National Government do not regard his people, the Somalilanders, as equals. He adds that ". . . the history of the Somali people is [that] they have never had a central authority".[50] To demonstrate its commitment to self-determination, the Somaliland administration held a referendum on 31 May 2001 in terms of which the residents of Somaliland were asked to vote on a new constitution that included an article on territorial independence. Ninety-seven percent of the voters endorsed the constitution. The TNG referred to the referendum as "bogus" and illegal. The TNG contended in an official statement that: "Mr Egal has no legal authority to unilaterally nullify the Act of Union of the Somali Republic, enacted as Law No. 5 of January 3, 1961 by the then National Assembly, which had forever bound together in a single unitary state the two former Italian and British Somali colonial territories."[51] The Somaliland referendum was also opposed by Puntland leaders who described it as "unwise and provocative".[52]

The Somali National Movement (SNM) is a staunch supporter of the anti-unification campaign. The SNM fought a successful insurgency against former president Siad Barre. After the declaration of independence, the SNM agreed to demobilise and support a civilian government. It threw its weight behind the former prime minister of Somalia, Mohamed Ibrahim Egal, resulting in his election as Somaliland's president in 1993. Subsequently, however, the SNM became one of Egal's critics – despite the fact that stability and resources had been brought to the territory under his leadership – for failing to secure international recognition. More importantly, the SNM feels that Egal has betrayed the course of their struggle,

Somaliland's independence. This was stated unequivocally by Abdirahman Awale, the member of the SNM leadership.[53] Consequently, the SNM seeks to form an alliance with all "progressive forces" in the country, especially the clans. Besides the SNM, Egal has been put under pressure by his Members of Parliament. It was reported on 22 August 2001 that 37 MPs had tabled a motion in parliament calling for Egal's impeachment on allegations of financial mismanagement and high treason, claiming that he had failed to pursue secession effectively. The motion was rejected.

Puntland has had its own share of problems. Under the Transitional Charter of Puntland, the mandate of the Puntland administration expired on 30 June 2001. Instead of undertaking mandated presidential and parliamentary elections, the administration, citing the unfavourable situation in Somalia, sought a three-year extension of its term. A group of traditional leaders referred the decision on the extension to the House of Representatives, which following a majority vote extended the terms of its office and the executive for three years.[54] The chairman of the Supreme Court declared the extension unconstitutional. Abdullahi Ahmed suspended the chairman on 29 June 2001 and the House of Representatives ratified the decision on the following day. However, the chairman maintained that the announcement of his removal was *ultra vires* and hence null and void. His position was upheld by a meeting of titled leaders. Abdullahi Ahmed argued that a decision of elders could not overturn a decision of the House of Representatives. Pursuant to unsuccessful attempts by elders and business people to promote a peaceful solution to the constitutional crisis, fighting broke out in Boosaaso on 6 August 2001. Abdullahi Ahmed retreated to his hometown, Gaalkacyo. The chairman of the Supreme Court stated that he had no political ambitions himself and that he would organise a community meeting, as provided for in the Charter, to set the future course of Puntland. The conference was opened in Garoowe, on 26 August 2001, with over 400 participants representing all five regions. At the time of writing, it was still in session. Meanwhile, Abdullahi Ahmed announced that he remained president of Puntland, claiming that Gaalkacyo was the interim capital and blaming "fundamentalists" and the TNG for his difficulties.[55] He has also publicly declared that the conference in Garoowe is illegal.

The constitutional crisis in Puntland has broken a decade of relative peace in the area. On 5 and 6 August 2001, fighting between Abdullahi Ahmed's forces and those of the chairman of the Supreme Court resulted in the relocation of United Nations humanitarian staff from Boosaaso and Hargeysa. Although staff were soon allowed to return, tensions remain high. On 23 August 2001, the relative stability of Somaliland was affected by the arrests of four sultans at a gathering of traditional leaders. There were clashes between government forces and sultan militias, resulting in five deaths and a brief suspension of United Nations activities.

In late 2001, the authority of the presidents of both Somaliland and Puntland has been challenged. This has led to uncertainty regarding the political stability of those regions. This does not appear to be something that might lead to the unification of these administrations with the larger state, despite the fact that this instability is viewed by some as an indication that the residents of these regions would like to see a unified Somalia.[56]

Apart from political concepts and structures, it seems clear that human resource development is a priority for government, NGOs and the private sector. The recently announced UNDP programme for identifying skilled Somalis abroad for short missions in Somalia is one initiative that, according to the UN and international agencies, deserves serious support. Another development worthy of serious support is the programmes sponsored by women's organisations in the NGO sector. Many argue that women are the pioneers for peace and development in Somalia and it is therefore essential that Somali women's NGOs and women politicians and activists be supported by both local and international communities.[57]

Present and Future Opportunities for Reconciliation

In Somalia, there is an apparent need for reconciliation at both local and national level. The former appears vital, especially as family members and schoolmates may belong to different factions. However, issues of truth, justice and reconciliation have, so far, not been addressed by the new government, which is attempting to create general political stability and generate international support for reforms. The appointment of a 25-member peace and reconciliation committee remains only a formality and has not been followed by substantial action.

During the 10 years of civil war, a culture of impunity has taken root in Somalia. Westernised courts (of varying quality) have been established in many parts of Somalia. If the courts are able to work at all, they often permit the transfer of complaints, even capital offences, to elders for settlement by customary law. Somali customary law, known as *heer*, has its own criminal and civil jurisprudence. *Heer* is established through ad hoc assemblies in which men deliberate on current problems. Judicial decisions are arrived at by consensus of elders representing the parties in a dispute. Contrary to western court systems, which penalise the individual financially or by incarceration, Somali traditional courts oblige a group from the offender's sub-clan to pay compensation. Shame is believed to deter recidivism.[58] However, militias fighting for political power have rarely been convicted by traditional courts and western courts often lack the power and resources to prosecute. In general, the court system in Somalia might work for small offences but not for gross human rights violations and war crimes. To change this, the UNDP for Somalia has decided to expand its Somali Civil Protection Programme. Already working in Somaliland, the UNDP now wants to cover the whole of Somalia with the aim of improving the judiciary's standards and practices, promoting law enforcement and the demobilisation of armed militia groups.

In terms of investigating the past, serious political observers in Mogadishu have argued throughout the Djibouti peace process that a truth commission is needed in Somalia and that persons known to have committed war crimes and other criminal offences should be blocked from participation in the political process and perhaps prosecuted. On 6 May 2001, the Transitional National Government (TNG), as provided for in Article 30 of the Transitional National Charter, appointed a 25-member National Commission for Reconciliation and Property Settlement (NCRPS). The committee was expected to send representatives to all regions of Somalia requesting recommendations on how the reconciliation process could be completed. Committee representatives had to act as intermediaries between the TNG and the existing regional administrations and factions. The committee had been tasked to define the most suitable way of establishing a federal system and to find methods of addressing property and land issues.

The NCRPS included representatives of most of Somalia's clans and some prominent individuals. It was to be chaired by Abdirazzaq Hajj Husayn, a respected former prime minister of Somalia; Abdiqadir Muhammad Zope, a former minister and Rahanweyn elder; and Somalia's internationally renowned novelist, Nuruddin Farah. In order for the committee to carry out its mandate effectively, it had to include missions to Somaliland and Puntland. Both administrations had rejected the TNG and therefore did not recognise the NCRPS. The Somali Reconciliation and Restoration Council (SRRC) also rejected the body.[59] When the SRRC was formed on 23 March 2001, it stated that its aim would be to hold an "all-inclusive national reconciliation conference within six months to form a representative Transitional Government of Unity".[60] Subsequently, the conference was postponed and it was said that it would be convened late in 2002.

Both the TNG and SRRC claim to be national, multi-clan alliances. Both have stated that they wish to pursue national reconciliation. Both include personalities who were prominent in the Barre regime. Neither seems to disagree on any major political issue, including such potentially divisive issues as the role of religion in the state or the relationships between central and local administrations. Clearly, the differences ought not to be irreconcilable. This is evidenced by the fact that the TNG has managed to bring on board two of the five faction leaders based in Mogadishu who were originally opposed to its formation. It has also held several positive discussions with another faction leader, Osman Hassan Ali "Atto". The TNG has extended its invitation to the other two faction leaders in Mogadishu, Mohammed Farah Aidid and Muse Sudi Yalahow. Both continue to challenge its authority. The TNG has appealed to "the opposition groups to lay down their arms and come to the negotiating table".[61] However, the TNG has had some setbacks. On 25 July 2001, Abdirazzaq Hajj Husayn resigned as the chairman of the NCRPS. He felt that he had not received the support of the prime minister and objected to the procedure adopted by the TNG in appointing members of the NCRPS and in announcing its establishment. Referring to Abdirazzaq's resignation, a Somali political analyst commented that he was "a highly respected, trusted and independent individual, and replacing him with someone acceptable will be difficult".[62]

There have also been reported differences between the prime minister of the TNG, Ali Khalif Galeyr and the president. Galeyr admitted as much on 22 September 2001 during his appearance on HornAfrik television. However, he stated that all the issues had been resolved.[63] On 11 October 2001, TNG MPs tabled a motion of no confidence in the TNG. This was confirmed by the TNA Deputy Speaker, Muhammad Abdi Yusuf. The motion accused the government of "dereliction of duty, and corruption". On 28 October 2001, the interim government was voted out of office. 174 members of the 245-seat assembly voted on the motion. 141 supported the government's sacking, with only 29 voting in support of the government. Four MPs abstained from the vote.[64]

Despite the problems confronting the TNG, it is regarded by the international community as an important milestone in the move toward peace and reconciliation. The UN has called on Somali leaders to put aside their narrow interests and work together for the interests of the people of Somalia at large. Similar sentiments were echoed by the League of Arab States at a summit meeting in March 2001, where it adopted a resolution which called on "all factions and sections of the Somali people to work for their utmost with the elected President and his Government to bring about security and stability, to safeguard Somalia's territorial integrity and to bring about the country's rehabilitation and reconstruction".[65]

Perhaps one of the most important issues to be addressed in Somalia today is the reintegration of children and young people who fought in the militias during the civil war. Other areas that require immediate attention include the right to free expression and protection of an independent press and media. This would necessitate training offered to newspaper and radio journalists. Reintegration, education and professional training are themselves not enough to ensure reconciliation, but are milestones on the way.

A number of international actors in and around Somalia are potential allies of those in Somalia who want to lead the transition process. Specifically, the Nairobi-based UN organisations involved in Somalia have several actors willing to put their weight behind viable political initiatives. To co-ordinate the UN help for Somalia, the Somalia Aid Coordination Body (SACB) provides an umbrella structure for the humanitarian operations of UN agencies and NGOs. It seems clear that were the UN, the EU and other organisations to make a choice between work that leads to a reunification of Somalia, or to exclusively local efforts, the former would be by far the more attractive. Indeed the UN aid co-ordinator Randolph Kent pledged that the new government was going to have a tremendous impact on the work of aid organisations. At present, the international NGOs capable of participating in and facilitating a process towards reconciliation include CARE, the International Committee of the Red Cross and Save the Children. Although the situation for NGOs in Somalia has become worse and, in 1999, humanitarian workers were the victims of numerous acts of violence and threats, all of these organisations are currently working in Somalia, promoting, among other things, different reconciliation programmes by providing training, improving education and respect for humanitarian rules and by trying to institute peace and conflict resolution activities.[66] Their objective is not necessarily to support the unification of the country but to help on whatever level seems reasonable and appropriate.

The government's capability and/or willingness to facilitate reconciliation initiatives with either the heads of Somaliland and Puntland or the major faction leaders is less clear. It seems that all of them would participate only under certain conditions. The new government is willing to meet at least some of its opponents, but certainly does not want to discuss the legitimacy of the transitional parliament, the elected interim president and the new constitution. Ibrahim Egal from Somaliland and Abdullahi

Yussuf Ahmed from Puntland appear open to reconciliation as long as peace and stability in their regions is not in danger and as long as Salat Hassan treats them duly, which in the case of Egal means that he wants to be seen as the president of an independent state. Last but not least, the position of the faction leaders remains difficult to assess. Some may be open to a process of reconciliation, but only if it comes with a chance to particpate in the political process.

NOTES

1 John Drysdale, *Stoics Without Pillows* (London: Haan Associates Publishing, 2000), 151.
2 There is no uniform spelling of the names. Other spellings are: Abdoulkassim Salat Hassan, Abdiqasim Salad Hasan and Alif Kalif Galaydh respectively.
3 Bernhard Helander, "Will There be Peace in Somalia Now?" Reprinted at www.somaliawatch.org/archiveoct00/001009401.htm (accessed 12 November 2000).
4 Integrated Regional Information Network (IRIN), "New Reconciliation Committee Formed." Reprinted at www.allafrica.com/stories/200105080180.html (accessed 10 May 2001).
5 William J. Durch, "Introduction to Anarchy: Humanitarian Intervention and 'State-Building' in Somalia," in *UN Peacekeeping, American Politics, and the Uncivil Wars of the 1990s*, ed. William J. Durch (London: Macmillan Press, 1997), 313.
6 Samuel M. Makinda, *Seeking Peace from Chaos: Humanitarian Intervention in Somalia* (London, New York: Lynne Rienner Publishers, 1993), 18.
7 Jos van Beurden, "Somalia: In a State of Permanent Conflict," in *Searching for Peace in Africa: An Overview of Conflict Prevention and Management Activities*, eds. Monique Mekenkamp, Paul van Tongeren and Hans van de Veen (Utrecht: European Platform for Conflict Prevention and Transformation, 1999), 157.
8 Maxamed D. Afrax, "The Mirror of Culture: Somali Dissolution Seen Through Oral Expression," in *The Somali Challenge: From Catastrophe to Renewal?*, ed. Ahmed I. Samatar (London, New York: Lynne Rienner Publishers, 1994), 233.
9 Makinda, *Seeking Peace from Chaos*, 25.
10 Daniel Compagnon, "Somali Armed Movements. The Interplay of Political Entrepreneurship & Clan-Based Factions," in *African Guerrillas*, ed. Christopher Clapham (Oxford: James Currey, 1998), 74.
11 IRIN, "Somalia: IRIN Guide to the Somali National Peace Conference." Reprinted at www.reliefweb.int/IRIN/cea/countrystories/somalia/20000630a.phtml (accessed 14 March 2001).
12 Different spellings: Husayn Mohamed Aydid, Hussein Mohamed Aideed.
13 Different spelling: Musa Sudi Yalahow.
14 IRIN, "Chairmanship of Opposition Council to Rotate." Reprinted at www.allafrica.com/stories/200103300569.html (accessed 30 March 2001).
15 Makinda, *Seeking Peace from Chaos*, 17.
16 Lee V. Cassanelli, "Explaining the Somali Crisis," in *The Struggle for Land in Southern Somalia: The War Behind the War*, eds. Catherine Besteman and Lee V. Cassanelli (London: Haan Associates Publishing, 2000), 23.

17 Cassanelli, "Explaining the Somali Crisis," 22.

18 IRIN, "Somalia: IRIN interview with Muhammad Ibrahim Egal, President of Somaliland, 28 May 2001." Reprinted at www.reliefweb.int/IRIN/cea/countrystories/somalia/20010528.phtml (accessed 11 October 2001).

19 IRIN, "Somalia: IRIN interview with Prime Minister Ali Khalif Galayhd, 14 May 2001." Reprinted at www.reliefweb.int/IRIN/cea/countrystories/somalia/20010528.phtml (accessed 11 October 2001).

20 IRIN. "Somalia: IRIN interview with Somali National Movement (SNM), 18 May 2001." Reprinted at www.reliefweb.int/IRIN/cea/countrystories/somalia/20010518.phtml (accessed 11 October 2001).

21 Bernhard Helander, "Will There be Peace in Somalia Now?"

22 Different spelling: Mohammed Ibrahim Igal.

23 Reuters, "Somaliland Leader Denounces New Mogadishu Government." Reprinted at www.cnn.com/2000/WORLD/africa/11/23/somalia.somaliland.reut (accessed 28 November 2000).

24 Drysdale, Stoics Without Pillows, 21.

25 African Newswire Network (ANN); IRIN, "Somalia: New Parliament Grapples with Somaliland and Puntland." Reprinted at www.africanewswire.com/annews/categories/djibouti/story3773.shtml (accessed 15 March 2001).

26 IRIN, "Interview with PM Ali Khalif Galeyr, Part 2." Reprinted at www.allafrica.com/stories/200011230036.html (accessed 29 November 2000).

27 Helander, "Will There be Peace in Somalia Now?"

28 IRIN, "Special Report on Interim Government of Somalia." Reprinted at www.somaliawatch.org/archiveoct00/001019401.htm (accessed 10 November 2000).

29 Helander, "Will There be Peace in Somalia Now?"

30 IRIN, "Interview with PM Ali Khalif Galeyr, Part 2."

31 IRIN, "Horn of Africa: IRIN Update, 6 December 2000." Reprinted at www.allafrica.com/stories/200012060235.html (accessed 10 December 2000).

32 Durch, "Introduction to Anarchy," 313.

33 Terrence Lyons and Ahmed I. Samatar, Somalia: State Collapse, Multilateral Intervention, and Strategies for Political Reconstruction (Washington, DC: The Brookings Institution, 1995), 11; see also Martin Doornbos, "Pasture and Polis: The Roots of Political Marginalization of Somali Pastoralism," in Conflict and the Decline of Pastoralism in the Horn of Africa, ed. John Markakis (London: Macmillan Press, 1993), 104–105.

34 Peter Woodward, The Horn of Africa: State Politics and International Relations (London, New York: Tauric Academic Studies, 1996), 65–67.

35 Durch, "Introduction to Anarchy," 314.

36 Lyons, Somalia: State Collapse, 14–15.

37 Amnesty International, "Amnesty International Annual Report 2000. Somalia." Reprinted at www.amnesty.org (accessed 20 November 2000).

38 Makinda, Seeking Peace from Chaos, 41–47.

39 Idil Salah and Bernard Taylor, "Peace and Development in Northern Somalia: Opportunities and Challenges." Reprinted at www.somaliawatch.org/archive/990908601.htm (accessed 15 November 2000).

40 IRIN, "Special Report on Interim Government of Somalia."

41 Different spellings: Ismael Hurreh, Isma'il Mahmud Hurre "Buba".

42 IRIN (Nairobi), "Somalia: SRRC to Organise Reconciliation Conference." Reprinted at www.allafrica.com/stories/200108080015.html (accessed 15 April 2001).

43 Woodward, The Horn of Africa, 84–85.

44 IRIN, "Somalia: IRIN Guide to the Somali National Peace Conference." Reprinted at www.reliefweb.int/IRIN/cea/countrystories/somalia/20000630a.phtml (accessed 13 November 2000).

45 Mohamed Sahnoun, *Somalia: The Missed Opportunities* (Washington DC: United States Institute of Peace Press, 1994), 10; Makinda, *Seeking Peace from Chaos*, 32.

46 IRIN, "Somalia: IRIN Horn of Africa Interview with the Chairman of the Somali Peace Conference, Hassan Abshire Farah, 1 July 2000." Reprinted at www.reliefweb.int/IRIN/cea/countrystories/somalia/20000701.phtml (accessed 19 October 2001).

47 IRIN, "IRIN Interview with Abdallah Derow Isaak, Speaker of Somalia's Transitional National Assembly, 4 September 2000." Reprinted at www.reliefweb.int/IRIN/countrystories/somalia/20000904a.phtml (accessed 18 October 2001); IRIN, "Somalia: IRIN Interview with Maryam Arif Qasim, a Member of Somalia's Transitional Parliament, 4 September 2000." Reprinted at www.reliefweb.int/IRIN/cea/ countrystories/somalia/20000904b.phtml (accessed 18 October 2001); IRIN, "Somalia: IRIN Horn of Africa Interview with the Chairman of the Somali Peace Conference, Hassan Abshire Farah, 1 July 2000." Reprinted at www.reliefweb.int/ IRIN/cea/countrystories/somalia/20000701.phtml (accessed 19 October 2001).

48 IRIN, "Somalia: Faction Leaders Reaffirm Opposition to Transitional Government, 1 March 2000." Reprinted at www.reliefweb.int/IRIN/cea/country stories/somalia/20010301.phtml (accessed 11 October 2001).

49 Helander, "Will There be Peace in Somalia Now?"

50 IRIN, "Somalia: Interview with Muhammad Ibrahim Egal, President of Somaliland, 28 May 2001." Reprinted at www.reliefweb.int/IRIN/cea/countrystories/somalia/20010528.phtml (accessed 11 October 2001).

51 Somalia Official Website, "Official Statement of the Transitional National Somali Government on the Bogus Referendum in Some of the Northwestern Regions of the Somali Republic, 4 June 2001." Reprinted at www.somaligov.com/dailynews/june/042001.html (accessed 10 October 2001).

52 IRIN, "Somalia: Puntland Challenges Neighbouring Referendum, 30 April 2001." Reprinted at www.reliefweb.int/IRIN/cea/countrystories/somalia/20010430.phtml (accessed 16 October 2001).

53 IRIN, "Yes. When he [Egal] says he is for independence, it is for local consumption only. He tells the people here one thing, but in his speeches elsewhere he has clearly declared that Somalia will unite one day. He says we will talk to the southerners when they make their home clean and negotiate with them . . . He says one thing to the public, and a different thing to the international community," "Somalia: IRIN Interview with the Somali National Movement (SNM), 18 May 2001." Reprinted at www.reliefweb.int/IRIN/cea/countrystories/somalia/20010518.phtml (accessed 11 October 2001).

54 IRIN, "Somalia: Puntland Administration Gets Extension, 25 June 2001." Reprinted at www.reliefweb.int/IRIN/cea/countrystories/somalia/20010625 (accessed 16 October 2001).

55 IRIN, "Somalia: Puntland Leader Refusing to Step Down, 9 August 2001." Reprinted at www.reliefweb.int/IRIN/cea/countrystories/somalia/20010807a.phtml (accessed 16 October 2001).

56 IRIN, "IRIN Interview with Prime Minister Ali Khalif Galaydh, 14 May 2001." Reprinted at www.reliefweb.int/IRIN/cea/countrystories/somalia/20010514.phtml (accessed 11 October 2001); realising this challenge, the Secretary-General of the UN, Kofi Annan, has contended in his latest report on the situation in Somalia that, "while

the search for a national solution continues, much more attention could be paid to local political settlements". He further argues that, "nevertheless, recent events have shown that disputes which often appear to be purely local cannot be solved by local actors alone at the local level. Thus, the process of rebuilding national institutions should go forward with strong and impartial efforts at local reconciliation. Ongoing United Nations Programmes to enhance local capacities should be strengthened as a parallel means to advance reconciliation at the local and national levels."

57 Salah, "Peace and Development in Northern Somalia."

58 Drysdale, *Stoics Without Pillows*, 3, 145; Woodward, *The Horn of Africa*, 24.

59 IRIN, "Somalia: SRRC Slams Reconciliation Committee, 10 May 2001." Reprinted at www.reliefweb.int/IRIN/cea/countrystories/somalia/20010510c.phtml (accessed 11 October 2001).

60 Reliefweb, "Report of the Secretary-General on the Situation in Somalia (S/2001/963), 11 October 2001." Reprinted at www.reliefweb.int/w/rw (accessed 16 October 2001).

61 IRIN, "Somalia: Interim Government Appeals to Opposition, 14 August 2001." Reprinted at www.reliefweb.int/IRIN/cea/countrystories/somalia20010814.phtml (accessed 9 October 2001).

62 IRIN, "Somalia: Chairman of Reconciliation Committee Resigns, 30 July 2001." Reprinted at www. reliefweb.int/IRIN/cea/countrystories/somalia/20010730b. phtml (accessed 9 October 2001).

63 FT.com, "Somalia: Prime Minister Admits Disagreements with President, Parliament, 24 September 2001." Reprinted at http://globalarchive.ft.com/globalarchive/articles.html (accessed 11 October 2001).

64 IRIN, "Somalia: Parliament Votes Out Interim Government, 29 October 2001." Reprinted at www.irinnews.org/report.asp (accessed 5 November 2001).

65 Reliefweb, "Report of the Secretary-General on the Situation in Somalia (S/2001/963), 11 October 2001." Reprinted at www.reliefweb.int/w/rw (accessed 16 October 2001).

66 International Committee of the Red Cross, "Annual Report 1999 of the Committee of the Red Cross." Reprinted at www.icrc.org/icrceng.nsf (accessed 4 December 2000).

Resources

Books, Articles, Current Media Reports

Cassanelli, Lee. "Explaining the Somali Crisis." In *The Struggle for Land in Southern Somalia: The War Behind the War.* Edited by Catherine Bestman and Lee V. Cassanelli. London: Haan Associates Publishing, 2000.

Compagnon, Daniel. "Somali Armed Movements. The Interplay of Political Entrepreneurship & Clan-Based Factions." In *African Guerrillas,* edited by Christopher Clapham, 73–90. Oxford: James Currey, 1998.

Doornbos, Martin. "Pasture and Polis: The Roots of Political Marginalization of Somali Pastoralism." In *Conflict and the Decline of Pastoralism in the Horn of Africa,* edited by John Markakis, 100–121. London: Macmillan Press, 1993.

Durch, William J. "Introduction to Anarchy: Humanitarian Intervention and 'State-Building' in Somalia." In *UN Peacekeeping, American Politics, and the Uncivil Wars of the 1990s,* edited by William J. Durch, 311–365. London: Macmillan Press, 1997.

Drysdale, John. *Stoics Without Pillows.* London: Haan Associates Publishing, 2000.

Helander, Bernhard, "Will There be Peace in Somalia Now?" Reprinted at www.somaliawatch.org/archiveoct00/001009401.htm (accessed 12 November 2000).

Lyons, Terrence and Ahmed I. Samatar. *Somalia: State Collapse, Multilateral Intervention, and Strategies for Political Reconstruction.* Washington, DC: The Brookings Institution, 1995.

Makinda, Samuel M. *Seeking Peace from Chaos: Humanitarian Intervention in Somalia.* International Peace Academy occasional paper. London, New York: Lynne Rienner Publishers, 1993.

Mekenkamp, Monique, Paul van Tongeren and Hans van de Veen, eds. *Searching for Peace in Africa: An Overview of Conflict Prevention and Management Activities.* Utrecht: European Platform for Conflict Prevention and Transformation, 1999.

Sahnoun, Mohamed. *Somalia: The Missed Opportunities.* Washington, DC: United States Institute of Peace Press, 1994.

Salah, Idil and Bernard Taylor. "Peace and Development in Northern Somalia: Opportunities and Challenges." Reprinted at www.somaliawatch.org/archive/990908601.htm (accessed 15 November 2000).

Samatar, Ahmed I., ed. *The Somali Challenge: From Catastrophe to Renewal?* London, New York: Lynne Rienner Publishers, 1994.

Woodward, Peter. *The Horn of Africa: State Politics and International Relations.* London, New York: Tauric Academic Studies, 1996.

Websites

Dhambaal, Somali newspaper, e-mail: dhambaal@mail.com; website: www.dhambaal.com

Puntin offers a wide range of historical information as well as news about the latest developments in northern Somalia and especially Puntland: www.puntin.org

Radio Voice of Peace/Somalia: Somali Radio Station: www.afriline.net/innovate.html

Somaliainter is a website offering news, reports and chat opportunities in Somali and English: www.somaliainter.com

Somalianews is a website in English which provides links to human rights reports about

Somalia, local and international newspapers and the latest news about Somalia: www.somalianews.com
Somalinet is Somalia's Internet Gateway – the largest Somalia-related portal: www.somalinet.com
Somalipress provides news in English and Somali: www.somalipress.com

Government, Intergovernmental Bodies and Political Parties

Somaliland.com offers information about the Somaliland government, the Somaliland constitution in Somali and English, Somaliland links and news and newspaper links: http://www.somaliland.com
United Nations Somalia provides news about the latest developments in Somalia and the wider Horn of Africa region, UN comment, online information database, etc.: http://www.unsomalia.org

Local NGOs

Peace and Human Rights Network is a non-clan-based organisation founded at a workshop in February 1997 to analyse the conflict situation, attended by about 20 organisations (among them the Somali Olympic Committee, other NGOs, journalists, teachers, community leaders and ex-militia members). PO Box 71335, Nairobi, Kenya. Tel/Fax: 252 121 5048. E-mail: phrn@compuserve.com
Sanaag Agricultural Development Organisation is based in Djibouti and operates in Somalia. Its main activities are training workshops to provide NGOs in Somalia with skills for handling and understanding conflicts and research, such as trends in pastoral institutions and livelihoods. Contact: Hassan Mohamed Ali, director. PO Box 10012, Djibouti, Djibouti. Tel: 253 340 749. Fax: 253 340 751.
Somalia Peace Line is working in Somalia and throughout the region trying to establish a culture of peace and to achieve the economic, cultural and social reconstruction of Somalia. Its programme includes local and regional mediation activities, research and conflict resolution training for leaders at the grassroots level. Contact: Abdullahi M. Shirwa, deputy chairman. Mogadishu, Somalia – S.B.195 – BC, c/o PO Box 3313, Dubai, United Arab Emirates. Tel: 252 (1) 658 325/ (59) 64 419. Fax: 252 (1) 657 600.
Somaliawatch Organisation focuses on the governance and human rights situation in Somalia: http://www.somaliawatch.org

International NGOs

Action Against Hunger has been working in Somalia since June 1992 and is one of the few humanitarian organisations left in Mogadishu: http://www.aah-usa.org
CARE has programmes (agriculture and food production, disaster and emergency relief, education, landmine awareness, etc.) in Somaliland and Puntland as well as in central and southern Somalia: http://www.care.org
International Committee of the Red Cross is based in Nairobi, Kenya, with expatriates and field officers conducting frequent trips to all parts of Somalia. ICRC's work focuses on an emergency response to the direct effects of conflict combined with natural disasters. It also has a tracing programme, essential for thousands of Somalis still displaced within their homeland or scattered throughout the world: http://www.icrc.org
Save the Children aims to improve education and institute peace and conflict resolution activities: http://www.savethechildren.org

SOMALIA COUNTRY INFORMATION

Geography
Location: Eastern Horn of Africa, bordering the Gulf of Aden and the Indian Ocean, east of Ethiopia.
Cities: *Capital:* Mogadishu. *Other cities:* Hargeysa, Kismaayo, Boosaaso, Baydhabo.

People
Nationality: *Noun:* Somali(s). *Adjective:* Somali.
Population (July 1995 est.): 7 347 554.
Population growth rate (1995 est.): 15.58%.
Ethnic groups: 85% Somali, 15% Bantu and Arabs.
Religion: 99% Muslim.
Languages: Somali (official), Arabic, Italian, English.
Education: *Literacy:* total population that can read and write, 24%; male 36%, female 14%.
Health: *Infant mortality rate:* 119.5/1 000. *Life expectancy:* 56 years. *HIV infection rate:* 0.25%.
Workforce: 2.2 million; very few are skilled workers. Pastoral nomad: 70%. Agriculture, government, trading, fishing, handicrafts, and other: 30%.

Economy
GDP (1985 at current prices): $1.8 billion.
GDP real growth rate: N/A.
Per capita income: N/A.
Inflation rate: N/A.
Natural resources: Undetermined quantities of various minerals, including petroleum.
Agriculture: 55% of GDP at factor cost. *Products:* livestock, bananas, corn, sorghum, sugar. *Arable land:* 13%, of which 1.2% is cultivated.
Industry: 7% of GDP. *Types:* sugar, textiles, packaging, oil refining.
Trade (1985): *Exports:* $110 million: livestock, bananas, hides and skins. *Major markets:* Saudi Arabia, Italy, North Yemen. *Imports:* $470 million: food grains, animal and vegetable oils, petroleum products, transport equipment. *Major suppliers:* Italy, Saudi Arabia, US, France, UK.
Economic aid recipient (1985): $400 million. *Primary donors:* Italy, Saudi Arabia, World Bank, US. *US aid:* $110 million.

Military
Military expenditure: Dollar figures: N/A.
Military expenditure: Percent of GDP: N/A.

Demographic information is drawn from that compiled by the United States Department of State. See http://www.state.gov/r/pa/ei/bgn

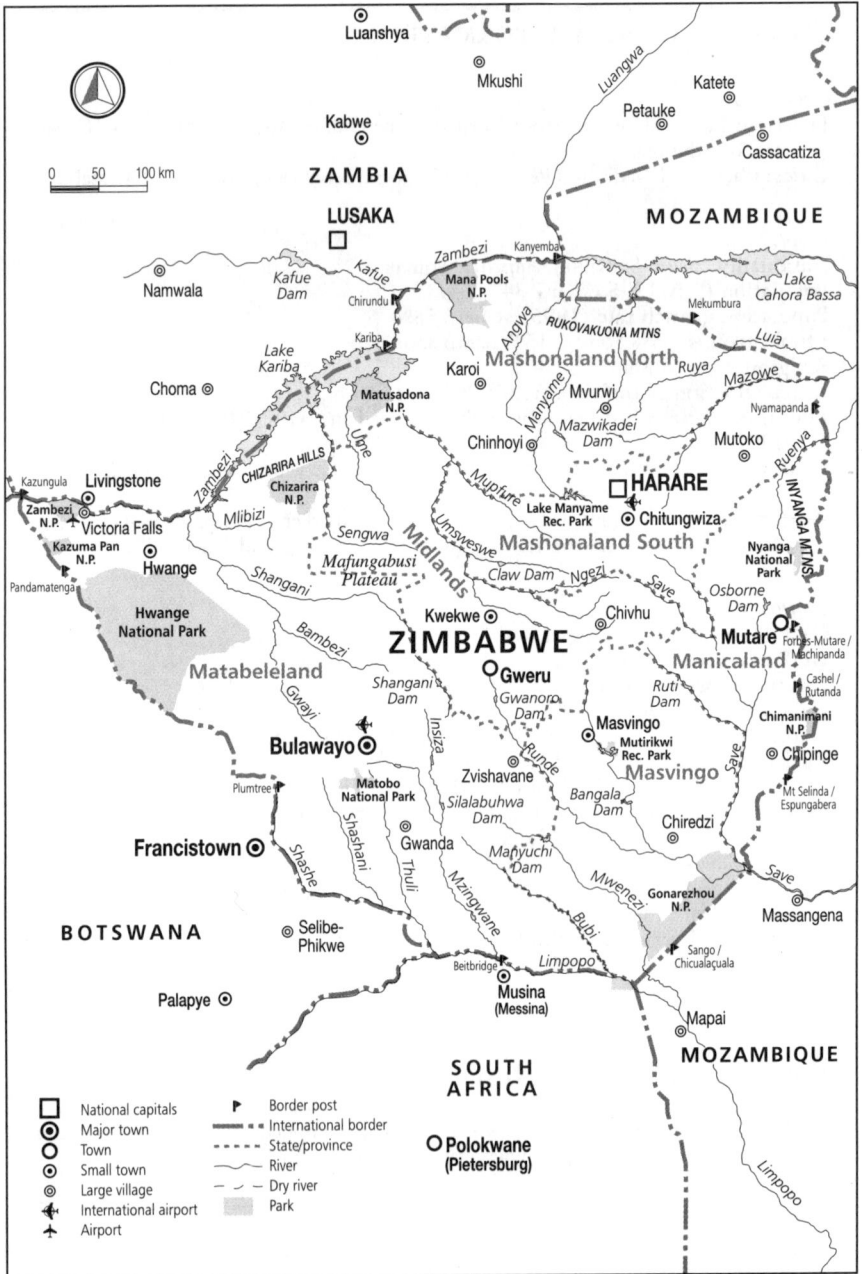

ZAMBIA

Luanshya

Mkushi

Kabwe

Katete

Petauke

Cassacatiza

0   50   100 km

LUSAKA

MOZAMBIQUE

Namwala

Kafue Dam

Kafue

Zambezi

Kanyemba

Mana Pools N.P.

Angwa

Lake Cahora Bassa

Chirundu

Mekumbura

Luia

RUKOVAKUONA MTNS

Choma

Lake Kariba

Kariba

Karoi

Mashonaland North

Ruya

Mazowe

Luangwa

Mvurwi

Matusadona N.P.

Mazwikadei Dam

Mutoko

Nyamapanda

Ruenya

CHIZARIRA HILLS

Chinhoyi

Mupfure

Chizarira N.P.

Kazungula

Livingstone

Zambezi

Mlibizi

Sengwa

Umsweswe

Midlands

Lake Manyame Rec. Park

HARARE

Chitungwiza

INYANGA MTNS

Zambezi N.P.

Victoria Falls

Mashonaland South

Nyanga National Park

Kazuma Pan N.P.

Hwange

Shangani

Mafungabusi Plateau

Claw Dam

Ngezi

Save

Osborne Dam

Pandamatenga

Kwekwe

Chivhu

Mutare

Forbes-Mutare / Machipanda

ZIMBABWE

Hwange National Park

Bambezi

Gweru

Manicaland

Cashel / Rutanda

Matabeleland

Shangani

Shangani Dam

Gwanoro Dam

Ruti Dam

Chimanimani N.P.

Gwayi

Insiza

Masvingo

Chipinge

Bulawayo

Mutirikwi Rec. Park

Mt Selinda / Espungabera

Plumtree

Matobo National Park

Zvishavane

Masvingo

Silalabuhwa Dam

Bangala Dam

Shashani

Gwanda

Runde

Chiredzi

Francistown

Thuli

Manyuchi Dam

Mwenezi

Gonarezhou N.P.

Save

Massangena

Shashe

Selibe-Phikwe

Mzingwane

Bubi

Sango / Chicualacuala

BOTSWANA

Limpopo

Beitbridge

Palapye

Musina (Messina)

Mapai

MOZAMBIQUE

SOUTH AFRICA

Polokwane (Pietersburg)

Limpopo

□	National capitals	▶	Border post
◎	Major town		International border
○	Town		State/province
◉	Small town		River
◎	Large village		Dry river
✈	International airport		Park
✈	Airport		

Chapter 8

Zimbabwe: A Hundred Years War

Tyrone Savage and Shupikayi Blessing Chimhini

The current conflict in Zimbabwe is the product of an incomplete and corrupted transition from colonial rule. In the aftermath of colonial dispossession and a brutal war against the white-minority Rhodesian regime, the establishment of Zimbabwe in 1980 seemed to hold the possibility of breaking with the coercive patterns of the past. Early on, the administration established by Robert Mugabe seemed promising. Educational reform was extremely successful, for example, and the process of integrating the warring armies and factions of the bush war into a national army (ZNA) went ahead uneventfully. Democratic representation formed an integral part of the political processes and Mugabe's rival as leader of the nationalist forces, Joshua Nkomo, was included in the first cabinet. Members of the defeated Rhodesian regime were permitted to retain their seats in parliament, where they participated freely in debates. Splits soon developed, however, leading to the expulsion of Nkomo and his closest aides from the cabinet. Reports emerged of large scale atrocities by government troops against "dissidents" and ex-combatants in Nkomo's home constituency based in the southwest of the country, Matabeleland. Moreover, reform of the country's land policy – a continual flashpoint in Zimbabwe's history – was much slower than initially projected.

The tensions resulting from an inchoate transition to thoroughgoing democracy have become conspicuous in the context of a severe economic crisis. Economic hardship, in turn, has exacerbated political tensions, leading to wide ranging protests, food riots, social unrest, and the emergence of political opposition. In response to this challenge, the Mugabe administration has conspicuously shed its rhetoric of inclusivity and reconciliation, cultivating a militant image that re-evokes its history as a liberation movement. The result has been a drastic erosion of political freedom, human rights and public life in Zimbabwe. Mugabe is patently using the institutions of the state, particularly the armed forces, in an effort to maintain his monopoly on power. Internationally, Zimbabwe is now perceived to be run by an administration that flagrantly flouts the rule of its own law. Within Zimbabwe, a prolific opposition movement has emerged, comprising labour, civil society and church organisations. Mugabe, in turn, has defended his policies as part of an historic struggle against the lingering presence of colonial institutions and contemporary neo-colonial forces.

It was in such conditions that the 2002 presidential elections were held, resulting in Mugabe's fifth term in office. The process was fraught with irregularities, however, producing a widely disputed outcome the social and political impact of which is yet to become fully apparent. What has become evident is a loss of public faith in democratic means of producing change. All this suggests that the conflict in Zimbabwe is reaching a critical mass. Questions about historical justice, economic equity, social reconciliation and accountable governance have become increasingly pressing. Conditions are now urgent for engagement with Zimbabweans about developing the means of translating the present crisis into transitional processes designed around the prospect of social reconciliation and democratic transformation.

In its first section, this profile examines the crisis that has emerged over the past five years. In the hope of discerning the deep-running roots of this crisis, the profile then turns to examine the patterns of conflict that have shaped Zimbabwe's history, noting in particular the role of land. The final sections outline possibilities for sustainable peace-building and reconciliation.

The Face of Conflict

Contemporary Zimbabwe is marked by worsening poverty, internal repression and widening social divisions, exacerbated by the processes and outcomes of the 2002 presidential elections. Relations between government-aligned forces, comprising the ZANU-PF party, the veterans' movement and portions of the Zimbabwean military, and the growing, hastily built coalitions that make up the opposition to Mugabe's regime have become increasingly polarised.[1] The present section charts the course of the crisis, setting it in the context of growing economic hardship. Particular concern is given to the level and scope of violence, the response of government, and the ways in which the crisis has eroded political freedom, human rights and public life in Zimbabwe.

The Zimbabwean economy is currently in a steep decline. It may still worsen. Unemployment, inflation and interest rates are all spiralling upward, prompting one international economist to describe the situation as "pre-revolutionary".[2] In January 1998, protests over worsening poverty deteriorated into food riots. The strife lasted three days, ending only when the army intervened with live ammunition. At least eight people died and dozens were injured. Food protests have recurred since. In October 2000, teargas was dropped on crowds from army helicopters and armoured cars were sent into the townships.[3] In September 2001, the Reserve Bank of Zimbabwe (RBZ) indicated that the country's economy was in a "downward spiral" and would probably shrink by around 8% that year. Sydney Mabika, an economist and assistant director at the RBZ, said initial forecasts of a 2.8% contraction for the year had been revised downward because of the knock taken by the country's agricultural sector.[4]

President Mugabe claims that Zimbabwe's economic situation owes much to the stranglehold that whites continue to exert on the Zimbabwean economy, particularly in the agricultural sector. He also points to the neo-colonial demands of the International Monetary Fund (IMF) and the World Bank. Attempting to consolidate the social gains made possible by liberation from white rule, in the early years of independence the Mugabe administration incurred loans that soon spiralled. Within four years, Zimbabwe's debt servicing consumed 37% of export earnings. Arrears on debt servicing are currently in the vicinity of US$1 billion, on a debt of US$4.5 billion.[5] According to Mugabe, the structural adjustments imposed by creditors are responsible for the hardships that currently engulf the country. Mugabe no longer has a working relationship with the IMF and the World Bank. In late 1999, the Bretton Woods institutions suspended their loans of US$193 million and US$140 million respectively after an incident in which Mugabe told IMF officials to "shut up" when they questioned Zimbabwe's engagement in the Congo. International support has since shrunk drastically. Mugabe's detractors span a broad range. International economists argue that the constraints imposed by the lending institutions are merely conditions Zimbabwe agreed to when accepting the loans. Most Western donors have frozen all aid. Disgruntled Zimbabweans from various sectors – opposition members, NGO workers, tobacco farmers – continue to voice their frustration over growing economic hardships, flagrant corruption in government and Zimbabwe's costly involvement in the war in the Democratic Republic of the Congo (DRC).

The Zimbabwean economy is in a dire condition, having tumbled into near freefall, with the price of basic foodstuffs beyond reach for many Zimbabweans. Poverty is now rampant. Reports are emerging that Zimbabwe may soon face starvation on a vast scale. A study compiled by experts from the World Food Programme (WFP), the Food and Agricultural Organisation (FAO) and the Southern African Development

Community's (SADC) early warning unit estimated that Zimbabwe's farming industry would face a 600 000 ton deficit of maize, its staple crop, in late 2002 and 2003 – fully a third of the country's annual needs. Similarly, wheat output is expected to be down by over 200 000 tons, almost half of Zimbabwe's needs. Imports are unaffordable, given the lack of foreign currency.[6]

The economic conflict has precipitated a crisis of governance. The Mugabe administration's legitimacy draws heavily on its role in the struggle for liberation from white rule. The possibilities at independence have not yet been realised in the form of a social order grounded in democratically accountable governance. On the contrary, whereas Zimbabwe enjoyed a measure of checks and balances in the first years of independence through a Westminster type of government, by 1987 a de facto one-party state was instituted. In 1985 and 1987 the Supreme Court held that the courts were competent to look into the exercise of presidential prerogatives.[7] The response by government was swift. Parliament, which had only three opposition members, rubber-stamped Amendment No. 7 to the constitution, declaring that the exercise of presidential prerogatives could not be challenged in court. This, and the gamut of constitutional amendments that followed, posed a clear affront to the democratic principles of checks and balances, giving the president vast powers – including the means of subverting mechanisms meant to curtail the excessive use of presidential powers. Given the overwhelming majority of ZANU-PF in parliament and the right of the executive president to hire and fire ministers at whim, parliament was reduced to a rubber stamp for executive decisions. In the unlikely event that the parliament moved a motion to impeach the president, the president could simply dissolve the parliament. If faced with severe and acute opposition, the president could declare a state of emergency and rule by decree without the inconvenience of having to give effect to the bill of rights. In addition to this, a number of draconian pieces of legislation inherited from the Smith regime had been kept on the statute books. One notable act was the Law and Order Maintenance Act, which allowed for detention without trial.

In this context, the state emerged as the centre of patronage politics, such that, until the recent crisis, proximity to those with access to state power was the main goal of political activity. In consequence, protest against economic hardship has readily translated into protest against government. In 1996, a wave of strikes ran through virtually every sector of the economy. One of the chief beneficiaries of government's patronage, the civil service, held firm in their demands and were eventually awarded wage increases of 35%. This victory set a precedent for popular protest in everyday political life in Zimbabwe. The most significant actors in these early protests were the veterans of Zimbabwe's *Second Chimurenga*, the war of liberation from the white Rhodesian regime. Since early 2000, the veterans have become a conspicuous and staunch ally of the Mugabe administration, which in turn has supported their campaign to evict white commercial farmers. Yet the present alliance is the product of compromises developed amid protests initially directed against Mugabe himself. In March 1997, a series of revelations emerged about fraudulent claims on the War Victims' Compensation Fund, in response to which the government abruptly and unilaterally suspended payments. The ensuing investigations revealed that many of the culprits were highly placed members of the government and ZANU-PF party, and that the amount plundered over a mere eight months was close on Z$450 million. Though the government had frequently pleaded lack of resources as the explanation for its failure to address pressing domestic needs, it was now perceived as having satisfied the material wants of its own leaders and their cohorts at the expense of Zimbabwe's veterans. Veterans protested that their welfare and public dignity had been undermined and demanded the reinstatement of the fund.

The veterans' protests had enormous symbolic significance. Though the fund was hastily reinstated on a case-by-case basis, Mugabe refused to meet the representatives of the veterans. Demonstrations for meaningful compensation turned violent. Veteran leaders abused Mugabe's representatives, marched on the president's residence, and, on Zimbabwe's most solemn public occasion, the Heroes' Day Commemoration (11 August), heckled and booed the president. On 21 August, veterans' representatives finally succeeded in gaining an audience with Mugabe. The outcome was a concession that each war veteran should receive Z$50 000 and a tax-free monthly pension of Z$2 000. As matters progressed, moreover, it became apparent that estimates of the number of former combatants had erred and that, instead of 32 000, the number of claimants would be twice that, a number that would rise as former detainees and auxiliaries came to press their cases. The total amount of unbudgeted funds required by the end of the year was in the vicinity of Z$5.3 billion. Eventually, Finance Minister Herbert Murerwa indicated that he would achieve savings in the published budget by reducing certain welfare expenditures, improving tax collection and borrowing Z$2 billion from domestic sources. By the end of September, the Zimbabwe dollar had begun a steep decline. In October, the World Bank announced the suspension of US$62.5 million in balance of payments support pending an explanation from the Zimbabwe government as to how it intended to fund the veterans' payouts. Similarly, the IMF insisted that the government raise additional taxes to pay the war veterans' gratuities. *Africa Confidential* commented at the time:

> War veterans are proving the most potent political and financial force in Zimbabwe this year. Their success, after one of the most strident campaigns since Independence, in negotiating compensation packages of Z$50,000 (US$ 3–4,000) each has brought into question the government's ability to finance its 18-month budget reduction programme.[8]

By instituting payouts, Mugabe won over the war veterans. The cost, however, was a significant worsening of the economic crisis. In the same month as the veterans' payouts, September 1997, Robert Mugabe made an executive decision to dispatch Zimbabwean forces to help defend the Congolese capital, Kinshasa. The city – and with it, the rule of President Laurent Kabila – looked to be within days of falling to Rwandan, Ugandan and Congolese troops. Kabila showed his gratitude by awarding what appeared to be lucrative business concessions to Zimbabwe, including diamonds and land – deals which have produced little or nothing in the way of benefits for the general population. Moreover, the excursion began an intervention with huge, growing costs: over 11 000 troops (a quarter of the Zimbabwean army) are now engaged in a complex and apparently unwinnable war. Even by government accounts, Zimbabwe's involvement cost over US$200 million in the first two years alone, large scale casualties in take-no-prisoner skirmishes have been substantial, and Mugabe has found his popularity at home deeply undermined. *Africa Confidential* describes the dilemmas the engagement has posed as follows:

> The economic cost of Zimbabwe's military involvement, with no immediate return, is a load which donors do not wish to lighten. And the human cost, in troops lost and resources diverted, is fertile ground for the political opposition. However, Mugabe is by no means free to drop the whole misconceived adventure. He himself, with a group of intimate supporters, would be the main beneficiary if things turned out as he hoped. Bringing home the troops would itself be risky. Although the figures are secret, it is widely believed that more than 200 Zimbabwean soldiers have been killed or wounded in Congo; if

the sacrifice turned out to be in vain, there is a real risk that the returning troops would join up with Mugabe's other critics.[9]

The gains from Zimbabwean engagement in the war have mostly taken the form of mining concessions to several private companies controlled by government ministers and military officers. To date, Zimbabwe's efforts in the Democratic Republic of the Congo have yielded little besides lucrative pickings for those officers running their own informal diamond mining operations in Congo's alluvial areas, most notably the Kasaï diamond fields.[10]

By late 1997, Zimbabweans were confronted with worsening economic hardships, discontent about state patronage, and embroilment in a costly, possibly unwinnable war abroad. In response, numerous groups from civil society, including NGOs, church groups and labour unions, began campaigning for constitutional reform that would reduce the power of the presidency and promote democratic accountability. The coalition named itself the National Constitutional Assembly (NCA). In reply, Mugabe established and appointed the Constitutional Commission to conduct a review and prepare a new draft constitution to be submitted to a national referendum. The NCA was openly critical of the Constitutional Commission, however, asserting that it was government-controlled and that its work could not reflect the will of the public. Moreover, the NCA conducted workshops around the country aimed at developing public awareness of constitutional reform. On 12–13 February 2000, a national referendum was held on a draft constitution that would maintain a strong presidency and moreover would risk reducing the independence of the judiciary. Though turnout was small, 55.9% of the votes cast were "against". The event handed Mugabe his first significant electoral defeat.[11] Its political significance was huge. The 1990 elections had resulted in an overwhelming victory for Mugabe and his party. Voter turnout, however, was only 54% and reports did emerge that the campaign was not free and fair. Mugabe won re-election in March 1996, receiving 93% of votes cast. However, less than one-third of eligible persons voted and his two main opponents withdrew from the race, alleging intimidation and harassment of their supporters. With the defeat of Mugabe in the constitutional referendum, there appeared the possibility to effect change through the polls.

In response to the growing crises, the Zimbabwe Council of Trade Unions (ZCTU) mounted protests against tax increases and levies designed to pay the war veterans' bill. These were partially successful and government was forced to rescind certain measures. Attention then shifted to the price of basic goods, many of which had increased by about 50% at a time when many Zimbabweans had seen their real earnings decline by 60% since 1991. From 19–21 January 1998, Harare and its townships saw food riots on a scale unprecedented in Zimbabwe. In February, the ZCTU mounted a national stay-away to protest tax increases. The unions also demanded a long-term solution to the problem of repeated increases in the price of basic foodstuffs, some of which had increased by as much as 70% over the previous three months. This season of protests drew widespread support for the union: amid serious and prolonged economic decline, the ZCTU gained significant political clout at the forefront of an energised labour movement. In September 1999, six months before the scheduled parliamentary elections, the ZCTU labour federation launched a new political party, the Movement for Democratic Change (MDC), appointing a former union leader, Morgan Tsvangirai, as its leader.

The 2000 elections saw the Mugabe regime subjected to unprecedented challenge from the MDC, which swept the urban vote and won 57 of the 120 contested seats. The elections were marred by violence, however. Zimbabwe's Human Rights NGO Forum's Political Violence Monitoring Project issued a report indicating that, in the run-up to the parliamentary elections, 13 000 people were affected by political violence. In all, more than 2 000 were assaulted and over 40 were killed. ZANU-PF militias were reportedly responsible for 93% of the violence. The opposition MDC has always claimed that it was this violence which enabled President Mugabe's ZANU-PF party to win, and accordingly, brought a legal challenge against 38 specific election contests. In December, Robert Mugabe issued a decree banning these challenges, but the Supreme Court ruled that losing candidates had a constitutional right to go to court if they were dissatisfied with the way the elections were conducted. Given the patterns of state-sponsored violence already evident, it has, predictably, been in these legally-disputed constituencies that disappearances, torture and summary executions have been evident. Moreover, in October 2000, all politically-motivated crimes committed in the run-up to the parliamentary elections were given indemnity in terms of a presidential amnesty.[12]

The conflict over land is central to both the economic crisis and the crisis of governance in Zimbabwe. Throughout its history, the country's political economy as well as conflicts around it have centred on ownership of the land. For now, it is important to note the re-emergence of the land question in the present crisis. In the aftermath of the referendum defeat, Mugabe resuscitated the land reform and redistribution issue, amending the existing constitution to allow the state to acquire commercial farms without compensation. Mugabe announced that if dispossessed white farmers were to be compensated, it would be up to Britain to provide the compensation, since the land had originally been seized from indigenous Africans by white settlers. International response was predictably unsympathetic. The British government immediately indicated that it would not be party to land expropriation and would not offer assistance for any land reform and resettlement programme that failed to address the needs of the landless poor. It pointed out that the resettlement programme Zimbabwe launched at independence had still failed to resettle more than 60 000 out of the original target of 152 000 and that the state had consistently underestimated the difficulties of resettling landless peasants and subsistence farmers on commercial or undeveloped farmland. As a consequence, much of the land already acquired by the Zimbabwean government was either lying fallow, had reverted to bush or had been overrun by squatters. Moreover, without technical assistance for new farmers, Zimbabwe's existing agricultural sector risked being significantly undermined, and food production, therefore, could be expected to plummet. The Commercial Farmers Union (CFU) calculated that the expropriation of these farms would reduce overall farm production from Z$14 billion to Z$8.3 billion. The Mugabe administration, on the other hand, has consistently refused to engage in such debate, arguing instead that the real agenda of the British is to protect the neo-colonialist agenda of expatriate agrobusiness.[13] The ensuing conflict has seen numerous violent invasions by actual veterans and many jobless, disenchanted urban youths.[14]

On 17 March 2000 the CFU, exercising their right to protection of the law under the constitution, obtained a High Court order declaring the invasions to be illegal. The police were ordered to evict the unlawful occupiers within 24 hours. To demonstrate the fact that the occupations were unlawful, the judge who made the order secured the consent of all the parties, including the police and the war veterans' leader. By December, however, the invaders had become even more brazen, with their leader quoted publicly as declaring that they were now fighting for land ". . . and whosoever is killed, it's tough luck". This proved to be no empty threat. Declaring that they would not obey any court order barring them from unlawfully occupying private property, the activities of the "war veterans" intensified. The police apparently made no attempt to comply with the order, arguing that it would be impossible, dangerous and counterproductive to do so. It is widely accepted that the acquiescence of the state made this possible.

The case was heard in Zimbabwe's High Court, where the judge noted that the invasions were of a violent and riotous nature, and directed that the Commissioner of Police had a clear duty to enforce the law and to afford the white commercial farmers the protection of the law enshrined in the constitution. Even after this judgment, however, which made clear the legal position regarding the invasions, the police evidently took no action to evict the occupiers and the invasions continued. The situation continued to deteriorate, and, in September 2000, the CFU challenged the legality of the land redistribution programme in the Supreme Court. There, the farmers argued on constitutional grounds in that the programme was politically and racially discriminatory. Moreover, the respondents, the Minister of Agriculture and the provincial governors, conceded that they had failed to comply with required procedures, prompting the court to observe that, although the land issue was a political matter, the political method of resolving the dispute was by enacting and complying with laws. The court went as far as stating that the government appeared "unwilling to carry out a sustainable land reform in terms of its own law". Moreover, the court observed, "a network of organisations, operating with complete disregard for the law, has been allowed to take over from government. War veterans, villagers and unemployed townspeople have simply moved onto farms. They have been supported, encouraged, transported and financed by party officials, public servants, the Central Intelligence Organisation and the Army. The rule of law has been overthrown in the commercial farming areas and farmers and farm workers on occupied farms had consistently been deprived of the protection of the law."

The decision by the Supreme Court was ominous, setting the judiciary and the executive in direct confrontation, with Mugabe declaring that the judiciary had no right to oppose the presidency. Similarly, when Mark Chavunduka, editor of the newspaper *The Standard*, and a senior reporter, Ray Choto, were apprehended and tortured in military detention, the High Court intervened and ordered their release on three separate occasions, pointing out that, under Zimbabwean law, the military has no powers to arrest or detain civilians. Defence Ministry officials ignored the rulings, however. The judges then asked Mugabe to reaffirm his commitment to the rule of law. His reply was that they should resign and that judges had no right to give instructions to the president. Mugabe has since replaced the country's Chief Justice, Anthony Gubbay, with Godfrey Chidyausiku, a strong supporter of the president.[15] Such incidents have prompted a perception, both locally and internationally, that Zimbabwe is governed by a regime that considers itself above its own laws.

As a result, relations between government, on the one side, and on the other, the international humanitarian community, select domestic institutions, local civil society and various sectors of the population, have become polarised. This deterioration in relations has been accompanied by a wave of violence. Local NGOs consistently report that since the government's loss in the constitutional referendum, intimidation by youth militias closely linked to ZANU-PF has proliferated in urban areas (against anti-government demonstrators, opposition members and civil rights activists) as well as in rural areas (against white farmers). Reports have emerged of attacks on opposition figures by shadowy urban militias in Harare's townships and by militias in military-style camps in the rural areas. Reports of government officials using harassment and torture for political ends have become commonplace. Labour rights, including freedom of association and the right to strike, have been systematically violated. Labour leaders have become the targets of severe police beatings. Foreign journalists have been expelled and local journalists detained and tortured. Supreme Court judges have been warned that their safety could not be assured if they chose to rule against presidential directives. NGO workers have been harassed and killed, as have opposition political candidates and their supporters.

It was in such conditions that the 2002 presidential elections were held. Mugabe set the tone for the presidential elections when, at the ZANU-PF congress in December 2001, he told party members to treat the following year's election campaign as "total war". He called on party members to regard themselves as soldiers. "Where we are going, it is not like the June 2000 parliamentary elections, which was like a football game where I was centre striker. This is total war, the *Third Chimurenga*." Disorder and violence increased in the months that followed. According to the Human Rights NGO Forum, at least 16 politically motivated murders were reported in January and February 2002. Ruling-party militias set up roadblocks in rural areas throughout the country, harassing travellers who were unable to produce party membership cards. Teachers were attacked, leading to the closing of 35 schools in Masvingo Province alone. In Bindura, opposition supporters were evicted from their homes by ZANU-PF militants, who then utilised the homes as bases for their own political activities. Over a million people were compelled to buy ZANU-PF party cards to avoid being beaten up for failing to produce one. Large parts of the country were declared "no-go" areas for MDC supporters. Militia bases were established in the run-up to the poll and remained operational with the acquiescence of the state. Nothing was done to ensure that these bases were dismantled and prosecutions were not instituted against those responsible for human rights violations committed in them.

The election itself failed to meet the requirements of international electoral norms or Zimbabwe's Constitution, which requires that Zimbabwe's president be chosen by the registered voters, according to procedures prescribed in an Act of Parliament. The elections were, however, marked by executive interference that left hundreds of thousands of registered voters stripped of their right to vote. Registered voters not residing in their constituency, for example, those from rural areas working in the cities as well as those residing outside the country, lost their right to vote. The only exceptions were armed forces, diplomats and polling officials. The number of polling stations in opposition strongholds was reduced drastically, resulting in long queues and the turning away, eventually, of thousands of voters. Mugabe personally ordered the wooden ballot boxes to only be sealed at the aperture on top, and not on the base, sides or hinges, despite a parliamentary vote against the changing of this law. In the lead-in to the elections, the heads of the security forces made it clear they would not accept the opposition candidate if he won the election; they then chose officers to help run the elections. The voters' roll was kept secret and often caused confusion, and counting was done in secret. Ultimately, there were indications of vote rigging on a large scale.

In such conditions, Robert Mugabe won his fifth term in office. The impact of the widely disputed process is yet to become apparent. What is evident, in addition to the growing economic crisis, is a pervasive gloom in Zimbabwean civil society resulting from a loss of faith in democratic processes and, in consequence, a lack of options. In short, the conflict in Zimbabwe is rapidly reaching a critical mass. Poverty is prolific and questions both about historical justice and democratically accountable governance have become pressing. Conditions are now urgent for engagement with Zimbabweans about developing the means of translating the present crisis into transitional processes designed around the prospect of social reconciliation, justice and the welfare of all Zimbabweans. Any thoroughgoing solution will, however, necessarily situate the present crisis within the patterns of conflict that have given shape to Zimbabwe's history. In particular, it may be useful to unpack the historical pattern of coercive rule around the country's land-based political economy.

The Historical Roots of Violence and Division

The divisions that mark the present conflict in Zimbabwe follow from a history of coercive governance and inequitable management of the country's land-based political economy. This section charts the trajectory of this struggle through successive governments – from the various mutations of colonial rule through to independent Zimbabwe – and highlights the racialised distribution of land resources in a country in which the bulk of the population is rural and well over 90% indigenous African.

Prior to colonial invasion, the population of present-day Zimbabwe comprised several ethnic groups, among them the Mashona (Shona speakers), who constitute about 75% of the population and have lived in the area the longest, and the Matabele (Sindebele speakers), a Zulu offshoot representing about 20% of the population and who are centred in the southwest around Bulawayo. In 1888, Cecil John Rhodes obtained a concession for mineral rights from local chiefs, enabling the British to proclaim a "sphere of influence" in the area it would name Southern and Northern Rhodesia. In 1890, the Pioneer column of colonists arrived, comprising 196 Pioneers and 500 police. At this time, there were approximately 700 000 Africans, mainly Shona and Sindebele speakers, in the territory. The British South African Company (BSAC), which had instigated the trek and was desperate for tangible results, was pressured by the would-be miners for compensation in the form of large grants of land that the company had no real authority to give. By 1893, the BSAC was already settling Pioneers on large tracts of land, without any obligation to actually do anything except make an annual payment of £1 "quit rent" per farm. Civilians followed the Pioneers and were given grants of 2 500 hectares under the Victoria agreement. This "land grab" precipitated a number of conflicts between settlers and locals, culminating in the Anglo-Ndebele war of 1893 which led to the removal and eventual destruction of the Ndebele monarchy. In 1895, the territory was formally named Rhodesia, and placed under the British South Africa Company's administration, an event which precipitated the *First Chimurenga* (war of liberation) of 1896 and 1897. It proved to be a vicious war, claiming 8 000 lives in 18 months. In its aftermath, the settlers created a colonial state, institutionalising a system of racialised land distribution that successive governments were to grapple with and which holds the roots of the present conflict. In 1899, the colonial administration indicated that it would "assign to the natives land sufficient for their occupation, whether as tribes or portions of tribes, and suitable for agriculture and pastoral requirement".[16] This was euphemism. The policy allowed the forcible resettling of defeated Africans in "reserves". By 1905, under this new land allocation policy, there were about 60 Native Reserves, occupying about 22% of Rhodesia. Nearly half of the African population of 700 000 now lived in reserves. By 1920, the Native Reserves constituted an area of 8.7 million hectares, while the number of white farms encompassed approximately 15 million hectares.[17]

Following the termination of the British South Africa Company's charter in 1923, Southern Rhodesia's white settlers were given the choice of being incorporated into the Union of South Africa or becoming a separate entity within the British Empire. The settlers rejected incorporation, and Southern Rhodesia was formally annexed by the United Kingdom. It became a self-governing colony with its own legislature, civil service, armed forces and police. As European immigrants sought to exploit the country's agricultural potential, their demand for more land led to the first of a series of racially-based land redistribution acts. These acts were designed to entrench the settler agricultural system and showed little grasp of demographic needs. Rather, the codification of the racial division of land, most notably through the Land Apportionment Act (LAA) of 1931, was an attempt to safeguard the interests of the single most powerful political constituency in the country, the white settler farming community.

The racial bias of state-imposed land allocation policies was one source of conflict. A second source of conflict was demography. In 1890, the African population in Rhodesia numbered about 700 000 in an area of 150 000 km.[18] By 1910, the African population of approximately 900 000 were restricted to Native Reserves comprising 70 000 km (or 8.7 million hectares). By contrast, the settlers, numbering about 20 000, occupied 60 000 km (6 million hectares) of prime farming land.[19] By 1930, the rural African population had grown to about 1.3 million. The effects of crowding in the Native Reserves were becoming evident, as conflicts erupted between the administration and peasants, between settlers and African farmers, and also between and among families, chiefs and headmen over rights to allocate, use and retain land. By 1945, the African population had increased to 4 million (with 2.8 million in the rural areas). The period 1935 to 1955 saw the forcible removal of 67 000 African families from their traditional lands into new Native Reserves to make way for white-owned farms.[20] Many displaced, dispossessed Africans now became farm-workers, only to find that, by living in farm compounds, they had apparently placed themselves outside the scope of traditional authorities for protection or redress. The outcome was a national legacy of abuse of African farm-workers by settlers.

In September 1953, Southern Rhodesia joined with the British protectorate of Northern Rhodesia and Nyasaland to form the Central African Federation. An effort to pool resources and markets, the federation flourished economically, but was opposed by the African population who feared they would not be able to achieve self-government with the federal structure dominated by white Southern Rhodesians. The federation was dissolved in 1963 and the following year, Northern Rhodesia and Nyasaland became the independent states of Zambia and Malawi. The white electorate in Southern Rhodesia, however, showed little willingness to accede to African demands for increased political participation. In 1963, the hardline conservative party of the settlers, the Rhodesia Front (RF), took office. Basing his campaign on a platform of rapid independence from the United Kingdom, Prime Minister Ian Smith led the RF to an overwhelming victory in the 1965 elections, winning all 50 of the first roll seats. On 11 November 1965, after lengthy and unsuccessful negotiations with the British government, Rhodesia issued a Unilateral Declaration of Independence (UDI) from the United Kingdom.

Though the British government considered the UDI unconstitutional and illegal, it nevertheless indicated that it would not use force to quell the rebellion. Instead, Britain imposed sanctions on Rhodesia and requested other nations to do the same. On 12 November 1965, the United Nations determined that the Rhodesian government and UDI were illegal and called on member states to refrain from assisting or recognising the Smith regime. On 16 December 1966, for the first time in its history, the UN Security Council imposed mandatory economic sanctions on a state. Shipments of arms, aircraft, motor vehicles, petroleum and petroleum products to Rhodesia were proscribed. On 29 May 1968, the Security Council unanimously voted to broaden the sanctions by imposing a total embargo on virtually all commercial relations with Rhodesia.

In response to the imposition of sanctions, the Rhodesian regime sought self-sufficiency in food production and raw materials. Accordingly, it encouraged white farmers to diversify production, in particular promoting maize, cattle and cotton. At the outbreak of war in the early 1970s, racial preferencing in agricultural policy was such that annual subsidies and loans averaged about R$8 000 per white farmer – and less than a single dollar per African farmer. Accordingly, white commercial agriculture increased its share of production from about 30% in the early 1960s to 75% in 1979.[21] In 1969, the Rhodesian government passed the Land Tenure Act (No. 55). Its primary aim was to update the LAA by imposing even more rigid regulations. Rhodesia was redivided into African and white settler areas. The latter were protected by a number of constitutional safeguards.[22] The development of these land policies was also supported by numerous repressive security laws, including the Law and Order (Maintenance) Act (1960) and the Emergency Powers Act (1960), each of which permitted the Rhodesian Security Forces (RSF) to carry out violent reprisals against guerrillas and civilians with impunity.

The *Second Chimurenga* began in the early 1960s as a largely urban protest against an increasingly repressive state. The Rhodesian Police responded aggressively, jailing hundreds. This repression, in turn, radicalised African nationalists, who began to consider armed resistance. During the *Second Chimurenga*, violence reached a peak. An estimated 50 000 people of all races (but mainly Africans) died in the war, with countless others injured.[23] The bulk of casualties occurred in the rural areas, most of which were operational sectors. The distinguishing feature of this conflict was the systematic and often arbitrary use of violence. Such violence took the form of whippings, beatings, torture and murder. The violence was mainly perpetrated upon civilians by RSF, police and the guerrillas. As the situation worsened, the RSF increasingly targeted civilians for torture and murder. The Rhodesian tactical doctrine called for a "body count" approach, in which success was measured by the number of enemy killed in battle. As guerrilla infiltration multiplied, state legislation and the size of the RSF increased. State control of the rural areas became increasingly problematical. "Protected villages" were established to monitor the peasants and prevent contact with the guerrillas. The entire country virtually became an operational zone, as order was enforced through violence and land became one of the rallying points of peasant conscientisation.

In the early 1970s, informal attempts at settlement were renewed between the United Kingdom and the Rhodesian administration. Following the April 1974 coup in Portugal and the resulting shifts of power in Mozambique and Angola, pressure on the Smith regime to negotiate a peaceful settlement began to increase. In addition, the sporadic anti-government guerrilla activity which had begun in the late 1960s intensified and became widespread after 1972. In 1974, the major African nationalist groups – the Zimbabwe African Peoples' Union (ZAPU) and the Zimbabwe African National Union (ZANU), which split away from ZAPU in 1963 – gathered their military forces under the rubric of the "Patriotic Front (PF)". In 1976, as the war worsened, the Smith government agreed in principle to majority rule and a meeting in Geneva with black nationalist leaders to negotiate a final settlement of the conflict. Blacks represented at the Geneva meeting included ZAPU leader Joshua Nkomo, ZANU leader Robert Mugabe, UANC Chairman Bishop Abel Muzorewa and former ZANU leader Rev. Ndabaningi Sithole. The meeting failed to find a basis for agreement, largely as a result of Rhodesian intransigence.

In May 1979, the British began a new round of consultations that culminated in deliberations on a settlement at Lancaster House in London.
On 12 December 1979, in preparation for the transition, British
Governor Lord Christopher Soames arrived in Salisbury. His arrival
signalled the end of the Rhodesian rebellion and the beginning of
Zimbabwe's independence. Several months of negotiations produced an
agreement that called for a cease-fire, a transition period under British rule
leading to full independence, new elections and a new constitution that
allowed majority rule while protecting minority rights. The UN Security
Council endorsed the settlement agreement and voted unanimously to call
on member nations to remove sanctions. During the transition period,
numerous political parties campaigned for the 27–29 February pre-
independence elections. Amid a mix of conciliatory and intimidatory
rhetoric, Robert Mugabe's ZANU-PF party won and set about forming
Zimbabwe's first government. Zimbabwe gained its independence on
18 April 1980.

The new government, anxious to attract foreign investment, articulated
a policy of reconciliation and declared that white farmers were a welcome
and integral part of the new Zimbabwe. The reconciliation policy was
generally successful during the country's first two years of independence,
as former political and military opponents began to work together. The
integration of Zimbabwe's then three armed forces – the existing
Rhodesian forces combined with the two guerrilla armies – went through
relatively uneventfully. Smith and many of his associates held seats in the
parliament where they participated freely in debates. Likewise, Joshua
Nkomo, Mugabe's rival as leader of the nationalist forces, was included in
the first cabinet along with several other members of PF-ZAPU.

Old rivalries soon re-emerged, however, leading to the expulsion of
Nkomo and his closest aides from the cabinet. Moreover, reports began to
emerge of atrocities in Nkomo's constituency, Matabeleland. During this
"dissident" war, government forces led by the Fifth Brigade committed
serious atrocities. In 1983–84, the government declared a curfew in areas
of Matabeleland and sent in the army to suppress dissidents. Credible
reports surfaced of widespread violence and disregard for human rights by
the security forces during these operations. Political tension rose in the
country as a result. This war, initially against ex-combatants, had by the
mid-1980s widened in scope to include traumatised peasants and jobless
youths. By the time of the Unity Accord in 1987, an estimated 6 000 rural
people in Matebeleland had became casualties in a war that represented
both a perpetuation of the ethnic and ideological conflict between ZAPU

and ZANU in independent Zimbabwe as well as a clamouring over resources.

At the Lancaster House Conference in 1979, it was agreed that the new constitution would remain inviolate for at least 10 years and that the property rights of commercial farmers would be protected. At independence, agriculture in Zimbabwe comprised three distinct sub-sectors: large-scale commercial farming, comprising 6 000 white farmers in possession of 46% of all arable land, most of it in the high rainfall regions with the greatest potential for agricultural production; small-scale commercial farming, comprising 8 500 African farmers in possession of 4.2% of all arable land, most of it in the drier, less productive regions; communal farming, comprising 4.3 million people occupying 49.3% of all arable land, three-quarters of it in drier, less productive regions. In this context, land redistribution proceeded under experimental models on land that the government had purchased at market rates from willing sellers. During the 1980s, however, the parameters of the land crisis widened considerably as government took on the problem of resettling thousands of displaced people. Resettlement had become an integral part of the land allocation problem. The government's plan was to resettle 18 000 families on about 1.2 million hectares of land that had been abandoned during the war. In 1982, however, the number targeted for resettlement was raised to 162 000 families on 10 million hectares. By 1990, the government had acquired 3.5 million hectares presumably for this purpose.[24] However, only 19% of the land acquired was prime land. The demographics were also unsettling. The population was growing rapidly, while poverty rose in the rural areas as a result of drought, fewer jobs on farms, low yields, lower prices for products, transport problems, lack of funds for equipment, infrastructure and security of tenure. Government, under pressure from its rural constituency, pushed through the Land Acquisition Act (1992), entitling the government to designate commercial farms for resettlement. Under the terms of the Act, the government gave notice that it would be acquiring mainly white-owned, commercial farms for redistribution purposes.

After almost 20 years of independence, the pace of land redistribution had been significantly slower than envisaged. In September 1998, the government convened an International Donors' Conference on Land Reform and Resettlement to mobilise financial resources for the resettlement programme. At the event, Mugabe set out a procedure that entailed "orderly" resettlement without lawlessness or environmental destruction. The donors committed to supporting an Inception Phase to be implemented over a period of 24 months. The initial phase was never implemented, however.

Government blamed donors for not keeping their promises, and donors blamed the government for not having even established a task force.

It has been against this historical backdrop, beginning from the racially skewed, demographically impractical land allocation policies of the early colonial government, that the present-day conflict over land in Zimbabwe has emerged. It was such disparities, reiterated through various stages of Zimbabwe's transition, that produced the conditions for the current land conflicts among Africans and white farmers. This crisis in turn has made manifest the tensions resulting from an inchoate transition to thorough-going democracy. In seeking to secure the cornerpiece of the Zimbabwean political economy – land – the Mugabe administration has conspicuously shed its earlier policies of inclusivity and reconciliation. The outcome has been a drastic erosion of political freedom, human rights and public life in Zimbabwe. Questions about historical justice, economic equity, social reconciliation and democratically accountable governance have become increasingly pressing, along with questions about the processes by which these questions should be addressed. Conditions are therefore fertile for discussion about the process of change in Zimbabwe and ways of trans-lating the present crisis into transitional processes designed around the prospect of social reconciliation and justice.

Prospects for Peace-building

The current crisis is evident on at least three levels: economics, gover-nance and land policy. Resolution of the land question is indispensable if a sustainable peace is to be established in Zimbabwe. As we have observed, throughout Zimbabwe's history, land has been a primary fault-line. It is the flashpoint for conflict in the present crisis. Sam Moyo, Director of the Southern African Regional Institute for Policy Studies, views the current difficulties as the result of the arrangements developed in the transitional negotiations that took place at Lancaster House. The agreements that emerged entailed a shared commitment by the Zimbabwean and British governments to provide matching funds for land acquisition. The turning point came in the early 1990s. As severe eco-nomic hardship took hold, the Zimbabwean leadership began to question the terms of this arrangement, arguing that paying for land returned to those disposed by colonialism should not be Zimbabwe's responsibility. The Zimbabweans went further, questioning Britain's right to place con-ditions on reparations. The British government in turn indicated that it would not be party to land expropriation. As these differences became entrenched, the reform process slowed down to a virtual standstill. The

full effects of this stoppage became evident in 1997 when poverty worsened drastically. Moyo goes on to argue that three compromises will be
necessary for sustainable resolution of the conflict: the government will
have to curtail violence on commercial farmland, the British government
will have to resume funding the programme, and white farmers will have
to give up about five million hectares of land.[25]

On 6 September 2001, an agreement was brokered in the Nigerian capital between the Zimbabwean and British governments that seemed to
address the first two of the conditions. In the Abuja agreement,
Zimbabwe committed itself to restoring the rule of law, ending farm occupations and removing squatters from white-owned farms not listed for
compulsory acquisition (see Appendix for the text of the Abuja agreement). In return, the British government agreed to fund the land reform
programme and made arrangements for the United Nations Development
Programme (UNDP) to work with Zimbabwe's government to pursue
"effective and sustainable land reform".[26]

Reaction in the region to the agreement was mixed. Some commentators said it remained to be seen whether Mugabe would keep his word.
Others noted that the accord created a basis on which southern African
leaders could build. Lindiwe Sisulu, Chief Director of Equatorial Africa
and Indian Ocean islands in South Africa's Department of Foreign Affairs,
commented that SADC leaders could work with what had been agreed to
and ask how to make it happen. Sisulu said that the SADC should set about
"cementing the agreement in Abuja and emerging with a programme satisfactory to all". Similarly, Eddie Maloka of the Africa Institute of South
Africa felt the SADC leaders would want "to get a sense of how Mugabe
is going to go about, not only dealing with the land issue, but also stabil-
ising the country politically – basically taking forward the Commonwealth
decision (the Abuja agreement) . . . Their challenge will be to come out of
the meeting with concrete steps creating the conditions for the agreement
to be implemented."[27]

Within Zimbabwe, commentators were generally dubious. Brian
Raftopoulos of the Zimbabwe Institute of Development Studies argued
that it would be virtually impossible for Mugabe to stay within the
conditions of the agreements made in Abuja and still contain the opposition in the country. According to Raftopoulos, since narrowly winning
parliamentary elections last year Mugabe and ZANU-PF have been building their political survival strategy around violence and intimidation.
"Fulfilling the Abuja and Harare agreements will create peace in the
country and therefore space for the opposition to build on widespread

discontent among Zimbabweans and mobilise against ZANU-PF,"
Raftopoulos said. "That is just too dangerous for Mugabe."[28]

In the weeks following the Abuja agreement, violent seizures of farms
continued unabated. By the end of September 2001, the CFU had reported
25 new farm invasions.[29] Government spokesperson Jonathan Moyo
announced that Zimbabwe did not commit in Abuja to curb violence on
white-owned farms. The agreement, Moyo said, only required the government to implement land reforms within its laws and its constitution.
He said the violence was a "side effect" of the land crisis and that it would
disappear "on its own" once the government resettled black farmers on
white-owned farms – "once there is recognition of the fundamental problem, the symptoms will disappear". Such rhetoric on the question of land
occurs in the context of a worsening crisis at the levels of economics and
governance. The economic crisis is rapidly taking the form of widespread
famine that was predicted to leave millions of Zimbabweans starving. At
the time of writing, at least six million people were facing famine in the
country as a result of a deficit of 1.6 million metric tons of maize. If
allowed, international NGOs could bring in about 500 000 metric tons –
but this would only partly address the crisis. What is needed is for the
Grain Marketing Board to engage with the problem as a public – rather
than a political – issue and to make a comprehensive assessment of the
present and impending crisis. Food itself has become a tool for induce-
ment or of mobilisation in that, according to the head of World Vision
(Zimbabwe), "whoever controls the distribution of food now has leverage
in the political control of the country".[30]

In such conditions, the prospects for peace are bleak. Moreover, in the
aftermath of the March 2002 elections a division has been widening in
public discourse about ways of resolving the conflict in Zimbabwe. On
one side, Mugabe's rhetorical defence of his policies as necessary in an
ongoing, historic struggle against residual colonialism and neo-colonial
forces is intensifying. On the other, his opponents argue that the principal
condition for recovery in Zimbabwe is a firm commitment – by all parties
– to democratic processes. Ahead of the 2002 presidential elections,
Andrew Nongogo of Transparency International (Zimbabwe) noted:
"There can be no meaningful development without peace, and no free and
fair elections can take place in a violent situation."[31] Without a firm commitment to stopping violence and adhering to democratic processes,
Mugabe's opponents argue, issues such as historical justice will continue
to be exploited by the Mugabe administration as it seeks to ensure its own
survival, heedless of the cost to the life of the nation.

Present and Future Possibilities for Reconciliation

Set against the backdrop of colonialism and its various mutations, the establishment of Zimbabwe in 1980 represented the possibility of reconciliation and a break with the coercive patterns of the past. The new government articulated a policy of reconciliation. Democratic representation formed an integral part of the political processes and former political and military opponents began to work together. Mugabe's rival among the nationalist forces, Joshua Nkomo, and several of his followers were included in the first cabinet. Moreover, education reform went ahead extremely successfully.

Reconciliation between Mugabe and his perceived rivals did not last long, however. Amid the push and pull of public life, Joshua Nkomo and numerous others were expelled. Moreover, in 1983–84, the government declared a curfew in areas of Nkomo's constituency, Matabeleland, and sent in elite forces to suppress dissidents. By the time peace was restored in 1987, thousands of civilians had been killed in a war waged in the name of national unity. Again, amid the public protest and food rioting that followed the economic crisis of the early 1990s, the Mugabe administration deployed troops against Zimbabwean citizens.[32] As disgruntled citizens developed coalitions to oppose the government, the Mugabe administration adopted a militant attitude, evocative of its history as a liberation movement, which allowed it to define its violence as an unfinished chapter in the national story. Following its referendum defeat in 2000, ZANU-PF "openly encouraged and covertly organised" the invasions of white-owned farms, allocating Z$20 million to the Zimbabwe National Liberation War Veterans Association (ZNLWVA) to spearhead its election campaign.[33] Africa Rights, in an open letter to President Bakili Muluzi, Chairman of SADC, puts it this way:

Under the smokescreen of asserting the rights of black Zimbabweans to the land stolen from them under colonialism, ZANU-PF presented the land invasions as a popular uprising against white domination. There was and remains a fundamental need to restore land rights to black Zimbabweans and to reverse the plight of the rural poor . . . But the land invasions were not directed at these aims. Instead, they were a key element of the ruling party's strategy to remain in power, providing a context in which human rights abuses could be perpetrated with impunity.[34]

This view is supported by evidence of complaints by farm invaders themselves. Clever Chakanyuka, a war veteran and leader of the farm invasions in Goromonzi, was quoted by the Integrated Regional Information Network (IRIN) as saying, "Since the beginning of the invasions, I was in the forefront, but I am living like a madman on Pashiro farm, where our headquarters is. I have no food and they haven't given us any land. I believe they have used us. People are starving out there on the farms. . . . We are just there. At times we are forced to go and beg for food from near-by homesteads. The government has abandoned us. . . ."[35]

The Mugabe administration has not only failed to redistribute resources. It has failed to turn Zimbabwe's history of economic inequity into a national question, an issue that draws Zimbabweans together around the prospect of a social order that breaks from the historical patterns of violence. Currently, Mugabe's ostensible commitment to righting historical wrongs takes the form of pitting Zimbabweans against each other and doing so in ways that undermine and scapegoat a sector integral to the country's macroeconomic stability, namely, the white commercial farmers. In March 2001, the CFU released a report entitled "Farming into the Future", which accepts the principle of redistribution of productive assets to correct historical imbalances. The Zimbabwean government's response has reflected an unwillingness to develop any sort of negotiated solution.

Opposition to Mugabe has gathered, at least for now, under the rubric of the MDC. The MDC poses an unprecedented challenge to the Mugabe regime. The MDC's strength derives from the breadth of the coalition it represents and, within that, there are numerous local organisations engaged in reconciliation work. Among these organisations are the Zimbabwe Human Rights Association (ZIMRIGHTS), Zimbabwe Lawyers for Human Rights, Bulawayo Legal Projects Centre (BLPC), the Association of Zimbabwe Journalists, the Zimbabwe Women's Resource Centre and Network, the Human Rights Research and Documentation Trust of Southern Africa and the National Association of NGOs (NANGO). The Catholic Commission for Justice and Peace Zimbabwe (CCJPZ) and the Legal Resources Foundation are also very involved and together brought out a report that detailed the massacres in Matabeland during the so-called "dissidents' war".

Amid the growing divide in Zimbabwean politics, the Zimbabwe Council of Churches (ZCC) has promoted the possibility of reconciliation. The ZCC played an integral role in the formation of the National Constitutional Assembly, which sought to bring about structural changes capable of promoting a culture of democratic accountability and human rights. Engagement by the ZCC has, at least under the presidency of Bishop Ambrose Moyo, been deliberately non-partisan, advocating constitutional reforms rather than outright opposition to the ruling party. The council even withdrew from the NCA once it became perceived as an opposition movement.[36]

From this position, the ZCC has remained actively committed to reconciliation. At a retreat held at Victoria Falls in mid-2001, the ZCC sought to develop dialogue with all parties to the crisis. The gathering, in its own words, "challenge[d] the nation to rise above party and petty politics and . . . be constructively engaged in finding positive approaches to nation-building for a just and sustainable society in Zimbabwe".[37] In the pastoral letter developed at the meeting, the ZCC sets out recommendations for peace and reconciliation, addressing them to each of the parties to the conflict, under various headings according to the areas of conflict. With regard to the political situation, the ZCC "call[s] upon political leadership to categorically condemn and desist from perpetrating political violence". With regard to law and order, the ZCC notes that, currently, "the law is selectively applied or not being applied in cases of political violence. The ZCC is deeply perturbed by the role given to the war veterans in 'resolving' national issues and by the violence surrounding their activities and the perception that they are above the law." Accordingly, the ZCC "call[s] upon the Government to apply the law impartially regardless of political affiliation" and to allow the judiciary to function independently of the executive. The ZCC "call[s] upon the war veterans to desist from perpetrating violence on the farms, refrain from industrial invasions as this is counter-productive [and] stop taking the law into their own hands and allow for the legal system to resolve industrial disputes". Detailed recommendations are provided with regard to the economy, the land and the elections.[38]

Such a non-partisan position has drawn both the ire of the Zimbabwean government, which wants active support, and of the opposition, which insists that, in the current climate of unmitigated government violence, political neutrality is not possible. This double-bind is symptomatic of the nature of the Zimbabwean crisis. Zimbabwe has never had the sort of open, democratic debate that is capable of promoting reconciliation amid transition and the prospect of justice for all. In the aftermath of the widely disputed 2002 presidential elections, the prospects for democratic debate around national issues have grown bleak. Such a debate would necessarily include all interested parties – dispossessed peasants, white farmers, civil society and government. A forum in which all such parties commit to engaging in dialogue – as emerged in South Africa in the form of "talks about talks" – may, however, be an unwelcome prospect for the Zimbabwean government. Numerous commentators have noted that open debate in contemporary Zimbabwe would have resulted in certain defeat for Mugabe in the 2002 elections; among the principal costs of that disputed process is now a lack of options for Zimbabweans committed to democratic means of producing change.

Amid the present crisis as well as in the long term, if Zimbabwe's hundred years of conflict is to find resolution, it will be necessary that historical and current grievances – in particular, the overriding issue of land – be addressed in ways capable of transforming the social and political landscape in Zimbabwe and creating conditions for a peaceful transition out of historical patterns of coercive rule. Restorative justice and social reconciliation will be integral to the establishment in Zimbabwe of what Mahmood Mamdani describes as a political order based not on conquest but consent. Such an order would entail a break from Zimbabwe's conflictual history and would be about establishing a political community of equal and consenting citizens. The precondition will be "survivors' justice" – a practical embodiment of empathy rather than the settling of a historical score.[39]

NOTES

1 See Chris McGreal, "In Defence of Power and Profit." *The Mail and Guardian*, 1–7 June 2001, 15.

2 David Hale, chief global economist for the Zurich Insurance Group in Chicago, "A View of Africa 2001 and Beyond." Speech presented at the Investing in Africa Mining Indaba 2001 Conference, Cape Town, 8 February 2001.

3 *Africa Confidential* 41:22 (10 November 2000).

4 Integrated Regional Information Network (IRIN), "Economy to Shrink 8 Percent – RBZ." Reprinted at http://www.reliefweb.int/IRIN/sa/countrystories/zimbabwe/20010920b.phtml

5 *Africa Confidential* 42:8 (20 April 2001).

6 Peta Basildon, "Early Warning of Mass Starvation in Zimbabwe: Farm Disruptions Result in Severe Shortfalls in Basic Foodstuffs." *The Sunday Independent*, 20 May 2001, 3.

7 PF-ZAPU v. Minister of Justice 1985(1) ZLR 305.

8 *Africa Confidential* 38:23 (21 November 1997).

9 *Africa Confidential* 41:9 (28 April 2000).

10 *Africa Confidential* 41:11 (26 May 2000).

11 1.3 million people voted out of an electorate of 5 million (*Africa Confidential* 41:4 (18 February 2000)).

12 Clemency Order No. 1 of 2000, published in General Notice 457A of 2000.
13 *The Herald*, 14 September 1997.
14 Tapera Knox Chitiyo, "Land Violence and Compensation: Reconceptualising Zimbabwe's Land and War Veterans' Debate." *Track Two* Vol. 9 No. 1, May 2000. Reprinted at http://ccrweb.ccr.uct.ac.za/two/9_1/zimbabwe.html (accessed 11 December 2001). Chitiyo notes "many of [the 'war veterans'] are clearly unemployed youths, some who were not even born at the time of the war of liberation". *Africa Confidential* 41:14 (7 July 2000) also reports that "actual veterans instigated court proceedings against Chenjerai 'Hitler' Hunzvi for misuse of their pension fund but amid the tumult of the farm occupations the corruption case against Hunzvi was delayed. Hunzvi also faces torture charges, substantiated by Amnesty International, for permitting his followers use of his doctor's surgery to torture opposition supporters." Hunzvi died, reportedly of cerebral malaria, on 6 June 2001.
15 IRIN, "Mugabe Makes Ally Chief Justice." Reprinted at http://www.reliefweb.int/IRIN/sa/countrystories/zimbabwe/20010821b.phtml (accessed 11 December 2001).
16 Palmer, 1977, cited in Chitiyo, "Land Violence and Compensation."
17 Rolin, 1978, and Palmer, 1977, cited in Chitiyo, "Land Violence and Compensation."
18 Rolin, 1978, cited in Chitiyo, "Land Violence and Compensation."
19 Palmer, 1977, cited in Chitiyo, "Land Violence and Compensation."
20 Magaya, 1981, cited in Chitiyo, "Land Violence and Compensation."
21 Ian Phimister, "The Combined and Contradictory Inheritance of the Struggle Against Colonialism," quoted in *Zimbabwe's Prospects: Issues of Race, Class, State, and Capital in Southern Africa*, ed. Colin Stoneman (London: Macmillan, 1988), 8.
22 Marshall, 1976, cited in Chitiyo, "Land Violence and Compensation."
23 Evans, 1982, cited in Chitiyo, "Land Violence and Compensation."
24 Moyo, 1987, cited in Chitiyo, "Land Violence and Compensation."
25 IRIN, "IRIN Interview with Land Expert Sam Moyo." Reprinted at http://www.reliefweb.int/IRIN/sa/countrystories/zimbabwe/20010814.phtml (accessed 11 December 2001).
26 IRIN, "All Heads Turn to SADC Indaba in Harare." Reprinted at http://www.reliefweb.int/IRIN/sa/countrystories/zimbabwe/20010907.phtml (accessed 11 December 2001).
27 Ibid.
28 IRIN, "IRIN Focus on Continuing Crisis." 17 September 2001. Reprinted at http://www.reliefweb.int/IRIN/sa/countrystories/zimbabwe/20010917.phtml (accessed 11 December 2001).
29 IRIN, "Land Talks 'Collapse'." 27 September 2001. Reprinted at http://www.reliefweb.int/IRIN/sa/countrystories/zimbabwe/20010927.phtml (accessed 11 December 2001).
30 Rudo Kwaramba, in a presentation at the Zimbabwe-South Africa Dialogue convened by the Institute for Justice and Reconciliation, Cape Town, July 2002.
31 IRIN, "Land Talks 'Collapse'."
32 African Rights Letter, 22 September 2001. Reprinted at http://www.africapolicy.org/docs01/zim0109.htm (accessed 11 December 2001).
33 Ibid.
34 Ibid.
35 IRIN, "Disgruntled War Vets Threaten to Join MDC," 22 May 2001. Reprinted at http://www.reliefweb.int/IRIN/sa/countrystories/zimbabwe/20010522b.phtml

(accessed 11 December 2001).

36 Bishop Ambrose Moyo, President of the Zimbabwe Council of Churches, Keynote Address delivered at the Preparatory Discussions for a South Africa-Zimbabwe Dialogue, held in Durban, 7–8 September 2001. Reprinted at www.ijr.org.za (accessed 11 December 2001).

37 ZCC Pastoral Letter, *The Truth Shall Make You Free . . .!* Reprinted at www.ijr.org.za (accessed 11 December 2001).

38 Ibid.

39 Mahmood Mamdani, *When Does a Settler Become a Native?: Reflections on the Colonial Roots of Citizenship in Equatorial and South Africa* (Cape Town: University of Cape Town, 1998).

40 "Text of Zimbabwe Agreement" BBC News, 7 September 2001. Reprinted at http://news.bbc.co.uk/hi/english/world/africa/newsid_1530000/1530132.stm (accessed 11 December 2001).

RESOURCES

Books, Articles, Current Media Reports

Amin, Nick. *Peasant Differentiation and Food Security in Zimbabwe*. Harare: UZD, 1991.

Astrow, Andre. *Zimbabwe: A Revolution that Lost its Way*. London: Zed, 1983.

Beach, David Nelson. "'Chimurenga', The Shona Rising of 1896–1897." *Journal of African History* 20:3 (1979).

———. *Zimbabwe Before 1900*. Gweru: Mambo, 1984.

Chitiyo, Tapera Knox. "Land Violence and Compensation: Reconceptualising Zimbabwe's Land and War Veterans' Debate." *Track Two* 9:1 (May 2000). Reprinted at http://ccrweb.ccr.uct.ac.za/two/9_1/zimbabwe.html (accessed 11 December 2001).

Cilliers, Jackie. *Dismissed: Demobilisation and Reintegration of Former Combatants in Africa*. South Africa: IDP, 1996.

Gann, Lewis H. and Thomas H. Henriksen. *The Struggle for Zimbabwe: Battle in the Bush*. New York: Praeger, 1981.

Gregory, M. "Zimbabwe 1980: Politicisation through Armed Struggle and Electoral Mobilisation." *Journal of Commonwealth and Comparative Politics*, March 1981.

Keppel-Jones, Arthur. *Rhodes and Rhodesia: The White Conquest of Zimbabwe 1884–1902*. Ontario: McGill-Queens University Press, 1993.

Kriger, Norma J. *Zimbabwe's Guerrilla War: Peasant Voices*. Cambridge: Cambridge University Press, 1992.

Leach, Melissa and Robin Means, eds. *The Lie of the Land: Challenging Received Wisdom of the African Environment*. Oxford: Oxford University Press, 1996.

Mamdani, Mahmood. *When Does a Settler Become a Native?: Reflections on the Colonial Roots of Citizenship in Equatorial and South Africa*. Cape Town: University of Cape Town, 1998.

Mandaza, Ibbo, ed. *Zimbabwe: The Political Economy of Transition 1980–1986*. Dakar: CODESRIA, 1986.

Martin, David and Phyllis Johnson. *The Struggle for Zimbabwe: The Chimurenga War*. Harare: ZPH, 1981.

Moyo, Sam. *The Land Question in Zimbabwe*. Harare: CODESRIA, Jongwe, 1987.

Palmer, Robin. *Land and Racial Domination in Rhodesia*. Berkeley: University of California Press, 1977.

Palmer, Robin and Neil Parson, eds. *The Roots of Rural Poverty in Central and Southern Africa*. London: Heinemann, 1977.

Ranger, Terence. *Revolt in Southern Rhodesia, 1896–7: A Study in African Resistance*. Evanston: Northwestern University Press, 1967.

———. *Peasant Consciousness and Guerrilla War in Zimbabwe: A Comparative Study*. Berkeley: University of California Press, 1975.

Riddell, Roger. *The Land Question: From Rhodesia to Zimbabwe*. London: Catholic Institute for International Relations, 1980.

Sithole, Masipula. *Zimbabwe: Struggles Within the Struggle*. Salisbury: Rujeko, 1978.

Stoneman, Colin, ed. *Zimbabwe's Prospects: Issues of Race, Class, State, and Capital in Southern Africa*. London and Bastingstoke: Macmillan, 1988.

Stromm, J. *Zimbabwe's Revolution*. Cambridge: Cambridge University Press, 1988.

Weinmann, J. *Zimbabwe's Land Crisis: A Reassessment*. Berkeley: University of California Press, 1996.

Primary Documents

Amani Trust, Network of Independent Monitors, Physicians for Human Rights. Analysis of Zimbabwe Presidential Election, 9 and 10 March 2002, in terms of SADC Parliamentary Forum Electoral Recommendations. Reprinted at http://www.ijr.org.za/zim_monitor/current/AmaniReport.htm

Zimbabwe Council of Churches Pastoral Letter, *The Truth Shall Make You Free . . .!* Reprinted at www.ijr.org.za

Government, Intergovernmental Bodies and Political Parties

ZANU-PF is the party that has ruled Zimbabwe since independence: http://www.zanupf.gov.zw

The Movement for Democratic Change (MDC) is Zimbabwe's most prominent opposition political party, and comprises a coalition of labour, business, church and women's organisations as well as student leaders, human rights and civic groups, and representatives of the impoverished rural population: http://www.mdczimbabwe.com

Local NGOs

The African Forum and Network on Debt and Development (AFRODAD) is a network comprising African NGOs, churches, labour unions and private citizens, promoting debt relief: http://www.irc-online.org/cbl/fairtrade/af/afrodad.html

Mass Public Opinion Institute is committed to democratic change and survey's public opinion in Zimbabwe.

The National Constitutional Assembly (NCA) is a conglomerate of human rights organisations, churches, trade unions, women's groups, professionals and interested individuals, all committed to a process aimed at entrenching democratic participation in the making of a new constitution and in the governance of Zimbabwe: http://www.nca.org.zw

Radio Voice of the People engages in media activities committed to promoting democracy in Zimbabwe.

The Zimbabwe Council of Churches is actively engaged in developing a non-partisan position on transition in Zimbabwe.

The Zimbabwe Liberation Platform comprises Zimbabweans committed to the ongoing establishment of freedom in Zimbabwe.

International NGOs

Media Institute of Southern Africa (Zimbabwe)

Transparency International: http://www.transparency.org

ZIMBABWE COUNTRY INFORMATION

Geography
Location: Southern Africa, between South Africa and Zambia.
Cities: *Capital:* Harare.

People
Nationality: *Noun:* Zimbabwean(s). *Adjective:* Zimbabwean.
Population (2000 est.): 11 342 521.
Population growth rate (2000 est.): 0.26%.
Ethnic groups: African 98% (Shona 71%, Ndebele 16%, other 11%), white 1%, mixed and Asian 1%.
Religions: Christian 25%, traditional African beliefs 24%, syncretic (part Christian, part traditional) 50%, Muslim and other 1%.
Languages: English (official), Shona, Sindebele (the language of the Ndebele, some-times called Ndebele), numerous but minor tribal dialects.
Education (1995 est.): *Literacy:* total population 85%; male 90%; female 80%.
Health (2000 est.): *Infant mortality rate:* 62.25/1 000. *Life expectancy:* 44 years. *HIV infection rate:* 25.84%.
Workforce (1996 est.): 5 million. Agriculture: 66%. Services: 24%. Industry: 10%.

Economy

GDP (1999 est.): $26.5 billion.
GDP real growth rate: 0%.
Per capita income: $2 400.
Inflation rate: 59%.
Natural resources: Coal, chromium, ore, asbestos, gold, nickel, copper, iron ore, vana-dium, lithium, tin, platinum group metals.
Agriculture: 28% of GDP. *Products:* corn, cotton, tobacco, wheat, coffee, sugar cane, peanuts, cattle, sheep, goats, pigs.
Industry: 32% of GDP. *Types:* mining (coal, gold, copper, nickel, tin, clay, numerous metallic and non-metallic ores), steel, wood products, cement, chemicals, fertiliser, clothing and footwear, foodstuffs, beverages.
Trade (1997 est.): *Exports:* $2 billion: tobacco, gold, ferroalloys, cotton. *Major markets:* South Africa, UK, Germany, Japan, US. *Imports:* $2 billion machinery and transport equipment, other manufactures, chemicals, fuels. *Major suppliers:* South Africa, US, UK, Japan, Germany.
Economic aid: Recipient (1995): $437.6 million.
Debt – external (1998): $5 billion.

Military
Military expenditure: Dollar figures: $127 million (FY99/00).
Military expenditure: Percent of GDP: 3.1% (FY99/00).

Demographic information is drawn from that compiled by the United States Department of State. See http://www.state.gov/r/pa/ei/bgn

Appendix: The Abuja agreement

The following is the text of the agreement, in full, as presented by the Nigerian government and signed by all parties.

The meeting recognised that as a result of historical injustices, the current land ownership and distribution needed to be rectified in a transparent and equitable manner. It also agreed on the following:

❑ Land is at the core of the crisis in Zimbabwe and cannot be separated from other issues of concern to the Commonwealth such as the rule of law, respect for human rights, democracy and the economy. A programme of land reform is, therefore, crucial to the resolution of the problem

❑ Such a programme of land reform must be implemented in a fair, just and sustainable manner, in the interest of all the people of Zimbabwe, within the law and constitution of Zimbabwe

❑ The crisis in Zimbabwe also has political and rule of law implications which must be addressed holistically and concurrently. The situation in Zimbabwe poses a threat to the socio-economic stability of the entire sub-region and the continent at large

❑ The need to avoid a division within the Commonwealth, especially at the forthcoming CHOGM [Commonwealth Heads of Government Meeting] in Brisbane, Australia, over the situation in Zimbabwe

❑ The orderly implementation of the land reform can only be meaningful and sustainable if carried out with due regard to human rights, rule of law, transparency and democratic principles. The commitment of the government of Zimbabwe is therefore crucial to this process.

The committee recognises the need for the adoption of confidence-building measures to ensure the implementation of the conclusions of the meeting. In this regard, the meeting welcomed assurances given by the Zimbabwe delegation as follows:

❑ Commitment to the Harare Commonwealth Declaration and the Millbrook Commonwealth Action Programme on the Harare Declaration

❑ There will be no further occupation of farm lands

❑ To speed up the process by which farms that do not meet set criteria are de-listed

❑ For farms that are not designated, occupiers would be moved to legally acquired lands

❑ Acceleration of discussions with the UNDP [United Nations Development Programme] with a view to reaching agreement as quickly as possible

❑ Commitment to restore the rule of law to the process of land reform programme

❑ Commitment to freedom of expression as guaranteed by the constitution of Zimbabwe and to take firm action against violence and intimidation

❑ Invitation by the foreign minister to the committee to visit Zimbabwe.

The meeting agreed, in the overall context of the statement, that the way forward is for Zimbabwe's international partners

❑ to engage constructively with the UNDP and the government of Zimbabwe in pursuing an effective and sustainable land reform programme on the basis of the UNDP proposals of December 2000

❑ to respond positively to any request from the government of Zimbabwe in support of the electoral process

❑ to continue to contribute to poverty reduction programmes for the benefit of the people of Zimbabwe and that those partners present (Australia, Canada and United Kingdom) would actively pursue these objectives.

The meeting also welcomed the re-affirmation of the United Kingdom's commitment to a significant financial contribution to such a land reform programme and its undertaking to encourage other international donors to do the same.

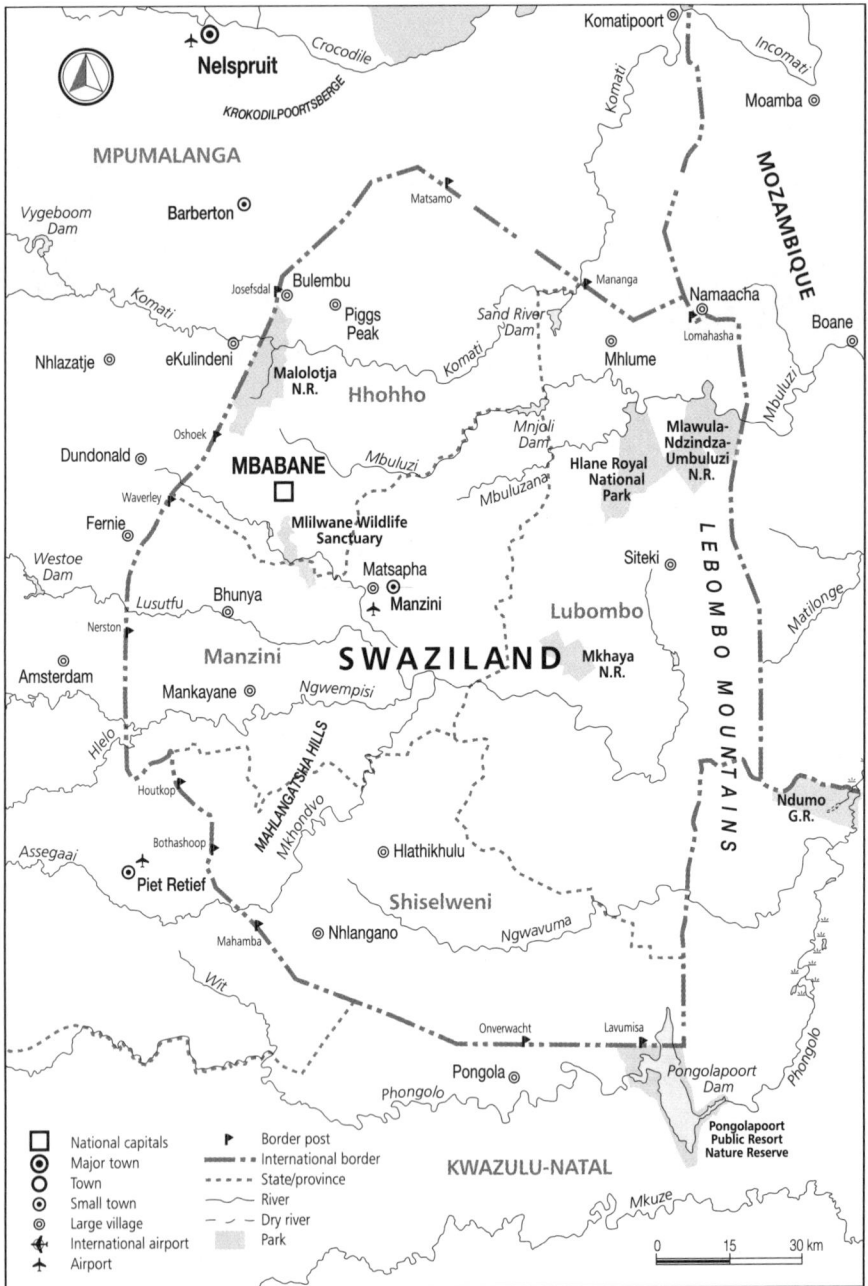

Map legend:

- ☐ National capitals
- ⊚ Major town
- ◎ Town
- ⊙ Small town
- ◉ Large village
- ✈ International airport
- ✈ Airport
- ▶ Border post
- ▬▬ International border
- ┄┄ State/province
- ―― River
- ― ― Dry river
- ▨ Park

Labels on map:

Nelspruit
Komatipoort
Incomati
Moamba
KROKODILPOORTSBERGE
Crocodile
MPUMALANGA
Komati
MOZAMBIQUE
Vygeboom Dam
Barberton
Matsamo
Mananga
Namaacha
Boane
Josefsdal
Bulembu
Piggs Peak
Sand River Dam
Lomahasha
Nhlazatje
eKulindeni
Komati
Mhlume
Mbuluzi
Malolotja N.R.
Hhohho
Mnjoli Dam
Mlawula-Ndzindza-Umbuluzi N.R.
Oshoek
MBABANE
Mbuluzi
Hlane Royal National Park
Dundonald
Mbuluzana
Waverley
Mlilwane Wildlife Sanctuary
Fernie
Matsapha
Siteki
Westoe Dam
Manzini
L E B O M B O   M O U N T A I N S
Lusutfu
Bhunya
Manzini
Matilonge
Nerston
Manzini
SWAZILAND
Lubombo
Amsterdam
Mankayane
Ngwempisi
Mkhaya N.R.
Hlelo
MAHLANGATSHA HILLS
Houtkop
Mkhondvo
Ndumo G.R.
Bothashoop
Hlathikhulu
Assegaai
Piet Retief
Shiselweni
Mahamba
Nhlangano
Ngwavuma
Wit
Onverwacht
Lavumisa
Pongolapoort Dam
Pongola
Phongolo
Pongolapoort Public Resort Nature Reserve
Phongolo
KWAZULU-NATAL
Mkuze

0   15   30 km

Chapter 9

Swaziland: Between Monarchy and Democracy

MANELISI GENGE

The current conflict in Swaziland is premised on popular demands for multi-party politics, democratisation and an end to an absolute monarchy. In southern Africa, Swaziland is the only country ruled by an absolute monarch. The monarchy governs the country through a state of emergency, passed by the late King Sobhuza II in 1973. The state of emergency banned multi-party politics. Prospects for reconciliation thus turn heavily on convincing the monarchy to relinquish absolute power and become a constitutional monarchy and permit multi-party politics in the context of a democratic Swaziland. This will not be achieved easily because, ever since the Swazi state was formed, the Dlamini royal family has enjoyed a monopoly on political power. Consequently, the monarchy has resisted demands for political power sharing.

Political analysts have tried to write off the Swazi monarchy as an institution on the verge of collapse.[1] Yet, the monarchy has retained its resilience and vigour as the absolute authority in the country. Part of the explanation for such endurance lies with its ability to forge links with constituencies outside Swaziland, while it simultaneously denies its subjects a similar ability. Therefore, the failure of the Swazi trade unions and civil society organisations to establish connections with like-minded institutions outside Swaziland has contributed to their ineffectiveness in realising their goals of abolishing the state of emergency, introducing multi-party politics within a democratic context and converting the monarchy to a constitutional one. In this context, reconciliation would entail exposing the pro-democracy formations in Swaziland to like-minded groups outside the country.

The Face of Conflict

The conflict is one of low intensity. Currently there is very minimal loss of life. In fact, the low casualty levels have resulted in a lack of concerted international attention to the country's present condition. According to the UN definition, there are few human rights violations. However, there are violations of human rights given the undemocratic nature of government. This is the main issue of contention in Swaziland: monarchical politics with a veneer of a Westminster-style parliamentary system versus the demand for democracy made by the Swaziland Federation of Trade Unions (SFTU), under the leadership of its General Secretary, Jan Sithole, Swaziland Federation of Labour (SFL) and the still banned People's United Democratic Movement (PUDEMO).[2] Yet, the government is still in a strong position in the sense that it has not been challenged to the point of losing credibility or legitimacy. Trade unions have not succeeded in defining their agenda to include a broad spectrum of political issues. Therefore, trade union movements in Swaziland have not even come close to what Morgan Tsvangirai, leader of the Movement for Democratic Change (MDC), a former trade unionist leader, did in Zimbabwe when he converted his trade union agenda from labour concerns to political concerns.

The government of Swaziland is a dual monarchy, meaning that it is presided over by an executive monarch, Ngwenyama (a king) and a queen mother, Indlovukati (the She-Elephant). The monarchy rules the country with its Swazi National Council (SNC), known in isiSwati as Labadzala. There is also a parliamentary system, the multi-party aspect of which was enshrined in the British-drawn constitution for an independent Swaziland, but which was compromised by the late King Sobhuza II when he issued the 1973 decree that banned all political party activity in Swaziland. Hence the current political system in the country is known as a non-party system. Most members of parliament are associated somehow with the Swazi monarchy. For example, the current prime minister, Dr Barnabas Sibusiso Dlamini, Prince Guduza Dlamini, Minister of Economic Planning and Development, Lufto Dlamini, Minister of Enterprise and Employment, and Phetsile Dlamini, Minister of Health and Social Welfare, are all related to the Swazi king. King Mswati III is head of state and has veto powers over the National Assembly. The Swazi monarchy appears to many as a kind of dictatorship. One commentator remarked: "The monarch retains full control of executive and legislative decisions, with the Cabinet and parliament merely endorsing royal decisions."[3] The totalitarian cast of the monarchy becomes noticeable when viewed in the context of the democratic governments that emerged during the 1990s in southern Africa.

Local government is based on the power of chiefs, exercised through the *tinkhundla* system introduced in 1978, which purports to be the "traditional" Swazi way of government. Most of the chiefs, especially those who occupy senior positions, are related to the royal house. Some scholars have pointed out that the mythology of the *tinkhundla* system serves Dlamini royal ideology: "Indeed, one of the underlying reasons for [the late] King Sobhuza's [II] success as a leader was his ability not only to modify and transform Swazi tradition when occasion demanded, but even to re-invent it."[4]

The current conflict in the country is waged by the "traditional" political elite against the popular masses and is political in nature. It is about power, that is, a popular demand for the democratisation of political space and power. It is mainly a domestic-centred conflict in the sense that it involves Swazi royalists and their government versus popular demands by Swazi citizens. However, the Swazi royalists and government are said to occasionally receive logistical and military support from the former colonial power, Britain, and from the declining South African Afrikaner Weerstands Beweging (AWB), a right-wing organisation.[5]

The Swazi monarchy still enjoys international support from the United Nations Development Programme. However, the international community has recently pressurised King Mswati's government to reform its political system. In early October 2001, Amnesty International and the International Labour Organisation (ILO) pressed the government to abolish the 1973 decree and other laws which "compel citizens to provide free labour for the king and other traditional rulers".[6] The US has threatened to exclude Swaziland from its Growth and Opportunity Act, intended for trade concessions for developing countries, over Swaziland's bad industrial relations record. The state does enjoy recognition from organisations on the continent such as the African Union and the Southern African Development Community (SADC). Birthday celebrations of King Mswati III still attract wide attention from governments in the southern African region and from the diplomatic community. This suggests that the monarchy as an institution in Swaziland still enjoys support from outside the country.

The trade unions, for their part, interact with the ILO and with the South African trade unions, such as the Congress of South African Trade Unions (COSATU). However, Swaziland's trade unions have not attracted or asked for international support of their views on the political affairs of the country. PUDEMO remains an underground movement and has so far failed to canvass political support from regional leaders for its programme. In fact, PUDEMO has not presented a programme of action for the governance of the country, should it become a ruling party. This is PUDEMO's major weakness in its fight for the restoration of party politics in Swaziland.

The main actors in the conflict are the monarchy and its government on the one side and the SFTU, SFL, PUDEMO and the banned Ngwane National Liberation Congress (NNLC) on the other. The monarchy as an institution enjoys a fair level of support in the country. Its longevity in Swazi politics and its ideology of Swaziness have given the monarchy a central place in Swazi politics.[7] In general, Swazi society is conservative in its outlook on life. However, trade unions, PUDEMO and the NNLC enjoy a degree of popular support in their demands for the democratisation of political power and the creation of a democratic space.[8]

The royalists and their government are in complete control of the trappings of state, such as the judiciary, police, military and the state treasury. Their opponents have none of these resources and are always harassed by the state through the use of the resources at its disposal. As mentioned above, the Swazi monarchy and its government still enjoy international and regional legitimacy. This is so despite its failure to open up a democratic space to its citizens and to those who aspire to multi-party politics. The opposition has so far even failed to influence the SADC to seriously consider its (Swazi opposition) grievances against the royalists and their government. It has also failed to sell its agenda either to the ruling parties or the opposition parties in the region. The donor community still provides financial support to the Swazi state for its projects.[9]

The Historical Roots of Violence and Division

Unlike many countries in the world, Swaziland is not composed of multi-ethnic groups. This is largely due to the way Swaziland, together with Botswana and Lesotho, were colonised by the British. In these countries, the British did not do what they were fond of doing in other colonies, that is, collapsing independent pre-colonial kingdoms into a single colonial state. The Dlamini conquest, which predates the advent of European colonialism, led to the formation of the Swazi state.[10] That state has evolved into the present-day Swaziland, a development that has entailed the weaving and crafting of the Dlamini ideology until it became acceptable to the conquered peoples.

Although Swazi society is not deeply divided as in, for example, Rwanda and Nigeria, there is a common perception among the amaSwati that, besides the royalty, the position of chief, and the highest position in western-style politics, that of a prime minister, are reserved for descendants of the Dlamini clan or its relatives.

There is only one local language, namely, isiSwati, which is an official language along with English. In the SADC region, only Swaziland,

Lesotho and Botswana can boast of having only one African language that is spoken by almost all residents.

There are few deep-seated sources of conflict in Swaziland. The primary area of contention is the need for the democratisation of politics by allowing a multi-party system. Both external and internal commentators consider the existence of an absolute monarch as the main source of contention in the country. The Swazi monarch uses the ideology of tradition as a mechanism to manipulate politics in the country.[11] Other external commentators have observed that the main historical origins of conflict in Swaziland have been the Swazi monarch's ownership and control of natural resources, namely land and cattle, which he claims to be keeping in trust for the nation. The opponents of this view have argued, "In practice, however, these national assets have been utilised to shore up the economic power of the king and his confidants."[12] The control of these natural resources and their use by the monarchy to boost its power may need to be part of negotiating a reconfiguration of political power toward a democratic dispensation.

The participants in the opposition argue that the absolute nature of the monarchy, the rule by decree which has been in place since 1973, and the ban on political activity by those who wish to create political parties, are the roots of the conflict. The opposition wants a constitutional monarchy, the unbanning of political parties and the introduction of a democratic process for popular participation in the politics of the country.[13] However, the major flaw of the pro-democracy formations, so far, is their failure to produce a programme of action, that is, a policy document. This has been interpreted by their opponents as an indication of their lack of preparedness for national governance.

The king and his government, for their part, want to maintain the *status quo*. Instead of democratising politics, they responded to popular demands with an unproductive Constitutional Review Commission (CRC). At its inception, in July 1996, the CRC comprised 31 persons. In constituting it the king cunningly attempted to undermine proponents of democracy by appointing to the CRC four conservative women, the then-PUDEMO's president Mario Masuku, and the deputy president of SFTU, among others. He appointed these persons as ordinary citizens, not as representatives of their structures or constituencies.[14] More importantly, many members of the CRC favoured the current political dispensation and were princes, chiefs, or relatives of the royal family. The CRC was chaired by a member of the royal family.[15] Even the terms of reference did not allow for submissions by organisations or structures. For example, one of the terms of reference stipulated that "no one may represent anyone or be represented in any capacity while making submissions to the commission".[16]

The CRC had the following mandate:

- ❑ Compile and document the current constitutional framework and circulate it to all *tinkhundla* centres.
- ❑ Review any legislation, decree or proclamation that has a bearing on constitutional and human rights matters.
- ❑ Consider the constitutions of other countries which the commission may consider appropriate for the purpose of obtaining any information, guidelines or principles.
- ❑ Receive oral submissions, representations and information from members of the general public, and for this purpose visit all *tinkhundla* centres to access such members as well as consider the 1992 Tinkhundla Review Commission Report.[17]

Furthermore, the CRC had a mandate to "consider and provide for appropriate provisions and entrenchment on the monarchy and other Swazi traditional institutions".[18] The members of the CRC were immune from ridicule, criticism or challenge during the life of the CRC. In protecting the members of the CRC, a clause stated, "no person may insult, disparage or belittle any member of the commission, or obstruct, interrupt, hinder or prejudice an officer, member of the commission or the commission in the performance of its functions".[19] Contravention of the stipulation was punishable with a maximum fine of R5 000 or five years imprisonment or both.[20] This stipulation received unanimous condemnation from the pro-democracy formations, including the media.[21] Of course, it did not take too long for some of the members of the CRC to notice the futility of its own mandate. By January 1997 Masuku of PUDEMO withdrew from the CRC claiming that, "it will be a treasonable offence to the people of Swaziland and the international democratic community if we are seen to be part of the process which is nothing but a miscarriage of democracy".[22] King Mswati seems to be prepared to cling to his role as an absolute executive monarch, in defiance of popular calls for a constitutional monarch and multi-party democracy in the country.

It is extremely difficult to comment on the opposition's views within Swaziland or those of third parties in the country regarding the nature of the conflict. There is little media freedom in the country. The monarchy and its government have the power to create effective propaganda. They are still in complete control of the state apparatus. They have persistently banned media from reporting on certain events in the country. The whole state machinery is at their disposal for their propaganda. Their opponents are constrained by logistical weaknesses and by the absence of a solid base of operation both inside and outside the country.

There is relatively limited cultural, racial and ethnic diversity in Swaziland. The country is predominantly populated by the amaSwati people. There are few white citizens (2% of the population), who are the descendants of the colonisers of Swaziland. These Europeans are of British and Afrikaner stock and are not a homogenous group either in their ethnic composition or in their views on the events in the country. There are also a few German descendants. The Afrikaner descendants are concentrated in agriculture and stock farming, whereas the British are more involved in the industrial sector. Unlike in other former colonies, where European colonisers were generally resented by the colonised, in Swaziland there was a closer co-operation or even collaboration between the Swazi monarchy and the colonisers against the Swazi masses.[23] At independence, the white population in Swaziland supported King Sobhuza II's Imbokodvo National Movement (INM), which contested and won the first independence parliamentary elections in 1967.[24] Other scholars have observed harmonious relations between the white citizens and the amaSwazi in general.[25]

The fact that the Swazi monarchy had collaborated with the European colonialists against the Swazi masses during the colonial period has led to a lack of support for the pro-democracy proponents from the white population in independent Swaziland. The monarchy has created a conducive atmosphere for white investors in Swaziland, to an extent that the king has turned a blind eye to racial and gender discrimination at the workplace.[26] Swaziland's lack of diversity has contributed to the conflict because the country has largely failed to draw the attention of those who are sympathetic to ethnically based conflicts.

Colonialism does not play an important role in Swazi society with regard to the current conflict. In 1973, when the late King Sobhuza II suspended the British-influenced 1968 constitution with its multi-party arrangements, he was in fact taking the country back to a precolonial political system. However, he did not alter the economic structure which he inherited from British colonialism. Hence there was a structural contradiction in the way political power and the economy functioned in postcolonial Swaziland.

Swaziland is currently ruled under the 1973 decree of emergency that outlawed political parties. Since then, Swaziland has had no constitution to guide the conduct of politics.[27] Electoral politics in the sense of competitive party politics does not exist in the country. Swaziland practises what is termed parliamentary "representation" without political parties. Parliament has two houses: the Assembly and the Senate. The Assembly has 50 members, of whom 40 are elected through a secret ballot by the Electoral College, while the other 10 members are the king's nominees. Senate is constituted by 20 members. It is constituted after the House of Assembly has been fully staffed. The Assembly elects 10 members of the Senate. The other 10 are nominated by the king. The Electoral College is composed through the elaborate *tinkhundla* system. The country is divided into 40 *tinkhundla* (electoral) districts. Then, each of the *tinkhundla* elects 2 representatives to form an 80 member Electoral College. The Electoral College then elects members of the House of Assembly. Candidates of the Electoral College and the House of Assembly have no party or organisational affiliation. The election of candidates to the Electoral College is shrouded in mystery since the electorate is not supposed to know anything about their political or class profiles. Members of the House of Assembly ostensibly represent national interests with no regard to any particular constituency or electoral district.

The electoral system does not enjoy popular support in the country. It is criticised for its undemocratic nature and for its lack of transparency. Members of both houses cannot be held accountable for their shortcomings to any particular constituency. In 1987, signs of public discontent about the *tinkhundla* system emerged, when people raised concerns about its composition and functions to Mndeni Shabalala, the *indvuna yetinkhundla* (electoral commissioner), who toured the country as part of an election campaign to "educate" the people on the *tinkhundla* system. At meetings held at the Mayiwane and Madlangempisi centres (electoral districts) his audience is reported to have pointed out to him that the procedures of the *tinkhundla* system were ignored with respect to the election of members of parliament. They wanted to know who really elected members of parliament.[28] They also asked "why it was that the two members elected at the *tinkhundla* level did not directly represent them in parliament, 'because we elected them as a result of trust and hope that they will represent [our] *Tinkhundla* in Parliament'".[29] A member of the audience articulated his concern about the lack of transparency in the election of parliamentarians and the need to change the system: "We do not know these members of Parliament because we do not elect them. When King Sobhuza II introduced these elections under the *tinkhundla* system, he said it was not permanent and that the system should be changed if it be proved unsatisfactory."[30] The views of this audience demonstrate that some people in Swaziland are dissatisfied with the current electoral politics and would change the *tinkhundla* system if given the chance. It is likely that if the citizens of Swaziland were allowed to elect their own representatives in a multi-party political context, they would not re-elect most of the current politicians. However, they would not necessarily vote against the institution of kingship, which is deeply ingrained in the political culture.

Notwithstanding the current popular demands for democratisation in the country, there is no danger of a coup. The banned PUDEMO is a popular alternative to the existing political authority. Civil society organisations are not well developed in the country. However, trade unions, such as the SFTU and SFL, are strong voices within the civil society constituency. Swaziland has a strong religious constituency. From the days of the late King Sobhuza II to the present king, royalists have maintained close ties with religious bodies without wanting to appear to be favouring any particular denomination.

Prospects for Peace-building

Since there is no open or fully-blown conflict or hostility in Swaziland, there have not been any peace talks as in traditional conflicts such as those of the Democratic Republic of the Congo, Burundi, Rwanda, Angola or Lesotho. The situation in Swaziland remains confined to the local participants, except for a few visits to the country by South African government officials, who are very cautious in their approach to the domestic affairs of Swaziland. The Swazi king does not address the issues directly, but instead stands behind the CRC, which the trade unions and civil societies disparagingly refer to as a "toy telephone".[31]

Some of the key fault-lines that prevent a resolution of the conflicting positions are the following: first, the continued existence of the 1973 decree muzzles attempts by the pro-democracy formations to table their demands for multi-party politics. The royalists use this decree to delegitimise or criminalise the concerns of the pro-democracy groups. Therefore, there is a need to persuade the government of Swaziland to lift the state of emergency. This would open up the political space for genuine talks about how to solve the current situation in the country. Second, PUDEMO remains banned and cannot participate in negotiations about the future of politics. With the 1973 decree in place, the necessary debate by a diversity of stakeholders, regarding the opening up of the democratic space and party politics versus the *tinkhundla* system, has been reduced to a private dialogue between individual citizens on the one hand, and the

CRC and the king on the other. The media is not permitted to report on the process. Third, the CRC appears to complicate if not confound negotiations for democratic rule. Fourth, the absence of a third party from outside Swaziland at intermittent peace talks to resolve contentious issues is a key fault-line. It seems that the Swazi king would not welcome such a third party, unless it worked on his terms. For example, when announcing the long-awaited results of the CRC, King Mswati III is reported to have said that "since this country had welcomed the report and identified with it, it would be unfortunate if outsiders punched holes in it".[32] The royalists have long prevented the involvement of any foreign third party which might be sympathetic to their opponents.

The deep division is the issue of rulers versus subjects, where the latter want to change an entrenched set of power relations. The Dlamini royalists have long established themselves as the sole political authority in Swaziland. This arrangement predates European colonialism in Swaziland and was never fundamentally undermined by British colonialism.[33] The history and the ideology of kingship in Swaziland have evolved to such an extent that the country is normally perceived by both the Dlamini monarchy and the rural masses as the property of the king. Now popular demands for democracy and mass participation in governance appear to be direct challenges to the dominance of the monarchy.

All parties want peace in the country. But the notion of peace means different thing to the royalists and the pro-democracy groups. For the royalists, peace means a conducive atmosphere for attracting foreign investors to the country, whereas for the pro-democracy groups peace means the establishment of multi-party politics, democracy and the lifting of the state of emergency.[34] Both parties believe in a negotiated resolution of their differences.

The first requirement for negotiated politics in Swaziland may be for regional powers to recognise the fact that there is political instability in the country which requires their intervention. Second, these regional powers ought to convince the Swazi monarch of the benefit to him and the country from such an intervention. Once this scenario becomes acceptable to the Swazi authorities, then the regional powers could devise a mechanism to resolve conflict or bring about negotiated politics in the country.

When announcing the results of the CRC, King Mswati III stated that the next step was to appoint a group of constitutional lawyers to draft a constitution based on the CRC's report.[35] Yet he was aware that the CRC report does not enjoy popular support in the country. He is reported to have said, "The recommendations contained in the report were made by

Swazis and we hope that dissenting voices will recognise the fact that whatever is in the report was consented to by the entire nation."[36] This statement flies in the face of the fact that some CRC members withdrew from the committee on the grounds that there was a conflict of interests. Instead of addressing the reasons for the withdrawal of such persons as Masuku, the king is reported to have said, "*kwase akusevakali kutsi labanye bashonephi*", meaning "they mysteriously disappeared from the CRC".[37] Therefore, what King Mswati perceives as progress towards resolving the political stalemate in the country is still a non-starter for the pro-democracy groups.

Present and Future Opportunities for Reconciliation

There are no immediate prospects for resolving the current situation in the country. One cannot expect the Swazi monarch to voluntarily limit the scope of his executive power. PUDEMO, trade unions and the NGOs, for their part, will continue to be outmanoeuvred by the monarchy as long as they treat their demands for multi-party politics, democratisation and a constitutional monarchy as domestic issues which are limited to internal players. Even the Swaziland Solidarity Network, a coalition of mainly South African labour groups, has not forged an effective strategy for collaboration with the pro-democracy formations in Swaziland.

Another major obstacle toward addressing the situation in Swaziland is the Southern African Development Community's (SADC) position. The government of Swaziland still enjoys support from the SADC. Pro-democracy groups, both in Swaziland and outside, have so far failed to present their concerns to the SADC leaders and appeal for either the isolation of Swaziland from the SADC or for the SADC's intervention to resolve the political situation in the country. They have also failed to take advantage of Masuku's arrest in November 2000 by using it as a rallying point for local and international support.

The government of Swaziland enjoys the logistical support of important political players in Africa. For example, Swaziland recently asked Nigeria to provide it with experienced legal practitioners to serve as magistrates in Swaziland. The Nigerian High Commissioner in South Africa, Tunji Olagunju, promised that such a request would be considered within the context of a soon-to-be-established bi-national commission between Nigeria and Swaziland. He also mentioned that Nigeria and Swaziland were about to enter into an economic, scientific and technical co-operation agreement in November 2001.[38]

Swaziland's pro-democracy groups have weak links with South Africa, because they limit their contacts to labour organisations and the South

African Communist Party (SACP). This is a weakness, for the political influence of labour organisations such as COSATU and the SACP in South Africa is questionable. Therefore, one would not expect such organisations to play an influential role in assisting the democratisation of Swaziland. For example, the SACP's condemnation of the undemocratic nature of Swaziland's government has not yielded much change.[39] The pro-democracy groups in Swaziland would stand a better chance of receiving assistance if they worked closely with political parties in South Africa, instead of only with labour organisations.

The situation in Swaziland appears to require a form of intervention to reconcile the views of the monarchy and those held by pro-democracy groups. However, there is no easy solution given that the Dlamini monarchy has historical claims to being the founder of the Swazi state. It withstood Boer and British colonialism, succeeded colonial power at independence in 1968, and enjoys substantial popular support in the country. Even the pro-democracy groups in the country do not envisage a democratic Swaziland without a monarch. Hence, their call for a constitutional monarchy. Both the monarchy and the pro-democracy formations could be persuaded to consider the British model of the co-existence of the monarchy and parliamentary politics. (Here one is mindful of the concerns in Britain about the relevance of the monarchy in present times.)

The main countries with some leverage to influence political change in Swaziland are South Africa and the US, because of their huge financial investment in the country. But South Africa does not appear to be willing to exercise such an influence. The US could play such a role should it wish to do so. For example, in July 2001, Prime Minister Barnabas Sibusiso Dlamini announced that the king had lifted a ban on the controversial royal decree that prohibited publication of printed material (books, magazines or newspapers) critical of the king. The decree had also prevented "anyone from impersonating, or ridiculing the king" and had prevented legal challenges to any of the monarch's executive decisions.[40] Dlamini informed the public that, in lifting the ban, the king had considered the views of the trade unions, the general public, employers and the diplomatic community. Dlamini's announcement was preceded by US criticism of the decree, which was contained in a letter published by the Swazi media a week before the announcement. It is reported that the US letter stated that if the decree were not lifted, Swaziland would be excluded from the African Trade Growth Opportunities Act (ATGOA).[41]

The pro-democracy formations' major weakness is that they do not seem to have a well-respected leader, one that could either lead an opposition party or form a ruling party in a multi-party Swaziland, with the exception of Masuku of PUDEMO. The pro-democracy groups ought to begin to position or package themselves as either an official opposition or a government-in-waiting. And they should begin to interact with influential power brokers in the region and worldwide.

NOTES

1 See, for example, John Daniel and Johnson Vilane, "Swaziland: Political Crisis, Regional Dilemma," *Review of African Political Economy* 35 (1986): 54–67; Augustine Oyowe, "Swaziland at the Crossroads," *The Courier* 147 (1994): 18–20; Kuseni Dlamini, "The Old Order is Dying: Worker Militancy in Swaziland," *South African Labour Bulletin* 19 (1995): 85–90; Philemon Lukhele, "Mswati goes too far," *The Sowetan*, Tuesday, 3 July 2001, 8.

2 Other formations are the Swaziland Youth Congress (SWAYOCO), the banned National Liberatory Congress (NLC), the Swaziland National Association of Unemployed People (SNAUP) and the Federation of Swaziland Employers (FSE).

3 Jabulane Matsebula, "Challenging the Royalty: Underground Politics in Swaziland," *SAPEM* (1991): 28.

4 Richard Cornwell, *Swaziland and Lesotho: The Political and Economic Arena* (Pretoria: Africa Institute of South Africa, 1994), 4–5; see Richard Levin, "Swaziland Tinkhundla and the Myth of Swazi Tradition," *Journal of Contemporary African Studies* 10 (1991): 1–23.

5 Kuseni Dlamini, "Swaziland: Edging Closer to Democracy?" *South African Labour Bulletin* 20 (1996): 70. Dlamini's works are insightful, but do not cite sources for their evidence. This is their major weakness and whatever value they have is undermined by this limitation.

6 Business Media Company, "Swaziland's draft constitution to be ready in October." Reprinted at www.bdfm.co.za/cgi-bin/pp-print.pl (accessed 12 December 2001).

7 This refers to an acceptance of the monarchy as the sole political authority in Swaziland and the acceptance of the role of tradition in Swazi life and politics. It is patriotism based on the primacy of kingship in Swazi politics. Usually any criticism of the institution of monarchy is perceived by the royalists and their followers as "unSwazi". And as one scholar has noted, "[b]eing labelled 'unSwazi' is a heavy stigma in traditional circles". See Dlamini, "Old Order," 89.

8 For a discussion on the effectiveness of each of these actors on the ground in Swaziland, see Kuseni Dlamini, "Politics of Change: Swaziland's Future in the Balance," *Indicator SA* 14 (1997): 17–21; Dlamini, "Swaziland: Edging Closer to Democracy?"; Matsebula, "Challenging the Royalty," 27–29, and Mohammed Motala, "Trade Unions in Swaziland," *South African Labour Bulletin* 24 (2000): 85–90.

9 For example, see Robert Schroeder, "Swaziland and the European Union," *The Courier* 147 (1994): 35–38.

10 After the conquest the Dlamini clan assumed the royal position in Swazi politics. For a discussion of the Dlamini conquest and its consequences, see Hilda Kuper, *An African Aristocracy: Rank Among the Swazi* (London: Oxford University Press, 1947, reprinted 1965); Hilda Kuper, *The Swazi: A South African Kingdom* (New York: Holt,

1963); Richard Levin, *When the Sleeping Grass Awakens* (Johannesburg: Witwatersrand University Press, 1997), Introduction and chapters 2 and 4.

11 For a discussion of this point, see Levin, "Swaziland," 1–23; Richard Levin, "Is this the Swazi Way? State, Democracy and the Land Question," *Transformation* 13 (1990): 46–66; Richard Levin, "Traditional Land Tenure in Swaziland: Technical Efficiency, Problems of Democratic Organisation and the Value of Legalistic Classifications," in *Social Relations in Rural Swaziland: Critical Essays*, ed. Michael Neocosmos (University of Swaziland: Social Science Research Unit, 1987): 151–170.

12 Levin, *Sleeping Grass*, 15. The scenario described by Levin existed in pre-colonial Swaziland and is still in existence in present-day Swaziland.

13 For these demands, see Matsebula, "Challenging the Royalty,"; Dlamini, "Politics of Change," and Dlamini, "Swaziland," 17–21.

14 Dlamini, "Politics of Change," 17.

15 Ibid 18.

16 Ibid 17–18.

17 Ibid 18.

18 Ibid.

19 Ibid.

20 Ibid.

21 Ibid.

22 Dlamini, "Politics of Change," 17.

23 For a discussion of the evolving relations and contestations between the Swazi monarchy and the European colonisers, see Manelisi Genge, "Law and the Imposition of Colonial Rule in Swaziland, 1890–1898" (MA thesis, Ohio University, Athens, 1992), and Manelisi Genge, "Power and Gender in Southern African History: Power Relations in the Era of Queen Labotsibeni Gwamile Mdluli of Swaziland, *ca.* 1875–1921" (Ph.D. dissertation, Michigan State University, East Lansing, 1999).

24 John Baloro, "The Human Rights to Free Association and Assembly and Multi-party Democracy: A Study of the Law and Practice in Swaziland," *Africa Insight* 22 (1992): 208.

25 See Hilda Kuper, *The Uniform of Colour: A Study of White-Black Relationships in Swaziland* (Johannesburg: Witwatersrand University Press, 1947, reprinted 1969).

26 Dlamini, "Old Order," 86.

27 For a discussion of the violations of human rights in Swaziland, see Baloro, "Human Rights," 206–11; Human Rights Watch, "An Africa Watch Report: Academic Freedom and Human Rights Abuses in Africa" (New York: Human Rights Watch, 1991): 97–107; Paul Bischoff, "Peace, Nationalism and the State of Human Rights in Swaziland," *Human and People's Rights Project Monograph No. 7* (Lesotho: National University of Lesotho's Institute of Southern African Studies, 1989); K. A. Maope, "Human Rights in Botswana, Lesotho and Swaziland: A Survey of the Boleswa Countries," *Human and People's Rights Monograph Series No. 1* (Lesotho: National University of Lesotho's Institute of Southern African Studies, 1986), and Steven Neff, "Human Rights in Botswana, Lesotho and Swaziland: Implications of Adherence to International Human Rights Treaties," *Human and People's Rights Monograph Series No. 1* (Lesotho: National University of Lesotho's Institute of Southern African Studies, 1986). For a comprehensive study of the human rights record in Swaziland, see a collection of essays in *Human Rights in Swaziland: The Legal Response*, eds. Chuks Okpaluba, Nkonzo Hlatshwayo and Bekithemba Khumalo (Kwaluseni, Swaziland: University of Swaziland, 1997).

28 Baloro, "Human Rights," 209.

29 Part of this quotation is quoted by Baloro, "Human Rights."

30 Baloro, "Human Rights."

31 University of Pennsylvania School of Arts and Sciences, "Swaziland: Constitutional Review [1999/06/02]." Reprinted at www.sas.upenn.edu/African_Studies/Newsletter/irinw6199b.html (accessed 12 December 2001).

32 Reported by Innocent Maphalala, "Swazis Have Spoken," *Swazi News*, Saturday, 11 August 2001, 8.

33 For a brief overview of this arrangement, see "Introduction," in *Swaziland: Contemporary Social and Economic Issues*, eds. Peter G. Forster and Bongani J. Nsibande (Aldershot, Burlington, USA: Ashgate, 2000), xvi–xix. The notion of kingship versus clans has long been a subject of scholarly interest among historians, see for example, David Newbury, *Kings and Clans: Ijwi Island and the Lake Kivu Rift, 1780–1840* (Madison, Wisconsin: The University of Wisconsin Press, 1991). More recently scholars of African politics have studied the notion of subjects versus citizens within a colonial context, see Mahmood Mamdani, *Citizen and Subject: Contemporary Africa and the Legacy of Late Colonialism* (Princeton, New Jersey: Princeton University Press, 1996).

34 See Ncamsile Mamba, "Don't Whisper in the Dark: King Calls on Nation to Speak Freely on National Issues," *Swazi News*, 15 September 2001, 4.

35 Maphalala, "Swazis Have Spoken," 8.

36 Ibid.

37 Ibid.

38 "Swaziland Seeks Nigerian Magistrates," *The Guardian*. Reprinted at www.ngrguardiannews.com/news2/nn836716.html (accessed 17 October 2001).

39 Alec Lushaba, "Swaziland: SA Party Call for Pressure on Undemocratic States." Reprinted at www.africaonline.com/site/Articles/1,34976.jsp (accessed 1 September 2001).

40 BBC News, "Swazi King Bows to Pressure." Reprinted at http://newssearch.bbc.co.uk/hi/english/world/africa/newsid_1456000/1456292.stm (accessed 12 December 2001).

41 Ibid. See also allafrica.com, "King Mswati III Repeals Controversial Decree." Reprinted at http://allafrica.com/stories/printable/200107250209.html (accessed 12 December 2001).

RESOURCES

Books, Articles, Current Media Reports

Baloro, John. "The Human Rights to Free Association and Assembly and Multi-party Democracy: A Study of the Law and Practice in Swaziland." *Africa Insight* 22 (1992): 206–211.

Bischoff, Paul. "Peace, Nationalism and the State of Human Rights in Swaziland." *Human and People's Rights Project Monograph No. 7.* Lesotho: National University of Lesotho's Institute of Southern African Studies, 1989.

Bonner, Philip. *Kings, Commoners and Concessionaires: The Evolution and the Dissolution of the Nineteenth-Century Swazi State.* Johannesburg: Ravan, 1983.

Daniel, John and Johnson Vilane. "Swaziland: Political Crisis, Regional Dilemma." *Review of African Political Economy* 35 (1986): 54–67.

Dlamini, Kuseni. "The Old Order is Dying: Worker Militancy in Swaziland." *South African Labour Bulletin* 19 (1995): 85–90.

———. "Swaziland: Edging Closer to Democracy?" *South African Labour Bulletin* 20 (1996): 67–72.

———. "Politics of Change: Swaziland's Future in the Balance." *Indicator SA* 14 (1997): 17–21.

Forster, Peter G. and Bongani J. Nsibande. "Introduction." In *Swaziland: Contemporary Social and Economic Issues*, edited by Peter G. Forster and Bongani J. Nsibande. Aldershot, Burlington, USA: Ashgate, 2000.

Genge, Manelisi. "Power and Gender in Southern African History: Power Relations in the Era of Queen Labotsibeni Gwamile Mdluli of Swaziland, *ca.* 1875–1921." Ph.D. dissertation, East Lansing: Michigan State University, 1999.

Kirya, George B. "The 'No Party' or 'Movement' Democracy in Uganda." In *The Evolving African Constitutionalism: Special Issue,* edited by Adama Dieng. International Commission of Jurists, June 1998: 79–89.

Kuper, Hilda. *An African Aristocracy: Rank Among the Swazi.* London: Oxford University Press, 1947, reprinted 1965.

———. *The Uniform of Colour: A Study of White-Black Relationships in Swaziland.* Johannesburg: Witwatersrand University Press, 1947, reprinted 1969.

———. *The Swazi: A South African Kingdom.* New York: Holt, 1963.

Levin, Richard. "Traditional Land Tenure in Swaziland: Technical Efficiency, Problems of Democratic Organisation and the Value of Legalistic Classifications." In *Social Relations in Rural Swaziland: Critical Essays,* edited by Michael Neocosmos, University of Swaziland: Social Science Research Unit, 1987: 151–170.

———. "Is this the Swazi Way? State, Democracy and the Land Question," *Transformation* 13 (1990): 46–66.

———. "Swaziland Tinkhundla and the Myth of Swazi Tradition." *Journal of Contemporary African Studies* 10 (1991): 1–23.

———. *When the Sleeping Grass Awakens.* Johannesburg: Witwatersrand University Press, 1997.

Motala, Mohammed. "Trade Unions in Swaziland." *South African Labour Bulletin* 24 (2000): 85–90.

Okpaluba, Chuks, Nkonzo Hlatshwayo and Bekithemba Khumalo, eds. *Human Rights in Swaziland: The Legal Response.* Kwaluseni, Swaziland: University of Swaziland, 1997.

SWAZILAND COUNTRY INFORMATION

Geography
Location: Southern Africa.
Cities: *Capital:* Mbabane (1996 pop. 58 096). *Other city:* Manzini (principal commercial city, pop. 64 842, 1996 est.).

People
Nationality: *Noun:* Swazi(s). *Adjective:* Swazi.
Population (1999 est.): 910 000.
Population growth rate: 3%.
Ethnic groups: The majority of the population is Swazi, the remainder is Zulu and the white population is 2%.
Religions: It is estimated that the population is 40% Zionist, 20% Roman Catholic, 10% Muslim, and the remaining 30% divided between other beliefs.
Languages: IsiSwati and English (official).
Education: *Years compulsory:* none. *Attendance:* 95% primary and 44% secondary. *Literacy:* 75%.
Health (1997): *Infant mortality rate:* 86.1/1 000. *Life expectancy:* 57.7 years. *HIV infection rate:* 18.5%.
Workforce: Agriculture and forestry: 28.3%. Construction: 6.3%. Distribution: 18.7%. Finance: 7.9%. Manufacturing: 27.4%. Mining and quarry: 1.8%. Services: 7.8%. Transport: 1.8%.

Economy
GDP (1998): $1.02 billion.
GDP real growth rate (1998): 2.3%.
Per capita income (1998): $1 300.
Inflation (1999): 5.9%.
Natural resources: Asbestos, coal, diamonds, quarry stone, timber, talc.
Agriculture: 9.6% of GDP. *Products:* sugar cane, corn, citrus fruits, livestock, wood, pineapples, tobacco, rice, peanuts.
Industry: 36% of GDP. *Types:* sugar refining, light manufactured goods, wood pulp, textiles, ginned cotton, processed foods, consumer goods.
Trade (1999): *Exports:* $634.5 million: soft drink concentrates, sugar, wood pulp, canned fruits, cotton yarn. *Major markets:* South Africa, EU, Mozambique, US. *Imports:* $753.7 million: chemicals, clothing, foodstuffs, machinery, motor vehicles, petroleum products.

Military
Military expenditure: Dollar figures: $23 million (FY95/96).
Military expenditure: Percent of GDP: 1.9% (FY95/96).

Demographic information is drawn from that compiled by the United States Department of State. See http://www.state.gov/r/pa/ei/bgn

238

Chapter 10

Uganda: Half Way to Democracy

SUSANNE STRELEAU

Uganda is a small landlocked country situated in East Africa, bordered by Sudan in the north, the Democratic Republic of Congo (DRC) in the west, Kenya in the east and Rwanda and Tanzania in the south. Over the last 20 years, the country called the "Pearl of Africa" by the British prime minister Winston Churchill has undergone a remarkable process of transformation. It has made its way from chaos and violence to relative stability, recovery and growth. Uganda's government has been one of the most consistent reformers in sub-Saharan Africa over the past decade. Still, there are many problems that remain unresolved. At a key point in its history, the consolidation of reform will depend heavily on whether Uganda can resolve several significant and protracted conflicts.

Established as a British protectorate in 1894, Uganda obtained independence in 1962 and, under President Milton Obote, became a republic in 1967. Idi Amin, a military commander who ruled Uganda for eight brutal years, deposed Obote in 1971. Amin's reign of terror resulted in the death of between 300 000 and 500 000 Ugandans. In 1980, Obote regained the presidency, but was soon ousted by Tito Okello. Six years later, then Defence Minister and current president Yoweri Museveni led his rebel National Resistance Army (NRA) into Kampala and took power. Under Museveni, Ugandans have negotiated a new constitution and seen significant economic growth. General elections were held in 1986, inflation continues to slow and the nation has taken bold steps to curb the spread of HIV/Aids. However, Museveni is not unchallenged. In today's Uganda, there are a number of groups that continue to work for the overthrow of Museveni's government. The more powerful of these factions have ties to Uganda's neighbours. In the northern region, the Lord's Resistance Army (LRA) and the Uganda National Rescue Front II (UNRF-II) are active and supported partially by Sudan. In the southwest and west, the government is opposed by the Allied Democratic Forces (ADF). The Uganda Salvation Army/Front (USA/F) operates primarily in the eastern regions.

Besides armed struggle, there are several other factors that hinder the development of Uganda, a country that might otherwise be seen as a model for development in Africa. Not all parts of Uganda have been able to participate in the reform process. There remains a striking gulf between the southern and northern regions. In the latter, the infrastructure lies in shambles and the majority of the population lives under rather dire and often violent conditions. Due to cultural and linguistic differences, as well as the danger of landmines and ambushes along northern roads, there is little social contact between southern and northern Ugandans.

Furthermore, Uganda continues to rank as one of the poorest countries in the world. It has one of the lowest life expectancies and a very high illiteracy rate. During the last few years, Uganda's involvement in the Congolese war, as well as general mismanagement and corruption, have complicated peace-making and reform.

With regard to conflict resolution and peace-building, it appears that President Museveni is less prepared to talk to the diverse rebel groups, especially those in the north, than to employ the military. Nevertheless, in early 2000, Museveni did offer a blanket amnesty to all rebels. Some have used this policy to return home. The main rebel leaders, however, appear less interested in indemnity than in inclusion in structures of political power. Nevertheless, throughout the country, reconciliation initiatives are being facilitated by church communities, district officials, the UN and both local and international NGOs. Many focus on reducing violence, creating dialogue between warring factions in the north and reintegrating child soldiers. However, these initiatives offer little immediate hope for a political solution to the larger conflict. A lasting peace will likely have to emerge from peace talks between rebel groups and the government.

The Face of Conflict

Uganda has set out on a promising path toward growth and peace. However, it faces a number of significant problems. Regional conflicts are destabilising the country, especially the war in the DRC. Economic growth, foreign investment and the privatisation process have slowed, in part because of mismanagement and corruption. Uganda carries an immense debt, roughly $3.2 billion. According to the World Bank and the International Monetary Fund, it will continue to depend on substantial external assistance for at least the next decade.[1]

Since the National Resistance Movement (NRM) of President Museveni took power in 1986, Uganda has enjoyed a kind of basic stability. However, there have been severe and violent conflicts in the northern, southwest and, more recently, eastern regions. The issues are complex, especially as participants hold conflicting views about the motives, purpose and extent of the fighting. Nevertheless, a common claim of all rebel groups in Uganda is that they are fighting the government, especially what they perceive to be Museveni's dictatorial nature. Peter Otia, leader of the currently inactive rebel movement, the Uganda People's Army, has claimed that his is a struggle for democracy in Uganda.[2]

The conflict in the northern region of Uganda has occupied centre-stage. It is a source of violence and instability that has the potential to undo many efforts at reform. Comprising almost a third of the country, the northern region has not shared the advances made in central and southern Uganda. Persistent conflict has taken place in two districts, Kitgum and Gulu, both of which are inhabited by the Acholi people. Since 1988, the LRA, led by Joseph Kony, has operated from bases in southern Sudan and enjoyed support from the Sudanese government.[3] In the same region, the UNRF-II has renewed its activity since March 1998. The UNRF-II has been accused of terrorist attacks and also appears to receive support from the Sudanese government.

The basic motive of the LRA and other rebel groups is political influence and the overthrow of the Ugandan government. The LRA aims to rule Uganda in accordance with its "Ten Point Programme" – a plan based on the ten biblical commandments. Supported by the militantly Islamic government of Sudan, the beliefs and practices of the ostensibly Christian LRA have changed over the years. In 1987, the LRA was closely identified with the Holy Spirit Movement of Alice Lakwena, a connection that bolstered Kony's popularity with the Acholi. More than 10 years later, with a shift toward Islamic beliefs and practices, the Acholi fear him.[4] The LRA has also built up a network of representatives outside Uganda. The LRA is supplied with weapons and transport by the Sudanese government in retaliation for the support that the Ugandan government gives to rebel groups in Sudan, especially to the Sudanese People's Liberation Army (SPLA). To achieve its aims, the LRA also co-operates with the West Nile Bank Front in northwest Uganda, to which former Ugandan president Idi Amin was closely connected, and which seeks to create an independent Islamic West Nile state.

The conflict has been waged with incredible brutality. Children have been abducted, trained as soldiers and forced to commit atrocities. The civilian population has been brutalised by rape, mutilation, torture and outright slaughter. Villages are raided, stores looted and houses and schools burned. The infrastructure has collapsed and in many areas agriculture and education have been affected.[5] Since 1995, when the Sudanese government began to support the LRA, rebels have been armed with machine guns and landmines instead of rifles and machetes. At about the same time, the Ugandan People's Defence Force (UPDF) started to move the Acholi people into so-called protected camps. This action is problematic, especially in light of the UPDF's record of human rights abuse. The Acholi do not trust the UPDF. There are reports of forced internment. Due to the conditions in the camps and the gross human rights violations committed by both sides, the situation represents nothing less than a humanitarian crisis. In early 2002, it was estimated that there are over 500 000 internally displaced persons in Uganda, a situation that threatens to undermine democratic reform and perpetuate the abuse of human rights.[6]

With respect to motives, the rebels in the north insist that a peace agreement was signed in December 1985 by then guerrilla leader Museveni during a brief period when the Acholi controlled the Ugandan government under President Okello. The claim is that Museveni abrogated the deal a mere two weeks after it was signed. In the period following Museveni's assumption of power, the rebels claim that the NRA occupied Acholi land and perpetrated human rights abuses. After fleeing to Sudan, the Ugandan-supported Sudanese rebel faction, the SPLA, destroyed their camps. According to the rebels, they were left with little choice but to re-enter Uganda to establish a defensible zone of occupation. Today, the LRA offers a message similar to other rebel factions. In a 1998 public meeting, convened in London, representatives of the LRA stated that they are fighting a liberation war to overthrow Museveni's dictatorship and establish a multi-party democracy in Uganda.[7]

The Acholi people provide a variety of reasons for the conflict. In June 1998, Acholi from all walks of life came together for a two-day meeting to discuss different aspects of the situation in Gulu and Kitgum. In their opinion, the foremost issue was the harassment, torture and killing of the Acholi civilian population by the NRA. However, Acholi support for the LRA has faded. The rebels are accused of terrorising civilians. Caught somewhere in the middle, distrustful of Museveni's government and threatened by the LRA, the Acholi have called on the government to end its support of the SPLA and demanded that Sudan disassociate itself from the LRA.[8] For his part, President Museveni takes the view that the original problem in the north was that the Acholi people were deprived of a chance to enrich themselves at the expense of other Ugandans.[9] The NRM has also argued that power and money motivate Kony and his LRA. With respect to ending the conflict, Museveni has stated that peace talks with

Kony, whom he calls a terrorist without a political agenda, are morally indefensible given Kony's alleged reign of terror against the people.[10] In 2002, fighting between the LRA and government forces continued. The latter, with the permission of the government, have taken their operation "Iron Fist" into Sudan. Uganda's Defence Minister recently claimed that he did not expect the LRA to survive to the end of 2002. Reports of the fighting are contradictory. Some claim that Sudan continues to support Kony even though it has allowed the Ugandan army into its territory. Reports in April 2002 indicated that Kony was on the run, if not under siege, in the mountains of southern Sudan. Also operating in the north-western part of Uganda, the UNRF-II appears to be moving on a different track. In June 2002, the group signed a cease-fire agreement with the government, paving the way for some form of political dialogue.

Another hazard zone is the northeast of Uganda, where the Karamojong, a semi-nomadic minority of about 100 000 people, have amassed substantial fire-power. They use these arms for cattle and vehicle raids into neighbouring districts, such as the Teso, Bugisu and Kapchorwa areas.[11] While the conflicts in the north and northwest are inextricably related to Sudan's past support for the LRA and UNRF-II, the difficulties in the Karamoja region (Kotido and Moroto districts) are internal and have larger implications on a regional level only occasionally when cattle and vehicle raids lead the heavily armed Karamojong into Kenya or Sudan. However, hundreds of people, including many children and women, have died in the fighting. Although the UPDF has intervened in the fighting with helicopters that have caused heavy casualties, they have, so far, failed to provide effective security and protection to the unarmed neighbouring districts against those wielding an estimated 30 000 illegal weapons. However, the Ugandan government intends to start a disarmament programme carried out by 7 000 UPDF soldiers, of whom 4 300 have already been deployed.[12] There is disagreement about the motives for the Karamojong's actions. Some view it as political while others argue that the cattle raids are a cultural tradition, a way of accumulating wealth and demonstrating masculinity.[13]

For the first time since the defeat of the Uganda People's Army by Museveni's troops in the late 1980s, rebel activity reappeared in eastern Uganda in mid-1998. A previously unknown rebel group, the USA/F, began carrying out attacks on prisons (for instance, the Mutufu local administration prison from where they abducted 70 inmates) and other government facilities. Other rebel groups in the area are the Citizens Army for Multiparty Politics and the Anti Referendum Army.[14]

The west and southwest of Uganda constitute another hotspot. There, the UPDF has been fighting the ADF. The ADF is led by Herbert Itongwa and is made up of ex-soldiers of the Mobutu regime, the defeated Rwandan Habyarimana regime and extreme elements of the Tabliq Muslim community.[15] The ADF has been engaged in a guerrilla war since 1996 and is operating in the Ruwenzori Mountains in western Uganda and eastern Congo. The districts mostly affected by this conflict are Bundibugyo and Kasese. In 2000 the ADF also launched attacks in Bushenyi, Hoima, Kibale and Mubende. The fighting has left the local population short of food, water, shelter and medical care.[16]

Like the LRA in the north, the ADF in the southwest has escalated its attacks against civilians. There are reports of massacres and mutilations and frequent decapitations. The abduction of children – from Uganda and the DRC – is an often-used means of supplying troops. On several occasions, the ADF has interrupted school to abduct a whole class of students. Due to the conflict, more than 100 000 civilians in this region have been internally displaced and are living in overcrowded camps. Although President Museveni recently declared the war over and the ADF defeated, the situation is far from being resolved. Some key rebel leaders are still in hiding in the DRC.[17]

Compared to the views and motives of the northern rebel groups, less is known about the combatants in the west and southwest. But the ADF has, like the LRA, claimed that it is fighting against Museveni's one-party state. To explain abductions, the ADF from time to time releases statements blaming the UPDF for terrorising citizens after being defeated by the ADF. The ADF says that the civilian population always pleads with the rebel fighters for help to avoid the government army. According to Human Rights Watch, these declarations are part of a well-targeted misinformation campaign.[18]

Along with these internal conflicts, Uganda is deeply entwined in the Congo war. The war in the DRC, which erupted in the summer of 1998, continues despite the Lusaka Agreement – involving six other African governments and rebel movements from Rwanda, Uganda and Burundi. Uganda's participation in the Congo war has to be seen in a regional context. Uganda and the neighbouring states, Burundi and Rwanda, contributed to the downfall of the Mobutu regime by supporting Laurent Kabila and his *Alliance des forces démocratiques pour la libération du Congo-Zaïre* (AFDL). Shortly after seizing power in May 1997, the new Congolese government was accused of being a puppet of Rwanda and Uganda. To prove the contrary, the late President Kabila tried to dilute the

influence of these countries, turning against them by ordering their troops
out of the DRC. He also charged that Uganda and Rwanda were plotting
to set up a Tutsi-Hima empire in the region. Coalitions shifted almost
overnight. By August 1998, yesterday's friends were enemies.

Uganda's expressed reason for intervention in the Congo war is "security". The government believes that the ADF uses Congolese territory as a
base. The official aim of the UPDF was the destruction of the ADF plat-
forms and preventing Sudan from taking advantage of the administrative
vacuum in eastern Congo to attack Uganda.[19] In the course of the war, the
allied Rwandan and Ugandan troops, the Rwandese Patriotic Army
(RPA) and the UPDF, began to fight among themselves in diamond-rich
Kisangani. The fighting severely damaged Uganda's reputation in the eyes
of the international community. Both Uganda and Rwanda were condemned by the US and the UN.[20] In the Ugandan-controlled Ituri region,
UPDF troops have also participated in fighting over land disputes
between the Hema and the Lendu over the last two years. While the
Lendu identify with the Tutsi, the Hema see themselves as kin to the
Hutu. The UPDF became involved and added fuel to the conflict by
recruiting and training both the Hema and the Lendu, but later were
alleged to favour the Hema and reportedly even helped them attack the
Lendu. These incidents resulted in an estimated 7 000 civilian deaths and
180 000 people being displaced, and struck another blow to Uganda's
image among the UN and donor countries.[21]

Often connected to the conflicts which trouble Uganda is the problem
of constant and grave abuse of human rights, including killings, child
abuse and torture. Of particular concern is the abduction of children in the
north and west of the country. The ADF, LRA and UNRF-II abduct children for training as guerrillas, and young girls are used as sex and labour
slaves. In the north, more than 10 000 children are estimated to have been
abducted since the beginning of the conflicts. Recently, the Ugandan government granted full access to a political and military training camp housing child soldiers from the DRC, and over 163 Congolese children have
subsequently been handed over to a UNICEF-led assessment team.[22]

The violence and abuse is compounded by a lack of civil rights protection. Citizens face arbitrary arrests as well as cruel, inhumane and degrading treatment in police stations. Even the formation of NGOs is restricted.
In addition to the violation of fundamental human rights, Ugandans
also lack full freedom of speech and press, the right of peaceful assembly
and association and the right to form political parties. Political and economic life is troubled by mismanagement and corruption. However, the

apparent lack of commitment to fighting corruption in the mid-1990s was followed by a more activist parliament in 1998. A number of ministers and high-ranking officials have been forced to resign after cases of power abuse and corruption have come to light. The human rights record has improved significantly over the last 15 years as well, mostly because the NRA and UPDF are more conscious of civilian rights than the security forces were under Idi Amin and Milton Obote.[23]

Early in 2000, Uganda was beset with a rather tumultuous presidential campaign. Newspapers published voter surveys, election-monitoring groups were set up and it was feared that refugees and foreigners would manage to register in the voters' lists. The election campaign included a significant number of incidents and riots, in particular violence incited or carried out by government agents. The leading challenger to President Museveni was Colonel Dr Kizza Besigye. Like Museveni, he ran for the NRM, in which he had held a number of positions. Because of the violence and intimidation that marked the election campaigns, Ugandans, along with the international community, worried over the security of the candidates and the voters. President Museveni sent additional troops to the north to ensure peaceful elections and stop LRA tampering. The situation calmed somewhat. Museveni was re-elected in March 2001 with about 70% of the vote.[24]

The international perception of the situation in Uganda is ambivalent. Since 1997, the international community has embraced the generation of so-called "new African leaders". With this expression, they describe the relatively young and often charismatic ex-guerrilla fighters who have turned statesmen. The presidents of Rwanda, Eritrea, Ethiopia and the DRC fall into this category. The motivation and energy of these politicians have raised hopes among western governments for an African Renaissance.[25] President Museveni also belongs to this group of leaders. Western leaders see him as one of the key figures in the Great Lakes region and a power broker in regional conflicts. Therefore, although united in condemning the violent conflicts and most of the rebel groups, the international community has been reluctant to call for democratic reforms and respect for human rights in Uganda. However, this does not mean that the political and human rights situation in Uganda has gone unnoticed.

The extensive coverage of human rights abuses in the US Department of State's annual *Human Rights Report* shows that it is not unaware of the situation's complexity and the fact that all sides have committed atrocities.[26] During the 1995 constitutional debates, the US took a critical position on Museveni's Movement System, a concept the president introduced intended to embrace the entire population within the NRM. The US stressed that governments that do not allow political competition and deny human rights are likely to fail at great human cost.[27] At the same time, the US embassy in Kampala issued a statement, noting that "the stage is being set for the entrenchment of a system of government which falls seriously short of full democracy and political enfranchisement".[28] In the following years, the US embassy continued to criticise the government. For instance, it questioned the credibility and fairness of the 1996 elections and indicated that it would not offer support for the 2000 referendum on Uganda's restrictive political system, saying that freedom of association and assembly were not voteable commodities.[29] In spite of that, the Museveni government remains relatively close to the US, especially as it toes American foreign policy in Sudan. While, for instance, the Kenyan and Zambian governments receive funding only on the condition of progress on democratisation and human rights, Uganda has successfully evaded such regulations. Although US criticism of Uganda has lessened, the US has also taken steps to distance itself from Museveni.[30]

The European Union (EU) is also rather silent on the issues of democratisation and human rights in Uganda. During Uganda's preparation for the 2000 referendum, the EU expressed concerns about lack of political freedom in Uganda. At a 1998 donor meeting in Kampala, the EU declared that it would closely monitor the coming referendum, and that it would look at the structures and activities of the movement as well as at the terms and applications of the referendum bill. The Netherlands was a bit more direct, criticising the Ugandan government for extending its transitional period. It dismissed the referendum as unfair and threatened to cut off Dutch aid if Uganda did not reduce defence expenditure. The position of the UK is less clear. The British Labour Party's secretary, Nick Sigler, viewed the referendum as a cause for concern and described the Movement System as worrying. This was in line with the British High Commissioner to Uganda, Michael Cook, who argued in favour of allowing political parties to campaign for the referendum.[31] In contrast, Clare Short, British Secretary of State for International Development, expressed support for the referendum, stating that the Ugandans have a right to choose what they want.[32]

The World Bank is among Museveni's strongest supporters. Uganda is one of the few African countries that has a sound economic record and that adheres strictly to the fiscal discipline requirements imposed by the Bank. It was also the first country to benefit from the Heavily Indebted Poor Countries (HIPC) initiative. Uganda has served as an important advocate for the World Bank in Africa. The relationship has offered important benefits for both.[33] The World Bank has therefore done little to address the need for political reform in Uganda. Its website indicates support for the present system in Uganda, stating that "economic reform has been accompanied by political reform" and that the Ugandan government is "composed of broad-based political groupings brought together under the country's no-party political system".[34] For its part, the UN has focused on Uganda's violent conflicts, especially the problem of child soldiers. In 1998, the UN Commission on Human Rights adopted a resolution on the abduction of children in northern Uganda, calling upon the LRA rebels to cease abductions and release children being held. Another UN Security Council Resolution, urging greater protection for children in armed conflicts, was mainly due to briefings by UN special representatives on rebel abuses against children in Uganda.[35]

The Historical Roots of Violence and Division

Towards the end of the nineteenth century, at the height of the scramble for Africa, the region known today as Uganda came under British influence. In 1894, a British protectorate was established. In determining the borders, the colonial powers had little respect for ethnic (inter) relations and cultural history. Like most African countries, Uganda's people represent a mixture of different tribes and religions. In the south, people had lived for centuries in centralised kingdoms with a hierarchy of chiefs as well as parliaments. In the north, most of the people were nomadic pastoralists. British rule initially focused on the Kingdom of Buganda in the south. In 1900, the Buganda land was divided equally between the British and its chiefs. Extension of colonial rule to the areas outside Buganda followed quickly. This caused problems as some of the neighbouring kingdoms had been Buganda's enemies. Tension increased partly because the Buganda often became British attendants, a position through which they were able to obtain something of a privileged position in society. The northern part of Uganda remained undeveloped during the colonial era. While the people from the south served the British as civil servants, the northerners were recruited as soldiers. The army was detested. Its composition stayed the same after independence and the rule of soldiers from the northern regions of Acholi, Teso, Lango and the West Nile was expanded under the Obote government from 1962 to 1971.[36]

Uganda gained independence in 1962 as a federation of five kingdoms, all under an alliance of the predominately Protestant Ugandan People's

Congress (UPC) and the *Kabaka Yekka*, the traditionalist political party of Buganda. A northerner, Milton Obote, became prime minister and the king *(Kabaka)* of Buganda was made president. This coalition did not last long. In 1964, an attempt to push Obote and his deputy army command-er, Idi Amin, out of power ended with the dethroning of the *Kabaka*, the promotion of Amin to army chief of staff and the suspension of Uganda's constitution. In the period that followed, the UPC ruled increasingly alone. In 1966–67, Obote imposed a new republican constitution on the country, establishing a strong executive presidency and weakening the influence of the traditional leaders. Buganda rejected the constitution and Obote ordered the army to attack the palace of the *Kabaka* in Mengo. The *Kabaka* fled to exile. The kingdoms were abolished and Uganda became a republic. In 1969, after an assassination attempt on Obote, the UPC banned all political opposition.[37]

While Obote was busy attempting to strengthen his political position, Amin used the time to gain control over part of the Ugandan armed forces. Since 1969, Obote had divided the army into two factions: the Nilotic soldiers, mostly Acholi and Lango, and the West Nilers, a group composed of Kakwa, Nubian, Lugban and Sudanese soldiers. Obote, him-self a Langi from the north, relied on the Nilotic soldiers, building them into the majority of the army, whereas Amin was supported by the West Nilers, especially the Nubian, who were the army's professional backbone. As Amin's influence grew, Obote tried to isolate and remove him from the army. Amin put a stop to these plans by ousting Obote while he was attending a conference in Singapore.

Initially, many Ugandans welcomed Amin's coup. Western powers saw Amin as a loyal ally in the fight against communism. After taking power, Amin embarked on a programme of populist gestures, including the release of many detainees and the return of the *Kabaka's* body from exile for burial. The enthusiasm soon turned into horror. As he started to elim-inate his opponents from the army, thousands of Acholi and Langi soldiers were brutally killed in massacres. In 1972, Amin delivered another bomb-shell: seeking friends in the Arab world, he became an outspoken critic of Israel and ordered all Israelis to leave the country. Later in the same year, he ordered all non-citizen Asians to leave as well. Eventually, many Europeans also left Uganda after Amin nationalised foreign-owned com-panies. With the economy in shambles and growing discontent among civilians and soldiers, Amin decided to preoccupy the army with an exter-nal enemy. Therefore, in 1978, he ordered the invasion of the Kagera Salient, a region in neighbouring Tanzania. Tanzania's president Julius

Nyerere responded with a counter invasion, joining the rebel Uganda National Liberation Army (UNLA).

Amin was overthrown in April 1979.[38] His rule was followed by the brief presidencies of the former Vice Chancellor of the Kampala Makerere University, Yusef Lule, and Godfrey Binaisa, the Attorney General under Obote. Both administrations were short-lived. However, it is remarkable that under Binaisa a ban on political parties was imposed. He argued that this would prevent the politics of religion, sectarianism, rivalry and hatred, and would lead Uganda toward consensus. Binaisa was removed from power by pro-Obote forces in the UNLA, the ban on political parties was cancelled and elections were scheduled for December 1980.[39] Among the candidates was ex-President Obote, and the young Museveni, the latter running for his Uganda Patriotic Movement (UPM). Museveni was then a minor player. Obote was declared the winner and immediately sworn in as president. Most international observers, as well as the participating parties, objected on the grounds that the elections were rigged by a corrupt and military-dominated pro-Obote system.

Museveni took the undemocratic elections as a reason for guerrilla warfare. He established the NRM, with its military wing, the NRA. Headquartered in Luwero, in southcentral Uganda, Museveni's declared aim was to free Uganda from the manipulations of elitist and non-representative political parties. The civil war that followed was only slightly less brutal than Amin's regime, killing more than 200 000 civilians.[40] Beside Museveni's NRA, which was strongly supported in the Buganda region, other rebel groups fought against Obote. In July 1985, the Acholi faction within UNLA, headed by Basilio and Tito Okello, ousted Obote and started peace talks with the NRA and NRM in Nairobi. Although Museveni and the new president, Tito Okello, signed a peace accord, Museveni continued his guerrilla war and finally overthrew the government in January 1986.[41]

When Museveni came to power, he suspended political party activity for a four-year transition period. The NRM established the National Resistance Council (NRC) to govern. Museveni's initial government embraced a wide political spectrum that narrowed as time passed. In 1989, Museveni extended the interim period for another five years, saying that the objectives of the NRM had not yet been met. In the same year, he appointed a Constitutional Commission to draft a new constitution for Uganda. The Commission, known as the Odoki Commission, after its chairman Justice Ben Odoki, finished its task in 1992. It issued a report that proposed a framework for a new constitution which reflected the attitudes of political parties in Uganda. Uganda's fourth constitution was enacted in September 1995. In 1996, Museveni won the race for the presidential elections against his Democratic Party (DP) opponent, Paul Ssemogerere.[42]

The impact of colonialism has continued to ripple through the fabric of Ugandan life. The ensuing conflicts are compounded and sometimes caused by ethnic and regional differences. In terms of culture, religion and economic activity, Uganda is not a homogeneous country. Its population of about 21 million is made up of more than 50 ethnic groups, which fall into four broad groups, namely the Bantu, Nilotics, Nilo-Hamites and Sudanic peoples. Each group speaks a different language. Luganda and Swahili are widely spoken and English is the official language. Uganda does not have a state religion. More than 80% of the population are Christian (Catholics 44%, Protestants 39%) and about 10% are Muslims. Religious groups must register with the government. There are several small sectarian communities. Some of these attracted special attention in March 2000 when mass graves were found to contain the remains of followers from the Movement for the Restoration of the Ten Commandments of God.[43]

Since Amin's regime, education has deteriorated, due mostly to political disturbances and subsequent economic problems. Although signs of renewal and improvements in the education sector can be seen, Uganda's adult literacy rate is still the lowest in East Africa. In recent years, the amount of money provided for education has fallen drastically. Parents have to pay for primary school education, which means that children from financially disadvantaged families do not have access to education. Altogether, only 53% of children attend school. Half drop out before they have mastered basic reading, writing and arithmetic.[44]

The most important sector of the economy in Uganda is agriculture, employing over 80% of the population. The economy depends especially on the exportation of coffee. Tea, tobacco and cotton are also key exports. Conditions for farming in Uganda are good, with fertile soils and regular rainfall. The economy was badly affected under the Amin regime. The inflation rate reached 1 000%, real wages dropped dramatically, the infrastructure deteriorated and tourism vanished. Today, economic development is steady but fragile. The economy grew at a rate of about 5% during 2000 and the pace of privatisation is increasing. However, the GDP remains at $330 per capita, a very low level, and foreign economic assistance still provides about 50% of government revenue. Furthermore, due to chronic corruption and continuing concerns about regional security in the wake of Uganda's involvement in the DRC, foreign investment remains weak, making up only 4% of GDP.[45]

Uganda's political situation is characterised by significant divisions. Museveni introduced the "no-party" system when his NRM took power in 1986. Parties could exist, but their members were not able to run as candidates in elections. The "no-party" system was entrenched by the 1995 constitution's prohibition on political party conferences, public rallies and campaigns. The NRM does not see itself as a political party but as a "Movement" representing the entire population. In theory, every Ugandan is a member of the Movement and can, as such, stand for any public office but cannot do so under the banner of the three existing political parties. The Movement system has been personified in an individual, President Museveni, who has for many years positioned himself as the guarantor of Uganda's stability.[46] This vision has led to at least one watchdog group claiming that "the Movement is a totalitarian regime under the control of one man".[47] The constitution stipulated that a referendum should be held in 2000 to decide whether a multi-party system would be used for the presidential and parliamentarian elections. The referendum was carried out in June 2000 and resulted in the indefinite extension of the Movement. The campaigns for the referendum were, of course, characterised by restrictions on political party activity as well as unequal funding. The state-owned media favoured the current system and activities by opposition parties and efforts to promote a multi-party system received minimal press coverage.[48]

The Ugandan constitution provides for a 281-member unicameral parliament. Ten seats in parliament are reserved for members of the Ugandan army, the UPDF. During the last few years, the Ugandan parliament has continued to assert its independence and role as an effective check and balance on the executive. However, Movement supporters remained in control of the legislative branch.[49] Uganda has embarked on a programme of government decentralisation, the aim of which is to increase the role of civilians in government. In 1998, local government elections seemed to indicate that the system was beginning to pay dividends. In February 2001, the Minister of Justice and Constitutional Affairs inaugurated a Commission of Inquiry charged with reviewing decentralisation and considering whether Uganda should move to a federalist system.[50]

The Movement is not only the leading political force in Uganda, but has also organised a number of organs that extend into civil society. The Movement established a National Association of Women's Organisation in Uganda (NAWOU), a Ugandan National Students' Association (UNSA) and Youth Councils. In addition, it resisted attempts by NGOs to organise themselves into a broader coalition. Since the elections in 1996, the Movement has also carried out political and military education, popularly known as *chaka mchaka*. These programmes take place throughout Uganda and provide the Movement with a platform to spread its political programme.[51] Unionisation has remained practically non-existent in Uganda and membership in the National Organisation of Trade Unions (NOTU) has declined steadily.

The right to freedom of association and assembly and the right to free speech are severely restricted by the Ugandan constitution. Many kinds of independent political activity are banned. Political events, seminars and rallies are often broken up by police. Such control also applies to media and civil society, although Museveni promised a free press when he took power in 1986. According to the Press and Journalists Statute of 1995, journalists need to apply for a licence on an annual basis and a Media Council observes and enforces the proper conduct of journalists. Nevertheless, Uganda does have an active civil society and a lively media. A number of independent newspapers, such as *The Monitor* and *The Citizen*, and some radio and television stations are highly critical of government policies. Journalists as well as opposition politicians are regularly detained and interrogated for their reporting. They are reportedly harassed, arrested on questionable sedition and incitement charges and sometimes tortured in so-called "safe houses". Uganda is also home to several human rights NGOs and the Makerere University in Kampala is considered to be one of the most important academic human rights institutions in Africa.[52] Like the press, NGOs also face constraints that hinder their activities. Since 1989, NGOs have required a certificate of registration, which can be revoked in the name of public interest. However, with the creation of new commissions, such as the Ugandan Human Rights Commission (UHRC), and a vocal and progressive parliament, Uganda has made important steps toward establishing a human rights culture in Uganda during the last few years.

Prospects for Peace-Building and Reconciliation

The road to peace in Uganda is fraught with obstacles. Over its 15 years in power, Museveni's government has approached the problem in a variety of ways, often tailoring its approaches to the particular region of the country in which it is engaged. Overall, the strategy has involved a combination of amnesty and armed engagement, a sort of carrot and stick approach that has sometimes worked and sometimes entrenched opposition. The matter is complicated by the international dimension of the conflict, the fact that some rebel forces are based in either Sudan or the DRC and that fighting has strained relations with Uganda's neighbours. At the time of writing, there are signs that certain key conflicts may soon end. However, these appearances do not represent guarantees.

The last serious attempt by the Museveni government to hold peace talks in the north was in 1994. The peace talks between the LRA and the NRM were facilitated by Betty Bigombe, then Minister for Pacification of the North. An Acholi, Bigombe appeared close to a breakthrough, but the talks ended abruptly when Museveni suddenly announced that the LRA would be given seven days to put down their arms and turn themselves over to the government. Opinions about why the peace talks failed vary. Some say that Bigombe should not be the one to receive the credit of bringing peace to the north. Others believe that Museveni gave Kony, the leader of the LRA, such a short ultimatum because Kony was stalling to buy time to gain support from Sudan. In 1997, Uganda's parliament voted to continue the use of military force to end the conflict.[53] Since then, Museveni has frequently emphasised this strategy by saying that he will not talk to the rebels and that the conflict will be resolved through military means. Recent reports indicate that the government has achieved some military success against Kony's forces. These gains, however, appear to beg the question of how to establish a sustainable peace in the north, a matter that turns heavily on how to create incentives for the rebels to disarm and enter into meaningful political dialogue.

A crucial part of the government's approach to peace-building has been amnesty. Passed in late 1999, the Amnesty Act offers indemnity to any and all individuals who "report" themselves to government officials and agree to disarm. The legislation was seen as a crucial step in promoting reconciliation in Uganda. In August 2000, African Rights issued a detailed report on the amnesty process, indicating that while amnesty had the support of citizens in Acholi, there were a number of impediments to its successful implementation.[54] The commission charged to oversee the process was slow to begin its work, especially with respect to publicising the nature and mechanisms of the amnesty. Continued fighting has undermined incentives for application. Among members of the LRA, there is substantial distrust of the amnesty, an indication that the amnesty may be successful only if there is a corresponding political dialogue on reintegration and reconciliation. The matter is complicated further by the government's continuing commitment to win a military battle over the LRA. With amnesty on one side and armed struggle on the other, the question of how peace will emerge in the north remains open. In the west, however, the approach seems to be paying off as the ADF appears willing to accept the amnesty in the face of growing military action by the government.

In the southwest, there have been few formal peace talks. However, human rights groups, local leaders and the churches have asked Museveni to consider negotiations with rebel groups and it seems that there is widespread support for peace talks within the civilian population. That the Movement prefers a military solution runs contrary to the views of analysts who argue that neither side of the respective conflicts is capable of winning. At this stage, the only concession Museveni is prepared to make is amnesty.[55]

Internationally, the 1999 Nairobi Accord appears to have reduced tensions between Uganda and Sudan. The matter of the DRC, however, is a different and much more complicated story. The DRC situation has multiple and complex implications for peace in Uganda. In recent years, tensions between Uganda and Rwanda have been very high. Each accuses the other of training armed opposition groups and coveting the DRC's natural resources. Before the 2001 elections, the Ugandan government named Rwanda a "hostile state". Over the last three years, each side has battled the other in Kisangani, battles that have cost hundreds if not thousands of lives. However, there have been positive measures taken to reduce tensions. In early 2002, Uganda and Rwanda signed a set of confidence measures that *inter alia* allowed each country's troops to move within the other's territory. These measures have been enhanced by a series of bilateral meetings designed to promote dialogue and crisis management. Still, the larger matter of the DRC remains. As of February 2002, it appeared Uganda continues to support Jean-Pierre Bemba's rival Congolese Liberation Movement. In the past this alliance has sparked significant clashes in the DRC, conflict that continues to complicate any attempt to resolve the Congolese war.

Reconciliation will be difficult in Uganda. However, a considerable number of local and international NGOs, as well as the UN and church communities, are involved in long-term reconciliation efforts. The UN, for instance, offers conflict resolution courses for both the public and the private sector at the Uganda Management Institute (UMI).[56] Traditional reconciliation methods have also been rediscovered by Ugandans and Western donors. Traditional leaders have been asked to reassume their role as mediators. In the north, for example, the Acholi culture uses the so-called *mato oput* ritual to achieve reconciliation between enemies. The

wrongdoer has to give a truthful account of what he did, accept responsibility and make a gesture of physical restitution. The wrongdoer and
the aggrieved party then share a drink made of bitter hops in front of
witnesses to signal that reconciliation has occurred.[57]

In the context of truth and justice, reconciliation entails the risk of creating a culture of impunity. The Ugandan judiciary does not have the
means to lead extensive judicial investigations. Although generally independent, the judiciary is weak compared to the executive. It is also under-
staffed which leads to prolonged pre-trial detentions, a poor judicial
administration and a large case backlog.[58] To find out the truth about what
happened in the past as well as about ongoing human rights abuses, the
Ugandan government established several commissions. In 1986, shortly
after gaining power, Museveni appointed the Commission of Inquiry into
Human Rights Violations. The task of the commission was to investigate
human rights abuses that occurred in the period 1962 to 1986. Its mandate was broad, but focused on arbitrary arrest and detention, torture and
killings by the government security forces. The commission's work was to
be completed by 1988, but due to financial constraints and lack of personnel the final report was only published in 1994. The commission went
all over Uganda to hear the testimonies of victims of human rights abuses.
Often the hearings were publicised via the media, especially the radio.[59]

More recently, in 1999, the judicial Commission of Inquiry into
Corruption in the Police Force began its operation. The commission
uncovered incidents of killings and brutality by the police. Several senior
officers were arrested on charges of extortion. The proceedings were open
to the public and received extensive press coverage.

Uganda has a vibrant landscape of local human rights groups that are
engaged in conflict resolution, peace-building and reconciliation. *Jamii Ya
Kupatanisha* (JYKA), the Ugandan branch of the International Fellowship
of Reconciliation, is one of the numerous domestic NGOs involved in
promoting reconciliation, tolerance and common understanding among
the different peoples, ideologies and cultures of Uganda by providing
training in peace and reconciliation. Another group is the Centre for
Conflict Resolution (CECORE). CECORE provides conflict resolution
programmes that link parties for mediated dialogue. It promotes various
methods of resolving conflicts, including traditional African methods.
Other local NGOs, such as the Foundation for African Development
(FAD) and the Foundation for Human Rights Initiative (FHRI), focus on
civic education, promoting better understanding of democratic values and
practices, including constitutionalism, the rule of law and voter education.

The most notable international NGOs in Uganda are the International Committee of the Red Cross (ICRC), USAID and World Vision Uganda. Perhaps more than ever before, there appears to be a significant interest in promoting reconciliation in Uganda. In part, the opportunity has been a by-product of the amnesty law and a sense among citizens in the north that it is time to move beyond decades of conflict. The clans of the Acholi have a long-standing and engrained approach to restorative justice, one that involves a process of testimony and reparations within local communities. The question, however, is whether these processes can develop and operate alongside the political machinations of the amnesty process. There is also a question of scale, of whether local groups will be able to handle the sheer number of perpetrators and rebels that need to be disarmed and reintegrated into Ugandan society. The Ugandan churches are playing an increasing role in resolving these problems but it is still early days. The reconciliation process will need to be supported by the international community but in a way that does not generate resentment or the perception of meddling. Accordingly, the Amnesty Commission faces some significant challenges, rallying support for its work in a manner that empowers communities and persuades rebels that it is possible to move Uganda further toward democratic consolidation.

NOTES

1 USAID, "Congressional Presentation FY 1997." Reprinted at www.usaid.gov/pubs/cp97/countries/ug.htm (accessed 5 February 2001).

2 Human Rights Watch, "Hostile to Democracy: the Movement System and Political Repression in Uganda, 1999." Reprinted at www.hrw.org/hrw/reports/1999/uganda/Uganweb-09.htm (accessed 25 January 2001).

3 Alfred Wasike and Justin Moro, "Museveni Warns Kony, Bashir." Reprinted at www.allafrica.com/stories/200102170111.html (accessed 20 February 2000).

4 Human Rights Watch, "The Scars of Death: Children Abducted by the Lord's Resistance Army, 1997." Reprinted at www.hrw.org/reports97/uganda (accessed 14 February 2001).

5 Barney Afako, *Northern Uganda: Justice in Conflict* (London: African Rights, 2000), 3–4; Amnesty International, USA, "Annual Report 1999: Uganda." Reprinted at www.amnestyusa.org/ailib/aireport/ar99/afr59.htm (accessed 5 February 2001); Heike Behrend, "War in Northern Uganda," in *African Guerrillas*, ed. Christopher Clapham (Oxford: James Currey, 1998), 115–18.

6 Amnesty International, USA, "Annual Report 1999: Uganda"; David Westbrook, "The Torment of Northern Uganda: A Legacy of Missed Opportunities," in *OJPCR: The Online Journal of Peace and Conflict Resolution* 3 (2000). Reprinted at www.trinstitute.org/ojpcr/p3_2westbrook.htm (accessed 27 January 2001); UN Office for

258   STRELEAU

the Co-ordination of Humanitarian Affairs, "Humanitarian Update – Uganda, April/ May 2002." Reprinted at www.reliefweb.int (accessed July 2002).

7 Human Rights Watch, "Hostile to Democracy"; David Westbrook, "The Torment of Northern Uganda."

8 David Westbrook, "The Torment of Northern Uganda."

9 Yoweri Museveni, *Sowing the Mustard Seed* (London: Macmillan, 1997), 178.

10 See the article by Museveni's press secretary, "Talk Peace with Kony? Why not Jack the Ripper?" *East African*, 22–28 February 1999.

11 MS Uganda, "Annual Report 1998." Reprinted at www.ms-dan.dk/uk/country/ ms-uga/Olddoc/Annual98.htm (accessed 18 December 2000); Monique Mekenkamp, Paul van Tongeren and Hans van de Veen, eds., *Searching for Peace in Africa: An Overview of Conflict Prevention and Management Activities* (Utrecht: European Platform for Conflict Prevention and Transformation, 1999), 260; Human Rights Watch, "World Report 2000, Uganda." Reprinted at www.hrw.org/hrw/wr2k/Africa-12.htm (accessed 2 February 2001).

12 Chris Osekeny Jamu, "7,000 UPDF To Disarm Karimojong." Reprinted at www.allafrica.com/stories/200102190177.html (accessed 21 February 2001).

13 USAID Uganda, "Northern Uganda Program." Reprinted at www.crosswinds. net/~usaid/uganda/northernuganda.html (accessed 12 February 2001).

14 Human Rights Watch, "World Report 2000, Uganda"; Mekenkamp et al., *Searching for Peace in Africa*, 261.

15 Aili Mari Tripp, *Women & Politics in Uganda* (Oxford: James Currey, 2000), 57–58.

16 Mekenkamp et al., *Searching for Peace in Africa*, 261; Human Rights Watch, "World Report 2000."

17 Allafrica.com, "ADF War Over, Says Museveni." Reprinted at www.allafrica.com/ stories/200102110112.html (accessed 9 February 2001); Integrated Regional Information network (IRIN), "ADF Still 'Force To Be Reckoned With'." Reprinted at www.allafrica.com/stories/200102220155.html (accessed 24 February 2001).

18 Human Rights Watch, "Hostile to Democracy."

19 Pascal Ngoga, "Uganda: The National Resistance Army," in *African Guerrillas*, ed. Christopher Clapham (Oxford: James Currey, 1998), 105; MS Uganda, "Annual Report 1998."

20 Filip Reyntjens, "Briefing: The Second Congo War: More than a Remake." *African Affairs* 98 (1999): 241–50; International Crisis Group, "Scramble for the Congo: Anatomy of an Ugly War, Dec. 2000." Reprinted at www.intl-crisis-group. org/projects/showreport.cfm?reportid=130 (accessed 2 February 2001); "Uganda and Rwanda: Friends or Enemies, May 2000." Reprinted at www.intl-crisis-group.org/ projects/showreport.cfm?reportid=37 (accessed 27 January 2001).

21 Human Rights Watch, "Background to the Hema-Lendu Conflict in Uganda-Controlled Congo." Reprinted at www.hrw.org/backgrounder/africa/hemabckg.htm (accessed 14 February 2001); note that the Hima and the Hema are two different ethnic groups.

22 Amnesty International USA, "Annual Report 1999: Uganda"; IRIN "Child Soldiers Identified In Kyankwanzi." Reprinted at www.allafrica.com/stories/ 200102230109.html (accessed 25 February 2001).

23 Human Rights Watch, "Hostile to Democracy"; US Department of State, "Country Reports on Human Rights Practice – 2000, February 25, 2001." Reprinted at www.state.gov/g/drl/rls/hrrpt/2000/af/index.cfm?docid=847 (accessed 2 March 2001).

24 Guardian Unlimited, "Museveni Declared Winner in Ugandan Elections." Reprinted at www.guardian.co.uk/international/story/0,3604,451704,00.html (accessed 25 March 2001).

25 Nicholas Kotch, "New Club of African Leaders the Event of 1997." Reuters World Service, 27 December 1997.

26 US Department of State, "Country Reports on Human Rights Practice"; see also John Kakande, "United States Attacks Uganda Over Human Rights." Reprinted at www.allafrica.com/stories/200102280054.html (accessed 2 March 2001).

27 Edmond Kizito, "US Urges Uganda to Build Full Democracy." Reuters World Service, 13 May 1995.

28 Deutsche Presse-Agentur, "US Warns that Kampala May Fall 'Short of Full Democracy'." Deutsche Presse-Agentur, 12 May 1995.

29 Ofwono Opondo, "US warns Uganda over Referendum." Sunday Vision, 20 July 1997, 1.

30 Human Rights Watch, "Hostile to Democracy."

31 New Vision, "UK Envoy Appeals on Referendum." New Vision, 25 June 1999; John Kakande, "DP Hosts African Parties." New Vision, 28 October 1997.

32 Erich Ogoso Opolot, "Britain Will Not Press for Parties." New Vision, 7 October 1997.

33 Human Rights Watch, "Hostile to Democracy."

34 World Bank, "Countries: Uganda." Reprinted at www.worldbank.org/afr/ug2.htm (accessed 1 March 2001).

35 United Nations, Press Release HR/CN/872, 24 April 1998, and Press Release HR/CN/935, 27 April 1999.

36 Phares Mutibwa, Uganda since Independence: A Story of Unfulfilled Hopes (London: Hurst & Company, 1992), 1–10; Mahmood Mamdani, Imperialism and Fascism in Uganda (London, Ibadan, Nairobi: Heinemann Educational Books, 1983), 5–12.

37 Human Rights Watch, "Hostile to Democracy"; Holger Bernt Hansen and Michael Twaddle, "The Issues," in From Chaos to Order: The Politics of Constitution Making in Uganda (London: James Currey, 1996), 1–17.

38 Mutibwa, Uganda since Independence, 71.

39 Ibid, 125.

40 Ibid, 125.

41 Tripp, Women & Politics in Uganda, 55–56; Mutibwa, Uganda since Independence, 125; Human Rights Watch, "Hostile to Democracy."

42 David Mukholi, A Complete Guide to Uganda's Fourth Constitution: History, Politics and the Law (Kampala: Fountain Publishers, 1995), 25.

43 World Vision, "Uganda Country Factfile." Reprinted at www.worldvision.org.uk/our_work/uganda.htm (accessed 2 February 2001); D. Wadada Nabudere, Imperialism and Revolution in Uganda (London: Onyx Press, 1980), 12–20.

44 USAID, "Basic Education Programs in Africa, Country Profiles, Uganda." Reprinted at www.usaid.gov/regions/afr/basiced/uganda/html (accessed 10 February 2001).

45 World Vision, "Uganda Country Factfile"; Tripp, Women & Politics in Uganda, 110–11.

46 The Mail and Guardian, "Ugandans Reject Multi-Party Democracy." Reprinted at www.mg.co.za/mg/za/archive/2000jul/01julpm-news.html (accessed 12 January 2001).

47 Human Rights Watch, "Hostile to Democracy."

48 Tripp, *Women & Politics in Uganda*, 58, 64; US Department of State "Country Reports on Human Rights Practice – 2000."

49 Ibid.

50 Katamba G. Mohammed, "Constitutional Review Commission Swears In." Reprinted at www.allafrica.com/stories/200102230428.html (accessed 26 February 2001).

51 Westbrook, "The Torment of Northern Uganda."

52 US Department of State, "Country Reports on Human Rights Practice – 2000."

53 Westbrook, "The Torment of Northern Uganda."

54 African Rights, "Striving for Justice: Preparations for the Amnesty in Northern Uganda," Discussion Paper No. 10, August 2000.

55 *New Vision*, "ADF War Over, Says Museveni." Reprinted at www.allafrica.com/stories/200102110112.html (accessed 11 February 2001).

56 *New Vision*, "UMI To Teach Conflict Resolution." Reprinted at URL: www.allafrica.com/stories/200102110117.html (accessed 13 February 2001).

57 Westbrook, "The Torment of Northern Uganda."

58 US Department of State, "Country Reports on Human Rights Practice – 2000"; Afako, *Northern Uganda: Justice in Conflict.*

59 Priscilla B. Hayner, "Fifteen Truth Commissions – 1974 to 1994: A Comparative Study," in *Transitional Justice Vol. I: General Considerations,* ed. Neil Kritz (Washington DC: United States Institute of Peace Press, 1995), 233–35; summary booklet, "Pearl of Blood." Reprinted at www.reconciliation.org.za/country/index.pl?&id=uganda02.htm (accessed 1 February 2001).

RESOURCES

Books, Articles, Current Media Reports

Afako, Barney. *Northern Uganda: Justice in Conflict*. London: African Rights, 2000.

Clapham, Christopher, ed. *African Guerrillas*. Oxford: James Currey, 1998.

Hansen, Holger Bernt and Michael Twaddle, eds. *From Chaos to Order: The Politics of Constitution Making in Uganda*. London: James Currey, 1996.

Hayner, Priscilla B. "Fifteen Truth Commissions – 1974 to 1994: A Comparative Study." In *Transitional Justice Vol I: General Considerations*, edited by Neil Kritz. Washington: United States Institute of Peace Press, 1995.

Mamdani, Mahmood. *Imperialism and Fascism in Uganda*. London, Ibadan, Nairobi: Heinemann Educational Books, 1983.

Mekenkamp, Monique, Paul van Tongeren and Hans van de Veen, eds. *Searching for Peace in Africa: An Overview of Conflict Prevention and Management Activities*. Utrecht: European Platform for Conflict Prevention and Transformation, 1999.

Mukholi, David. *A Complete Guide to Uganda's Fourth Constitution: History, Politics and Law*. Kampala: Fountain Publishers, 1995.

Museveni, Yoweri. *Sowing the Mustard Seed*. London: Macmillan, 1997.

Mutibwa, Phares. *Uganda since Independence: A Story of Unfulfilled Hopes*. London: Hurst & Company, 1992.

Nabudere, D. Wadada. *Imperialism and Revolution in Uganda*. London: Onyx Press, 1980.

Ngoga, Pascal. "Uganda: The National Resistance Army." In *African Guerrillas*, edited by Christopher Clapham. Oxford: James Currey, 1998.

Reyntjens, Filip. "Briefing: The Second Congo War: More than a Remake." *African Affairs* 98 (1999): 241–50.

Tripp, Aili Mari. *Women & Politics in Uganda*. Oxford: James Currey, 2000.

Westbrook, David. "The Torment of Northern Uganda: A Legacy of Missed Opportunities." In *OJPCR: The Online Journal of Peace and Conflict Resolution* 3 (2000). Reprinted at http://www.trinstitute.org/ojpcr/p3_westbrook.htm (accessed 27 January 2001).

Primary Documents

Commission of Inquiry into Human Rights Violations – The report of the commission was produced in October 1994. Available on the internet is a pamphlet which contains highlights of the commission's findings, conclusion's and recommendations: http://www.reconciliation.org.za/country/index.pl?&id=uganda00.htm

Makerere University, Kampala: http://www.imul.com/muk

The Monitor, the most widely read non-governmental newspaper: http://www.monitor.co.ug

New Vision is a government-owned countrywide newspaper: http://www.newvision.co.ug

Government, Intergovernmental Bodies and Political Parties

Buganda homepage provides information about news, history, language, culture etc. of
    Buganda: http://www.buganda.com
Government of Uganda homepage provides information about the executive, constitu-
    tion, parliament, 2001 election campaign, ministries, judiciary and districts of
    Uganda: http://www.government.go.ug
Uganda Human Rights Commission (UHRC) is an independent body established
    under the Constitution of Uganda to promote and protect human rights:
    http://www.uhrc.org

Local NGOs

Action for Development (ACFODE) is a voluntary, non-profit, civil society women's
    organisation, formed in 1985. It seeks to create and stimulate awareness of the
    needs, problems and rights of women in Uganda: http://www.acfode.or.ug
African Centre for Rehabilitation, Treatment and Torture of Victims (ACTV),
    established in 1993 by Samuel L. Nsamba, is a human rights NGO:
    http://www.actv.or.ug
Centre for Conflict Resolution (CECORE) is involved in education and training
    regarding conflict prevention and peace-building. Having joined with other
    NGOs in the Great Lakes region, it focuses not only on Uganda but also on
    border-crossing conflicts: http://www.cecore.org/index.html
Foundation for African Development (FAD) is a non-political, non-profit, adult
    education NGO focusing on the field of civic education, promoting better under-
    standing of democratic values and practices, including constitutionalism, rule of
    law, and voter education: http://www.uganda.co.ug/fad/index.htm
Foundation for Human Rights Initiative (FHRI) seeks to enhance the knowledge,
    respect and observance of human rights, and to encourage exchange of informa-
    tion and experiences through training, education, research, advocacy, lobbying and
    networking: http://www.hri.ca/partners/fhri
The Human Rights Network – Uganda (HURINET-U) is a coalition of 13 organi-
    sations based and operating in Uganda. It promotes networking through public
    lectures, seminars and conferences etc. and offers training programmes for staff
    and volunteers of member organisations to improve their knowledge and skills for
    effective implementation of human rights programmes: http://www.uganda.
    co.ug/hurinet
Jamii Ya Kupatanisha (JYKA) founded in 1988, promotes reconciliation, tolerance
    and common understanding among the different peoples, ideologies and cultures
    of Uganda by providing educational training in peace and reconciliation, organis-
    ing youth work camps, arranging peace prayer festivals and exchanging visits
    between people of different tribes: http://www.peacelink.it/afrinews/29_issue/
    p10.html
Makerere University Human Rights and Peace Centre (HURIPEC) was estab-
    lished in 1993 and is the first research and academic-based institution in the east
    African region. It is devoted to teaching, researching and the compilation of
    local/regional materials relating to human rights: http://www1.umn.edu/
    humanrts/africa/huripec.htm
The Uganda Human Rights and Documentation Centre (UHEDOC) aims to iden-
    tify and gather data on human rights issues, to carry out education on human

rights, to initiate and conduct research on various aspects of human rights, to monitor, investigate and document human rights abuses and to make referrals of persons whose rights have been violated: http://www.imul.com/muk/uhedoc

International NGOs

International Committee of the Red Cross (ICRC) covers a wide spectrum of humanitarian programmes, including assistance to civilians affected by conflicts, emergency assistance, support for health facilities, training to local nurses, visits to detainees to check on their material and psychological conditions, and the promotion and facilitation of educational seminars to spread the rules of international humanitarian law and principles: http://www.icrc.org

World Vision Uganda is a Christian organisation receiving financial support from the UK government and the European Union. World Vision's work in Uganda started in 1979 with a relief and rehabilitation programme after the overthrow of Amin. Today, the organisation has 80 projects in 19 districts, including an HIV/Aids prevention and control project, a child survival project, a Sudanese refugees project and various development projects: http://www.worldvision. org.uk

UGANDA COUNTRY INFORMATION

Geography
Location: Eastern Africa, west of Kenya.
Cities: *Capital:* Kampala (1991 pop. 774 214). *Other cities:* Jinja, Mbale, Mbarara.

People
Nationality: *Noun:* Ugandan(s). *Adjective:* Ugandan.
Population (2000): 23 000 000.
Population growth rate (1999): 2.7%.
Ethnic groups: African 99%, European, Asian, Arab 1%.
Religions: Christian 66%, Muslim 16%, traditional and other 18%.
Languages: *English* (official); Luganda and Swahili widely used; other Bantu and Nilotic languages.
Education (1993): *Literacy:* 62%.
Health: *Infant mortality rate:* 81/1 000. *Life expectancy:* 37 years. *HIV infection rate:* 9.51%.

Economy
GDP (1999): $24 billion.
Inflation rate (December 1999): Approx. 7%.
Natural resources: Copper, cobalt, limestone.
Agriculture: *Cash crops:* coffee, tea, tobacco, sugar cane, cut flowers, vanilla. *Food crops:* banana, corn, cassava, potatoes, millet, pulses (largely self-sufficient in food). *Livestock and fisheries:* beef, goat meat, milk, Nile perch, tilapia.
Industry: *Types:* processing of agricultural products (cotton ginning, coffee curing), cement production, light consumer goods, textiles.
Trade (1995–96): $624.5 million: coffee, cotton, tobacco, tea. *Major market:* EU. *Imports (1994–95):* $1.193 billion: petroleum products, machinery, cotton, textiles, metals, transportation equipment. *Major suppliers:* OPEC countries, EU.

Military
Military expenditure: Dollar figures: $95 million (FY98/99).
Military expenditure: Percent of GDP: 1.9% (FY98/99).

Demographic information is drawn from that compiled by the United States Department of State. See http://www.state.gov/r/pa/ei/bgn

Map of South Africa and surrounding countries showing national capitals, major towns, towns, small towns, large villages, international airports, airports, border posts, international borders, state/province borders, rivers, dry rivers, and parks.

MOZAMBIQUE

Limpopo

MAPUTO

Cape Vidal

ZIMBABWE

Beitbridge
Musina
(Messina)

Krugér
National
Park

Lebombo

Nelspruit

SOUTPANSBERGE

Polokwane
(Pietersburg)

Ulundi

Pietermaritzburg

*KwaZulu-
Natal*

Durban

*INDIAN
OCEAN*

Groblér's
Bridge

Limpopo

Lephalale
(Ellisras)

Limpopo

PRETORIA

Mpumalanga

Oshoek

**SWAZI-
LAND**

Gauteng

Johannesburg

Piet Retief

E. Cape

Kopfontein

North West

Bethlehem

LESOTHO

Umtata

East London

Welkom

Free State

Ramatlabama

Mafikeng

Bloemfontein

Maseru
Bridge

Bisho

GABORONE

Vaal

Kimberley

Orange

Middelburg

Grahamstown

Eastern Cape

Port Elizabeth

BOTSWANA

Vryburg

SOUTH AFRICA

De Aar

Beaufort
West

*Cape
St Francis*

KALAHARI

Northern Cape

GREAT KAROO

Knysna

Mossel Bay

Kgalagadi
Transfrontier
Park

Orange

Upington

Nakop

Onseepkans

LANGEBERGE

Oudtshoorn

LITTLE KAROO

Western Cape

Robertson

Calvinia

Cape Agulhas

WINDHOEK

Orange

Vioolsdrif

CEDARBERG

Paarl

Springbok

*St Helena
Bay*

CAPE
TOWN

Cape Point

NAMIBIA

**Walvis
Bay**

*ATLANTIC
OCEAN*

National capitals
Major town
Town
Small town
Large village
International airport
Airport
Border post
International border
State/province
River
Dry river
Park

0 100 200 km

Chapter 11

South Africa: Beyond the "Miracle"

CHARLES VILLA-VICENCIO AND S'FISO NGESI*

After almost 10 years of non-racial democracy, South Africa finds itself in the latter phase of a remarkable transition – shaped by a progressive constitution and two democratic elections. The election of Thabo Mbeki as president in 1999 and the recent completion of the work of the Truth and Reconciliation Commission (TRC) signal the beginning of consolidation, within which the demands for human dignity, freedom and equality that lie at the heart of our constitutional order must be realised. Should these demands not be met the acclaim that greeted this new democracy in 1994 will have a hollow ring.

At both the material and socio-political levels, there remain deep divisions in South Africa. These structural and attitudinal divides continue to fuel conflict and animosity. Despite the overtures of the African National Congress (ANC) to the largely white and coloured New National Party, and more specifically those of President Mbeki to white Afrikaner leaders, political parties remain split largely along racial-ethnic lines. The economy continues to depend on white capital, with reform efforts caught on the horns of a dilemma: whether to promote business confidence with a neo-liberal economic plan or assist the millions of citizens who need basic housing and jobs.

The TRC process brought both healing and dispute. Its recommendations about reparations are only beginning to be partially implemented by the government after a long delay. At a subjective and social level, the Commission's work has underscored the point that the process of reconciliation and reconstruction is a long-term project. It is a collective effort designed to translate the miracle of 1994 into a lasting and stable democracy.

It may be argued that the South African settlement is better understood not as a miracle but as a contested process – driven as much by pragmatic needs and rugged compromise as by high ideals and moral intent. And yet, Archbishop Desmond Tutu's sense of the South African transition being a

* The initial research assistance of Bonnie Berkowitz is gratefully acknowledged.

miracle provides an important insight into the South African settlement when compared with many countries undergoing transition in other parts of Africa, the Balkans, Russia and elsewhere. The danger is that idealistic perceptions of the South African transition can underestimate the levels of resentment, alienation, disappointment and compromise that are perhaps an inevitable part of a political compromise of the magnitude of the South African settlement. This settlement was probably the only alternative to the escalation of violence and the destruction of any realistic possibility of reconstruction. Justice Richard Goldstone puts it thus: "The decision to opt for a Truth and Reconciliation Commission was an important compromise. If the ANC had insisted on Nuremberg-style trials for the leaders of the former apartheid government, there would have been no peaceful transition to democracy, and if the former government had insisted on a blanket amnesty then, similarly, the negotiations would have broken down. A bloody revolution sooner rather than later would have been inevitable. The Truth and Reconciliation Commission is a bridge from the old to the new."[1]

The major challenge facing South Africa now is to strike a balance between reconstruction and reconciliation so that the country can have a stable democracy. This apparently insurmountable challenge has been highlighted by President Thabo Mbeki who contends that:

> It's a very delicate thing to handle the relationship between [transformation and reconciliation] . . . It's not a mathematical thing; it's an art . . . If you handle the transformation in a way that doesn't change a good part of the status quo, those who are disadvantaged will rebel, and then goodbye reconciliation.[2]

This profile aims not simply to understand the promises and pitfalls of South Africa's democratic consolidation, but also the ways in which the present is being shaped by a history of racial and economic domination. It further reflects on the apartheid system and the road to a negotiated settlement. In these terms, the future of reconciliation may have much to do with the ways in which South Africans are able to fashion the culture of reconciliation into forms of material empowerment.

The Face of Conflict

The ANC's victory at the polls in the 1994 elections was not just the triumph of a political party. It signified the triumph of a broader liberation movement whose constituents include the ANC itself, the South African

Communist Party (SACP), the Congress of South African Trade Unions (COSATU) and a range of organisations of civil society. This was a civil society that was central to forging the terms of "people's power", the community politics that sustained the United Democratic Front in the 1980s and helped bring about the "negotiated revolution".

Few predicted that South Africa would avoid civil war and undertake a (relatively) peaceful transition to democracy. Many within the faith communities and in secular society, understandably and with justification, called on apartheid leaders to submit to unconditional repentance and surrender. This, it was insisted, was the only legitimate and realistic way to move forward. The breakthrough, however, came not as a result of any Damascus Road experience or capitulation of the old regime. It came as a result of a series of encounters within which protagonists on opposing sides began to make contact with one another. Tentative, fragile steps were taken that led to "talks about talks". In the process, cautious relationships were forged. This paved the way for a search for peace and the beginning of a reconciliation process.

Talks About Talks

Reflecting on the early stages of negotiations is both a therapeutic and pedagogical exercise.[3] This stage was difficult and dangerous. It was an initiative spurned by many – indeed most. The talks were "on" and then they were "off". There were "talks about talks about talks", there were "talks about talks" and there were "talks". ANC records show that in 1986 separate formal talks took place in Lusaka and Harare between the ANC leadership and six South African-based organisations: the Inyandza National Movement, COSATU, the National Union of South African Students (NUSAS), the South African Catholic Bishops' Conference (SACBC), the National African Federated Chambers of Commerce (NAFCOC) and the Northern Diocese of the Evangelical Lutheran Church in South Africa (ELCSA). These were followed by a historic meeting in Dakar in June 1987, hosted by President Abdou Diouf of Senegal. Led by Frederik van Zyl Slabbert and Alex Boraine, the delegation comprised 61 people, mostly white Afrikaans-speaking South Africans. The list of organisations and people who later travelled to Lusaka and elsewhere "to meet with the ANC" is a long and impressive one. They included Pieter de Lange, chairperson of the Afrikaner Broederbond; Danie Craven, chairperson of the South African Rugby Board; Gavin Relly, chairperson of Anglo American Corporation; church leaders, academics, women, men and youth. Covert meetings were held in London, New York, Lucerne, Berne, Geneva and elsewhere. They met with Oliver Tambo, Thabo Mbeki, Alfred Nzo, Jacob Zuma and other ANC leaders. There were, at the same time, emissaries moving between Pretoria and Lusaka. These included a University of Cape Town and University of the Western Cape delegation; Stellenbosch University academics, Willie Esterhuyse and Sampie Terreblanche; Cape Town-based lawyer, Richard Rosenthal; a Department of Constitutional Development and Planning official, Cobus Jordaan; and National Intelligence Service functionaries, Niel Barnard, Mike Louw and Maritz Spaarwater. Suffice it to say rapprochement began with contact and exploratory talks.

The Commonwealth Eminent Persons Group got involved. Minister of Justice Kobie Coetsee was holding regular meetings with Mandela in prison, in the Volks Hospitaal where Mandela was undergoing surgery, and on visits around Cape Town. Eventually, a historic meeting was held between Nelson Mandela and South African State President P. W. Botha at the latter's official residence, Tuynhuis. Mandela was given access to his lawyers, George Bizos, Ismail Ayob, Dullah Omar and others, while being allowed occasional telephone contact with ANC leadership in exile.

The carefully structured politics of "total strategy" to counter a "total onslaught" of the Botha regime was undermined daily by contact between adversaries. The demonising of opponents was giving way to dialogue. There was talking, listening and searching for ways forward. The drastic problems that needed urgent attention were beginning to be faced within a new social context – a new kind of relationship.

And yet this too was a contested process, with armed conflict and deep suspicion continuing to be the order of the day. Assassinations, cross-border raids and armed attacks on white farms, military targets and other venues continued. Within this context substantial issues were dealt with in formal negotiations and constitutional talks. In between, there was the *Harare Declaration*, in which the ANC declared it was possible to "end apartheid through negotiations". The unbanning of political organisations and the release of Mandela and other political prisoners followed. Next came the *Groote Schuur Minute*, the *Pretoria Minute* and the ANC's *Constitutional Principles and Structures for a Democratic South Africa*. The outcome was what Willem de Klerk called the emergence of a new "political ecology"[4] of discourse that gave momentum to the prevailing dialogue. The bellicose rhetoric that was rapidly taking South Africa into what Mandela called "the spectre of a South Africa split into two hostile camps; blacks on the one side and whites on the other, slaughtering one another",[5] was giving way to a different kind of encounter.

The South African reconciliation process began with contact – and yet this "contact" was itself grounded in a long history that shifted between social and economic engagement on the one hand and suspicion, alienation and political conflict on the other. This nation of strangers, torn apart by generations of colonialism and decades of statutory apartheid, did not resort to genocide as was the case in Rwanda, nor to the kind of slaughter that characterised the wars of Latin America or the ethnic cleansing of the former Yugoslavia. Why? This is a tantalising question on which major work needs to be done. The "miracle" of the peaceful transition was indeed impressive. However, the transition did not resolve all the fundamental causes of the conflict, although it provided a new context within which to deal with them. Racism and fear of "majority domination" continue to define white politics, whereas the majority of blacks believe that the transformation of an essentially white-owned economy is happening too slowly. The divide between rich and poor remains one of the worst in the world. The country's economy shows promise but has yet to meet the expectations of both policy-makers and citizens.[6]

Economic Disparity

Since the 1980s, it is generally acknowledged that South African economic performance has rated only fair to poor. Per capita income has dropped by at least 15% in real terms, and there has been no growth in total employment, with unemployment rates among the economically active black population exceeding 50% in some areas. Ratios of both investment and saving to national income have fallen dramatically and there has been substantial capital outflow every year since 1985 through a combination of capital flight and debt repayment. Further, urban migration has put increasing pressure on both housing and infrastructure. In the 1980s and early 1990s, the productivity of new government investment continued to fall, mainly because of investment in "strategic" industries, which the apartheid government considered to be important to combat sanctions, and of other related costs of maintaining the apartheid system.[7]

With the advent of democracy in 1994, the ANC-led government inherited these problems, plus a range of additional economic challenges, which some believe should have been given more attention in an overt and explicit manner in the negotiations that ended apartheid. The Mandela government confronted a lack of local and foreign investment. The talk of foreign aid and western-led economic empowerment remained largely a promise. The newly elected democratic government had to face impoverished citizens who had high and frequently unrealistic expectations about the fruits of democracy. In 1993, the South African Living Standards and Development Survey compiled a profile of basic needs in South Africa. It noted that about 25% of children under the age of five suffered from malnutrition; that nearly 25% of households did not have running water; that nearly 45% of all households did not have access to grid electricity; and that just under one million households lived in shacks or informal dwellings, a condition that has much to do with the low life expectancy for blacks in South Africa. The fact that there are historical and contemporary economic divisions between white, coloured, Indian and black South Africans complicates the situation. There is also a clear gap between rural and urban dwellers.

The new government had to address these factors, particularly with respect to the issues of unemployment, income distribution, land redistribution and education. Historically, racist employment legislation and educational exclusion effectively limited the entry of black South Africans into a large number of occupations.[8] Realising that repealing apartheid employment legislation could not on its own redress its legacies, the government passed the Employment Equity Act in 1998, as a way to achieve equality in the workplace by eliminating unfair discrimination and implementing positive measures to redress disadvantages experienced by black people,[9] women and the disabled to ensure equitable representation in all occupational categories and levels in the workforce. This piece of legislation was criticised by the official opposition, the Democratic Party, which accused the ANC of the "creeping reintroduction of race policies".[10] Since then, economic reform has continued to be a contested terrain. Further legislation has been introduced, compromises have been found and new ways sought to redress an economic imbalance that has the capacity to undermine the progress made since 1994. The outcome has been tension not only between the government and business but also between the government and trade unions. The latter tension, some suggest, contains the seeds to undo the ANC-SACP-COSATU alliance that constitutes the majority in government.

This said, the government has taken several significant steps to promote labour rights. These include procedures for dealing with labour disputes through the Commission of Conciliation, Mediation and Arbitration (CCMA); the extension of the right to negotiate to all workers; the protection of basic employment rights; skills development and related matters. On the other hand, unemployment continues to increase and prices of basic foods and commodities continue to rise, requiring government to find ways of translating good policy into practices that ensure the basic needs of the poor are met. While black people now make up a larger proportion of South Africa's middle class, the gap between the upper and lower ends of the black community is increasing.[11] So, although there has been a decline in inter-racial inequality, intra-racial inequality has increased. Indeed, a recent report ranked South Africa as the country with the most skewed income distribution in the world, second only to Brazil.[12]

The historical exclusion of blacks from land ownership has further drastically limited development in rural areas. Today, the government continues with the struggle to process land claims and return sites that were appropriated under apartheid laws. The slow pace of this reform has left many frustrated and led to calls by some, including the Pan Africanist Congress (PAC), for citizens to appropriate land in a manner resembling the take-overs in Zimbabwe. President Mbeki and the courts have stated that land grabs will not be tolerated. The issue remains unresolved and will remain a key source of tension in coming years.

In addition to these economic reform initiatives, the question of consolidation has focused on the development of legitimate democratic institutions, defined partly by regular and fair polls and by a set of rights that ensure the freedoms of opposition, speech and association. Given the country's history, however, the problem of legitimacy looms large, particularly as citizens vacillate between very high expectations for reform and distrust of government's power and intentions. The situation is further complicated by the fact that the ANC strikes many as intolerant of criticism, a problem that has fed concern over racial tensions and distrust.[13]

Identity

The common view is that in a divided society, people identify primarily with their own ethnic group rather than the nation. In a survey conducted by Idasa, only 13% of South African citizens in 1994 identified themselves as "South Africans". Most people chose instead a wide range of racial, linguistic and religious identifications. Some question whether the ANC has moved away from its non-racial policies in favour of programmes that highlight racial and ethnic distinction. The claim is arguable and the subject of significant controversy. Viewed as a whole, the debate indicates that there remain significant rifts in South Africa, forms of distrust and mental balkanisation that thwart community and nation-building efforts.[14] This said, President Mbeki's "I am an African"[15] speech allays fears pertaining to national inclusivity. Mbeki unequivocally demonstrates "Africanism" as an inclusive concept. And more recently, responding in parliament to the use of the "kill the farmer, kill the Boer" slogan at the funeral of ANC MP Peter Mokaba, he insisted "those farmers and Boers are as much South African and African as I am".[16]

Mbeki believes that the ideal of a non-racial society is doomed if millions of people – most of them black – continue to languish in degrading poverty. Should they come to identify the "new South Africa" with the preservation of the glaring inequalities of the "old South Africa" then, he warns, a social explosion may loom on the horizon. Thus, the building of a non-racial society is inextricably linked to wider social transformation and the overriding government priority is to address the awesome legacy of apartheid.[17]

Democratic Debate

Having won 66.36% of the vote in 1999, the ANC enjoys a significant majority in parliament. Some have argued that this dominance has the potential to undermine hopes for a strong and independent parliament. In fact, many commentators – across the political spectrum – argue that many in the ANC are intolerant of criticism, showing little interest in open debate about the issues facing the country. Some political commentators have claimed that the ANC leadership has tended to regard opposition through an explicitly racial lens. The ANC's displeasure with the white opposition and a press that it considers insufficiently sympathetic was significantly evident in Mandela's opening address to the fiftieth ANC National Conference – significant because the former president is perceived as more tolerant toward criticism. In this speech he identified sections of the media and white opposition parties as "counter-revolutionary forces" that had "essentially decided against the national agenda" and wanted to "propagate a reactionary, dangerous and opportunist position". This dangerous position, according to Mandela, assumed the existence of a stable democracy and assumed that opposition parties only "have a democratic obligation merely to discredit the ruling party so that they may gain power after the next elections".[18] The issues embedded in this claim are pertinent and yet difficult to unravel. The ANC has been confronted with an opposition that has done little to smooth its transition to power. Nor has the opposition even acknowledged that it may take time to establish an effective government. Internally, the ANC remains relatively stable and seems set to continue to attract the lion's share of the electoral support for some time to come. There is increasing but still rather indefinite talk about a future split in the ANC, which may result in an opposition party to the left of the current government. Recent developments in South African politics have raised some concerns regarding the tenets of democracy, particularly a credible opposition. The dissolution of the alliance between the Democratic Party and the New National Party has produced mixed feelings. While the ANC and the New National Party contend that their "co-operative government" reflects their commitment to non-racial politics as well as to attending to the needs of the poor, the question arises as to whether this is not an attempt by the ANC to weaken the opposition. Differently put, does this "co-operative government" augur well for the consolidation of democracy? In a similar vein, Mandela's endeavours to lure the former ANC stalwart, Bantu Holomisa, to rejoin the ANC have been met with scepticism. Subsequently, Holomisa's party, the United Democratic Movement, and the PAC have "agreed on the establishment of the strategic co-operative agreement . . . [that] will result in promoting National Unity among South Africans and to realign politics in order to complete the process of transformation".[19] It remains to be seen whether this arrangement will provide a credible black-led opposition.

The above tensions reflect vibrant political debate, within a context where the fundamentals created by the constitution remain firmly in place. Despite the political dominance of the ANC, there has been no attempt to revise the constitution. Several elections at national, regional and local levels have been held since 1994, and contestants have accepted the outcomes. Judiciary rulings have been independent and unchallenged. So-called Chapter Nine institutions, including the Human Rights Commission, the Public Protector and the Commission on Gender Equality, and a vibrant civil society all suggest a maturing constitutional democracy founded on a Bill of Rights. The sustainability of this birthright will in the long run no doubt be severely tested as the impact of poverty, unemployment, crime and HIV/Aids and related problems begin to be felt.

Reconstruction

In the face of substantial economic problems and political division, South African democratisation made steady, if not always consistent, progress. Despite apartheid policies that ensured the exploitation of human resources, under-investment in human capital, labour rigidities, large budgetary outlays for duplicate layers of government and facilities, governmental interventions into the economy and lack of foreign investment, the South African economy responded with a 1.1% growth in 1993. Although slow and limited, this was the first positive growth in four years. The election of Nelson Mandela in early 1994 saw an even greater improvement with 2.3% growth – with not insignificant growth being predicted for the following few years.[20] It was evident that the primary objective of President Mandela's Government of National Unity (GNU) was to address the historical inequities in political, economic and social opportunities between black and white South Africans.

In 1994, the Reconstruction and Development Programme (RDP) was launched as part of the ANC's election programme. As defined by President Mandela, the RDP encompassed not only socio-economic pro- grammes designed to redress imbalances in living conditions, but also institutional reform, educational and cultural programmes, employment generation and human resources development. As a policy framework, the RDP targeted donor aid and guided the government's budgetary process, leading to significant shifts in government expenditure.[21] At the same time, a special RDP fund, composed of several billion rands annually, financed high-profile "presidential projects", such as free medical care for children under the age of six and pregnant mothers, a school feeding scheme programme, electrification of poor homes and public works pro- jects for unemployed youths. A separate RDP office was set up to admin- ister the fund and co-ordinate the different facets of the programme in the various ministries. In 1996, however, the RDP lost its most visible public face when its director was assigned to other ministerial duties. Thereafter, the RDP was eliminated as a separate entity, with its co-ordinating func- tions subsumed into the office of then Deputy President Thabo Mbeki.

In 1995, South Africa achieved an economic growth rate of 3.3%. High consumer confidence and a demand for durable and semi-durable goods led to an increase in private consumption, which exceeded the growth in real personal disposable income. Private consumption, then, was partly financed by an expansion of credit at the cost of domestic savings. The agricultural sector of the economy grew considerably, 82.3% in real terms. However, the overall upturn in economic activities was not accompanied by employment growth.[22] In the wake of the RDP, the South African gov- ernment adopted a new macro-economic strategy that was to drive a 6% GDP growth by 2000 and an increase in employment. This new policy, the Growth, Employment and Redistribution Strategy (GEAR), placed an emphasis on market forces, with the government playing a reduced eco- nomic role.[23] The government gradually eliminated measures to protect the currency and implemented trade liberalisation policies.[24] Furthermore, the reform of the labour market was identified as a crucial factor in creat- ing a more flexible employment environment. GEAR faced a number of teething problems. It was a noticeable move away from the previous ANC policy regarding the need to nationalise large-scale industry and undertake a basic redistribution of wealth from whites to blacks. To many critics on the left, it smacked of acquiescence to the World Bank and International Monetary Fund, especially as the ANC came to accept privatisation in principle and dropped talks of regulating foreign investment and currency exchange.[25]

GEAR has generated substantial political controversy within the COSATU-ANC-SACP alliance. In 1997, the then Secretary General of COSATU, Sam Shilowa, said of the GEAR policy: "We will lobby, fight, convince, negotiate, twist around, do everything possible for our position."[26] Responding to critics who detected an overall shift in focus from aggressively tackling social concerns to relying on orthodox macroeconomic remedies, Pundy Pillay, who headed the RDP policy unit within the President's Office, insisted that the RDP remained an important component of government policy. According to him, the RDP was not incompatible with GEAR; the two polices required each other to work.[27] More recently, there has been a governmental shift away from GEAR, although this has done little to satisfy those who claim that the ANC remains uncommitted to the masses and detached from its historical promise of pursuing material equality for all citizens.

Much depends now on the success of the New Partnership for Africa's Development (Nepad), which links good governance to economic development. The advent of the African Union, with the initial stage of leadership being placed in the hands of President Mbeki, places huge responsibilities on the president and South Africa to ensure reconstruction both in South Africa and the continent as a whole.

Crime

Tied directly to the problems of reforming the South African economy, crime is a significant concern, affecting both domestic stability and the perceptions of international investors. In the first three years after South Africa's political transition overall crime levels seemed to stabilise. While crime levels increased marginally in 1996–97, the increase was 4.8% in 1997–98 and reached a peak of 7% in 1998–99.[28] Between 1994 and 1999 violent crime increased by 21.6%. Property crime increased by 14.9% over the same period, followed by commercial crime at 6.7% and violent crime against property 6.6%. According to the Human Sciences Research Council survey data, almost three times as many South Africans felt unsafe in 1999 compared to 1994. Much of this is attributable to the country's extraordinarily high levels of violent crime. According to the most recently available Interpol figures, in 1996 South Africa had the highest per capita murder, rape, robbery and violent theft levels of the 114 countries surveyed. Perceptions of crime vary substantially according to the race, income and geography of respondents.[29]

HIV/Aids

Perhaps more than any other country in the region, South Africa confronts an enormous threat in the form of HIV/Aids. The disease is rampant throughout the country. Studies suggest that between 25 and 35% of the adult population is HIV-positive. This implies that in some regions over 50% of citizens will fall victim to the virus. Within a matter of years, the country is likely to lose an entire generation, a tragedy that will have a tremendous impact on its socio-political fabric. Tens if not hundreds of thousands of children will be orphaned. The economy will bear the weight of caring for those who fall ill. Recently, the issue of HIV/Aids sparked much controversy in both scientific and political circles in South Africa and abroad. Mbeki's questioning of the causation between HIV and Aids provoked the debate. This created an impression that the ANC government was not fully committed to dealing with the Aids epidemic. Arguably, the issue has been misrepresented by all sides, particularly as Mbeki has been slow to clarify his position and the "mainstream" scientific community has been willing to concede no ground on the question of whether anti-retrovirals are always effective. Mandela also stepped into the fray, questioning whether the government was doing enough about the problem. The government has faced and lost several lawsuits regarding its obligation to provide drugs to pregnant women to prevent mother-to-child transmission. The government has since dropped its controversial hardline stance on Aids drugs, unveiling new plans to provide anti-retroviral medication at state hospitals. Announcing the plans after a cabinet meeting, the government for the first time clearly acknowledged that anti-retroviral drugs can help prevent the transmission of the disease. It has decided that rape victims will now be entitled to the therapy to reduce the chance of the transmission of the virus. Moreover, it has pledged to provide the anti-retroviral drug, Nevirapine, to HIV-positive pregnant women, perhaps by December 2002. The turnaround follows a Constitutional Court ruling that the government must follow a High Court order compelling it to provide Nevirapine to HIV-positive pregnant women at suitably equipped state hospitals. Aids activists have welcomed this turnabout, particularly the Treatment Action Campaign which launched the court case against the government.[30]

The Historical Roots of Violence and Division

The divide and rule of apartheid took many forms, some emerging from the halls of parliament, others growing from the barrels of guns. However, it may be argued that the source of South Africa's violent and divided past was colonialism. Details aside, both the British and the Afrikaners shared a belief in the total separation, on every level, of black and white South Africans. Although this belief became official policy only after the National Party had ascended to power, its foundation had been laid nearly half a century previously, in a policy of racial segregation. This policy was based on the fallacy that whites were of "superior intellect". Tied to colonial racism, Afrikaner nationalism grew from a number of sources and culminated in the 1948 election of the National Party. The architects of the apartheid system sought to create the grounds for the separate development of the peoples that inhabited South Africa. The implicit and explicit racism of the vision was covered with the veneer that all the nation's races could realise their potential if left to their own devices. Judged by the world as a crime against humanity, apartheid was a vicious system, one that became more violent as the ideal was slowly exposed as the evil that it was. Its origins and implementation shed substantial light on the deep divisions that now pervade South African society.[31]

Separating Black from White

The Prohibition of Mixed Marriages Act of 1949 was the first major piece of apartheid legislation. It made marriages between whites and members of other racial groups illegal. The Immorality Act of 1950 extended an earlier ban on sexual relations between whites and blacks (the Immorality Act of 1927) to a ban on sexual relations between whites and any non-whites.[32] The Population Registration Act of 1950 provided the basis for separating the population of South Africa into different races. Under the terms of this Act, all residents of South Africa were classified as white, coloured or native (later called Bantu) people. Indians, whom the Herenigde (Reunited) National Party in 1948 had refused to recognise as permanent inhabitants of South Africa, were included under the category "Asian" in 1959. The act required that people be classified primarily on the basis of their "community acceptability". Later amendments placed greater stress on "appearance" to deal with the practice of light-coloured blacks "passing" as whites. The Act also provided for the compilation of a population register for the whole country and for the issuing of identity cards.

Other laws provided for geographic, social and political separation. The Group Areas Act of 1950 extended the provisions of the Natives Land Act of 1913, and later laws divided South Africa into separate areas for whites and blacks (including coloureds), and gave the government power to conduct forced removals, events that devastated communities and splintered families. In 1954, the Tomlinson Commission concluded that the areas set aside for Africans would support no more than two-thirds of their intended inhabitants even under the best of conditions. The government ignored its recommendation that more land be allocated to the reserves and began removing Africans from designated white areas.[33] The Bantu Authorities Act of 1951 established Bantu tribal, regional and territorial authorities in the regions set out for Africans under the Group Areas Act, and it abolished the Natives' Representative Council. The Bantu authorities were to be dominated by chiefs and headmen appointed by the government. The government also sought in 1951 to remove coloured voters in the Cape Province from the common voters' roll and place them onto a separate roll by which they would elect white representatives (Separate Representation of Voters Act of 1951). The Supreme Court declared the Act invalid on constitutional grounds. Reluctant to concede defeat, the government resorted to Draconian measures. It increased the size of the Appellate Division from five to eleven judges. It also increased the size of the Senate, while changing the method of electing senators. The outcome was a sympathetic Appellate Division and the necessary two-thirds National Party majority in a joint sitting of both Houses of Parliament. The South Africa Act of 1956 was passed with the necessary unicameral majority and the Separate Representation of Voters Act was revalidated. Coloured citizens were removed from the common voters' roll.[34]

Separate and Unequal

The unequal allocation of resources and exploitation of labour were central premises of apartheid, evident in legislation on general facilities, education and jobs. The Reservation of Separate Amenities Act of 1953 stated that all races should have separate amenities – such as toilets, parks and beaches – and that these need not be of an equivalent quality. Under the provisions of this act, apartheid signs were erected throughout South Africa. The Bantu Education Act of 1953 decreed that blacks should be provided with separate educational facilities under the control of the Ministry of Native Affairs, rather than the Ministry of Education. The pupils in these schools would be taught their Bantu cultural heritage and, in the words of Hendrik F. Verwoerd, then Minister of Native Affairs, they would be trained "in accordance with their opportunities in life".[35] These he considered to be not "above the level of certain forms of labour". The

Act also removed state subsidies from denominational schools with the result that most of the mission-run African schools were sold to the government or closed. The Extension of University Education Act of 1959 prohibited blacks from attending white institutions, with few exceptions, and established separate universities and colleges for Africans, coloureds and Indians.

The perversely titled Industrial Conciliation Act of 1956 enabled the Minister of Labour to reserve categories of work for members of specified racial groups. In effect, if the Minister felt that white workers were being pressured by "unfair competition" from blacks he could re-categorise jobs for whites only and increase their rates of pay. Under the terms of the Native Laws Amendment Act of 1952, African women as well as men were made subject to influx control and the pass laws and, under Section 10 of the Act, neither men nor women could remain in urban areas for longer than 72 hours without a special permit stating that they were legally employed. Also misnamed, the Abolition of Passes and Co-ordination of Documents Act of 1952 was designed to make the policy of pass restrictions easier to enforce. It abolished the old pass, replacing it with a document known as a reference book. The act stated that all Africans had to carry a reference book containing their photograph, address, marital status, employment record, list of taxes paid, influx control endorsements and rural district where they were officially resident; not having the reference book on one's person was a criminal offence punishable by a prison sentence. In 1955, the Minister of Native Affairs stated that African women would be issued with passes with effect from January 1956. Up until then, only African men had been obliged to carry passes. Outraged by the government's intention, women of all races launched the Women's Anti-Pass Movement, with the first protest taking place in October 1955. Protests grew all over the country and culminated in a mass demonstration at the Union Buildings in Pretoria on 9 August 1956.[36] Since 1994 this day has been celebrated as "Women's Day" in South Africa.

Sovereign Security

Apartheid's desire to classify and regulate bred the conditions for a militaristic police state. As separate development took shape, the powers of the police and security forces grew. The Suppression of Communism Act of 1950 declared the Communist Party and its ideology illegal. Among other features, the Act defined communism as any scheme that aimed "at bringing about any political, industrial, social, or economic change within the Union by the promotion of disturbance or disorder" or that encouraged "feelings of hostility between the European and the non-European races of the Union the consequences of which are calculated to further . . . disorder". These very broad terms allowed the Minister of Justice to list and ban members of such organisations, usually for five-year periods, from holding public office, attending public meetings or residing in specified areas. The Public Safety Act of 1953 gave the British Governor-General power to suspend all laws and proclaim a state of emergency. The Criminal Law Amendment Act of 1953 stated that anyone accompanying a person found guilty of offences committed while "protest[ing], or in support of any campaign for the repeal or modification of any law" would also be presumed guilty and would have the burden of proving his or her innocence. The Native Administration Act of 1956 permitted the government to "banish" Africans, essentially exiling them to remote rural areas far from their homes. The Customs and Excise Act of 1955 and the Official Secrets Act of 1956 gave the government power to establish a Board of Censors to censor books, films and other materials imported into or produced in South Africa. During the 1950s, enforcement of these various laws resulted in approximately 500 000 pass law arrests annually, the listing of more than 600 people as communists, the banning of nearly 350 people and the banishment of more than 150 other people. The enforcement of pass laws, in particular, led to the Sharpeville massacre on 20 March 1960, where 69 people died when police opened fire on peaceful protesters.

By definition, the system of apartheid caused deep division within the country, specifically along race and class lines. In response, resistance forces that had been operating peacefully turned to military opposition and underground tactics. The ANC, which aimed to create a non-racial democracy for all South African citizens, was banned in 1960. Shortly thereafter, its armed wing, *Umkhonto we Sizwe* (MK – Spear of the Nation), was formed. Its opening manifesto declared that the repression of apartheid had come to justify an armed response. MK targeted strategic sites – police stations and power plants. Similarly, although enjoying less support and wielding less power, *Poqo* (Blacks Only), the militant wing of the PAC, engaged in a campaign of targeting and killing in particular African chiefs and headmen believed to be collaborating with the government. Some young white students and professionals established their own organisation, the African Resistance Movement, and carried out bomb attacks on strategic targets.

By 1964, the police had succeeded in repressing much of these efforts. Seventeen MK leaders were arrested at a farmhouse at Rivonia near

Johannesburg in July 1963 and, along with Nelson Mandela – who had already been imprisoned on other charges – tried for treason. Eight, including Mandela, were sent to prison for life. Oliver Tambo escaped from South Africa and became president of the ANC in exile. Robert Sobukwe of *Poqo* was jailed on Robben Island until 1969 and then placed under a banning order and house arrest in Kimberley until his death in 1978. Furthermore, in 1963, the General Law Amendment Act allowed the police to detain people for 90 days without charging them and without allowing them access to a lawyer. At the end of that period, the police could re-arrest and re-detain them for a further 90 days. During the period of detention, no court could order a person's release; only the Minister of Justice had that authority.

In the years that followed, opposition remained alive, even as the government took further steps to entrench apartheid. It established alternative political structures for Africans in the homelands or reserves. In 1963, the Transkei homeland, poverty-stricken and overpopulated, was made self-governing. Other homelands were even less economically viable. Bophuthatswana consisted of 19 separate pieces of land spread hundreds of kilometres apart, and KwaZulu (formed out of Zululand and other parts of Natal in 1972) was divided into at least 11 fragments interspersed with white farms and coastal land allocated to whites. Under the provisions of the Group Areas Act, urban and rural areas in South Africa were divided into zones in which members of only one racial group could live. In practice, it was blacks who had to move, often under the threat or use of force. Between 1963 and 1985, approximately 3.5 million blacks were removed from areas designated for whites and were sent to the homelands. However, even though the homeland population rose by 69% between 1970 and 1980, the numbers of blacks in the cities continued to rise through natural growth and evasion of influx control. By 1980, after 20 years of removals, there were twice as many blacks in South Africa's towns as there were whites.

By the middle of the 1970s, apartheid was clearly under strain. The appeal of black consciousness and the levels of participation in the Soweto demonstrations of 1976 illustrated a profound discontent and a call for "people's power". Violence finally erupted in the sprawling township of Soweto, situated on the outskirts of Johannesburg. On 16 June 1976, a group of students protesting against the government's imposition of Afrikaans as a medium of instruction in African schools were met by a contingent of the South African police. In the ensuing mêlée, over 500 young people were killed, including 13-year-old Hector Peterson.[37]

Following the Soweto uprisings, hundreds of young Africans slipped across South Africa's northern borders and volunteered to fight as guerrilla soldiers for the ANC and the PAC. In the late 1970s, some of these people began to re-enter South Africa secretly to carry out sabotage attacks on various targets that were seen as symbols of apartheid.

Labour discontent also grew. The combination of discriminatory legislation and employer reliance on the use of inexpensive labour meant that African workers were poorly paid and were subjected to an enormous number of restrictions. Economic recession in the early 1970s, followed by inflation and a contraction in the job market, resulted in a dramatic upsurge in labour unrest. In the first three months of 1973, some 160 strikes involving more than 60 000 workers took place in Durban; in the early 1970s, no more than 5 000 African workers had struck annually and in the 1960s the average had been closer to 2 000. Labour unrest spread to East London and the Rand and continued.

Urban-based strikes drew attention to the fact that, despite the ambitions of apartheid, the South African economy was failing. Nearly three-quarters of South Africa's urban population in 1980 were black. Only half of the African population lived in the homelands, and even then the rural land available was so inadequate that population densities were far greater than they were in the rest of the country. At least four-fifths of the homeland dwellers lived in poverty. Yet the South African government persisted in arguing that Africans were really rural dwellers and that they should exercise political rights only in the homelands. In 1976 the government proclaimed the Transkei an independent nation-state and followed this move by granting independence to Bophuthatswana in 1977, Venda in 1979 and Ciskei in 1981. Citizens of these states, including the half who lived outside their borders, were then deemed aliens in South Africa. Another six ethnically based homelands were granted limited self-government in preparation for eventual independence: they were Kwa-Zulu, Lebowa, Gazankulu, QwaQwa, KaNgwane and KwaNdebele.

Internationally, the 1970s saw increasing opposition to the apartheid regime. The administrations of US presidents Richard Nixon and Gerald Ford, including US Secretary of State Henry Kissinger, had favoured working with the National Party government. They saw South Africa as a key strategic ally in the cold war and had both encouraged the invasion of Angola and promised US military support. President Jimmy Carter, however, considered South Africa a liability for the west. His vice president, Walter Mondale, told then South African prime minister John Vorster that the United States wanted South Africa to adopt a policy of one person, one vote. Anti-apartheid sentiments also grew in Britain and Europe, while the UN, composed of a majority of third world states, in 1973 declared apartheid "a crime against humanity" and in 1977 declared the existing embargo on the sale of arms to South Africa to be mandatory. Such criticism had a considerable material impact. South Africa had to invest large sums in the development of its own armaments industry. Because of an embargo by the Organisation of the Petroleum Exporting Countries (OPEC), it also had to pay more for oil and purchased most of its supplies from the Shah of Iran until his overthrow in 1979. Foreign investment in South Africa, on which the country depended for much of its economic growth, also became increasingly expensive and uncertain in the second half of the 1970s. A growing sluggishness in the South African economy, coupled with concerns about the country's political stability in light of the Soweto demonstrations, caused most investors to seek more attractive ventures for their capital in other countries. Foreign capital still flowed into South Africa, but it was primarily in the form of short-term loans rather than investments. In 1976, for example, two-thirds of the foreign funds entering South Africa were in short-term loans, usually of 12 months' duration.

International pressure on the South African government intensified further in the mid-1980s. Anti-apartheid sentiment in the US, fuelled in large part by television coverage of the ongoing violence in South Africa, heightened demands for the removal of US investments and for the imposition of official sanctions. In 1984, 40 US companies pulled out of South Africa, with another 50 following suit in 1985. In July 1985, Chase Manhattan Bank caused a major financial crisis in South Africa by refusing to roll over its short-term loans, a lead that was soon followed by most other international banks, fuelling inflation and eroding South African living standards. In October 1986, the US Congress, overriding a presidential veto, passed legislation implementing mandatory sanctions against South Africa; these included banning all new investments and bank loans, ending air links between the US and South Africa and banning many South African imports. Calls for economic sanctions also came from the Commonwealth, with only British prime minister Margaret Thatcher, a firm non-believer in sanctions, holding off severe economic action. International banks, at the same time, continued to underwrite apartheid government loans and many nations continued to trade with South Africa. Limited sanctions were also imposed by the European Economic Community, including a ban on the sales of gold Krugerrands in Europe and the import of South African coal. Some European countries imposed further restrictions, including a total trade ban by Sweden and Denmark.

President P. W. Botha activated security legislation to deal with these crises. In mid-1985 he imposed the first of what would become a series of states of emergency in various parts of South Africa. This was the first time such laws had been used since the Sharpeville violence in 1960. The state of emergency was extended throughout the nation the following year. The emergency regulations gave the police powers to arrest without warrants and to detain people indefinitely without charging them or even allowing lawyers or next of kin to be notified. It also gave the government even greater authority than the considerable powers it already possessed to censor radio, television and newspaper coverage of the unrest. Botha deployed police and more than 5 000 troops in African townships to quell the spreading resistance. By February 1987, unofficial estimates claimed that at least 30 000 people had been detained, many for several months at a time. South Africa's complex and fragmented society became increasingly polarised around anti-apartheid groups who expressed a growing sense of urgency in their demands for an end to the failed system of racial separation, and white conservative defenders of apartheid who intensified their resistance to change. Facing mounting international disapproval, economic stagnation and a campaign of ungovernability by liberation forces, the government tentatively began to signal that apartheid would have to be substantially altered or abandoned. In January 1986, President Botha shocked conservatives in the all-white House of Assembly with the statement that South Africa had "outgrown the outdated concept of apartheid". The government undertook tentative, incremental change at a carefully controlled pace, while at the same time it severely limited the activities of anti-apartheid agitators. The government tightened press restrictions, effectively banned the United Democratic Front mass movement and other activist organisations and continued to renew the state of emergency throughout the rest of the 1980s.

In February 1986 President Botha agreed to a visit of the Commonwealth Eminent Persons Group (EPG), a group of Commonwealth leaders who had been charged by the October 1985 Commonwealth Conference with seeking a solution to the South African impasse. He also allowed them to have meetings with Mandela in Pollsmoor Prison. The issues they discussed involved violence, negotiations and international sanctions.[38] They were then convinced that peace could only be achieved with Mandela's release and they reported that black support for the ANC was now widespread and growing. In the meantime, the South African Defence Force, under the orders of President Botha, launched air raid and commando attacks on ANC bases in Botswana, Zambia and Zimbabwe. This action sabotaged whatever goodwill had been engendered by the Commonwealth visitors. Consequently, the EPG left South Africa. It was at that time that Mandela began secret talks with Botha's ministers, from his private quarters in prison, culminating in a meeting with Botha himself.

President Botha suffered a stroke in January 1989. Although the process of choosing a successor almost split the National Party, the Minister of Education F. W. de Klerk was elected to succeed him. President De Klerk indicated that he intended to undertake major reforms, deviating from the piecemeal process initiated by his predecessor. He had held secret talks with the imprisoned Mandela, who by then had been transferred to Victor Verster prison in December 1988 in order to make preliminary discussions easier. The sea change came on 2 February 1990. Surprising many, De Klerk announced the impending release of Mandela in a speech that also unbanned the ANC, the PAC and the SACP. Going further, De Klerk also lifted media restrictions and claimed that he was interested in convening negotiations designed to write a fully democratic constitution. He pledged that his government would investigate alleged human rights abuses by the security forces. He also sought improved relations with the rest of Africa by proposing joint regional development planning with neighbouring states and by inviting other African leaders to increase trade with South Africa.

After much internal discussion, the ANC resolved in March 1990 that it should meet face-to-face with the government. These were to be the first official or open "talks about talks", with the meetings planned for early April. However, this plan was disrupted by violence that erupted towards the end of March between the police and ANC demonstrators. After con-sultation with the ANC's National Executive Committee, Mandela announced the suspension of the talks. He told De Klerk that the govern-ment could not "talk about negotiations on the one hand and murder our people on the other".[39] However, despite the suspension of the official talks, Mandela, with the approval of the ANC leadership, met privately to keep up the momentum of the negotiations. Their discussion centred pri-marily on finding a new date. Hence, the first round of talks was held in May 1990 in Groote Schuur, resulting in the *Groote Schuur Minute*.[40]

In terms of the *Minute*, a working group was established to make re-commendations on *inter alia* a definition of political offences in the South African situation and to advise on norms and mechanisms to deal with the release of political prisoners. On 21 May, the working group found that, while there was legislation allowing for the pardon or release of people who had already been sentenced or were awaiting appeals, new legislation would be required for people who had not yet been charged. This resulted in the Indemnity Act No. 35 of 1990. This was followed by the Further Indemnity Act No. 151 of 1992. The legislation was broad.

The National Council on Indemnity was established to advise De Klerk on possible amnesties, with all members thereof being appointed by the president and all sittings held *in camera*. In the words of Jody Kollapen: "The Act is nothing more than an attempt on the part of the government to create a mechanism whereby it can forgive itself and those acting under its command, instructions or authority for the grossest of human rights violations."[41]

It was in a sense reminiscent of the *Punto Final*, in which the Argentinean junta in 1983 provided itself with amnesty.[42] In fact De Klerk later suggested that there ought to be a blanket amnesty for all political offenders. He further granted 3 500 members and ex-members of the police indemnity on the eve of the South African general election. Although the validity of this action was widely questioned by a number of senior officials in the present government, the legislation of 1990 and 1992 was validated by the Promotion of National Unity and Reconciliation Act No. 34 of 1995, which governed the TRC.[43] Recently, the issue of indemnity and amnesty has again come to the fore. This follows the granting of "presidential pardon" by President Mbeki to 33 individuals, most of whom were denied amnesty by the TRC[44] – suggesting that this issue, central to the final phases of the potential settlement, will haunt the nation for some time to come.

In August 1990, during the *Pretoria Minute* meeting, Mandela announced the suspension of the ANC's 30-year armed struggle.[45] The government continued lifting apartheid restrictions, and in October – at De Klerk's prompting – the National Party opened its ranks to all races. On 15 October 1990 parliament repealed the Reservation of Separate Amenities Act of 1953.

The talks were threatened by escalating violence throughout 1990, and Mandela accused the government of doing little to end it. De Klerk and Mandela continued their political tug-of-war. De Klerk sought domestic and international approval for the changes already under way, while Mandela pressed for change at a faster pace. A series of legislative decisions and political breakthroughs in 1990 moved South Africa closer to non-racial democracy, but at the end of the year, it was clear that many obstacles remained.

The National Peace Accord of September 1991 was a critical step toward formal negotiations. The 33-page accord was signed by representatives of 27 political organisations and national and homeland governments. It set codes of conduct for all parties to the process, including the police. The accord also established a network of "peace committees" to contain the violence that continued to plague the townships. One of the most important results of the National Peace Accord turned out to be the establishment of networks of committed individuals, the opening of communications channels and the trust that began to be sown through discussion. The accord itself failed to accomplish its immediate goal; the violence continued and increased sporadically throughout 1992.

The first forum for writing a democratic constitution, the Convention for a Democratic South Africa (CODESA), convened in late 1991. The talks at CODESA produced both steady progress and bitter debate. The National Party continued to believe that it could control the ANC and retain a measure of power in the new dispensation. Debate centered on the form of the new government, the procedures for writing a new constitution, and the question of power-sharing. The talks also illustrated the deep political divisions in the country, particularly in the east where ANC and Inkatha Freedom Party forces clashed regularly. It was discovered that the government was supporting the Inkatha Freedom Party, a link that led Mandela to rebuke the National Party and threaten to withdraw from the negotiations. Unable to reach agreement on several key issues, neither side was ready yet to compromise. In June 1992, residents of the Boipatong hostel were killed by Inkatha Freedom Party followers who were thought to be working with the government. Enraged at the National Party's apparent unwillingness to control violence, the ANC withdrew from all talks and began a winter of mass action.

Private talks led to a Memorandum of Understanding in November, an agreement in which De Klerk agreed both to the principle of majority rule and the procedures for writing the country's new constitution. With respect to the latter, it was agreed that negotiators would write an interim constitution that would become the basis for free elections. Only then would the final constitution be written, crafted by leaders who had been elected by all the people of South Africa. The negotiations that followed – the Multiparty Negotiating Forum – took place over the course of 1993. They illustrated that the country was far from unified. In an odd alliance, the Afrikaner right wing and the Inkatha Freedom Party both opposed the form and content of the talks, each threatening to boycott the election scheduled for April 1994. Last-minute negotiations brought both into the fold but demonstrated that the new government would face the task of trying to heal very deep divisions and distrust.

Installed in May 1994, the Government of National Unity faced significant challenges. Although it was one of the most progressive constitutions in the world, the new constitution took shape in talks that did little to address the country's rich-poor gap. Thus, some have concluded that the transition allowed for blacks to rule while whites kept (economic) power. Expectations for reform ran high, too high for a liberation movement that was now focused on converting itself into a political party. However, the Mandela administration made significant headway in building a unified vision of South Africa. Symbols of reconciliation, not the least of which was Mandela himself, defused some tensions even as they left others unresolved. Indeed, the legacy of apartheid left bitter scars in people as well as within all structures of government. In 1999, Thabo Mbeki became president, inheriting these problems.

Mbeki provides a different kind of leadership. Although he does not always exude the warmth and charismatic leadership of his predecessor, he shows a great capacity for pragmatic problem-solving and policy-making. This has been his administration's strength – a virtue that has left it somewhat distant from the people but which has started to yield substantial reform.

In a survey done by Stephen Rule in 1999, empirical evidence showed that there was much dissatisfaction within the South African citizenry over a number of issues. The survey showed that satisfaction with the general economic situation in South Africa ranged from 11% in KwaZulu-Natal to 40% in Mpumalanga. Satisfaction levels in the three provinces with large metropolitan populations were all lower than the national average of 23%. What was evident was that the voters of the economic core areas in the country were thus more dissatisfied with the state of the economy than those of the economically peripheral regions. A slightly higher proportion, 28%, indicated satisfaction with the financial situations of their own households and only one in five adults felt that government policies during the preceding 12 months had been beneficial to the economy of the country.[46]

This aside, the ANC continues to enjoy the support of the vast majority of South African voters. Despite the high levels of crime and unemployment, a remarkable two-thirds of the survey population indicated their trust in the national government.[47] Furthermore, respondents were asked whether they thought that relations between the different races of South Africa had improved since the first democratic elections in April

1994. More than half replied in the affirmative. However in the Western Cape, only three out of ten thought that race relations had improved. Although this survey showed some positive aspects about the transition in post-apartheid South Africa, other surveys gave a more negative view on some aspects. In reports done by the British Broadcasting Corporation, issues such as education, housing and crime were among some of the areas that were seen as problematic. The report made mention of housing promises not fulfilled, sprawling squatter camps and lack of amenities. It spoke of the extent of violent crime in the cities and its link to poverty. Furthermore, it spoke of huge classroom shortfalls, lack of electricity for schools, unaffordable school fees and job losses for teachers.

Reconciliation and the Potential for Nation-building

Following the negotiated revolution, the South African TRC has both captured the world's attention and generated substantial controversy. Born of an agreement in the country's interim constitution, the Commission has adopted a victim-centred approach to the problems of recovering a lost history and healing the deep divisions that separate citizens, communities and institutions. It is a body designed to remake the country's future through reviewing the past. In the words of its chairperson, Archbishop Emeritus Desmond Tutu: "Having looked the beast of the past in the eye . . . let us shut the door on the past."

The TRC was established as a statutory body designed to promote a culture of human rights. It had precious little time to conduct its work – a mere 18 months. Eventually, the mandate was extended, particularly to accommodate the slow pace of hearings and the processing of amnesty applications from perpetrators of gross human rights violations. Throughout its existence, the body generated both hope and disputes. Its hearings opened a window into a past filled with violence, revealing government hit squads and atrocities committed by all parties in the conflict. Indeed, a key problem for the Commission was how to fulfil its mandate of completing as full a picture as possible of the events that occurred between 1960 and the early 1990s. Many argued that the Commission conflated the evils of apartheid with the excesses of a just liberation struggle. Others argued that the body was engaged in a witch-hunt, eager to rewrite history in the ANC's favour. What is clear is both that the TRC has made an important contribution to healing deep divisions and that there is much work still to be done.[48]

The TRC had the widest mandate of any truth commission to date. Its authorising legislation set important parameters for its work, defined its goals and objectives and articulated the means through which they were to be pursued. The following tasks were central to its work:

- establishing as complete a picture as possible of the causes, nature and extent of the gross violations of human rights during a 34-year period;
- facilitating the granting of amnesty to persons who make full disclosure of all relevant facts relating to acts associated with a political objective;
- making known the facts and whereabouts of victims and restoring their dignity by affording them the opportunity to relate their own accounts of violations that they had suffered; and
- producing a report that included recommendations for the prevention of future human rights violations and what reparations might be granted to victims.[49]

In South Africa today, there are perhaps as many views on the TRC as there are people. The same can be said about what it means to engage in reconciliation. For example, there are at least three divergent schools of thought when it comes to how South Africa should approach its past. There are those, especially in the ranks of the National Party and the Inkatha Freedom Party, who hold that the country should draw a line and move forward, allowing the past to remain in the past. In this way, it is argued, old wounds will not unravel the tasks of nation-building. Others hold the opposite view. It is important, they argue, that the wounds of the past should be opened to allow for proper catharsis. The legislation governing the Commission speaks to this view directly. The third school of thought, heard frequently from the ranks of those in the PAC, contends that there should be an unconditional release of those now imprisoned who fought against apartheid. They also argue that the country should undertake to prosecute those who committed crimes in the name of supporting apartheid.

One of the clear benefits of the TRC process was its ability to demonstrate the violence of the past. No longer could anyone deny what the country had been through. The process also seemed to give witnesses some measure of relief from their pain through public testimony. In some way, the TRC offered the chance for public ownership of the transition, arguably a key aspect of democratisation. In particular, it was the human rights violations hearings that made the TRC most accessible to the average South African. TRC representatives travelled throughout the country to take statements from victims of gross human rights violations. Of the 21 300 victims who came forward, approximately 2 000 were invited to testify in public hearings. For many, these highly charged hearings were the centrepiece of the Commission. Those who had been victims of political violence were given a platform from which they could recount their personal histories. On this basis a common understanding of South Africa's history during this turbulent period was started, if not built. Extensive media coverage was instrumental in keeping the public informed. In particular, daily South African Broadcasting Corporation radio coverage of the TRC hearings, in South Africa's indigenous languages, made the TRC highly accessible.

Did the TRC work? At some level it is too early to tell. However, in a national survey conducted in 2001, despite concerns expressed on a range of issues that continue to divide the nation, South Africans across the colour line indicated that they thought the country would be a poorer place if there were no other racial groups in the country.[50] A significant result, considering the prominence of racial tension in South Africa. The survey further shows that South Africans are ready to find compromise solutions to such divisive issues as amnesty and reparations. Black and white South Africans indicated that amnesty for perpetrators of gross violations of human rights in the apartheid context was morally unjust, and yet 65% of black South Africans conceded that amnesty was a price that needed to be paid to secure a peaceful transition to democratic rule in South Africa. Interestingly, only 18% of whites saw it as such! Black South Africans, in particular, were also ready to accept that the inherent injustice of amnesty could be compensated for in different ways. Payment of money as compensation was not seen as the *only* such palliative. A sincere apology and an opportunity for victims to relate the stories of their suffering in public were cited as important alternatives to normative forms of retribution and even reparation.[51] Of course, these results can be challenged. The above results do, however, suggest that the incredible amount of goodwill and willingness to find a formula for coexistence in the South African situation should not be squandered. And yet the same survey shows that while the majority of South Africans of all races support the payment of reparations to apartheid's victims, only 10% of whites indicate that they are personally ready to contribute to such payments.[52]

The TRC generated support from many sectors but also significant criticism, some of which re-inscribed old divisions and animosities. Many did not participate in the process. This is most apparent when one looks at the paucity of high-level apartheid leaders who refused to apply for amnesty. The TRC was attacked for its work from all sides of the political spectrum. It was accused of bias at different stages and seemed to struggle with how to communicate the message that reconciliation was something that all citizens needed to work towards. Part of the difficulty was that the Commission had limited resources, which barred it from creating programmes for community-building, anti-racism education and economic reform. The Commission was obliged to content itself with making extensive recommendations on these and other related concerns. Ironically, the success or failure of the Commission is no longer in its hands. Government, business and society as a whole are required to respond to the recommendations – correcting, augmenting and bringing to completion the unfinished work of the Commission. This said, the pointed criticism of the Commission from some politicians, activists and scholars needs to be heard.

A list of literature is provided in the resources section of this profile and constitutes vital reading for those interested in understanding the ways in which the Commission worked and what it attempted to accomplish. For example, Mahmood Mamdani argues that the TRC focused on a very narrow sense of truth. For him there is not a single truth of apartheid, but many truths. Furthermore, the Commission's view of South African history was established through very narrow lenses, crafted to reflect the experience of a tiny minority: state perpetrators on the one hand, and victims, such as political activists, on the other hand.[53] He also suggests that the TRC's view of human rights violations led it to exclude the experience of those millions of ordinary people who lived and laboured under the violence of the apartheid system.

Supporters of the Commission have argued that these criticisms may be valid but not always fair, especially in light of the amount of work that confronted the TRC and the short time in which it had to be accomplished. As the process was a publicly oriented attempt to recognise the terms of the past and create the basis not for retribution but reconciliation, the Commission did much good even as it could not do everything. In the present day, the question thus becomes what might have been done differently, particularly in terms of recognising victims, creating sustainable reconciliation programmes and avoiding the legal-political controversy that slowed the Commission in its efforts. One obvious answer appears around the reparation process, a source of continuing concern. The matter plays directly into larger questions of how to allocate resources in the wake of authoritarian regimes, a matter that the ANC has struggled with at broader levels. The country also now faces the question of whether to prosecute those who failed to receive or did not apply for amnesty. Legal trials promise great costs with uncertain results. They may serve the interests of justice even as they undo some of the conciliation achieved by the Commission.

The TRC has had a basic effect on the lives of South Africans. There are a number of organisations that have taken its lead and continued work in the field of reconciliation and transition in South Africa. Some of their projects have concentrated on racism, nation-building and transitional justice. Although the TRC infiltrated the lives of ordinary South African citizens for a number of years, its work still needs to be carried forward, particularly in the field of education. According to Naledi Pandor, the TRC Report states that admitting the truth restores one's dignity and identity, confirms experience as real and not illusory and affirms one's sense of self. For Pandor, the report encourages South Africans not to seek amnesia as a means of confronting the past, because the past refuses to lie down quietly. School curriculum planners should reflect on her words, and ensure that curricula make reference to the positive values that should be inculcated in society as a whole: democracy, an appreciation of human rights, problem-solving, tolerance, respect for diversity, non-sexism and non-racism.

What of reconciliation beyond the work of the TRC? Today it appears that one of the central tasks facing South Africa is to use the bedrock established by the Commission to address other problems that continue to divide the country. Most notably, the question of material redistribution and poverty alleviation continues to haunt the country and its leadership. There are increasing efforts to place these issues within a framework of reconciliation, particularly with respect to how citizens can begin to negotiate their interests and share finite resources. In any event, the process will be slow, a consolidation effort that will take years, if not generations. There is much hope in South Africa, but there is also significant despair and material inequality that has the potential to undo the miracle. South Africa, however, is not Zimbabwe. The ANC-led government appears to have a solid base of support and a clear vision for reform. Its reluctance to listen to criticism may need to lessen if channels of democratic governance are to fulfil their potential. In these terms, it is safe to say that the South African transition is ongoing, a delicate process of balancing nation-building and justice.

With the TRC having submitted its final report to the government, there is likely to be an intense national debate around reparations and prosecutions for years to come. Human rights groups have called for the prosecution of those who were denied amnesty by the TRC and those who failed to apply for amnesty. The Department of Justice has, in turn, indicated the need for a mechanism designed to advance the cause of nation-building, suggesting the need for the historic bridge of compromise to be crossed yet again. The nation is confronted once more with the kind of moral and legal concerns that it faced with the enactment of the Promotion of National Unity and Reconciliation Act No. 34 of 1995 that required the TRC to "facilitate the granting of amnesty to persons who make full disclosure of all relevant facts relating to acts associated with a political objective and comply with the requirements of this Act".

Few will contest the need for national healing and reconciliation. The question is *how*? There is a need, on the one hand, to restore confidence in the rule of law and a need, on the other, to bring closure to a dark chapter in South African history. The prospect of indefinite prosecutions does not augur well for national healing. The state lacks the capacity to prosecute all who should perhaps be prosecuted. It is also very difficult to prove according to court procedure the guilt beyond all reasonable doubt of high-ranking officers who were allegedly behind past gross violations of human rights. The court cases involving the former Minister of Defence, General Magnus Malan, and the South African architect of chemical and biological warfare, Dr Wouter Basson, vividly illustrate this point. It is not easy to cross the bridge of compromise or to restore a nation. Once again a balance has to be struck between the needs of the victims and survivors on the one hand, and the dire need for national healing and reconciliation on the other. Ultimately the success of South Africa, like that of other African countries, is directly linked to the success of the continent as a whole in overcoming war, bad governance, under-development and economic growth. The leadership task facing President Mbeki in establishing the credibility of the African Union and Nepad is huge.

NOTES

1 Richard Goldstone, *The Hauser Lecture*, New York University, January, 1997.

2 Quoted in an interview with Ingrid Uys in *Millenium Magazine*, May 1996.

3 See Allister Sparks, *Tomorrow is Another Country* (Sandton: Struik Book Distributors, 1994); Richard Rosenthal, *Mission Impossible: A Piece of South African History* (Cape Town & Johannesburg: David Philip Publishers, 1998).

4 Willem de Klerk, "The Process of Political Negotiations," in *Birth of a Constitution*, ed. Bertus de Villiers (Cape Town: Juta, 1994), 1–11.

5 The Mandela Page, "The Mandela Document: A document presented by Nelson Mandela to PW Botha before their meeting on 5 July 1989." Reprinted at www.anc.org.za/ancdocs/history/mandela/doc890705.html (accessed 15 February 2002).

6 Tom Lodge, *Consolidating Democracy: South Africa's Second Democratic Election*

(Johannesburg: EISA, Witwatersrand University Press, 1999), 64.

7 Heather Deegan, *South Africa Reborn: Building a New Democracy* (Pittsburgh, Pa.: University of Pittsburgh Press, 1999).

8 Anton D. Lowenberg and William H. Kaempfer, *The Origins and Demise of South African Apartheid: A Public Choice Analysis* (Ann Arbor: University of Michigan Press, 2001).

9 In terms of the Employment Equity Act No. 55 of 1998, "black people" is a generic term referring to Africans, coloureds and Indians.

10 *The Cape Times*, 3 February 1998.

11 Hennie Kotze, *Elite Perspectives on Policy Issues in South Africa* (Stellenbosch: Stellenbosch University, 2001), 69; Andrew Whiteford and Dirk Ernst van Seventer quoted in Nicoli Nattrass and Jeremy Seekings, "Race and Economic Inequality in South Africa Today," *Daedalus* 131, 1.

12 *The Mail and Guardian*, 28 July 2000.

13 Larry Diamond, ed., *Democratization in Africa* (Baltimore: John Hopkins University Press, 1999).

14 A study conducted in 2001 by the Institute for Justice and Reconciliation illustrates these opinions. See www.ijr.org.za.

15 The Mbeki Page, "Statement of Deputy President TM Mbeki, on behalf of the African National Congress, on the occasion of the adoption by the Constitutional Assembly of The Republic of South Africa Constitution Bill 1996, Cape Town, 8 May 1996." Reprinted at www.anc.org.za/ancdocs/history/mbeki/1996/sp960508.html (accessed 10 June 2002).

16 *Business Day*, 20 June 2002.

17 The Mbeki Page, "Statement of Deputy President Thabo Mbeki at the opening of the debate in the National Assembly on Reconciliation and Nation-Building, Cape Town, 29 May 1998." Reprinted at www.anc.org.za/ancdocs/history/mbeki/1998/sp980529.html (accessed 10 June 2002). This speech is also known as the "Two-Nations" speech.

18 The Mandela Page, "Report by the President of the ANC, Nelson Mandela to the 50th National Conference of the African National Congress, Mafikeng, 16 December 1997." Reprinted at www.anc.org.za/ancdocs/history/mandela/1997/sp971216.html (accessed 27 May 2002).

19 United Democratic Movement, "Joint Press statement between the UDM and PAC, 9 June 2002." Reprinted at www.udm.org.za/media_dir2002/20020609_udm&pac_aftertalks.htm (accessed 11 June 2002); Victor Mecoamere, "PAC, UDM in slow dance: Parties outline details of anti-ANC pact." *The Sowetan*, 10 June 2002.

20 US Department of State, "Country Reports, 1995." Reprinted at www.state.gov/www/issues/economic/trade_reports/africa95/SAFRICA.html (accessed 25 February 2002).

21 *Africa Recovery Online: A United Nations Publication*, "South Africa Tackles Social Inequities." Reprinted at www.un.org/ecosocdev/geninfo/afrec/subjindx/144soafr.htm (accessed 25 February 2002).

22 Deegan, *South Africa Reborn*.

23 Ibid, 139.

24 *Africa Recovery Online*, "South Africa Tackles."

25 Ibid.

26 See Eddie Webster and Glenn Adler, "Towards a Class Compromise in South Africa's 'Double Transition': Bargained Liberalism and the Consolidation of Democracy." Reprinted at www.columbia.edu/itc/seminars/671/article.html (accessed

22 July 2002).

27 Ibid.

28 Bill Dixon, "Cloud over the Rainbow: Crime and Transition in South Africa." Unpublished paper, 21.

29 Crime information drawn from Nedcor, "A Battle Lost? Violent Crime Trends in 1999," *Nedcor ISS Crime Index* 4 (2000).

30 *The Guardian*, 19 April 2002.

31 There is a vast literature on the rise and development of apartheid. For general and accessible accounts see Allister Sparks, *The Mind of South Africa* (New York: Alfred A. Knopf, 1990); see also *Truth and Reconciliation Commission of South Africa Report 1* (1998): 95.

32 *Reader's Digest: Illustrated History of South Africa* (Cape Town: The Reader's Digest Association of South Africa, 1988), 375.

33 Deborah Posel, *The Making of Apartheid, 1948–1961: Conflict and Compromise* (New York: Clarendon Press, 1991).

34 Charles Villa-Vicencio, "Whither South Africa: Constitutionalism and Law-Making," *Emory Law Journal* 40 (1991): 141–62.

35 Edgar H. Brookes, *Apartheid: A Documentary Study of Modern South Africa* (London: Routledge and Kegan Paul, 1968), 50.

36 African National Congress, "The Demand of the Women of South Africa for the Withdrawal of Passes for Women and the Repeal of the Pass Laws: Petition presented to the Prime Minister, Pretoria, 9 August 1956." Reprinted at www.anc.org.za/ancdocs/history/women/petition560809.html (accessed 27 June 2002).

37 Keith Maguire, *Politics in South Africa: From Vorster to De Klerk* (Edinburgh: W & Chambers, 1991), 24.

38 Nelson Mandela, *Long Walk to Freedom: The Autobiography of Nelson Mandela* (Randburg: Macdonald Purnell, 1994), 516–17.

39 Ibid, 568.

40 African National Congress, "The Transition: Minutes and Accords between the ANC and the South African Government, May 1990–February 1991." Reprinted at www.anc.org.za/ancdocs/history/transition/minutes.html (accessed 7 January 2002).

41 Jody Kollapen, "Accountability: The Debate in South Africa," *Journal of African Law* 73 (1993): 4–5.

42 Neil Kritz, ed., *Transitional Justice Vol. II: Country Studies* (Washington DC: United States Institute of Peace Press, 1995), 11, 326, 487.

43 Charles Villa-Vicencio, "A Different Kind of Justice: The South African Truth and Reconciliation Commission," *Contemporary Justice Review* 1 (1999): 407–28.

44 *The Star*, "Mbeki's secret amnesty list revealed, May 13, 2002." Reprinted at www.ijr.org.za/pardonart.html (accessed 14 June 2002).

45 Whether the ANC's decision to suspend the armed struggle was done in good faith remains a moot point. This stems from the fact that the announcement was made after the Security Branch of the then South African Police had discovered Operation Vula, an ANC/SACP plot aimed at utilising the space and freedom of movement created by the negotiation process to bring about a revolutionary overthrow of the government of the day. See Jim Jenkin, "Talking to Vula: The Story of the Secret Underground Communications Network of Operation Vula." Reprinted at www.softwar.net/vula.html (accessed 27 June 2002); H. D. Stadler, *The Other Side of the Story: A True Perspective* (Pretoria: Contact Publishers, 1997), 90–98.

46 Stephen Rule, *Electoral Territoriality in Southern Africa* (Aldershot: Ashgate Publishers, 2000), 226–28.

47 Ibid, 228.
48 Richard A. Wilson, *The Politics of Truth and Reconciliation in South Africa: Legitimising the Post-Apartheid State* (Cambridge: Cambridge University Press, 2001).
49 *Truth and Reconciliation Commission of South Africa Report 1* (1998): 117–34.
50 Survey undertaken by Dr James Gibson. See Institute for Justice and Reconciliation website at http://www.ijr.org.za. Altogether 62% of blacks, 64% of whites, 79% of coloureds and 76% of people of Asian origin indicated their preference for a country of racial diversity.
51 James Gibson, "Truth, Justice and Reconciliation: Judging Amnesty in South Africa," develops this argument further. An unpublished paper, 5 June 2001.
52 91% of blacks, 54% of whites, 64% of coloureds and 90% of South Africans of Asian origin support the payment of direct compensation to victims by government.
53 Mahmood Mamdani, "Reconciliation without Justice," *Southern African Political and Economic Monthly* 10 (1997): 22–25.

RESOURCES

Books, Articles, Current Media Reports

Africa Recovery Online: A United Nations Publication. "South Africa Tackles Social Inequities." Reprinted at www.un.org/ecosocdev/geninfo/afrec/subjindx/ 144soafr.htm (accessed 25 February 2002).

African National Congress. "The Transition: Minutes and Accords between the ANC and the South African Government, May 1990–February 1991." Reprinted at www.anc.org.za/ancdocs/history/transition/minutes.html (accessed 7 January 2002).

Biggar, Nigel, ed. *Burying the Past: Mercy, Peace and Democratic Justice After Civil Conflict.* Washington: Georgetown University Press, 2001.

Bizos, George. *No One To Blame: In Pursuit of Justice in South Africa.* Cape Town: David Philip Publishers, 1998.

Boraine, Alex. *A Country Unmasked.* Oxford: Oxford University Press, 2000.

Boraine, Alex et al. *Dealing with the Past: Truth and Reconciliation in South Africa.* Cape Town: Idasa, 1997.

Davenport, Thomas Rodney H. *South Africa: A Modern History.* London: Macmillan, 2000.

De Klerk, Willem. "The Process of Political Negotiations." In *Birth of a Constitution,* edited by Bertus de Villiers. Cape Town: Juta, 1994.

Deegan, Heather. *South Africa Reborn: Building a New Democracy.* Pittsburgh: University of Pittsburgh Press, 1999.

Diamond, Larry, ed. *Democratization in Africa.* Baltimore: John Hopkins University Press, 1999.

Dyzenhaus, David. *Truth, Reconciliation and the Apartheid Legal Order.* Cape Town: Juta, 1998.

Hadland, Adrian and Jovial Rantao. *The Life and Times of Thabo Mbeki.* Rivonia: Zebra Press, 1999.

James, Wilmot and Linda van de Vijver. *After the TRC: Reflections on Truth and Reconciliation in South Africa.* Cape Town: David Philip Publishers, 2000.

Jenkin, Jim. "Talking to Vula: The Story of the Secret Underground Communications Network of Operation Vula." Reprinted at www.softwar.net/vula.html (accessed 27 June 2002).

Lodge, Tom. *Consolidating Democracy: South Africa's Second Democratic Election.* Johannesburg: EISA, Witwatersrand University Press, 1999.

Lowenberg, Anton D. and William H. Kaempfer. *The Origins and Demise of South African Apartheid: A Public Choice Analysis.* Ann Arbor: University of Michigan Press, 2001.

Mamdani, Mahmood. "Reconciliation without Justice." *Southern African Political and Economic Monthly* 10 (1997): 22–25.

Mandela, Nelson. *Long Walk to Freedom.* Randburg: Macdonald Purnell, 1994.

Mandela Page, The. "The Mandela Document: A document presented by Nelson Mandela to PW Botha before their meeting on 5 July 1989." Reprinted at www.anc.org.za/ancdocs/history/mandela/doc890705.html (accessed 15 February 2002).

———. "Report by the President of the ANC, Nelson Mandela to the 50th National Conference of the African National Congress, Mafikeng, 16 December 1997."

Reprinted at www.anc.org.za/ancdocs/history/mandela/1997/sp971216.html (accessed 27 May 2002).

Mbeki Page, The. "Statement of Deputy President TM Mbeki, on behalf of the African National Congress, on the occasion of the adoption by the Constitutional Assembly of The Republic of South Africa Constitution Bill 1996, Cape Town, 8 May 1996." Reprinted at www.anc.org.za/ancdocs/history/mbeki/1996/sp960508.html (accessed 10 June 2002).

————. "Statement of Deputy President Thabo Mbeki at the opening of the debate in the National Assembly on Reconciliation and Nation-Building, Cape Town, 29 May 1998." Reprinted at www.anc.org.za/ancdocs/history/mbeki/1998/sp980529.html (accessed 10 June 2002).

Meiring, Piet. *Chronicle of the Truth Commission*. Vanderbijlpark: Carpe Diem, 1999.

Nina, Daniel. "Popular Justice in Transition to a 'New' South Africa: Alexandra, A Case Study." Institute for African Alternatives Occasional Papers No. 2, Durban, South Africa, May 1992.

Rotberg, Robert and Dennis Thompson, eds. *Truth v. Justice: The Morality of Truth Commissions*. Princeton: Princeton University Press, 2000.

Rosenthal, Richard. *Mission Impossible: A Piece of South African History*. Cape Town: David Philip Publishers, 1998.

Rule, Stephen. *Electoral Territoriality in Southern Africa*. Aldershot: Ashgate Publishers, 2000.

Saunders, Christopher. *Historical Dictionary of South Africa*. Lanham: Scarecrow, 2000.

Sparks, Allister. *Tomorrow is Another Country*. Sandton: Struik Book Distributors, 1994.

Star, The. "Mbeki's secret amnesty list revealed, May 13, 2002." Reprinted at www.ijr.org.za/pardonart.html (accessed 14 June 2002).

Tutu, Desmond. *No Future Without Forgiveness*. London: Rider, 1999.

United Democratic Movement. "Joint Press Statement between the UDM and PAC, 9 June 2002." Reprinted at www.udm.org.za/media_dir2002/20020609_udm&pac_aftertalks.htm (accessed 11 June 2002).

Villa-Vicencio, Charles and Erik Doxtader, eds. (forthcoming) *Memory, Justice and Impunity: Amnesty in South Africa*. Cape Town: David Philip Publishers.

Villa-Vicencio, Charles and Wilhelm Verwoerd, eds. *Looking Back Reaching Forward: Reflections on the Truth and Reconciliation Commission of South Africa*. Cape Town: David Philip Publishers, 2000.

Wilson, Richard A. *The Politics of Truth and Reconciliation in South Africa: Legitimising the Post-Apartheid State*. Cambridge: Cambridge University Press, 2001.

Primary Documents

Truth and Reconciliation Commission of South Africa Report, Vols. 1–5. (1998). All the volumes are also accessible at: www.polity.org.za/govdocs/commissions/1998/trc

Government, Intergovernmental Bodies, Political Parties

African National Congress (ANC): http://www.anc.org.za
Democratic Party (of South Africa): http://www.da.org.za
Freedom Front: http://www.vryheidsfront.co.za
Human Sciences Research Council (HSRC): http://www.hsrc.ac.za
Inkatha Freedom Party (IFP): http://ifp.org.za
New National Party: http://www.natweb.co.za

Pan Africanist Congress of Azania (PAC): http://paca.org.za
South African Communist Party (SACP): http://www.sacp.org.za
South African government news and information website: http://www.gov.za

Local NGOs

Africa Institute for South Africa (AISA) is an independent organisation focusing on
Africa in its research, publications and resource library: http://www.ai.org.za

Centre for Conflict Resolution (CCR) aims at contributing toward a just and
sustainable peace in South Africa and other African countries by promoting
constructive, creative and co-operative approaches to the resolution of conflict and
the reduction of violence: http://ccrweb.ccr.uct.ac.za

Centre for Policy Studies (CPS) is an independent policy research institution committed to producing original and thought-provoking research on South Africa's
most pressing political and social issues: www.cps.org.za

Centre for the Study of Violence and Reconciliation (CSVR) is a multi-disciplinary
South African NGO dedicated to making a meaningful contribution to peaceful
and fundamental transformation in South Africa and in the southern African
region: http://www.csvr.org.za

Institute for Democracy in South Africa (Idasa) is committed to promoting a sustainable democracy in South Africa and elsewhere by building democratic institutions, educating citizens and advocating social justice: http://www.idasa.org.za

Institute for Healing of Memories is a trust that seeks to contribute to the healing
journey of individuals, communities and nations: http://www.healingmemories.
co.za

Institute for Justice and Reconciliation (IJR) was launched in May 2000 and is self-
consciously located in post-apartheid South Africa. It is committed to using the
insights generated through its work in South Africa to engage in dialogue with
other African countries: http://www.ijr.org.za

SOUTH AFRICA COUNTRY INFORMATION

Geography
Location: Southern Africa, at the southern tip of the continent of Africa.
Cities: *Capitals:* Administrative, Pretoria; Legislative, Cape Town; Judicial, Bloemfontein. *Other cities:* Johannesburg, Durban, Port Elizabeth.

People
Nationality: *Noun:* South African(s). *Adjective:* South African.
Population (2000): 43 000 000.
Population growth rate (2000): 1.5%.
Ethnic groups: Black 77.6%, white 10.3%, coloured 8.7%, Indian 2.5%, other 0.9%.
Religions: Christians 68%, Muslim 2%, Hindu 1.5%, traditional African 28.5%.
Languages: Afrikaans, English, Ndebele, Pedi, Sotho, Swazi, Tsonga, Tswana, Venda, Xhosa, Zulu (all official languages).
Education: *Years compulsory:* 7–15 years of age for all children. The Schools Act of 1996 aims to achieve greater educational opportunities for black children, mandating a single syllabus and more equitable funding for schools. *Literacy:* total population that can read and write 81.8%; male 81.9%, female 81.7% (1995 est.).
Health (official): *Infant mortality rate:* 24.6/1 000. Estimates from international organisations range from 50 to 60/1 000. *Life expectancy:* 62 years for women; 52 years for men. *HIV infection rate:* 12.91%.

Economy
GDP (2000): $126 billion.
GDP real growth rate (2000): 3.1%.
Per capita income (2000): $2 900.
Inflation rate (2000): 5.3%.
Unemployment rate (2000): 30%.
Natural resources: Almost all essential commodities, except petroleum products and bauxite. Only country in the world that manufactures fuel from coal.
GDP composition (2000): *Agriculture and mining:* 9.7%. *Industry:* 24.4%. *Services:* 65.9%. World's largest producer of platinum, gold and chromium; also significant coal production.
Industry: *Types:* minerals, mining, motor vehicles and parts, machinery, textiles, chemicals, fertilisers, information technology, electronics, other manufacturing and agro-processing.
Trade (2000): *Exports:* $31.5 billion: gold, other minerals and metals, agricultural products, motor vehicles and parts. *Major markets:* UK, US, Germany, Italy, Japan, East Asia, sub-Saharan Africa. *Imports:* $27.3 billion: machinery, transport equipment, chemicals, petroleum products, textiles and scientific instruments. *Major suppliers:* Germany, US, Japan, UK, Italy.
Economic aid: Recipient: $676.3 million.

Military
Military expenditure: Dollar figures: $2 billion (FY 00/01).
Military expenditure: Percent of GDP: 1.5% (FY 99/00).

Demographic information is drawn from that compiled by the United States Department of State. See http://www.state.gov/r/pa/ei/bgn

Map of Mozambique showing scale 0–75–150 km. Surrounding countries: TANZANIA, ZAMBIA, MALAWI, ZIMBABWE, SOUTH AFRICA, SWAZILAND. Provinces: Cabo Delgado, Niassa, Nampula, Tete, Zambézia, Manica, Sofala, Inhambane, Gaza, Maputo.

Towns and features: Songea, Mtwara, Quionga, Mzuzu, Lake Malawi, Kasungu, Lichinga, Gomba/Masuguru, Pemba, Chipata, LILONGWE, Cassacatiza/Katete, Mandimba/Namwera, Cuamba, Nacala, Nampula, Zobué/Mwanza, Zomba, Zumbo/Kanyemba, Lake Cahora Bassa, Mecumbura/Mukumbura, Tete, Blantyre, Milange/Mlanje, MOZAMBIQUE, Cochemane/Nyama-Panda, Nsanje, Mocuba, Zambézia, HARARE, Quelimane, ZIMBABWE, Machipanda/Forbes-Mutare, Chimoio, Gorongosa N.P., Mutare, Sofala, Beira, Masvingo, Chibabava, INDIAN OCEAN, Gonarezhou N.P., Save, Massangena, Zinave N.P., Sango/Chicualacuala, Vilanculos, Banhine N.P., Inhambane, Kruger National Park, Gaza, Inhambane, Lebombo, Inharrime, Xai-Xai, Quissico, Manhiça, SOUTH AFRICA, MAPUTO, Namaacha, Bela Vista, SWAZILAND, Manhoca. Rivers: Luangwa, Lugenda, Messalu, Rovuma, Lúrio, Zambezi, Manica, Limpopo, Maputo.

Legend:
- ☐ National capitals
- ◉ Major town
- ○ Town
- ◎ Small town
- ⊙ Large village
- ✈ International airport
- ✈ Airport
- ▶ Border post
- ▪ ▪ International border
- ---- State/province
- ～ River
- ～ Dry river
- Park

Chapter 12

Mozambique: Making Peace – The Roots of the Conflict and the Way Forward

IRAÊ BAPTISTA LUNDIN AND ANTÓNIO DA COSTA GASPAR

Every conflict has its own history and development. The armed conflict in Mozambique had its own source and dynamic, emerging in a specific historical context. Consequently, the peace-building process has taken its own specific way; it does not offer a blueprint for other war-torn countries engaged in the search for peace. The Mozambican peace process has been successful so far; it is considered a "good example" within the United Nations Peacekeeping Operations framework.

The experience in Mozambique is linked to the nature of its internal conflict as well as to the cold war environment. Multi-track diplomacy and initiatives carried out by civil society were important in sustaining dialogue and reconciliation among Mozambicans. The commitment demonstrated by civil society was useful in building trust based on tolerance and mutual understanding. A dialogue was not only possible but also fruitful; the parties learned that give and take is the best way to construct a common ground. The existing social differentiations between people and regions and cultural diversity were not used in a prejudicial manner. However, the issue of power relations between the former opponents still hampers the reconciliation process. The main question is how to enlarge the political and social space to include people who were previously excluded. The principles of the General Peace Accord (GPA) signed in 1992 between the two parties to the conflict, proved to be more idealistic than functional. The war ended but a number of crucial questions related to the future participation of people in the political and economic life of the country were not properly addressed. The matter has much to do with the need to include more people from the Mozambique National Resistance Movement (RENAMO) in state affairs and the national economy, both of which are open but arguably dominated by those from the Front for the Liberation of Mozambique (FRELIMO). In the end, it is a question about the state- and nation-formation process in that all Mozambican people are supposed to participate in the process of development, regardless of their ethnic identity, religious beliefs or political affiliation.

This work reviews the internal and external roots and causes of the conflict. It introduces the process of searching for peace and the actions aimed at promoting reconciliation in the country from the early 1980s to the early 1990s. The path of peaceful settlement includes the Nkomati Accord signed between the governments of Mozambique and South Africa in 1984, and the GPA reached between the Mozambican government and RENAMO in 1992. Finally, it considers the peace-building process and prospects for reconciliation.

The Face of Conflict

The GPA was signed on 4 October 1992 between the government and the rebel movement RENAMO, ending almost 30 years of armed conflict. The three decades of conflict included the struggle for national liberation (1964–74) and the war waged by RENAMO after independence (1976–92). However, even though the peace-building process was successfully constructed, some crucial issues that sustained the conflict have yet to be settled. The most difficult issues at present are power relations and how to establish a reliable and functional mechanism for including the people in socio-economic areas strongly dominated by neo-liberal economic policies. In fact, any measures intended to reconstruct and reduce absolute poverty are directly challenged by the external conditions imposed on the Mozambican economy by international financial institutions.[1]

As part of the peace-building measures and reconciliation, the government introduced deep institutional reforms. The 1990 constitution is a good example in that it paved the way for a multi-party democratic system. The abolition of the death penalty and adoption of a law guaranteeing press freedom illustrate the reach of this new dispensation. Pluralism, in terms of culture, religious diversity and other forms of identity, is respected and encouraged by the new democratic state. The traditional elite became a valid partner for the state – at the level of local (rural) dialogue.[2] Traditional healers, through their national association, are interacting with the modern health sector, sharing their experiences. Religious beliefs and practices are freely practised across the country by all citizens, including the political elite.[3]

Changes were also introduced at legal and administrative levels of governance. Decentralisation is part of the political agenda, encouraging and enhancing the participation of citizens in state affairs at a community level. The process provides and enlarges the space for parties to participate in political life. Besides strengthening civil society, the process gives a voice to traditional leaders, another purpose of decentralisation, in turn strengthening the state authorities.

Many argue that a strong functional state needs to address carefully and comprehensively the roots and sources of insecurity facing the state and ordinary citizens. The new democratic state aims to function under the rule of law, with executive, legislative and judiciary powers working alongside the responsible participation of ordinary citizens. The space for people's participation is ensured through legislation, and ordinary citizens are actively engaged in reconstruction and reconciliation in the country.

The GPA paved the way for stability and reconciliation. However, it has proved to be more idealistic than functional. Among other issues, it created and sustains an asymmetrical power relation between the two former opponents, and at present the centre of the dispute lies in the power-sharing between FRELIMO and RENAMO, an issue not yet agreed upon or even on the table for discussion. Legally, it appears that no such arrangement is forthcoming, a problem that according to the government makes it impossible to move toward satisfying RENAMO's claims.

The challenge ahead lies in the need to absorb RENAMO's partisans in state affairs. Other unfinished business in this matter – left over from the war of liberation – is the future status of ex-combatants from the colonial war. According to the government, ex-combatants include only those who participated in the struggle against the colonial power, whereas RENAMO argues that government legislation should also include people other than FRELIMO freedom fighters.

The ongoing power-sharing issue and the asymmetrical power relations constitute a major bottleneck in the process of reconciliation between the two major political parties. President Joaquim Chissano of FRELIMO and Afonso Dhlakama of RENAMO met officially three times in 2001, accompanied by senior officials from both sides, to search for peaceful solutions to the existing political crisis. RENAMO argued FRELIMO was not taking the case seriously enough. But indications are that the door for dialogue is still open.

Civil society has been putting pressure on President Chissano and Dhlakama to together resolve the stalemate that exists. An acute stalemate emerged after the 1999 general elections when the RENAMO-Electoral Union contested the results. RENAMO argued that the results were fraudulent and asked for a re-count. The High Court turned down RENAMO's appeal, aggravating the political crisis. In response, the RENAMO-Electoral Union boycotted the first session of parliament. As a solution to the crisis, the opposition vindicated the office of the governor in the six provinces where they received the majority of votes – in the centre and north of the country – but this finding was not well received by the ruling party.

The situation worsened when direct dialogue between the government and RENAMO, led by Chissano and Dhlakama, failed again, mainly because of the ongoing problem of lack of consensus on power-sharing issues. RENAMO carried out demonstrations in November 2000 to protest against the results of the elections across the country. In some parts of the country, the demonstrations turned into acts of vandalism in which state property was destroyed and state buildings occupied. In the central and northern regions of the country police intervened, and some demonstrators were killed. One of the worst hit was the office of the administration of the District of Montepuez in the province of Cabo Delgado. Six policemen were killed in Montepuez and many more were injured. About 80 RENAMO militants imprisoned in the town died of asphyxiation. This incident has not yet been fully explained. Two local police officers were given long sentences along with five RENAMO activists who were found guilty of allegedly "participating and inciting the public to break the law". The government said the demonstrations were illegal,[4] while RENAMO claimed the right of freedom of expression and the right of manifestation envisaged by the 1990 constitution.

This episode illustrates the difficult road ahead for conflict resolution and demonstrates that the reconciliatory discourse that dominated the country at the time of the signing of the NPA is no longer widespread. The government has hardened its position and RENAMO has adopted a discourse of inciting the population to civil unrest on the basis of ethnic and regional identities, pointing to existing unequal development and lack of opportunities.[5] This discourse may polarise society along ethnic regional lines, with serious consequences for peace and reconciliation in a country where 70% of the population live below the absolute poverty level.

The regions where RENAMO has its strongest social basis are less developed (with higher levels of absolute poverty), a fact which may be used against the government's programmes and activities. In spite of the government's efforts, there are at present many institutional constraints to "humanising" the impact of micro-economic policies on ordinary citizens. The new practices are not only connected to factors of the past but also, particularly at present, to the neo-liberal model of development in an increasingly globalised world. Therefore, there is a need to improve the state's ability to provide for its citizens' needs through strengthening its dialogue with international partners.

Crime is also an issue of concern. It is widespread and includes high levels of violence against ordinary citizens. This is not directly connected to the outcome of ending the conflict, i.e. demobilised soldiers are not the major source of crime. Many believe that the rise in crime has more to do with the negative impact of the Structural Adjustment Programme (SAP) in force since 1987. The SAP has pushed the state to embark on privatisation, neglecting the social and economic effects of this on the labour force. As a consequence the rate of unemployment has increased, which in turn may have led to the rise in crime across the country, notably in the urban areas.

Summing up, the current political scenario in Mozambique clearly shows the complexities of a peace-building process, particularly in a post-conflict phase. The conflict of the past has shifted in nature and form. The sources of insecurity are no longer based on violence but rather lie with the high rate of absolute poverty, aggravated by dependence on external aid and loans. The conditions under the macro-economic policies supported by the international financial institutions will continue to be an obstacle to the country's development and the consolidation of peace, national reconciliation and democracy.

The Historical Roots of Violence and Division

The roots of the conflict in Mozambique are varied, and may be traced from pre-colonial, colonial and post-independence history. They are also connected to structural and circumstantial causes and their internal and external dimensions. The internal causes of the conflict are directly connected to the process of nation and state formation in a very complex territory in terms of ethnic and linguistic groups and religious pluralism. The policies, actions and attitudes of the ruling elite toward political, economic and social domains within the state formation framework contributed to some extent to the rise and consolidation of the conflict in the country. The external cause of conflict has to do with the destabilising role of the former Rhodesian and South African regimes in undermining the majority government in Mozambique.

The origin of RENAMO as the Mozambican National Resistance Movement (MNR) is well known, and has been well documented as the outcome of interrelated internal and external causes. The movement was initially established by the Rhodesian security forces to undermine Mozambican support for Zimbabwean nationalists. However, RENAMO was also a result of internal factors such as "errors" made by the ruling elite, for example a number of ex-commanders were expelled from

FRELIMO and sent to prison or re-education camps. Those who were discontented decided to cross the Zimbabwean border where they were recruited and integrated into the anti-FRELIMO fifth column operating in Mozambique.[6]

There was not just one conflict in Mozambique but many, which led to a war which lasted 16 years after independence. For analytical purposes we identify socio-cultural, socio-economic and administrative factors behind the internal sources of the conflict in Mozambique.

The socio-cultural factors are closely linked to the nature and complexity of Mozambican society. This includes the matri- and patrilineal systems of filiation, the multiplicity of ethnic and linguistic group identities, the differences between urban and rural areas and the differentiated contacts of the social groups with "outsider" culture. The process of internalising western values was not uniform across different geographic zones, which allowed the colonial power to divide and rule. This made it difficult to harmonise any political administrative power, although pluralism in a territory does not constitute a source of conflict *per se*. The sources of conflict revolve around state policies of exclusion toward some people based on race, ethnic group, religion and ideological motivation.

In the process of state and nation formation, FRELIMO tended to view its values as universal and tried to impose them on all social groups.[7] The ruling elite attempted, for example, to mould the family according to patrilineal rules and under a socialist regime with a centralised government. This generated resistance among people. The socialist regime discouraged other cultural ideological practices. FRELIMO also adopted a hostile attitude toward African cultural practices then labelled obscurantism. The traditional elite, especially the chiefs and traditional healers, was also excluded from social political life, which alienated many people especially in the rural areas.

The socio-economic factors behind the conflict have different elements. The genesis of FRELIMO helps explain the internal political conflict in the country. The front was created out of three nationalist movements based in neighbouring countries (Rhodesia, Tanzania and Malawi), essentially on an ethnic basis.[8] This process was sponsored by the then president of Tanzania, Julius Nyerere, and the presidency of FRELIMO was handed to Eduardo Mondlane,[9] then a senior officer in the United Nations. The leadership was formed in a controversial climate among the members, which led to divergences of opinion and conflicts of interest. As a result, some prominent leaders from the three movements were excluded from FRELIMO and moved into exile to continue their fight.

Socio-economic factors also refer to the consequences of the socialist system and regional asymmetries in development which are useful in understanding persisting animosities between individuals and groups in Mozambique. The development in the south is the result of proximity to the South African economic system and of the former presence of the colonial power in Maputo, which worked to the detriment of those in the north and centre. Twenty-five years of political independence have not been able to eliminate this inherited unequal development in the country. Moreover, there is a strong perception among ordinary citizens that FRELIMO has a deep connection to the south and RENAMO to the centre and north of the country. This perception may be justified by the fact that the south has superior regional development, investment and opportunities for individuals and social groups to participate in the process of reconstruction and nation building.

Political independence opened up an opportunity to build the new society from "Rovuma to Maputo",[10] a process conceived under a single-party democracy where Mozambicans were supposed to be equal before the law, regardless of their ethnic group, religion and social status. However, in practice some of the adopted policies were exclusionary. The elite that emerged under the one-party socialist democracy gave primacy to political affiliation. In short, FRELIMO dominated politics and the economy, and controlled the mechanisms of indirect participation of the population in all spheres of social, political, administrative and cultural life.

We now turn to administrative factors. In the course of the state-building process, the dismantling of the administrative structures of the colonial state without creating workable non-partisan structures created a power vacuum in the rural areas. This development spurred the entrance of the MNR.[11] The movement took over efforts to destabilise the country, attacking the provinces of Manica and Tete. It grew considerably and started to conduct armed resistance to the government using external military and logistical support. Inside the country the movement got help from a group of discontents, among them the traditional leadership that provided a solid rear-guard in the rural areas.

In this context, it became easier for RENAMO to take over large areas in the rural areas because of its policy of terror and destruction. It engaged in kidnapping people and forcing them to engage in acts of cruelty toward their own people, thereby preventing them from returning to their own communities and forcing them to stay with RENAMO.

In sum, these dynamics constituted the major internal sources of the armed conflict in Mozambique. A set of old and new hierarchical factors created animosities after independence, which have been aggravated by the new social exclusion that has emerged in the context of democratisation and the introduction of the neo-liberal economy.

The external roots of the conflict in Mozambique have to do with domestic, regional and international factors strongly influenced by cold war discourse. For the purposes of analysis, we have grouped them into three categories: the national development strategy adopted in 1977 based on the socialist model; post-independence external policy toward the southern Africa region; and the hostile regional environment under racist and minority regimes. These factors were intimately linked.

In 1977 when FRELIMO declared itself a Marxist-Leninist party, the right to "build socialism" in the country was conceived by the ruling elite in Mozambique as an act of sovereignty. However, it underestimated and ignored regional interdependence and the force of the prevailing "white supremacy" minority regimes. The socialist model clearly demarcated the country's future orientation in opposition to the prevailing capitalist system in the region. This paved the way for concern within western policy circles as well as within the regional minority regimes. In hindsight, FRELIMO's most serious error was to assume that it would be allowed to pursue a non-aligned foreign policy and a socialist economy. The mistake was to believe that it had real freedom of choice to decide state affairs. Many political analysts now believe this view was naive.

The post-independence external policy toward the southern African region took into account the need to back the liberation struggle. Regional security and political and economic interdependence were seen as the bottom line for stability and the sustainability of political independence in Mozambique. As Mozambique president at the time, Samora Machel, pointed out several times, Mozambique would not be "truly independent" unless external threats from the minority regimes were eliminated. Indeed, the interdependence of the liberation struggles in the region became clear as the wars intensified: Rhodesian military operations deep inside Mozambique underlined for FRELIMO the need to reinforce the Zimbabwean nationalist movements opposing the Ian Smith regime in then Rhodesia. Mozambique stepped up its support for the Zimbabwean guerrillas and, in March 1976, closed the border with Rhodesia. The Rhodesian Security Forces began to recruit in the mid-1970s for the MNR.

When Rhodesia became Zimbabwe in 1980, the external focus of the MNR was transferred to the apartheid regime of South Africa. The immediate and more tangible effect of Zimbabwe's independence was the removal of military threats from Mozambique's borders. However, the transference of the MNR's attention from Zimbabwe to South Africa was not seriously taken into account by the Mozambican authorities. They also underestimated the military and logistical support from South Africa to RENAMO.

The hope that the end of Rhodesia would imply the end of the MNR was not to be fulfilled. In fact, its real political meaning and far-reaching strategic implications were not anticipated. Mozambique's backing of the nationalist movements in South Africa and Zimbabwe was clearly not welcomed in those countries. Mozambique's actions were perceived as a threat to the national security and vested interests of the South African apartheid regime.

In response to the perceived threat, South Africa increased its air raids, posing new and unpredictable challenges to the Mozambican army. South African military support to RENAMO increased substantially. Mozambique faced dual threats – from the South African regime and from RENAMO. In short, the country was exposed to South Africa's "total strategy".

The minority regimes were a primary source of permanent instability and tension in the region. The black majority-ruled state and socialist model in Mozambique created a precedent that could not be tolerated by its hostile neighbours. The perceived risk was that the eventual success of a black majority-ruled government in Mozambique would have a direct influence on South Africa and Rhodesia.

Prospects for Peace-building

The ruling elite held that, in regard to the termination of war in Mozambique, negotiations with RENAMO were an "unacceptable course of action".[12] The zero-sum approach, that war could only be terminated by a victory, dominated the political discourse. However, the devastation of civil war exacerbated by a prolonged drought, coupled with military stalemate for both parties, led to a re-evaluation of this view.

The need for peace, co-existence and co-operation in southern Africa was of paramount importance for the Mozambican leadership under Machel in the early 1980s. There was a need "to achieve peace (and) normalise life . . . paving the way for economic restoration and progress in the country".[13] It was taken for granted that the major impediment to national development was the ongoing war against the state backed by the apartheid regime via the MNR. By the early 1980s the Mozambican government initiated an effort to find peace through politics. However, the ongoing conflict was conceived in classical inter-state terms, recognising the Mozambican and South African authorities as the main parties to the conflict. The MNR was neglected, which made it difficult to recognise the movement as a valid partner in discussions on the settlement of the conflict. In fact, according to some analysts Machel "appeared not to be worried about the MNR in those days. He seemed to think that it would disappear along with its creator, the Rhodesian regime."[14]

The first sign of a political settlement came when President Machel and South African prime minister P. W. Botha signed the Nkomati Accord on 16 March 1984. Under the terms of the Nkomati Accord, South Africa undertook to halt its support for RENAMO and Mozambique agreed to close down the ANC's military operations in the country. The Nkomati Accord was a clear indication of the "survival policy" pursued by the Mozambican ruling elite which was characterised by a carrot and stick approach.

At this point it appeared that there was greater incentive for peace than war. However, the zero-sum solution was not totally ruled out from FRELIMO's calculations. It stated that, "all political and diplomatic actions were complemented by military actions on the ground".[15] On the one hand, the military operations on the ground were under way, notwithstanding the deep logistical problems. On the other hand, diplomatic actions led some western countries to provide military assistance to the country.

The accord was seen as a way of keeping peace and stability in the region through "non-aggression and good neighbourliness" between Mozambique and South Africa. However, the expected climate of non-aggression, co-existence and co-operation between the two states failed. The war not only carried on but also essentially assumed the "highest physical, psychological and unprecedented cruelty in Africa and elsewhere in the world".[16] Children were used to commit crimes beyond human imagination. Citizens were kidnapped in urban and rural areas, tortured, mutilated or murdered. After the Nkomati Accord, RENAMO, far from reducing its actions, intensified its campaign, seemingly "provisioning itself from the Mozambican Army"[17] and from South African military forces.[18]

In the post-Nkomati atmosphere, the South African authorities tried to bring together the government of Mozambique and RENAMO for the first face-to-face negotiations in Pretoria in October 1984. The effort was premature. In the end, the Pretoria Declaration was issued, in which the South African government apparently committed itself to bringing peace to the southern African region, particularly Mozambique, but it was peace *à la* Pretoria. For a number of reasons these talks soon collapsed. Firstly, the South African military intelligence clearly sabotaged any peace effort. Secondly, the white settlers in Mozambique were not prepared to discuss peace with the government of FRELIMO. Thirdly, the government's army was in a better position than RENAMO's forces.

The conflict continued to destabilise the government, drain the country's resources and halt development. The conflict reached its apex in 1986, by which time the war had devastated the Mozambican economy and the country had become increasingly dependent on foreign assistance. Furthermore, on 19 October 1986 the government of Mozambique suffered a major blow when President Machel died in an aircraft crash on his return to Maputo following a regional summit meeting in Zambia. FRELIMO appointed Joaquim Chissano, then Minister for Foreign Affairs, as president.

While the war continued, with neither side able to achieve military victory, the government launched a comprehensive political and economic reform process in the form of the Structural Adjustment Programme. Constitutional changes, which included replacing single-party democracy with a multi-party system based on general elections for the presidency and parliament, came into effect in 1990, when the government decided to undertake far-reaching political and economic reforms, abandoning its Marxist philosophy. The principles of a more market-oriented approach under the guidelines of international financial organisations were introduced. This political move enabled the government to gain further financial and political support from western governments and, to an extent, kept RENAMO politically isolated. The government's economic and political reforms enhanced the prospects of political accommodation. For its part, RENAMO, also at a military stalemate, organisationally weak and with its external material support uncertain, was also being pushed toward negotiations.

Tentative negotiations through the intermediaries of the Catholic Church began seriously in 1988. They developed rapidly. Establishing a basis for negotiations between the government and RENAMO was a very difficult task. This phase was mainly characterised by informal and explorative meetings between the antagonists through the facilitation of Mozambican churches. In February 1989, a delegation of Mozambican Anglican and Catholic bishops travelled to Nairobi, Kenya to meet senior RENAMO leaders. They returned to Maputo to tell Chissano that "they believed RENAMO was also tired of the war and therefore peace negotiations were possible". Informal negotiations began to turn into a basis for formal talks.

As a result, the government drew up a "twelve-point position paper" which called on RENAMO to halt its attacks and offered "a dialogue about the ways to end the violence, establish peace and normalise the life of everyone in the country". This document marked FRELIMO's first concrete steps on the road to a negotiated settlement. The RENAMO leadership also drew up a "sixteen-point paper", expressing a desire to bring an end to the war. These two unpublished documents were welcomed within the national and international community as they increased the possibility for peace and reconciliation in the country.

The search for common ground between the two parties showed that while both sides had a strong interest in peace, each remained highly "distrustful of the other and could not accept the other's claim to legitimacy". For example, RENAMO's demand for equal status with the government in any direct negotiations was "unacceptable to the authorities in Maputo".[19] Furthermore, for negotiations to begin it was essential to identify mutually acceptable mediators. Here again the distrust between the parties was noticeable. RENAMO was willing to accept Kenya or Portugal as mediators. The government favoured joint mediation by Zimbabwe and Kenya. The first attempt to bring the parties to a face-to-face meeting hosted by Malawi in 1990 failed.[20] The Catholic Community of Santo Egídio offered Rome as an alternative, with the approval of the Italian government. Both sides accepted the offer.[21] Negotiations began in July 1990. On the one side was a government that had 15 years of experience of governing in a single-party system. On the other side was a "proxy guerrilla organisation, with [apparently] a vaguely identified leadership, carrying no societal administrative experience and with no political/organisational structure".[22]

The negotiations in Rome were marked by distrust, even if there was a strong mutual desire to end the war. According to the first joint communiqué of 10 July 1990, there was political will not only to terminate the military hostilities but essentially "to create the necessary political, economic and social conditions for building a lasting peace and normalising the life of all Mozambican citizens".[23] The peace-building process was not only an end in itself but also a means to create an environment for national development and reconciliation among people, to move toward political stability and progress.

Over time the spirit of mutual tolerance gradually increased, which opened up the possibility for consensus. There existed an awareness of belonging to the same motherland and, above all, the sense of a common "Mozambican identity", of being part of the same geographic territory and the same family of citizens. The feeling of commonness was expressed by public statements and finally through the accords and consensus reached in the different phases of the process.

After formal talks began, a partial cease-fire agreement was reached. This accord sought to protect highly vulnerable corridors important for the Mozambican economy and for the economy of other Southern African Development Co-ordination Conference (SADCC) member states. Its impact was apparently limited, since Zimbabwean troops continued to operate elsewhere in Mozambique.[24]

During 1991, RENAMO's refusal to recognise the legitimacy of the government slowed progress toward peace. An agenda for full peace negotiations was agreed to on 28 May 1991. It consisted of six areas: the law of political parties, the electoral system, military issues, guarantees, a cease-fire and a donor conference.

The GPA deals with military, political and humanitarian issues. It consists of seven protocols agreed upon in the negotiation process, and a number of joint communiqués and declarations. The key stipulations were that all armed forces were to be demobilised under UN supervision and a small portion of them incorporated into the new 30 000-strong armed forces, and that presidential and parliamentary elections were to be held before 4 October, also under UN supervision.

With the Peace Accord, the two signatories promised, before the Mozambican people and the international community, to undertake difficult and complex activities toward its successful implementation. There were, however, forces opposing the settlement. According to the Italian politician Aldo Ajello, the special representative of the UN General Secretary in Mozambique, the war in the country was a profitable business for some people, but they were the "minority and [. . .were] neutralised".[25] The so-called "peace spoilers"[26] were thus unable to change the course of history because of the popular desire for peace, heavily supported by the international community.

The international community, through the United Nations Operations in Mozambique (UNOMOZ), was responsible for the implementation and supervision of the GPA which, in our view, was facilitated by the nature and political will of the Mozambican people to end the war. The success of the UNOMOZ was also due to the skilful manoeuvring of Aldo Ajello, who used his personal diplomatic and political experience to push things forward. However, several aspects of the peace agreement were not satisfactorily implemented. For instance, the integration of the zones under RENAMO's influence into a single state remained a remote goal.

In general, the cease-fire held but implementation of the accord was delayed by about a year. Nevertheless, elections were held in October 1994 and FRELIMO won a majority in the 250-member assembly, 129 seats against 112 for RENAMO. Chissano was elected president with 53% of the vote against 34% for RENAMO's leader. A coalition of three small parties won nine seats, helping to ease polarisation in the parliament between the ex-opponents.[27]

The Mozambican case reveals that peace-building is a complex process requiring a strong will and commitment from the parties in the conflict. Without those elements, the best mediator will fail. The former UN General Secretary, Boutros Boutros-Ghali, through his work, *An Agenda for Peace*, has made a valuable contribution to understanding both the content and scope of the peace-building processes, particularly in the post-conflict situation. He pointed out that peace-building consists of "sustained, co-operative work to deal with underlying economic, social, cultural and humanitarian problems".[28] The "sustainable and co-operative work" should ensure successful disarming, restoring order, destroying weapons, repatriating refugees, training the military and the security forces, monitoring elections, and promoting the political participation of citizens. It entails, among other things, patience, tolerance, political will and a permanent dialogue among the parties involved. How much demilitarisation has contributed to peace-building is a very important question.

The presence of the UN through the UNOMOZ for two years no doubt contributed to peace-building in Mozambique. The operation was set up after the UN Security Council approved an amount of US$260 million covering a troop contingent of up to 7 500 military personnel and 354 observers.[29] The mission was regarded as one of the most complex ever undertaken. It ensured the maintenance of a cease-fire, with few serious violations, and undertook the disarmament of some 80 000 combatants and facilitated their return to civilian life. In this context, the former opposing forces were demobilised, as well as the paramilitary forces, most of them from the government side. This may have reduced the possibility of new military hostilities. Co-ordinated humanitarian relief efforts, in the course of which about four million refugees and displaced people returned to their homes, highlight the work of the UNOMOZ. The success of the electoral process, in which citizens freely and democratically exercised their right to determine their future government, is also the outcome of the presence of the UNOMOZ.

There is no doubt that the presence of the UN through the UNOMOZ contributed to peace and stability in Mozambique. However, it is also important to emphasise that the determining factor behind successful peace-building was and is related to the strong will for peace among ordinary citizens as well as the FRELIMO and RENAMO leadership. The process of "disarming the minds" of ordinary citizens was crucial for the demilitarisation of the society – and it is still ongoing.

Present and Future Opportunities for Reconciliation

Peace-building and reconciliation concern many in Mozambique. They require endurance, determination and persistence. The state and civil society are playing an encouraging role, combining efforts to keep the peace and promote development. The state has provided a legal framework that enables citizens to take part in the process of transforming a divided society into one based on solidarity, reconciliation, tolerance and national unity. The first National Human Development Report (1998) produced in the country also recognised this joint effort by the state and civil society.[30]

Besides the new legislation creating a democratic dispensation, state institutions for training and research are building capacity for popular participation in democracy. Traditional structures, religious groups and other civil society organisations are also playing a role in consolidating peace and promoting reconciliation. The Centre for African Studies (CEA) at the University Eduardo Mondlane (UEM) and the Centre for Strategic and International Studies (CEEI) at the Higher Institute of International Relations (ISRI) are both state research institutions working on conflict prevention, management and resolution, and development. The CEA was created after independence as a think-tank and is used to provide political and economic support to the government. It has been running a comprehensive programme on Women and Law, addressing the causes of gender-based violence and conflict. The CEEI was officially set up in 1992, having advised the government in the course of the peace process. It is involved in conflict resolution processes both domestically and externally, notably in Angola and Burundi, advising Mozambican government officials. The two centres are presently working with civil society, at local and national levels. They are doing research on several issues, particularly the processes of state formation, land issues, ethnicity and the structure of new social groups.

Traditional structures are also contributing to peace and reconciliation, using notions embedded in African culture to reconcile and reintegrate, for instance, former soldiers. In local rural areas reconciliation is conducted according to African traditional rituals. According to one demobilised soldier, "coming back after the war my father took me to a traditional healer. [. . .] Because in my zone there is a tradition saying that 'when someone leaves the military life, coming home, in the first place, before eating anything, your father has to take you to the house of a traditional doctor to treat your head. So it may stop going round as it used to do when in the army'. A ceremony has to be performed in order to slow down the rhythm the heart used to beat when in the bush, to make it normal again."[31]

According to Baptista Lundin, "The ritual of social integration [. . .] is divided into three parts. [. . .] The *first* part is designed to help the ex-soldier overcome his acquired identity (military) as 'a killing machine' and regain a civilian identity after which he 'becomes a person again'. The ceremony is meant to cleanse both physically and spiritually, so the individual first takes a steam bath, and then washes afterwards in water fortified with various herbs. The *second* aspect of the ritual is the propitiation of the spirits to announce to the dead relatives that the 'lost sheep' is back home. In this ceremony thanks are given for the protection that made possible his safe return home. The *third* and last part of the ritual is reconciliation with the spirits of the dead persons killed by the ex-soldier, a symbolic 'encounter' with his victims. In this last moment, forgiveness is requested and is backed by a show of remorse.

"Compensation usually requested by the 'dead', speaking through the traditional healer [the official of the ceremony], comes in the form of cash or goods. This ritual of cleansing includes sessions where former enemies, in person or represented by relatives, are brought together and put through rituals in order to reconcile them. In some regions a collective meal is served, and everybody eats together as a sign of reconciliation."

The number of civil society organisations is growing in Mozambique. According to a 1997 survey by KULIMA, there were 788 NGOs in Mozambique. Many of them conduct peace and reconciliation programmes and promote socio-economic activities from a national to a local level. Religious groups are also working to restore the basic values disrupted during the armed conflict. For instance, the Christian Council of Churches (CCM) is known for its work in peace, social and economic justice, and in advocating debt relief through the Jubilee movement. The CCM has a programme (TAE) to transform weapons into productive materials. The programme converts arms into agriculture materials such as hoes, spades, axes, cutlasses, as well as other productive equipment such as sewing machines, carpentry tools, etc. The TAE project has made possible the destruction of hundreds of thousands of weapons in the country, while promoting development in the rural areas by handing over agricultural tools and machinery to rural communities.

The Anglican Church is running a project caring for the street children of Maputo, especially those displaced by the war. The United Methodist Church has a programme called JUSTAPAZ (Just Peace), and a Centre for the Study and Transformation of Conflicts in Maputo for promoting civic education and peace in Mozambique. The Christian Mission for Rural Development works mainly in the central and northern provinces, as well as in Inhambane and Maputo in the south, and is engaged in civic education, human rights and conflict resolution as well as emergency relief.

The Catholic Church, which was involved in the peace process in Mozambique from the very beginning until the signing of the Rome accord in 1992,[32] has been working through its organisation, Caritas, as well as through pastoral activities, trying to promote reconciliation within and between communities.

Besides the religious organisations, there are many other civil society associations involved in promoting peace and reconciliation in Mozambique. Among others are the Associations of War Veterans, the Mozambican Organisation of the Demobilised Soldiers (AMODEG) and the Mozambican Organisation of the Handicapped Demobilised Soldiers (ADENIMO).

The AMODEG and ADENIMO were created in 1992 to represent the interests of ex-soldiers from both sides of the armed conflict. The basic purpose of these two organisations is to protect the rights of their members, while working in community-based conflict resolution. REDIPAZ (Peace Network), a network of seven Mozambican groups and organisations still in its early stages, develops activities in the field of conflict transformation and peace. REDIPAZ is supposed to be part of a broader regional movement for peace and reconciliation. LINK is a forum of national and international NGOs established in 1996 to introduce and promote conflict resolution within NGOs through training Mozambican staff. It has encouraged local NGOs to develop strategic plans of their own, and the Organisation for Conflict Resolution (OREC) is an outcome of that effort.

The League of Human Rights and the Association of Human Rights and Development deal with human rights issues and with peace-building and reconciliation, but in a very specific field. There are also powerful organisations in Mozambican society that play an active role in monitoring dissent. Peace Observatory emerged around the time of the first anniversary of the violence in Montepuez. Its ultimate goal is to try to prevent the re-escalation of violent conflicts. It also aims to carry out activities that help install an enduring peace grounded in the recognition of differences and diversity.

In conclusion, the most important factor in the success of the peace process in Mozambique was the will for peace among Mozambicans and their commitment to the GAP. This will for peace was demonstrated by the leadership of the parties to the conflict, but more especially by ordinary Mozambicans. The spontaneous return of hundred of thousands of refugees from neighbouring countries (Malawi, South Africa, Zimbabwe, Swaziland and Zambia) confirmed a deep and general feeling of "war fatigue" among the population. The spirit of reconciliation and tolerance was one of the most powerful driving forces for consolidating peace in the country. The leader of RENAMO, Dhlakama, has several times declared his commitment to peace, stating that his party will not "resort to war", even in the face of its ongoing lack of consensus with the government on many issues, such as power-sharing.

Nevertheless, the peace and development efforts are still far from complete. For the time being, as argued by Martinho Chachiua, the "peace dividend" has been peace itself across the country.[33] In spite of all setbacks, the general spirit of peace and reconciliation resides among the political elite, the political leaders and the ordinary people. But, peace in Mozambique means the absence of hostility between FRELIMO and RENAMO. In other words it is a negative peace because the roots of the conflict are still present in social life. This points to the need for close monitoring of the peace process and the creation of dialogue at all levels of society. It is important that the "dialogue initiated at the time of the peace talks [. . .] continues as long as necessary in order to monitor the dynamics of change of the society in peacetime".[34]

NOTES

1 Considering that 60% of Mozambique's national budget is based on external aid and loans, the role of the International Monetary Fund and the World Bank, as well as bilateral donors, in state affairs is paramount.

2 The Decree 15/2000 regulates the interaction between the state at local level and community leaders.

3 President Chissano recently married his wife of many years according to Catholic ritual.

4 The law that made the demonstrations illegal was later amended by parliament.

5 The government's programme for 2000–04 anticipated the questions of imbalances and unevenness of development in the regions and participation of social groups, and opens up possibilities for reducing people's sense of exclusion.

6 The early recruits were disgruntled settlers who had fled from Mozambique, black Mozambican soldiers who had served with the Portuguese Army, former members of FRELIMO who had been expelled from the Front and, finally, FRELIMO soldiers who had been imprisoned for crimes committed after independence. There was also recruitment among Mozambican miners working in South Africa.

7 Recent history has connected the south of the country with the power to decide and rule in state affairs. This is well illustrated by the fact that the three presidents that FRELIMO has had so far all originated from the province of Gaza in the south, from areas within about 50 km from one another.

8 The Mozambican African National Union (MANU) based in Tanzania, the Democratic Union of Mozambique (UDENAMO) based in Rhodesia and the National Union for Mozambican Independence (UNAMI) based in Malawi.

9 Contradictory opinions have recently appeared in the debate on the role of Eduardo Mondlane in the foundation of FRELIMO. According to FRELIMO's arguments, Mondlane was the "architect of national unity" because he managed to unite the three nationalist movements. However, at present there is a long way to go in forming an objective reading and interpretation of facts to understand what really happened in the course of the war for national liberation.

10 "From Rovuma to Maputo" was the slogan used by Machel to indicate national unity. Rovuma is the name of the river that forms the border with Tanzania and Maputo is the capital in the south and also a river in the province with the same name.

11 Political secretaries answering centrally to FRELIMO were appointed to take the place of the traditional elite, and the rural zones were left in the hands of the political nomenclature. At present, the rural zones are still not included in the state administration. However, there is reform of the administrative apparatus under way, including a draft of the law to re-insert the rural settlements into the state-organised administration.

12 UN, *The United Nations: Mozambique 1992–1995* (New York: United Nations, 1995), 14.

13 FRELIMO, *Relatório do Comité Central ao V Congresso* (Maputo: Partido FRELIMO, 1989), 5.

14 Thomas Ohlson, *Power Politics and Peace Policies: Intra-State Conflict Resolution in Southern Africa* (Uppsala: Uppsala University, Department of Peace and Conflict Research, 1998).

15 FRELIMO, *Relatório do Comité Central ao V Congresso*, 156.

16 FRELIMO, *Relatório do Comité Central ao V Congresso*.

17 UN, *The United Nations: Mozambique 1992–1995*, 14.

18 As a matter of fact, the evidence post-Nkomati revealed that the war intensified in Mozambique, but South African diplomats continued to deny the government's claim that support was being given to the MNR.

19 UN, *The United Nations: Mozambique 1992–1995*.

20 The meeting failed because of the lack of consensus on the locale of talks. Moreover, the process of building trust and co-operation was still fragile. Besides, the government insisted on Blantyre, Malawi, as an ideal place for talks considering both economic cost and communications facilities, whereas RENAMO proposed Nairobi, claiming there was a lack of security in Malawi, ironically in a country where it enjoyed support and sympathy from local authorities.

21 Both President Chissano and Dhlakama are Catholic.

22 Anders Nilsson, *Peace in Our Time: Towards a Holistic Understanding of World Society Conflicts* (Gothenburg: Gothenburg University, 1999).

23 UN, *The United Nations: Mozambique 1992–1995.*

24 The Zimbabwean troops were deployed in Mozambique from 1984 and by 1990 constituted about 10 000 military personnel (Goran Lindgren, Kjell-Åke Nordquist and Peter Wallerstein, *Peace Process in the Third World* (Uppsala: Uppsala University, Department of Peace and Conflict Research, 1991)).

25 Aldo Ajello, "The Role of UNOMOZ in the Pacification Process." In *Mozambique: Elections, Democracy and Development,* ed. Brazão Mazula (Maputo: Inter-Africa, 1996), 118.

26 Immanuel Wallerstein, *Preventing Violent Conflicts: Past Records and Future Challenges* (Uppsala: Uppsala University, Department of Peace and Conflict Research, 1998).

27 The Liberal Party of Mozambique (PALMO), the Democratic and National Party (PANADE) and the Mozambican National Party (PANAMO) built a coalition, the Democratic Union (UD).

28 Boutros Boutros-Ghali. *An Agenda for Peace* (New York: United Nations, 1992).

29 UN, *The United Nations: Mozambique 1992–1995.*

30 UNDP, "Mozambique National Human Development Report 1998." In *Peace and Economic Growth: Opportunities for Human Development,* ed. by A. Gumede (Johannesburg: Creda Press, 1998).

31 A demobilised soldier, 25 years old, from Nicoadala-Zambezia (NOTICIAS, "Entrevista com Soldados Desmobilisados, Maputo, April 28, 1993"), 3.

32 The Church through its programmes is active throughout the country with 23.8% of Mozambicans embracing the faith, 24% in the north, 23% in the central region and 18% in the south (Instituto Nacional de Estatística, "Instituto Nacional de Estatística 1997." Reprinted at www.ine.gov.mz). Note that the majority of the population of Mozambique is Catholic, and "throughout the country, where the Catholic religion is not the first in terms of followers, it is the second" (UNDP, "Mozambique National Human Development Report 1999"), 23.

33 Irae Baptista Lundin, Martinho Chachiua, António Gaspar, Habiba Guebuza and Guilherme Mbilana, "Reducing Costs through an Expensive Exercise: The Impact of Demobilisation in Mozambique." In *Demobilisation in Sub-Saharan Africa: The Development and Security Impacts,* ed. by Kees Kingma (London: Macmillan Press, 2000).

34 Irae Baptista Lundin, "Will Mozambique Remain a Success History?" *African Security Review* 9 (2000): 88.

RESOURCES

Books, Articles, Media Reports

Ajello, Aldo. "The Role of UNOMOZ in the Pacification Process." In *Mozambique: Elections, Democracy and Development*, edited by Brazäo Mazula. Maputo: Inter-Africa, 1996.

Baptista Lundin, Iraê. "Mechanisms of Community Reception of Demobilised Soldiers in Mozambique." *African Journal of Political Science* 3 (1998): 104–18.

———. "Will Mozambique Remain a Success History?" *African Security Review* 9 (2000): 79–88.

———. *Reflections on the Dynamics of a Nation Building Process under Stress: The Case of Mozambique 1993–1998*. Gothenburg: Gothenburg University, 2001.

———. (forthcoming) "Reflections on Conflict Resolution and 'Prevention': The State and Citizens in Mozambique." In *Demilitarisation and Peace-Building in Southern Africa*, edited by Kees Kingma and Peter Batchelor. Bonn: Bonn International Center for Conversion.

Baptista Lundin, Iraê, Martinho Chachiua, António Gaspar, Habiba Guebuza and Guilherme Mbilana. "Reducing Costs through an Expensive Exercise: The Impact of Demobilisation in Mozambique." In *Demobilisation in Sub-Saharan Africa: The Development and Security Impacts*, edited by Kees Kingma. London: Macmillan Press, 2000.

Boutros-Ghali, Boutros. *An Agenda for Peace*. New York: United Nations, 1992.

Farinha, F. *An Assessment for Mozambican NGOs Working on Conflict Transformation, Social and Economic Justice and Capacity Building*. Mieo: DIAKONIA-Southern Africa, 2001.

Lindgren, Goran, Kjell-Åke Nordquist and Peter Wallerstein. *Peace Process in the Third World*. Uppsala: Uppsala University, Department of Peace and Conflict Research, 1991.

Mazula, Brazäo. *Educaçao, Cultura e Ideologia em Moçambique: 1975–1985*. Lisboa: Ediçoes Afrontamento, 1995.

Mazula, Brazäo, ed. *Mozambique: Elections, Democracy and Development*. Maputo: Inter-Africa, 1996.

Nilsson, Anders. *Peace in Our Time: Towards a Holistic Understanding of World Society Conflicts*. Gothenburg: Gothenburg University, 1999.

Ohlson, Thomas. *Power Politics and Peace Policies: Intra-State Conflict Resolution in Southern Africa*. Uppsala: Uppsala University, Department of Peace and Conflict Research, 1998.

UN. *The United Nations: Mozambique 1992–1995*. New York: United Nations, 1995.

UNDP. "Mozambique National Human Development Report 1998." In *Peace and Economic Growth: Opportunities for Human Development*, edited by A. Gumede. Johannesburg: Creda Press, 1998.

———. "Mozambique National Human Development Report 1999." In *Economic Growth and Human Development: Progress, Obstacles and Challenge*, edited by A. Gumede. Johannesburg: Creda Communications, 2000.

Wallerstein, Immanuel. *Preventing Violent Conflicts: Past Records and Future Challenges*. Uppsala: Uppsala University, Department of Peace and Conflict Research, 1998.

Zartman, I. William. *Ripe for Resolution: Conflict and International Intervention in Africa*. New York: Oxford University Press, 1989.

Government, Intergovernmental Bodies and Political Parties

FRELIMO: http://dana.ucc.nau.edu/~nm5/Frelimo.html
RENAMO: http://dana.ucc.nau.edu/~nm5/Renamo.html

International NGOs

Human Rights Watch has an Africa section that monitors human rights developments in Mozambique and brings out annual and periodic reports: http://www.hrw.org

United Nations Development Programme (UNDP) is committed to the UN principle that development is inseparable from the quest for peace and human security and that the UN must be a strong force for development as well as peace: http://www.undp.org.za

MOZAMBIQUE COUNTRY INFORMATION

Geography
Location: Southern Africa, bordering the Mozambique Channel, between South Africa and Tanzania.
Cities: *Capital:* Maputo. *Other towns:* Cabo, Delgado, Gaza, Manica, Nampula, Sofala, Tete.

People
Nationality: *Noun:* Mozambican(s). *Adjective:* Mozambican.
Population (July 2000 est.): 19 104 696.
Population growth rate: 1.47%.
Ethnic groups: Africans 99.66% (Shangaan, Chokwe, Manyika, Sena, Makua and others), Europeans 0.06%, Euro-Africans 0.2%, Indians 0.08%.
Religions: Traditional African 50%, Christian 30%, Muslim 20%.
Languages: *Official:* Portuguese. *Other:* indigenous languages.
Education: *Literacy:* total population that can read and write 40.1%; male 57.7%, female 23.3%.
Health (2000 est.): *Infant mortality rate:* 139.86/1 000. *Life expectancy:* 37.52 years. *HIV infection rate:* 14.17%.
Workforce: Figures not available. Agriculture: 81%. Industry: 6%. Services: 13%.

Economy
GDP (1999 est.): $18.7 billion.
GDP real growth rate: 10%.
Per capita income: $1 000.
Inflation rate: 4%.
Natural resources: Coal, titanium, natural gas, hydropower.
Agriculture: (34% of GDP). *Products:* cotton, cashew nuts, sugar cane, tea, cassava (tapioca), corn, rice, tropical fruits; beef, poultry.
Industry: (18% of GDP). *Types:* food, beverages, chemicals (fertiliser, soap, paints), petroleum products, textiles, cement, glass, asbestos, tobacco.
Trade (1999): *Exports:* $300 million: prawns, cashews, cotton, sugar, copra, citrus, coconuts, timber. *Major markets* (1996 est.): Spain, South Africa, Portugal, Japan, Malawi, India, Zimbabwe. *Imports:* $1.6 billion: food, clothing, farm equipment, petroleum, transport equipment. *Major suppliers:* South Africa, Zimbabwe, Saudi Arabia, Portugal, United States, Japan, India.
Economic aid: Recipient (1995): $1.115 billion.
Debt – external (1999): $4.8 billion.

Military
Military expenditure: Dollar figures: $72 million (FY97).
Military expenditure: Percent of GDP: 4.7% (FY 97).

Demographic information is drawn from that compiled by the United States Department of State. See http://www.state.gov/r/pa/ei/bgn

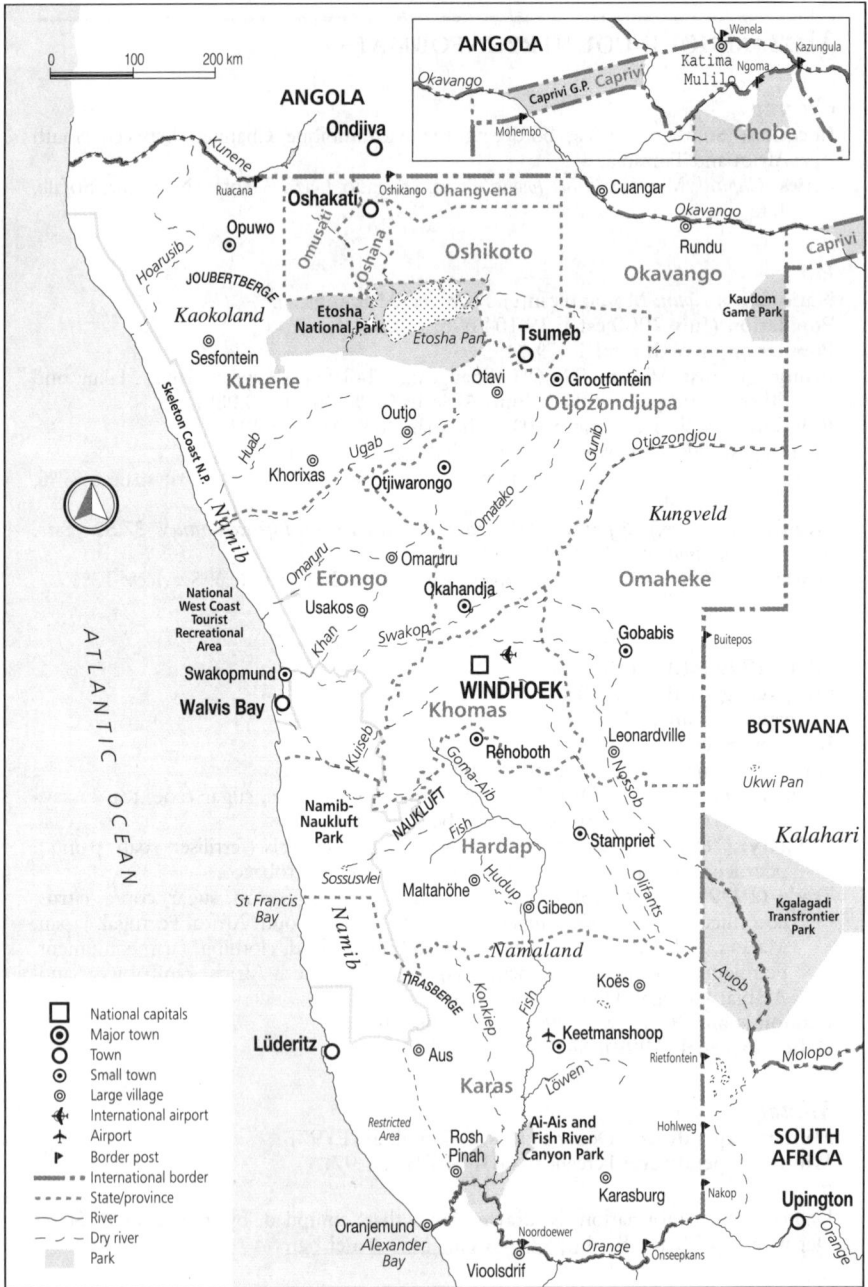

ANGOLA

Wenela
Kazungula
Katima
Mulilo
Ngoma
Okavango
Caprivi G.P. Caprivi
Mohembo
Chobe

ANGOLA
Ondjiva

Ruacana
Oshikango Ohangvena
Oshakati
Opuwo
Omusati Oshana
Oshikoto
Cuangar
Okavango
Rundu
Caprivi
Okavango
Kaudom
Game Park

JOUBERTBERGE
Hoarusib
Kaokoland
Etosha
National Park
Etosha Pan
Tsumeb

Sesfontein
Kunene
Otavi
Grootfontein
Otjozondjupa

Huab
Outjo
Ugab
Khorixas
Otjiwarongo
Omatako
Guinb
Otjozondjou
Kungveld

Omaruru
Omaruru
Erongo
Okahandja
Omaheke

National
West Coast
Tourist
Recreational
Area
Usakos
Khan
Swakop
Gobabis
Buitepos

Swakopmund
WINDHOEK
Khomas

Walvis Bay

ATLANTIC OCEAN

Réhoboth
Goma-Alb
Leonardville
BOTSWANA

Ukwi Pan

Namib-
Naukluft
Park
NAUKLUFT
Fish
Hardap
Stampriet
Kalahari

Sossusvlei
Maltahöhe
Hudup
Gibeon
Olifants
Kgalagadi
Transfrontier
Park

St Francis
Bay
Namaland
Koës

Namib
TIRASBERGE
Konkiep
Fish
Auob

National capitals
Major town
Town
Small town
Large village
International airport
Airport
Border post
International border
State/province
River
Dry river
Park

Lüderitz
Aus
Karas
Keetmanshoop
Rietfontein
Molopo

Restricted
Area
Rosh
Pinah
Ai-Ais and
Fish River
Canyon Park
Hohlweg
SOUTH
AFRICA

Karasburg
Nakop
Upington

Oranjemund
Alexander
Bay
Noordoewer
Orange
Onseepkans
Orange
Viooldrif

Chapter 13

Namibia: The Jigsaw Puzzle of Democracy

EDMOND TIKU AND ERIK DOXTADER

After 23 years of armed struggle, Namibia achieved its independence on 21 March 1990. The United Nations Security Council Resolution 435 of 1978 paved the way for the establishment of a Constituent Assembly to draft a new constitution, organise elections and prepare the territory for independence. This was a great victory for the Organisation of African Unity (OAU) and the people of Namibia as it signalled the end of external decolonisation on the African continent. However, 12 years after independence, Namibia still seems steeped in its past. In Windhoek, significant traces of German colonial rule and South African occupation remain. Afrikaans, a language associated with past oppression, has the awkward status of *lingua franca*. A testament to the lasting divisiveness of apartheid, Katura Township in Windhoek still has houses marked according to the ethnic roots of their inhabitants.[1] All of this is strange to many Namibians; it was not what they expected in 1990. While there has been relative peace in the country over the last decade, Namibia continues to sort the puzzle pieces of democracy, struggling to see what the picture should look like and how it is best put together.

The Namibian transition to democracy has been bedevilled with a number of political and socio-economic problems. Many can be linked directly to issues that the Namibian government inherited from the German and South African colonial administrations. Independently, none of these problems may be enough to fundamentally destabilise the country. Together, however, their synergy represents a source of concern. Firstly, Namibia continues to suffer under the yoke of unequal land distribution.[2] This disparity is not unrelated to ethnic animosity and division, much of it linked to the dynamics of colonialism. In particular, the Ovambos, who were a privileged ethnic group during the colonial era, have used their political party, the South West African People's Organisation (SWAPO), to rule the country in a way that has fostered perceptions and feelings of domination. Such dissatisfaction is fed by significant unemployment and a relatively weak economy. HIV/Aids threatens to tear deeply into the social fabric. The country's borders also remain a cause of controversy. The

Angolan civil war has brought conflict and human rights violations into the country. Meanwhile, the government continues to struggle with the question of how to handle the Caprivi Strip and the call by some of its inhabitants for secession. Reconciliation over the matter is not assured. All told, there are no quick solutions to these problems. They have produced obvious frustration, evident in what seems to be the government's growing intolerance of criticism. Some have wondered if the struggles may develop into opportunities for third forces to meddle in Namibia's internal affairs. This profile examines the current face and historical roots of Namibia's struggle to consolidate democracy. It also considers ways in which the country is attempting to resolve conflict and how these efforts may give way to reconciliation and stability.

The Face of Conflict

Led by President Sam Nujoma, the Namibian government has emphasised the need to replace the remnants of colonialism that fostered ethnic division and inequality with a new and just society. The prominent theme in this process is *national reconciliation among the country's people* – a theme that marks a shift from ethnic polarity to co-operative nation-building. Success will depend on the resolution of several significant and urgent problems. However, unlike many of its neighbours, Namibia is not in the midst of civil war. Its problems are diverse and sometimes difficult to pin down. There is evidence that significant numbers of citizens are disillusioned with the state of the country and the government. The reasons for the dissatisfaction appear to vary, ranging across issues of ethnicity, economic inequality, access to land and power-sharing within government. There is not one face to the conflict in Namibia but many, each linked to the others and each capable of generating significant obstacles to democratic nation-building.

Namibia is a multi-party republic. A president, who is directly elected for a five-year term, holds executive authority. The constitution is based on Roman-Dutch law and includes significant measures for the protection and promotion of human rights. The country is divided into 13 administrative regions. The liberation movement that fought for independence, SWAPO, now the ruling party, enjoys tremendous popular support. In each election since independence, SWAPO has maintained its power, amassing electoral support that has ranged from a low of 57% to a high of 76%.[3] This has allowed the party to control the country's legislative bodies, especially at the national level. One can rightly say that the most prominent feature of post-independence politics in Namibia has been the consolidation of single-party rule, although the dominant opposition political parties – the Democratic Turnhalle Alliance (DTA), the Congress of Democrats (CoD) and the United Democratic Front (UDF) do enjoy some support.[4]

The electoral dominance of SWAPO highlights ethnic differences in Namibia. The ruling elite is composed mainly of people from the Ovambo tribe. Namibia has 11 ethnic groups, among them the Ovambos, Kavangos, Hereros, Namas and Khoikhoi.[5] Of these groups, the Ovambos constitute more than 52% of the population. The majority of people in Namibia speak their language. The dominance of the Ovambos in the political scene is viewed by some as unfair and anti-democratic. This has fed a struggle for power in recent years. Members of other ethnic groups do not foresee any possibility of playing a significant role in Namibian politics.

Before the 1999 National Assembly elections in Namibia, Mafwe Mwilima of the Caprivi region and a supporter of the DTA said, "People [in the Caprivi region] are being denied the right to vote. Very few or none will turn up. DTA supporters are not going to vote."[6] The DTA has accused SWAPO of attempting to win elections in the Caprivi to consolidate its power. The DTA claimed in a press statement: "SWAPO is in a hurry to have the election take place in the Caprivi so that it can win the region by default, because it has been their principle objective since independence to take the Caprivi away from the DTA at all costs."[7] The significance of this claim is difficult to assess. There is growing evidence, however, that those outside the corridors of power are alienated and increasingly hostile toward Ovambos and SWAPO. This is particularly true in the Caprivi Strip where minority political leaders, like Mishake Muyongo and Ben Ulenga, believe that the government is ignoring the needs of many citizens. Muyongo is a past president of the DTA. He played a pivotal role in the independence struggle and served as vice president of SWAPO for 16 years before joining the DTA. He later served for years as the president of the DTA before he led a secessionist movement in Caprivi to free his people from what he calls the stigma of being "second class citizens".[8]

Like most of its neighbours, Namibia faces a daunting task of redistributing wealth. Income disparities are dramatic and skewed along racial lines. Along with Ulenga, the leader of the CoD, Muyongo is concerned that the government does not recognise or represent the economic interests of all ethnic groups. Presently, blacks earn an average annual per capita income of US$750 as compared to the US$16 500 earned by whites.

Almost all of Namibia's arable land is in the hands of whites, who form just 6% of the population.[9] The land issue has created substantial bitterness. Many of the landless believed that SWAPO would restore the holdings lost during colonial appropriations.[10] Yet, the majority of those who labour on white-owned farms and mines live in anguish and abject poverty. Since independence, no workable land redistribution plan has been forthcoming, a failure that has brokered animosity. Some commentators argue that if redistribution is not rapid, Namibia's future may look something like Zimbabwe's present. Prime Minister Hage Geingob admits the government is worried about the land issue, noting that it is an issue that could undermine Namibia's peace: "We know that we are sitting on a powder keg. It is an emotive issue. But it has to be handled by the leadership with care and in a fair way."[11]

One commentator, Paul Vleermuis of the Namibian National Farmers' Union, also claims that there will be a lot of social dissatisfaction if there is not speedy progress on the land question. He adds: "We might have something like what is happening in Zimbabwe now. But we are not saying it will happen. It is now the right time to pro-actively look at alternative ways of land distribution."[12] There are many who urgently want equitable and prompt redistribution of land and other resources. As the deprivation is extreme, delays fuel resentment.

There is also increasing criticism of the government's willingness to use domestic resources for the wars in Angola and the Democratic Republic of Congo (DRC), conflicts that are far removed from the ordinary citizen. There is a wide belief that land redistribution will reduce poverty, raise the standards of living and restore the dignity of citizens. Given recent trends in Zimbabwe, some farm owners appear willing to participate in a land redistribution scheme.

Against this backdrop, the Namibian government is struggling to resolve disputes over the status and secession of the Caprivi region.[13] The Caprivi Strip constitutes 400 of Namibia's 824 290 square kilometres. The Caprivians represent a total of 4% of the population found in Namibia. This piece of land is a territorial anomaly, a tiny piece of land stretching northeastwards into Botswana and Zimbabwe. Despite its small size, it represents a substantial conflict. The move to create a Caprivi State was immediately followed by a state of emergency in the region, especially in the capital, Katima Mulilo.[14] This move led to a massive exodus of ordinary Caprivians (especially women and children) to Botswana, 342 deaths and the Caprivian separatist leaders fleeing into exile. The government is now in control of the Caprivi Strip and some of the separatists who fled are returning. At present, 128 Namibians face charges of high treason for their role in the Caprivi unrest. The trial has been a stop and start affair, due largely to the fact that the defendants have won a court claim mandating the state to provide and pay for their legal representation. Meanwhile, a number of those being held have lodged complaints of torture by government officials.

The leaders of the Caprivi Liberation Movement argue that the Namibian government neglects the region to a degree that warrants secession. They hold that the Caprivi Strip is an artificial appendix of Namibia and that it does not belong to the mainland. Its marginal status is given as the reason for increasing unemployment and the government's neglect of its crumbling infrastructure. Muyongo, the secessionist leader, has argued that the people have "no choice if they are to end their long years of suffering under the government of President Sam Nujoma". The Caprivi Strip, he continues, "has been described by a recent United Nations report as Namibia's poorest region and support for economic development is not commensurate to its resource contribution". To the Caprivians their fight is a just one. In contrast, the Namibian government views the residents of the Strip as disloyal, especially as they have allied themselves with the DTA.

Namibia's natural and climatic conditions have provoked uprisings in certain areas and exacerbated the conflict in Caprivi, especially as the government has seemed unwilling or unable to help citizens with basic subsistence requirements. Namibia incorporates two deserts – the Namib Desert to the west and the Kalahari Desert to the east. In each, there is little possibility for cultivation. The risk of famine is thus high. The leader of the Khoisan people in northern Namibia has indicated that many in the region face starvation and that the problem is made worse by the secessionist conflict.[15] The acting chief, Thadeus Chadau, also said the failure of rains had meant there was no harvest, and Namibian soldiers were preventing them from leaving their villages in the Caprivi Strip in search of wild food because of the security situation.

Internationally, Botswana, South Africa and much of the world community have condemned the separatists' actions and supported the efforts of President Nujoma to maintain the country's territorial integrity. At present, there is stalemate in the region as the separatists, assisted by the National Union for the Total Independence of Angola (UNITA), conduct sporadic attacks in the northern area of Kavango. Also, the United Nations High Commissioner for Refugees (UNHCR) has asked the Caprivians seeking asylum in Botswana to renounce their separatist claims.

While there are some external forces feeding tensions in the Caprivi Strip, it is also clear that the Namibian government's involvement in the DRC and Angola has not been popular with citizens or opposition parties. Namibia sent approximately 2 000 Namibian soldiers to defend the government of the DRC against the "rebels". This involvement is costing millions of Namibian dollars, resources that critics would like to see spent on development. By the same token, Namibia's Mines Minister, Jesaya Nyamu, admitted that the country has commercial interests in a diamond mine in the DRC.[16] Conscientious objectors who refuse to participate in the war in the DRC have been held at military bases and barred from speaking to human rights groups.[17] Thus, the Namibian National Society for Human Rights has called on the government to end the secrecy surrounding Namibia's involvement in the war in the DRC and to provide the public with casualty statistics. Particularly disturbing is the fact that Namibian children are being allowed to fight in the Angolan civil war. This has fed popular unhappiness, fuelling the call for a withdrawal from both theatres.[18] For its part, the government contends that national security justifies the Angolan intervention, especially given that UNITA rebels are using Namibian soil as a base of operations. There are indications that UNITA and an opposition party from the south of Zambia are assisting the people of Caprivi.[19] UNITA has responded to the direct involvement of Namibian security forces in Angola with violence that has destabilised the northern areas. There have been reports of abductions, the murder of innocent civilians and looting.[20]

Resentment over the flow of money and resources into external conflicts highlights Namibia's fragile economic situation. Unlike many African countries, Namibia has not been forced to implement stabilisation and structural adjustment programmes. It is not threatened by an impending economic collapse. Still, Namibia faces considerable economic challenges. For example, productive capacity in Namibia remains concentrated in primary sector activities like mining, commercial livestock farming and fishing. The manufacturing base remains small. The service sector, dominated by the government, accounts for over half of GDP.[21] Today, the country shows an enormous disparity of income and wealth, gaps that reflect the legacy of apartheid. The GDP per capita in Namibia was N$9 615 (US$1 753) in 1998. This, however, masks the uneven distribution of wealth within the country. Indeed a recent report by the Southern African Development Community notes that 11% of the population in Namibia, including most white citizens, earn 51.5% of the total income. Namibia's racially linked inequality, coupled with an estimated unemployment rate of 40%, appears to threaten Namibia's young democracy.[22]

Since independence, the government has sought to sustain economic growth, diversify a narrow production base and attract foreign investment in the manufacturing sector. Poverty alleviation has been addressed by increasing spending on public health, education and social infrastructure. At the same time, the government has committed itself to fiscal stability and reducing the budget deficit to 3% of GDP. The latter task is proving difficult and creating conflict, especially as ministries continue to overspend budget allocations. Most recently, the Namibian government's military role in the DRC forced the Finance Minister to seek an additional N$173 million (US$27 million) for defence. This increased total expenditure on defence for 1999/2000 to N$732 million, or 10.3% of total expenditure, representing a 65% increase over the defence allocation for 1998/99.[23]

Thanks to South Africa, Namibia's pre-independence debt was recently forgiven. However, Namibia does not qualify for "least developed country" status and so is not able to make use of certain multilateral credits. Namibia recorded an average annual real GDP growth rate of 5% during the first half of the 1990s. Since then, GDP growth has declined, dropping to 2.4% between 1996 and 1998. The Economic Intelligence Unit estimates a real GDP growth of 4.5% for the year 2000, up from an estimated 3% in 1999.

The growing HIV/Aids crisis is impacting on the Namibian economic and cultural fabric in a substantial way. According to the Aids Care Trust, which is co-financed by the state, Namibia has a national HIV infection rate of about 23% among adults. The government has treated the fight against HIV/Aids as a priority. To fight this pandemic, the government has diverted funds for economic development. This decision has caused some friction.[24] The opposition parties blame the infection rate on the government's inability to create jobs for the country.

Many commentators have placed their faith in Namibia's post-independence constitution. A progressive document, the constitution guarantees freedom of association, expression and press. It bars arbitrary arrest, detention without trial and the death penalty while safeguarding the right of individual property ownership and the payment of just compensation for any expropriated property. Until recently, the ruling party has observed the provisions of the constitution. Critics were worried, however, when SWAPO tabled a constitutional amendment to extend the presidential term limit from two to three. With a two-thirds majority of SWAPO members in both houses of parliament, the constitutional amendment was approved. The outcome of increasing the presidential term has been a noticeable concentration of power.

President Nujoma has appeared to keep challengers at bay with periodic cabinet shuffles. Nonetheless, he enjoys substantial support. In the last elections, the ruling party won 10 out of the 13 local councils, including the Caprivi Strip, and a clear majority of the seats in parliament. If elections were held today, SWAPO would win easily. Its support owes something to the perception that it guided the country to independence. SWAPO also appears increasingly ready to enter power-sharing arrangements with the opposition. For example, the official opposition party, the CoD, has been given official status in parliament.

Despite popular support, there are many who believe that the president has become intolerant if not autocratic. There is a growing disrespect for certain groups, especially those in the media sector. While freedom of speech and press are generally respected in Namibia, there has been increasing pressure placed on reporters of government-owned media. The privately owned press has come under steady attack from the president and others for allegedly covering sensitive news stories, leaking confidential policy documents and having a "hostile" attitude toward the executive. Government leaders have also lashed out at and restricted foreign journalists. Namibian Broadcasting Corporation (NBC) radio and television talk show hosts have been removed from their positions, allegedly for political reasons, and NBC reporters are said to "exercise considerable self-censorship on certain controversial issues". In April 2000, a Namibian cabinet member, accompanied by two police officers, barred an NBC news team from covering a news conference on a CoD decision to walk out of parliament. The government has defended its position by arguing that criticism is coming from those nostalgic for colonial days. Still, the restrictions have led both the Media Institute of Southern Africa and the Journalist Association of Namibia to issue action alerts.

Government intolerance has appeared in other forms as well. Recently, the Southern African Human Rights NGO Network held a demonstration in order to "take a public stand" against the "attacks on human rights" by the state. The National Co-ordinator, Jotham Rwamiheto, said "the march was the first step . . . when democracy is in danger, it affects everybody. As civil society we feel we have a role to play in maintaining democracy, peace and stability." He further objected to attacks by the state that consisted of calls to dismiss judges, a ban on government advertising in the independent *The Namibian* newspaper and incitement to purge homosexuals.[25] Also cited were calls to stop teaching Afrikaans, calls for Namibians not to marry foreigners, the labelling of white Namibians as "racists" and "colonialists". In short, the organisation argued that the "policy of reconciliation is being replaced by a policy of confrontation and outright disregard for the democratic constitution and institutions of this country".[26] The Black Radical Congress, based at Columbia University in New York, also criticised Nujoma's attacks on gays and lesbians: "Given that he is a former freedom fighter and the Head of State, Nujoma's homophobic and discriminatory actions are particularly repugnant."[27]

Amnesty International has not been silent on the human rights situation in Namibia. In a published report, it urged the office of the Ombudsman in Namibia to investigate reports of widespread human rights violations.[28] Before its request to the Ombudsman, in a report published in March 2000, it accused the Namibian security forces of killing and injuring Caprivi secessionists. The report also said that the Namibian authorities have breached international and national law in their treatment of Angolan refugees housed in Osire Refugee Camp. It also reported that the Namibian Defence Force has forcibly deported prisoners.

Portraits of Namibia show a country with enormous potential but whose politics and economic situation risk the development and consolidation of democracy. Growing worries about the dominance of SWAPO, Namibia's involvement in two outside wars and the secession problems in Caprivi all signal possible threats to stability. All these problems have their roots in the country's history.

The Historical Roots of Violence and Division

Namibia is located in the southwestern part of the African continent, between Angola to the north and South Africa to the south. It stretches northeastwards where it shares boundaries with Botswana, Zambia and Zimbabwe. It comprises a total surface area of 824 269 square kilometres.[29] Included is the strategic enclave of Walvis Bay, an area that was long disputed and only returned by South Africa in 1994. Namibia can be divided into three broad regions, the Namib, the Central Plateau and the Kalahari Desert. Of these regions, the largest is the Central Plateau, which covers 50% of the entire territory and lies east of the Namib Desert. These geographic divisions were used by the South African administration to entrench its policy of ethnic division for political purposes.

Namibia has been directly shaped by the long struggle of the indigenous people against colonial intrusion, first by Germany and later South Africa. As early as the sixteenth century, the region's indigenous people confronted a large-scale foreign presence, contact that gave way to colonial rule. The expanding Dutch colony at the Cape spread far into the southern African interior in the late sixteenth and seventeenth centuries. As it involved the expropriation of land and water by the Dutch, the expansion forced the local Khoisan people to migrate.[30] The Germans employed various methods to acquire land and cattle from the indigenous population. These included offers of protection against other ethnic groups or clans, raiding campaigns, building forts, outright purchase of land and extension of credit. Settlers were encouraged to move from Germany and smaller numbers came from South Africa. African migrant labour further distorted population settlement. In 1900, there were attempts to push Africans into reserves. In 1902, despite opposition, the Hoachanas reserve was established, covering an area of 50 000 hectares. By the start of World War I, the settler population was estimated at 20 000.

The German administration's land policy distorted local politics, particularly as it disrupted the succession of traditional chiefs. It also altered the class configuration of the society. Political and economic power was racialised, as white settlers became employers, entrepreneurs, investors and decision-makers, while the indigenous people remained unskilled and semi-skilled labourers. These class distinctions were institutionalised. Native commissioners were charged to oversee particular issues like health, clothing, payment of wages, creating service contracts and the provision and distribution of black labour for white farmers. Another feature of the German administration that has had a devastating impact on peace in the country was a territory swap between Britain and Germany in 1890. Britain acquired Zanzibar in East Africa, while Germany got the slice of land that later became known as the Caprivi Strip – giving it access to the Zambezi River – along the border of what is now Zambia.

The German colonial occupation did not go unchallenged. The local people resisted, despite the superior strength of the German forces. The Herero rose against the Germans in 1904. The Nama people of the south and the Damara joined them. To suppress the resistance, the Germans undertook a systematic and repressive military campaign. The Herero and Nama uprisings resulted in troop reinforcements from Germany. Over 10 000 well-equipped German soldiers were in the territory by the end of 1904.[31] It would be three years before the colonial masters could declare the region pacified.

The outbreak of World War I opened a new chapter in Namibia's history. During the war, South Africa aligned itself with other countries against Germany. A year later, German forces surrendered the territory to

South Africa. Following the provisions of the 1919 Peace Treaty of Versailles, the League of Nations entrusted the territory (under the name South West Africa) as a C-Mandate to the Union of South Africa. In terms of the mandate, the Union was charged to administer Namibia in accordance with the objectives set up under the Principal and Associated Allied Powers. These goals concerned the protection of indigenous peoples, the creation of an administrative system to ensure this protection and measures to prevent annexation by former enemies or other colonial powers. Of particular importance was the prohibition of annexation, especially in light of attempts by South Africa's General Jan Smuts to incorporate the region. The mandate was seen as largely impractical, particularly as the South African government viewed the indigenous people as politically and economically backward. Thus, despite promises by the Union to promote the material, moral and social well-being of the indigenous people, the latter were denied basic economic, educational, social and political opportunities and any right to self-determination. Political segregation meant that they had no right to vote or hold public office. Structural and attitudinal race discrimination resulted in their exclusion from education, technical and professional training, marketing arrangements, provision of credit and the disposal of land and mineral rights. After uprisings by the Namibians in 1922 and 1925 in opposition to the imposition of tax on dogs, the League of Nations severely criticised the South African administration.

The founding of the United Nations in 1945 brought potential for change in Namibia. The League's mandate policy was replaced by a trusteeship system, the latter being a new structure of international tutelage. More important, however, was the growing concern for social, economic, educational and political institutions. The Namibian issue became a moral question as concern for human rights grew. Still, South Africa continued its efforts to incorporate the territory. It held that the territory was incapable of developing and maintaining separate administrative and economic structures. South African administrators claimed that the indigenous people desired and supported incorporation. The UN rejected these arguments. South Africa continued to challenge the legal status of the trusteeship policy, arguing that it was under no obligation to place the territory under this system and maintaining that the requirement to submit annual reports constituted no legal acknowledgement of UN power. For neither the first nor the last time, South Africa refused to cede any ground to the international community.

From the 1960s, South Africa began to pursue what were in effect policies of ethnic fragmentation. Following the "vision" of grand apartheid, it argued that each population group should develop separately within its own "homeland". The Development of Self-Government for Native Nations in the South West Africa Act, No. 54 of 1968 was passed by the South African parliament to set this process into motion. Damaraland, Hereroland, Kaokoland, Okavangoland, Eastern Caprivi and Ovamboland were set up as separate territories for "native nations". However, South Africa's attempt to control internal politics in Namibia faced opposition. SWAPO launched a political and diplomatic campaign against South African rule. Besides SWAPO, other groups like the South West Africa National Union (SWANU) petitioned for the territory's independence at international forums. On 26 August 1966, SWAPO formally launched an armed struggle against the Republic's occupation of the territory. The South African government began to use the Caprivi Strip as a launching pad for operations against SWAPO and opposition movements in neighbouring Angola. This was the start of a long and bloody conflict.

The international committee lost little time in denouncing South Africa's actions in Namibia. This was aptly illustrated by the 1971 Advisory Opinion given by the International Court of Justice in which, by a vote of thirteen to two, the Court declared the South African occupation illegal and demanded its immediate withdrawal. The South African government rejected the ruling. SWAPO was encouraged by this declaration as it offered official recognition of Namibia's claims for independence and legitimacy for the struggle.[32] The deadlock in the territory, coupled by the armed confrontation between SWAPO and South African forces, prompted five western powers – Britain, France, United States, Canada and West Germany – to launch diplomatic initiatives intended to facilitate a settlement. These efforts were unsuccessful. South Africa continued to control the country's internal political process through the unrepresentative Constituent Assembly, a body dominated by the DTA.

UN Security Council Resolution 435 of 1978 called for territorial independence and free elections. Although both parties agreed in principle to the resolution, South Africa objected to the UN's plans for implementation. SWAPO and the South African administrators disagreed over the terms laid down by the resolution. The impasse continued into the 1980s. The introduction of the Reagan administration's "linkage" policy further complicated the plan as it made Namibia's independence conditional on the withdrawal of Cuban troops from neighbouring Angola. This issue, along with foot-dragging, outright resistance by South Africa and the continuation of warfare, brought a delay of nearly a decade to the move to independence.

The dramatic political realignments of the late 1980s, coupled with intense instability within South Africa, created room to break the stalemate. Dialogue about the actual implementation of Resolution 435 took place in 1988. Late in the year, two agreements were signed. Angola, Cuba and South Africa signed the first agreement, which set 1 April as the start of the move to Namibian independence and provided for the deployment of UN peace-keeping forces to monitor the transition. The second agreement provided for the staged withdrawal of Cuban troops from Angola by July 1991.[33] As a result, the war that had ravaged the territory for over two decades came to an end.

Prospects for Peace-building

The problems that confront Namibia are perceived and interpreted differently by Namibians and the international community. Obstacles to stability appear to include the insurrection in Caprivi and differences about how to nurture a human and civil rights culture, especially as it bears on the problem of how government represents and sometimes dominates the country's various ethnic groups. The fact that the government, opposition political parties, NGOs and the international community have divergent views on these issues suggests that consensus and conflict resolution will have to be forged across a number of lines and intersecting issues.

The problem of the Caprivi territory constitutes a central problem for the leadership and citizens of Namibia, a matter that raises significant questions about what counts as good governance and respect for ethnic-cultural difference. The government appears to view the demand for a separate state by the Caprivians as treason. It has thus attempted to arrest and try those connected with the separatist movement.[34] The DTA, the CoD and other political parties have overtly condemned the actions of the Caprivians. The DTA has dismissed Mujongo for the role he played in the secession. On the other hand, the Caprivians view the government as an oppressor. They claim that the government has neglected the region and treated residents as second-class citizens. The leadership of the Caprivi Liberation Army appears determined to forge an autonomous country and claims that peace depends on their regional autonomy.

The international support Namibia receives from organisations like the International Committee of the Red Cross and the UNHCR has helped to alleviate factionalism, especially in the Caprivi insurrection. These organisations have provided relief to Namibia's civilian population and refugees suffering in the northern area of Namibia, in Botswana and in the Caprivi Strip. Moreover, during the crisis in Caprivi the Legal Assistance Centre

and other groups such as the Council of Churches in Namibia played a pivotal role in asserting the legal rights of detained Namibians, contesting the
government's interpretation of its own state of emergency regulations and
monitoring human rights abuses. Indeed, government leaders ultimately
conceded that human rights violations were committed and undertook to
put an end to any mistakes made. The government also lifted the state of
emergency within the required 30 days, although not before it was challenged in court. Botswana and the UNCHR have requested a guarantee of
safety from the government for the return of Caprivian refugees and assurances that they will be treated fairly upon arrival.[35]

However, some argue that the government's position is obscuring
important issues that bear directly on how Namibians can heal the wounds
of the past. In attempting to resolve sources of tension, the government
has refused to heed many calls from the international community, local
NGOs and opposition political parties for an investigation into human
rights abuses and violations that took place during the colonial administration and the war for independence. As part of its programme of nation-
building, the leadership of SWAPO formulated and adopted a policy of
national reconciliation in 1989. The policy was intended to guard against
revenge and retribution, the consequences of which were held to undermine peace and stability. The Breaking the Wall of Silence (BWS) movement that represents former detainees of SWAPO has been vocal in this
matter, vowing that it will continue to press SWAPO for an acknowledgement of its pre-independence record of human rights abuse.[36] BWS
chairperson, Pauline Dempers, has accused SWAPO of "ostrich-like
behaviour – of burying its head in the sand about the SWAPO ex-detainee
issue". Dempers, at a BWS press conference in Windhoek, reacted to a
SWAPO press release headed "It is either reconciliation or the opening of
old wounds" by saying, "[The] SWAPO leadership may wish to die without addressing the issue, as some did, [but] the issue will remain with your
children and our children and the future generations . . . The issue will be
there until the whole Namibian population becomes extinct and no
human beings remain in Namibia any more." In the press release issued by
the office of the SWAPO Secretary-General, the party referred to a "chain
of attacks on SWAPO", saying "the most vituperative is the demand that
SWAPO should engage in a process of public confession and apologise to
those who were detained during the liberation struggle". It stated that if
BWS or the National Society for Human Rights "prefer that old wounds
be opened up and that the policy of national reconciliation be buried,
SWAPO will be adequately prepared to join the battle". In response,

Dempers claimed that for SWAPO "reconciliation means stone-cold silence should prevail in a zombie-like manner. In the minds of SWAPO chieftains, reconciliation means 'we have not seen anything, we have not heard anything and we must not say anything'". She explained that BWS wanted SWAPO to admit that it had detained, abducted and killed people and to explain why these actions were taken and under what conditions. Other members of BWS have added that the former detainees' names need to be cleared and restored through openness on the part of SWAPO about its treatment of detainees. Dempers concluded: "There are no old wounds or new wounds. The wounds are just there and they are visible and need healing. To think that silence will heal wounds is daydreaming."

Debate over the nature of past violence is tied closely to the problem of post-independence power-sharing. As is frequently the case, different ethnic groups, political parties and local NGOs have different views of this concept. Nujoma's government, in an effort to maintain its popular support, has courted and sometimes co-opted independent national-level organisations like religious bodies, student unions and trade unions. Despite the ruling party's best efforts to keep such organisations within SWAPO's ambit, some have resisted. The Namibian National Student Organisation (NANSO) voted in 1991 to disaffiliate from SWAPO. Those who led the move to disaffiliate were labelled as "foreign agents" by the SWAPO leadership. Soon after, a splinter national student organisation, NANSO-affiliated, was formed with assistance from the ruling party.[37] Similar pressures have been exerted on the major trade union federation, the National Union of Namibian Workers (NUNW). In the early years of independence, affiliation was a key issue for the NUNW, with repeated unsuccessful attempts by member unions to move the federation away from the ruling party.[38] Indeed, the NUNW has been one of the few organisations to support both a third term for President Nujoma and Namibian military involvement in the DRC. Within government, President Nujoma has also courted opposition parties, offering some of them positions in government. For example, the CoD has been recognised as the official opposition party in parliament and the speaker of parliament is from the CoD. The other political parties, like the DTA and UDF, are compelled to accept their junior position because of the tremendous support and popularity that SWAPO enjoys.

Like student and union federations, the major church federation in Namibia, the Council of Churches in Namibia (CCN), has encountered pressure from the ruling party. The CCN has longstanding ties with SWAPO. However, in recent years it has come under attack for confronting the "detainee issue" – the detention and killing of SWAPO cadres in Angolan exile camps during the 1980s. Indeed, the ruling party attempted to prevent the CCN from holding a national conference on reconciliation to discuss unresolved issues concerning the detainees. The CCN held a Conference on National Reconciliation in March 1998 to which SWAPO sent no delegates. Church leaders in Namibia have been vocal in calling for a dialogue rather than war as a means for ending the armed conflicts in which Namibia has become embroiled.[39]

In Namibia, the struggle over the last 11 years has been largely against foreign and vanquished opponents. And the struggle against white minority South African rule did not generate the same level of boycotts and uprisings as it did in South Africa. Instead, outright war and international diplomacy were the primary means by which the struggle was waged. To date, with few exceptions, there does not appear to be significant anger and alienation against those who hold power in Namibia. Rather there appears to be eagerness on the part of many organisations to engage the state, despite resistance from some political leaders to such engagement and the considerable inexperience of many groups. The media, meanwhile, remains committed to "telling it like it is". The existence of a functional civil society has created a favourable atmosphere where disgruntled parties can assemble to sort out their differences. The manner in which civil society tackles problems that disturb the consolidation of democracy in Namibia, and the positive way in which the factions involved react, are compelling indicators that there is a potential for sustainable peace in Namibia. Organisations representing more than 60% of NGOs in Namibia play a role in monitoring government policy and performance. These groups have co-sponsored workshops on topics like "How Civil Society Can Effectively Influence Public Policy Formulation" and "International Human Rights Standards and Procedures". The Namibian Institute for Democracy is active in civic education. In the 1999 national elections, the Namibian Non-Governmental Organisation Forum (NANGOF) and CCN stationed trained election monitors at polling stations around the country, as part of the Namibian Civil Society Elections Monitoring Project.[40] These and other groups have adopted important watchdog roles. For example, the Namibian National Farmers' Union and the NUNW have been particularly outspoken on the government's failure to move quickly on the land issue. The Namibian National Teachers' Union, NANSO, the CCN and NANGOF have been particularly strong in their condemnation of Namibian intervention in the DRC and Angolan wars.

With this progress, many have expressed concern over the government's apparent intolerance of opposition and political criticism. Indeed, the state has been accused of being increasingly autocratic. Over the last 11 years, high-ranking government leaders have frequently attacked the constitution, the judiciary and civil society actors, as well as leaders of opposition political parties. These groups are often branded as foreign, unpatriotic, un-African, enemies, traitors and spies. Vitriolic attacks have also been directed at traditional leaders who are not politically affiliated to the ruling party, as well as foreigners, academics, indigenous minority groups and sexual minorities. The 1999 general and presidential elections saw unprecedented acts of political intolerance and physical intimidation directed against civil society, opposition political parties and gays and lesbians.[41] Some feel that public debate occurs only when Nujoma or his ruling SWAPO leadership allow it. Critical issues, such as the 1998 constitutional amendment and the military involvement of Namibia in the DRC and Angola, are not open for discussion. The alleged non-compliance of the Namibian government with constitutional provisions and international human rights treaties is attributed to its autocratic behaviour and reliance on centralised, top-down, highly personalised and winner-takes-all forms of political rule.

The government of Namibia controls substantial media resources, outlets that critics claim have been used to disseminate propaganda, distort information and censor critical or opposing views. Although it has a tradition of vibrancy, the country's media has little history of inclusiveness, impartiality and independence. Prior to independence both the print and electronic media were perceived to be partisan – either pro- or anti-government. This trend continues. Part of the problem is attributable to the fact that white Namibians control the country's private media while SWAPO controls state-owned media. White Namibians are inherently vulnerable to government attacks and, as such, are easily demonised and discredited by being branded as racists, foreigners, the enemy or associated with the former apartheid regime. Although true in some cases, such attacks are usually made only when they criticise the government.

Politicised ethnicity, weak or partisan civil society and fractured labour unions are factors that contribute to the problem of real and perceived intolerance. Like many other sub-Saharan countries, Namibian society is tribally, culturally and linguistically heterogeneous, with one numerically dominant ethnic group. With more than 11 ethnic groups, the country's political parties are either regionally or ethnically based. Domination of the civil service by members of particular ethnic groups has led to charges of marginalisation and persecution of members of minority groups in the country. The recent secessionist uprising in Eastern Caprivi and the simmering ethnic discontent in Kavango and Western Caprivi could be used as pointers in this regard. In short, Namibia is not without ethnic tensions, conflicts that bear directly on controversies over how it is governed. The relative weakness of civil society organisations and labour unions contributes to the problem. Many lack the ability to challenge the autocratic behaviour of leaders, especially given that some have long-standing affiliations with SWAPO. Criticism is frequently co-opted.

The progressive nature of the Namibian constitution may offer a way out of these troubles. It is a document that includes significant protections for human and civil rights. There are some who argue that Namibia would do well to establish a truth commission, but this is a move that the government currently opposes. In any case, the ongoing problems about how to balance nation-building and pluralism will likely require the continued growth of civil society and a widespread commitment to turn the promise of constitutional rights into policies that promote tolerance, respect and political participation.

Present and Future Opportunities for Reconciliation

What conclusions can be drawn about the prospects of reconciliation in Namibia? Clearly, there are reasons for concern, prime among them SWAPO's political dominance. Moreover, this has been accompanied by a notable concentration of power within the executive branch of the government and considerable evidence of opposition to democratic debate by some Namibian leaders and citizens. The goal of reconciliation would be to consolidate democracy by engendering accountability, and respect for the rule of law and human rights, and ensuring high living standards for citizens. Although Namibia is not experiencing a "hot war", the work of reconciliation may need to focus directly on the conflict in the Caprivi Strip, the land redistribution issue and Namibia's involvement in Angola and the DRC.

The stalemate over the Caprivi Strip issue remains. Many Caprivians want autonomy and blame the government for their situation. But the position of the Caprivians is exceptionally fragile as they do not have a substantial platform from which to negotiate. They have been purged, detained and forced to flee the Caprivi Strip. Many of those prepared to pursue secession are in exile. The Namibian Security Force is in total control of the Strip. The government does not appear prepared to negotiate with those it terms "traitors" or "rebels". It has requested that Botswana and Denmark repatriate those secessionists who have been granted refugee status so that they might face trial in Namibia. The international community has urged the warring parties in Namibia to stop hostilities in the Caprivi Strip. The UNHCR has asked secessionists to renounce their position. While the efforts of international organisations have helped lessen the effects of the Caprivi conflict, the larger issues of political representation and resource-sharing remain largely unresolved.[42]

Redistribution of land is a central concern for those working toward peace and reconciliation. The Namibian government is preoccupied with seeking a solution to the land issue.[43] Eleven years after independence, thousands of Namibians remain landless and poor. The problem is so sensitive that Nujoma recently said that failure to immediately address the need for land redistribution could lead to a second revolution in the country. In the face of conflicting social and political pressures, however, the government is pursuing a careful and measured course. Anxious to avoid chaos during the process of land distribution, it has attempted to devise systematic programmes of land acquisition and distribution, a process that Nujoma has conceded to be "painfully slow". Given the numerous unresolved questions about land resettlement in Namibia, a committee has been established, chaired by President Nujoma himself. According to Geingob, this is so that "the land question can be revisited again, involve all the players and [to] come up with some solutions".[44] The government has been buying land from white farmers on a "willing-seller, willing-buyer" basis. This attempt to resettle poor and landless Namibians has proven slow and expensive. According to some, not enough white farmers have been willing to sell their farms to the government at reasonable rates. At the end of 1997, the Deputy Lands Principal Secretary in the Namibian Ministry of Lands, John Mbango, complained that the ministry is experiencing difficulties buying enough land due to "inflated and unrealistic" prices set by white farmers. Such difficulties have fuelled sharp criticisms of the government's methodical approach. Mike Venaani, Secretary-General of the DTA, has warned that the land issue has whipped up enormous emotions since independence in 1990. If incorrectly handled, he said, the problem could transform a peaceful Namibia into "a sea of flames overnight".

Trade unions associated with the ruling party have also called for the restitution of land. They have called on the government to seize land without paying compensation, since the land was "stolen" by the colonisers. This would require changing Article 16 of the constitution. NUNW president Ponhele ya France says the constitution was made by the people and should be changed by the people. "To pay for our own land is a waste of money," he says. "We are opposed to it. The land was given to generals of the [colonial occupation] wars as compensation. We also have our generals. The land must be appropriated." However, the Namibian constitution – widely hailed as a model for other African countries – entrenches property rights, including the right of all people to own land and bequeath it to their heirs. Therefore, land can only be expropriated by the state "in the public interest" and "subject to the payment of just compensation, in accordance with requirements and procedures to be determined by Act of parliament".

The government is averse to grabbing land, Geingob told *Africa Recovery Online* in an interview: "I ask people who are saying change the constitution: What constitution are you going to change? The constitution talks about property rights. We are honouring property rights. I ask them: Do you want me to come to your house and grab your suits? The moment you bring it down to the basics, they don't know what they are talking about. And we are going to have lawlessness the moment you start dishonouring property rights. You grab today from this one, tomorrow we grab from you." Geingob emphasised: "We have to be leaders, even when people are shouting about grabbing land. Leaders have to be fair, provide justice. They must lead." He added: "You should know that some people are shouting because they want to come into power. They are failing to see weaknesses in the government, so they must pick up something to get us. They just want to make noise so that they may be voted in." Soon after independence, Geingob organised a land conference with participants from all sections of Namibian society. "We debated and debated and came to a very good understanding," he said. The conference agreed that land belonging to absentee landlords would be seized and redistributed to the poor and landless. Land that was idle or under-utilised would be the next target. But grabbing under-utilised land was not a straightforward matter, Geingob noted. "How do you determine something is under-utilised? This year you had rain, therefore the land is utilised. The following year you have drought, and it is not utilised. Are you going to grab it?" The conference did not resolve the problem of ancestral land. "Those who claim ancestral land say they are the original owners of the country, as their ancestors lived in certain areas," the prime minister said. "Now, who do we give it to? To the Hereros? To the San people? Land in Windhoek [the capital] did belong to some people. Do we give it back to them? Certain things are impractical."[45] The Namibian Society for Human Rights argues that it will be difficult to determine the rightful owners. Most Namibians moved into the country from the Great Lakes region around the 14th century, while others arrived between the sixteenth and nineteenth centuries. If anything, the Namibian Society for Human Rights says, the San people are the rightful owners of the land, since "they have been living here for at least 30 000 years, but they are discriminated against by everyone". The San were driven into the arid lands by the newcomers and today only about 70 000 or so have survived in the Kalahari Desert in Botswana and Namibia. Of the 30 000 San in Namibia, the bulk are landless, except for some 2 000 who live in Bushmanland. The conference faced similar problems with "stolen land" – farms acquired by white colonists. "People say stolen land cannot be bought; grab it," Geingob noted. "Now, we took an oath as leaders to do justice. Everybody has human rights, including the whites. If a white person 100 years ago stole the land, is it fair to grab that land from [the descendant of] that white person because it happens to be stolen land? Are you going to visit the sins of the father on the child?"

President Nujoma has called on white farmers to be "bold and sincere" in how they offer their land for sale: "It will not contribute to the success of equitable land redistribution if farmers and other land owners are only prepared to offer land that is less economical, or when prices for the farms or the improvements made to the land are inflated beyond their real cost." Such actions, he said, are hindering the government's efforts to acquire land, and thwarting national reconciliation. Geingob has also been appealing to white farmers to voluntarily give up their underused or unused lands for resettlement: "To the white people we say: Look, we talk about reconciliation. You are also in this country; you must do something, meet us half way. Why don't you also give up some land voluntarily?" One rich man, after talking to Nujoma, gave six farms to the government for settlement. "So sometimes it's a question of convincing people to do the right thing," Geingob remarked.[46]

However, the main organisation of commercial farmers, the Namibian Agricultural Union, has remained critical of the resettlement programme, accusing the government of turning productive commercial farming land into communal areas. It says this not only destroys the fragile ecology of the land, but also exacerbates poverty. Productivity, it argues, will not be achieved by expanding the land farmed under conditions similar to those in the communal areas. The government agrees that productivity is crucial to the success of resettlement. Geingob said that the government must convince "those who are land hungry that it is not just a question of having the land and sitting and saying, aha, I have land now -- but of working on it. Productivity is very important."[47]

Preserving access to communal lands is another unresolved issue in the land controversy. In fact, the problem of redistribution also involves the communal lands that are under the control of chiefs who traditionally allocate territory to their subjects. Before the government stopped the practice, well-to-do individuals were fencing off large chunks of land, thereby excluding other users. Some government ministers were accused of this practice. "If a minister goes back home, he can get a piece of land from the chief," Geingob explained. "Not only ministers, everybody. But of course, there is the pretension that ministers getting anything is corruption. We have solved the problem of fencing off communal land by saying only a maximum of 10 hectares can be fenced – if you want to have a little place you can call your own. That is reasonable. But if you want to get rich, get a big farm, then go and buy commercial land."[48]

Namibia's involvement in the DRC and Angola will play a role in Namibia's future economic and political development. Presently, the conflicts are costing the country millions of Namibian dollars yearly. Reconciling the perceptions held by the government, local NGOs and opposition parties on the involvement of their country in these armed conflicts has been the preoccupation of internal and external groups. In this vein, the international assignment that the former president of Botswana, Sir Ketumile Masire, has been accorded to mediate in the DRC crisis may broker a peace that will end Namibia's involvement in the civil war in that country.[49] According to the international community, if the Lusaka Peace Accord is implemented, Namibia will have no justification for pursuing activities in the DRC. The opposition parties and local NGOs see the government involvement as a waste of the country's resources and they urge the Namibian government to withdraw its troops from the DRC. At the time of writing, it appeared that a withdrawal would be likely.

To achieve the goals of national development based on equity, growth and justice, it appears that the people of Namibia will need to continue the work of dismantling colonial structures and institutions that have brought so much conflict and suffering. Independence in Namibia – Africa's last colony – took place after intense international negotiations. Though it has one of the most progressive democratic constitutions on the African continent, the true potential of this document has yet to be realised. The country is plagued by many political and socio-economic problems that it inherited from the German and South African colonial administrations. These problems are aggravated by the country's involvement in two neighbouring civil wars and the uncertain plan for the redistribution of land. To alleviate the problems facing the country, especially with a view to uplifting the living standards of citizens, civil society has been vocal about the government's so-called high-handed way of resolving these problems. Such criticism has met with mixed response. "National reconciliation amongst the country's people" was a prominent theme at independence, designed to overcome ethnic polarity and to further nation-building. These objectives created an aspiration among Namibians to move from the past to the future, dismantling the old in the name of creating a new democratic dispensation. Some remain disappointed with the progress made. They see a civil society that has yet to gain the ear of government and a society that has not yet taken the promise of its progressive constitution and translated it into a basis for tolerance, respect and equality. In large measure, the optimal use of the opportunities available for reconciliation and long-term political stability in Namibia have much to do with the political will of the government of Namibia and the values and respect Namibians have for the constitution. The puzzle pieces, however, are not always so easy to fit together. The process continues, work that contains much promise and which will not be completed without time for healing and reconstruction.

Notes

1 Despite the more than 10 languages spoken and the predominance of Afrikaans, English was adopted as the official language in Namibia.

2 Johnny Pitswane, "Namibia: Challenges of the First Decade," in *Southern Africa at the Crossroads?*, eds. Larry Benjamin and Christopher Gregory (Rivonia: Justified Press, 1992), 114.

3 Christiaan Keulder, *Voting Behaviour in Namibia II: Regional Councils 1998* (Windhoek: Friedrich Ebert Stiftung, 1999), 61.

4 In the December 1999 National Assembly elections the DTA scored 9.4%, the CoD 9.9% while the UDF scored 2.9%.

5 Philippe Gervais-Lambony, *L'Afrique du Sud et les Etats Voisins* (Paris: Armand Colin, 1997), 217–18.

6 Chrispin Inambao, "Caprivi Latest – Poll Fears, Mafwe feels Sidelined, November 27, 1998." Reprinted at www.namibian.com.na (accessed 25 September 2001).

7 Ibid.

8 Chris Talbot, "Civil War in Namibia." Reprinted at www.wsws.org/articles/ 1999/ aug1999/nami-a13_prn.shtml (accessed 25 September 2001).

9 Gretchen Bauer, "Namibia in the First Decade of Independence: How Democratic?" *Journal of Southern African Studies* 27 (2001): 52.

10 George Eyknyn, "Namibia's Burning Land Issue." Reprinted at http:// news.bbc.co.uk/hi/english/world/africa/newsid_866000/866019.stm (accessed 25 September 2001).

11 Ibid.

12 Ibid.

13 *The Namibian*, "The Caprivi – a Legacy of Colonialism, 6 August 1999." Reprinted at www.namibian.com.na/Focus/Caprivi/legacy.htm (accessed 1 October 2001); Anne Pitsch, "East Caprivians, Namibia." Reprinted at www.bsos.umd.edu/cidcm/mar/namcapri.htm (accessed 26 September 2001). The leader of Zambia's Lozi separatist movement, Akashambatwa Lewanika, has announced his support for the secessionists in the Caprivi Strip of Namibia.

14 John Qwelane, "Rumbles of a Past Scramble." Reprinted at www.suntimes.co.za/1999/08/08/news/news08.htm (accessed 26 September 2001).

15 BBC News, "World: Africa Caprivi Unrest leaves Namibian Bushmen Hungry." Reprinted at http://news.bbc.co.uk/hi/english/world/africa/newsid_450000/450685.stm#top (accessed 27 September 2001).

16 Africaonline.com, "Bribery, Corruption and Nepotism: The Corruption Case in Lesotho has Broadened its Scope." Reprinted at www.africaonline.com.na/news13.html (accessed 26 September 2001). Allegations that presidents Robert Mugabe of Zimbabwe and Sam Nujoma of Namibia have personally been granted diamond mines in the DRC continue to surface, possibly explaining the involvement of the two countries in that war. See Integrated Regional Information Network (IRIN), "Namibia: Namibia has Mine in the DRC – Minister." Reprinted at www.reliefweb.int/IRIN/sa/countrystories/namibia/20010222.phtml (accessed 26 September 2001).

17 Tangeni Amupadhi, "NDF Mum on 'Conscientious Objectors'." Reprinted at www.namibian.com.na/Netstories/2000/August/News/009758F1EB.html (accessed 26 September 2001). The Namibian Defence Force has refused to confirm or deny reports that it has detained 22 soldiers for refusing to fight against UNITA in Angola.

18 IRIN, "Namibia: Government says 'No' to Child Soldiers." Reprinted at www.reliefweb.int/IRIN/sa/countrystories/namibia/20010430a.phtml (accessed 26 September 2001).

19 The majority of Caprivi's 100 000 people are Lozi-speaking and share more in common with fellow Lozi-speaking people in neighbouring Zambia than Namibians.

20 Chris McGreal, "Angolan Rebels accused of Killing French Children." Reprinted at www.mg.co.za/mg/news/2000jan1/5jan-namibia.html (accessed 26 September 2001).

21 Economic Intelligence Unit, *Country Profile 1997–98* (London: EIU, 2000), 11.

22 Economic conditions are considered to have significant implications for the prospects of reconciliation in Namibia. The argument for this is that a market economy and a higher level of economic development provide the most propitious circumstances for nurturing and sustaining democracy. Of the new democracies in Africa, only Namibia, South Africa and Seychelles are economically prepared for democracy. This assessment is based on the countries' relatively favourable per capita incomes, resource endowments and socio-economic indicators. Michael Bratton and Nicholas van de Walle, *Democratic Experiments in Africa: Regime Transitions in Comparative Perspective (Cambridge Studies in Comparative Politics)* (Cambridge: Cambridge University Press, 1997), 39–240.

23 Economic Intelligence Unit, *Country Report April 2000* (London: EIU, 2000), 18.

24 IRIN, "Namibia: Register Prostitutes, Urges Namibian Health Minister." Reprinted at www.reliefweb.int/IRIN/sa/countrystories/namibia/20010417.phtml (accessed 26 September 2001).

25 Media Institute of Southern Africa, "Namibian Government Refuses to Advertise in Independent Newspaper." Reprinted at www.dfn.org/focus/namibia/namibian.htm (accessed 26 September 2001).

26 Max Mahatma and Jean Sutherland, "Namibians Rally on Rights, 30 April 2001." Reprinted at www.namibian.com.na (accessed 1 October 2001).

27 Human Rights Watch, "Special Issues and Campaigns: Lesbian and Gay Rights." Reprinted at www.hrw.org/wr2k1/special/gay.html (accessed 26 September 2001). In Namibia, President Sam Nujoma was regularly quoted as calling lesbians and gays "unnatural" and against the will of God. State television reported in October 2000 that Home Affairs Minister Jerry Ekandjo urged new police officers to "eliminate" lesbians and gays "from the face of Namibia".

28 Inter-Church Coalition on Africa, "Angola Urgent Action Bulletin Child Soldiers." Reprinted at www.web.net/iccaf/humanrights/angolainfo/urgangolachildsoldiers0300.htm (accessed 26 September 2001).

29 Andre du Pisani, *South West Africa/Namibia: The Politics of Continuity and Change* (Johannesburg: Jonathan Ball, 1986), 6.

30 Pitswane, "Namibia: Challenges of the First Decade," 114.

31 Klaus Dierks, "Namibian Library of Dr. Klaus Dierks: From Pre-colonial Times to Independent Namibia." Reprinted at www.klausdierks (accessed 21 September 2001).

32 Africa South of the Sahara, "Countries: Namibia." Reprinted at www.sul.stanford.edu/depts/ssrg/africa/namibia.html (accessed 27 September 2001).

33 Geoffrey Berridge, *Return to the UN: UN Diplomacy in Regional Conflicts* (London: Macmillan, 1991), 71.

34 Werner Menges, "Treason Trial Put Off, August 23, 2001." Reprinted at www.namibian.com.na (accessed 26 September 2001).

35 Anne Pitsch, "East Caprivians, Namibia"; IRIN, "Namibia: More Caprivi Refugees Return." Reprinted at www.reliefweb.int/IRIN/sa/countrystories/namibia/19990707htm (accessed 28 September 2001).

36 Werner Mender, "We Won't Be Silenced, Vow Former Detainees, 12 July 1999." Reprinted at www.namibian.com.na (accessed 26 September 2001).

37 Gretchen Bauer, "Challenges to Democratic Consolidation in Namibia," in *State, Conflict and Democracy in Africa*, ed. Richard Joseph (Boulder: Lynne Rienner, 1999), 437–38. In August 1997, NANSO-affiliated also disaffiliated from SWAPO, renaming itself Mighty NANSO. The group stated that it was disaffiliating because it had to achieve its goal of helping SWAPO to win a two-thirds majority in the December 1994 elections and because it wished to obtain donor funds. Mighty NANSO leader Abraham Ndumbu was expelled from SWAPO in late 1996 after urging the party to come clean on the detainee issue and calling for greater government action to curb corruption.

38 Ibid, 437–38.

39 Tangeni Amupadhi, "Churches Lobby Nujoma, 10 February 2000." Reprinted at www.namibian.com.na (accessed 1 October 2001).

40 Christof Maletsky, "Civil Society to Monitor Polls, 7 October 1999." Reprinted at www.namibian.com.na (accessed 1 October 2001).

41 Chrispin Inambao, "NSHR Says Rights Abuses Escalating, Wednesday, August 1, 2001." Reprinted at http://www.namibian.com.na (accessed on 11 October 2001).

42 Anne Pitsch, "East Caprivians, Namibia"; IRIN, "Namibia: More Caprivi Refugees Return."

43 Peter Mwaura, "Namibia Moves Cautiously on Land Deals," *Africa Recovery Online: A United Nations Publication*. Reprinted at www.un.org/ecosocdev/geninfo/afrec/subjindx/123land2.htm (accessed 9 August 2001).

44 Ibid.

45 Quoted in Peter Mwaura, "Namibia Moves Cautiously on Land Deals."

46 Peter Mwaura, "Namibia Moves Cautiously on Land Deals."

47 Ibid.

48 Ibid.

49 Namibian Government website, "Lusaka Agreement to be Reviewed." Reprinted at www.grnnet.gov.na/News/Archive/2001/May2001/Week3/lusaka.htm (accessed 1 October 2001).

Resources

Books, Articles, Media Reports

Appiah, Anthony and Henry Gates. *Africana: The Encyclopedia of the African and African American Experience*. New York: Basic Books, 1999.

Bauer, Gretchen. "Challenges to Democratic Consolidation in Namibia." In *State, Conflict and Democracy in Africa*, edited by Richard Joseph. Boulder: Lynne Rienner, 1999.

———. "Namibia in the First Decade of Independence: How Democratic?" *Journal of Southern African Studies* 27 (2001): 33–55.

Bratton, Michael and Nicholas van de Walle. *Democratic Experiments in Africa: Regime Transitions in Comparative Perspective (Cambridge Studies in Comparative Politics)*. Cambridge: Cambridge University Press, 1997.

Cliffe, Lionel. *The Transition to Independence in Namibia*. Boulder: Lynne Rienner, 1994.

Du Pisani, Andre. *South West Africa/Namibia: The Politics of Continuity and Change*. Johannesburg: Jonathan Ball, 1986.

Du Toit, Pierre. "Bridge or Bridgeheads: Comparing the Party Systems of Botswana, Namibia, Zimbabwe, Zambia and Malawi." In *The Awkward Embrace: One-Party Domination and Democracy*, edited by Hermann Giliomee and Charles Simkins. Cape Town: Tafelberg, 1999.

Eyknyn, George. "Namibia's Burning Land Issue." Reprinted at http://news. bbc.co.uk/hi/english/world/africa/newsid_866000/866019.stm (accessed 25 September 2001).

Gervais-Lambony, Philippe. *L'Afrique du Sud et les Etats Voisins*. Paris: Armand Colin, 1997.

Henrichsen, Dag. Namibia Bibliographical Update, A Source of New Monographs, Journals, Articles, Theses etc. on Namibia. Reprinted at http://www.baslerafrika. ch/Bibliographical/Update.html

Ihonvbere, Julius. "On the Threshold of Another False Start? A Critical Evaluation of Pro-democracy Movements in Africa." *Journal of Asian and African Studies* 33 (1996): 125–42.

Leys, Colin and John S. Saul. *Namibia's Liberation Struggle: The Two-edged Sword*. Columbus: Ohio University Press, 1995.

Monga, Celestin. "Civil Society and Democratization in Francophone Africa." *Journal of Modern African Studies* 33 (1995): 362

Moorsom, Richard. "Namibia's Economy at Independence: Report on Potential Norwegian-Namibian Industrial Co-operation." Reprinted at www.cmi.no/ public/pub1990htm

Omar, Gasan, Stare Katjiuanjo and Elias Kanguatjivi. "An Introduction to Namibia's Political Economy." Saldru Working Paper 75. Cape Town: University of Cape Town, 1990.

Pitsch, Anne. "East Caprivians, Namibia." Reprinted at www.bsos.umd.edu/cidcm/ mar/namcapri.htm (accessed 26 September 2001).

Pitswane, Johnny. "Namibia: Challenges of the First Decade." In *Southern Africa at the Crossroads?*, edited by Larry Benjamin and Christopher Gregory. Rivonia: Justified Press, 1992.

Primary Documents

Dierks, Klaus. "Namibian Library of Dr. Klaus Dierks: From Pre-colonial Times to Independent Namibia." Reprinted at www.klausdierks (accessed 21 September 2001).

The Namibian: http://www.namibian.com.na

Governmental, Intergovernmental Bodies, Political Parties

Democratic Turnhalle Alliance (DTA): http://www.framework.co.za/dua/namibia/dta.html

Media Institute for Southern Africa (MISA) is a non-governmental organisation promoting media freedom and diversity in the Southern Africa Development Community: http://www.freemedia.at/misa.htm

Namibian government official news and information website: http://www.grnnet.gov.na/intro.htm

South West Africa People's Organisation (SWAPO): http://www.swapo.org.na

Southern Africa Human Rights (NGO) Network (SAHRINGON) is a multi-country, cross-cultural network of human rights organisations that aims to create a dynamic human rights movement in a democratic southern Africa: http://www.unam.na/166/namibia/NGOs-/SAHRINGON.htm

Local NGOs

Council of Churches in Namibia (CCN). Director: Nangula E. Kathindi, email: ccwindhoek@iafrica.com.na

Legal Assistance Centre (LAC) is a non-profit public interest law centre in Namibia. It litigates only in the public interest, where a case is likely to have an impact beyond the people directly involved: http://www.lac.org.na/default.htm

Namibia Institute for Democracy (NID) is an independent, non-profit organisation which develops educational programmes and utilises the media, seminars, discussion groups and community information programmes to educate and inform Namibians about the Namibian constitution and principles of multi-party democracy: http://www.iwwn.com.na/nshr

National Society for Human Rights (NSHR) is a private, non-profit, non-partisan and paralegal human rights monitoring group and advocacy organisation in Namibia: http://nshr.namweb.com.na/old site http://www.iwwn.com.na/nshr

International NGOs

Chr. Michelsen Institute (CMI) is a private social science research foundation working on issues of development and human rights, primarily in sub-Saharan Africa, Asia and the Middle East.

The Human Rights Committee of South Africa (HRCSA) is an NGO based in South Africa. Its objective is to monitor and advocate human rights issues and ensure the promotion and protection of human rights.

Inter-Church Coalition on Africa (ICCAF) is a Canadian ecumenical forum rooted in the biblical prophetic tradition that calls for justice and peace for all people. It carries out specific and specialised work of common concern to its member churches and their African partners.

NAMIBIA COUNTRY INFORMATION

Geography
Location: Southern Africa, bordering the south Atlantic Ocean, between Angola and South Africa.
Cities: *Capital:* Windhoek. *Other towns:* Keetmanshoop, Lüderitz, Oranjemund, Swakopmund, Tsumeb, Walvis Bay, Oshakati, Otjiwarongo.

People
Nationality: *Noun:* Namibian(s). *Adjective:* Namibian.
Population (July 2000 est.): 1 771 327.
Population growth rate (2000 est.): 1.57%.
Ethnic groups: Black 87.5%, white 6%, mixed 6.5%. About 50% of the population belong to the Ovambo tribe and 9% to the Kavango tribe. Other ethnic groups are: Herero 7%, Damara 7%, Nama 5%, Caprivian 4%, Bushmen 3%, Baster 2%, Tswana 0.5%.
Religions: Christian 80% to 90% (Lutheran at least 50%), traditional African 10% to 20%.
Languages: English 7% (official), Afrikaans – common language of most of the population and about 60% of the white population, German 32%, indigenous languages: Oshivambo, Herero, Nama.
Education (2000 est.): *Literacy:* whites 100%; others 30%.
Health (2000 est.): *Infant mortality rate:* 70.88/1 000. *Life expectancy:* 42.46 years.
Workforce (1999 est.): 500 000. Agriculture: 47%. Industry: 25%. Services: 28%.

Economy
GDP (1999 est.): $7.1 billion.
GDP real growth rate: 3%.
Per capita income: $4 300.
Inflation rate: 8.5%.
Natural resources: Diamonds, copper, uranium, gold, lead, tin, lithium, cadmium, zinc, salt, vanadium, natural gas, hydropower, fish, suspected deposits of oil, coal and iron ore.
Agriculture: 12% of GDP. *Products:* millet, sorghum, peanuts, livestock, fish.
Industry: 30% of GDP. *Types:* Meat packaging, fish processing, dairy products, mining (diamond, lead, zinc, tin, silver, tungsten, uranium, copper).
Trade (1999): *Exports:* $1.4 billion: diamonds, copper, gold, zinc, lead, uranium, cattle, processed fish, karakul skins. *Major markets:* UK, South Africa, Spain, France, Japan. *Imports:* $1.5 billion: foodstuffs, petroleum products and fuel, machinery and equipment, chemicals. *Major supplies:* South Africa, Germany, US, Japan.
Economic aid: Recipient (1998): $127 million.
Debt – external (1999): $127 million.

Military
Military expenditure: Dollar figures: $90 million (FY97/98).
Military expenditure: Percent of GDP: 2.6% (FY97/98).

Demographic information is drawn from that compiled by the United States Department of State. See http://www.state.gov/r/pa/ei/bgn

Chapter 14

Lesotho: Political Conflict, Peace and Reconciliation in the Mountain Kingdom

MOKETE LAWRENCE PHERUDI

The Basotho emerged out of the demographic turmoil of the Difaqane in the 1820s.[1] In 1868, the territory became a colonial possession of the British crown. Its loss of political sovereignty and cultural independence was explicit in the Annexation Proclamation, bringing the Basotho and their land under the direct rule of Britain and subjecting them to a system of hut and head taxes. The tax collected was used not to develop the Basotho and their country but as a tool to sustain and prolong colonial rule. The Basotho communal subsistence economy was destroyed and the Basotho became wage earners who had to pay tax. Under British rule, Lesotho was a source of forced labour.

The Basotho are a homogenous people, sharing a common language, culture and history of struggle to preserve their national identity against all odds. They have a strong tradition of protecting their human rights, including the indigenous concept of free speech at the *pitso* (open air assembly), equal justice and accountability. The Basotho have an unusually high level of literacy, due in great part to the presence of missionaries for over a century: the French Protestant Church (now known as the Church of Lesotho or the Lesotho Evangelical Church), the Roman Catholic Church and the Church of England. Today 90% of the cost of education is borne by the government, but schooling is not yet free and compulsory. The National University of Lesotho (formerly known as Pius XII College) is at Roma, near Maseru.[2]

Lesotho is very small, one of the smallest political units in Africa. It is the same size as Belgium and has a population of 2 200 000 (2000 estimate), spread over an area of about 11 716 square kilometres.[3] The country is landlocked, as it is surrounded by South Africa. Its boundaries are the Drakensberg Mountains and the Caledon and Orange rivers. These waterways also provide the Basotho with fresh water. The territory has 10 districts, all named after their chief towns, except Berea chief town, Teyateyaneng.[4]

A British colony for 98 years, Lesotho was granted independence on

4 October 1966. Because it was a kingdom, the new dispensation brought complications of a political nature. Independence was granted in the face of the opposition's protest and general tension. The first general elections were held in 1965 and the Basotholand National Party (BNP) won, defeating the Basotholand Congress Party (BCP) and the Marematlou Freedom Party (MFP). The next election was held in 1970 and the BNP lost but refused to hand over power to the victorious BCP.[5] The political instability and constitutional crisis that ensued was contained largely by dictatorial rule and patronage politics. Since then, politics in Lesotho have been marked by repression and intrigue on the part of the political elite, working within a highly polarised society, with weak political institutions and paltry economic resources. When the 1985 elections were aborted due to the intrigues of the BNP, the executive organ of the state locked horns in a fierce political battle with the armed forces, resulting in the military putsch of 1986. As in previous political conflicts, a South African role could be seen in the coup.

The Face of Conflict

The military withdrew gracefully to the barracks in 1993, thus allowing free competition for state power. Elections were held shortly thereafter. The BCP's victory and the nature of Lesotho's electoral system meant that the results produced a de facto one-party state. Rok Ajulu remarked, "it was probably the first time in African politics when a one party government came about freely and fairly through the box".[6] Not all contestants accepted the outcome of the 1993 elections. The BNP claimed that the elections were rigged and that in no circumstances would the party allow Ntsu Mokhehle of the BCP to rule.[7] Although its attempts to have the outcome declared null and void failed, the BNP attempted to destabilise the BCP government until 1997.

In December 1993, Lesotho Defence Force (LDF) members demanded a 100% salary increase as well as a number of other allowances. In response to the LDF's demand, Prime Minister Mokhehle stated, "the issue of salaries of all Public Servants, including those of the army, is being considered and a decision will be taken at the appropriate time. There will be no preferential treatment on the issue of salaries of the Public Servants."[8] Mokhehle's response did not satisfy some LDF members and they split into two factions, the loyalist (Ratjomose-based, pro-government group) and the rebels (Makoanyane-based, government antagonists). This development produced tensions within the army and between the army and the government.

Conflict between the factions broke out on 14 January 1994 at Makoanyane Barracks. Patrick Majara, the Chief of the Lesotho Defence Air Force Squadron, was attacked and critically injured by the opposition forces. The Ratjomose faction perceived the attack on Majara as cause for retaliation. The two factions began to position themselves on the hilltops around Maseru, preparing for combat. The Makoanyane faction occupied the Makoanyane and Lithabaneng hilltops and the Ratjomose faction occupied Thetsane's Hill. A total of 750 soldiers out of 2 000 were involved in the skirmishes. The two groups engaged in sustained gun and mortar battle. Five soldiers died and eleven civilians were wounded. As the skirmishes continued, lawlessness within the LDF escalated.

The demand for a salary increase was not the sole reason for the dispute. There were other simmering issues in the background. There were past hostilities between the BCP's military wing, the Lesotho Liberation Army (LLA), and the pro-BNP LDF who suspected that the ruling party would soon use the LLA against them. Moreover, the BCP Minister of Agriculture, Co-operatives, Marketing and Youth Affairs, Ntsukunyane Mphanya, declared that the "Lesotho Liberation Army will be integrated into the country's armed force, regardless of whether or not the opponents of the regime like it".[9] Such utterances sowed the seeds of conflict, political hatred, suspicion and distrust between the LDF and the BCP-led government.

After a brief and superficial stability, chaos broke out when 2 500 of the 3 000 Lesotho Mounted Police (LMP) demanded a salary increase of 60%. With its weak economy, the government could not afford to meet the demand. On 16 May 1994, police attacked a Member of Parliament, Ramakatsa of Mpharane. On 17 May, shots were fired at the BCP offices. The house of another MP, Ntsukunyane Mphanya, was also attacked. The Information Minister and the Acting Minister of Finance, Mpho Malie, was kidnapped and tortured for his alleged support of the government before being released the following day.[10]

The long-standing dispute continued simmering. On 6 February 1997, eight members of the LMP, led by Second Lieutenant Pakiso Molise and backed by two-thirds of the 3 000 members, seized the police headquarters in Maseru. They were due to stand trial for the 1995 murder of their colleagues and they were seeking amnesty in terms of Lesotho's Pardon Act of 1995, which stipulated that security force members could not be charged for crimes committed between 1993 and 1995.[11] Police work was brought to a halt throughout the country, paving the way for lawlessness. For days the government of the ageing and sick Mokhehle failed to act.

Given the LMP's refusal to vacate the headquarters, the government sent the LDF to remove them by force on 16 February 1997. Gunfire and explosions rocked Maseru. The police headquarters was the scene of intermittent artillery fire and automatic gunfire. The battle was one-sided, with the police offering weak resistance to the onslaught.[12] Khoabane Cheko, one of the chiefs who visited the shooting scene, commented that "the military action was a disgrace to Lesotho". He argued that such an action was not appropriate while there were ongoing attempts to negotiate a solution and that the government was politically inflexible.[13] After the episode, Molapo Qhobela, the BCP leader, observed that whether the prime minister liked it or not, he had wittingly or unwittingly sown seeds of dissension between the army and the police and made the army aware of its power, a strength that it could use against him.

In 1998, the following parties contested the elections: the ruling Lesotho Congress for Democracy (LCD), the BCP, the MFP, the BNP, the Sefate Democratic Party, the National Progressive Party, the Christian Democratic Party, the National Independent Party, the Lesotho Labour Party, the United Democratic Party and the Independents. The political atmosphere in the country was characterised by significant tension between the LCD, just eight months' old at the time of the elections, and the major opposition parties. At the heart of this tension was the manner in which the LCD had assumed power, a move which opponents dubbed a parliamentary coup. Mokhehle had resigned from the BCP and with 41 loyal members transferred to the new party. This gave him a majority in parliament (41 out of 64 MPs).[14] When attempts to unseat the LCD government through various forms of protests, including appeals from the king and the Southern Africa Development Community (SADC), failed, the opposition parties thought they could dislodge it through an electoral contest.

This was not to be, as the LCD won 79 out of 80 seats. This was unexpected because the LCD was a new party on Lesotho's political scene and, more importantly, its emergence had triggered unprecedented bitterness among the political elite and the electorate, all of which suggested that it would not perform well. However, this view ignored the fact that Lesotho politics is largely driven by personality cults, which means that confidence in an individual politician stems from their perceived political influence in the country. For example, Mokhehle was a commoner when he appealed for the emancipation of the Basotho from British rule. He was perceived to be the man who saved the Basotho from the violence of colonialism and political oppression. Even after his death, voters continued to vote for his party in large numbers and it can be argued that Mokhehle's legacy did generate some support for the LCD.

The new landscape did not improve Lesotho's politics. However, the current conflict in Lesotho is not related only to the 1998 elections and their outcome. The conflict is fairly complex and, broadly, has the following elements. Firstly, the split in the BCP that resulted in the formation and rise to power of the LCD, fuelled anger within the BCP because it was reduced to an opposition party. Secondly, the LDF and the LMP wanted their party, the BNP, to assume power because it was thought that the LLA still posed a threat. Thirdly, there were power struggles among politicians of the same parties, particularly within the ruling party, as the prime minister, Pakalitha Mosisili, and his deputy, Kelebone Maope, pulled in different directions. The latter resigned from the LCD in March 2001 to form his own political party, called the Lesotho People's Congress (LPC). In the BNP, there was also a power struggle between Metsing Lekhanya and Majara Molapo and in the BCP Molapo Qhobela was engaged in a power struggle with Tseliso Makhakhe. After the 1998 elections, the opposition parties formed an alliance, but this did not survive due to schisms within the political parties themselves.[15] All told, these developments have deepened the political polarisation among the Basotho and have fostered an unprecedented sense of bitterness and heightened political intolerance. The opposition parties joined forces to protest the outcome of the elections. These parties, joined by five smaller parties, such as the Sefate Democratic Party, marched to the palace to hand over a petition requesting that King Letsie III dissolve the LCD government and organise fresh elections. They charged that the elections had been rigged.[16]

The protesting parties managed to render the country ungovernable when for the better part of August and September 1998 they camped at the palace in Maseru, organised stay-aways and paralysed the normal business of parliament by closing offices, confiscating government vehicles, preventing government officials from discharging their duties and hijacking the state-run Radio Lesotho. Things came to a head on 10 August 1998 when the protesters called a stay-away in Maseru, barricaded the entire town, harassed street vendors and brought the town to a standstill. The security establishment was reluctant to intervene and armed conflict ensued between supporters of the ruling party and the opposition. At least five people died and fifteen others were seriously injured. These developments effectively paralysed the LCD government. Prime Minister Mosisili called for help from the SADC, especially from the troika countries, South Africa, Botswana and Zimbabwe, without consulting the king. This was a sign of the ice-cold relations between the two arms of the state's executive. The troika delegation came to Lesotho with a view to help quell the turmoil and it was finally agreed that a commission headed by South African Justice Pius Langa should be formed to look into allegations of election fraud.[17]

The Langa commission released its report on 17 September and it was brought to Lesotho by a delegation of officials from the troika countries headed by Sydney Mafumadi, the then South African Minister of Safety and Security. The findings of the commission were summarised as follows: "We are unable to state that the invalidity of the elections has been conclusively established. We point out, however, that some of the apparent irregularities and discrepancies are of sufficiently serious concern. We cannot however postulate that the result does not reflect the will of the Lesotho electorate."[18] This conclusion did not sit well with the opposition groups. To some extent they had lost confidence in the report because of the long delay before its release, the fundamental contradictions between the preliminary report and the final version, and its circulation among the troika governments long before the conflicting parties even had a glance at it.

After the handing over of the Langa report, events took a new turn in Lesotho. There was a complete collapse of law and order and increased anarchy. The prime minister and the parliamentarians were vulnerable to attack by the opposition. The government was rendered ineffective and the prime minister appealed for SADC military assistance through a letter which stated: "The only intervention I can and do request is of a military nature . . . . This morning, the situation has worsened . . . furthermore serious threats are being made including abducting ministers, killing the Prime Minister and Foreign Affairs Minister at any time. The most serious tragedy is that the police and in particular the army are at best spectators . . . . We have a coup on our hands."[19] This passage graphically painted a picture of impending civil war in Lesotho and a covert military coup in the making. The importance of the prime minister's allegation of a coup lies in the fact that it invoked Article 5 Section 2 (ib) of the Protocol on Politics, Defence and Security in the Southern African Development Community, which states that one of the intra-state conflicts which could warrant regional intervention is a "threat to the legitimate authority of the government (such as a military coup by the armed or paramilitary forces)". So when the Lesotho prime minister mentioned a coup, South Africa saw red, fearing for its Lesotho Highlands Water Project and anticipating an influx of refugees and cross-border trafficking of narcotics.[20]

Under the auspices of the SADC, South Africa responded by sending a contingent of 600 heavily armed soldiers into Lesotho on 22 September 1998. On 28 September 450 troops reinforced this group and 750 more arrived on 8 October. The skirmishes between the South African National Defence Force and the LDF forces lasted two days. In the process, roughly 113 people were reported killed and about 20 injured. The Lesotho police counted 47 civilians dead and 15 injured, whereas the SADC counted 58 civilians and 8 of their members dead, not counting the 68 bodies collected by Red Cross officials in various parts of the country. Neither the Lesotho government nor the Red Cross has confirmed the final civilian death toll. Many families are believed to have buried their dead without notifying the country's shaky civil authorities.[21]

The economic impact of this conflict has been disastrous for Lesotho. Looters helped themselves to merchandise from all kinds of retailers. Mamello Morrison said at the time, "but now look at our city, it has been destroyed".[22] A building known as Mokorotlo, which was a tourist attraction at the entrance to Maseru, was looted and burned. Indeed Maseru was gutted. Its burned and ravaged skyscrapers, the ruins of the business centres, were evidence of what was once a thriving capital. According to Molopo Notshi, the Minister of Employment and Labour, the arson and looting had a significant impact on employment. In Maseru, 141 businesses, which had employed 1 707 people, were burned and looted. These were fruit and vegetable shops, furniture dealers, grocery shops, pharmacies, electronic and music centres, supermarkets, butcheries, clothing and textile stores, as well as salons and beauty treatment shops. In Mafeteng, 87 businesses, which employed 702 persons, were burned and looted. In Mohale's Hoek, 16 business establishments, employing a total of 150 people, were looted. In Butha-Buthe, two business enterprises were looted, resulting in the loss of 46 jobs. Overall, 246 business enterprises were burned and looted, resulting in the loss of 2 609 jobs. Molopo further argued that the average monthly earnings lost amounted to M2 548 990 million.

Despite the damage done in Lesotho, the SADC forces succeeded in restoring law and order, protecting democracy and preventing a coup. South Africa succeeded in protecting its interests in the Lesotho Highlands Water Project. Even though the SADC helped Lesotho a great deal, certain sectors were critical of SADC involvement in the domestic affairs of Lesotho. Lesotho's government was entitled to invite SADC forces to intervene under Article 2(7) of the United Nations Charter. International law regards the recognised government of the day as the external expression of the state. The government constituted by the ruling party, the LCD, was therefore legally competent to request external diplomatic and military assistance. The present constitutional arrangements in Lesotho do not give the monarch, King Letsie III, such an executive function.

It does not, however, follow automatically that the Lesotho government's request had to be accommodated and acted upon by foreign governments. This is where legality and legitimacy intersect. Was it legal or legitimate for South Africa and its SADC partners to accede to the Lesotho government's request for intervention? Beyond what regional and international law arrangements provide, it is also important to consider the self-interest of the intervening state. For South Africa, it is the product of history that Lesotho is situated within its belly. This is one of the consequences of the application of the international law of *uti possidetis* (retention of colonial borders). Although the official South African position has so far not highlighted this, it would be naive not to view this fact of geographical and territorial connectedness as having played some role in the decision. Any widespread chaos in Lesotho would necessarily translate into considerable problems inside South Africa. Whatever the other justifications, it was a matter of "self-defence" for South Africa. The extent to which instability in Lesotho places serious responsibilities on South Africa is illustrated by the fact that South Africa was subsequently called on to help in the rebuilding of Maseru. The local communities and the Department of Welfare cared for the refugees who spilled over into the Free State. Of course, such assistance was in line with South Africa's international obligation under the 1951 Geneva Convention, as well as the 1969 Refugee Convention of the Organisation of African Unity.

The Historical Roots of Conflict

The Basotho and the proto-state came into being in the first half of the nineteenth century. Moshoeshoe the Great or Chief of the Mountain (*c*. 1785–1870) was proclaimed the founder and father of the Basotho nation. He was engaged in nation-building, a process involving the Basia, Batlokoa, Bakubung, Bakoena, Bamokoteli, Bakhatla, Baphuthi and Nguni. The "Basotho of Moshoeshoe" were of divergent ethnic backgrounds and circumstances, which is frequently cited as a reason why the Basotho have still not forged a strong unity and why factions and political quarrels are common features of the nation.

A root cause of the crisis in Lesotho is the role of European colonialists and missionaries. Missionary bodies, notably the Paris Evangelical

Missionary Society (1833), the Roman Catholic Church (1860s) and the Anglicans (1875) undermined the social fabric of the Basotho nation by forcing them to renounce their customs and adopt a western lifestyle. As if that was not enough, the missionaries of one congregation taught their followers to regard the followers of other denominations as enemies. South Africa's Cape colonial government colluded with the missionaries to teach distorted political ideas, a defective education that was in practice worse than illiteracy because of its misleading effects. Lesotho school text-books were full of political fallacies designed to rationalise the Basotho's exclusion from politics.[23]

Missionaries influenced the birth of the political parties in Lesotho, especially the BNP. Initially called the Christian Democratic Party when it was formed in 1958, the BNP was associated with the Roman Catholic Church and the Catholic bishops did everything in their power to discredit the BCP. The BCP challenged the missionaries' work as attempts to keep the Basotho perpetually oppressed, subservient, self-ridiculed and ex-ploited. The Church did little to promote reconciliation in Lesotho politics, but instead created political divisions among the Basotho, divisions that became evident in the proliferation of political parties. Thus, political awareness grew accompanied by division and distrust.

Intolerance among Lesotho politicians has also contributed to destabil-isation in the country. This view was clearly espoused in *Work for Justice* (a newsletter produced by the Maseru-based Transformation Resource Centre), which argues that the long-established parties have only sparked confusion, hatred, inter-party fights and killings.[24] The three long-established political parties – the BCP, the BNP and the MFP – were each rooted firmly in the history and traditions of Lesotho. Each drew on dif-ferent elements of those traditions and appealed to different constituencies. Although they had much in common, each tended to emphasise its own distinctive interpretation of Lesotho's past and how Lesotho could regain its sense of internal unity, break out of its extreme dependence upon South Africa and move forward to claim its place among the family of nations.

The BCP, MFP and BNP contested the 1960 elections. There were also many independent candidates. Most observers interpreted the elections as a landslide victory for the BCP, but appearances were deceptive. The next five years saw the other parties sabotaging the efforts of the BCP. The BCP victory brought more frustration than successful pluralism.[25]

Not all of Lesotho's political problems come from internal factors. Lesotho's unique geographical position has often resulted in South Africa holding the territory hostage and supporting the BNP against the BCP.

During the 1965 elections, South African prime minister H. F. Verwoerd granted Lesotho a significant amount of maize to help the country through its food crisis and to solicit votes for the BNP. Such efforts increased division among Basotho politicians.[26] The first post-independence elections were held in 1970. When the BNP appeared to be losing against the BCP, BNP leader Leabua Jonathan suspended the constitution and launched a coup. Jonathan declared a five-year "holiday" from democratic rule. Immediately thereafter, B. J. Vorster, Verwoerd's successor, put his weight behind Jonathan's regime by stating that "despite the 1970 coup, I am prepared to continue the good relations with Leabua".[27] This created a precedent whereby authority and constitutional order rested on guns. Toward the late 1970s, it was payback time for Lesotho. South Africa demanded that Lesotho expel the African National Congress (ANC) and the Pan Africanist Congress (PAC) and recognise the independence of the Transkei. Jonathan's refusal to comply portended what has been called South Africa's imperialism-destabilisation programme.

In 1974, the BCP attempted a coup and failed, a failure that sparked a reign of terror. BCP party members went into exile and formed the LLA. The LLA, with the help of South Africa, destabilised the BNP government through what they termed a civil war against Jonathan, based on General André Beaufre's (the former commander of the French Forces in Algeria) "interior manoeuvre". The LLA's attacks increased. The training of the LLA was undertaken at the security base at Dithotaneng in QwaQwa (then a South African "homeland") and at a camp on Ferndale Farm, near Bergville, KwaZulu-Natal. Some training was also done at Vlakplaas, a notorious establishment of the South African security establishment. South African support of the LLA thus contributed directly to political tension and conflict in Lesotho.

Jonathan's unwillingness to accept South African demands resulted in an intensification of the conflict. South Africa used bullyboy tactics and in 1986 Lesotho's borders were closed. The direct impact of closing the borders was the 1986 coup by the LDF, an event that resulted in a military government under Major General Justin Metsing Lekhanya, a leader who maintained amicable relations with South Africa. As a power consolidation strategy, the military government passed Order No. 4 of 1986, an act that banned all political activity in Lesotho. Its stipulations were less concerned with restoring democracy and promoting reconciliation than with sowing discord. The order cast suspicion upon the opposition parties. With "no party politics", citizens had no formal means to articulate interests or needs. The military rulers felt that this vacuum served the nation's interest.

On 24 January 1986, as chairperson of the Military Council, Lekhanya announced to the nation that, "For a long time this nation had been plunged into a political quagmire by politicians whose actions did not necessarily align themselves with national interests . . . We therefore decided that there should be no more political activity which has been the root cause of internal problems in Lesotho."[28]

Lekhanya seemed to regard politicians with contempt. However, banning political activities was a recipe for future conflict. Ayittey argues that: "The politics of exclusion has been the source of Africa's political instability, civil strife, wars and chaos." He further states that two factors underlie Africa's (including Lesotho's) unending political violence and civil wars: the absence of mechanisms for the peaceful transfer of political power and for the peaceful resolution of conflict.[29] After tasting power, the government, led by Lekhanya, became reluctant to hold elections. Some members of the LDF began to insinuate that it was best to "do it yourself", meaning that anyone who toppled the government did so for personal gain.[30] Some claimed that they did not topple Jonathan because the alternative was civilian rule.

Lesotho presents one of the more bizarre political complexities in southern Africa. Its politics since independence have been clearly characterised by missionary dictates, a deep constitutional crisis, lack of popular elected government (hence the severe legitimacy crisis of the state) and rule by brute force, all of which has undermined human rights and accountability. This was evident when the BNP government created an armed youth league, which terrorised, tortured and killed the government's opposition. For example, Desmond Sixishe, Vincent Makhele and their wives were killed during the military rule in 1986. LDF members shot Selometsi Baholo, then Minister of Finance, for refusing a pay increase. Anyone opposing or suspected of opposing the government was killed. Gross violations of human rights became the norm.

This lack of accountability has been one of the major sources of conflict in Lesotho. Almost every party that has been in power has been struck by rifts and intra-party disputes that have compromised their responsibilities to the people. What is more, there has been a lack of popular, co-ordinated strategies designed to exert pressure for democratic transformation such as power-sharing, participative democracy and reconciliation. Every government has threatened civil servants with retrenchments and all parties have seemed to promote division more than unity. This situation has created hostility, uncertainty and a persistent need to mobilise against the government.

The culture of rejecting election outcomes and resorting to violence has created a serious conflict situation in Lesotho. The very first election results were disputed in 1965 by the BCP. Before the 1970 elections, the BCP was confident that it was going to win, a prediction that was confirmed by one of its leaders, Chief Maseribane of Quthing, when he declared: "How can we lose the match? The ball is ours, the jerseys are ours, the field is ours and more importantly, the referee too is ours."[31] Yet when the BCP showed signs of winning the vote, the BNP launched a coup, the first in the history of Lesotho. For almost 23 years (1970–92) no elections were held. Lesotho became a one-party dictatorship under Jonathan. In 1993, the second post-independent elections were held and the BCP emerged victorious, but the BNP disputed the outcome. In 1998, an eight-month-old party, the LCD, won the elections and for the first time the opposition parties joined forces to oppose the election outcome. This culture of dispute has deep roots and is coupled with violence.

The formation and existence of a partisan army is one cause of political instability. Initially, card-carying members of the BNP were recruited into the army, through the *sephephechana* system (paying money/joining fee of a party). Therefore, the LDF was formed along party lines. Aristotle never liked professional soldiers, saying that they only serve their master. The assertion is relevant to the LDF and the LMP. The army's loyalty to the BNP has long been evident. In 1994, the army mutinied, something that had not happened during the BNP's 16 years of oppressive rule (1970–86). They also did not defend the constitution when King Letsie III dissolved the BCP government in 1994 or when they became spectators while opposition parties – including the BNP – rendered the country ungovernable. Other state institutions, like the police and the civil servants, underwent a similar transformation, as if no other party could take power in Lesotho.[32] Jonathan warned civil servants that no promotion of any political party would be tolerated. Anyone interested in politics was asked to resign. This warning was an attempt to discourage political alignment within the work environment and a message to the opposition that they could not exploit civil servants for their political objectives. In 1998, the LCD government did likewise by issuing a strong warning and threat to civil servants that "it has come to the attention of the government that some of your officers have been engaging in inappropriate political gatherings . . . this is viewed as a serious breach of discipline by the Public Servants . . . failure to resign would lead to dismissal in which case one would forfeit terminal benefits".[33] This warning to civil servants created a clear impression that each party had to intimidate them in the name of efficiency, a policy that resulted in suspicion, distrust and hatred.

In 1997 police seized control of the police headquarters in Maseru and mutinied because Second Lieutenant Molise and seven others refused to stand trial for the 1995 murder of their colleagues and demanded amnesty in terms of Lesotho's Pardon Act of 1995. Molise submitted that, "the crisis was caused by an attempt of the ruling party to crack down on its perceived political opponents, including churches, teachers and medical workers".[34]

The external dependence of Lesotho has also been a source of conflict.[35] On more than one occasion, the BCP government has invited the intervention of South Africa without consultation with other stakeholders. In 1998, the LCD invited SADC intervention. The opposition groups were not satisfied and Molapo Qhobela, the BCP leader, warned that, "the allied forces were betrayed by the battle-shy ruling LCD who had lost touch with what was happening in the country. He [President Mandela] is honestly deceiving himself. As soon as the SANDF/SADC leaves, we go back to square one. I am not going to disclose what we are going to do."[36]

There are civil societies in Lesotho, some of which remain outside the conflict. But their role has been fairly marginal because the troika countries (South Africa, Botswana and Zimbabwe) of the SADC have played the leading role in the Lesotho political and constitutional crisis in recent years.

The other source of conflict in Lesotho is the pursuit of power and control by politicians. Too many have used this power for self-enrichment through corruption and profiteering at the public's expense. Party activists have shown a lack of tolerance and justice, with little knowledge of or commitment to the party's constitution and rules. The tendency to refer disputes to the courts has meant that minimal effort has been given to a negotiated settlement within the parties concerned.

Prospects for Peace-Building

Lesotho is a country torn by dissension, ravaged by political violence, and still walking a narrow line between reconciliation and civil war. Although the future remains uncertain, there is cause for optimism. In 1994, the army mutiny triggered a reaction from other stakeholders inside and outside Lesotho. The NGOs, businesspeople of Lesotho, the Lesotho Council of Churches and trade unions appealed with one voice to soldiers to stop their skirmishes because the conflict was affecting the lives and property of the Basotho as a whole. At that time, the BCP-led government was powerless to intervene and appealed for foreign help. Mokhehle appealed to Ketumile Masire, the chairperson of the SADC, and Chief Emeka Anyaoku, the Secretary General of the Commonwealth of Nations, to send a peace-keeping force.[37] The opposition parties in Lesotho (the BNP, the United Democratic Party, Hareeng Basotho and Kopanang Basotho) sent a statement addressed to the SADC's Executive Secretary, Kaire Mbuende, which argued that: "We urge all outside military inter-ventionists whose interests are not affected at this stage to know that should they be tempted with intervention, they would be doing so against a unified political expression of an entire nation. Their action will be understood by Basotho and the sovereign Lesotho as a naked interference and a rape against our nation."[38] The opposition parties' request was not considered because the SADC was more concerned about regional stabil-ity than the political contest among the parties in Lesotho.

Two diplomats from the Commonwealth Secretariat, Ghanaian Moses Anafu and Maxwell Gayland of Australia, arrived in Lesotho on 25 January 1994 to negotiate a cease-fire and assess the political crisis that was engulfing the mountain kingdom. The pair could not succeed in their mission because they did not win the confidence of the opposition parties. At the same time, the then leader of the BNP, Retshelisitsoe Sekhonyana, fuelled the conflict by publicly declaring that: "because of the political crisis in Lesotho, peace has been threatened by a government failure to bring the LLA under control. The LLA was being armed with AK47 auto-matic machine guns . . . and it constitutes a serious threat to peace . . . the BNP will fight LLA until we are all killed if need be."[39] The BCP's response to Sekhonyana's utterances was firm and presented by Mpho Malie, the then Minister of Information: "The BCP-led government would like to strongly advise the political parties which are bent on sow-ing seeds of confusion which threaten peace and stability to refrain from such. The aim of these people is mainly to instil fear in Basotho in order to disrupt peace . . . Government's patience is unfortunately sometimes interpreted as weakness. These people, we know, were bitter about the BCP landslide victory during the elections and were defeated in court while contesting the election outcome. Government, therefore, appeals to Basotho people to stay calm and dissociate themselves from instigation by opportunists."[40]

On 28 January 1994, a delegation from the Commonwealth Secretariat and the SADC arrived in Lesotho on a fact-finding mission. They con-sulted various stakeholders. The ensuing report was given to presidents Robert Mugabe and Ketumile Masire. After familiarising themselves with the report, they arrived in Lesotho on 10 February 1994 and received a resounding welcome from the people of Lesotho. They consulted with all the stakeholders. At the end of their mission, the two presidents observed that the BCP government had not made a serious commitment to national reconciliation and its implementation. Their observation was as follows: "It was and still remains our very clear impression that, notwithstanding a recognised need for national reconciliation, little if any progress had been made towards the implementation of such policy or towards the promotion of a truly national dialogue."[41] However, the two presidents did not define the crisis simply as a struggle between the BCP government and the LDF. They recognised its broader dimensions, specifying that since the LDF was formed to counteract the activities of the BCP, it was difficult to be loyal to such a government. Again the skirmishes between the BCP's military wing, the LLA, and the LDF were still fresh in the minds of the LDF members, who also feared that they would lose their jobs under BCP rule. As such, they emphasised the importance of a national dialogue. On 13 February 1994, the army laid down its weapons and returned to the barracks under the deal brokered by the Commonwealth and the SADC. They agreed to surrender their weapons before talks resumed with the government.

After the cease-fire, the United Nations Development Programme (UNDP) held a seminar with LDF members. The UNDP facilitator, John O. Kakonge, outlined the responsibilities of the disciplined forces. Their defined role was to contribute toward nation-building, maintain law and order, protect lives and property, defend sovereignty and territorial integrity, and comply with peace support obligations under the United Nations.[42] In his conclusion, Kakonge quoted Robert McNamara: "Security means development. Security is not military hardware, though it may include it. Security is not military force, though it may include it. Security is not traditional military activity, though it may encompass it. Security is development and without development there can be no security."[43]

Dr Kakonge's emphasis was on the positive role that the army could play in building a peaceful co-existence in Lesotho. In his terms, all government institutions, including the army, were responsible for finding lasting peace in the country.

After the military crisis, conflict ensued between the BCP government and Moshoeshoe II over his reinstatement after his 1990 deposition by the military government. Instead of negotiating the reinstatement process, the BCP government launched an inquiry into the activities of Moshoeshoe II from before independence. In taking this direction, the government did not consult with Letsie III who was then head of state. Seeing the refusal of the BCP government to reinstate his father, he dissolved the BCP government on 17 August 1994. In so doing, Letsie III suspended certain sections of the Lesotho constitution with Order Nos. 1 and 2 of 1994, which indicated that the government of Lesotho, which hitherto existed prior to 17 August 1994, was dissolved. King Letsie III toppled the BCP government, betraying the scale of instability in Lesotho. After the coup, Letsie III merely cited what he termed a petition by thousands of the Basotho as the reason for his decision. Thereafter, he instituted an Interim Council of Ministers.

Civil society in Lesotho condemned King Letsie III's action, but could not convince him to change his decision. Mokhehle appealed to SADC for his reinstatement. On 25 August 1994, both Mokhehle and King Letsie III were invited to SADC talks in Pretoria. The deliberations went on without significant success. Both the King and Mokhehle were encouraged to hold talks and resolve the impasse as soon as possible. After long talks, on 14 September 1994, a Statement of Understanding was signed between King Letsie III and Mokhehle in the presence of presidents Nelson Mandela, Mugabe and Masire. The three "Ms" were guarantors of the agreement. It signalled the end of hostilities between the BCP government and Letsie III, reinstated Mokhehle as prime minister and made Moshoeshoe II the head of state. Lastly, no one was supposed to be prosecuted for his or her role in the 1994 royal coup.[44] After the signing of the document, the Basotho left their offices and celebrated in the streets of Maseru. They danced on the pavements and motor vehicles hooted along the main street. Mokhehle told the cheering crowd that he thanked them and the presidents of South Africa, Botswana and Zimbabwe for their efforts to defend the constitution and democracy.

In his speech at the reinstatement of Moshoeshoe II, President Mugabe encouraged a national dialogue among Lesotho's leaders, one that would involve consultation and interaction between the people, the government and its monarchy, with each respecting the other's responsibility in nation-building. He concluded: "Now is the time for countries of our region to close the chapter of internal crisis and work for the improvement of the lives of our people; no meaningful development can occur if there is no peace and stability."[45]

In 1998, Lesotho held elections. The LCD achieved a landslide victory, taking 79 out of 80 seats in the National Assembly. The opposition parties, consisting of the BCP, the BNP, the MFP and other small parties, joined forces to contest the fairness of the election. They were determined to unseat the government or at least render the country ungovernable in response to what they perceived as a conspiracy between the LCD and the Independent Electoral Commission. Molapo Qhobela, the BNP leader and the spokesperson of the opposition, declared that the elections were rigged (*li pheuoe, li a nkha*). Under troika leadership, several groups from the SADC arrived in Lesotho to broker an amicable solution. All the stakeholders finally agreed to a commission of inquiry under the headship of Justice Pius Langa, the Deputy President of the South African Constitutional Court. The commission had serious concerns about apparent irregularities and discrepancies, but was unable to say conclusively that the elections should be declared invalid. As noted earlier, this was an unpopular finding for the opposition groups and led to protest. President Mosisili appealed for SADC assistance. The response was the start of Operation Boleas in Lesotho, which facilitated talks over issues such as holding new elections, drafting a code of conduct for political parties and taking steps to improve police professionalism and army discipline. Finally, the parties concluded a Memorandum of Agreement, which called for elections to be held within 15 to 18 months. It was also agreed that the parties that contested the elections would form an Interim Political Authority (IPA) which would lead the country into the election process.[46]

All the parties were satisfied with the arrangement because it accommodated them in the interim governance of the country. Since the formation of the IPA there has been stability in Lesotho. Charles Mofeli, the former leader of the United Democratic Party in Lesotho, argued that peace is a necessity in the country: "Lesotho cannot afford to be at war against itself when other nations are busy setting up the goals of national peace and reconciliation . . . I call upon all Basotho, of all political, religious and social persuasions to stand up and shout with one voice that Lesotho declares a truce on all internal hostilities and recrimination."[47] According to Mofeli, no individual can bring peace in Lesotho. Instead, collective efforts are important in restoring lasting peace in the territory. Basotho should continue their rise from the ashes of conflict. Whatever the difficulties, Lesotho continues to strive for peace.

Elections were held on 23 May 2002, as decided and agreed upon within the IPA. The IPA had scrapped the old system of elections and introduced a new system that contained a mixture of a first-past-the-post system and proportional representation. This system was the innovation of the Basotho themselves. It was a home-brewed alternative to the electoral crisis that has engulfed Lesotho for many decades. Under the new electoral system, voters cast two ballots, one for a local candidate, another for one of the 19 parties running in the election.

On 30 June, the election results were announced as follows: LCD 54%, the BNP 22%, and the LPC 7%. The LCD won 77 out of 80 contested seats in the 120 seat parliament. The LPC secured one seat, while the results in other seats were invalidated because candidates had died. Under the new system assigning 40 seats based on proportional representation, the opposition BNP secured 21 seats while the LCP got 4 seats. The rest were shared among the remaining opposition parties. About 10 parties form the Lesotho parliament. It was the first time that more than one political party has been represented in Lesotho's parliament. This is a foundation for a lasting political solution in the country. The international and SADC observers declared the election free and fair. Despite that, the main opposition party, the BNP, under the leadership of Lekhanya, asked for an audit of the results, suggesting that the 2002 general elections may have been rigged. (In fact only the BNP and the LPC were not satisfied with the election outcome.) The reaction of Lekhanya can be attributed to two factors. Firstly, despite having been the chairperson of the Military Council (1986–91), he did not come to power through an election, but through a coup. Secondly, he lost power through a coup, before the elections in Lesotho. Therefore, the electoral process has not been part of his political career.

On 4 June 2002, Lesotho's prime minster, Mosisili, was sworn in for a second five-year term following his party's victory in an election rejected by the opposition. In his inaugural speech, he noted that his government faced the challenge of continuing to promote stability and democracy. Lekhanya commented about the inauguration that "this is [an] illegal ceremony. We still insist that pending the finalization of our forensic audit test we are not in a position to say the elections were free and fair." Despite his defiant attitude, at the time of writing Lekhanya had confirmed that the opposition parties would take their seats in parliament, which is a hopeful sign for political stability in the country.

The 2002 election in Lesotho was relatively more acceptable than other elections held since independence because of the following:

❑ The collaboration of Basotho politicians within the IPA.
❑ The transparency, trust and appreciation of political differences that was promoted during the period leading up to the election.
❑ All the parties had constant discussions with the Independent Electoral Commission (IEC), which built trust and confidence in the IEC.
❑ The electoral model was a home-brewed innovation of the Basotho themselves and they all had ownership of it.

❏ Lastly, the Basotho were tired of the endless political chaos, particularly that of 1998 which resulted in the destruction of Maseru city centre and other towns, and in job losses and disinvestment by some foreign investors.

The general reaction to the outcome of the 2002 elections gives hope for optimism, peace and stability in Lesotho.

Present and Future Opportunities for Reconciliation

Despite substantial political turmoil, Lesotho has not experienced the levels of violence found in many other African countries. At present, there is a favourable platform for reconciliation. The LDF and the LLA have reason for reconciliation in the wake of their past conflict. The LDF was protecting the BNP government whereas the LLA fought to topple the BNP government so that the BCP could take over. Ordinary civilians also suffered at the hands of both the LDF and the LLA. In 1970, the BNP denied the BCP an opportunity to rule, an event that continues to foster animosity. Politicians thus have occasion to become reconciled with each other, especially if the process can help resolve differences about what counts as a fair election. This suggests that a crucial area for reconciliation is the dispute over leadership and the problem of how to facilitate political participation and a culture of questioning that has been absent since the 1998 destruction of Maseru.

The sons and daughters of Moshoeshoe are bound together by the concept "we are one nation – *re bana ba thari*".[48] The Basotho remain a single group with a sense of their common identity. The notion of family is strongly embraced and there is little emphasis on ethnic diversity. Lesotho is a small country and families have links in other constituencies or villages because of inter-marriages. When political turmoil breaks out, it is often perceived as a family feud rather than political conflict. Conflict is frequently perceived as something that creates enemies among families. It is also believed to retard collective progress and advancement. The means to resolve conflict vary. In the rural areas, the interventions of chiefs are still valued – through holding open air assemblies and collective deliberations about the causes of conflict and their solutions. The level of political involvement in rural areas is relatively low, a tendency that reduces party power in particular areas. In urban areas, the situation is different. Political parties like the BCP and BNP initially start protests with court petitions. When they do not succeed, they resort to violence, especially if this can dent the image of the ruling government. As was evident during the looting and destruction of property after the 1998 elections, violence is also used by criminal elements to advance their interests. The majority of Lesotho's civilians do not have access to lethal weapons, a situation that helps promote peace and reconciliation.

Peace is a central concern to the Basotho themselves. Both the Lesotho coat of arms and the national anthem emphasise the need to preserve, sustain and respect peace, with the latter calling for "*Khotso, Pula, Nala* – Peace, Rain and Prosperity*". To find a lasting solution to Lesotho's political problems, the country's leadership has agreed to resolve their differences at the negotiating table. This approach was facilitated by the SADC after the 1998 election where all parties were accommodated in the IPA. The inclusive character of the IPA has been described as the primary basis for reconciliation and the creation of tolerance. Article 13 of the IPA Act prescribes that decisions shall be taken by consensus. This appears vital to avoid the charges of majority domination that have led to acrimony in the past.[49] The IPA can also use arbitration as a means of resolving specific log-jams. Despite the IPA's consistently difficult relationship with the executive and legislature, it continues to pursue the objectives of reconciliation, consensus and tolerance. New political institutions, including the IPA and the IEC, designed to provide political peace and reconciliation in Lesotho, have proven valuable and resilient.

Laurie Nathan, the director of the Centre for Conflict Resolution in Cape Town, has argued that there are a number of elements involved in the creation of peace and reconciliation. To varying degrees, these elements are beginning to appear in Lesotho. Firstly, there needs to be political will; the main parties must be committed to peace and accept that reconciliation is not the responsibility of one party but all stakeholders. Secondly, all sides should also work toward collaborative problem-solving. Compromise has become a "dirty word" to politicians, a sign of weakness. It need not be. The main parties to the dispute must be willing to accommodate each other. In the past, both the LCD and the BCP have approached each other as adversaries, bargaining in win-lose terms. This has led to escalating animosity. Thus, there is some concern not to look for zero-sum solutions to the present troubles. Using a win-win approach, parties may begin to recognise their common interests and establish the grounds for interaction, if not alliance. This work will have to be inclusive, especially if future accords are to be implemented and sustained. This need was a key concern in the 1998 Statement of Agreement.[50]

To achieve peace and reconciliation in Lesotho, it may be important to have external support. Few long-standing national disputes are resolved without some kinds of technical advice, mediation or facilitation. The form of this assistance, however, has proven controversial, especially given that in 1994, during the LDF mutiny, the BCP government's appeal for SADC intervention led opposition parties to request SADC not to intervene. From 1998, the ruling LCD also relied heavily on foreign assistance, something the BCP objected to: "Any intervention from outside will be interpreted by our people as aggression against King Letsie and his Kingdom. So whatever happens from now, we are ready. Lesotho is a sovereign state and not a SADC colony." This history suggests that there will need to be local ownership of the process. Those giving external support cannot prescribe or impose a solution. The solutions must come from parties involved in the dispute themselves. During the LDF mutiny in 1994, the BCP government was not prepared to negotiate with the opposition parties to find the solution to the problems. Because it suspected the BNP of fuelling the conflict within the LDF, the BCP appealed for SADC intervention without consulting parliament, the National Security Council, the king and other opposition parties. In their findings of the root cause of the LDF conflict, both presidents Mugabe and Masire confirmed that this unilateral action hampered reconciliation and national dialogue.

Civil societies and non-partisan facilitation and mediation must also be engaged in the process. It is not enough for the political elite to broker a settlement. All the parties in Lesotho have endorsed this view. That is why after the disputed election outcome of 1998, the opposition alliance (BNP, BCP, MFP, etc.) went to court and made submissions to the Langa Commission and the Leon Commission. To greater and lesser degrees, parties have recognised the potential role of non-partisan institutions, bodies that can assist participants to understand the position of the other sides and help establish the rules of the negotiating game. The latter is crucial to Lesotho given the long history of parties agreeing to enter elections and then contesting their outcome on sometimes dubious grounds. As disputes are inevitable, there is increasing support for management mechanisms provided by institutions like the Lesotho Network for Conflict Management. The constitution, the courts and the legal system may also come to play a role. In a conflict-ridden society, local peace committees that take into account all parties may help individuals and groups to adhere to codes of conduct. The parties in Lesotho have recognised the importance of direct, face-to-face dialogue. This is evident in the terms of the IPA, which is directly promoting dialogue among Lesotho politicians. Though there are differences, parties have accepted that the destiny of the country is not an individual but a collective effort. The international community can help, but the initiative has to come from the Basotho themselves. Some appropriate solutions can be found in Lesotho's own indigenous systems, which are almost everywhere castigated as backward and primitive. But the solution lies with the people of Lesotho themselves, a position echoed by Ayittey: "The time has come for African leaders to re-examine themselves and find out whether they are prepared to face and overcome the challenges facing the continent to make it what the founding fathers had meant it to be."[51] Basotho themselves have to decide the future of their own state and they will have to do this against the powerful forces of globalisation and regionalism. Lesotho has reached the crossroads where the centripetal forces of nationhood and nationalism are pitted against the centrifugal forces of globalism and regionalism. The nature of the response to this challenge by both political and civil society will be critical in reshaping Lesotho's future. Conflict resolution skills are needed (and civil society has an important role to play here) to heal divisions in society and to bring antagonistic factions back into constructive dialogue with one another.

Participants at a recent workshop on justice and reconciliation agreed in principle that Lesotho may have cause to form a kind of Truth and Reconciliation Commission, similar to that adopted in South Africa but tailored to the express needs and interests of the Basotho. However, a TRC-like structure will not be popular with some elements of the LDF, BNP, LLA and BCP (including the police) to the degree that they have been implicated in the violation of human rights. Both the police and army mutinies of 1994, among others, were instigated by the BCP government's commissions of inquiry into their activities. This view was clearly confirmed by M. J. Lekhanya, the BNP leader, when he said: "*re mabitla a liketsahalo tse nyalosang*" [we are the graves of the unpleasant events]. An investigation of the past does run the risk of creating further division.

In a 2000 address, South African Justice Langa illustrated the complex demands of reconciliation when he argued, "a strong programme for reconciliation must include strong efforts to address the sense of grievance in the victim community . . . reconciliation and forgiveness must never be taken for granted . . . somebody must surely take responsibility and everyone else must recognise that we are all part of this nation in which these things have happened . . . reconciliation is not an event. It will require the on-going commitment of all levels of society . . . what was deeply divided must be united."[52] The submission by Justice Langa is true; reconciliation is not automatic. It requires hard work and that participants be able to make genuine attempts to understand those from whom they are alienated. It is evident from some of the controversies that have surrounded the IPA that this work will be difficult for the political parties.

There are risks with reconciliation in Lesotho. The spirit of give and take is not and has not been part of Lesotho's history. Reconciliation requires true openness. Most of the critical issues in Lesotho politics are regarded as "classified, top secret – *pinyane*", and the Basotho themselves do not feel free to talk about them, making the situation more complicated. The depoliticisation of government institutions like the army and the police also carries risks. The army has tasted power and is aware of its strength. A shift in mindset will be important but difficult to achieve. It will take time to build trust and institutions of accountability. There will also be a need to overcome the frequent conflation of national and self-interest that has been evident in the actions of some politicians.

According to those at a workshop held in Lesotho in 2001, there is a shared sense that peace, justice and reconciliation must start in the heart of the individual, the family, the community, then the nation. This movement takes time and depends on the open collaboration of everyone, from the individual to the government. It was also agreed that it is important to invest resources in education for peace and reconciliation. The education should be for all – young and old, members of political parties, the community and government institutions. Peace, justice, reconciliation, conflict avoidance and conflict management all go together. In the end, the people of Lesotho are on their own. They cannot always depend on international intervention when peace is threatened.[53]

The nation and its people must create peace and reconciliation together, borrowing lessons from others only when appropriate. This work will most likely call for significant interventions from the NGO community, most of which works under the umbrella body of the Lesotho Council of Non-Governmental Organisations (LCN). This structure is relatively young, as it was founded in May 1990.[54]

There are various type of NGOs in Lesotho. On the one side are institutional bodies, many of which are foreign-controlled, owned and initiated. Their senior staff tend to be expatriates. They also have good management systems although some lack stability and strong links to the international community. They show a strong interest in local resource development and tend to have a high degree of stability in terms of performance and sustainability. On the other hand, there are local groups that can be classified under two sub-categories: community based organisations (CBOs) that operate at grassroots, village and community levels, and supra-local groups that operate at district, regional and national levels. Both kinds are locally controlled, owned and influenced. There is a degree of concern for local resource development. Both groups tend to have low levels of organisational stability and viability. CBOs outnumber other types and show the greatest diversity in terms of stability and viability. Some are active and indicate some potential for growth, while some are just organisations in name with very little activity. It is still relatively early days for civil society in Lesotho.

NOTES

1 The wars and the migrations of the Difaqane were a by-product of socio-political revolution within communities and wider loyalties. It was a genuine process of nation-building among the tribes.

2 B. Makalo Khaketla, *Lesotho 1970: An African Coup under the Microscope* (Morija: Morija Printing Works, 2000), viii.

3 Geoffrey Tylden, *The Rise of the Basuto* (Cape Town: Juta, 1950), ix.

4 Mokete L. Pherudi, The Mountain Kingdom of Lesotho, 1986–1997: A Democracy in Crisis (Bloemfontein: Unpublished Ph.D. Thesis, Free State University, 2000), 3–5.

5 Mokete L. Pherudi, "Intolerance Elections Outcome: Focus on Africa," *UNIQWA Research Chronicle* 2 (2000): 2–5.

6 Rok Ajulu, "From Collaboration to Dilemma: A Historical Background to Lesotho's Election of 1993," in *Democratisation and Demilitarisation in Lesotho: The General Election of 1993 and its Aftermath*, eds. Roger Southall and T. Petlane (Pretoria, Colorpress: 1995), 16.

7 *The Weekly Mail*, 30 April–03 May 1992, 17.

8 *Lesotho Today*, 13–19 Jan 1994, 1–2.

9 *Mo-Africa*, 7 October 1994, 1. Both the LDF and the LLA served different parties, the BNP and BCP respectively. They were arch rivals, particularly because the LDF was formed to counteract the activities of the LLA. After the BCP victory in the 1993 elections there was a fear among LDF members that the BCP would seek revenge by sacking and replacing them with the members of the LLA.

10 K. Makoa, "The Political Crisis in Lesotho and the Role of External Forces," *Africa Insight* 24 (1994): 226.

11 "Lesotho Policemen Seize HD," *The Citizen*, 8 February 1997, 15.

12 "Mutiny Ends after Police Station is Seized by Lesotho Army," *Business Day*, 17 February 1997.

13 "30 Arrested and a Police Mutiny Ends," *Pretoria News*, 17 February 1997.

14 "Bizarre Move by Lesotho Leader," *Pretoria News*, 10 June 1997.

15 Khabele Matlosa, "Lesotho after 1998 Elections: What Went Wrong?" *Southern Africa Political and Economic Monthly* 11 (1998): 5; interview with Sekara Mafisa, chairperson of the Independent Electoral Commission during the 1998 general elections, 4 July 2001.

16 It is worth noting that in 1994, when the king dissolved the BCP government,

Retshelisitsoe Sekhonyana, leader of the BNP, and Vincent Malebo, leader of the MFP, were part of the interim government which was vehemently criticised by Molapo Qhobela, leader of the BCP, as unconstitutional and tantamount to a coup. Ironically, in 1998 the three leaders spoke with one voice, arguing that the king should dissolve a constituted government and establish a government of national unity that could arrange new elections.

17 Commission of inquiry into conduct of the Lesotho General Elections, 23 May 1998, 1.

18 Ibid, 28.

19 Sechaba ka'Nkosi and Howard Barrell, "SA Troops Alert as Maseru Mutinies," *The Mail and Guardian*, 18–24 September 1998. Reprinted at www.mg.co.za/mg/news/98sep2/18sep-lesotho.html (accessed 25 October 2001).

20 Matlosa, "Lesotho after 1998 elections," 17.

21 Pherudi, *The Mountain Kingdom of Lesotho*, 253; Institute of Southern African Studies-National University of Lesotho (ISAS-NUL), "Lesotho Clippings: Post-Electoral Crisis," 2 November 1998, 71.

22 S. L. Barnard and Mokete L. Pherudi, "The Dawn of the Political Cloud over Lesotho 1998 Elections," *Journal for Contemporary History* 24 (1999): 51.

23 Robert Edgar, *Prophets with Honour: A Documentary History of Lekhotla la Bafo* (Johannesburg: Ravan Press, 1998).

24 "Do We Need a Peace Process in Lesotho?" *Work for Justice – Newsletter of Transformation Resource Centre – Maseru* 32 (1992): 7.

25 Stephen J. Gill, *A Short History of Lesotho* (Morija: Morija Printing Works, 1993), 213.

26 Khaketla, *Lesotho*, 175.

27 "The Case of Lesotho," *The Cape Times*, 3 February 1970, 1.

28 Ponts'o Sekatle, "King or Country: The Lesotho Crisis of August 1994," *Indicator South Africa* 12 (1994): 68.

29 George B. N. Ayittey, *Africa in Chaos* (London: Macmillan, 1998), 50, 75.

30 Winston C. M. Maqutu, *Constitutional History of Lesotho* (Mazenod: Mazenod Institute, 1990), 74.

31 Mokete L. Pherudi and S. L. Barnard, "Lesotho coup d'états: Political decay and erosion of democracy," *Journal for Contemporary History* 26, No. 1 (June 2001), 73.

32 Pherudi, *The Mountain Kingdom of Lesotho*, 134.

33 *Mo-Africa*, 9 October 1998, 7.

34 "Lesotho Mutineers Vow to Fight SA Intervention Forces," *The Sunday Independent*, 16 February 1997.

35 Khabele Matlosa, "The Post Election Crisis in Lesotho," *African Association of Political Science* 4 (1999): 2.

36 ISAS-NUL, "Lesotho Clippings," 2 November 1998, 36.

37 "Army Mutiny in Lesotho," *The Citizen*, 27 January 1994.

38 Transformation Resource Centre – Maseru, Statement by Political Leaders on the Crisis in Lesotho, 26 January 1994.

39 Interview with Retshelisitsoe E. Sekhonyana, the then leader of the BNP, 17 October 1998.

40 Pherudi, *The Mountain Kingdom of Lesotho*, 138.

41 Lesotho National Archives, Report on Presidential Visit to the Kingdom of Lesotho, 16.

42 John O. Kakonge, (UNDP) Resident Representative – Seminar on the Role of the Disciplined Forces, 4–6 July 1995.

43 Robert McNamara, *The Essence of Security* (New York: Harper and Row, 1968), 251.

44 Lesotho National Archives, Statement of Understanding between His Majesty Letsie III and Dr Ntsu Mokhehle, 14 September 1994.

45 Ibid, Speech Delivered by His Excellency the President, Cde R. G. Mugabe, at the Occasion Marking the Reinstatement of His Majesty King Moshoeshoe II of the Kingdom of Lesotho, 25 January 1995.

46 *Mololi*, "Memorandum of Agreement," 2(14), 14 October 1998.

47 "Lekhanya Will Not Step Down," *The Mirror*, 14 July 1989.

48 Interview with N. C. Ntsane, former Secretary General of the BNP and the present Director of Agriculture in the Eastern Free State, 1 December 1997.

49 "The IPA's Experiences in the Promotion of Political Reconciliation and Tolerance," Workshop on Justice and Reconciliation in Lesotho, 29–31 October 2001.

50 "Do We Need a Peace Process in Lesotho?" *Work for Justice – Newsletter of Transformation Resource Centre – Maseru*, 55 (2001): 3.

51 Attiyey, *Africa in Chaos.*

52 Pius N. Langa, "Transcending a Century of Injustice," in *Transcending a Century of Justice,* ed. Charles Villa-Vicencio (Cape Town: IJR, 2001), 20–21.

53 "Some Lessons Learned," Workshop on Justice and Reconciliation in Lesotho, 29–31 October 2001.

54 Maria Motebang, "Lesotho's Non-Governmental Organisation: Competent Watch-Dogs for Democracy?" *Review of Southern African Studies* 3 (1999): 2–14.

RESOURCES

Books, Articles, Media Reports

Ajulu, Rok. "From Collaboration to Dilemma: A Historical Background to Lesotho's Election of 1993." In *Democratisation and Demilitarisation in Lesotho: The General Election of 1993 and its Aftermath*, edited by Roger Southall and T. Petlane. Pretoria, Colorpress: 1995.

Ayittey, George B. N. *Africa in Chaos*. London: Macmillan, 1998.

Barnard, S. L. and Mokete L. Pherudi. "The Dawn of the Political Cloud over Lesotho 1998 Elections," *Journal for Contemporary History* 24 (1999).

Edgar, Robert. *Prophets with Honour: A Documentary History of Lekhotla la Bafo*. Johannesburg: Ravan Press, 1998.

Gill, Stephen J. *A Short History of Lesotho*. Morija: Morija Printing Works, 1993.

Institute of Southern African Studies-National University of Lesotho (ISSA-NUL). Lesotho Clippings: Post Electoral Crisis, 2 November 1998.

Khaketla, B. Makalo. *Lesotho 1970: An African Coup under the Microscope*. Morija: Morija Printing Works, 2000.

Langa, Pius N. "Transcending a Century of Injustice." In *Transcending a Century of Justice,* edited by Charles Villa-Vicencio. Cape Town: IJR, 2001.

Lesotho National Archives. "Statement of Understanding between His Majesty Letsie III and Dr Ntsu Mokhehle, 1994."

———. "Speech Delivered by His Excellency the President, Cde R. G. Mugabe, at the Occasion Marking the Reinstatement of His Majesty King Moshoeshoe II of the Kingdom of Lesotho, 25 January 1995".

Makoa, K. "The Political Crisis in Lesotho and the Role of External Forces," *Africa Insight* 24 (1994).

Maqutu, Winston C. M. *Constitutional History of Lesotho*. Mazenod: Mazenod Institute, 1990.

Matlosa, Khabele. "Lesotho after 1998 Elections: What Went Wrong?" *Southern Africa Political and Economic Monthly* 11 (1998).

———. "The Post Election Crisis in Lesotho," *African Association of Political Science* 4 (1999).

McNamara, Robert. *The Essence of Security*. New York: Harper and Row, 1968.

Motebang, Maria. "Lesotho's Non-Governmental Organisation: Competent Watch-Dogs for Democracy?" *Review of Southern African Studies 3 (1999)*.

Pherudi, Mokete L. The Mountain Kingdom of Lesotho, 1986–1997: A Democracy in Crisis. Bloemfontein: Unpublished Ph.D. Thesis, Free State University, 2000.

———. "Intolerance Elections Outcome: Focus on Africa," *UNIQWA Research Chronicle* 2 (2000): 2–5.

Sekatle, Ponts'o. "King or Country: The Lesotho Crisis of August 1994," *Indicator South Africa* 12 (1994).

Tylden, Geoffrey. *The Rise of the Basuto*. Cape Town: Juta, 1950.

Weisfelder, Richard F. *Political Contention in Lesotho 1952–1965*. Morija: Morija Printing Works, 1999.

Local NGOs

Lesotho Network for Conflict Management: PO Box 988, Maseru, 100 Lesotho. Phone: 09622 322038. Fax: 09266 310228. Contact person: S. Santho.

Transformation Resource Centre (TRC): PO Box 1388, Carlton Centre, Third Floor, Kings Way, Maseru, 100 Lesotho. Phone: 09622 322038. Fax: 09622 32279. Contact persons: M. Senyane and K. Matlosa.

LESOTHO COUNTRY INFORMATION

Geography
Location: Southern Africa, an enclave of South Africa.
Cities: *Capital:* Maseru (1997 pop. 386 000). *Other cities:* Teyateyaneng (240 754), Leribe (300 160), Mafeteng (211 970), Mohale's Hoek (184 034).

People
Nationality: *Noun:* Mosotho (sing.); Basotho (pl.). *Adjective:* Basotho.
Population (2000 est.): 2 202 954.
Annual growth rate (2000 est.): 1.4%.
Ethnic groups: Basotho 99.7%; white 1 600; Asian descent 800.
Religions: 80% Christian, including Roman Catholic (majority), Lesotho Evangelical, Anglican, other denominations.
Languages: *Official:* Sesotho and English. *Others:* Zulu, Xhosa.
Education (1998): *Years compulsory:* None. *Literacy:* 71.3%.
Health (1997 est.): *Infant mortality rate:* 80.3/1 000. *Life expectancy:* 51.66 years. *HIV infection rate:* 8.35%.
Workforce (1997 est.): 689 000. 86% subsistence agriculture.

Economy
GDP (1997 est.): $5.1 billion.
GDP real growth rate (1997 est.): 9% (although this decreased significantly in 1998 because of political unrest).
Per capita income (1997 est.): $2 500.
Inflation rate (1998 est.): 8.7%.
Natural resources: Water, agricultural and grazing land, some diamonds and other minerals. Lesotho is an exporter of excess labour.
Agriculture (1997 est.): 14% of GDP. *Products:* corn, wheat, sorghum, barley, peas, beans, asparagus, wool, mohair, livestock. *Arable land:* 11%.
Industry (1997 est.): 46% of GDP. *Types:* food, beverages, textiles, handicrafts, construction, tourism.
Trade (1996 est.): *Exports:* $218 million: clothing, furniture, footwear and wool. *Major markets:* South Africa, Botswana, Swaziland, Namibia, North America. *Imports:* $1.1 billion: corn, clothing, building materials, vehicles, machinery, medicines, petroleum products. *Major suppliers:* South Africa, Asia.
Economic aid (1998): *Primary donors:* World Bank, International Monetary Fund, European Union, United Nations, United Kingdom, other bilateral donors. *US aid:* $400 000.

Military
Military expenditure: Dollar figures: N/A.
Military expenditure: Percent of GDP: N/A.

Demographic information is drawn from that compiled by the United States Department of State. See http://www.state.gov/r/pa/ei/bgn

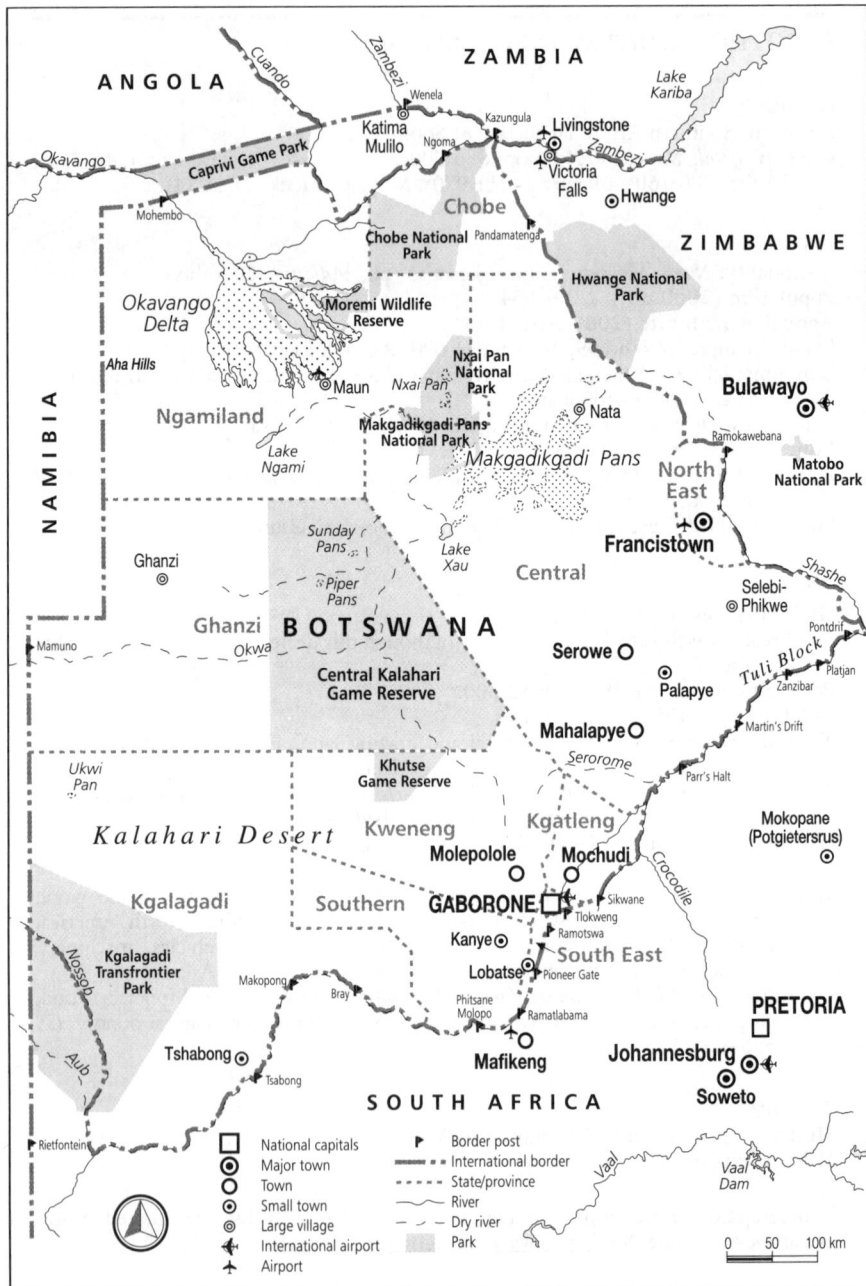

ANGOLA

ZAMBIA

Cuando

Zambezi

Wenela

Katima
Mulilo

Ngoma

Kazungula

Livingstone

Lake
Kariba

Okavango

Caprivi Game Park

Zambezi

Mohembo

Victoria
Falls

Chobe

Hwange

Okavango
Delta

Chobe National
Park

Pandamatenga

ZIMBABWE

Aha Hills

Moremi Wildlife
Reserve

Hwange National
Park

Ngamiland

Maun

Nxai Pan

Nxai Pan
National
Park

Nata

Bulawayo

Makgadikgadi Pans
National Park

Makgadikgadi Pans

Ramokawebana

NAMIBIA

Lake
Ngami

Lake
Xau

North
East

Matobo
National Park

Ghanzi

Sunday
Pans

Central

Francistown

Ghanzi

Piper
Pans

BOTSWANA

Serowe

Selebi-
Phikwe

Shashe

Pontdrif

Mamuno

Okwa

Palapye

Tuli Block

Platjan

Central Kalahari
Game Reserve

Mahalapye

Zanzibar

Martin's Drift

Ukwi
Pan

Khutse
Game Reserve

Serorome

Parr's Halt

Kalahari Desert

Kweneng

Kgatleng

Mokopane
(Potgietersrus)

Kgalagadi

Molepolole

Mochudi

Southern

GABORONE

Sikwane

Kgalagadi
Transfrontier
Park

Makopong

Bray

Kanye

Tlokweng

Ramotswa

South East

Crocodile

Nossob

Phitsane
Molopo

Lobatse

Pioneer Gate

Ramatlabama

PRETORIA

Aub

Tshabong

Tsabong

Mafikeng

Johannesburg

Rietfontein

SOUTH AFRICA

Soweto

Vaal

Vaal
Dam

National capitals
Major town
Town
Small town
Large village
International airport
Airport

Border post
International border
State/province
River
Dry river
Park

0   50   100 km

Chapter 15

Botswana: The Hopes and Fears of Consolidation

GAPE KABOYAKGOSI

While its critics have rightly pointed out various anomalies, Botswana's democratic system is one of the best examples of stability in Africa.[1] A combination of circumstances accounts for this success. The country has had multi-party politics since its independence from Britain in 1966. Mineral-led economic growth averaged nine percent annually over the entire post-colonial period, returns from which were invested in assisting the country's poor. The country's governing elite has shared a commitment to astute economic management of the country's resources, a concern for human rights and a foreign policy based strongly on non-aggression in the unstable southern African region. However, in the 1990s, Botswana's democracy encountered obstacles and lately the country has found itself faced with a host of problems that require decisive, proactive thinking on the part of the leadership. Some of these challenges, such as the rise in acrimonious ethnic sentiment and HIV/Aids, are relatively new. Others – like the decline in ethical and accountable governance, voter apathy, a highly fragmented opposition, threats to the economic base, growing inequalities and poverty levels, and rising unemployment – have a longer history.

The basic thrust of this chapter is that, while Botswana has made recognisable achievements in the economic, social and political spheres, such advances are now under serious threat of reversal. The leadership and the nation of Botswana face the challenge of reinvigorating the country's democratic institutions and making the system open for all citizens. Botswana must look beyond what it has achieved in past decades, into a future of more participation by citizens in the political and economic spheres of the country.

The Face of Conflict

While the conflict in Botswana is not a hot, open war, there are problems that the country has no experience in dealing with and which threaten its stability. An important challenge is the highly fragmentary nature of political opposition. The opposition's weakness is long-standing and means that voters lack credible alternatives to the ruling party. Since the late pre-independence days, the opposition showed tendencies to self-destruction, a characteristic that continues. Before the first election in 1965, two parties were the major contestants for state control in Botswana. Besides the Botswana Democratic Party (BDP), there was the Botswana People's Party (BPP). The BPP split up because of the influence of two factions in the South African struggle. Its leader Phillip Matante, who had attachments to the African National Congress, had disagreements with Motsamai Mpho, who had connections with the Pan Africanist Congress. Mpho then left to form the Botswana Independent Party (BIP). From then on, and up to 1994, the BIP's electoral performances were largely insignificant, gaining on average only four seats in the National Assembly.

After years of toil as a party with only three members of parliament, the Botswana National Front (BNF) numbers in parliament rose to 13 in 1994. This gain was attributed to the newly delimited electoral regions, which allotted eight more constituencies in the urban areas, the BNF's electoral mainstay. It was also helped by corruption scandals that rocked the BDP government in the early 1990s. Rising unemployment and the economic downturn in the same period, as well as the government's low civil service wage, also influenced the opposition's gains. These gains turned to losses in 1999, when the BNF had another split. Eleven of the members present in parliament left the party to form the Botswana Congress Party (BCP), which became the official opposition in parliament, despite the fact that no party of this name had ever contested elections. However, the BCP performed poorly in the 1999 elections, where they gained only one seat to the BNF's six.

The BNF's organisational dysfunctions cripple the party's operations. It is faced with the prospect of electing a new leader, with the impending resignation of Dr Kenneth Koma. The party is divided over a successor, with one faction supporting Peter Woto, Koma's current deputy. The other supports Otsweletse Moupo's bid for leadership. What has made this situation more precarious is that Koma's public support for Woto is regarded as a manoeuvre to ensure his control of the party even in retirement. In a recent show of defiance, one of the factions in the BNF youth wing organised a youth congress in Kang, where elections were held without the sanction of the mainly Koma-loyal central committee.[2]

In this environment, voter apathy is a significant problem. Since Botswana's first general elections in 1965, voter turnout has been, for the most part, on a downward trend. In 1965, the turnout was 69.4% of the registered population. In 1969, the turnout was only 37.5% and, in 1974, 26.2%. The trend of low voter turnout has continued, a malady for a young democracy. The president of the Botswana Christian Council, in an attempt to explain the low voter turnout, argued that citizens are making statements in not voting, possibly to show a need for systematic reform.[3]

After three decades of self-rule as a unitary state and a unified nation, there are indications that Botswana's ethnic harmony might now be in danger, and thus the country's continued existence as a unified entity could be under threat. Having governed with the constitution that was partly drafted by the British in 1966, Botswana now finds that the same constitution is a great source of ethnic discontent. The constitution does not recognise the existence of certain ethnic groups. Instead, it gives primacy to eight tribes whose major source of identity and commonality is the Setswana language, one of the two official languages in the country (the other being English). In 2000, President Festus Mogae appointed a commission to investigate the alleged discriminatory aspects of the constitution. The commission came about after parliament adopted a motion that requested the government "in order to promote Nation Building to amend Sections 77, 78, and 79 of the constitution, to make it tribally neutral".[4] Among the many findings by the commission was that the composition of the House of Chiefs should be rethought with a view to include all the other tribes. The commission also recommended that "no tribe or ethnic community should be named in the Constitution". The commission also went on to find that the naming in the constitution of the eight so-called major tribes, while others were not so named, had the import of relegating the other tribes "to the inferior status of *merathswana* (minor and/or subordinate tribes)". Added to that, the commission, whose findings emanated from a national consultative process, also found that "the constitution condones and legitimises the discrimination of the unlisted tribes with all its perceived consequences, including the marginalisation of their cultures, languages and identities".[5]

What would probably have been the usual political haggles in retooling the constitution became a major source of ethnic tension, especially given the recent formation of *Pitso Ya Batswana* (PYB). PYB seized, as their first major task, the challenge of swaying Batswana to vote against some suggested changes to the judiciary. PYB opposed the "yes" vote, which was encouraged by Mogae, citing allegations that one ethnic group, the Kalanga, dominates the judiciary. The Kalanga are incidentally one of the groups that the constitution fails to mention. PYB's contention was that voting "yes" would be tantamount to an endorsement of domination.

PYB also claimed that the president was silently endorsing ethnic domination of the Kalanga in the judiciary.[6] PYB met their match in the Society for the Promotion of Ikalanga Language (SPIL). SPIL is an association formed for the promotion of Kalanga culture. The public exchanges between SPIL and PYB in recent times have been anything but harmonious. For instance, at a recent workshop organised by the Botswana Centre for Human Rights, representatives of the two groups apparently refused to shake hands, despite being urged to do so by other participants. Both camps argue that President Mogae has offered only silence while the nation is embroiled in a potentially destructive dialogue. One SPIL member said that the president's silence legitimised hate speech aimed at the Kalangas. PYB, on the other hand, said the president had "snubbed" their request for a meeting while he had honoured a SPIL function with his presence.

Recently, ethnic disputes have lessened. PYB lost their case to stop the referendum. Mogae addressed the problem during his recent state of the nation address, where he blamed a group of "urban elites who seem poised to poison the atmosphere in pursuit of their narrow, sectarian and selfish interests" for the problem of rising ethnic tensions.[7]

Botswana has a decentralised form of government. Yet the most potent criticism against the Botswana-type system is that it is a somewhat hesitant arrangement. Instead of emphasising the devolution of power, decentralisation in Botswana is, at best, an agency model. Under the current arrangement, central government has a significant say in the running of local government affairs, especially through central control over sources of finance. Mfundisi makes this point by stating that the BDP has used the poor fiscal stance of local government to "stifle political opposition at the local level".[8] This can be blamed partly on Botswana's relatively good economic performance, where there is very little pressure on local government agencies to raise their own funds to support local services. Central government raises revenues, mostly out of mining, which are then distributed to local government agencies. Thus, creative ways to raise finances are not encouraged. In this way, local government agencies have potential sources of revenues taken over by national government, making fiscal independence hard to achieve. In a sense, this also works to the detriment of local democratic consolidation. Another negative feature of the current model is that the district councils, the city councils and town councils are statutory organisations. This means that parliament can revoke their existence. While this possibility seems far-fetched under the current regime, there is still concern that there is not constitutional provision for the existence of local government institutions. Unlike in South Africa, where the provinces are constitutionally provided for, Botswana's constitution does not assure local government. At some level, this is because Botswana's decentralisation process has not been crisis driven and therefore the government has not felt any pressure to decentralise politically. This form of decentralisation can be disadvantageous to local populations as the councils are the final points of service delivery.

Another measure that gives central government the means to control local authorities is the right bestowed on the Minister of Local Government to handpick individuals to sit on the councils and land boards. There is a reduction of opposition majorities through this process, a matter that is tantamount to vote stealing by the ruling party, at least in so far as opposition parties are concerned. For instance Holm makes the point that this practice did take away the opposition majority in Jwaneng, where defections from the opposition-held council led to the council shifting control to the BDP, owing to the "specially elected" councillors together with the defectors making majority numbers.[9] Many feel that this practice effectively subverts the will of the voters.

In his recent state of the nation address, President Mogae made the claim that Botswana's most challenging problem is Acquired Immune Deficiency Syndrome (Aids). He described Botswana's battle with HIV/Aids as so serious that the nation is faced with the risk of extinction.[10] From being a country with one case of HIV infection in 1985, a few years after HIV/Aids was recognised as a major public health challenge, the infection rate has climbed to a world-leading 35% in the adult population.[11] As well as leading to many deaths, HIV/Aids also redefines social relationships through the stigmatisation of those infected. In economic terms, it reduces productivity. While the pandemic is not expected to destroy Botswana's economy, it will have several profound ill effects on the country's social fabric. Economically speaking, the government will have to increase its expenditure as the need to care for those infected with the virus grows.[12]

While few fault the government for lack of effort, some accuse it of failing to arrest the spread of the virus in its earliest stages. The Botswana National Policy on HIV/Aids came only in 1993. Once the policy was in place, it took another five years to create the National Aids Co-ordinating Agency (NACA). This is despite recognition in the policy of the need for a "multi-sectoral approach" and for many players to fight the virus.[13] Regarding the government's intention to provide anti-retroviral drugs to all HIV-positive citizens, there are concerns as to its ability to carry out such a large-scale public health programme.

A prominent HIV/Aids activist in Botswana, Billy Mosedame, high-lighted this problem, saying that the delayed supply of anti-retroviral drugs was evidence of a lack of concern for victims by the government. He claims that, while the government "shows us off at Aids conferences and proclaims to the world that 'these are people living with HIV/Aids, we love them, care for them, support them'", appeals for drugs to the Minister of Health have not been acted on.[14] However, the problem seems to be more linked to the intricacies and inefficiency of the policy process, rather than ill will on the part of the government.[15] That aside, the gov-ernment has set up comprehensive programmes to address the needs of people affected by, but not necessarily infected with, HIV/Aids. For instance, the government has begun a process of registering and caring for orphans in the country.

Botswana has been recognised as a country that has consistently main-tained and respected the human rights of its citizens.[16] In 1989, however, Attaliah Molokomme made the point that Botswana's state often takes advantages of loopholes in the constitution to deprive citizens of their constitutionally-guaranteed human rights.[17] Some 10 years later, this assessment still holds true. Currently, such rights as the right to freedom of association are tampered with by the state to its advantage, at the expense of institutionalising democratic governance. Molokomme gives the example of trade unions, where government has laws that make it illegal for people to be fully employed, therefore ensuring that trade unions may not fully develop into a force strong enough to engage the state. Monageng Mogalakwe, on the same issue, points to the fact that, despite Botswana's membership of the International Labour Organisation, the country has not ratified the organisation's conventions.[18]

A further example of the state's alleged human rights shortfall appears around the issue of citizenship. Before *Dow v. the Government of Botswana*, a landmark case whose ending warranted a constitutional amendment, the right of citizenship was just one of those denied to some citizens by the state. Children born of female citizens of Botswana with expatriate fathers could not have their mothers' citizenship bestowed on them. This practice was in line with Botswana's largely patriarchal culture, something that per-meates policy.[19] Ms Dow, now a judge on the Botswana bench, success-fully challenged this law. Yet another example is that the penal code still outlaws homosexuality while the constitution provides the right to priv-acy. In an evident attack on the right to privacy, a Motswana man is cur-rently expected to come to trial because he was found having carnal knowledge "against the order of nature".

Another illustration of human rights under unnecessary duress in Botswana is demonstrated by the suppression of the right to freedom of speech and freedom of the press. Botswana's media is often made to feel that its very existence is a favour by the government. Despite arguments for press freedom, Botswana's recent history is one of consistent harassment of the media by the government. There have been actions by the government, either in their official capacities or on behalf of the state, which smack of interference with press freedom. While in the past the government has used "national security" as a measure of control, lately there has been a further series of actions seen to restrict freedom of the press. In government-owned media organs, top officials apparently suppress opinions contrary to those of the state. The most recent and perhaps most significant example of this is the case of the news editor of Botswana Television, a government-owned television station, who resigned citing official interference with his duties. In a report published in a local newspaper, news editor Chris Bishop cited interference from the Vice President's Office as the reason why the station could not run a feature on Marietta Bosch, who was then a death row inmate and the first person of European descent to fall victim to Botswana's capital punishment law.[20] Another example of the government's antagonism to the press came during the recent World Press week. The government proceeded to punish two newspapers, the *Botswana Guardian* and the *Midweek Sun*, by withdrawing government advertisements from their pages, saying that they were not reporting on the government in a favourable light.[21] The sister newspapers took the government to court over the advertisement ban and won their case. These actions by the state, where the government is clearly prepared to use public money to deprive the public of its right to information, places a question mark over the government's commitment to freedom of speech.

It is now 10 years since corruption scandals put a huge blot on the image of Botswana as an accountable, ethically governed state.[22] Most of those implicated in the scandals were high-level government officials and leaders in the ruling BDP. Writing on this issue, Kenneth Good observed that corruption in Botswana was nothing new, adding credence to another claim by Kempe Ronald Hope Sr, which implies indirectly that Botswana, perhaps like many other African countries, is plagued with a highly parasitical elite that preys on state resources for its own gain.[23] Good's more disconcerting hypothesis, however, was that this type of activity "was unlikely to be eliminated".[24] Lepetu Setshawaelo, leader of the opposition Botswana Alliance Movement, expressed the view that the BDP is not doing enough to root out corruption.

Similar concerns about the state's commitment to combating corruption were raised at a recent conference held by the Transparency International Botswana Chapter (TIBOT). Writing at the conference, Good described Botswana's governing elite as using their influence and positions of authority to "entrench their political power and to enrich themselves at the expense of the majority of the people".

What is more disconcerting than corruption is the erosion of accountability in government work. For instance, there is a trend towards a silent acceptance of huge cost overruns and lack of proper accountability practices in the public service. Some examples from the recent past include the case of Botswana Telecommunications Corporation, a state-owned communications parastatal, where poor management led to the procurement of an inappropriate billing system, leading to "a number of grievances and decline in customer satisfaction, besides loss of revenue for the corporation".[25] While no wilful wrongdoing is suggested or even apparent in the alleged cases, what is disconcerting is that they are becoming commonplace in an environment of scarce economic resources.

On the international scene, Botswana continues to play an active role in regional affairs. One such significant step is the country's role in bringing peace to the Democratic Republic of the Congo (DRC). Former Botswana president, Sir Ketumile Masire, now plays the role of facilitator in the Congolese peace process. His role in the process has not been without its opponents, especially in Botswana, where citizens felt that the former president was perhaps risking his life for people who were not ready to embrace the need for peace. This was not an unfounded concern as the then president of the DRC, Laurent Kabila, had expressed an unwillingness to accept Masire as facilitator, accusing the former president of bias and requesting a different person to facilitate the Inter-Congolese Dialogue. Recently, however, the former president has managed to bring the warring factions to dialogue in Gaborone, Botswana. The *Botswana Guardian*, in its weekly commentary, commended "the effort and patience of the Inter-Congolese Dialogue facilitator Sir Ketumile Masire who, despite so many odds, remained convinced that peace is possible".[26]

In the region however, Botswana's relations with its neighbours remain somewhat bumpy. The early 1990s brought renewed hopes for peace in southern Africa, with the decolonisation of Namibia and the fall of apartheid in South Africa. However, relations between Botswana and Namibia, a long-time beneficiary of Botswana's neighbourliness during its liberation struggle, have been mired in several diplomatic and near military skirmishes. The most widely known of these is the Sedudu Island case that both countries took to the International Court of Justice.[27] Some weeks before the release of the judgment, there was a reported military build-up in the disputed area, with the media in Namibia playing an especially inflammatory role in raising hostilities. This love-hate relationship between neighbours was not improved by Namibia's successful lobbying of the German government, a former colonial master, to stop the Dutch government from selling Botswana long-range leopard tanks.

Another potentially explosive area in Botswana's relations with her neighbours is over international sources of fresh water. Southern Africa is home to the Kalahari Desert, the world's second largest desert. Water resources are a very ripe source for both latent and open conflict.[28] For instance, Botswana and Namibia disagreed over Namibia's intentions to dredge the Okavango River in 1997.

The Historical Roots of Violence and Division

The nomadic Khoi and San tribes of southern Africa originally inhabited the physical place that is now called Botswana. The more politically and militarily organised pastoralist communities of the Tswana displaced these tribes and pushed them into the hinterland of the Kalahari Desert, where they now mostly reside. In 1885, during the scramble for Africa, Britain came to colonise what was then a loose federation of Tswana-speaking tribes. These tribal groups existed in what came to be known as the Bechuanaland Protectorate. Britain was apparently reluctant to colonise the Tswana territories. The British had a belief that their interests north of the Limpopo "were limited", thus they saw very little sense in making many investments, even in the protectorate.[29]

Throughout the protectorate era, the British did not establish direct rule in the colony. Rather they practised indirect rule, letting the chiefs dictate the affairs of the territory. The British had minimal input into the daily affairs of the colony and the chiefs of the various Tswana tribes continued to have a lot of say in the running of the tribes. This is probably one explanation for Botswana's stability. Succession in chieftainship is one of the surviving institutions of the pre-colonial Tswana that has persisted. Another is the *kgotla* form of democracy. Tswana tribes reputedly practised democratic governance where, in a forum called the *kgotla* ("a gathering of people in the world"), male adults were allowed to take part in village affairs.

Upon independence in 1966, the British left without much bloodshed and struggle. The Bechuanaland Protectorate became the Republic of Botswana. The new post-colonial government, led by Sir Seretse Khama (later knighted by the British, like his successor Masire), was based on the principles of Westminster-type governance. To date, the government of Botswana has the form of a republic with three branches of government – the legislature, judiciary and executive. The legislature is a unicameral House of Parliament, made up of elected representatives. Forty-four of the representatives are directly elected in elections and four of the members are "specially elected" members of parliament. The executive consists of the cabinet and presidency. The president is, however, not elected by popular vote. The task of electing the president rests with the party that holds a majority in parliament. The civil service, too, is part of the executive. Some critics of the Botswana system have pointed out that the current system does not really favour democratic representation. The argument is that the civil service, with their ability to control information and their superior skills compared to the legislature, are the de facto policy makers. Hence, parliament's role strikes some as mere rubber-stamping. The judiciary consists of judges who are expected to be politically neutral. Blending traditional Tswana institutions into government, the customary court system is part of the judiciary. The chiefs are the heads of the customary court system, which operates on the basis of traditional legal principles.

As far back as 1964, the government of Botswana was predisposed toward a certain form of decentralisation, which has evolved into deconcentration of power, as opposed to political devolution. This has enabled the state to have a presence in most rural areas. What must be noted, however, is that the institutions of decentralisation are not institutions of political independence from the centre. Rather, they are objects of central government's delivery strategy for the rural populace.

Local government structures ensure that the traditional forms of governance are incorporated into the modern post-colonial state. Through membership in the House, the chiefs are a part of the new dispensation. This is more so in the rural areas, where their constituents and the majority of Botswana's population reside. In this way, the chiefs, who command a loyal following at local level, have helped ensure stability and legitimacy for the post-colonial government of Botswana. The one notable defect of the chieftaincy institution in Botswana, however, is that some of the tribes in the country are not represented.

Despite the anomaly of elections having always been won by only one party, elections are free and fair. The ruling BDP has been in power since 1966, and has never refused to accede to electoral contest at the end of the normal five-year term of government. The BPP has faded in national prominence and the BNF now serves as the main opposition. While the

BDP is seen as a liberal party, the BNF has social democratic leanings. Derided as "communist" in the 1970s, the BNF is an offshoot of Marxist politics and Koma, its leader, was educated in the former Soviet Union. Like other opposition parties in Botswana, the BNF has a rather dismal internal administrative system. In the last general election, Botswana had as many as seven political parties vying for electoral power, but most of these did not earn a seat. Only the BNF and its offshoot, the BCP, gained seats in the National Assembly. The BNF won six seats and the BCP won only one seat in the National Assembly.

Southern Africa's pre-colonial history consists of wars of displacement and highly militarised societies. In its immediate post-colonial period, Botswana was a prime candidate for instability due to the actions of racist regimes in the then Rhodesia, later Zimbabwe, South Africa, and the latter's then colony Namibia. Botswana, though, never went into open warfare with any of her aggressor neighbours. Botswana's army, the Botswana Defence Force, is a tightly controlled, highly disciplined army that is mostly involved in anti-poaching activities, protecting the country's bountiful wildlife resources, and performing humanitarian activities. The BDF has come to be a symbol of the country's commitment to Botswana's ideals for peace and stability, taking part in peace-keeping activities in Somalia, Mozambique and Lesotho, all assignments in which they were commended by other peace-keepers for their disciplined, professional approach to their duties.

In 1976, Botswana discovered diamonds in the town of Orapa and, soon after this, another rich kimberlite deposit was discovered in Jwaneng. For the next 20 years, Botswana's was among the fastest growing economies in the world. Up until 2000, it averaged over nine percent growth rate per annum. In 1998, the country's per capita Gross Domestic Product was $3 300. Botswana's is a liberal, open economic system and the country has never indulged in a closed economic strategy or a nationalistic economy. Botswana's challenge is to sustain its economic growth at a time when the economy is over-reliant on mineral wealth, especially diamond sales. The future of diversification, however, looked bright in the late 1990s, when there was growth in the non-mining share of the GDP. Since then, the divestment by Motor Company of Botswana, a group that assembled Hyundai and Volvo cars, has led to a decline. Botswana's employment problems stem from a lack of modernisation in the rural sector. This includes an underdeveloped road network, lesser-developed marketing capacities, an urban bias in development and persistent drought. The unemployment trend is generally on the rise.[30]

In Botswana, around half the population lives below the poverty datum line. In the rural areas, 64% of families are under the poverty line. The gender aspect of poverty is such that more women are poverty-stricken than men. Also, children are more impoverished than adults. As a separate issue, land ownership is likely to become a major point of contention in Botswana. In southern Africa, land is a flash-point. In Botswana, the most disposed tribe territorially is the Basarwa. This nomadic tribe's lifestyle conflicts with the government's economic development strategies. The government's rural development strategy has always encouraged tribes to come together in one place where social services can be developed collectively.

Present and Future Opportunities for Reconciliation

While Botswana has enjoyed a period of uninterrupted political stability and economic growth, the time has perhaps come for the country to move toward reinvigorating the democratic system that has led to that stability. The time has also come to strengthen citizens' ability to partake in the economic gains that the country has made in the past and which are expected to continue in the near future.

The signs are clear. Batswana do not go to the polls in the numbers one could hope for. This must be taken as a worrying signal. Part of the reason is that electoral contests have now become a de facto one-party race in Botswana, with the BDP expected to win every contest it enters. Coupled with this, the same reasons that make the BDP the only viable competitor during elections, are circumstances that disproportionately favour the ruling party's chances of winning an election. One of these includes lopsided campaign finance regulations. Campaign finance is one area where opposition parties have been getting a raw deal. In the past election, the BDP got campaign sponsorship to the tune of two million pula, while the opposition got none. If this was entirely due to the inability of the opposition to raise money, that would perhaps be understandable, but the reality is that parties are forbidden from raising money from foreign sources. The question then is, did the BDP play by the rules? And even if so, electoral reform is needed to bolster equality of competition and lend credence to Botswana's electoral system. Either all parties need to be allocated a certain amount of money out of the public coffers, using past electoral performance to gauge the allocations, or alternatively, all parties must be allowed to raise campaign monies in and out of the country to the best of their abilities.

Another way in which citizens can be given a voice in the political process is by increasing effective representation by the members of parliament. Parliament's ability to voice the aspirations of the ordinary citizenry is weakened by its weakness vis-à-vis the executive. Part of ensuring effective representation will entail increasing parliament's access to crucial information. In its current state, parliament is ineffective. Even MPs' input into budgetary processes is very limited since, like ordinary citizens, they have little knowledge of the data that go into annual budgets. Like the citizens they represent, members of parliament only get to see budgets when the Minister of Finance announces them at the beginning of every financial year. Decentralisation is another area at which government might look to make the existing democratic dispensation more meaningful to citizens. Political devolution is a type of decentralisation in which districts are given more political autonomy. While Botswana is effectively a unitary state, more devolution will ensure more effective representation.

A way to deal with inefficiency in Botswana's public enterprises is to privatise them. In their current state, they lack competition and thus accountability. Monopolisation of the market makes some of them impervious to calls for improvement. It is comforting to note that the government is proceeding with privatisation, with the release of the privatisation white paper and its approval by parliament. It is also commendable that the government is taking precautions to ensure that the process is as free from possible failure as it can be. However, such a venture needs to be quickly executed. While privatisation will most likely improve the efficiency of public economic institutions, it could backfire if citizens' stake in the economy is paid only lip service. It is thus commendable that the government is proceeding with the Citizen Entrepreneurial Development Agency (CEDA), an empowerment strategy that will make available some credit to citizens.

The income redistribution challenge has recently come under duress with the possibility that the education budget may be reduced. Botswana's legislators are currently touring the country, consulting citizens on the need to cut back education expenditures and raising the likelihood that free universal education may be discontinued. This will defeat income redistribution as education has been one way that government has helped reduce poverty.

Tribalism as a "new" problem in Botswana ought not to have reached the proportions that it has recently. This is just one example of how perhaps the country's legislative branch fails to take the initiative in keeping the constitution in harmony with changing times. The country's legislative community needs to actively engage in reviewing the constitution and not wait for discontent to simmer before taking action.

The HIV/Aids pandemic is certainly one of Botswana's foremost challenges. People continue to be infected despite the government's efforts at encouraging prevention. Despite free distribution of condoms and high awareness rates in the population about HIV/Aids, it seems difficult to reverse the trend of high infection rates. It is thus commendable that the government is undertaking to supply anti-retroviral drugs to HIV-positive citizens. As with other government programmes, however, implementation could become a problem. As a way to augment the government's capacity to implement programmes concerning HIV/Aids, the state must also consider contracting some of the activities to NGOs or perhaps financially empowering NGOs to engage in HIV/Aids care and mitigation activities.

NOTES

1 Samuel Huntington, *Third Wave: Democracy in the Late Twentieth Century* (Norman: University of Oklahoma Press, 1991), 24–25.

2 Tebogo Kethamile, "BNF youth defy Koma," *The Botswana Gazette*, 10 October 2001.

3 "Botswana Cannot Afford to Throw Away Three Decades of Nation-Building – BCC President," *The Botswana Gazette*, 7 November 2001.

4 Government of Botswana, *Report on the Presidential Commission of Inquiry into Sections 77, 78 and 79 of the Constitution of Botswana* (Gaborone: Government Printer, 1997), 1.

5 Government of Botswana, *Report on the Presidential Commission of Inquiry*, 95.

6 Bashi Letsididi, "Mogae, PYB on Collision Course," 12 October 2001.

7 F. G. Mogae, president of the Republic of Botswana, "State of the Nation Address to the First Meeting of the Third Session of Parliament," 29 October 2001.

8 A. Mfundisi, "The Formation and Structure of Central Government and its Institutional Relationship with Local Government in Botswana," in *Botswana: Politics and Society*, eds. Wayne Edge and M. Lekorwe (Pretoria: Van Schaik, 1998).

9 John Holm, "Elections and Democracy in Botswana," in *Democracy in Botswana: The Proceedings of a Symposium held in Gaborone*, eds. John Holm and Patrick Molutsi (Gaborone: Macmillan Botswana, 1989), 197.

10 Anton La Gardia, "A Nation on the Brink of Extinction by HIV/AIDS." Reprinted at www.smh.com.au/news (accessed 24 October 2001).

11 Government of Botswana, Botswana National Policy on HIV/AIDS, Gaborone, 1993, 3.

12 The government of Botswana has put in place several bold initiatives to arrest the impact of the epidemic on the nation. The boldest of this is the planned supply of free anti-retroviral drugs on a universal scale to the infected population. This initiative, which is the first of its type in sub-Saharan Africa, demonstrates the government's commitment to alleviating the problems of those infected. The government has also

initiated a programme called the Prevention of Mother to Child Transmission that aims at helping alleviate the problem of infecting unborn infants.

13 Ministry of Health (1997), Botswana HIV/AIDS Medium Term Plan II 1997–2002, NACP, 38.

14 "AIDS Activist Betrayed," *The Botswana Guardian*, 10 October 2001, 1.

15 "Long-term Vision for Botswana: Towards Prosperity for All," Presidential Task Group for a Long-term Vision for Botswana, September 1997, 21.

16 Attaliah Molokomme, "Political Rights in Botswana: Regression or Development?" in *Democracy in Botswana: The Proceedings of a Symposium held in Gaborone*, eds. John Holm and Patrick Molutsi (Gaborone: Macmillan Botswana, 1989).

17 Ibid.

18 Monageng Mogalakwe, *The State and Organized Labour in Botswana: "Liberal Democracy" in Emergent Capitalism* (Brookfield: Ashgate, 1997), 94.

19 Women in Botswana still have to ask their husbands for permission if they want to sell their joint property, while the males may proceed to do so without their wives' consent.

20 "Khama stopped Bosch Feature," *The Botswana Guardian*, 13 July 2001.

21 "Newspaper Hounded as Press Freedom Week Ends," Integrated Regional Information Network (IRIN), 12 May 2001. Reprinted at http://allafrica.com/stories/2000105120013/html (accessed 25 May 2001).

22 This section is based heavily on Kenneth Good, "Corruption and Mismanagement in Botswana: Best-Case Example?" *Journal of Modern African Studies* 32 (1994): 499–521.

23 Kempe Ronald Hope Sr., ed., *Corruption and Development in Africa* (London: Macmillan, 2000).

24 Kenneth Good, "Corruption and Mismanagement in Botswana, Best-Case Example?"

25 Baledzi Gaolathe, Minister of Finance and Development Planning (Budget Speech), Republic of Botswana, FY 2001/2002, 10.

26 "Comment," *The Botswana Guardian*, 20 August 2001.

27 Namibia and Botswana both lay claim to an island in the north of Botswana.

28 Lekopanyane Mooketsi, "Namibian Relations get Frostier with Botswana over the Okavango." Reprinted at www.mg.coza/mg/news/97jan2/28jan-okavango.html (accessed 20 May 2001).

29 J. Ramsay, "The Establishment and Consolidation of the Bechuanaland Protectorate, 1870–1910," in *Botswana: Politics and Society*, eds. Wayne Edge and M. Lekorwe.

30 Kempe R. Hope Sr, "Growth, Unemployment and Poverty in Botswana," in *African Political Economy* (London: M. E. Sharpe, 1997), 21.

RESOURCES

Books, Articles and Media Reports

Edge, Wayne and M. Lekorwe, eds. *Botswana: Politics and Society*. Pretoria: Van Schaik, 1998.

Good, Kenneth. "The State and Extreme Poverty in Botswana: The San and Destitutes." *Journal of Modern African Studies* 37 (1999): 185–205.

Government of Botswana. *Report on the Presidential Commission of Inquiry into Sections 77, 78 and 79 of the Constitution of Botswana*. Gaborone: Government Printer, 1997.

Holm, John. "A Paternalistic Democracy," in *Democracy in Developing Countries*, edited by Larry Diamond et al. London: Adamantine Press, 1988.

Holm, John and Patrick Molutsi, eds. *Democracy in Botswana: The Proceedings of a Symposium held in Gaborone*. Gaborone: Macmillan Botswana, 1989.

Mogalakwe, Monageng. *The State and Organized Labour in Botswana: "Liberal Democracy" in Emergent Capitalism*. Brookfield: Ashgate, 1997.

Stedman, Stephen J., ed. *Botswana: The Political Economy of Democratic Development*. London: Lynne Rienner, 1993.

Government

The Government of Botswana website: http://www.gov.bw

Local NGOs

Botswana Confederation of Commerce, Industry and Manpower is an umbrella body of various private sector organisations in the country: http://www.newafrica.com//boccim

Botswana Council of Non-Government Organisations (BOCONGO) is the umbrella body that acts as a linking organisation to all the NGOs in Botswana: http://www.bocongo.bw

Botswana Exports Development and Investment Agency (BEDIA) acts as a focal point for businesspeople who want to source manufactured goods from Botswana: http://www.bedia.bw

The Botswana Gazette: http://www.gazette.bw

Botswana Institute for Development Policy Analysis (BIDPA) deals with economic issues and does consultancy for government, the private sector and other international NGOs: http://www.bidpa.bw

Botswana Media Consultative Council (BMCC) works toward the promotion of a free, ethnic, democratic and productive media in Botswana: http://www.ibis.bw/~botswanamedia/body.html

The University of Botswana is the only university in the country: http://www.ub.bw

International NGOs

Political Resources on the Net – Botswana is a website with a comprehensive number of links to resources of international and local political organisations in Botswana: http//www.politicalresources.net/botswana.htm

United Nations in Botswana has a website with links to all the UN organisations operating in Botswana: http://www.unbotswana.org.bw

BOTSWANA COUNTRY INFORMATION

Geography
Location: Southern Africa.
Cities: *Capital:* Gaborone (pronounced ha-bo-ro-neh), 2000 pop. 213 017. *Other towns:* Francistown (101 805), Selebi-Phikwe (49 017), Molepolole (47 094), Kanye (36 877), Serowe (33 335), Mahalapye (32 047), Lobatse (32 075), Maun (31 260), Mochudi (30 671).

People
Nationality: *Noun and adjective:* Motswana (sing.); Batswana (pl.).
Population (1999): 1 610 000.
Population growth rate (1999): 2.3%.
Ethnic groups: Tswana 55%–60%, Kalanga 25%–30%, Kgalagadi, Herero, Basarwa ("Bushmen"), Khoi, whites 5%–10%.
Religions: Christianity 60%, traditional African 40%.
Languages: English (official), Setswana, Ikalanga.
Education: *Literacy:* 68.9%.
Health (1999): *Infant mortality rate:* 59/1 000. *Life expectancy:* 39.9 years. *HIV infection rate:* 35%.
Workforce (1999): 255 618.

Economy
GDP (1999): $5.2 billion.
GDP real growth rate (1998–99): 4.5%.
Per capita income (1999): $3 200.
Natural resources: Diamonds, copper, nickel, coal, soda ash, salt, gold, potash.
Agriculture (1998–99): 2.8% of GDP. *Products:* livestock, sorghum, white maize, millet, beans.
Industry: *Types:* mining (35% of GDP): diamonds, copper, nickel, coal, textiles, construction, tourism, beef processing, chemical products production, food and beverage production.
Trade (1995): *Exports:* $4.5 billion: diamonds, nickel, copper, meat products, textiles, hides, skins, and soda ash. *Major markets:* South Africa, Zimbabwe, UK. *Imports:* $1.8 billion: machinery, transport equipment, manufactured goods, food, chemicals, fuels. *Major suppliers:* South Africa, Zimbabwe, EU.
Economic aid: Recipient of $25 million in US aid.

Military
Military expenditure: Dollar figures: $61 million (FY99/00).
Military expenditure: Percent of GDP: 1.2% (FY99/00).

Demographic information is drawn from that compiled by the United States Department of State. See http://www.state.gov/r/pa/ei/bgn